T0202976

Lecture Notes in Computer Science   11696

More information about this series at http://www.springer.com/series/7409

Fabio Crestani · Martin Braschler ·
Jacques Savoy · Andreas Rauber ·
Henning Müller · David E. Losada ·
Gundula Heinatz Bürki ·
Linda Cappellato · Nicola Ferro (Eds.)

Experimental IR Meets Multilinguality, Multimodality, and Interaction

10th International Conference of the CLEF Association, CLEF 2019
Lugano, Switzerland, September 9–12, 2019
Proceedings

 Springer

Editors
Fabio Crestani (iD)
Universita della Svizzera Italiana
Lugano, Switzerland

Jacques Savoy (iD)
University of Neuchâtel
Neuchâtel, Switzerland

Henning Müller (iD)
HES-SO Valais-Wallis
Sierre, Switzerland

Gundula Heinatz Bürki
Swiss Alliance for Data-Intensive Services
Thun, Switzerland

Nicola Ferro (iD)
University of Padua
Padua, Italy

Martin Braschler
Zurich University of Applied Sciences
Winterthur, Switzerland

Andreas Rauber
Technische Universität Wien
Vienna, Austria

David E. Losada (iD)
University of Santiago de Compostela
Santiago de Compostela, Spain

Linda Cappellato (iD)
University of Padua
Padua, Italy

ISSN 0302-9743   ISSN 1611-3349   (electronic)
Lecture Notes in Computer Science
ISBN 978-3-030-28576-0   ISBN 978-3-030-28577-7   (eBook)
https://doi.org/10.1007/978-3-030-28577-7

LNCS Sublibrary: SL3 – Information Systems and Applications, incl. Internet/Web, and HCI

This Springer imprint is published by the registered company Springer Nature Switzerland AG
The registered company address is: Gewerbestrasse 11, 6330 Cham, Switzerland

Preface

Since 2000, the Conference and Labs of the Evaluation Forum (CLEF) has played a leading role in stimulating research and innovation in the domain of multimodal and multilingual information access. Initially founded as the Cross-Language Evaluation Forum and running in conjunction with the European Conference on Digital Libraries (ECDL/TPDL), CLEF became a standalone event in 2010 combining a peer-reviewed conference with a multi-track evaluation forum. The combination of the scientific program and the track-based evaluations at the CLEF conference creates a unique platform to explore information access from different perspectives, in any modality and language.

The CLEF conference has a clear focus on experimental information retrieval (IR) as seen in evaluation forums (CLEF Labs, TREC, NTCIR, FIRE, MediaEval, RomIP, TAC, etc.) with special attention to the challenges of multi-modality, multilinguality, and interactive search ranging from unstructured, to semi-structured and structured data. CLEF invites submissions on significant new insights demonstrated by the use of innovative IR evaluation tasks or in the analysis of IR test collections and evaluation measures, as well as on concrete proposals to push the boundaries of the Cranfield/TREC/CLEF paradigm.

CLEF 2019[1] was organized and hosted by the Università della Svizzera italiana in Lugano, Switzerland, during September 9–12, 2019. The conference format consisted of keynotes, contributed papers, lab sessions, and poster sessions, including reports from other benchmarking initiatives from around the world.

CLEF 2019 marks a special edition as it is the 20th anniversary of CLEF, since its establishment in 2000. We celebrated this event by organizing a session devoted to the past and, especially, the future of CLEF. We also prepared a book[2] focusing on the lessons learnt in the 20 years of CLEF, and its impact over time.

CLEF 2019 introduced several novelties. First, we setup a mentorship program to support the preparation of lab proposals for newcomers to CLEF. The CLEF newcomers mentoring program offered help, guidance, and feedback on the writing of draft lab proposals by assigning a mentor to proponents, who helped them in preparing and maturing the lab proposal for submission. If the lab proposal fell into the scope of an already existing CLEF lab, the mentor helped proponents to get in touch with the lab organizers and team up forces.

Second, CLEF 2019 hosted an Industry Day for the first time, jointly organized with the Swiss Alliance for Data-Intensive Services. The goal was to further open CLEF to a wider, industrial community through demo sessions, panels, and special keynotes

---

[1] http://clef2019.clef-initiative.eu/.

[2] Ferro, N., Peters, C. (eds.): *Information Retrieval Evaluation in a Changing World – Lessons Learned from 20 Years of CLEF*, The Information Retrieval Series, vol. 41. Springer International Publishing, Germany (2019).

where the best and most pertinent work of CLEF participants would be made publicly visible.

Lastly, for the first time, the European Conference for Information Retrieval (ECIR) and CLEF joined forces: ECIR 2019 hosted a special session dedicated to CLEF Labs where lab organizers present the major outcomes of their Labs and their plans for ongoing activities, followed by a poster session to favor discussion during the conference. This was reflected in the ECIR 2019 proceedings, where CLEF Lab activities and results were reported as short papers. The goal was not only to engage the ECIR community in CLEF activities but also to disseminate the research results achieved during CLEF evaluation cycles as submission of papers to ECIR.

The following scholars were invited to give a keynote talks at CLEF 2019: W. Bruce Croft (University of Massachusetts at Amherst, USA) delivered a talk entitled "The Relevance of Answers," which focused on information retrieval tasks that involve retrieving answers rather than documents in response to users' questions with the aim of identifying some of the key aspects of answers that should be studied to support the ongoing development of more effective search systems. Yair Neuman (Ben Gurion University of the Negev, Israel) gave a speech on "Automatic Analysis of Personality Dimensions through Digital Signatures: Vision, Achievements and Challenges," presenting the vision of computational personality analysis and its relevance for current challenges in various fields, including a critical examination of some ventures, such as those developed by IBM Personality Insights and the late Cambridge Analytica, and finally pointing to the challenges facing those who are interested in advancing the field.

CLEF 2019 received a total of 30 submissions, of which a total of 15 papers (7 long, 8 short) were accepted. Each submission was reviewed by three Program Committee (PC) members, and the program chairs oversaw the reviewing and follow-up discussions. In total, 13 countries were represented in the accepted papers. This year, many contributions tackled the social networks with the detection of stances or early identification of depression signs on Twitter in a cross-lingual context. Web data is also analyzed in an information diffusion perspective as to discover the main factors explaining a higher probability of being retweeted. More directly related to information retrieval, one study investigates the challenge of tuning parameters for different collections, and another analyzes how kids would use a vocal assistant for performing a search task.

Like in previous editions since 2015, CLEF 2019 continued inviting CLEF lab organizers to nominate a "best of the labs" paper that was reviewed as a full paper submission to the CLEF 2019 conference according to the same review criteria and PC. Seven full papers were accepted for this "best of the labs" section.

The conference integrated a series of workshops presenting the results of lab-based comparative evaluations. CLEF 2019 was the 10th year of the CLEF Conference and the 20th year of the CLEF initiative as a forum for IR Evaluation. The labs were selected in peer review based on their innovation potential and the quality of the resources created. The labs represented scientific challenges based on new data sets and real world problems in multimodal and multilingual information access. These data sets provide unique opportunities for scientists to explore collections, to develop solutions for these problems, to receive feedback on the performance of their solutions, and to discuss the issues with peers at the workshops.

In addition to these workshops, the nine benchmarking labs reported results of their year-long activities in overview talks and lab sessions. Overview papers describing each of these labs are provided in this volume. The full details for each lab are contained in a separate publication, the Working Notes, which are available online[3].

The nine labs running as part of CLEF 2019 were as follows:

CLEF/NTCIR/TREC Reproducibility – CENTRE@CLEF[4] aims to run a joint CLEF/NTCIR/TREC task on challenging participants: (1) to re-produce best results of best/most interesting systems in previous editions of CLEF/NTCIR/TREC by using standard open source IR systems; (2) to con-tribute back to the community the additional components and resources devel-oped to reproduce the results in order to improve existing open source systems.

Identification and Verification of Political Claims – CheckThat![5] aims to foster the development of technology capable of both spotting and verifying check-worthy claims in political debates in English and Arabic.

CLEF eHealth[6] aims to support the development of techniques to aid laypeople, clinicians, and policy-makers in easily retrieving and making sense of medical content to support their decision making. The goals of the lab are to develop processing methods and resources in a multilingual setting to enrich difficult-to-understand eHealth texts, and provide valuable documentation.

Early Risk Prediction on the Internet – eRisk[7] explores challenges of evaluation methodology, effectiveness metrics, and other processes related to early risk detection. Early detection technologies can be employed in different areas, particularly those related to health and safety. For instance, early alerts could be sent when a predator starts interacting with a child for sexual purposes, or when a potential offender starts publishing antisocial threats on a blog, forum or social network. The main goal is to pioneer a new interdisciplinary research area that would be potentially applicable to a wide variety of situations and to many different personal profiles.

Multimedia Retrieval – ImageCLEF[8] provides an evaluation forum for visual media analysis, indexing, classification/learning, and retrieval in medical, nature, security and lifelogging applications with a focus on multimodal data, so data from a variety of sources and media.

Biodiversity Identification and Prediction – LifeCLEF[9] aims at boosting research on the identification and prediction of living organisms in order to solve the taxonomic

---

[3] http://ceur-ws.org/Vol-2380/.

[4] http://www.centre-eval.org/clef2019/.

[5] https://sites.google.com/view/clef2019-checkthat/.

[6] http://clef-ehealth.org/.

[7] http://erisk.irlab.org/.

[8] https://www.imageclef.org/2019.

[9] http://www.lifeclef.org/.

gap and improve our knowledge of biodiversity. Through its biodiversity informatics related challenges, LifeCLEF is intended to push the boundaries of the state-of-the-art in several research directions at the frontier of multimedia information retrieval, machine learning, and knowledge engineering.

Digital Text Forensics and Stylometry – PAN[10] is a networking initiative for the digital text forensics, where researchers and practitioners study technologies that analyze texts with regard to originality, authorship, and trust-worthiness. PAN provides evaluation resources consisting of large-scale corpora, performance measures, and web services that allow for meaningful evaluations. The main goal is to provide for sustainable and reproducible evaluations, to get a clear view of the capabilities of state-of-the-art-algorithms.

Personalised Information Retrieval – PIR-CLEF[11] provides a frame-work for the evaluation of Personalised Information Retrieval (PIR). Current ap-proaches to the evaluation of PIR are user-centric, mostly based on user studies, i.e., they rely on experiments that involve real users in a supervised environment. PIR-CLEF aims to develop and demonstrate a methodology for the evaluation of personalised search that enables repeatable experiments. The main aim is to enable research groups working on PIR to both experiment with and provide feedback on the proposed PIR evaluation methodology.

Extracting Protests from News – ProtestNews[12] aims to test and improve state-of-the-art generalizable machine learning and natural language processing methods for text classification and information extraction on English news from multiple countries such as India and China for creating comparative databases of contentious politics events (riots, social movements), i.e. the repertoire of contention that can enable large scale comparative social and political science studies.

The picturesque lakeside city of Lugano is famous for its beautiful quasi-Mediterranean climate and is a popular destination for its lovely scenery and its laid back lifestyle. The conference dinner, which took place on the second evening, enabled the participants to enjoy the scenery from Monte San Salvatore, on the lake shore just opposite to Lugano, dining and drinking in good company. The first evening was devoted to welcoming CLEF participants to the conference, with a reception at the Universitá della Svizzera Italiana (USI), which hosted CLEF. The third evening, on the other hand, saw academic and industry participants happily getting to know each other over an aperitif at the Villa Ciani, right in the center of Lugano, in the lovely Parco Ciani.

The success of CLEF 2019 would not have been possible without the huge effort of several people and organizations, including the CLEF Association[13], the Program Committee, the Lab Organizing Committee, the local Organization Committee in

---

[10] http://pan.webis.de/.

[11] http://www.ir.disco.unimib.it/pir-clef2019/.

[12] https://emw.ku.edu.tr/clef-protestnews-2019/.

[13] http://www.clef-initiative.eu/association.

Lugano, the reviewers, and the many students and volunteers who contributed. Finally, we thank ACM SIGIR (who provided funding for students travel) and Innosuisse (who provided general funding support) for the generous support.

July 2019

Fabio Crestani
Martin Braschler
Jacques Savoy
Andreas Rauber
Henning Müller
David E. Losada
Gundula Heinatz
Linda Cappellato
Nicola Ferro

Organization

CLEF 2019, Conference and Labs of the Evaluation Forum – Experimental IR meets Multilinguality, Multimodality, and Interaction, was hosted by the University of Lugano, Switzerland.

General Chairs

Fabio Crestani	Universitá della Svizzera Italiana (USI), Switzerland
Martin Braschler	Zurich University of Applied Sciences (ZHAW), Switzerland

Program Chairs

Jacques Savoy	Université de Neuchâtel, Switzerland
Andreas Rauber	Vienna University of Technology (TU Wien), Austria

Lab Chairs

Henning Müller	University of Applied Sciences Western Switzerland (HES-SO), Switzerland
David E. Losada	University of Santiago de Compostela, Spain

Lab Mentorship Chair

Lorraine Goeuriot	Université Grenoble Alpes, France

Industry Chair

Gundula Heinatz	Swiss Alliance for Data-Intensive Services, Switzerland

Proceedings Chairs

Linda Cappellato	University of Padua, Italy
Nicola Ferro	University of Padua, Italy

Local Organization

Monica Landoni	USI, Switzerland
Ali Bahrainian	USI, Switzerland
Mohammad Alian Nejadi	USI, Switzerland
Maram Barifah	USI, Switzerland

| Manajit Chakraborty | USI, Switzerland |
| Esteban Andrés Ríssola | USI, Switzerland |

CLEF Steering Committee

Steering Committee Chair
Nicola Ferro — University of Padua, Italy

Deputy Steering Committee Chair for the Conference
Paolo Rosso — Universitat Politècnica de València, Spain

Deputy Steering Committee Chair for the Evaluation Labs
Martin Braschler — Zurich University of Applied Sciences, Switzerland

Members

Khalid Choukri	Evaluations and Language resources Distribution Agency (ELDA), France
Paul Clough	University of Sheffield, UK
Norbert Fuhr	University of Duisburg-Essen, Germany
Lorraine Goeuriot	Université Grenoble Alpes, France
Julio Gonzalo	National Distance Education University (UNED), Spain
Donna Harman	National Institute for Standards and Technology (NIST), USA
Djoerd Hiemstra	Radboud University, The Netherlands
Evangelos Kanoulas	University of Amsterdam, The Netherlands
Birger Larsen	University of Aalborg, Denmark
Mihai Lupu	Vienna University of Technology, Austria
Josiane Mothe	IRIT, Université de Toulouse, France
Henning Müller	University of Applied Sciences Western Switzerland (HES-SO), Switzerland
Jian-Yun Nie	Université de Montréal, Canada
Maarten de Rijke	University of Amsterdam, The Netherlands
Eric SanJuan	University of Avignon, France
Giuseppe Santucci	Sapienza University of Rome, Italy
Jacques Savoy	University of Neuchêtel, Switzerland
Laure Soulier	Pierre and Marie Curie University (Paris 6), France
Christa Womser-Hacker	University of Hildesheim, Germany

Past Members

Jaana Kekäläinen	University of Tampere, Finland
Séamus Lawless	Trinity College Dublin, Ireland
Carol Peters	ISTI, National Council of Research (CNR), Italy (Steering Committee Chair 2000–2009)

Emanuele Pianta   Centre for the Evaluation of Language and
                    Communication Technologies (CELCT), Italy
Alan Smeaton   Dublin City University, Ireland

Sponsors

Università della Svizzera italiana

Zürcher Hochschule
für Angewandte Wissenschaften

Swiss Alliance for
Data-Intensive Services

SIGIR
Special Interest Group
on Information Retrieval

Schweizerische Eidgenossenschaft
Confédération suisse
Confederazione Svizzera
Confederaziun svizra

Swiss Confederation

Innosuisse – Swiss Innovation Agency

FNSNF
FONDS NATIONAL SUISSE
SCHWEIZERISCHER NATIONALFONDS
FONDO NAZIONALE SVIZZERO
SWISS NATIONAL SCIENCE FOUNDATION

Contents

CLEF 2019 Lab Overviews

History

What Happened in CLEF... For a While?

Nicola Ferro$^{(\boxtimes)}$

Department of Information Engineering, University of Padua, Padua, Italy
ferro@dei.unipd.it

Abstract. 2019 marks the 20th birthday for CLEF, an evaluation campaign activity which has applied the Cranfield evaluation paradigm to the testing of multilingual and multimodal information access systems in Europe. This paper provides a summary of the motivations which led to the establishment of CLEF, and a description of how it has evolved over the years, the major achievements, and what we see as the next challenges.

1 Introduction

Performance measuring is a key to scientific progress. This is particularly true for research concerning complex systems, whether natural or human-built. Multilingual and multimedia information systems are particularly complex: they need to satisfy diverse user needs and support challenging tasks. Their development calls for proper evaluation methodologies to ensure that they meet the expected user requirements and provide the desired effectiveness.

Large-scale worldwide experimental evaluations provide fundamental contributions to the advancement of state-of-the-art techniques through the establishment of common evaluation procedures, the organisation of regular and systematic evaluation cycles, the comparison and benchmarking of proposed approaches, and the spreading of knowledge.

The *Conference and Labs of the Evaluation Forum (CLEF)*[1] is a large-scale *Information Retrieval (IR)* evaluation initiative organised in Europe but involving researchers world-wide. CLEF shares the stage and coordinates with the other major evaluation initiatives in the field, namely: the *Text REtrieval Conference (TREC)*[2] [182], the first large-scale evaluation activity in the field of IR, which began in 1992; the *NII Testbeds and Community for Information access Research (NTCIR)*[3], which promotes research in information access technologies with a special focus on East Asian languages and English; and the *Forum for Information Retrieval Evaluation (FIRE)*[4], whose aim is to encourage research in Indian languages by creating a platform similar to CLEF, providing data and a common forum for comparing models and techniques applied to these languages.

---

[1] http://www.clef-initiative.eu/.
[2] http://trec.nist.gov/.
[3] http://research.nii.ac.jp/ntcir/.
[4] http://fire.irsi.res.in/.

© Springer Nature Switzerland AG 2019
F. Crestani et al. (Eds.): CLEF 2019, LNCS 11696, pp. 3–45, 2019.
https://doi.org/10.1007/978-3-030-28577-7_1

This year marks the 20th birthday of CLEF, which began as an independent activity in 2000. The goal of this report is to provide a short overview of what motivated the setting up of CLEF, what has happened in CLEF during these years, and how CLEF has evolved to keep pace with emerging challenges.

I was a bit reluctant to write this paper since Carol Peters, who established CLEF and coordinated it for the first ten years, wrote a series of "What Happened in CLEF" papers [347–352] where she was used to welcome readers and introduce them to the main outcomes and news of a CLEF edition. So, putting myself within the wake of this tradition seemed a bit bold but a 20th anniversary is a so special event that it is worth the risk and the attempt.

The paper is organized as follows: Sect. 2 describes the beginning and the first period of CLEF, the so-called "CLEF Classic" period; Sect. 3 introduces the second (and current) period of CLEF, known as the "CLEF Initiative" period; Sects. 4 and 5 give an idea of the spread and extension of CLEF activities by providing a short account of the topics addressed in the conference, tracks and labs over the years together with pointers to papers providing more details; Sect. 6 attempts to provide an assessment of the status of CLEF in the IR community; Sect. 7 presents the book we have prepared for celebrating the 20th anniversary of CLEF; Sect. 8 remembers friends and colleagues who have greatly contributed to CLEF but, sadly, are no more with us; Sect. 9 presents the CLEF Association, the no-profit legal entity committed to sustaining and running CLEF; finally, Sect. 10 discusses some news in the CLEF eco-system and how to look for future research directions.

2   CLEF "Classic": 2000–2009

The *Cross-Language Evaluation Forum* (CLEF) began as a cross-lingual track at TREC in 1997 [421], moving to an independent activity in 2000 [345], since Europe was felt as a more suitable environment than USA for fully empowering multilinguality.

The underlying motivation for CLEF was the "Grand Challenge" formulated at the *Association for the Advancement of Artificial Intelligence (AAAI)* 1997 Spring Symposium on Cross-Language and Speech Retrieval [189]. The ambitious goal was the development of fully multilingual and multimodal information access systems capable of:

- processing a query in any medium and any language;
- finding relevant information from a multilingual multimedia collection containing documents in any language and form;
- presenting it in the style most likely to be useful to the user.

The main objective of CLEF has thus been to promote research and stimulate development of multilingual and multimodal IR systems for European (and non-European) languages [346], through:

- the creation of an evaluation infrastructure and the organisation of regular evaluation campaigns for system testing;

- the building of a multidisciplinary research community;
- the construction of publicly available test-suites.

CLEF has pursued this objective by attempting to anticipate the emerging needs of the R&D community and to promote the development of multilingual and multimodal systems that fulfil the demands of the AAAI 1997 Grand Challenge. However, while the first three editions of CLEF were dedicated to mono- and multilingual ad-hoc text retrieval, gradually the scope of activity was extended to include other kinds of text retrieval across languages (i.e., not just document retrieval but question answering and geographic IR as well) and on other media (i.e., collections containing images and speech).

During what is jokingly referred to as the "classic" period of CLEF (2000–2009), several important results were achieved: research activities in previously unexplored areas were stimulated, permitting the growth of IR for languages other than English; evaluation methodologies for different types of *Cross Language Information Retrieval (CLIR)* as well as *MultiLingual Information Access (MLIA)* systems, operating in diverse domains, were studied and implemented; a large set of empirical data about multilingual information access from the user perspective was created; quantitative and qualitative evidence with respect to best practices in cross-language system development was collected; reusable test collections for system benchmarking were developed; language resources for a wide range of European languages, some of which had been little studied, were built. CLEF activities have resulted in the creation of a considerable amount of valuable resources, also for under-represented languages, extremely useful for many types of text processing and benchmarking activities in the IR domain. Perhaps, most important, a strong, multidisciplinary, and active research community focussed mainly, but not only, on IR for European languages came into being.

If we had to summarize the major outcome of CLEF in this period with just one sentence, we could safely say that CLEF has made multilingual IR for European languages a reality, with performances as satisfactory as monolingual ones.

3 The CLEF Initiative: 2010 Onwards

3.1 Scope

The second period of CLEF started with a clear and compelling question: after a successful decade studying multilinguality for European languages, what were the main unresolved issues currently facing us? To answer this question, CLEF turned to the CLEF community to identify the most pressing challenges and to list the steps to be taken to meet them.

The discussion led to the definition and establishment of the *CLEF Initiative*, whose main mission is to promote research, innovation, and the development of information access systems with an emphasis on multilingual and *multimodal* information with various levels of structure.

In the CLEF Initiative an increased focus is on the *multimodal* aspect, intended not only as the ability to deal with information coming in multiple media but also in different modalities, e.g. the Web, social media, news streams, specific domains and so on. These different modalities should, ideally, be addressed in an integrated way; rather than building vertical search systems for each domain/modality the interaction between the different modalities, languages, and user tasks needs to be exploited to provide comprehensive and aggregated search systems.

The continuity with the first period of CLEF on multilinguality and this increased attention for multimodality has led to the definition of a set of action lines for the CLEF Initiative:

- multilingual and multimodal system testing, tuning and evaluation;
- investigation of the use of unstructured, semi-structured, highly-structured, and semantically enriched data in information access;
- creation of reusable test collections for benchmarking;
- exploration of new evaluation methodologies and innovative ways of using experimental data;
- discussion of results, comparison of approaches, exchange of ideas, and transfer of knowledge.

The new challenges and the new organizational structure, described below, have motivated a change of name for CLEF: from the *Cross-Language Evaluation Forum*, of the "classic" period, to *Conference and Labs of the Evaluation Forum*, which now reflects the widened scope.

3.2 Structure

The new challenges for CLEF also called for a renewal of its structure and organization. The annual CLEF meeting is no longer a Workshop, held in conjunction with the European Conference on Digital Libraries (ECDL, now TPDL – Theory and Practice of Digital Libraries), but has become an independent event, held over 3.5–4 days and made up of two interrelated activities: the *Conference* and the *Labs*. As shown in Fig. 1, the *Conference* and the *Labs* are expected to interact together and mutually reinforce each other, bringing new interest and new expertise into CLEF.

More in detail, the *Conference* is a peer-reviewed conference, open to the IR community as a whole and not just to *Lab* participants, and aims at stimulating discussion on innovative evaluation methodologies, fostering a deeper analysis and understanding of experimental results, and promoting multilingual and multimodal information access at large. The *Labs* are the core of the evaluation activities; they are selected on the basis of topical relevance, novelty, potential research impact, the existence of clear real-world use cases, a likely number of participants, and the experience of the organizing consortium. We allow also for a special case of pilot lab activities, called *Workshops*, whose goal is to explore new and "risky" evaluation activities, which are not ready yet for

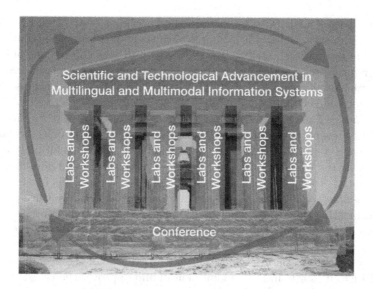

Fig. 1. Structure of the CLEF Initiative.

being shipped as full-fledged *Labs* and benefit from an incubation and discussion period to better tune them.

The *Conference* and the *Labs* originate two streams of peer-reviewed publications. The *CLEF Proceedings*[5] are published in the Springer Lecture Notes in Computer Science (LNCS) series and contain full and short papers submitted to the *Conference*, condensed overviews of the *Lab* activities, and revised and selected "best of labs" papers from labs in the previous edition of CLEF. The *CLEF Working Notes* are published in the CEUR Workshop Proceedings (CEUR-WS.org)[6] series and contain extended lab overviews and detailed papers from the participants in the lab activities. The peer-review process for the *CLEF Proceedings* is ensured by a Programme Committee, which is established for each CLEF edition; the review process for the *CLEF Working Notes* is ensured by dedicated Programme Committees, which are setup separately for each lab of each CLEF edition.

3.3 Organization

In order to favour participation and the introduction of new perspectives, CLEF has introduced a new open-bid process which allows research groups and institutions to bid to host the annual CLEF event and to propose themes. Initially, the bidding process followed a one-year ahead cycle but now, thanks to the interest in and the engagement with CLEF, it follows a three-years ahead cycle, i.e. we are now managing the bids for hosting CLEF 2022.

---

[5] https://link.springer.com/conference/clef.
[6] http://ceur-ws.org/.

While in the CLEF "Classic" period the governing body of CLEF was the *Steering Committee*, which was in charge of the overall coordination of CLEF, of selecting the evaluation activities to be carried out in each edition, and of looking ahead for future research directions, the new participatory approach called for a more articulated organization and for a better separation of concerns.

Each edition of CLEF appoints its own *General Chairs, Programme Chairs*, and *Lab Chairs*. The General Chairs are responsible for the overall running of the annual CLEF event, i.e. *Conference* and *Labs* meetings, and serve as the chairs of the organizing committee. The Program Chairs are responsible for planning and implementing the technical program of the *Conference*, and therefore their main responsibility is to ensure that the scientific quality of the *Conference* is at the highest possible level. The Labs Chairs are responsible for selecting, planning, and implementing the focused benchmarking activities, and therefore their main responsibility is to ensure that the scientific and technical quality of the *Labs* is at the highest possible level.

Finally, as before, the *Steering Committee* is charge of the overall coordination of CLEF: it assists in the appointment of and approves the General Chairs, the Program Chairs and the Labs Chairs for the annual CLEF edition; it devises improvements to the CLEF structure and organization; it manages the bidding process; and, it looks ahead for future research directions to be pursued.

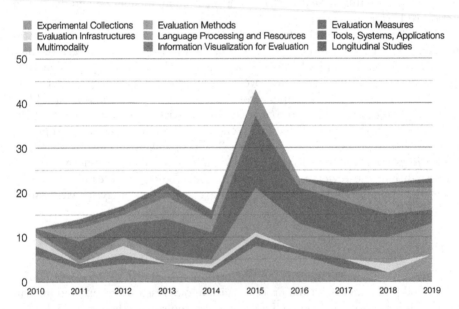

Fig. 2. Topics addressed by the CLEF conference over the years and number of submissions for each topic.

4   The Conference

Figure 2 gives an overview of the topics addressed by the CLEF conference over the years, together with the number of submissions for each topic. Figure 2 clearly shows there is a constant stream of papers in the two core areas of CLEF, namely *evaluation* – broken down into "Experimental Collections", "Evaluation Methods", "Evaluation Measures", and "Evaluation Infrastructures" – and *multilinguality and multimodality* – broken down into "Language Processing and Resources", "Tools, Systems, Applications", and "Multimodality". Moreover, we also have a third focus on less mainstream topics – broken down into "Information Visualization for Evaluation" and "Longitudinal Studies".

We briefly summarize below these topics with pointers to the main references:

Experimental Collections explored different issues concerning experimental collections such as: the creation of collections for Persian and Arabic languages; resource-effective creation of pseudo-test collections for specialised tasks; log-based experimental collections; collections for specific domains, e.g. question answering, plagiarism detection, social image tagging; gamification for relevance judgments; early risk detection, such as depression prediction; collections of query features; social media cross-domain corpora [37, 44, 45, 145, 147, 155, 186, 192, 222, 254, 275, 290, 298, 312, 377, 420, 461, 472];

Evaluation Methods studied core problems related to evaluation methodologies and proposed new methods, such as: the reliability of relevance assessments; living labs for product search tasks; evaluation of information extraction and entity profiles; semantic-oriented evaluation of machine translation and summarization; search snippet evaluation and query simulators; news recommendation; teaching; study of long tails in relevance judgments; crowdsourcing; definition of transactional tasks; component-based evaluation; methodologies for authorship verification; accounting for bias; evaluation of user models; creation of ground-truth in text classification and question answering; impact of gold standards on evaluation [31, 34, 43, 91, 118, 133, 176, 191, 218, 221, 236, 266, 295, 297, 328–330, 399, 416, 418, 419, 426, 471, 480, 487, 490];

Evaluation Measures dealt with the analysis of the features of the evaluation measures and the proposal of new measures such as: formal properties of measures for document filtering; robustness of metrics for patent retrieval; problems with ties in evaluation measures; effort-based measures and measures for speech retrieval; extension of measures to graded relevance; click models; text interestingness and diversity; measures for real-life categorisation and hierarchical clustering [19, 22, 32, 66, 122, 146, 171, 225, 280, 300, 331];

Evaluation Infrastructures investigated how to design and develop shared infrastructures to support different aspects of IR evaluation such as: automating component-based evaluation; managing and providing access to the experimental outcomes and the related literature; using cloud-base approaches to offer evaluation services in specialised domains; developing proper ontologies to describe the experimental results; and exploiting map-reduce techniques for effective IR evaluation; frameworks for question-answering; tools for replicability and reproducibility [7, 39, 110, 179, 180, 185, 269];

Language Processing and Resources continued the CLEF interest in multilinguality by dealing with tools, algorithm, and resources for multiple languages such as: lemmatizers, decompounders and normalizers for underrepresented resources using statistical approaches; statistical stemmers; named entity extraction, linking and clustering in cross-lingual settings; exploitation of multiple translation resources; language-independent generation of document snippets; language variety identification; gender identification; text alignment; Web genre identification; sentiment analysis and opinion mining; personality and author profiling; mixed-code script analyzers; text clustering; language and terminology analysis, also for query suggestion; microblog contextualization; early depression detection; personality recognition; stance detection in social media; readability; fact checking [1, 25, 33, 50, 52, 65, 74, 79, 89, 90, 93, 95, 96, 141, 149, 153, 217, 248, 253, 257, 268, 270, 274, 294, 327, 336, 391, 394, 395, 408, 410, 412, 415, 427, 440, 449, 450, 455, 477, 482, 491];

Tools, Systems, and Applications covered the design and development of various kinds of algorithms, systems, and applications focused on multilinguality and specialised domains such as: semantic discovery of resources in cloud-based systems; Arabic question answering; cross-language similarity search using thesauri; automatic annotation of bibliographic references; exploitation of visual context in multimedia translation; sub-topic mining in Web documents and query interpretation; exploiting relevance feedback for building tag-clouds in image search; query expansion for image retrieval; transcript-based video retrieval; *Peer-To-Peer (P2P)* information retrieval; event detection in microblogs; medical information retrieval; citation for scientific publication; news recommendation; image decomposition and captioning; ranking products in e-commerce; conversational search; mathematical retrieval; systematic reviews; data fusion [2, 3, 11–13, 29, 38, 47, 51, 76, 88, 92, 98, 104, 114, 116, 119, 135, 148, 150, 156, 157, 164, 170, 173, 177, 183, 197, 229, 235, 240, 245, 247, 255, 256, 263, 264, 267, 273, 292, 293, 296, 302, 323, 382, 396, 398, 402, 411, 422, 425, 428, 429, 432, 446, 448, 475, 476, 481, 483–485, 487, 489];

Multimodality explored multimodality in the sense described in Sect. 3 above, i.e. the aggregation and integration of information in multiple languages, media, and coming from different domains, such as: semantic annotation and question answering in the biomedical domain; selecting success criteria in an academic library catalogue; finding similar content in different scenarios on the Web; interactive information retrieval and formative evaluation for medical professionals; microblog summarization, disambiguation and expansion; multimodal music tagging; multi-faceted IR in multimodal domains; ranking in faceted search; domain adaptation; cross-domain vertical search; prediction of venues in social media; query expansion for speech retrieval; neural networks for medical image classification; vocal assistant-mediated search; lifelogging; voice question answering [21, 46, 63, 64, 78, 80, 82, 100, 111, 174, 175, 178, 184, 211, 219, 226, 231, 232, 241, 258, 262, 271, 279, 288, 324, 325, 406, 424, 434, 437, 438, 447, 488];

Information Visualization for Evaluation opened up a brand new area concerned with exploiting information visualization and visual analytics techniques not only for presenting the results of a search system but also for improving interaction with and exploration of experimental outcomes such as exploiting visual analytics for failure analysis; comparing the relative performances of IR systems; and visualization for sentiment analysis; visualization for patterns; data analytics and visualization for system settings [24, 99, 105, 252, 409, 465];

Longitudinal Studies conducted various kinds of medium and long term analyses such as: the scholarly impact of evaluation initiatives; lessons learned in running evaluation activities and in specific domains; performance trends over the years for multilingual information access; and, component-level analysis across different system configurations [112, 113, 123, 132, 291, 316, 456, 459, 479].

5 Tracks and Labs

Figure 3 provides an overview of the tracks and labs offered by CLEF over the years; these are briefly summarized below together with some pointers to relevant literature.

Multilingual Text Retrieval (Ad-hoc, 2000–2009) focused on multilingual information retrieval on news corpora, offering monolingual, bilingual and multilingual tasks, and developed a huge collection in 14 European languages [4, 5, 56–60, 106–108, 128];

Domain Specific Cross-Language IR (DS, 2000–2008) dealt with multilingual information retrieval on structured scientific data from the social sciences domain [57–59, 237–239, 369, 370, 439];

Interactive Cross-Language IR (iCLEF, 2001–2006, 2008–2009) explored different aspects of interactive information retrieval on multilingual and multimedia collections, also using gamification techniques [165–169, 223, 320, 321];

Spoken Document/Speech Retrieval (CLEF SR, 2002–2007) investigated speech retrieval and spoken document retrieval in a monolingual and bilingual setting on automatic speech recognition transcripts [120, 121, 208, 322, 335, 478];

Question Answering (QA@CLEF, 2003–2015) examined several aspects of question answering in a multilingual setting on document collections ranging from news, legal documents, medical documents, linked data [81, 140, 154, 281–283, 299, 337–341, 343, 344, 401, 414, 462–464];

Multimedia Retrieval (ImageCLEF, 2003–2019) studied the cross-language annotation and retrieval of images to support the advancement of the field of visual media analysis, indexing, classification, and retrieval [28, 72, 73, 83–86, 101–103, 158, 159, 172, 194–196, 212, 265, 289, 304, 305, 307–309, 311, 317–319, 381, 392, 393, 451, 453, 457, 458, 460, 466–468, 486];

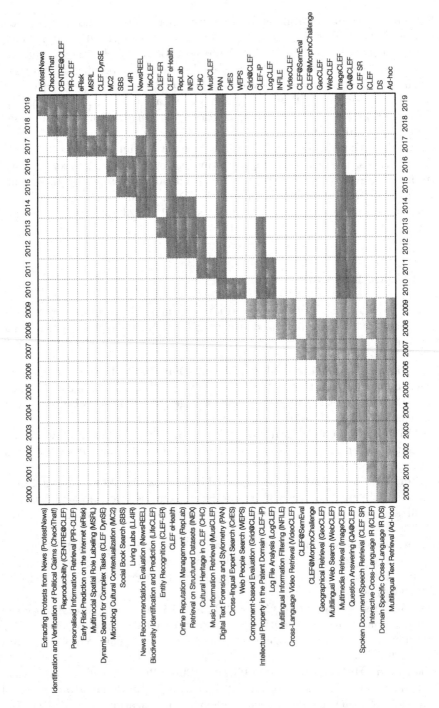

Fig. 3. Labs offered by CLEF over the years (CLEF "Classic" period in green; the CLEF Initiative period in blue). (Color figure online)

Multilingual Web Search (WebCLEF, 2005–2008) addressed multilingual Web search, exploring different faces of navigational queries and known-item search [35,198,199,430];

Geographical Retrieval (GeoCLEF, 2005–2008) evaluated cross-language *Geografic Information Retrieval (GIR)* against search tasks involving both spatial and multilingual aspects [151,152,285,287];

CLEF@SemEval (2007) explored the impact of *Word Sense Disambiguation (WSD)* on multilingual information retrieval [6]; it continued as a sub-task of the Ad Hoc lab in 2008 and 2009;

CLEF@MorphoChallenge (2007–2009) assessed unsupervised morpheme analysis algorithms using information retrieval experiments with the goal of designing statistical machine learning algorithms that discover which morphemes make up words [249–251];

Cross-Language Video Retrieval (VideoCLEF, 2008–2009) aimed at developing and evaluating tasks related to the analysis of and access to multilingual and multimedia content with a special focus on video retrieval [260, 261]; it went on to become the *MediaEval Benchmarking Initiative for Multimedia Evaluation*[7] successful series, dedicated to evaluating new algorithms for multimedia access and retrieval;

Multilingual Information Filtering (INFILE, 2008–2009) experimented with cross-language adaptive filtering systems on news corpora [48,49];

Log File Analysis (LogCLEF, 2009–2011) investigated the analysis and classification of queries in order to understand search behavior in multilingual contexts and ultimately to improve search systems by offering openly-accessible query logs from search engines and digital libraries [109,284,286];

Intellectual Property in the Patent Domain (CLEF-IP, 2009–2013) focused on various aspects of patent search and intellectual property search in a multilingual set using the MAREC collection of patents, gathered from the European Patent Office [375,378–380,400];

Component-based Evaluation (Grid@CLEF, 2009) piloted component-based evaluation by allowing participants to exchange the intermediate state of their systems in order to asynchronously compose components coming from different systems and experiment with a larger grid of possibilities [126];

Web People Search (WEPS, 2010) focused on person name ambiguity and person attribute extraction on Web pages and on online reputation management for organizations [17,30]; the activity continued in the RepLab lab;

Cross-lingual Expert Search (CriES, 2010) was run as a brainstorming workshop and addressed the problem of multi-lingual expert search in social media environments [433];

Digital Text Forensics and Stylometry (PAN, 2010–2019) studied plagiarism, authorship attribution, social software misuse, different types of profiling [20,26,97,163,193,210,383–386,388–390,404,435,436];

Music Information Retrieval (MusiCLEF, 2011) was run as a brainstorming workshop to aid the development of novel methodologies for both content-

---

[7] http://www.multimediaeval.org/.

based and contextual-based (e.g. tags, comments, reviews, etc.) access and retrieval of music [326]; this activity has continued as part of MediaEval;

Cultural Heritage in CLEF (CHiC, 2011–2013) promoted systematic and large-scale evaluation of digital libraries and, more in general, cultural heritage information access systems, using the huge Europeana dataset, aggregating information from libraries, museums, and archives [144, 371, 372];

Retrieval on Structured Datasets (INEX, 2012–2014) was a stand-alone initiative pioneering structured and XML retrieval from 2002[8]; it joined forces with CLEF in 2012 to further promote the evaluation of focused retrieval by providing large test collections of structured documents [40, 41, 77, 244, 413, 454, 474];

Online Reputation Management (RepLab, 2012–2014) has been a competitive evaluation exercise for online reputation management systems; the lab focused on the task of monitoring the reputation of entities (companies, organizations, celebrities) on Twitter [15, 16, 18];

CLEF eHealth (2012–2019) focused on *Natural Language Processing (NLP)* and IR for clinical care, such as annotation of entities in a set of narrative clinical reports or retrieval of web pages based on queries generated when reading the clinical reports [160, 161, 227, 228, 441, 443–445];

Entity Recognition (CLEF-ER, 2013) was a brainstorming workshop on the multilingual annotation of named entities and terminology resource acquisition with a focus on entity recognition in biomedical text, in different languages and on a large scale [397];

Biodiversity Identification and Prediction (LifeCLEF, 2014–2019) aimed at evaluating multimedia analysis and retrieval techniques on biodiversity data for species identification, namely images for plants, audio for birds, and video for fishes [200–202, 204–206];

News Recommendation Evaluation (NewsREEL, 2014–2017) focused on evaluation of news recommender systems in real-time by offering access to the APIs of a commercial system [188, 233, 234, 272]

Living Labs (LL4IR, 2015–2016) dealt with evaluation of ranking systems in a live setting with real users in their natural task environments, acting as a proxy between commercial organizations (live environments) and lab participants (experimental systems) [423];

Social Book Search (SBS, 2015–2016) investigated techniques to support users in complex book search tasks that involve more than just a query and results list [242, 243].

Microblog Cultural Contextualization (MC2, 2016–2017) investigated techniques to support users in complex book search tasks that involve more than just a query and results list [117, 162].

Dynamic Search for Complex Tasks (CLEF DynSE, 2017–2018) promoted the development of both algorithms which interact dynamically with user (or other algorithms) towards solving a task and of evaluation methodologies to quantify their effectiveness [214, 215].

[8] https://inex.mmci.uni-saarland.de/.

Multimodal Spatial Role Labeling (MSRL, 2017) explored the extraction of spatial information from two information resources that is image and text, which is importa in various applications such as semantic search, question answering, geographical information systems and even in robotics for machine understanding of navigational instructions or instructions for grabbing and manipulating objects [246].

Early Risk Prediction on the Internet (eRisk, 2017–2019) explored the evaluation methodology, effectiveness metrics and practical applications (particularly those related to health and safety) of early risk detection on the Internet [276–278].

Personalised Information Retrieval (PIR-CLEF, 2017–2019) provided a framework for evaluation of *Personalized Information Retrieval (PIR)* by developing a methodology for evaluation PIR which enables repeatable experiments to enable the detailed exploration of personal models and their exploitation in IR [332–334].

Reproducibility (CENTRE@CLEF, 2018–2019) run a joint task across CLEF, NTCIR, and TREC on challenging participants to reproduce best results of the most interesting systems submitted in previous editions of CLEF/NTCIR/TREC and to contribute back to the community the additional components and resources developed to reproduce the results [125,127].

Identification and Verification of Political Claims (CheckThat!, 2018–2019) aimed to foster the development of technology capable of spotting check-worthy claims in English political debates in addition to providing evidence-supported verification of Arabic claims [115,313].

Extracting Protests from News (ProtestNews, 2019) aimed to test and improve state-of-the-art generalizable machine learning and natural language processing methods for text classification and information extraction on English news from multiple countries such as India and China for creating comparative databases of contentious politics events (riots, social movements), i.e. the repertoire of contention that can enable large scale comparative social and political science studies [190].

6   Trends

We present here some data on CLEF; the aim is to attempt an informal assessment of its impact on the research community.

Figure 4 shows the participation in CLEF over the years. A positive growth trend is exhibited, a possible consequence of the capacity of CLEF to renew itself and to attract new communities and expertise in addition to core information retrieval activities. In particular, since 2014, CLEF is no more backed by any direct project funding and runs on a completely voluntary-effort basis, still keeping levels of participation comparable to the previous ones.

Figure 5 shows the number of Labs offered by CLEF over the years. It can be noted how the new mechanism introduced for selecting labs is proving effective in restricting the number of Labs run annually, with an average of about 8 Labs

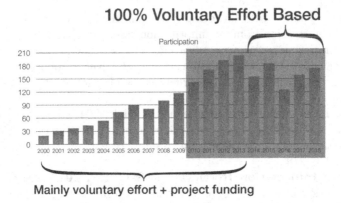

Fig. 4. Participation in CLEF over the years (CLEF "Classic" period un-shaded; CLEF Initiative period shaded).

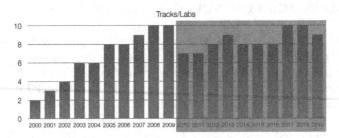

Fig. 5. Number of labs offered by CLEF over the years (CLEF "Classic" period un-shaded; the CLEF Initiative period shaded).

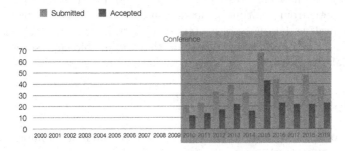

Fig. 6. Number of papers submitted and accepted in the CLEF conference over the years (CLEF "Classic" period un-shaded; the CLEF Initiative period shaded).

per year which allows CLEF to continue successful activities for more than one cycle, typically three years, but also to introduce new activities every year. Also note that we put a cap on a maximum of 10 labs per edition, in order to avoid dispersion into too many activities.

Figure 6 shows the number of papers submitted and accepted in the CLEF Conference over the years. We see that the number of accepted papers has changed slightly over the years, almost stabilizing in the last two years, while the number of submitted papers has grown, allowing us to increase the selectivity and quality of the Conference.

The Conference part of CLEF still needs to be improved and strengthened. The challenge is to define its scope clearly so as to guarantee high quality but to avoid useless overlap with both the major venues in the field, like SIGIR, ECIR and CIKM, and also the fast growing ones, like ICTIR. However, a problem we are still facing is related to communication: CLEF is still mostly associated with its core evaluation activities and therefore, when information is circulated about the conference, it is often viewed as just concerning the evaluation labs even though it actually represents a wider opportunity.

Assessing the impact of an evaluation activity is a very demanding task and it can be done from multiple points of view, e.g. economic impact, industrial impact, scholarly impact, and so on.

In 2010, TREC conducted a deep study on its economic impact [405]. One of goals of CLEF has been to impact not only academia but also industrial research and society in a broader sense. Indeed, IR research can never be considered only at the theoretical level, clearly the overriding factors are the requirements of society at large. An important step in this direction, which began in "CLEF Classic" with ImageCLEF medical retrieval experiments but has certainly been increasingly reinforced in the "CLEF Initiative", is the involvement of real world user communities. Thus, just to cite a few examples, we have seen collaborations with the intellectual property and patent search domain in CLEF-IP, with health specialists in E-Health, with news portals in the NewsREEL project, until the very recent developments for early risk detection in social media as well as fact checking and trustworthiness.

When it comes to the scientific and scholarly impact, we enter the realm of bibliometrics: *TREC Video Retrieval Evaluation (TRECVID)* conducted a study on its scholarly impact [452] and some steps in this direction have been performed for CLEF as well [23,456,459]. However, analysing the impact of evaluation activities on system performances longitudinally over the years is still a research challenge, even if some attempts have been made for both TREC [27,230] and CLEF [132,134].

Such rigorous studies are beyond the scope of the present report, here we concentrate on identifying rough indicators with respect to the maturity and liveliness of the scientific production originated by CLEF. Therefore, as proxy for a more rigorous scholarly impact study, we can look at some statistics gathered from Google Scholar.

The query "CLEF evaluation" returns 53,300 hits which is comparable to the 53,000 hits of the query "TREC evaluation" (run in June 2019), suggesting a lively research community.

Figure 7 shows the trends of the h5-index, i.e. the h-index of the papers published in the last 5 years, and the h5-median, i.e. the the median number of

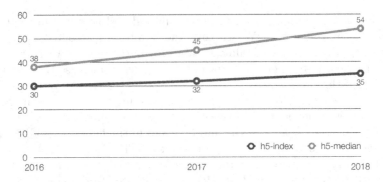

Fig. 7. Google Scholar Metrics for "Cross-Language Evaluation Forum": h5-index (blue) and h5-median (green). (Color figure online)

citations for the articles that make up the h5-index, from 2016 to 2018 taken from Google Scholar Metrics. We can observe a steady increase trend for both indicators, suggesting a positive scholarly impact for the research outcomes of the CLEF community.

As far as maturity is concerned, an indicator might be found in publications critically analysing, systematizing, and digesting the achievements, outcomes and experience; this has been done both for TREC [181,182,469] and CLEF [62,303,353], with a special publication for the 20th anniversary of CLEF, as discussed in the next section.

7 The CLEF Book

To celebrate the 20th anniversary of CLEF, we have prepared a book [130] which accounts for the evolution of CLEF over the years, its contribution to the advancement of research in multilingual and multimodal information access, and its perspectives for the future.

In order to do this, the volume is divided into six parts. The first three chapters in Part I "Experimental Evaluation and CLEF" explain what is intended by experimental evaluation and the underlying theory [470], describing how this has been interpreted in CLEF and in other internationally recognized evaluation initiatives [407]. In addition, the introductory chapter illustrates the activity and results of CLEF over the years in some detail [129]. Part II "Evaluation Infrastructure" presents research architectures and infrastructures that have been developed to manage experimental data [8] and to provide evaluation services in CLEF and elsewhere [306,387].

Parts III, IV and V represent the core of the volume, consisting of a series of chapters presenting some of the most significant evaluation activities in CLEF, ranging from the early multilingual text processing exercises to the later, more sophisticated experiments on multimodal collections in diverse genre and media. In all cases, the focus has not only been on describing "what has been achieved" but most of all on "what has been learnt". Part III "Multilingual and Multi-media Information Retrieval" focuses on multilinguality [417] and the impact of languages on information access [224]; it then addresses multimodality from the perspective of both images [87,310,374,473] and sound and vision [207]. Part IV "Retrieval in New Domains" deals with the medical domain [442], the intellectual property and patent domain [376], the biodiversity domain [203], and the structured data and semantic search domains[10] [213]. Part V "Beyond Retrieval" covers information access tasks other than pure retrieval, namely question answering [342], digital text forensics [403], online reputation management [10], and continuous evaluation and living labs [187].

The final Part VI "Impact and Future Challenges" is dedicated to examining the impact CLEF has had on the research world and to discussing current and future challenges, both academic and industrial. We conduct a proper scholarly impact analysis [259] and we discuss open issues and areas for future development, such as reproducibility and validity [142] and *Visual Analytics (VA)* for experimental evaluation [131]. In particular, the concluding chapter discusses the relevance of IR benchmarking in an industrial setting [220].

8   In Memoriam

This 20th anniversary is not only an opportunity to celebrate the achievements of CLEF but also, sadly, an occasion for remembering friends and colleagues who greatly contributed to what CLEF is today and inspired all of us.

In 2013 Emanuele Pianta, Fondazione Bruno Kessler (FBK) and Centre for the Evaluation of Language and Communication Technologies (CELCT), Trento, Italy, passed away in a car accident close to home. Emanuele, member of the CLEF Steering Committee, greatly contributed to the transition from "CLEF Classic" to the "CLEF Initiative", putting a lot of effort, ideas, and enthusiasm in this new project.

In 2017 Ray Larson, UC Berkeley, USA, passed away following a struggle with cancer. Ray was a dedicated scholar and innovator for CLEF since the early days, bringing in new activities and new research horizons, such as the geographic information retrieval tasks.

Very recently, in 2019, Séamus Lawless, Trinity College Dublin, Ireland, fell during a descent of Mount Everest, after having achieved his dream of reaching the peak. Séamus, member of the CLEF Steering Committee, greatly contributed to CLEF with his research talent and generosity of spirit by opening new research collaborations with the adaptivity and personalisation communities.

9   The CLEF Association

The CLEF Association[9] is an independent no-profit legal entity, established in October 2013 as a result of activity of the PROMISE[10] Network of Excellence which backed CLEF from 2010 to 2013.

---

[9] http://www.clef-initiative.eu/association.
[10] http://www.promise-noe.eu/.

Fig. 8. Pillar activities of the CLEF Association.

The CLEF Association has scientific, cultural and educational objectives and operates in the field of information access systems and their evaluation. Its mission is:

– to promote access to information and use evaluation;
– to foster critical thinking about advancing information access and use from a technical, economic and societal perspective.

Within these two areas of interest, the CLEF Association aims at a better understanding of the use and access to information and how to improve this. The two areas of interest stated in the the above mission translate into the following objectives:

– *clustering stakeholders* with multidisciplinary competences and different needs, including academia, industry, education and other societal institutions;
– *facilitating medium/long-term research* in information access and use and its evaluation;
– increasing, *transferring* and applying *expertise.*

As Fig. 8 shows, the CLEF Association pursues its mission and objectives via four pillar activities:

– *CLEF*: sustains and promotes the popular CLEF evaluation series as well as providing support for its coordination, organisation, and running;
– *Collections and Experimental Data*: fosters the adoption and exploitation of large-scale shared experimental collections, makes them available under appropriate conditions and trusted channels, and shares experimental results and scientific data for comparison with state-of-the-art and for reuse;
– *Infrastructure*: supports the adoption and deployment of software and hardware infrastructures which facilitate the experimental evaluation process, the sharing of experimental collections and results, and interaction with and understanding of experimental data;

– *Education and knowledge transfer*: organises educational events, such as summer schools, and knowledge transfer activities, such as workshops, aimed not only at spreading know-how about information access and use but also at raising awareness and stimulating alternative viewpoints about the technical, economic, and societal implications.

In it initial phase, the CLEF Association has been focused mainly on the first pillar, i.e. ensuring the continuity and self-sustainability of CLEF. CLEF 2014 was the first edition of CLEF not supported by a main European project,but run on a totally volunteer basis with only the support of the CLEF association membership fees paid by its multidisciplinary research community.

Moreover, the CLEF association plans to continue the already initiated activities for promoting and developing shared infrastructures and formats in IR evaluation [431] by also joining forces with relevant stakeholders in the fields as well as stimulating and contributing critical thinking about large-scale evaluation initiative and IR evaluation more in general.

10   Beyond CLEF

As it should have emerged across this paper, we constantly strive for improving CLEF and opening up new perspectives and collaborations.

In this respect, CLEF 2019 will host for the first time an Industry Day, jointly organized with the Swiss Alliance for Data-Intensive Services. The goal is to further open CLEF to a wider, industrial community through demo sessions, panels and special keynotes where the very best and most pertinent work of CLEF participants will be made more publicly accessible.

An aspect of CLEF of which we are particularly proud is the consolidation of a strong community of European researchers in the multidisciplinary context of IR. This year, for the first time, the *European Conference for Information Retrieval (ECIR)* and CLEF have joined forces: ECIR 2019 hosted a session dedicated to CLEF Labs where lab organizers present the major outcomes of their Labs and plans for ongoing activities, followed by a poster session in order to favour discussion during the conference. This is reflected in the ECIR 2019 proceedings, where CLEF Lab activities and results are reported as short papers. Similar plans are already in place for CLEF 2020 and ECIR 2020. The goal is not only to engage the ECIR community in CLEF activities, but also to disseminate the research results achieved during CLEF evaluation cycles at ECIR. This collaboration will of course strengthen European IR research even more. However, this European community should not be seen in isolation. CLEF is part of a global community; we have always maintained close links with our peer initiatives in the Americas and Asia. There is a strong bond connecting TREC, NTCIR, CLEF and FIRE, and a continual, mutually beneficial exchange of ideas, experiences and results.

On a closing note, there have been very recent brainstorming workshops [14, 124] to devise a future research agenda in IR for the coming years and they also touched upon evaluation topics. However, after 20 years of activities, the time may be ripe also for CLEF to organize a brainstorming event to envision the next decade of evaluation challenges.

Support for the Central Coordination of CLEF

CLEF 2000 and 2001 were supported by the European Commission under the Information Society Technologies programme and within the framework of the DELOS Network of Excellence for Digital Libraries (contract no. IST-1999-12262).

CLEF 2002 and 2003 were funded as an independent project (contract no. IST-2000-31002) under the 5th Framework Programme of the European Commission.

CLEF 2004 to 2007 were sponsored by the DELOS Network of Excellence for Digital Libraries (contract no. G038-507618) under the 6th Framework Programme of the European Commission.

Under the 7th Framework Programme of the European Commission, CLEF 2008 and 2009 were supported by TrebleCLEF Coordination Action (contract no. 215231) and CLEF 2010 to 2013 were funded by the PROMISE Network of Excellence (contract no. 258191).

CLEF 2011 to 2014 also received support from the ELIAS network (contract no. 09-RNP-085) of the European Science Foundation (ESF).

Over the years CLEF has also attracted industrial sponsorship: from 2010 onwards, CLEF has received the support of Google, Microsoft, Yandex, Xerox, Celi as well as publishers in the field such as Springer and Now Publishers.

Note that, beyond receiving the support of all the volunteer work of its community, CLEF tracks and labs have often received the support of many other projects and organisations; unfortunately, it is impossible to list them all here.

Acknowledgements. CLEF would not be possible without all the effort, enthusiasm, and passion of its community: lab organizers, lab participants, and attendees are the core and the real success of CLEF.

Many friends and colleagues – too many to mention them all but I sincerely thank all of them – have shared with me this journey through CLEF and their work, passion, ideas, expertise and wisdom have shaped what CLEF is today.

However, all of this would have not even been possible without Carol Peters, who established CLEF back in 2000, made it grown over the years with constant care, and put into CLEF her secret ingredient which makes it so special: a very friendly environment where everybody feels to be welcome and comfortable in sharing ideas and contributions. Carol has had the generosity of sharing her experience with me and teaching me a lot about how to run an evaluation initiative and grow a healthy research community: I will never thank her enough for this.

References

1. Abnar, S., Dehghani, M., Shakery, A.: Meta text aligner: text alignment based on predicted plagiarism relation. In: Mothe et al. [301], pp. 193–199
2. Adams, J., Bedrick, S.: Automatic indexing of journal abstracts with latent semantic analysis. In: Mothe et al. [301], pp. 200–208
3. Afzal, Z., Akhondi, S.A., van Haagen, H.H.H.B.M., van Mulligen, E.M., Kors, J.A.: Concept recognition in French biomedical text using automatic translation. In: Fuhr et al. [143], pp. 162–173
4. Agirre, E., Di Nunzio, G.M., Ferro, N., Mandl, T., Peters, C.: CLEF 2008: ad hoc track overview. In: Peters et al. [359], pp. 15–37
5. Agirre, E., Di Nunzio, G.M., Mandl, T., Otegi, A.: CLEF 2009 ad hoc track overview: robust-WSD task. In: Peters et al. [360], pp. 36–49
6. Agirre, E., de Lacalle, O.L., Magnini, B., Otegi, A., Rigau, G., Vossen, P.: SemEval-2007 task 01: evaluating WSD on cross-language information retrieval. In: Peters et al. [366], pp. 908–917
7. Agosti, M., Di Buccio, E., Ferro, N., Masiero, I., Peruzzo, S., Silvello, G.: DIREC-Tions: design and specification of an IR evaluation infrastructure. In: Catarci et al. [75], pp. 88–99
8. Agosti, M., Di Nunzio, G.M., Ferro, N., Silvello, G.: An innovative approach to data management and curation of experimental data generated through IR test collections. In: Ferro and Peters [130]
9. Agosti, M., Ferro, N., Peters, C., de Rijke, M., Smeaton, A. (eds.): CLEF 2010. LNCS, vol. 6360. Springer, Heidelberg (2010). https://doi.org/10.1007/978-3-642-15998-5
10. Carrillo-de Albornoz, J., Gonzalo, J., Amigó, E.: RepLab: an evaluation campaign for online monitoring systems. In: Ferro and Peters [130]
11. Alfalahi, A., Eriksson, G., Sneiders, E.: Shadow answers as an intermediary in email answer retrieval. In: Mothe et al. [301], pp. 209–214
12. Alharbi, A., Stevenson, M.: Improving ranking for systematic reviews using query adaptation. In: Crestani et al. [94]
13. Alkhawaldeh, R.S., Jose, J.M.: Experimental study on semi-structured peer-to-peer information retrieval network. In: Mothe et al. [301], pp. 3–14
14. Allan, J., et al.: Research frontiers in information retrieval - report from the third strategic workshop on information retrieval in Lorne (SWIRL 2018). In: SIGIR Forum, vol. 52, no. 1, pp. 34–90 (2018)
15. Amigó, E., et al.: Overview of RepLab 2013: evaluating online reputation monitoring systems. In: Forner et al. [138], pp. 333–352
16. Amigó, E., et al.: Overview of RepLab 2014: author profiling and reputation dimensions for online reputation management. In: Kanoulas et al. [216], pp. 307–322
17. Amigó, E., Artiles, J., Gonzalo, J., Spina, D., Liu, B., Corujo, A.: WePS3 evaluation campaign: overview of the on-line reputation management task. In: Braschler et al. [61]
18. Amigó, E., Corujo, A., Gonzalo, J., Meij, E., de Rijke, M.: Overview of RepLab 2012: evaluating online reputation management systems. In: Forner et al. [137]
19. Amigó, E., Gonzalo, J., Verdejo, M.F.: A comparison of evaluation metrics for document filtering. In: Forner et al. [136], pp. 38–49
20. Anderka, M., Stein, B.: Overview of the 1st international competition on quality flaw prediction in Wikipedia. In: Forner et al. [137]

21. Andrearczyk, V., Müller, H.: Deep multimodal classification of image types in biomedical journal figures. In: Bellot et al. [42], pp. 3–14

22. Angelini, M., et al.: Cumulated relative position: a metric for ranking evaluation. In: Catarci et al. [75], pp. 112–123

23. Angelini, M., et al.: Measuring and analyzing the scholarly impact of experimental evaluation initiatives. In: Agosti, M., Catarci, T., Esposito, F. (eds.) Proceedings of the 10th Italian Research Conference on Digital Libraries (IRCDL 2014), vol. 38, pp. 133–137. Procedia Computer Science (2014)

24. Angelini, M., Ferro, N., Santucci, G., Silvello, G.: Improving ranking evaluation employing visual analytics. In: Forner et al. [138], pp. 29–40

25. Antunes, H., Lopes, C.: Analyzing the adequacy of readability indicators to a non-English language. In: Crestani et al. [94]

26. Argamon, S., Juola, P.: Overview of the international authorship identification competition at PAN-2011. In: Petras et al. [373]

27. Armstrong, T.G., Moffat, A., Webber, W., Zobel, J.: Improvements that don't add up: ad-hoc retrieval results since 1998. In: Cheung, D.W.L., Song, I.Y., Chu, W.W., Hu, X., Lin, J.J. (eds.) Proceedings of the 18th International Conference on Information and Knowledge Management (CIKM 2009), pp. 601–610. ACM Press, New York (2009)

28. Arni, T., Clough, P., Sanderson, M., Grubinger, M.: Overview of the ImageCLEF-photo 2008 photographic retrieval task. In: Peters et al. [359], pp. 500–511

29. Arora, P., Foster, J., Jones, G.J.F.: Query expansion for sentence retrieval using pseudo relevance feedback and word embedding. In: Jones et al. [209], pp. 97–103

30. Artiles, J., Borthwick, A., Gonzalo, J., Sekine, S., Amigó, E.: WePS-3 evaluation campaign: overview of the web people search clustering and attribute extraction tasks. In: Braschler et al. [61]

31. Azarbonyad, H., Marx, M.: How many labels? Determining the number of labels in multi-label text classification. In: Crestani et al. [94]

32. Azarbonyad, H., Saan, F., Dehghani, D., Marx, M., Kamps, J.: Are topically diverse documents also interesting? In: Mothe et al. [301], pp. 215–221

33. Azarbonyad, H., Shakery, A., Faili, H.: Exploiting multiple translation resources for English-Persian cross language information retrieval. In: Forner et al. [138], pp. 93–99

34. Azzopardi, L., Balog, K.: Towards a living lab for information retrieval research and development - a proposal for a living lab for product search tasks. In: Forner et al. [136], pp. 26–37

35. Balog, K., Azzopardi, L., Kamps, J., de Rijke, M.: Overview of WebCLEF 2006. In: Peters et al. [357], pp. 803–819

36. Balog, K., Cappellato, L., Ferro, N., Macdonald, C. (eds.): CLEF 2016 Working Notes. CEUR Workshop Proceedings (CEUR-WS.org) (2016). ISSN 1613-0073. http://ceur-ws.org/Vol-1609/

37. Baradaran Hashemi, H., Shakery, A., Feili, H.: Creating a Persian-English comparable corpus. In: Agosti et al. [9], pp. 27–39

38. Basile, A., Dwyer, G., Medvedeva, M., Rawee, J., Haagsma, H., Nissim, M.: Simply the best: minimalist system trumps complex models in author profiling. In: Bellot et al. [42], pp. 143–156

39. Baudis, P., Sedivý, J.: Modeling of the question answering task in the YodaQA system. In: Mothe et al. [301], pp. 222–228

40. Bellot, P., et al.: Overview of INEX 2014. In: Kanoulas et al. [216], pp. 212–228

41. Bellot, P., et al.: Overview of INEX 2013. In: Forner et al. [138], pp. 269–281

42. Bellot, P., et al. (eds.): CLEF 2018. LNCS, vol. 11018. Springer, Cham (2018). https://doi.org/10.1007/978-3-319-98932-7
43. Beloborodov, A., Braslavski, P., Driker, M.: Towards automatic evaluation of health-related CQA data. In: Kanoulas et al. [216], pp. 7–18
44. Bensalem, I., Rosso, P., Chikhi, S.: A new corpus for the evaluation of Arabic intrinsic plagiarism detection. In: Forner et al. [138], pp. 53–58
45. Berendsen, R., Tsagkias, M., de Rijke, M., Meij, E.: Generating pseudo test collections for learning to rank scientific articles. In: Catarci et al. [75], pp. 42–53
46. Berlanga Llavori, R., Jimeno-Yepes, A., Pérez Catalán, M., Rebholz-Schuhmann, D.: Context-dependent semantic annotation in cross-lingual biomedical resources. In: Forner et al. [138], pp. 120–123
47. Berlanga Llavori, R., Pérez Catalán, M., Museros Cabedo, L., Forcada, R.: Semantic discovery of resources in cloud-based PACS/RIS systems. In: Forner et al. [138], pp. 167–178
48. Besançon, R., Chaudiron, S., Mostefa, D., Hamon, O., Timimi, I., Choukri, K.: Overview of CLEF 2008 INFILE pilot track. In: Peters et al. [359], pp. 939–946
49. Besançon, R., Chaudiron, S., Mostefa, D., Timimi, I., Choukri, K., Laïb, M.: Information filtering evaluation: overview of CLEF 2009 INFILE track. In: Peters et al. [360], pp. 342–353
50. Bhaskar, P., Bandyopadhyay, S.: Language independent query focused snippet generation. In: Catarci et al. [75], pp. 138–140
51. Blinov, V., Mishchenko, K., Bolotova, V., Braslavski, P.: A pinch of humor for short-text conversation: an information retrieval approach. In: Jones et al. [209], pp. 3–15
52. Bordea, G., Thiessard, F., Hamon, T., Mougin, F.: Automatic query selection for acquisition and discovery of food-drug interactions. In: Bellot et al. [42], pp. 115–120
53. Borri, F., Nardi, A., Peters, C., Ferro, N. (eds.): CLEF 2008 Working Notes. CEUR Workshop Proceedings (CEUR-WS.org) (2008). ISSN 1613-0073. http://ceur-ws.org/Vol-1174/
54. Borri, F., Nardi, A., Peters, C., Ferro, N. (eds.): CLEF 2009 Working Notes. CEUR Workshop Proceedings (CEUR-WS.org) (2009). ISSN 1613-0073. http://ceur-ws.org/Vol-1175/
55. Borri, F., Peters, C., Ferro, N. (eds.): CLEF 2004 Working Notes. CEUR Workshop Proceedings (CEUR-WS.org) (2004). ISSN 1613-0073. http://ceur-ws.org/Vol-1170/
56. Braschler, M.: CLEF 2000 - overview of results. In: Peters [345], pp. 89–101
57. Braschler, M.: CLEF 2001 - overview of results. In: Peters et al. [354], pp. 9–26
58. Braschler, M.: CLEF 2002 - overview of results. In: Peters et al. [355], pp. 9–27
59. Braschler, M.: CLEF 2003 - overview of results. In: Peters et al. [356], pp. 44–63
60. Braschler, M., Di Nunzio, G.M., Ferro, N., Peters, C.: CLEF 2004: ad hoc track overview and results analysis. In: Peters et al. [358], pp. 10–26
61. Braschler, M., Harman, D.K., Pianta, E., Ferro, N. (eds.): CLEF 2010 Working Notes. CEUR Workshop Proceedings (CEUR-WS.org) (2010). ISSN 1613-0073. http://ceur-ws.org/Vol-1176/
62. Braschler, M., Peters, C.: Cross-language evaluation forum: objectives, results, achievements. Inf. Retrieval **7**(1–2), 7–31 (2004)
63. Braslavski, P., Verberne, S., Talipov, R.: Show me how to tie a tie: evaluation of cross-lingual video retrieval. In: Fuhr et al. [143], pp. 3–15
64. Budíková, P., Batko, M., Botorek, J., Zezula, P.: Search-based image annotation: extracting semantics from similar images. In: Mothe et al. [301], pp. 327–339

65. Buraya, K., Farseev, A., Filchenkov, A.: Multi-view personality profiling based on longitudinal data. In: Bellot et al. [42], pp. 15–27

66. Cabanac, G., Hubert, G., Boughanem, M., Chrisment, C.: Tie-breaking bias: effect of an uncontrolled parameter on information retrieval evaluation. In: Agosti et al. [9], pp. 112–123

67. Cappellato, L., Ferro, N., Goeuriot, L., Mandl, T. (eds.): CLEF 2017 Working Notes. CEUR Workshop Proceedings (CEUR-WS.org) (2017). ISSN 1613-0073. http://ceur-ws.org/Vol-1866/

68. Cappellato, L., Ferro, N., Halvey, M., Kraaij, W. (eds.): CLEF 2014 Working Notes. CEUR Workshop Proceedings (CEUR-WS.org) (2014). ISSN 1613-0073. http://ceur-ws.org/Vol-1180/

69. Cappellato, L., Ferro, N., Jones, G.J.F., SanJuan, E. (eds.): CLEF 2015 Working Notes. CEUR Workshop Proceedings (CEUR-WS.org) (2015). ISSN 1613-0073. http://ceur-ws.org/Vol-1391/

70. Cappellato, L., Ferro, N., Losada, D.E., Müller, H. (eds.): CLEF 2019 Working Notes. CEUR Workshop Proceedings (CEUR-WS.org) (2019). ISSN 1613-0073. http://ceur-ws.org/Vol-2380/

71. Cappellato, L., Ferro, N., Nie, J.Y., Soulier, L. (eds.): CLEF 2018 Working Notes. CEUR Workshop Proceedings (CEUR-WS.org) (2018). ISSN 1613-0073. http://ceur-ws.org/Vol-2125/

72. Caputo, B., et al.: ImageCLEF 2014: overview and analysis of the results. In: Kanoulas et al. [216], pp. 192–211

73. Caputo, B., et al.: ImageCLEF 2013: the vision, the data and the open challenges. In: Forner et al. [138], pp. 250–268

74. Cassidy, T., Ji, H., Deng, H., Zheng, J., Han, J.: Analysis and refinement of cross-lingual entity linking. In: Catarci et al. [75], pp. 1–12

75. Catarci, T., Forner, P., Hiemstra, D., Peñas, A., Santucci, G. (eds.): CLEF 2012. LNCS, vol. 7488. Springer, Heidelberg (2012). https://doi.org/10.1007/978-3-642-33247-0

76. Chaa, M., Nouali, O., Bellot, P.: Combining tags and reviews to improve social book search performance. In: Bellot et al. [42], pp. 64–75

77. Chappell, T., Geva, S.: Overview of the INEX 2012 relevance feedback track. In: Forner et al. [137]

78. Chidlovskii, B., Csurka, G., Clinchant, S.: Evaluating stacked marginalised denoising autoencoders within domain adaptation methods. In: Mothe et al. [301], pp. 15–27

79. Chikka, V.R., Mariyasagayam, N., Niwa, Y., Karlapalem, K.: Information extraction from clinical documents: towards disease/disorder template filling. In: Mothe et al. [301], pp. 389–401

80. Chuklin, A., Severyn, A., Trippas, J., Alfonseca, E., Silen, H., Spina, D.: Using audio transformations to improve comprehension in voice question answering. In: Crestani et al. [94]

81. Cimiano, P., Lopez, V., Unger, C., Cabrio, E., Ngonga Ngomo, A.C., Walter, S.: Multilingual question answering over linked data (QALD-3): lab overview. In: Forner et al. [138], pp. 321–332

82. Clough, P., Goodale, P.: Selecting success criteria: experiences with an academic library catalogue. In: Forner et al. [138], pp. 59–70

83. Clough, P., Grubinger, M., Deselaers, T., Hanbury, A., Müller, H.: Overview of the ImageCLEF 2006 photographic retrieval and object annotation tasks. In: Peters et al. [357], pp. 223–256

84. Clough, P., et al.: The CLEF 2005 cross-language image retrieval track. In: Peters et al. [365], pp. 535–557

85. Clough, P., Müller, H., Sanderson, M.: The CLEF 2004 cross-language image retrieval track. In: Peters et al. [358], pp. 597–613

86. Clough, P., Sanderson, M.: The CLEF 2003 cross language image retrieval track. In: Peters et al. [356], pp. 581–593

87. Clough, P., Tsikrika, T.: Multi-lingual retrieval of pictures in ImageCLEF. In: Ferro and Peters [130]

88. Clough, P., Willett, P., Lim, J.: Unfair means: use cases beyond plagiarism. In: Mothe et al. [301], pp. 229–234

89. Coello-Guilarte, D.L., Ortega Mendoza, R.M., Villaseñor-Pineda, L., Montes-y Gómez, M.: Cross-lingual depression detection in Twitter using bilingual word-level alignment. In: Crestani et al. [94]

90. Collovini, S., Marcelo de Bairros Filho, P., Vieira, R.: Analysing the role of representation choices in portuguese relation extraction. In: Mothe et al. [301], pp. 105–116

91. Conlan, O., Fraser, K., Kelly, L., Yousuf, B.: A user modeling shared challenge proposal. In: Crestani et al. [94]

92. Corezola Pereira, R., Pereira Moreira, V., Galante, R.: A new approach for cross-language plagiarism analysis. In: Agosti et al. [9], pp. 15–26

93. Cossu, J.V., Ferreira, E., Janod, K., Gaillard, J., El-Bèze, M.: NLP-based classifiers to generalize expert assessments in e-reputation. In: Mothe et al. [301], pp. 340–351

94. Crestani, F., et al. (eds.): CLEF 2019. LNCS, vol. 11696. Springer, Heidelberg (2019)

95. Custódio, J., Paraboni, I.: An ensemble approach to cross-domain authorship attribution. In: Crestani et al. [94]

96. Dadashkarimi, J., Esfahani, H.N., Faili, H., Shakery, A.: SS4MCT: a statistical stemmer for morphologically complex texts. In: Fuhr et al. [143], pp. 201–207

97. Daelemans, W., et al.: Overview of PAN 2019: bots and gender profiling, celebrity profiling, cross-domain authorship attribution and style change detection. In: Crestani et al. [94]

98. Dehghani, M., Azarbonyad, H., Kamps, J., Marx, M.: Two-way parsimonious classification models for evolving hierarchies. In: Fuhr et al. [143], pp. 69–82

99. Déjean, S., Mothe, J., Ullah, M.Z.: Studying the variability of system setting effectiveness by data analytics and visualization. In: Crestani et al. [94]

100. Deneu, B., Servajean, M., Botella, C., Joly, A.: Evaluation of deep species distribution models using environment and co-occurrences. In: Crestani et al. [94]

101. Deselaers, T., Deserno, T.M.: Medical image annotation in ImageCLEF 2008. In: Peters et al. [359], pp. 523–530

102. Deselaers, T., Hanbury, A.: The visual concept detection task in ImageCLEF 2008. In: Peters et al. [359], pp. 531–538

103. Deselaers, T., et al.: Overview of the ImageCLEF 2007 object retrieval task. In: Peters et al. [366], pp. 445–471

104. Devezas, J., Nunes, S.: Index-based semantic tagging for efficient query interpretation. In: Fuhr et al. [143], pp. 208–213

105. Di Buccio, E., Dussin, M., Ferro, N., Masiero, I., Santucci, G., Tino, G.: To Re-rank or to re-query: can visual analytics solve this dilemma? In: Forner et al. [136], pp. 119–130

106. Di Nunzio, G.M., Ferro, N., Jones, G.J.F., Peters, C.: CLEF 2005: ad hoc track overview. In: Peters et al. [365], pp. 11–36

107. Di Nunzio, G.M., Ferro, N., Mandl, T., Peters, C.: CLEF 2006: ad hoc track overview. In: Peters et al. [357], pp. 21–34

108. Di Nunzio, G.M., Ferro, N., Mandl, T., Peters, C.: CLEF 2007: ad hoc track overview. In: Peters et al. [366], pp. 13–32

109. Di Nunzio, G.M., Leveling, J., Mandl, T.: LogCLEF 2011 multilingual log file analysis: language identification, query classification, and success of a query. In: Petras et al. [373]

110. Di Nunzio, G.M., Vezzani, F.: Using R markdown for replicable experiments in evidence based medicine. In: Bellot et al. [42], pp. 28–39

111. Dicente Cid, Y., Batmanghelich, K., Müller, H.: Textured graph-based model of the lungs: application on tuberculosis type classification and multi-drug resistance detection. In: Bellot et al. [42], pp. 157–168

112. Dietz, F., Petras, V.: A component-level analysis of an academic search test collection. Part I: system and collection configurations. In: Jones et al. [209], pp. 16–28

113. Dietz, F., Petras, V.: A component-level analysis of an academic search test collection.- Part II: query analysis. In: Jones et al. [209], pp. 29–42

114. Domann, J., Lommatzsch, A.: A highly available real-time news recommender based on apache spark. In: Jones et al. [209], pp. 161–172

115. Elsayed, T., et al.: Overview of the CLEF-2019 CheckThat!: automatic identification and verification of claims. In: Crestani et al. [94]

116. Ermakova, K.: A method for short message contextualization: experiments at CLEF/INEX. In: Mothe et al. [301], pp. 352–363

117. Ermakova, L., Goeuriot, L., Mothe, J., Mulhem, P., Nie, J.Y., SanJuan, E.: CLEF 2017 microblog cultural contextualization lab overview. In: Jones et al. [209], pp. 304–314

118. Esuli, F., Sebastiani, F.: Evaluating information extraction. In: Agosti et al. [9], pp. 100–111

119. Ezzeldin, A.M., Kholief, M.H., El-Sonbaty, Y.: ALQASIM: Arabic language question answer selection in machines. In: Forner et al. [138], pp. 100–103

120. Federico, M., Bertoldi, N., Levow, G.A., Jones, G.J.F.: CLEF 2004 cross-language spoken document retrieval track. In: Peters et al. [358], pp. 816–820

121. Federico, M., Jones, G.J.F.: The CLEF 2003 cross-language spoken document retrieval track. In: Peters et al. [356], p. 646

122. Ferrante, M., Ferro, N., Maistro, M.: Rethinking how to extend average precision to graded relevance. In: Kanoulas et al. [216], pp. 19–30

123. Ferro, N.: What happened in CLEF… for a while? In: Crestani et al. [94]

124. Ferro, N., et al.: Manifesto from Dagstuhl Perspectives Workshop 17442 - From Evaluating to Forecasting Performance: How to Turn Information Retrieval, Natural Language Processing and Recommender Systems into Predictive Sciences, vol. 7, no. 1, pp. 96–139. Dagstuhl Manifestos, Schloss Dagstuhl-Leibniz-Zentrum für Informatik, Germany (2018)

125. Ferro, N., Fuhr, N., Maistro, M., Sakai, T., Soboroff, I.: CENTRE@CLEF 2019. In: Azzopardi, L., Stein, B., Fuhr, N., Mayr, P., Hauff, C., Hiemstra, D. (eds.) ECIR 2019, Part II. LNCS, vol. 11438, pp. 283–290. Springer, Cham (2019). https://doi.org/10.1007/978-3-030-15719-7_38

126. Ferro, N., Harman, D.: CLEF 2009: Grid@CLEF pilot track overview. In: Peters et al. [360], pp. 552–565

127. Ferro, N., Maistro, M., Sakai, T., Soboroff, I.: CENTRE@CLEF2018: overview of the replicability task. In: Cappellato et al. [71]

128. Ferro, N., Peters, C.: CLEF 2009 ad hoc track overview: TEL & Persian tasks. In: Peters et al. [360], pp. 13–35
129. Ferro, N., Peters, C.: From multilingual to multimodal: the evolution of CLEF over two decades. In: Information Retrieval Evaluation in a Changing World - Lessons Learned from 20 Years of CLEF [130]
130. Ferro, N., Peters, C.: Information Retrieval Evaluation in a Changing World - Lessons Learned from 20 Years of CLEF. The Information Retrieval Series, vol. 41. Springer, Cham (2019). https://doi.org/10.1007/978-3-030-22948-1
131. Ferro, N., Santucci, G.: Visual analytics and IR experimental evaluation. In: Ferro and Peters [130]
132. Ferro, N., Silvello, G.: CLEF 15th birthday: what can we learn from ad hoc retrieval? In: Kanoulas et al. [216], pp. 31–43
133. Ferro, N., Silvello, G.: The CLEF monolingual grid of points. In: Fuhr et al. [143], pp. 16–27
134. Ferro, N., Silvello, G.: 3.5K runs, 5K topics, 3M assessments and 70M measures: what trends in 10 years of Adhoc-ish CLEF? Inf. Process. Manag. **53**(1), 175–202 (2017)
135. Fontanella, S., Rodríguez-Sánchez, A.J., Piater, J., Szedmak, S.: Kronecker decomposition for image classification. In: Fuhr et al. [143], pp. 137–149
136. Forner, P., Gonzalo, J., Kekäläinen, J., Lalmas, M., de Rijke, M. (eds.): CLEF 2011. LNCS, vol. 6941. Springer, Heidelberg (2011). https://doi.org/10.1007/978-3-642-23708-9
137. Forner, P., Karlgren, J., Womser-Hacker, C., Ferro, N. (eds.): CLEF 2012 Working Notes. CEUR Workshop Proceedings (CEUR-WS.org) (2012). ISSN 1613-0073. http://ceur-ws.org/Vol-1178/
138. Forner, P., Müller, H., Paredes, R., Rosso, P., Stein, B. (eds.): CLEF 2013. LNCS, vol. 8138. Springer, Heidelberg (2013). https://doi.org/10.1007/978-3-642-40802-1
139. Forner, P., Navigli, R., Tufis, D., Ferro, N. (eds.): CLEF 2013 Working Notes. CEUR Workshop Proceedings (CEUR-WS.org) (2013). ISSN 1613-0073. http://ceur-ws.org/Vol-1179/
140. Forner, P., et al.: Overview of the Clef 2008 Multilingual Question Answering Track. In: Peters et al. [359], pp. 262–295
141. Franco-Salvador, M., Rangel Pardo, F.M., Rosso, P., Taulé, M., Martí, M.A.: Language variety identification using distributed representations of words and documents. In: Mothe et al. [301], pp. 28–40
142. Fuhr, N.: Reproducibility and validity in CLEF. In: Ferro and Peters [130]
143. Fuhr, N., et al. (eds.): CLEF 2016. LNCS, vol. 9822. Springer, Cham (2016). https://doi.org/10.1007/978-3-319-44564-9
144. Gäde, M., Ferro, N., Lestari Paramita, M.: CHiC 2011 - cultural heritage in CLEF: from use cases to evaluation in practice for multilingual information access to cultural heritage. In: Petras et al. [373]
145. Gäde, M., Stiller, J., Petras, V.: Which log for which information? Gathering multilingual data from different log file types. In: Agosti et al. [9], pp. 70–81
146. Galuscáková, P., Pecina, P., Hajic, J.: Penalty functions for evaluation measures of unsegmented speech retrieval. In: Catarci et al. [75], pp. 100–111
147. Ganguly, D., Jones, G.J.F.: A gamified approach to relevance judgement. In: Fuhr et al. [143], pp. 214–220
148. Ganguly, D., Leveling, J., Jones, G.J.F.: Simulation of within-session query variations using a text segmentation approach. In: Forner et al. [136], pp. 89–94

149. Ganguly, D., Leveling, J., Jones, G.J.F.: A case study in decompounding for Bengali information retrieval. In: Forner et al. [138], pp. 108–119

150. Gebremeskel, G.G., de Vries, A.P.: Random performance differences between online recommender system algorithms. In: Fuhr et al. [143], pp. 187–200

151. Gey, F., et al.: GeoCLEF 2006: the CLEF 2006 cross-language geographic information retrieval track overview. In: Peters et al. [357], pp. 852–876

152. Gey, F.C., Larson, R.R., Sanderson, M., Joho, H., Clough, P., Petras, V.: Geo-CLEF: the CLEF 2005 cross-language geographic information retrieval track overview. In: Peters et al. [365], pp. 908–919

153. Ghosh, S., Singhania, P., Singh, S., Rudra, K., Ghosh, S.: Stance detection in web and social media: a comparative study. In: Crestani et al. [94]

154. Giampiccolo, D., et al.: Overview of the CLEF 2007 multilingual question answering track. In: Peters et al. [366], pp. 200–236

155. Gînsca, A.L., Popescu, A., Lupu, M., Iftene, A., Kanellos, I.: Evaluating user image tagging credibility. In: Mothe et al. [301], pp. 41–52

156. Glinos, D.G.: Discovering similar passages within large text documents. In: Kanoulas et al. [216], pp. 98–109

157. Gobeill, J., Gaudinat, A., Ruch, P.: Instance-based learning for tweet monitoring and categorization. In: Mothe et al. [301], pp. 235–240

158. Goëau, H., et al.: The CLEF 2011 plant images classification task. In: Petras et al. [373]

159. Goëau, H., et al.: The ImageCLEF 2012 plant identification task. In: Forner et al. [137]

160. Goeuriot, L., et al.: Overview of the CLEF eHealth evaluation lab 2015. In: Mothe et al. [301], pp. 429–443

161. Goeuriot, L., et al.: CLEF 2017 eHealth evaluation lab overview. In: Jones et al. [209], pp. 291–303

162. Goeuriot, L., Mothe, J., Mulhem, P., Murtagh, F., SanJuan, E.: Overview of the CLEF 2016 cultural micro-blog contextualization workshop. In: Fuhr et al. [143], pp. 371–378

163. Gollub, T., et al.: Recent trends in digital text forensics and its evaluation - plagiarism detection, author identification, and author profiling. In: Forner et al. [138], pp. 282–302

164. Gómez-Adorno, H., Martín-del Campo-Rodríguez, C., Sidorov, G., Alemán, Y., Vilariño, D., Pinto, D.: Hierarchical clustering analysis: the best-performing approach at PAN 2017 author clustering task. In: Bellot et al. [42], pp. 216–223

165. Gonzalo, J., Clough, P., Karlgren, J.: Overview of iCLEF 2008: search log analysis for multilingual image retrieval. In: Peters et al. [359], pp. 227–235

166. Gonzalo, J., Clough, P., Vallin, A.: Overview of the CLEF 2005 interactive track. In: Peters et al. [365], pp. 251–262

167. Gonzalo, J., Oard, D.W.: The CLEF 2002 interactive track. In: Peters et al. [355], pp. 372–382

168. Gonzalo, J., Oard, D.W.: iCLEF 2004 track overview: pilot experiments in interactive cross-language question answering. In: Peters et al. [358], pp. 310–322

169. Gonzalo, J., Peinado, V., Clough, P., Karlgren, J.: Overview of iCLEF 2009: exploring search behaviour in a multilingual folksonomy environment. In: Peters et al. [368], pp. 13–20

170. Goodwin, T., Harabagiu, S.M.: The impact of belief values on the identification of patient cohorts. In: Forner et al. [138], pp. 155–166

171. Grotov, A., Chuklin, A., Markov, I., Stout, L., Xumara, F., de Rijke, M.: A comparative study of click models for web search. In: Mothe et al. [301], pp. 78–90

172. Grubinger, M., Clough, P., Hanbury, A., Müller, H.: Overview of the ImageCLEF-photo 2007 photographic retrieval task. In: Peters et al. [366], pp. 433–444

173. Gupta, P., Barrón-Cedeño, A., Rosso, P.: Cross-language high similarity search using a conceptual thesaurus. In: Catarci et al. [75], pp. 67–75

174. Hagen, M., Glimm, C.: Supporting more-like-this information needs: finding similar web content in different scenarios. In: Kanoulas et al. [216], pp. 50–61

175. Hall, M., Toms, E.: Building a common framework for IIR evaluation. In: Forner et al. [138], pp. 17–28

176. Halvani, O., Graner, L.: Rethinking the evaluation methodology of authorship verification methods. In: Bellot et al. [42], pp. 40–51

177. Hammarström, H.: Automatic annotation of bibliographical references for descriptive language materials. In: Forner et al. [136], pp. 62–73

178. Han Lee, S., Loong Chang, Y., Seng Chan, S., Alexis, J., Bonnet, P., Goëau, H.: Plant classification based on gated recurrent unit. In: Bellot et al. [42], pp. 169–180

179. Hanbury, A., Müller, H.: Automated component-level evaluation: present and future. In: Agosti et al. [9], pp. 124–135

180. Hanbury, A., Müller, H., Langs, G., Weber, M.A., Menze, B.H., Salas Fernandez, T.: Bringing the algorithms to the data: cloud-based benchmarking for medical image analysis. In: Catarci et al. [75], pp. 24–29

181. Harman, D.K.: Information Retrieval Evaluation. Morgan & Claypool Publishers, San Rafael (2011)

182. Harman, D.K., Voorhees, E.M. (eds.): TREC. Experiment and Evaluation in Information Retrieval. MIT Press, Cambridge (2005)

183. Harris, C.G., Xu, T.: The importance of visual context clues in multimedia translation. In: Forner et al. [136], pp. 107–118

184. Hasan, S.A., et al.: Attention-based medical caption generation with image modality classification and clinical concept mapping. In: Bellot et al. [42], pp. 224–230

185. Hiemstra, D., Hauff, C.: MapReduce for information retrieval evaluation: "let's quickly test this on 12 TB of data". In: Agosti et al. [9], pp. 64–69

186. Hoang, T.B.N., Mothe, J., Baillon, M.: TwitCID: a collection of data sets for studies on information diffusion on social networks. In: Crestani et al. [94]

187. Hopfgartner, F., Balog, K., Lommatzsch, A., Kelly, L., Kille, B., Schuth, A., Larson, M.: Continuous evaluation of large-scale information access systems: a case for living labs. In: Ferro and Peters [130]

188. Hopfgartner, F., Kille, B., Lommatzsch, A., Plumbaum, T., Brodt, T., Heintz, T.: Benchmarking news recommendations in a living lab. In: Kanoulas et al. [216], pp. 250–267

189. Hull, D.A., Oard, D.W.: Cross-Language Text and Speech Retrieval - Papers from the AAAI Spring Symposium. Association for the Advancement of Artificial Intelligence (AAAI), Technical report SS-97-05 (1997). http://www.aaai.org/Press/Reports/Symposia/Spring/ss-97-05.php

190. Hürriyetoğlu, A., et al.: Overview of CLEF 2019 lab ProtestNews: extracting protests from news in a cross-context setting. In: Crestani et al. [94]

191. Huurnink, B., Hofmann, K., de Rijke, M., Bron, M.: Validating query simulators: an experiment using commercial searches and purchases. In: Agosti et al. [9], pp. 40–51

192. Imhof, M., Braschler, M.: Are test collections "real"? Mirroring real-world complexity in IR test collections. In: Mothe et al. [301], pp. 241–247

193. Inches, G., Crestani, F.: Overview of the international sexual predator identification competition at PAN-2012. In: Forner et al. [137]

194. Ionescu, B., et al.: ImageCLEF 2019: multimedia retrieval in medicine, lifelogging, security and nature. In: Crestani et al. [94]

195. Ionescu, B., et al.: Overview of ImageCLEF 2017: information extraction from images. In: Jones et al. [209], pp. 315–337

196. Ionescu, B., et al.: Overview of ImageCLEF 2018: challenges, datasets and evaluation. In: Bellot et al. [42], pp. 309–334

197. Jabeur, L.B., Soulier, L., Tamine, L., Mousset, P.: A product feature-based usercentric ranking model for e-commerce search. In: Fuhr et al. [143], pp. 174–186

198. Jijkoun, V., de Rijke, M.: Overview of WebCLEF 2007. In: Peters et al. [366], pp. 725–731

199. Jijkoun, V., de Rijke, M.: Overview of WebCLEF 2008. In: Peters et al. [359], pp. 787–793

200. Joly, A., et al.: Overview of LifeCLEF 2018: a large-scale evaluation of species identification and recommendation algorithms in the era of AI. In: Bellot et al. [42], pp. 247–266

201. Joly, A., et al.: Overview of LifeCLEF 2019: identification of Amazonian plants, south & north American birds, and niche prediction. In: Crestani et al. [94]

202. Joly, A., et al.: LifeCLEF 2017 lab overview: multimedia species identification challenges. In: Jones et al. [209], pp. 255–274

203. Joly, A., et al.: Biodiversity information retrieval through large scale content-based identification: a long-term evaluation. In: Ferro and Peters [130]

204. Joly, A., et al.: LifeCLEF 2014: multimedia life species identification challenges. In: Kanoulas et al. [216], pp. 229–249

205. Joly, A., et al.: LifeCLEF 2015: multimedia life species identification challenges. In: Mothe et al. [301], pp. 462–483

206. Joly, A., et al.: LifeCLEF 2016: multimedia life species identification challenges. In: Fuhr et al. [143], pp. 286–310

207. Jones, G.J.F.: 'Bout sound and vision: CLEF beyond text retrieval tasks. In: Ferro and Peters [130]

208. Jones, G.J.F., Federico, M.: CLEF 2002 cross-language spoken document retrieval pilot track report. In: Peters et al. [355], pp. 446–457

209. Jones, G.J.F., et al. (eds.): CLEF 2017. LNCS, vol. 10456. Springer, Cham (2017). https://doi.org/10.1007/978-3-319-65813-1

210. Juola, P.: An overview of the traditional authorship attribution subtask. In: Forner et al. [137]

211. Jürgens, J., Hansen, P., Womser-Hacker, C.: Going beyond CLEF-IP: the 'Reality' for patent searchers. In: Catarci et al. [75], pp. 30–35

212. Kalpathy-Cramer, J., Müller, H., Bedrick, S., Eggel, I., Garcia Seco de Herrera, A., Tsikrika, T.: Overview of the CLEF 2011 medical image classification and retrieval tasks. In: Petras et al. [373]

213. Kamps, J., Koolen, M., Geva, S., Schenkel, R., SanJuan, E., Bogers, T.: From XML retrieval to semantic search and beyond. In: Ferro and Peters [130]

214. Kanoulas, E., Azzopardi, L.: CLEF 2017 dynamic search evaluation lab overview. In: Jones et al. [209], pp. 361–366

215. Kanoulas, E., Azzopardi, L., Hui Yang, G.: Overview of the CLEF dynamic search evaluation lab 2018. In: Bellot et al. [42], pp. 362–371

216. Kanoulas, E., et al. (eds.): CLEF 2014. LNCS, vol. 8685. Springer, Cham (2014). https://doi.org/10.1007/978-3-319-11382-1
217. Karadzhov, G., Mihaylova, T., Kiprov, Y., Georgiev, G., Koychev, Y., Nakov, P.: The case for being average: a mediocrity approach to style masking and author obfuscation. In: Jones et al. [209], pp. 173–185
218. Karan, M., Snajder, J.: Evaluation of manual query expansion rules on a domain specific FAQ collection. In: Mothe et al. [301], pp. 248–253
219. Karisani, P., Oroumchian, F., Rahgozar, M.: Tweet expansion method for filtering task in Twitter. In: Mothe et al. [301], pp. 55–64
220. Karlgren, J.: Adopting systematic evaluation benchmarks in operational settings. In: Ferro and Peters [130]
221. Karlgren, J.: How lexical gold standards have effects on the usefulness of text analysis tools for digital scholarship. In: Crestani et al. [94]
222. Karlgren, J., et al.: Evaluating learning language representations. In: Mothe et al. [301], pp. 254–260
223. Karlgren, J., Gonzalo, J., Clough, P.: iCLEF 2006 overview: searching the Flickr WWW photo-sharing repository. In: Peters et al. [357], pp. 186–194
224. Karlgren, J., Hedlund, T., Järvelin, K., Keskustalo, H., Kettunen, K.: The challenges of language variation in information access. In: Ferro and Peters [130]
225. Karlsson, V., Herman, P., Karlgren, J.: Evaluating categorisation in real life - an argument against simple but impractical metrics. In: Fuhr et al. [143], pp. 221–226
226. Kavallieratou, E., del Blanco, C.R., Cuevas, C., García, N.: Interactive learning-based retrieval technique for visual lifelogging. In: Crestani et al. [94]
227. Kelly, L., Goeuriot, L., Suominen, H., Névéol, A., Palotti, J., Zuccon, G.: Overview of the CLEF eHealth evaluation lab 2016. In: Fuhr et al. [143], pp. 255–266
228. Kelly, L., et al.: Overview of the ShARe/CLEF eHealth evaluation lab 2014. In: Kanoulas et al. [216], pp. 172–191
229. Keszler, A., Kovács, L., Szirányi, T.: The appearance of the giant component in descriptor graphs and its application for descriptor selection. In: Catarci et al. [75], pp. 76–81
230. Kharazmi, S., Scholer, F., Vallet, D., Sanderson, M.: Examining additivity and weak baselines. ACM Trans. Inf. Syst. (TOIS) 34(4), 23:1–23:18 (2016)
231. Khwileh, A., Ganguly, D., Jones, G.J.F.: An investigation of cross-language information retrieval for user-generated internet video. In: Mothe et al. [301], pp. 117–129
232. Khwileh, A., Way, A., Jones, G.J.F.: Improving the reliability of query expansion for user-generated speech retrieval using query performance prediction. In: Jones et al. [209], pp. 43–56
233. Kille, B., et al.: Overview of NewsREEL'16: multi-dimensional evaluation of real-time stream-recommendation algorithms. In: Fuhr et al. [143], pp. 311–331
234. Kille, B., et al.: Stream-based recommendations: online and offline evaluation as a service. In: Mothe et al. [301], pp. 497–517
235. Kim, S.J., Lee, J.H.: Subtopic mining based on head-modifier relation and co-occurrence of intents using web documents. In: Forner et al. [138], pp. 179–191
236. Kliegr, T., Kuchar, J.: Benchmark of rule-based classifiers in the news recommendation task. In: Mothe et al. [301], pp. 130–141
237. Kluck, M.: The domain-specific track in CLEF 2004: overview of the results and remarks on the assessment process. In: Peters et al. [358], pp. 260–270

238. Kluck, M., Gey, F.C.: The domain-specific task of CLEF - specific evaluation strategies in cross-language information retrieval. In: Peters [345], pp. 48–56
239. Kluck, M., Stempfhuber, M.: Domain-specific track CLEF 2005: overview of results and approaches, remarks on the assessment analysis. In: Peters et al. [365], pp. 212–221
240. Kocher, M., Savoy, J.: Author clustering with an adaptive threshold. In: Jones et al. [209], pp. 186–198
241. Koitka, S., Friedrich, C.M.: Optimized convolutional neural network ensembles for medical subfigure classification. In: Jones et al. [209], pp. 57–68
242. Koolen, M., et al.: Overview of the CLEF 2016 social book search lab. In: Fuhr et al. [143], pp. 351–370
243. Koolen, M., et al.: Overview of the CLEF 2015 social book search lab. In: Mothe et al. [301], pp. 545–564
244. Koolen, M., Kazai, G., Kamps, J., Preminger, M., Doucet, A., Landoni, M.: Overview of the INEX 2012 social book search track. In: Forner et al. [137]
245. Koops, H.V., Van Balen, J., Wiering, F.: Automatic segmentation and deep learning of bird sounds. In: Mothe et al. [301], pp. 261–267
246. Kordjamshidi, P., Rahgooy, T., Moens, M.F., Pustejovsky, J., Manzoor, U., Roberts, K.: CLEF 2017: multimodal spatial role labeling (mSpRL) task overview. In: Jones et al. [209], pp. 367–376
247. Kosmopoulos, A., Paliouras, G., Androutsopoulos, I.: The effect of dimensionality reduction on large scale hierarchical classification. In: Kanoulas et al. [216], pp. 160–171
248. Kumar, N.K., Santosh, G.S.K., Varma, V.: A language-independent approach to identify the named entities in under-resourced languages and clustering multilingual documents. In: Forner et al. [136], pp. 74–82
249. Kurimo, M., Creutz, M., Varjokallio, M.: Morpho challenge evaluation using a linguistic gold standard. In: Peters et al. [366], pp. 864–872
250. Kurimo, M., Turunen, V.T., Varjokallio, M.: Overview of morpho challenge 2008. In: Peters et al. [359], pp. 951–966
251. Kurimo, M., Virpioja, S., Turunen, V.T., Blackwood, G.W., Byrne, W.: Overview and results of morpho challenge 2009. In: Peters et al. [360], pp. 587–597
252. Kürsten, J., Eibl, M.: Comparing IR system components using beanplots. In: Catarci et al. [75], pp. 136–137
253. Kvist, M., Velupillai, S.: SCAN: a swedish clinical abbreviation normalizer - further development and adaptation to radiology. In: Kanoulas et al. [216], pp. 62–73
254. de Pertile, S.L., Pereira Moreira, V.: A test collection to evaluate plagiarism by missing or incorrect references. In: Catarci et al. [75], pp. 141–143
255. de Pertile, S.L., Rosso, P., Pereira Moreira, V.: Counting co-occurrences in citations to identify plagiarised text fragments. In: Forner et al. [138], pp. 150–154
256. Lagopoulos, A., Anagnostou, A., Minas, A., Tsoumakas, G.: Learning-to-rank and relevance feedback for literature appraisal in empirical medicine. In: Bellot et al. [42], pp. 52–63
257. Lai, M., Tambuscio, M., Patti, V., Ruffo, G., Rosso, P.: Extracting graph topological information and users' opinion. In: Jones et al. [209], pp. 112–118
258. Landoni, M., Matteri, D., Murgia, E., Huibers, T., Soledad Pera, M.: Sonny, Cerca! evaluating the impact of using a vocal assistant to search at school. In: Crestani et al. [94]
259. Larsen, B.: The scholarly impact of CLEF 2010–2017. In: Ferro and Peters [130]

260. Larson, M., Newman, E., Jones, G.J.F.: Overview of VideoCLEF 2008: automatic generation of topic-based feeds for dual language audio-visual content. In: Peters et al. [359], pp. 906–917

261. Larson, M., Newman, E., Jones, G.J.F.: Overview of VideoCLEF 2009: new perspectives on speech-based multimedia content enrichment. In: Peters et al. [368], pp. 354–368

262. Lasseck, M.: Towards automatic large-scale identification of birds in audio recordings. In: Mothe et al. [301], pp. 364–375

263. Leiva, L.A., Villegas, M., Paredes, R.: Relevant clouds: leveraging relevance feedback to build tag clouds for image search. In: Forner et al. [138], pp. 143–149

264. Leong, C.W., Hassan, S., Ruiz, M.E., Rada, M.: Improving query expansion for image retrieval via saliency and picturability. In: Forner et al. [136], pp. 137–142

265. Lestari Paramita, M., Sanderson, M., Clough, P.: Diversity in photo retrieval: overview of the ImageCLEFPhoto task 2009. In: Peters et al. [368], pp. 45–59

266. Li, P., Jiang, X., Kambhamettu, C., Shatkay, H.: Segmenting compound biomedical figures into their constituent panels. In: Jones et al. [209], pp. 199–210

267. Li, W., Jones, G.J.F.: Enhancing medical information retrieval by exploiting a content-based recommender method. In: Mothe et al. [301], pp. 142–153

268. Linhares Pontes, E., Huet, S., Torres-Moreno, J.M.: Microblog contextualization: advantages and limitations of a multi-sentence compression approach. In: Bellot et al. [42], pp. 181–190

269. Lipani, A., Piroi, F., Andersson, L., Hanbury, A.: An information retrieval ontology for information retrieval nanopublications. In: Kanoulas et al. [216], pp. 44–49

270. Litvinova, T., Seredin, P., Litvinova, O., Ryzhkova, E.: Estimating the similarities between texts of right-handed and left-handed males and females. In: Jones et al. [209], pp. 119–124

271. Liu, F., Peng, Y., Rosen, M.P.: An effective deep transfer learning and information fusion framework for medical visual question answering. In: Crestani et al. [94]

272. Lommatzsch, A., et al.: CLEF 2017 NewsREEL overview: a stream-based recommender task for evaluation and education. In: Jones et al. [209], pp. 239–254

273. Lommatzsch, A., Werner, S.: Optimizing and evaluating stream-based news recommendation algorithms. In: Mothe et al. [301], pp. 376–388

274. Loponen, A., Järvelin, K.: A dictionary- and corpus-independent statistical lemmatizer for information retrieval in low resource languages. In: Agosti et al. [9], pp. 3–14

275. Losada, D.E., Crestani, F.: A test collection for research on depression and language use. In: Fuhr et al. [143], pp. 28–39

276. Losada, D.E., Crestani, F., Parapar, J.: eRISK 2017: CLEF lab on early risk prediction on the internet: experimental foundations. In: Jones et al. [209], pp. 346–360

277. Losada, D.E., Crestani, F., Parapar, J.: Overview of eRisk: early risk prediction on the internet. In: Bellot et al. [42], pp. 343–361

278. Losada, D.E., Crestani, F., Parapar, J.: Overview of eRisk 2019: early risk prediction on the internet. In: Crestani et al. [94]

279. Mackie, S., McCreadie, R., Macdonald, C., Ounis, I.: Comparing algorithms for microblog summarisation. In: Kanoulas et al. [216], pp. 153–159

280. Magdy, W., Jones, G.J.F.: Examining the robustness of evaluation metrics for patent retrieval with incomplete relevance judgements. In: Agosti et al. [9], pp. 82–93

281. Magnini, B., et al.: Overview of the CLEF 2006 multilingual question answering track. In: Peters et al. [357], pp. 223–256

282. Magnini, B., et al.: The multiple language question answering track at CLEF 2003. In: Peters et al. [356], pp. 471–486
283. Magnini, B., et al.: Overview of the CLEF 2004 multilingual question answering track. In: Peters et al. [358], pp. 371–391
284. Mandl, T., et al.: LogCLEF 2009: the CLEF 2009 multilingual logfile analysis track overview. In: Peters et al. [360], pp. 508–517
285. Mandl, T., et al.: GeoCLEF 2008: the CLEF 2008 cross-language geographic information retrieval track overview. In: Peters et al. [359], pp. 808–821
286. Mandl, T., Di Nunzio, G.M., Schulz, J.M.: LogCLEF 2010: the CLEF 2010 multilingual logfile analysis track overview. In: Braschler et al. [61]
287. Mandl, T., et al.: GeoCLEF 2007: the CLEF 2007 cross-language geographic information retrieval track overview. In: Peters et al. [366], pp. 745–772
288. Manotumruksa, J., Macdonald, C., Ounis, I.: Predicting contextually appropriate venues in location-based social networks. In: Fuhr et al. [143], pp. 96–109
289. Martínez-Gómez, J., García-Varea, I., Caputo, B.: Overview of the ImageCLEF 2012 robot vision task. In: Forner et al. [137]
290. Mayfield, J., Lawrie, D., McNamee, P., Oard, D.W.: Building a cross-language entity linking collection in twenty-one languages. In: Forner et al. [136], pp. 3–13
291. McCreadie, R., Macdonald, C., Ounis, I., Brassey, J.: A study of personalised medical literature search. In: Kanoulas et al. [216], pp. 74–85
292. McMinn, A.J., Jose, J.M.: Real-time entity-based event detection for Twitter. In: Mothe et al. [301], pp. 65–77
293. Medvedeva, M., Haagsma, H., Nissim, M.: An analysis of cross-genre and in-genre performance for author profiling in social media. In: Jones et al. [209], pp. 211–223
294. Miftahutdinov, Z., Tutubalina, E.: Deep learning for ICD coding: looking for medical concepts in clinical documents in English and in French. In: Bellot et al. [42], pp. 203–215
295. Mirsarraf, M.R., Dehghani, N.: A dependency-inspired semantic evaluation of machine translation systems. In: Forner et al. [138], pp. 71–74
296. Mitrovic, S., Müller, H.: Summarizing citation contexts of scientific publications. In: Mothe et al. [301], pp. 154–165
297. Molina, A., SanJuan, E., Torres-Moreno, J.M.: A Turing test to evaluate a complex summarization task. In: Forner et al. [138], pp. 75–80
298. Molina, S., Mothe, J., Roques, D., Tanguy, L., Ullah, M.Z.: IRIT-QFR: IRIT query feature resource. In: Jones et al. [209], pp. 69–81
299. Morante, R., Daelemans, W.: Overview of the QA4MRE pilot task: annotating modality and negation for a machine reading evaluation. In: Petras et al. [373]
300. Moreno, R., Huáng, W., Younus, A., O'Mahony, M.P., Hurley, N.J.: Evaluation of hierarchical clustering via markov decision processes for efficient navigation and search. In: Jones et al. [209], pp. 125–131
301. Mothe, J., et al. (eds.): CLEF 2015. LNCS, vol. 9283. Springer, Cham (2015). https://doi.org/10.1007/978-3-319-24027-5
302. Mulhem, P., Goeuriot, L., Dogra, N., Amer, N.O.: TimeLine illustration based on microblogs: when diversification meets metadata re-ranking. In: Jones et al. [209], pp. 224–235
303. Müller, H., Clough, P., Deselaers, T., Caputo, B. (eds.): ImageCLEF - Experimental Evaluation in Visual Information Retrieval. Springer-Verlag, Heidelberg (2010). https://doi.org/10.1007/978-3-642-15181-1
304. Müller, H., Deselaers, T., Deserno, T.M., Clough, P., Kim, E., Hersh, W.R.: Overview of the ImageCLEFmed 2006 medical retrieval and medical annotation tasks. In: Peters et al. [357], pp. 595–608

305. Müller, H., Deselaers, T., Deserno, T.M., Kalpathy-Cramer, J., Kim, E., Hersh, W.R.: Overview of the ImageCLEFmed 2007 medical retrieval and medical annotation tasks. In: Peters et al. [366], pp. 472–491

306. Müller, H., Hanbury, A.: EaaS: evaluation-as-a-service and experiences from the VISCERAL project. In: Ferro and Peters [130]

307. Müller, H., Garcia Seco de Herrera, A., Kalpathy-Cramer, J., Demner-Fushman, D., Antani, S., Eggel, I.: Overview of the ImageCLEF 2012 medical image retrieval and classification tasks. In: Forner et al. [137]

308. Müller, H., et al.: Overview of the CLEF 2009 medical image retrieval track. In: Peters et al. [368], pp. 72–84

309. Müller, H., et al.: Overview of the CLEF 2010 medical image retrieval track. In: Braschler et al. [61]

310. Müller, H., Kalpathy-Cramer, J., Garcia Seco de Herrera, A.: Experiences from the ImageCLEF medical retrieval and annotation tasks. In: Ferro and Peters [130]

311. Müller, H., Kalpathy-Cramer, J., Kahn, C.E., Hatt, W., Bedrick, S., Hersh, W.: Overview of the ImageCLEFmed 2008 medical image retrieval task. In: Peters et al. [359], pp. 512–522

312. Murauer, B., Specht, G.: Generating cross-domain text corpora from social media comments. In: Crestani et al. [94]

313. Nakov, P., et al.: Overview of the CLEF-2018 CheckThat! Lab on automatic identification and verification of political claims. In: Bellot et al. [42], pp. 372–387

314. Nardi, A., Peters, C., Ferro, N. (eds.): CLEF 2007 Working Notes. CEUR Workshop Proceedings (CEUR-WS.org) (2007). ISSN 1613-0073. http://ceur-ws.org/Vol-1173/

315. Nardi, A., Peters, C., Vicedo, J.L., Ferro, N. (eds.): CLEF 2006 Working Notes. CEUR Workshop Proceedings (CEUR-WS.org) (2006). ISSN 1613-0073. http://ceur-ws.org/Vol-1172/

316. Nordlie, R., Pharo, N.: Seven years of INEX interactive retrieval experiments - lessons and challenges. In: Catarci et al. [75], pp. 13–23

317. Nowak, S., Dunker, P.: Overview of the CLEF 2009 large-scale visual concept detection and annotation task. In: Peters et al. [368], pp. 94–109

318. Nowak, S., Huiskes, M.J.: New strategies for image annotation: overview of the photo annotation task at ImageCLEF 2010. In: Braschler et al. [61]

319. Nowak, S., Nagel, K., Liebetrau, J.: The CLEF 2011 photo annotation and concept-based retrieval tasks. In: Petras et al. [373]

320. Oard, D.W., Gonzalo, J.: The CLEF 2001 interactive track. In: Peters et al. [354], pp. 308–319

321. Oard, D.W., Gonzalo, J.: The CLEF 2003 interactive track. In: Peters et al. [356], pp. 425–434

322. Oard, D.W., et al.: Overview of the CLEF-2006 cross-language speech retrieval track. In: Peters et al. [357], pp. 744–758

323. Oh, H.S., Jung, Y., Kim, K.Y.: A multiple-stage approach to re-ranking medical documents. In: Mothe et al. [301], pp. 166–177

324. Olvera-Lobo, M.D., Gutiérrez-Artacho, J.: Multilingual question-answering system in biomedical domain on the web: an evaluation. In: Forner et al. [136], pp. 83–88

325. Orio, N., Liem, C.C.S., Peeters, G., Schedl, M.: MusiClef: multimodal music tagging task. In: Catarci et al. [75], pp. 36–41

326. Orio, N., Rizo, D.: Overview of MusiCLEF 2011. In: Petras et al. [373]

327. Ortega-Mendoza, M., Franco-Arcega, A., López-Monroy, A.P., Montes-y Gómez, M.: I, me, mine: the role of personal phrases in author profiling. In: Fuhr et al. [143], pp. 110–122

328. Otterbacher, J.: Addressing social bias in information retrieval. In: Bellot et al. [42], pp. 121–127

329. Pääkkönen, T., et al.: Exploring behavioral dimensions in session effectiveness. In: Mothe et al. [301], pp. 178–189

330. Palotti, J., Zuccon, G., Bernhardt, J., Hanbury, A., Goeuriot, L.: Assessors agreement: a case study across assessor type, payment levels, query variations and relevance dimensions. In: Fuhr et al. [143], pp. 40–53

331. Parks, M., Karlgren, J., Stymne, S.: Plausibility testing for lexical resources. In: Jones et al. [209], pp. 132–137

332. Pasi, G., et al.: Evaluation of personalised information retrieval at CLEF 2018 (PIR-CLEF). In: Bellot et al. [42], pp. 335–342

333. Pasi, G., Jones, G.J.F., Goeuriot, L., Kelly, L., Marrara, S., Sanvitto, C.: Overview of the CLEF 2019 personalised information retrieval lab (PIR-CLEF 2019). In: Crestani et al. [94]

334. Pasi, G., Jones, G.J.F., Marrara, S., Sanvitto, C., Ganguly, D., Sen, P.: Overview of the CLEF 2017 personalised information retrieval pilot lab (PIR-CLEF 2017). In: Jones et al. [209], pp. 338–345

335. Pecina, P., Hoffmannová, P., Jones, G.J.F., Zhang, Y., Oard, D.W.: Overview of the CLEF-2007 cross-language speech retrieval track. In: Peters et al. [366], pp. 674–686

336. Pellegrin, L., et al.: A two-step retrieval method for image captioning. In: Fuhr et al. [143], pp. 150–161

337. Peñas, A., Forner, P., Rodrigo, A., Sutcliffe, R.F.E., Forascu, C., Mota, C.: Overview of ResPubliQA 2010: question answering evaluation over European legislation. In: Braschler et al. [61]

338. Peñas, A., et al.: Overview of ResPubliQA 2009: question answering evaluation over european legislation. In: Peters et al. [360], pp. 174–196

339. Peñas, A., et al.: Overview of QA4MRE at CLEF 2011: question answering for machine reading evaluation. In: Petras et al. [373]

340. Peñas, A., Hovy, E.H., Forner, P., Rodrigo, A., Sutcliffe, R.F.E., Morante, R.: QA4MRE 2011–2013: overview of question answering for machine reading evaluation. In: Forner et al. [138], pp. 303–320

341. Peñas, A., et al.: Overview of QA4MRE at CLEF 2012: question answering for machine reading evaluation. In: Forner et al. [137]

342. Peñas, A., et al.: Results and lessons of the question answering track at CLEF. In: Ferro and Peters [130]

343. Peñas, A., Unger, C., Ngonga Ngomo, A.C.a.: Overview of CLEF question answering track 2014. In: Kanoulas et al. [216], pp. 300–306

344. Peñas, A., Unger, C., Paliouras, P., Kakadiaris, I.A.: Overview of the CLEF question answering track 2015. In: Mothe et al. [301], pp. 539–544

345. Peters, C. (ed.): CLEF 2000. LNCS, vol. 2069. Springer, Heidelberg (2001). https://doi.org/10.1007/3-540-44645-1

346. Peters, C.: Introduction. In: Cross-Language Information Retrieval and Evaluation: Workshop of Cross-Language Evaluation Forum (CLEF 2000) [345], pp. 1–6

347. Peters, C.: What happened in CLEF 2004? In: Peters et al. [358], pp. 1–9

348. Peters, C.: What happened in CLEF 2005? In: Peters et al. [365], pp. 1–10

349. Peters, C.: What happened in CLEF 2006? In: Peters et al. [357], pp. 1–10
350. Peters, C.: What happened in CLEF 2007? In: Peters et al. [366], pp. 1–12
351. Peters, C.: What happened in CLEF 2008? In: Peters et al. [359], pp. 1–14
352. Peters, C.: What happened in CLEF 2009? In: Peters et al. [360], pp. 1–12
353. Peters, C., Braschler, M., Clough, P.: Multilingual Information Retrieval. Springer, Heidelberg (2011). https://doi.org/10.1007/978-3-642-23008-0
354. Peters, C., Braschler, M., Gonzalo, J., Kluck, M. (eds.): CLEF 2001. LNCS, vol. 2406. Springer, Heidelberg (2002). https://doi.org/10.1007/3-540-45691-0
355. Peters, C., Braschler, M., Gonzalo, J., Kluck, M. (eds.): CLEF 2002. LNCS, vol. 2785. Springer, Heidelberg (2003). https://doi.org/10.1007/b12018
356. Peters, C., Gonzalo, J., Braschler, M., Kluck, M. (eds.): CLEF 2003. LNCS, vol. 3237. Springer, Heidelberg (2004). https://doi.org/10.1007/b102261
357. Peters, C., et al. (eds.): CLEF 2006. LNCS, vol. 4730. Springer, Heidelberg (2007). https://doi.org/10.1007/978-3-540-74999-8
358. Peters, C., Clough, P., Gonzalo, J., Jones, G.J.F., Kluck, M., Magnini, B. (eds.): CLEF 2004. LNCS, vol. 3491. Springer, Heidelberg (2005). https://doi.org/10.1007/b138934
359. Peters, C., Deselaers, T., Ferro, N., Gonzalo, J., Jones, G.J.F., Kurimo, M., Mandl, T., Peñas, A., Petras, V. (eds.): CLEF 2008. LNCS, vol. 5706. Springer, Heidelberg (2009). https://doi.org/10.1007/978-3-642-04447-2
360. Peters, C., Di Nunzio, G.M., Kurimo, M., Mandl, T., Mostefa, D., Peñas, A., Roda, G. (eds.): CLEF 2009. LNCS, vol. 6241. Springer, Heidelberg (2010). https://doi.org/10.1007/978-3-642-15754-7
361. Peters, C., Ferro, N. (eds.): CLEF 2000 Working Notes. CEUR Workshop Proceedings (CEUR-WS.org) (2000). ISSN 1613-0073. http://ceur-ws.org/Vol-1166/
362. Peters, C., Ferro, N. (eds.): CLEF 2001 Working Notes. CEUR Workshop Proceedings (CEUR-WS.org) (2001). ISSN 1613-0073. http://ceur-ws.org/Vol-1167/
363. Peters, C., Ferro, N. (eds.): CLEF 2002 Working Notes. CEUR Workshop Proceedings (CEUR-WS.org) (2002). ISSN 1613-0073. http://ceur-ws.org/Vol-1168/
364. Peters, C., Ferro, N. (eds.): CLEF 2003 Working Notes. CEUR Workshop Proceedings (CEUR-WS.org) (2003). ISSN 1613-0073. http://ceur-ws.org/Vol-1169/
365. Peters, C., et al. (eds.): CLEF 2005. LNCS, vol. 4022. Springer, Heidelberg (2006). https://doi.org/10.1007/11878773
366. Peters, C., et al. (eds.): CLEF 2007. LNCS, vol. 5152. Springer, Heidelberg (2008). https://doi.org/10.1007/978-3-540-85760-0
367. Peters, C., Quochi, V., Ferro, N. (eds.): CLEF 2005 Working Notes. CEUR Workshop Proceedings (CEUR-WS.org) (2005). ISSN 1613-0073. http://ceur-ws.org/Vol-1171/
368. Peters, C., et al. (eds.): CLEF 2009. LNCS, vol. 6242. Springer, Heidelberg (2010). https://doi.org/10.1007/978-3-642-15751-6
369. Petras, V., Baerisch, S.: The domain-specific track at CLEF 2008. In: Peters et al. [359], pp. 186–198
370. Petras, V., Baerisch, S., Stempfhuber, M.: The domain-specific track at CLEF 2007. In: Peters et al. [366], pp. 160–173
371. Petras, V., et al.: Cultural heritage in CLEF (CHiC) 2013. In: Forner et al. [138], pp. 192–211
372. Petras, V., et al.: Cultural heritage in CLEF (CHiC) overview 2012. In: Forner et al. [137]
373. Petras, V., Forner, P., Clough, P., Ferro, N. (eds.): CLEF 2011 Working Notes. CEUR Workshop Proceedings (CEUR-WS.org) (2011). ISSN 1613-0073. http://ceur-ws.org/Vol-1177/

374. Piras, L., Caputo, B., Dang-Nguyen, D.T., Riegler, M., Halvorsen, P.: Image retrieval evaluation in specific domains. In: Ferro and Peters [130]
375. Piroi, F.: CLEF-IP 2010: retrieval experiments in the intellectual property domain. In: Braschler et al. [61]
376. Piroi, F., Hanbury, A.: Multilingual patent text retrieval evaluation: CLEF-IP. In: Ferro and Peters [130]
377. Piroi, F., Lupu, M., Hanbury, A.: Effects of language and topic size in patent IR: an empirical study. In: Catarci et al. [75], pp. 54–66
378. Piroi, F., Lupu, M., Hanbury, A.: Overview of CLEF-IP 2013 lab - information retrieval in the patent domain. In: Forner et al. [138], pp. 232–249
379. Piroi, F., Lupu, M., Hanbury, A., Sexton, A.P., Magdy, W., Filippov, I.V.: CLEF-IP 2012: retrieval experiments in the intellectual property domain. In: Forner et al. [137]
380. Piroi, F., Lupu, M., Hanbury, A., Zenz, V.: CLEF-IP 2011: retrieval in the intellectual property domain. In: Petras et al. [373]
381. Popescu, A., Tsikrika, T., Kludas, J.: Overview of the Wikipedia retrieval task at ImageCLEF 2010. In: Braschler et al. [61]
382. Potha, N., Stamatatos, E.: An improved impostors method for authorship verification. In: Jones et al. [209], pp. 138–144
383. Potthast, M., Barrón-Cedeño, A., Eiselt, A., Stein, B., Rosso, P.: Overview of the 2nd international competition on plagiarism detection. In: Braschler et al. [61]
384. Potthast, M., Eiselt, A., Barrón-Cedeño, A., Stein, B., Rosso, P.: Overview of the 3rd international competition on plagiarism detection. In: Petras et al. [373]
385. Potthast, M., et al.: Overview of the 4th international competition on plagiarism detection. In: Forner et al. [137]
386. Potthast, M., Gollub, T., Rangel Pardo, F., Rosso, P., Stamatatos, E., Stein, B.: Improving the reproducibility of PAN's shared tasks: plagiarism detection, author identification, and author profiling. In: Kanoulas et al. [216], pp. 268–299
387. Potthast, M., Gollub, T., Wiegmann, M., Stein, b.: TIRA integrated research architecture. In: Ferro and Peters [130]
388. Potthast, M., Holfeld, T.: Overview of the 2nd international competition on Wikipedia vandalism detection. In: Petras et al. [373]
389. Potthast, M., Rangel Pardo, F.M., Tschuggnall, M., Stamatatos, E., Rosso, P., Stein, B.: Overview of PAN'17 - author identification, author profiling, and author obfuscation. In: Jones et al. [209], pp. 275–290
390. Potthast, M., Stein, B., Holfeld, T.: Overview of the 1st international competition on Wikipedia vandalism detection. In: Braschler et al. [61]
391. Pritsos, D.A., Stamatatos, E.: The impact of noise in web genre identification. In: Mothe et al. [301], pp. 268–273
392. Pronobis, A., Fornoni, M., Christensen, H.I., Caputo, B.: The Robot Vision Track at ImageCLEF 2010. In: Braschler et al. [61]
393. Pronobis, A., Xing, L., Caputo, B.: Overview of the CLEF 2009 robot vision track. In: Peters et al. [368], pp. 110–119
394. Raghavi, K.C., Chinnakotla, M.K., Black, A.W., Shrivastava, M.: WebShodh: a code mixed factoid question answering system for web. In: Jones et al. [209], pp. 104–111
395. Ragheb, W., Azé, J., Bringay, S., Servajean, M.: Language modeling in temporal mood variation models for early risk detection on the internet. In: Crestani et al. [94]
396. Rangel Pardo, F., Rosso, P.: On the multilingual and genre robustness of EmoGraphs for author profiling in social media. In: Mothe et al. [301], pp. 274–280

397. Rebholz-Schuhmann, D., et al.: Entity recognition in parallel multi-lingual biomedical corpora: the CLEF-ER laboratory overview. In: Forner et al. [138], pp. 353–367

398. Rekabsaz, N., Lupu, M.: A real-world framework for translator as expert retrieval. In: Kanoulas et al. [216], pp. 141–152

399. de Rijke, M., Balog, K., Bogers, T., van den Bosch, A.: On the evaluation of entity profiles. In: Agosti et al. [9], pp. 94–99

400. Roda, G., Tait, J., Piroi, F., Zenz, V.: CLEF-IP 2009: retrieval experiments in the intellectual property domain. In: Peters et al. [360], pp. 385–409

401. Rodrigo, A., Peñas, A., Verdejo, M.F.: Overview of the answer validation exercise 2008. In: Peters et al. [359], pp. 296–313

402. Roller, R., Stevenson, M.: Self-supervised relation extraction using UMLS. In: Kanoulas et al. [216], pp. 116–127

403. Rosso, P., et al.: Evolution of the PAN lab on digital text forensics. In: Ferro and Peters [130]

404. Rosso, P., Rangel, F., Potthast, M., Stamatatos, E., Tschuggnall, M., Stein, B.: Overview of PAN'16. In: Fuhr et al. [143], pp. 332–350

405. Rowe, B.R., Wood, D.W., Link, A.L., Simoni, D.A.: Economic Impact Assessment of NIST's Text REtrieval Conference (TREC) Program. RTI Project Number 0211875, RTI International, USA, July 2010. http://trec.nist.gov/pubs/2010.economic.impact.pdf

406. Sabetghadam, S., Bierig, R., Rauber, A.: A hybrid approach for multi-faceted IR in multimodal domain. In: Kanoulas et al. [216], pp. 86–97

407. Sakai, T.: How to run an evaluation task. In: Ferro and Peters [130]

408. Saleh, S., Pecina, P.: Reranking hypotheses of machine-translated queries for cross-lingual information retrieval. In: Fuhr et al. [143], pp. 54–68

409. Samuel, J.: Analyzing and visualizing translation patterns of Wikidata properties. In: Bellot et al. [42], pp. 128–134

410. Sánchez-Junquera, J., Villaseñor-Pineda, L., Montes-y Gómez, M., Rosso, P.: Character N-grams for detecting deceptive controversial opinions. In: Bellot et al. [42], pp. 135–140

411. Sanchez-Perez, M.A., Gelbukh, A.F., Sidorov, G.: Adaptive algorithm for plagiarism detection: the best-performing approach at PAN 2014 text alignment competition. In: Mothe et al. [301], pp. 402–413

412. Sanchez-Perez, M.A., Markov, I., Gómez-Adorno, H., Sidorov, G.: Comparison of character n-grams and lexical features on author, gender, and language variety identification on the same Spanish news corpus. In: Jones et al. [209], pp. 145–151

413. SanJuan, E., Moriceau, V., Tannier, X., Bellot, P., Mothe, J.: Overview of the INEX 2012 tweet contextualization track. In: Forner et al. [137]

414. Santos, D., Cabral, L.M.: GikiCLEF: expectations and lessons learned. In: Peters et al. [360], pp. 212–222

415. Ramos dos Santos, W., Paraboni, I.: Personality facets recognition from text. In: Crestani et al. [94]

416. Savenkov, D., Braslavski, P., Lebedev, M.: Search snippet evaluation at Yandex: lessons learned and future directions. In: Forner et al. [136], pp. 14–25

417. Savoy, J., Braschler, M.: Lessons learnt from experiments on the ad-hoc multilingual test collections at CLEF. In: Ferro and Peters [130]

418. Schaer, P.: Better than their reputation? On the reliability of relevance assessments with students. In: Catarci et al. [75], pp. 124–135

419. Schaer, P., Mayr, P., Sünkler, S., Lewandowski, D.: How relevant is the long tail?: a relevance assessment study on million short. In: Fuhr et al. [143], pp. 227–233

420. Schaer, P., Neumann, M.: Enriching existing test collections with OXPath. In: Jones et al. [209], pp. 152–158

421. Schaüble, P., Sheridan, P.: Cross-language information retrieval (CLIR) track overview. In: Voorhees, E.M., Harman, D.K. (eds.) The Sixth Text REtrieval Conference (TREC-6), pp. 31–44. National Institute of Standards and Technology (NIST), Special Publication 500-240, Washington, USA (1997)

422. Schubotz, M., Krämer, L., Meuschke, N., Hamborg, F., Gipp, B.: Evaluating and improving the extraction of mathematical identifier definitions. In: Jones et al. [209], pp. 82–94

423. Schuth, A., Balog, K., Kelly, L.: Overview of the living labs for information retrieval evaluation (LL4IR) CLEF Lab 2015. In: Mothe et al. [301], pp. 484–496

424. Schuth, A., Marx, M.: Evaluation methods for rankings of facetvalues for faceted search. In: Forner et al. [136], pp. 131–136

425. Shen, W., Nie, J.Y.: Is concept mapping useful for biomedical information retrieval. In: Mothe et al. [301], pp. 281–286

426. Shepeleva, N., Balog, K.: Towards an understanding of transactional tasks. In: Fuhr et al. [143], pp. 234–240

427. Sherkat, E., Velcin, J., Milios, E.E.: Fast and simple deterministic seeding of KMeans for text document clustering. In: Bellot et al. [42], pp. 76–88

428. Shing, H.S., Barrow, J., Galuščáková, P., Oard, D.W., Resnik, P.: Unsupervised system combination for set-based retrieval with expectation maximization. In: Crestani et al. [94]

429. Sierek, T., Hanbury, A.: Using health statistics to improve medical and health search. In: Mothe et al. [301], pp. 287–292

430. Sigurbjörnsson, B., Kamps, J., de Rijke, M.: Overview of WebCLEF 2005. In: Peters et al. [365], pp. 810–824

431. Silvello, G., Bordea, G., Ferro, N., Buitelaar, P., Bogers, T.: Semantic representation and enrichment of information retrieval experimental data. Int. J. Digit. Libr. (IJDL) **18**(2), 145–172 (2017)

432. Singh, G., Mantrach, A., Silvestri, F.: Improving profiles of weakly-engaged users: with applications to recommender systems. In: Fuhr et al. [143], pp. 123–136

433. Sorg, P., Cimiano, P., Schultz, A., Sizov, S.: Overview of the cross-lingual expert search (CriES) pilot challenge. In: Braschler et al. [61]

434. Spina, D., Amigó, E., Gonzalo, J.: Filter keywords and majority class strategies for company name disambiguation in Twitter. In: Forner et al. [136], pp. 38–49

435. Stamatatos, E., Potthast, M., Rangel Pardo, F.M., Rosso, P., Stein, B.: Overview of the PAN/CLEF 2015 evaluation lab. In: Mothe et al. [301], pp. 518–538

436. Stamatatos, E., et al.: Overview of PAN 2018. In: Bellot et al. [42], pp. 267–285

437. Stathopoulos, S., Kalamboukis, T.: Medical image classification with weighted latent semantic tensors and deep convolutional neural networks. In: Bellot et al. [42], pp. 89–100

438. Stefanov, V., Sachs, A., Kritz, M., Samwald, M., Gschwandtner, M., Hanbury, A.: A formative evaluation of a comprehensive search system for medical professionals. In: Forner et al. [138], pp. 81–92

439. Stempfhuber, M., Baerisch, S.: The domain-specific track at CLEF 2006: overview of approaches, results and assessment. In: Peters et al. [357], pp. 163–169

440. Suchomel, S., Brandejs, M.: Determining window size from plagiarism corpus for stylometric features. In: Mothe et al. [301], pp. 293–299

441. Suominen, H.: CLEFeHealth2012 - the CLEF 2012 workshop on cross-language evaluation of methods, applications, and resources for eHealth document analysis. In: Forner et al. [137]

442. Suominen, H., Kelly, L., Goeuriot, L.: The scholarly impact and strategic intent of CLEF eHealth labs from 2012–2017. In: Ferro and Peters [130]

443. Suominen, H., et al.: Overview of the CLEF eHealth evaluation lab 2018. In: Bellot et al. [42], pp. 286–301

444. Suominen, H., et al.: Overview of the CLEF eHealth evaluation lab 2019. In: Crestani et al. [94]

445. Suominen, H., et al.: Overview of the ShARe/CLEF eHealth evaluation lab 2013. In: Forner et al. [138], pp. 212–231

446. Tannebaum, W., Mahdabi, P., Rauber, A.: Effect of log-based query term expansion on retrieval effectiveness in patent searching. In: Mothe et al. [301], pp. 300–305

447. Tannebaum, W., Rauber, A.: Mining query logs of USPTO patent examiners. In: Forner et al. [138], pp. 136–142

448. Teixeira Lopes, C., Almeida Fernandes, T.: Health suggestions: a chrome extension to help laypersons search for health information. In: Fuhr et al. [143], pp. 241–246

449. Teixeira Lopes, C., Ribeiro, C.: Effects of language and terminology on the usage of health query suggestions. In: Fuhr et al. [143], pp. 83–95

450. Teixeira Lopes, C., Ribeiro, C.: Effects of language and terminology of query suggestions on the precision of health searches. In: Bellot et al. [42], pp. 101–111

451. Thomee, B., Popescu, A.: Overview of the ImageCLEF 2012 Flickr photo annotation and retrieval task. In: Forner et al. [137]

452. Thornley, C.V., Johnson, A.C., Smeaton, A.F., Lee, H.: The scholarly impact of TRECVid (2003–2009). J. Am. Soc. Inf. Sci. Technol. (JASIST) **62**(4), 613–627 (2011)

453. Tommasi, T., Caputo, B., Welter, P., Güld, M.O., Deserno, T.M.: Overview of the CLEF 2009 medical image annotation track. In: Peters et al. [368], pp. 85–93

454. Trappett, M., Geva, S., Trotman, A., Scholer, F., Sanderson, M.: Overview of the INEX 2012 snippet retrieval track. In: Forner et al. [137]

455. Trotzek, M., Koitka, S., Friedrich, C.M.: Early detection of depression based on linguistic metadata augmented classifiers revisited. In: Bellot et al. [42], pp. 191–202

456. Tsikrika, T., Garcia Seco de Herrera, A., Müller, H.: Assessing the scholarly impact of ImageCLEF. In: Forner et al. [136], pp. 95–106

457. Tsikrika, T., Kludas, J.: Overview of the WikipediaMM task at ImageCLEF 2008. In: Peters et al. [359], pp. 539–550

458. Tsikrika, T., Kludas, J.: Overview of the WikipediaMM task at ImageCLEF 2009. In: Peters et al. [368], pp. 60–71

459. Tsikrika, T., Larsen, B., Müller, H., Endrullis, S., Rahm, E.: The scholarly impact of CLEF (2000–2009). In: Forner et al. [138], pp. 1–12

460. Tsikrika, T., Popescu, A., Kludas, J.: Overview of the Wikipedia image retrieval task at ImageCLEF 2011. In: Petras et al. [373]

461. Turchi, M., Steinberger, J., Alexandrov Kabadjov, M., Steinberger, R.: Using parallel corpora for multilingual (multi-document) summarisation evaluation. In: Agosti et al. [9], pp. 52–63

462. Turmo, J., et al.: Overview of QAST 2009. In: Peters et al. [360], pp. 197–211

463. Turmo, J., Comas, P., Rosset, S., Lamel, L., Moreau, N., Mostefa, D.: Overview of QAST 2008. In: Peters et al. [359], pp. 296–313

464. Vallin, A., et al.: Overview of the CLEF 2005 multilingual question answering track. In: Peters et al. [365], pp. 307–331
465. Valverde-Albacete, F., Carrillo de Albornoz, J., Peláez-Moreno, C.: A proposal for new evaluation metrics and result visualization technique for sentiment analysis tasks. In: Forner et al. [138], pp. 41–42
466. Villegas, M., et al.: General overview of ImageCLEF at the CLEF 2015 labs. In: Mothe et al. [301], pp. 444–461
467. Villegas, M., et al.: General overview of ImageCLEF at the CLEF 2016 labs. In: Fuhr et al. [143], pp. 267–285
468. Villegas, M., Paredes, R.: Overview of the ImageCLEF 2012 scalable web image annotation task. In: Forner et al. [137]
469. Voorhees, E.M.: TREC: continuing information retrieval's tradition of experimentation. Commun. ACM (CACM) 50(11), 51–54 (2007)
470. Voorhees, E.M.: The evolution of cranfield. In: Ferro and Peters [130]
471. Wakeling, S., Clough, P.: Integrating mixed-methods for evaluating information access systems. In: Mothe et al. [301], pp. 306–311
472. Walker, A., Starkey, A., Pan, J.Z., Siddharthan, A.: Making test corpora for question answering more representative. In: Kanoulas et al. [216], pp. 1–6
473. Wang, J., Gilbert, A., Thomee, B., Villegas, M.: Automatic image annotation at ImageCLEF. In: Ferro and Peters [130]
474. Wang, Q., et al.: Overview of the INEX 2012 linked data track. In: Forner et al. [137]
475. Wang, X., Guo, Z., Zhang, Y., Li, J.: Medical image labeling and semantic understanding for clinical applications. In: Crestani et al. [94]
476. Wang, X., Wang, X., Zhang, Q.: A web-based CLIR system with cross-lingual topical pseudo relevance feedback. In: Forner et al. [138], pp. 104–107
477. Weitzel, L., Bernardini, F., Quaresma, P., Alves, C.A., Zacharski, W., de Figueiredo, L.G.: Brazilian social mood: the political dimension of emotion. In: Fuhr et al. [143], pp. 247–255
478. White, R.W., Oard, D.W., Jones, G.J.F., Soergel, D., Huang, X.: Overview of the CLEF-2005 cross-language speech retrieval track. In: Peters et al. [365], pp. 744–759
479. Wilhelm-Stein, T., Eibl, M.: A quantitative look at the CLEF working notes. In: Forner et al. [138], pp. 13–16
480. Wilhelm-Stein, T., Eibl, M.: Teaching the IR process using real experiments supported by game mechanics. In: Mothe et al. [301], pp. 312–317
481. Wilhelm-Stein, T., Herms, R., Ritter, M., Eibl, M.: Improving transcript-based video retrieval using unsupervised language model adaptation. In: Kanoulas et al. [216], pp. 110–115
482. Xu, K., Feng, Y., Huang, S., Zhao, D.: Question answering via phrasal semantic parsing. In: Mothe et al. [301], pp. 414–426
483. Yan, X., Gao, G., Su, X., Wei, H., Zhang, X., Lu, Q.: Hidden Markov model for term weighting in verbose queries. In: Catarci et al. [75], pp. 82–87
484. Yang, H., Gonçalves, T.: A compound model for consumer health search. In: Bellot et al. [42], pp. 231–236
485. Zamani, H., Esfahani, H.N., Babaie, P., Abnar, S., Dehghani, M., Shakery, A.: Authorship identification using dynamic selection of features from probabilistic feature set. In: Kanoulas et al. [216], pp. 128–140
486. Zellhöfer, D.: Overview of the personal photo retrieval pilot task at ImageCLEF 2012. In: Forner et al. [137]

487. Zhang, L., Rettinger, A., Färber, M., Tadic, M.: A comparative evaluation of cross-lingual text annotation techniques. In: Forner et al. [138], pp. 124–135

488. Ziak, H., Kern, R.: Evaluation of pseudo relevance feedback techniques for cross vertical aggregated search. In: Mothe et al. [301], pp. 91–102

489. Zingla, M.A., Latiri, C., Slimani, Y.: Tweet contextualization using association rules mining and DBpedia. In: Mothe et al. [301], pp. 318–323

490. Zlabinger, M., Rekabsaz, N., Zlabinger, S., Hanbury, A.: Efficient answer-annotation for frequent questions. In: Crestani et al. [94]

491. Zuo, C., Karakas, A., Banerjee, R.: To check or not to check: syntax, semantics, and context in the language of check-worthy claims. In: Crestani et al. [94]

Full Papers

Crosslingual Depression Detection in Twitter Using Bilingual Word Alignments

Laritza Coello-Guilarte$^{(\boxtimes)}$, Rosa María Ortega-Mendoza,
Luis Villaseñor-Pineda, and Manuel Montes-y-Gómez

Instituto Nacional de Astrofísica, Óptica y Electrónica,
Santa María Tonantzintla, Puebla, Mexico
{laritza.coello,rmortega,villasen,mmontesg}@inaoep.mx

Abstract. Depression is a mental disorder with strong social and economic implications. Due to its relevance, recently several researches have explored the analysis of social media content to identify and track depressed users. Most approaches follow a supervised learning strategy supported on the availability of labeled training data. Unfortunately, acquiring such data is very complex and costly. To handle this problem, in this paper we propose a crosslingual approach based on the idea that data already labeled in a specific language can be leveraged to classify depression in other languages. The proposed method is based on a word-level alignment process. Particularly, we propose two representations for the alignment; one of them takes advantage of the psycholinguistic resource LIWC and the other uses bilingual word embeddings. For evaluating the proposed approach, we faced the detection of depression by employing English and Spanish tweets as the source and target data respectively. The results outperformed solutions based on automatic translation of texts, confirming the usefulness of the proposed approach.

1 Introduction

Depression is among the most frequent mental disorders. It can have a big impact on both physical and mental health, leading in severe cases to suicide. Therefore, depression is a mental condition requiring special attention. Recently, social media have become the main communication channel in modern societies, where users share thoughts, emotions and activities among other information that can be used to reveal and track their mental state. Based on the known relationship between language use and mental health [7], some works have proposed using text classification techniques to analyze social media texts and to detect possible depressed users.

Most approaches for depression detection based on text classification have addressed the problem from a supervised perspective, supported on the availability of labeled training data [19]. Unfortunately, the process of collecting and labeling data is usually difficult and time-consuming, and, therefore, annotated corpora are scarcely available, especially in languages other than English. However, we considered that data already labeled in a specific language can be leverage to classify depression in other (resource-poor) languages. Our hypothesis is

F. Crestani et al. (Eds.): CLEF 2019, LNCS 11696, pp. 49–61, 2019.
https://doi.org/10.1007/978-3-030-28577-7_2

that, despite of their cultural diversity, people with depression tend to share similar information and to express in an analogous way. Therefore, under this hypothesis, in this paper we propose a new approach for depression detection based on crosslingual classification, which assigns classes to documents written in a target language using training data in a different language [8].

Approaches based on crosslingual classification have been successfully applied in text classification and sentimental analysis [1,16,23], but, as far as we know, there is not any research in crosslingual depression detection from texts. Hence, this work opens new opportunities in this research field.

It is well known that the main challenge for crosslingual classification is the vocabulary gap between source and target languages. The most basic strategy to transform the data into the same language is by applying machine translation [2]. This strategy is simple and straightforward, but it faces a lot of problems when dealing with social media texts, since they used to contain a lot of misspellings, slang words and acronyms. Recently, with the aim of reducing these problems, some strategies based on word embeddings have emerged to model relationships between words from different languages [18,25]. They map similar and *related* words from different languages to similar representations in a common embedding space, allowing to carry out a soft alignment of words [12].

The proposed approach is based on a soft word-level alignment for capturing correspondences between both languages. Particularly, we devise two representations for this alignment; one of them uses the psycholinguistic resource *Linguistic Inquirer and Word Count* (LIWC), taking advantage of the correspondence between their concepts in different language versions [15]. The other one uses word embeddings pretrained in social media texts, and a process for their bilingual alignment [4], which enables to find sets of related words by means of a similarity measure.

For evaluating the proposed approach, we consider the detection of depression by employing English and Spanish tweets as the source and target data respectively. The obtained results are encouraging, they give some evidence that the depression detection can be addressed from a crosslingual perspective, and that it is better handled by a soft word-level alignment approach than by applying an automatic translation procedure.

2   Related Work

Recent studies about depression detection coincide that social media users reveal their mental state through shared content [21,24]. Therefore, the automatic analysis of this content provides elements for detecting signs of depression. Traditionally, the analysis has been tackled from a text classification perspective. Several methods have been proposed. Furthermore, recent shared tasks such as CLEF eRisk [10,11] and CLPsych [6] have included depression-oriented challenges. In general, it has been established that there are features that capture differences between healthy and sick users. For example, [7] and [5] analyzed emotions from psycholinguistic resources as ANEW and LIWC. In this regard, [20] proposed a multimodal approach that combines emotional features, personal information of users, topics, domain-specific words about treatments and symptoms, as well as, information about the profile image of the users. Overall, most of the work has shown that topics and words are very useful elements for identifying depression. Particularly, signs highly associated with depressed people have been found in their social media communications, such as negative expressions, name of drugs as well as symptoms of the disease [9,17].

For this task, several representations have been used, from the traditional bag of words (BoW) [13] to more sophisticated representations such as those based on topics. For example, [22] represented tweets through topics extracted with LDA, whereas [14] used decision lists based on word n-grams. As far as we know, all proposed methods for depression detection are restricted to one single language; there is no solution based on crosslingual classification taking advantage of previously labeled data. It is worth noting that, in other tasks such as sentiment analysis, crosslingual approaches have achieved very successful results.

In sentiment analysis, several works have proposed domain adaptation techniques. One example is SCL (Structural Correspondence Learning) [16,23], which aims to model the relationship between features in different languages from a given set of pivot words [23]. On the other hand, [2] explored the ability of automatic machine translation to generate a reliable training corpus. They obtained reasonable results, nevertheless, exposed that different alternatives should be found to minimize the errors introduced by the translator. Searching a solution, [1,25] proposed the use of bilingual word embeddings for capturing semantic relationships between words, and so, for reducing the differences between languages.

The effectiveness of crosslingual approaches in sentiment analysis has motivated our interest in exploring the detection of depression from a crosslingual perspective. Hence, this paper introduces an approach for depression detection using English data to classify Spanish documents. The approach is characterized by the use of word-level alignments for mapping knowledge between both languages.

3 The Proposed Approach

This section describes the proposed crosslingual approach for detecting users with depression in Twitter. It basically uses an annotated corpus in one language for doing the detection in another language.

More formally, based on [16], let $D^s = \{d_1^s, ..., d_{|D^s|}^s\}$ denotes the collection of labeled documents (training set). Also, let $D^t = \{d_1^t, ..., d_{|D^t|}^t\}$ represents the set of unlabeled documents (test set). These sets of documents are written in different languages. Commonly, the language of training and test documents are referred as source and target languages respectively. In this crosslingual context, the vocabulary V is divided into $V^s = \{w_1^s, ...w_{|V^s|}^s\}$ and $V^t = \{w_1^t, ...w_{|V^t|}^t\}$, called vocabulary of the source language and vocabulary of the target language.

That means that a classifier Φ_s generated from D^s with V^s cannot be directly applied to classify documents from the target language. To face the gap between languages, the automatic translation of documents is an obvious but basic solution with several drawbacks. In particular, to address the language barrier we propose two crosslingual representations, one based on a multilingual psycholinguistic resource and other on bilingual word alignments. The idea behind both representations is allowing to capture soft word correspondences between languages. Following we describe these representations.

3.1 Representation Based on LIWC

LIWC is a pysycholinguistic resource coming from the field of psychology [15]. Currently, it is available in several languages. This resource allows to analyze emotional, cognitive, and structural components present in texts. Broadly speaking, it classifies the words into several linguistic and psychological categories. More formally, let $C^s = \{C_1^s, ..., C_{|C^s|}^s\}$ and $C^t = \{C_1^t, ..., C_{|C^t|}^t\}$ represent the set of categories of LIWC in the source language and the target language versions respectively. Each category is a set of words (lexical unigrams) denoted by $C_f = \{w_1, ..., w_{|C_f|}\}$.

Alignment. We observed that English and Spanish LIWC versions present a direct correspondence between knowledge in both languages. Specifically, the categories of the English version share the same index with the categories of the Spanish version. That means that C_1^s corresponds to (the translation of) C_1^t, and so on. We use the indexes of categories to align and create the vector of the unlabeled documents. For example, in the Spanish version, the indexes of the categories: $futuro_{15}$ and $negación_{19}$ correspond to their respective English categories: $future_{15}$ and $negate_{19}$.

Train and Test Representations. In this representation each labeled document (training instance) d_i^s is represented by a vector $\mathbf{d_i^s}$, whose feature space is determined by the categories compressed in LIWC:

$$\mathbf{d_i^s} = <v_{i,1}, ..., v_{i,|C^s|}> \tag{1}$$

where $v_{i,j} = \sum_{\forall w \in C_j^s} f(w, d_i^s)$ represents the sum of occurrences of words belonging to category C_j^s of the dictionary in the document d_i^s.

Considering the alignment mechanism, each unlabeled (test) document d_i^t is represented by a feature vector $\mathbf{d_i^t}$, which is in the same dimensional space of the training documents:

$$\mathbf{d_i^t} = <v_{i,1}, ..., v_{i,|C^t|}> \tag{2}$$

where $v_{i,j} = \sum_{\forall w \in C_j^t} f(w, d_i^t)$ represents the sum of occurrences of words belonging to category C_j^t of the dictionary from the target language. As the indexes of the categories from the source and target languages' dictionaries perfectly match, it can be assumed that vectors for training and test documents are represented in the same space.

3.2   Representation Based on Bilingual Word Embeddings

In this representation, bilingual word embeddings are used as strategy to align data between languages. We consider that they are an effective strategy due to their capacity to relate similar contexts and to find analogies between words. In this case, the proposed representation is based on the well known bag of words model. In order to obtain the same dimensional space, the words of unlabeled documents are mapped to the source language by the alignment process, as described below.

Alignment. We used the method described in [4] to align word embeddings from two different languages. The entries of this method are X_i, Z_j and D, where X_i and Z_j are the n-dimensional vectors of words in source and target language respectively, which will participate in the mapping process. D is a seed dictionary that acts as bilingual basic knowledge of the languages, it is a set of word pairs (w_i^s, w_i^t), where w_i^s is a word in the source language and w_i^t is its translation to the target language[1]. For example: (*depression, depresión*), (*movie, pelicula*), (*yesterday, ayer*). The output are word embeddings in both languages, which have been mapped to the same space. Then, we used these vectors to find related words. That is, for each word in the target language, its vector is compared with the vectors for each word in the source language using the cosine similarity, then the n most similar words from the source language are selected as candidate translations of the target word. The n value can be manually established or automatically determined by considering a similarity threshold δ.

Train and Test Representations. In this proposal, each labeled (training) document d_i^s is modeled by a feature vector $\mathbf{d_i^s}$ as follows:

$$\mathbf{d_i^s} = <v_{i,1}, ..., v_{i,|V^s|}> \tag{3}$$

where $v_{i,j} = f(w_j^s, d_i^s)$ represents normalized frequency of the word w_j^s in the document d_i^s.

On the other hand, for building the representation of test documents is necessary to first map each word from the target language to its n most similar words from the source language, in accordance to the alignment mechanism. For example, considering the Spanish and English as source and target languages respectively, and using $n = 3$, the words in the following sentence in Spanish language: "el *dolor explota* en mi *alma*", are transformed(mapped) to[2]: (*pain, fear, emptiness*), (*explode, combust, suffocate*), (*soul, heart,mind*), which represents the three most similar English words to *dolor, explota* and *alma* respectively. The transformed document is denoted as $\breve{d}_i^t$, whose maximum length is $n * |d_i^t|$.

The representation of test documents is built from the transformed documents, which now contain terms from the source language. Specifically, each $\breve{d}_i^t$ is modeled by a vector $\mathbf{d_i^t}$:

$$\mathbf{d_i^t} = <v_{i,1}, ..., v_{i,|V^s|}> \tag{4}$$

---

[1] In the experiments, the translation of the seed words was done by means of Google Translator.

[2] We are interested in using content features, therefore the stop words are ignored.

where $v_{i,j}$ represents the *weight* of word w_j^s in the transformed document $\breve{d}_i^t$. We consider two different kinds of weights, one based on frequency and other one based on similarity. Following we describe these two variants, which are normalized by the sum of weights of vector $\mathbf{d_i^t}$.

Frequency-Based Weight: in this case, $v_{i,j} = f(w_j^s, \breve{d}_i^t)$ represents the occurrences of the word w_j^s in the $\breve{d}_i^t$.

Similarity-Based Weight: as previously described, each word from the target language could be mapped to *several* words from the source language; in consequence, each word w_j^s from the source language is linked to a set of words from the target language denoted as Q_j. Given that each mapping pair has different confidence since the similarity of their words is different, the weight of word w_j^s in the transformed document $\breve{d}_i^t$ could be computed as follows: $v_{i,j} = \sum_{\forall w \in Q_j} sim(w, w_j^s)$, where $sim(w, w_j^s)$ represents the cosine similarity of the embedding vectors of the words $w \in d_i^t$ and w_j^s.

4   Experiments

4.1   Experimental Settings

Datasets. For evaluating the proposed method, we used data collected from Twitter. Particularly, we used the English dataset gathered in [20]. According to the authors, users were labeled as depressed if any of their posts matched with this expression (*"I'm/I was/I've been)...diagnosed with depression"*. The non-depressed label was assigned to users whose posts did not contain the string "depress". Following this methodology, we obtained data in Spanish[3], considering the following phrases: (*"Me diagnosticaron/He sido diagnosticado con/Me han diagnosticado)...depresión"* and the absence of the word *"depresión"* for depressed and non-depressed labels, respectively. Table 1 summarizes some statistics of these datasets.

Classification. For classification we used a Support Vector Machine (SVM). For evaluation, we applied a four cross-fold validation approach. Similar to most of the state-of-the-art works, we used F1-measure over the depressed class as main evaluation measure.

Alignment with Word Embeddings. As mentioned before, the alignment method based on word embedding requires vectors of words in the source and target languages as well as a seed dictionary. In particular, English and Spanish vectors were calculated over 60,000 and 10,000 Twitter user histories[4], respectively. The embeddings were learned with the Word2Vec (skip-gram model); we

---

[3] https://ccc.inaoep.mx/~mmontesg/resources/CrossLingualDepression.zip.
[4] English data was taken from [20] and Spanish data was taken from [3].

Table 1. Description of English and Spanish datasets

Language	Class	Number of users	Vocabulary size	Average tweets per user (standard deviation)
English	Depressed	2626	15239	220 (339)
	Non-depressed	5367	70258	1115(1866)
Spanish	Depressed	91	14410	4147(2138)
	Non-depressed	225	25231	3844 (3802)

learned 200-dimensional vectors. On the other hand, we built three different seed dictionaries selecting some words from the English corpus: **d-500** containing 500 words selected randomly, **d-1000** with 1000 words selected randomly, and **d-depression** containing the 200 most frequent words in the texts from depressed users. To form the words pairs we translated the seed words with the help of Google Translator.

Upper-Bound and Baseline Methods. The upper-bound method idealize the expected performance when training is done with documents from the target language. In other words, it considers a *monolingual* setting. As crosslingual baseline method, we consider a straightforward solution to the problem of crosslingual classification [16]: we used an automatic machine translation approach. Particularly, documents from the target language (Spanish in our case) were translated to the source language (English) by means of Google Translator. Then, a classifier is learned on the labeled English documents and tested on the unlabeled Spanish-translated documents. We explored this baseline method using two representations: BoW and LIWC. The first one corresponds to the traditional bag of words using normalized term frequency as weighting. The second one is based on LIWC, where features correspond to categories from this resource. In this case, the weights correspond to percentage of words from each category occurring in the document.

4.2 Results

Experiment 1: Overall Performance Evaluation

The purpose of this experiment is to provide a general perspective on the performance of the proposed approach, considering the two different ways of generating the bilingual alignments. In this experiment we referred as BA-LIWC to the crosslingual representation based on LIWC and as BA-BOW to the representation based on bilingual word embeddings. For the last one, we applied a basic configuration setting: a dictionary of 500 seed word pairs, $n = 1$, and frequency-based weights.

Accordingly, we compare the classification performance from the proposed representations against: (i) the upper-bound method, which is addressed by a monolingual setting using traditional BOW and LIWC representations, and (*ii*) the crosslingual baseline, based on machine translation and also considering the BOW and LIWC representations. We refer to this approaches as AT-BOW and AT-LIWC respectively. Results are showed in Table 2.

Table 2. Comparison of results from the proposed approach, the upper-bound and the crosslingual baseline methods.

Approach	Alignment	Representation	F1	Representation	F1
Monolingual	-	BOW	0.78	LIWC	0.72
Crosslingual	Translation	AT-BOW	0.52	AT-LIWC	0.61
	Alignment	BA-BOW	0.61	BA-LIWC	0.65

Results show an important drop in performance for crosslingual experiments with respect to the monolingual exercise, indicating that there are certain language dependent peculiarities in the expression of depression. Regarding the crosslingual experiments, it is important to point out that the lost of performance introduced by the translation process is greater than that from the proposed representations. This suggest that automatic text translations are not good enough to transfer ideas and sentiments from one language to another, and, at the same time, that the proposed soft-alignment based representations are helpful and appropriate for this task.

In addition, it can be observed that in the monolingual experiment the results with BOW outperformed those with LIWC, whereas in the crosslingual experiments happened the opposite. This suggests that aligning concepts between languages is more suitable than word to word alignments. Supported on these observations, we considered that the representation based on word embeddings should take advantage of aligning several words in English to each word in Spanish. Next experiments focus on this analysis.

Experiment 2: Parameterization of the Alignment Approach

This experiment aims to evaluate different configurations of the representation based on the alignment of bilingual embeddings; described in Sect. 3.2 and referred as BA-BOW in the previous experiment. Particularly, the following experiments evaluate the influence in the performance of the approach of two aspects: the seed dictionary, on the one hand, and the number of words involved in the mapping to the source language, on the other hand. The experiments also consider the two already proposed weighting schemes.

The influence of the dictionary was explored varying its size (number of seeds) and domain (seeds randomly selected vs related to the depression domain). The purpose is to identify the dictionary's characteristics that help to maximize the performance of the approach. Accordingly, we evaluated several dictionaries: **d-500** and **d-1000** whose seeds, 500 and 1000 respectively, were chosen randomly, as well as, **d-depress**, where 200 specific words from the depression domain were used as seeds. Results from Table 3 show that the BA-BOW representation takes advantage of domain specific dictionaries regardless of the term weighting. In other words, it is more important to have good (domain specific) seeds than a large number of them.

To evaluate the influence of the number of aligned words to each target language word, we considered different values of n. Specifically, we took the top-1 and top-5 most similar words from the source language to each word from the target language, that is, we used $n = 1$ and $n = 5$ respectively. In addition, we consider a dynamic selection criteria, which selects all word mappings having a similarity above a given threshold δ. The threshold δ was defined as follows: we computed the average of the top-1 similarities for each target (Spanish) word with the English words, and to this value we subtracted their standard deviation. This threshold has two advantages, it restricts itself to select words with high similarity, and it is flexible enough to retrieve many words for those words having many related words in the source language.

In general, results from Table 3 show that the approach takes advantage of having multiple mappings for each target language word. There are notable the improvements obtained with the similarity-based weights. The best results with this weighting scheme considerably outperformed the baseline results based on automatic machine translation (BOW-AT, from Table 2). Furthermore, it is important to mention that these results are very close to the upper-bound results (also shown in Table 2), which gives evidence of the suitability of this proposed representation.

Table 3. Results of the proposed cross-lingual representation, which is based on bilingual word embeddings for aligning concepts.

Term weighting scheme	Seed-Dictionary	n-values		
		$n = 1$	$n = 5$	δ
Frequency	d-500	0.58	0.61	0.61
	d-1000	0.58	0.62	0.63
	d-depress	0.58	**0.62**	**0.65**
Similarity	d-500	0.62	0.64	0.66
	d-1000	0.62	**0.67**	**0.69**
	d-depress	0.62	**0.67**	**0.69**

5 Analysis of the Alignment Process

In order to deepen the analysis of results, we explored the word alignments generated by the used process. Some examples are shown in Table 4. It is notorious the advantage of the alignment of word embeddings against the automatic translation. Firstly, it is possible to observe that the translator was unable to correctly translate (or even to translate) some casual words commonly used in social media, whereas the word alignment could find some related words. For example, the translator has problems to recognize the word *pendeja*[5] when it was used as a noun word, but when it acted as an adjective a suitable translation was obtained. Similarly, the expression *no manches, which is used by Mexican people for expressing surprise, was translated in a different context.*

In contrast, the proposed approach finds alignments to several English words expressing the similar emotions. Secondly, there are several words that were correctly translated by the automatic machine translation, but also in these cases the proposed bilingual alignment showed some benefits, since it considered more related words. For example, *chido* is an adjective used for Mexican people to refer to good things, and it was associated to other English words used to express a similar feeling. Table 4 also shows some Spanish words related to depression that were aligned to several English words used in similar contexts.

Table 4. Examples of some words and its aligned terms

Spanish word	Method of alignment	
	Translator	Embeddings
pendeja	*asshole, *pendeja*[a]	*bitch, stupid, crazy*
no manches	*do not stain*	*omg, wow, oh*
chido	*cool*	*cool, cute, nice, good, awesome*
tristeza	*sadness*	*sadness, depression, pain, anxiety, loneliness*
ansiedad	*anxiety*	*anxiety, depression, stress, frustration*
miedo	*fear*	*fear, doubts, weakness, frustration*
amarte	*loving you*	*die, cry, disappear*
llorar	*cry*	*signs*
ausencia	*absence*	*presence*

[a]The translation *asshole* was only obtained when the word *pendeja* was used as an adjective.

As a general conclusion of this analysis we can say that automatic translations are not good enough to transfer ideas and sentiments from one language to another. Furthermore, the generated bilingual word alignment tends to enrich the translation of words. Nevertheless, despite of the effectiveness of alignments generated by the word embeddings, we also could track some errors that affect the performance of the depression detection. Specifically, we found some misaligned words such as the ones showed in the last three rows of Table 4.

---

[5] An offensive term in Spanish.

6 Conclusions and Future Work

Current research in depression detection has been addressed from a monolingual perspective. This paper is supported on the idea that data already labeled in a specific language can be leverage to identify depression in other languages. Particularly, we introduced a crosslingual approach for depression detection. The proposed approach is based on a word-level alignment process aimed to transfer knowledge from one language to another. For this alignment, we proposed two representations. The first one is based on the use of LIWC, where the categories' indexes were used for alignment. The second one takes advantage of the structural similarity from the embedding space to induce the translation of source language words to target language words. The results showed that depression can be detected applying a crosslingual text analysis. This suggests that, in social media, depressive users tend to express their depression in a similar way despite of their language. We consider this finding opens new opportunities in this research field. Furthermore, we observed that the alignment process is of critical importance. In this context, automatic translation is not good enough to transfer ideas and sentiment from one language to another language, whereas the results of classification are improved when more contextual elements are considered.

As future work, we are interested in exploring the proposed approach for depression detection using other datasets and even other languages. On the other hand, the obtained conclusions have motivated us to study the application of crosslingual approaches for detecting other mental disorders in languages other than English.

Acknowledgments. This work was partially supported by CONACYT under scholarship 869498, postdoctoral fellowship CVU-174410 and project grant CB-2015-01-257383.

References

1. Abdalla, M., Hirst, G.: Cross-lingual sentiment analysis without (good) translation. arXiv preprint arXiv:1707.01626 (2017)
2. Al-Shabi, A., Adel, A., Omar, N., Al-Moslmi, T.: Cross-lingual sentiment classification from english to arabic using machine translation. Int. J. Adv. Comput. Sci. Appl. (IJACSA) **8**(12), 434–440 (2017)
3. Álvarez-Carmona, M.Á.: Author profiling in social media with multimodal information. Ph.D. thesis, Instituto Nacional de Astrofísica, Óptica y Electrónica (2019)
4. Artetxe, M., Labaka, G., Agirre, E.: Learning bilingual word embeddings with (almost) no bilingual data. In: Proceedings of the 55th Annual Meeting of the Association for Computational Linguistics (Volume 1: Long Papers), vol. 1, pp. 451–462 (2017)
5. Coppersmith, G., Dredze, M., Harman, C.: Quantifying mental health signals in Twitter. In: Proceedings of the Workshop on Computational Linguistics and Clinical Psychology: From Linguistic Signal to Clinical Reality, pp. 51–60 (2014)

6. Coppersmith, G., Dredze, M., Harman, C., Hollingshead, K., Mitchell, M.: Clpsych 2015 shared task: depression and PTSD on Twitter. In: Proceedings of the 2nd Workshop on Computational Linguistics and Clinical Psychology: From Linguistic Signal to Clinical Reality, pp. 31–39 (2015)
7. De Choudhury, M., Gamon, M., Counts, S., Horvitz, E.: Predicting depression via social media. In: Seventh International AAAI Conference on Weblogs and Social Media (2013)
8. Gliozzo, A., Strapparava, C.: Exploiting comparable corpora and bilingual dictionaries for cross-language text categorization. In: Proceedings of the 21st International Conference on Computational Linguistics and the 44th Annual Meeting of the Association for Computational Linguistics, pp. 553–560. Association for Computational Linguistics (2006)
9. Guntuku, S.C., Yaden, D.B., Kern, M.L., Ungar, L.H., Eichstaedt, J.C.: Detecting depression and mental illness on social media: an integrative review. Curr. Opin. Beha. Sci. **18**, 43–49 (2017)
10. Losada, D.E., Crestani, F., Parapar, J.: eRISK 2017: CLEF lab on early risk prediction on the internet: experimental foundations. In: Jones, G.J.F., et al. (eds.) CLEF 2017. LNCS, vol. 10456, pp. 346–360. Springer, Cham (2017). https://doi.org/10.1007/978-3-319-65813-1_30
11. Losada, D.E., Crestani, F., Parapar, J.: Overview of eRisk: early risk prediction on the internet. In: Bellot, P., et al. (eds.) CLEF 2018. LNCS, vol. 11018, pp. 343–361. Springer, Cham (2018). https://doi.org/10.1007/978-3-319-98932-7_30
12. Mikolov, T., Le, Q.V., Sutskever, I.: Exploiting similarities among languages for machine translation. arXiv preprint arXiv:1309.4168 (2013)
13. Nadeem, M.: Identifying depression on Twitter. arXiv preprint arXiv:1607.07384 (2016)
14. Pedersen, T.: Screening Twitter users for depression and PTSD with lexical decision lists. In: Proceedings of the 2nd Workshop on Computational Linguistics and Clinical Psychology: From Linguistic Signal to Clinical Reality, pp. 46–53 (2015)
15. Pennebaker, J.W., Booth, R.J., Francis, M.E.: LIWC2007: linguistic inquiry and word count. LIWC.net, Austin (2007)
16. Prettenhofer, P., Stein, B.: Cross-language text classification using structural correspondence learning. In: Proceedings of the 48th Annual Meeting of the Association for Computational Linguistics, pp. 1118–1127 (2010)
17. Reece, A.G., Reagan, A.J., Lix, K.L., Dodds, P.S., Danforth, C.M., Langer, E.J.: Forecasting the onset and course of mental illness with twitter data. Sci. Rep. **7**(1), 13006 (2017)
18. Ruder, S.: A survey of cross-lingual word embedding models. CoRR abs/1706.04902 (2017)
19. Sebastiani, F.: Machine learning in automated text categorization. ACM Comput. Surv. (CSUR) **34**(1), 1–47 (2002)
20. Shen, G., et al.: Depression detection via harvesting social media: a multimodal dictionary learning solution. In: IJCAI, pp. 3838–3844 (2017)
21. Stankevich, M., Isakov, V., Devyatkin, D., Smirnov, I.: Feature engineering for depression detection in social media. In: ICPRAM, pp. 426–431 (2018)
22. Tsugawa, S., Kikuchi, Y., Kishino, F., Nakajima, K., Itoh, Y., Ohsaki, H.: Recognizing depression from Twitter activity. In: Proceedings of the 33rd Annual ACM Conference on Human Factors in Computing Systems, pp. 3187–3196 (2015)
23. Wei, B., Pal, C.: Cross lingual adaptation: an experiment on sentiment classifications. In: Proceedings of the ACL 2010 Conference Short Papers, pp. 258–262. Association for Computational Linguistics (2010)

24. Wolohan, J., Hiraga, M., Mukherjee, A., Sayyed, Z.A., Millard, M.: Detecting linguistic traces of depression in topic-restricted text: attending to self-stigmatized depression with NLP. In: Proceedings of the First International Workshop on Language Cognition and Computational Models, pp. 11–21 (2018)
25. Yang, X., McCreadie, R., Macdonald, C., Ounis, I.: Transfer learning for multi-language Twitter election classification. In: Proceedings of the 2017 IEEE/ACM International Conference on Advances in Social Networks Analysis and Mining, pp. 341–348 (2017)

Studying the Variability of System Setting Effectiveness by Data Analytics and Visualization

Sébastien Déjean[1], Josiane Mothe[2], and Md. Zia Ullah[3(✉)]

[1] IMT, UMR5219 CNRS, UPS, Univ. de Toulouse,
118 Route de Narbonne, Toulouse, France
`sebastien.dejean@math.univ-toulouse.fr`
[2] IRIT, UMR 5505 CNRS, ESPE, Univ. de Toulouse,
118 Route de Narbonne, Toulouse, France
`josiane.mothe@irit.fr`
[3] IRIT, UMR 5505 CNRS, UPS, Univ. de Toulouse,
118 Route de Narbonne, Toulouse, France
`mdzia.ullah@irit.fr`

Abstract. Search engines differ from their modules and parameters; defining the optimal system setting is challenging the more because of the complexity of a retrieval stream. The main goal of this study is to determine which are the most important system components and parameters in system setting, thus which ones should be tuned as the first priority. We carry out an extensive analysis of 20,000 different system settings applied to three TREC ad-hoc collections. Our analysis includes zooming in and out the data using various data analysis methods such as ANOVA, CART, and data visualization. We found that the query expansion model is the most significant component that changes the system effectiveness, consistently across collections. Zooming in the queries, we show that the most significant component changes to the retrieval model when considering easy queries only. The results of our study are directly re-usable for the system designers and for system tuning.

Keywords: Information retrieval · Data analytics ·
Retrieval system modules · Effectiveness

1 Introduction

Search engines aim at retrieving the documents that will fit the user's expectations which he/she expresses through a query. Search engines vary according to various components and thus the way they handle the document indexing, the query/document matching model, the automatic query expansion, the document ranking, etc. For example, regarding the matching model, among the most popular models we can quote VSM [20], Probabilistic model [18], LSI [9], or Language model [17]; each model has in turn internal parameters that can be

© Springer Nature Switzerland AG 2019
F. Crestani et al. (Eds.): CLEF 2019, LNCS 11696, pp. 62–74, 2019.
https://doi.org/10.1007/978-3-030-28577-7_3

varied. When handling a new collection, finding the most appropriate component/parameter to tune as the first priority is not obvious. This is a challenging problem since many factors influence the system effectiveness, such as the system components, their parameters, the document collection, the queries, and the considered effectiveness measures while a few studies help in understanding this influence. In IR, most of these modules and parameters are tuned on a per-collection basis to optimize the system effectiveness [13]. This is the case in the evaluation campaign series[1] although IR research looks also for modules and parameters (methods) which work best on real-world search tasks.

While it is well-acknowledged that the system should be tuned according to the collection, there are a few studies that tackle the problem of the way to proceed. Grid search is such a method that determines the best value for each parameter to maximize the system effectiveness of a query set where a set of values is defined for each parameter [23]; this method is very resource demanding when there are many possible system settings[2]. It results in providing the optimized values of the system parameters, but neither offer explanations of these results nor cues on their transferability from one collection to another. Another recent approach is Random search [2] which can randomly explore the space of the possible system settings; it thus can be quicker than grid search but does not guarantee the optimal setting and does not solve the other drawbacks of grid search.

In this paper, we analyze which modules and parameters that influence system effectiveness the most. This analysis is worth to be conducted at various levels in order to get different types of information; this is done by zooming in and out the data set. The results of this study could be then used to know which component/parameter should be tuned as the first priority for achieving the best system effectiveness on a new collection. The results could also be used to better drive grid search or similar methods when optimizing systems to avoid exploring settings that are unlikely to be effective. This analysis is worth to be based on various data analysis methods; each one is appropriate to reveal different aspects of the problem. We use Analysis of variance (ANOVA) to reveal the components that significantly influence the effectiveness, CART (classification and regression tree) [5] to model the impact of the different component modalities, and data visualization. Finally, this analysis has to be made on a large scale so that the results could be reliable.

We used more than 20,000 different system settings, applied to three TREC ad-hoc collections and the associated queries that we will detail later on in this paper. Not surprisingly, we show that the most significant influencing factor is the query set.

Considering the system components, the most significant component is the query expansion model when zooming out (all collections together) and when considering each collection individually, although the optimal modality can differ

---

[1] https://trec.nist.gov/data.html.

[2] A system setting refers to an IR system configured with a retrieval model and an optional query expansion model with its parameters.

from one collection to another. More unexpected, when zooming in the queries and considering classes of query difficulties, we found out that the most significant module is the retrieval model for easy queries and the query expansion model for hard queries. Therefore, system components should be designed with the options of choosing from retrieval and query expansion models at run time based on the query difficulty level and be tuned accordingly.

The rest of the paper is organized as follows: related work is discussed in Sect. 2. Section 3 presents the specific objectives, we pursued, the methods and data that we used to achieve our goals. Experimental results are described and discussed in Sect. 4. Finally, Sect. 5 concludes this paper and mentions future work.

2   Related Work

Several studies used descriptive analysis to understand better the results obtained with various IR systems. In their earlier work, Banks et al. [1] considered two parameters (topic and system) and analyzed the results using variance analysis, cluster analysis, correlation, and a few other methods. The authors stated that the results were inconclusive and that none of these methods had yielded any substantial new insights.

Chrisment et al. [7] and Dinçer [10] revisited this topic and compared the performances of various search strategies by means of principal component analysis (PCA); both analyzed the participants' runs and showed that PCA can reveal the peculiarities of some runs and of some topics. Bigot et al. [3] conducted a similar analysis on TREC 7 ad-hoc collection considering Benzecri's χ^2 correspondence analysis rather than the PCA and suggested a system fusion method which improves about 20% compared to the best system at TREC. Mizzaro and Robertson [16] used network analysis to distinguish good systems from bad systems by defining a minimal subset of queries and concluded that "easy" queries perform the best in this task.

In these studies, the authors use the participants' run and systems which are considered to be black boxes. Other studies went deeper in the system parameter analysis. Compaoré et al. [8] analyzed two indexing parameters (Block size and IDF) and retrieval modules to determine which parameters significantly affect the system performance on TREC7-8 collection. They concluded that the retrieval model is more important than the indexing module. Bigot et al. [4] enlarged the analysis with regard to the number of parameters considering four different stemming algorithms, twenty-one retrieval models, seven combinations of topic fields as queries, six query expansion models, and other query expansion parameters.

In the same vein, Ferro et al. introduced the grid of points (GOP) to analyze the main and interaction effects of topics, indexing, and retrieval modules on system performance [12]. Using ANOVA, they found that having a stopword list in the indexing module has the biggest positive impact, then the stemmer, and retrieval model; the stopword list has also a significant interaction effect with the retrieval model. However, they did not consider the query expansion component in their study and their analysis of the indexing module was conducted on four small TREC collections (TREC 05, 06, 07, and 08). Moreover, varying the indexing module would be very costly to conduct for larger collections because it requires to construct many indexes. Therefore, it is unlikely that real-world systems implement several indexes of their collections. On the contrary, varying retrieval and query expansion modules would be easily done at run time only.

Our study is much ampler than related work; first, in terms of system components/parameters analyzed since the data set is composed of a total of more than 20,000 system settings including the query expansion module and in terms of collections that include larger collections than previous studies; second, in terms of the variability of the methods used to analyze the results; and third because we consider various levels of analysis (zooming in and out in the collections and query sets). We focus on the significant influential modules and parameters on system effectiveness and analyze whether they differ across the collections, across query difficulty level, and considering different evaluation measures.

3 Objectives, Methods, and Data

3.1 Data Analysis Objectives and Methods

The main objective of this study is to identify which is the most significant component/parameter of the system that influences the system effectiveness. This analysis is worth to be conducted at various levels in order to extract different types of information: (1) at the collection level, identifying which component significantly influence the system effectiveness the most can help the developers when tuning the system on a per-collection basis. The results could be used to anticipate transferability. Let us say that the most significant component is the same across collections, this is the ones that should be tuned first for any new collection; (2) zooming out and considering the queries of all the collections together would explore the more general trends, more independent to the considered queries. Results are likely to be less collection-biased; (3) Since the query set has a strong significant impact on the system effectiveness, zooming in the query sets is worth exploring. To do so, we consider the level of query difficulty since this is an active research direction [6,19,22]. Zooming in and considering individual query or groups of queries could help in understanding what are the main system failures and how to avoid them.

Various data analysis methods could reveal different aspects of the problem. Among the large set of possible methods, we select the Analysis of VAriance (ANOVA). ANOVA is a statistical method which is used to check if the means of two or more groups are significantly different from each other. It was widely used in the 1990s to explore the TREC IR runs results [21,25] and has recently been revived [12,24]. For a thorough understanding of the ANOVA, we would refer the readers to Miller's book [15] or Ferro et al. [12]. ANOVA can be designed as One-way (i.e. if there is a significant effect of an independent variable on a continuous dependent variable) or N-way with/without interaction (i.e. if there exist a significant interaction effect between N independent variables on a continuous dependent variable). In its application to IR, it has the interesting power of being able to show both the main effect of the components and also the interaction effects; however, it can not be used to decide which levels (modalities) of the factor (component) are the most significant. We also use CART (classification and regression tree) [5], which is appropriate to consider cross-effect of components but also to extract readable models from the data that could explain the results. Finally, this analysis has to be made on a large scale so that the results could be reliable; the collections and settings are presented in the next sub-sections.

3.2 Data Collections

We use three standard TREC collections, namely TREC7-8, WT10G, and GOV2. TREC7-8 consists of 528k documents and a total of 100 topics, WT10G consists of 1,692k documents and 100 topics, and GOV2 consists of 25 million documents and 150 topics. Indeed, when a document collection has been used for different sets of queries, we merged the queries in the experiments. We consider the title part of the topics as queries. The collections come with *qrels*, that is to say, judged documents (relevant or non-relevant) for each topic. Qrels are used by the evaluation program *trec_eval*[3] to calculate system effectiveness. We use the well-known AP (Average Precision) and P@10 (Precision at 10) as the evaluation measures. We use Terrier IR [14] to index the collections and retrieve the results for the queries from the three collections.

3.3 System Components, Parameters, and Settings

Previous studies have focused on the indexing components including the stoplists, the stemming algorithms used, and the retrieval component [8,11]. Having in mind the system setting optimization, adapting the indexing component is very resource demanding since several indexes need to be built and stored. Although it is feasible for small collections, it is more demanding for large collections and unrealistic for real-world systems.

In this study, we thus choose to consider the core IR system components that can be combined at run time: the retrieval module and the query expansion module (See Table 1).

Each retrieval module has its proper inner parameters that could be tuned in turn; however, these parameters vary from one model to another (e.g. it is k_1 and b parameters in the BM25 retrieval model, but it is μ in Language model). We keep the study of the variability of internal parameters of the retrieval model for future work. We thus rather consider in this study a single version of each of the 20 retrieval models and choose its default setting (e.g., BM25 ($k_1 = 1.2$, $b = .75$), DirichletLM ($\mu = 2500$), and PL2 (c = 1)) in Terrier [14][4]. We also

---

[3] http://trec.nist.gov/trec_eval/.
[4] http://terrier.org/docs/current/javadoc/org/terrier/matching/models/package-summary.html.

Table 1. System components and variants.

Component	Modalities
Retrieval model (RMod)	BB2, BM25, DFRBM25, DFRee, DLH, DLH13, DPH, DirichletLM, HiemstraLM, IFB2, InB2, InL2, InexpB2, InexpC2, JsKLs, LGD, LemurTFIDF, PL2, TFIDF, XSqrAM
Query expansion (QE)	0 (no expansion), Bo1, Bo2, Information, KL, KLCorrect, KLComplete

consider the 6 query expansion models implemented in Terrier which is optional when combined with the retrieval model (making 7 modalities for this variable).

To have the first look on the influence of the variables, we consider the three-way ANOVA test that estimates the main effects of the query, query expansion (QE), and retrieval model (RMod) factors on AP measure and report the preliminary evaluation result in Table 2.

Table 2. Three-way ANOVA considering the main effects of Query, QE, and RMod factors on AP for TREC7-8, WT10G, and GOV2 collections, independently. Columns refers to Df (Degree of freedom), SS (Sum of square), MS (Mean of square), F-val (F-value), P (P-value), and R (Rank in terms of F-value (higher is better)) of each factor; P of .00 refers to P-value $< 2e\text{-}9$.

	Factors	\multicolumn{6}{c}{TREC7-8}	\multicolumn{6}{c}{WT10G}	\multicolumn{6}{c}{GOV2}
		Df	SS	MS	F-val	P	R	Df	SS	MS	F-val	P	R	Df	SS	MS	F-val	P	R
AP	Query	99	52669	532	80735	.00	1	99	50614	511	45881	.00	1	148	85430	577	46288	.00	2
	QE	6	2074	346	52467	.00	2	6	1961	327	29324	.00	2	6	9377	1563	125328	.00	1
	RMod	19	489	26	3908	.00	3	19	2352	124	11110	.00	3	19	10573	557	44624	.00	3
	Error	2.5M	16811	0				2.4M	27170	0				3.7M	47102	0			

Columns of the Table 2 refers to the degree of freedom (DF), sum of square (SS), mean square (MS), F-value (F-val), P-value (P), and Rank (R, the order of importance in terms of F-value) of each factor. The higher the F-value (the ratio of between-group variability to within-group variability), the higher the effect of the factor on the response variable (say, AP).

From the SS, MS, and F-value of each factor in Table 2, we can observe that the most significant factor is generally the query apart from the GOV2 where the query is the second most significant component. Having a closer looks at the variance of the system effectiveness (AP) for GOV2 queries (not reported because of page limit), we observed that it was much higher on GOV2 than on other collections.

The most significant factor when not considering the query factor is consistently the query expansion (QE) component[5]. While some related work did not consider the query expansion component [12], we show here that it is of huge importance. We thus gave a closer look at the QE component.

Moreover, since any QE models have the same three high-level parameters: the number of documents used, the number of added terms, and the minimal number of documents where the considered terms should occur, we also consider these three parameters (see their description on Table 3).

Table 3. Parameters of the query expansion (QE) component.

Parameters	Modalities
Number of expansion documents (NED)	2, 5, 10, 20, 50, 100
Number of expansion terms (NET)	2, 5, 10, 15, 20
Minimum number of documents (MND)	2, 5, 10, 20, 50

We finally built numerous system settings; each system setting is being composed of a retrieval model among the 20 (Terrier default inner parameters for each of them) and optionally one of the 6 query expansion models; the latter is configured with one modality (level) for each of the three parameters (factors). We build as many systems as there are possible meaningful[6] combinations of module/parameter values (i.e. modalities); a system results from setting one of the modules/parameters to one of the modalities from Tables 1 and 3; that makes more than 20,000 systems treating each query.

4 Experimental Results and Discussion

Our experiments are three-fold. First, we consider each collection individually to identify which component significantly influence system effectiveness. The result can be useful for the developers when tuning their system on a per-collection basis and can be used to anticipate transferability issue across collections. Second, we zoom out the collections by considering the queries of all collections together to perceive the general effect of components on system effectiveness. Third, we zoom in by considering the groups of queries.

---

[5] We also calculated the Two-way ANOVA considering the main and interaction effects of query expansion (QE) and retrieval model (RMod) factors on AP; query expansion is consistently ranked first as well across the collections.

[6] Some combinations are not meaningful and thus were not used (e.g., using 5 documents in query expansion while the "expansion model" used is none).

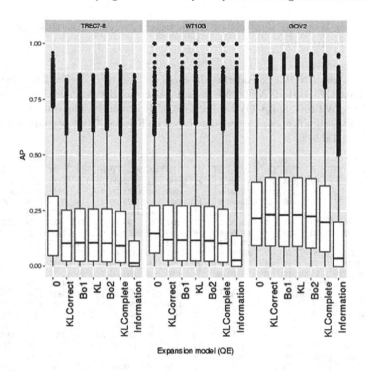

Fig. 1. Distribution of AP values considering the 7 query expansion (QE) modules on TREC7-8, WT10G, and GOV2 collections. Within a collection, boxplots are ordered by decreasing median on TREC7-8 collection

4.1 Significant Component Per-Collection

Our preliminary analysis (Table 2) shows that the most significant factor (when apart from queries) is the query expansion (QE). We visualize the distribution of AP measure for the 7 query expansion (QE) modules in Fig. 1 ("0" means no expansion). Each boxplot corresponds to an individual query expansion model and shows the distribution of AP values obtained for the various systems (all parameters vary except the query expansion for a boxplot) for each query individually. We ordered the box-plots in decreasing order based on the median of AP values on TREC7-8 collection. We can see that "Information" QE module performs the worst across collections (right sidebar of each sub-figure). On the contrary, no expansion ("0") is likely to perform better than any query expansion module in average at least on TREC7-8 and WT10G collections since it obtained the best median and Q3 (first left sidebar of each sub-figure). The chance of no expansion performing better than query expansion is higher, although there are some appropriate combinations for various expansion models that perform about the same. We can see that several models have similar shapes (2nd to 6th bars). This comment holds specifically well for WT10G collection where the maximum AP is the same and bar plots are very similar from one QE model to the other.

Moreover, we keep the analysis of more selective system settings (e.g., good systems) as future work.

Table 4. Six-way ANOVA considering the main and interaction effects (second order) of the Query, QE, RMod, NED, NET, and MND on the AP and P@10 measures for TREC7-8, WT10G, and GOV2 collections, independently. The results are ordered according to the significance of the module based on F-value. Other legends and settings are similar to Table 2.

	Factors	\multicolumn{6}{c}{TREC7-8}						\multicolumn{6}{c}{WT10G}						\multicolumn{6}{c}{GOV2}					
		Df	SS	MS	F-val	P	R	Df	SS	MS	F-val	P	R	Df	SS	MS	F-val	P	R
AP	Query	99	52668	532	82785	.00	1	99	50616	511	47632	.00	1	148	85430	577	49325	.00	2
	QE	6	2075	345	53812	.00	2	6	1960	326	30434	.00	2	6	9377	15639	133551	.00	1
	RMod	19	490	25	4013	.00	3	19	2350	123	11523	.00	3	19	10573	556	47551	.00	3
	NED	5	48	9	1479	.00	4	5	201	40	3738	.00	4	5	127	25	741	.00	6
	RMod*NET	20	152	7	1183	.00	5	24	257	10	998	.00	5	24	970	40	1177	.00	5
	RMod*QE	30	130	4	676	.00	6	36	349	9	902	.00	6	36	1460	40	3465	.00	4
	MND	4	9	2	339	.00	7	5	3	.7	62	.00	9	4	3	.8	70	.00	10
	NED*MND	20	26	1	199	.00	8	20	30	1	138	.00	8	20	30	1	126	.00	9
	QE*MND	20	17	.8	130	.00	9	20	13	.6	59	.00	10	20	44	2	188	.00	8
	RMod*NED	25	12	.5	72	.00	10	30	86	3	265	.00	7	30	74	2	209	.00	7
	Err	2.5M	16393	.0				2.4M	26170	.0				3.7M	44199	0			
P@10	Query	99	166129	1678	59602	.00	1	99	124620	1258	48305	.00	1	148	235832	1593	30300	.00	2
	QE	6	7077	1179	41894	.00	2	6	4107	684	26267	.00	2	6	25300	4217	80183	.00	1
	RMod	19	2004	105	3745	.00	3	19	3437	181	6941	.00	3	19	16708	879	16722	.00	3
	NED	5	264	52	1874	.00	4	5	140	28	1072	.00	4	5	291	58	1108	.00	5
	RMod*QE	30	640	21	758	.00	5	36	645	18	687	.00	5	36	3569	99	1885	.00	4
	RMod*NET	20	210	10	372	.00	6	24	215	9	344	.00	6	24	933	39	739	.00	6
	NED*MND	20	96	5	170	.00	7	20	86	4	165	.00	8	20	218	11	207	.00	8
	QE*MND	20	53	2	94	.00	8	20	30	1	58	.00	10	20	129	6	123	.00	10
	MND	4	7	2	64	.00	9	5	18	3	140	.00	9	4	31	8	148	.00	9
	RMod*NED	25	29	1	41	.00	10	30	223	7	285	.00	7	30	426	14	270	.00	7
	Err	2.5M	71820	.1				2.4M	63533	.1				3.7M	198619	0			

To analyze the system effectiveness into the main and interaction effects of system components, we estimated the Six-way ANOVA with second-order interaction and described the summary in Table 4. The higher the F-value and the lower the P-value (<0.001), the more significant the factor is. Whatever the collection, the query expansion (QE) component is the most significant factor when query effect is moved aside. Regardless of measures and collections, the next most significant modules are the retrieval module (RMod).

We can observe that the retrieval model (RMod) has a significant interaction effect with the expansion model (RMod*QE) and the number of expansion terms (RMod*NET) across collections and measures. Query expansion (QE) has a significant interaction effect with the minimum number of documents (QE*MND). Moreover, we observed the most significant interaction effects of the query with the expansion model (Query*QE) first and retrieval model (Query*RMod) second [not report]; we have also not reported some least influential factors [because of page limit].

4.2   Zoom-Out on Three Collections Altogether

To perceive a general tread from all the collections, we accumulated the queries and system settings from the three collections altogether, zoomed out on the parameter space, and estimated the Six-way ANOVA to break down both the AP and P@10 measures into the query, QE, RMod, NED, NET, and MND modules. The results are described in Table 5.

Table 5. Six-way ANOVA for the main effect of Query, QE, RMod, NED, NET, and MND when accumulating the three collections altogether for AP and P@10 measures, respectively. Other legends and settings are similar to Table 2.

Factors	AP						P@10					
	Df	SS	MS	F-val	P	R	Df	SS	MS	F-val	P	R
Query	348	201754	579	53640	.00	2	348	599241	1722	43243	.00	2
QE	6	12398	2066	191188	.00	1	6	33702	5617	141059	.00	1
RMod	19	10453	550	50901	.00	3	19	17971	946	23752	.00	3
NED	5	281	56	5205	.00	4	5	641	128	3220	.00	4
NET	4	12	3	274	.00	5	4	51	13	320	.00	5
MND	5	12	2	226	.00	6	5	50	10	253	.00	6
Err	8.7M	94751	.011				8.7M	349089	0			

Not surprisingly, we can see that the most significant component covering high variability is query expansion (QE) module. The next most significant modules are the query, retrieval model (RMod), and the number of expansion documents (NED) (in decreasing order). Therefore, we can deduce that the query expansion module should be given the first priority to tune for a new large collection.

4.3   Zoom-In the Collections - Groups of Queries

At first, we defined the groups of queries. Given three collections altogether, we calculated the average of AP (AAP) across systems for each query [16], then labeled the queries based on the quantile distribution of AAP. Queries having AAP higher than Q_3 (75%) are considered as easy, lower than Q_1 (25%) are considered as hard, and the remaining queries are considered as the medium. After defining the difficulty level of a query, we investigated the effectiveness each system achieved for that query and decided if the query is the easy, medium, or hard for that system. To explore the most important modules and their modalities, we employed the CART with a pruning parameter (i.e. cp) of 0.001 for the systems of all, easy, and hard queries, respectively. We visualized the CART for all queries in Fig. 2. The labels in the tree correspond to the modalities of the modules in Tables 1 and 3. We can clearly see that query expansion (QE) is the most important module in this case. This is consistent with the ANONA analysis in Sects. 4.1 and 4.2.

Figure 3 displays the resulting CARTs, in one hand for easy queries from the three collections altogether (left part) and on the other hand for hard queries

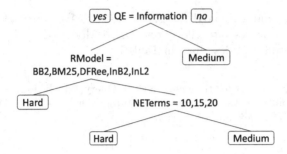

Fig. 2. CART for zooming out on the parameters space of systems of all queries.

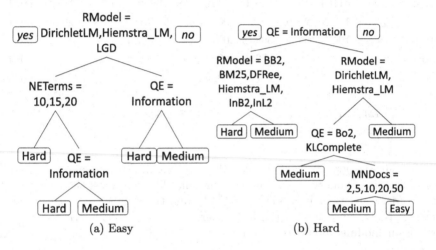

(a) Easy   (b) Hard

Fig. 3. CART visualization on zooming in the parameters space of systems for Easy (a) and Hard (b) queries.

(right part). We can clearly see that the trees are very different when considering either easy or hard queries of the collections altogether. We also observed this difference across collections [not plotted].

We can also observe that the most significant module (the top parameter for each tree) differs from easy queries to hard queries. For easy queries, the retrieval model (RMod) is the most significant module while the query expansion (QE) is for hard queries. Thus, system components should be designed with the options of choosing from retrieval and query expansion models at run-time and be tuned according to the query difficulty level.

5 Conclusion

In this paper, we have studied the problem of identifying which is the most significant component/parameter that influences the system effectiveness. We have conducted a large-scale analysis of more than 20,000 system settings that treated 350 queries from three different TREC ad-hoc collections. Using data analysis methods, we found that query expansion is the most significant system component when considering the three collections altogether. Zooming in the query set, we found that the most significant module differs according to the query difficulty class. For easy queries, the retrieval model is the most significant component to tune for optimal performance; this extends the analysis of Mizzaro and Robertson [16] where it was shown that easy query performs well to differentiate the good systems from bad systems. The query expansion is the most significant component for hard queries. These results imply that the transfer of parameter settings can be applied based on the query difficulty class and researchers can use our findings when designing and tuning their systems. These findings could be useful to develop adaptive systems based on the query difficulty classes.

As future work, we would like to study in deeper the interaction of the parameter settings with the characteristics of document collections, types of information needs, and suitability of retrieval methods across different search tasks. We also would like to investigate other effectiveness measures as well as a larger number of collections or collection shards in order to extract general trends. For example, we would like to observe if a certain type of collections (e.g., web collections) is homogeneous in terms of their parameter settings or if the parameter setting is completely collection dependent. Another track would be to define the minimum number of queries we would need to decide which will be the most important parameter for a given collection. Finally, we would like to apply other models than the decision tree.

References

1. Banks, D., Over, P., Zhang, N.F.: Blind men and elephants: six approaches to trec data. Inf. Retrieval **1**(1–2), 7–34 (1999)
2. Bergstra, J., Bengio, Y.: Random search for hyper-parameter optimization. J. Mach. Learn. Res. **13**(Feb), 281–305 (2012)
3. Bigot, A., Chrisment, C., Dkaki, T., Hubert, G., Mothe, J.: Fusing different information retrieval systems according to query-topics: a study based on correlation in information retrieval systems and trec topics. Inf. Retrieval **14**(6), 617 (2011)
4. Bigot, A., Déjean, S., Mothe, J.: Learning to choose the best system configuration in information retrieval: the case of repeated queries. J. Univ. Comput. Sci. **21**(13), 1726–1745 (2015)
5. Breiman, L.: Classification and Regression Trees. Routledge, Abingdon (2017)
6. Chifu, A.G., Laporte, L., Mothe, J., Ullah, M.Z.: Query performance prediction focused on summarized letor features. In: The 41st International ACM SIGIR Conference, pp. 1177–1180. ACM (2018)
7. Chrisment, C., Dkaki, T., Mothe, J., Poulain, S., Tanguy, L.: Recherche d information - analyse des résultats de différents systèmes réalisant la même tâche. Rev. Sci. Technol. l'Inf. **10**(1), 31–55 (2005)
8. Compaoré, J., Déjean, S., Gueye, A.M., Mothe, J., Randriamparany, J.: Mining information retrieval results: significant IR parameters. In: Advances in Information Mining and Management, October 2011

9. Deerwester, S., Dumais, S.T., Furnas, G.W., Landauer, T.K., Harshman, R.: Indexing by latent semantic analysis. J. Am. Soc. Inf. Sci. **41**(6), 391 (1990)

10. Dinçer, B.T.: Statistical principal components analysis for retrieval experiments. J. Assoc. Inf. Sci. Technol. **58**(4), 560–574 (2007)

11. Ferro, N.: What does affect the correlation among evaluation measures? ACM Trans. Inf. Syst. **36**(2), 19:1–19:40 (2017). https://doi.org/10.1145/3106371

12. Ferro, N., Silvello, G.: A general linear mixed models approach to study system component effects. In: Proceedings of the 39th International ACM SIGIR Conference, pp. 25–34. ACM (2016)

13. Harman, D., Buckley, C.: Overview of the reliable information access workshop. Inf. Retrieval **12**(6), 615 (2009)

14. Macdonald, C., McCreadie, R., Santos, R., Ounis, I.: From puppy to maturity: experiences in developing terrier. In: Proceedings of OSIR at SIGIR, pp. 60–63 (2012)

15. Miller Jr., R.G.: Beyond ANOVA: Basics of Applied Statistics. Chapman and Hall/CRC, London (1997)

16. Mizzaro, S., Robertson, S.: Hits hits trec: exploring IR evaluation results with network analysis. In: Proceedings of the 30th ACM SIGIR, pp. 479–486. ACM (2007)

17. Ponte, J.M., Croft, W.B.: A language modeling approach to information retrieval. In: Proceedings of the 21st ACM SIGIR Conference, pp. 275–281. ACM (1998)

18. Robertson, S., Zaragoza, H., et al.: The probabilistic relevance framework: BM25 and beyond. Found. Trends Inf. Retrieval **3**(4), 333–389 (2009)

19. Roy, D., Ganguly, D., Mitra, M., Jones, G.J.: Estimating gaussian mixture models in the local neighbourhood of embedded word vectors for query performance prediction. Inf. Process. Manag. **56**(3), 1026–1045 (2019)

20. Salton, G.: The SMART Retrieval System-Experiments in Automatic Document Processing. Prentice-Hall Inc., Upper Saddle River (1971)

21. Schutze, H., Hull, D.A., Pedersen, J.O.: A comparison of classifiers and document representations for the routing problem (1995)

22. Shtok, A., Kurland, O., Carmel, D.: Query performance prediction using reference lists. ACM Trans. Inf. Syst. **34**(4), 19:1–19:34 (2016)

23. Taylor, M., Zaragoza, H., Craswell, N., Robertson, S., Burges, C.: Optimisation methods for ranking functions with multiple parameters. In: Proceedings of the 15th ACM International Conference on Information and Knowledge Management, pp. 585–593. CIKM (2006)

24. Voorhees, E.M., Samarov, D., Soboroff, I.: Using replicates in information retrieval evaluation. ACM Trans. Inf. Syst. (TOIS) **36**(2), 12 (2017)

25. Zobel, J.: How reliable are the results of large-scale information retrieval experiments? In: Proceedings of the 21st Annual International ACM SIGIR Conference, pp. 307–314. ACM (1998)

Stance Detection in Web and Social Media: A Comparative Study

Shalmoli Ghosh[1](✉), Prajwal Singhania[1], Siddharth Singh[1], Koustav Rudra[2],
and Saptarshi Ghosh[1]

[1] Department of Computer Science and Engineering,
Indian Institute of Technology Kharagpur, Kharagpur, India
shalmolighosh94@gmail.com
[2] L3S Research Center, Hannover, Lower Saxony, Germany

Abstract. Online forums and social media platforms are increasingly
being used to discuss topics of varying polarities where different people
take different stances. Several methodologies for automatic stance detection from text have been proposed in literature. To our knowledge, there
has not been any systematic investigation towards their reproducibility,
and their comparative performances. In this work, we explore the reproducibility of several existing stance detection models, including both neural models and classical classifier-based models. Through experiments on
two datasets – (i) the popular SemEval microblog dataset, and (ii) a set
of health-related online news articles – we also perform a detailed comparative analysis of various methods and explore their shortcomings.

1 Introduction

Online platforms such as Twitter, Facebook and discussion forums, have become
popular platforms for discussing and expressing opinions about various inci-
dents/topics. In this context, *stance* is basically an opinion expressed by an individual towards some topic or event or personality. For instance, in the context of
a socio-political issue such as legalizing abortion in a country, some people can
support the issue while some others can oppose it, and yet others can be neutral. In today's Web, automatically identifying stance of a person from an online
post authored by the person, is an important problem (which is called *stance
detection*). Automatic stance detection has several applications [18], including
understanding the public opinion towards a specific socio-political issue, understanding the credibility of an online post based on whether it is supported by
authentic users, and so on.

According to earlier works, stance detection can be of two types – (i) Multi-
target Stance Detection, and (ii) Target (single) specific Stance Detection. Multi-
target stance detection aims at jointly detecting stances towards multiple related

S. Ghosh, P. Singhania and S. Singh—Equal contribution by authors.
K. Rudra—The work was done when the author was a Research Associate at IIT
Kharagpur.

F. Crestani et al. (Eds.): CLEF 2019, LNCS 11696, pp. 75–87, 2019.
https://doi.org/10.1007/978-3-030-28577-7_4

targets. This problem was introduced by Sobhani *et al.* [21] and has been studied by many later works [17,22,26]. In target-specific stance detection, the targets are considered separately and individually. In this work, we will be focusing on the problem of target-specific stance detection. Many algorithms have been proposed for target-specific stance detection; see Sect. 2 for a survey on such methods. However, to our knowledge, there has neither been any systematic comparison of these methods, nor any investigation of how reproducible these methods actually are. The present paper attempts to bridge this gap.

In this work, we explore *seven* target-specific stance detection models, out of which we implemented six (and publicly available code was used for the other model). We first investigate the reproducibility of the models. We then apply them on two datasets – (1) the standard SemEval microblog dataset, and (2) a formal text dataset of health-related articles. We also develop a new method that applies the recently developed BERT model [4] for stance detection, and compare its performance to that of the existing methods. Implementations of all algorithms discussed in this paper are available at https://github.com/prajwal1210/Stance-Detection-in-Web-and-Social-Media.

2   Related Work

In recent times, various works have tackled stance classification in different fields such as controversy detection [13], news articles [9], student essays [8], and so on. A reecent work [16] also studied stance detection from a diachronic perspective. The earlier models used traditional feature engineering-based methods, while the more recent models use deep neural architectures. We survey some stance detection models in this section.

Stance Detection Using Traditional Feature Engineering: Various works on stance detection use traditional feature engineering. For instance, Sen *et al.* [20] proposed a novel set of features with SVM model and a feedforward neural network model. HaCohen-kerner *et al.* [10] used 18 features including character skip-ngrams and character ngrams. Küçük *et al.* [15] used unigrams, bigrams, hashtags, external links, emoticons, and named entities as features to a SVM model. Dey *et al.* [5] proposed a two-phase SVM architecture with borrowed and novel feature sets.

It can be seen that most of the feature engineering based methods – including the baseline methods given by SemEval challenge [18] (that standardized the problem of stance detection over microblogs) – use SVM as a classifier. Hence, for our comparative analysis, we have chosen two SVM-based models.

Stance Detection Using Neural Models: In recent years, there have been many works using neural models for stance detection. Du *et al.* [7] used an attention based model for stance classification. Zarrella and Marsh [28], the winning team of the SemEval 2016 Task 6 A challenge, proposed a transfer learning method with features learned via distant supervision on two large unlabelled datasets. Wei *et al.* [27]), the second position holders of SemEval 2016 Task 6 A challenge, used Kim's CNN. Chen *et al.* [3] applied neural network model to classify stance of social media posts by considering users' taste, topics' taste and user comments on posts, whereas Dey *et al.* [6] used a two phase LSTM model.

Neural models for stance detection can be divided into a few informative categories like attention-based [7], convolution-based [27] and word embedding-based models [12]. For our comparative analysis, we have chosen one representative from each category, along with a recent pre-trained model named BERT [4].

Surveys on Stance Detection Models: There have been some relevant surveys as well. Zubiaga *et al.* [29] discussed various stance detection approaches for rumour detection and resolution. Several stance detection approaches were compared on Spanish and Catalan datasets in the StanceCat task [24]. Wang *et al.* [25] analysed the shortcomings of different stance detection models. But this survey did *not* actually compare performances of different methods over specific datasets, and also did not explore the reproducibility of different models, as is done in the present paper.

3 Dataset and Preprocessing

In this section, we describe the datasets used for the comparative analysis, and the preprocessing used over the datasets.

3.1 Datasets

We have used two types of publicly available stance-detection datasets:

(1) SemEval 2016 Task 6A Dataset [18]: contains microblogs (tweets) data related to the following 5 topics – (i) Atheism (AT), (ii) Climate Change is a real concern (CC), (iii) Feminist Movement (FM), (iv) Hillary Clinton (HC), and (v) Legalization of Abortion (LA). For each topic, we have used the official train-test split, as used in the SemEval 2016 challenge.

(2) Multi Perspective Consumer Health Query (MPCHI) Data: This dataset, taken from [20], comprises of formal texts (sentences collected from top-ranked articles corresponding to queries issued on a specific Web search engine) corresponding to the following 5 queries (claims) – (i) MMR vaccination can cause autism (MMR), (ii) E-cigarettes are safer than normal cigarettes (EC), (iii) Women should take HRT post menopause (HRT), (iv) Vitamin C prevents common cold (VC), (v) Sun exposure leads to skin cancer (SC). We split each dataset of MPCHI into train and test sets in the same proportion as in the SemEval data.

Each dataset contains texts annotated with one of three classes – Favor (supports the topic/claim), Against (opposes the topic/claim), and None (neutral to the topic/claim). Table 1 reports the statistics of all 10 datasets, and Table 2 shows some example posts from the datasets.

Table 1. Statistics of the datasets (divided into training and test sets).

Dataset	Topic	# Training instances			# Test instances		
		FAVOR	AGAINST	NONE	FAVOR	AGAINST	NONE
SemEval	AT	92	304	117	32	160	28
	CC	212	15	168	123	11	35
	FM	210	328	126	58	183	44
	HC	112	361	166	45	172	78
	LA	105	334	164	46	189	45
MPCHI	MMR	48	61	72	24	33	21
	SC	68	51	117	35	26	42
	EC	60	118	111	33	47	44
	VC	74	52	68	37	16	31
	HRT	33	95	44	9	41	24

Table 2. Examples of posts from some of the datasets

Tweet/Text	Label
Tweets from SemEval Dataset AT (Atheism)	
All that is needed for God for something to happen is to say "#Be" and it is; for God is capable of all things. #God created #trinity #SemST	AGAINST
Absolutely fucking sick & tired of the religious and their "We're persecuted" bollocks So f**king what? Pissoff! #SemST	FAVOR
In other related news. Boko Haram has killed over 200 people in the last 48hrs. #SemST	NONE
Texts from MPCHI Dataset HRT	
A 2002 study called the Women's Health Initiative (WHI), designed to explore the benefits and risks of combined estrogen-progestin HRT was halted three and a half years before the intended end of the study period, because researchers observed a 26% increase in the relative risk of breast cancer	AGAINST
HRT can also help to lower the risk of osteoporosis and prevent some of the long term health problems associated with early menopause	FAVOR
Ovarian cancer is the fifth most common cause of cancer death among women in the UK, accounting for six per cent of all female deaths from cancer	NONE

3.2 Preprocessing Methodology

Different prior works have used different preprocessing methods. To ensure a fair comparison among different models, we apply the same preprocessing before applying the models.

Standard Preprocessing: We perform standard preprocessing steps such as case-folding, stemming (using Porter stemmer), and stopword removal. However, note that stemming and stop-word removal are *not* performed while using neural models that rely on pre-trained embeddings (since the stemmed versions of terms would not probably be found in the pre-trained embeddings).

Exclusive Preprocessing for Microblogs: We perform the following preprocessing only for the microblog datasets (across all stance detection models):

(1) Normalization: We normalize the text using the method proposed by Han *et al.* [11]. This helps us to deal with abbreviations and out-of-vocabulary words. For example, the term '*aaf*' is expanded as '*as a friend*'.

(2) Hashtag Preprocessing: Users primarily use hashtags in tweets to convey their sentiments [11]. Hashtags are often created by concatenating several individual words. For example, #powertowomen is a popular hashtag used during the 'Feminist Movement'. Such hashtags are usually marked as OOV (Out Of Vocabulary) words by standard NLP tools. In this paper, we have used Word-ninja package[1] to split such combined texts into most probable constituent word sequences. For example, '**#powertowomen**' may be splitted as '**# power to women**' or '**# power tow omen**'. However, the algorithm returns the first one because it is more probable than the later one.

Incorporating the tweet normalization and hashtag preprocessing steps in this work have resulted in improved performance of existing models. Later in Sect. 7, we have shown the effect of this preprocessing.

4   Reproducing a Selection of Stance Detection Methods

For our present study, we selected a few representative methods from the two groups of methods stated in Sect. 2. In this section, we describe the challenges in reproducing the methods and possible ways to overcome the challenges. Note that, we used codes provided by the authors for the first model, while all the other models were reproduced by us.

(1) Convolutional Neural Networks: This method [27], which uses Kim's 1-D CNN-based sentence classification model [14], performed second-best in the SemEval stance detection task (Task 6A). We used the code that has been made available by the authors.[2] Note that, we applied our pre-processing techniques on the dataset before applying this model, and this step significantly improves the performance (see Sect. 7).

(2) Target-Specific Attention Neural Network [TAN]: Du *et al.* [7] proposed a novel bidirectional LSTM-based attention mechanism. We briefly describe the architecture below. A target sequence of length N is represented as $[z_1, z_2, \ldots, z_N]$ where $z_n \epsilon R^{d'}$ is the d'-dimensional vector of the n-th word in the target sequence. The target-augmented embedding of a word t for a specific

---

[1] https://github.com/keredson/wordninja.
[2] https://github.com/nestle1993/SE16-Task6-Stance-Detection.

target z is $e_t^z = x_t \odot z$ where $\odot$ is the vector concatenation operation. The dimension of e_t^z is $(d + d')$. An affine transformation maps the $(d + d')$-dimensional target-augmented embedding of each word to a scalar value as per Eq. 1:

$$a_t' = W_a e_t^z + b_a \tag{1}$$

where W_a and b_a are the parameters of the bypass neural network. The attention vector $[a_1', a_2', \ldots, a_T']$ undergoes a softmax transformation to get the final attention signal vector (Eq. 2):

$$a_t = softmax(a_t') = \frac{e^{a_t'}}{\sum_{i=1}^{T} e^{a_i'}} \tag{2}$$

Challenges in Reproducibility: Du *et al.* [7] mentioned that they trained embeddings on a manually scraped corpus, but they neither released the corpus nor the embeddings. We have used the pre-trained Glove 6B 300d embeddings for this purpose.[3] Additionally, whether dropout is used and what activation function is used in the middle layers were not mentioned in [7]. We have used dropout and ReLU activation function.

An observation About the TAN Model: Du *et al.* [7] claim that using the target-augmented embeddings enable the model to make *"full use of the target information in stance detection"* (quoted from [7]). However, we believe that this architecture does *not* take advantage of the target information at all. We give a simple proof for our claim:

Theorem 1. *The bypass neural network in the TAN is unaffected by the target information, i.e.,* $\frac{da_t}{dz} = 0$.

Proof: From Eq. (1), we have: $a_t' = W_a e_t^z + b_a \implies a_t' = W_a (x_t \odot z) + b_a$

$$\because W_a = W_{ax} \odot W_{az} \text{ (where } W_{ax} \epsilon R^d \text{ and } W_{az} \epsilon R^{d'}) :$$

$$\therefore a_t' = W_{ax} \cdot x_t + W_{az} \cdot z + b_a$$

Now, from Eq. (2), we have:

$$a_t = \frac{e^{a_t'}}{\sum_{i=1}^{T} e^{a_i'}} = \frac{e^{W_{ax} \cdot x_t + W_{az} \cdot z + b_a}}{\sum_{i=1}^{T} e^{W_{ax} \cdot x_i + W_{az} \cdot z + b_a}} = \frac{e^{W_{ax} \cdot x_t}}{\sum_{i=1}^{T} e^{W_{ax} \cdot x_i}}$$

$$\therefore \frac{da_t}{dz} = 0$$

We also back our claim with an empirical experiment, wherein we do *not* augment the target embeddings to the word-embeddings in the bypass neural network, i.e., we use $e_t^z = x_t$ (instead of $e_t^z = x_t \odot z$ in the original model). We call this

---

[3] https://nlp.stanford.edu/projects/glove/.

architecture the **TAN-**. We show later in the paper that results obtained by both the TAN and TAN- architectures are very similar.

(3) Recurrent Neural Network with Long Short Term Memory(LSTM): In the earlier TAN paper [7], one of the baselines was LSTM without target-specific embedding and target-specific attention. In this work we have also reproduced this LSTM-based method.

Challenges in Reproducibility: The challenges faced were same as TAN model and we took the same steps as for the TAN model [7].

(4) SVM-Based SEN Model: Sen *et al.* [20] proposed a SVM based stance detection model using five sets of features – stance vector, textual entailment, sentiment, medical knowledge based feature and a standard context based BoW feature. The stance vector is created on a sentence level based on an assumption [1] that the main information present in a sentence revolves around some particular parts-of-speech like the Nouns, Adjectives, Verbs, Adverbs. Thus these parts-of-speech are the main building blocks of the stance expressed by a sentence towards a particular claim. To identify the sentiment feature (positive or negative or neutral), we used a standard sentiment analyzer given in Stanford CoreNLP Toolkit to obtain the sentiment for a sentence.

Note that, we made one change while implementing this model. For the textual entailment feature, the original paper [20] used the Excitement Open Platform (EOP) [19]. We initially tried using EOP, but later we observed that results improve if textual entailment is estimated with Tensor Flow[4] where textual entailment is estimated using word vectorization, recurrent neural networks with LSTM and dropout as a regularization method.

Finally, the medical knowledge-based features were extracted using a tool called SemRep (https://semrep.nlm.nih.gov) along with the help of a medical knowledge-base called UMLS [2]. This feature is specifically for use with the MPCHI datasets (on which Sen *et al.* [20] performed their experiments). The medical feature is not used for SEMEVAL dataset as it is not related to health informatics.

Challenges in Reproducibility: In the BoW feature, we used word-unigrams, since the exact value of n for n-grams was not mentioned in the original paper [20].

(5) Two-Step SVM: Dey *et al.* [5] proposed a two-step stance detection approach. In the first step, they find whether a tweet is relevant to the given claim, and in the next step they detect the stance (if the tweet is relevant). The first step uses features such as Weighted MPQA Subjectivity-Polarity Classification and Wordnet Based Potential Adjective Recognition, whereas the second phase comprises of Sentiwordnet and MPQA Based Sentiment Classification, Frame Semantics, Target Detection, Word n-Grams and Character n-Grams.

---

[4] https://github.com/Steven-Hewitt/Entailment-with-Tensorflow/blob/master/Entailment%20with%20TensorFlow.ipynb.

Challenges in Reproducibility: According to Dey *et al.* [5], the two most important features are (i) Wordnet Based Potential Adjective Recognition and (ii) Frame Semantics. Especially, in the second phase, frame semantics is the most decisive feature. This feature attempts to estimate the relative importance of multiple clauses present in a tweet, where the clauses are considered to be separated by 'connector words'. However, there is lack of clarity about this feature. It is written that "We assign more weightage to the more important clause, in case connector words are present in the sentence." (quoted from [5]). But it is not clarified how exactly the relative weights of the clauses are decided. Due to this lack of clarity, we could not implement the frame semantics feature of this model. We have implemented all other features except frame semantics.

A General Challenge in Reproducibility Across all Models: Almost none of the prior works described in this section stated the exact values of the hyperparameters in the models. Hence, we adopted the same approach as Du *et al.* [7] – hyperparameters were tuned using 5-fold cross-validation on the training set (of each dataset).

5   Using BERT for Stance Detection

Apart from experimenting with existing stance detection methods, we have applied a recently developed deep learning model named BERT [4] (Bidirectional Encoder Representations from Transformers - developed by Google AI Language group) for stance detection. To the best of our knowledge, no prior work has applied BERT for stance detection.

BERT models pre-trained on large unlabeled corpora using bidirectional language modelling have been released by Google. This training is made possible by masking 15% of the input words, and using the corresponding final layer hidden states to predict these words. The pre-trained BERT model can be fine-tuned with just one additional output layer to create state-of-the-art models for a wide range of tasks, such as question answering and language inference, without substantial task-specific architecture modifications.

In this work, we used a pre-trained BERT (Large-Uncased) model. The input text is fed to the BERT model which generates representations of the words in the text through multiple transformer layers. We have then fed the output of the first head of the final layer of BERT through a randomly initialized feed-forward layer along with softmax and fine-tuning the network on the task-specific data.

6   Experimental Setup

Hyper-Parameter Tuning: As stated in Sect. 4, almost none of the prior works specify all the hyperparameter values. We tuned all hyperparamters (that are not stated in the respective papers) using 5-fold cross-validation on the training set. In case a hyperparameter value is specified in a paper, the said value is used. Model-wise hyperparameter values that were tuned by us are mentioned

Table 3. Hyperparameters of the models. For some hyperparameters, the values are different for different datasets.

Model	Hyperparameters
TAN and TAN-	Learning_rate: 5e-4, batch_size:50, dropout: 0.5, L2:[(AT, HRT):1.25, (CC, LA, HC):1, FM:0.75, (MMR, SC, VC, EC):0.25], epochs:[(AT, LA, VC):40-50,(CC, FM, HC, MMR, HRT, SC, EC):50-60]
LSTM	Learning_rate: 5e-4, batch_size:50, dropout: 0.5, L2:[(AT, HC, VC, EC):0.25, (CC, LA, MMR, HRT, SC):0.5, FM:0.75], epochs:[(AT, CC, FM, LA, HC, SC):50-60, (MMR, HRT, VC, EC):30-40]
CNN	Dropout: 0.5, Learning_rate_decay: 0.95, Squared norm limit:[(AT, FM, LA, MMR, VC, EC):7, (CC, HC, HRT):8, SC:9]
BERT	Learning_Rate:2e-5, Num_Train_Epochs:50, Warmup_Proportion:0.1, Max_Seq_Length:128
SEN	gamma:0.001(for both MPCHI and SemEval), rest as in paper [20]
Two-step SVM	As given in paper [5]

Table 4. Results showing the effect of our preprocessing on previous models (computed over all the datasets of SEMEVAL)

Method	Metric value reported by original paper	Metric value with our preprocessing
TAN	0.6879 [7]	**0.690**
LSTM	0.6321 [7]	**0.687**
CNN	0.6733 [27]	**0.706**

in Table 3 (using same notations as in our codes (for those not mentioned in the respective papers)).

Vote Scheme: We use the vote scheme proposed in [27] for prediction on the test set. For each model, we run ten parallel epochs, whose validation sets are randomly selected from the training set and are non-overlapping. According to [27], in each epoch, some iterations are deliberately chosen to predict the test set. Then, when this epoch ends, for every sentence in the test set, the label which appears most frequently in these predictions as the result of this epoch is appointed. Finally, when ten epochs end, voting happens within results of these ten epochs by the same method described above to determine the final labels. Performing multiple times independently and voting twice provides a robust mechanism for predicting. Note that the voting scheme is used for TAN, TAN-, CNN and LSTM models only.

Performance Metric: To evaluate the performance of all models, we use the same metric as used by the official SemEval 2016 Task A [18] – the macro-average of the F1-score for 'favor' and 'against' classes.

Table 5. Stance classification results on SEMEVAL datasets. Highest values marked in blue and boldface.

Model	AT	CC	LA	FM	HC	Total
TAN [7]	0.628	0.430	0.567	0.590	**0.728**	0.690
TAN-	0.638	0.440	0.572	0.542	0.724	0.692
LSTM [7]	0.629	0.429	0.628	0.571	0.611	0.687
SEN [20]	0.590	0.39	0.575	0.510	0.565	0.630
CNN [27]	0.641	0.445	**0.684**	0.552	0.675	0.706
BERT [4]	**0.743**	**0.446**	0.657	**0.650**	0.713	**0.751**
Two-step SVM (without Frame Semantics)	0.410	0.419	0.436	0.496	0.488	0.631
Two-step SVM (as reported in [5])	0.725	0.535	0.836	0.787	0.797	0.744

Table 6. Stance classification results on MPCHI datasets. Highest values marked in blue and boldface.

Model	HRT	EC	VC	SC	MMR	Total
TAN [7]	0.347	0.580	0.421	0.507	0.671	0.586
TAN-	0.569	0.583	0.578	0.468	0.608	0.589
LSTM [7]	0.464	0.609	0.592	0.575	0.665	0.631
SEN [20]	0.480	0.605	0.405	0.445	0.615	0.540
CNN [27]	0.359	0.539	0.524	0.252	0.524	0.551
BERT [4]	**0.669**	**0.780**	**0.647**	**0.769**	**0.782**	**0.756**
Two-step SVM (without Frame Semantics)	0.470	0.297	0.409	0.293	0.455	0.519

7   Results and Analysis

This section describes the comparative analyses of the different stance detection models, and also reports some error analysis.

Effect of Preprocessing on Existing Methods: In this work, we applied some tweet-specific preprocessing (tweet normalization and hashtag preprocessing) on the SemEval datasets (as stated in Sect. 3). Table 4 reports the performance of some of the models, as reported in the original paper (that proposed a model) and after this tweet-specific preprocessing. We see that the performance of the existing methods improves significantly due to this preprocessing.

Comparative Analysis: Tables 5 and 6 describe the performances of all models on SemEval dataset and MPCHI dataset respectively. Since we could not reproduce the Frame Semantics feature of the two-step SVM model [5], we have reported both the performances of our implementation and that reported in the original paper [5] for the SemEval datasets (the original paper worked only on the SemEval datasets, not the MPCHI datasets).

Table 7. Examples of tweets/texts misclassified by all models

Reason	Dataset	Tweet/Text
Sarcasm	FM	I like girls. They just need to know there place. #SemST
	CC	@JustinTrudeau Hey Justin I will give you 50 cents if you stop talking about climate 'Change' #Ottawa #davidsuzuki #cbc #SemST
Question	HC	Do you Progressives know how dangerously close you are to suppressing free speech? Stop it. #inners #readyforhillary #SemST
	FM	@BOZARbrussels is this how UN_Women sees #genderequality ? Only #women with arms like #men ?#stopmarriagebill #fakecases UN #SemST
Insufficient signal to target	EC	E-Cigarettes contain ONLY nicotine
	HRT	There are also ne therapies, such as progestogens and testosterone
	EC	Public health officials counter that it's too early to know very much about the health effects of e-cigarettes, especially on young people

It is clearly seen that the overall metric of BERT model is far better than that of other competing models. Apart from the BERT model, all other models perform better in case of SemEval dataset consistently. This is possibly because the size of MPCHI dataset is much smaller than that of SemEval dataset, and thus neural models might not train well over such small datasets. Also we observed that the CNN model performs well for shorter tweets (of length 5–10 words) while BERT works well for longer ones, since BERT is developed to capture context information over longer texts (details omitted due to lack of space).

Note that the results of TAN and TAN- models are very comparable as claimed in Sect. 4; in fact, as per the overall metric, the TAN- model performs slightly better than TAN for both types of datasets.

Where all Models Fail: We have considered the labels predicted by all the seven models, and checked those tweets/texts where all the models fail (i.e., no model was able to give the correct label). In total, there are 72 tweets (across all SemEval datasets) and 42 posts (across all MPCHI datasets) where all models classified wrongly; Table 7 shows some examples of such tweets/text. We manually observed these misclassified tweets and text, and made the following observations.

- In case of tweets (the SemEval datasets) the errors were mostly on tweets that contain (i) sarcastic comments [23], and (ii) questions.
- In case of the MPCHI dataset, there were some posts containing health-related facts, which actually express no stance w.r.t the target. All the models were unable to capture this notion.

  It is possible that the stance can be understood by a human having a lot of contextual background knowledge; however, it is difficult to understand the stance just from what is mentioned in the tweet/text.

8   Conclusion

To our knowledge, this is the first analysis of reproducibility of existing stance detection methods, as well as a systematic comparison of stance detection methods over two different type of datasets. We observed that the BERT pre-trained model can perform better stance detection than many existing methods. We see that no single method is able to give very high metric value over all datasets; this observation motivates us to explore some combination of methods (ensemble methods) for stance detection in future.

Acknowledgement. The work is partially supported by a project titled "Building Healthcare Informatics Systems Utilising Web Data" funded by Department of Science & Technology, Government of India.

References

1. Agrawal, A., An, A.: Unsupervised emotion detection from text using semantic and syntactic relations. In: Proceedings of the IEEE/WIC/ACM Joint Conferences on Web Intelligence and Intelligent Agent Technology (2012)
2. Bodenreider, O.: The unified medical language system (UMLS): integrating biomedical terminology. Nucleic Acids Res. **32**(Suppl. 1), D267–D270 (2004)
3. Chen, W.F., Ku, L.W.: UTCNN: a deep learning model of stance classification on social media text. arXiv preprint arXiv:1611.03599 (2016)
4. Devlin, J., Chang, M.W., Lee, K., Toutanova, K.: BERT: pre-training of deep bidirectional transformers for language understanding. arXiv preprint arXiv:1810.04805 (2018)
5. Dey, K., Shrivastava, R., Kaushik, S.: Twitter stance detection - a subjectivity and sentiment polarity inspired two-phase approach. In: Proceedings of the IEEE Conference on Data Mining Workshops (ICDMW) (2017)
6. Dey, K., Shrivastava, R., Kaushik, S.: Topical stance detection for Twitter: a two-phase LSTM model using attention. In: Pasi, G., Piwowarski, B., Azzopardi, L., Hanbury, A. (eds.) ECIR 2018. LNCS, vol. 10772, pp. 529–536. Springer, Cham (2018). https://doi.org/10.1007/978-3-319-76941-7_40
7. Du, J., Xu, R., He, Y., Gui, L.: Stance classification with target-specific neural attention networks. In: Proceedings of the International Joint Conferences on Artificial Intelligence (IJCAI) (2017)
8. Faulkner, A.: Automated classification of stance in student essays: an approach using stance target information and the Wikipedia link-based measure. Science **376**(12), 86 (2014)
9. Ferreira, W., Vlachos, A.: Emergent: a novel data-set for stance classification. In: Proceedings of the NAACL-HLT (2016)
10. HaCohen-kerner, Y., Ido, Z., Ya'akobov, R.: Stance classification of tweets using skip char ngrams. In: Altun, Y., et al. (eds.) ECML PKDD 2017. LNCS (LNAI), vol. 10536, pp. 266–278. Springer, Cham (2017). https://doi.org/10.1007/978-3-319-71273-4_22
11. Han, B., Baldwin, T.: Lexical normalisation of short text messages: makn sens a# twitter. In: Proceedings of the Annual Meeting of the Association for Computational Linguistics: Human Language Technologies (2011)

12. Hochreiter, S., Schmidhuber, J.: Long short-term memory. Neural Comput. **9**(8), 1735–1780 (1997)
13. Jang, M., Allan, J.: Improving automated controversy detection on the web. In: Proceedings of the ACM SIGIR Conference (2016)
14. Kim, Y.: Convolutional neural networks for sentence classification. CoRR abs/1408.5882 (2014). http://arxiv.org/abs/1408.5882
15. Küçük, D., Can, F.: Stance detection on tweets: an SVM-based approach. arXiv preprint arXiv:1803.08910 (2018)
16. Lai, M., Patti, V., Ruffo, G., Rosso, P.: Stance evolution and Twitter interactions in an italian political debate. In: Silberztein, M., Atigui, F., Kornyshova, E., Métais, E., Meziane, F. (eds.) NLDB 2018. LNCS, vol. 10859, pp. 15–27. Springer, Cham (2018). https://doi.org/10.1007/978-3-319-91947-8_2
17. Liu, H., Li, S., Zhou, G.: Two-target stance detection with target-related zone modeling. In: Zhang, S., Liu, T.-Y., Li, X., Guo, J., Li, C. (eds.) CCIR 2018. LNCS, vol. 11168, pp. 170–182. Springer, Cham (2018). https://doi.org/10.1007/978-3-030-01012-6_14
18. Mohammad, S., Kiritchenko, S., Sobhani, P., Zhu, X., Cherry, C.: Semeval-2016 task 6: detecting stance in tweets. In: Proceedings of the International Workshop on Semantic Evaluation (SemEval-2016), pp. 31–41 (2016)
19. Padó, S., Noh, T.G., Stern, A., Wang, R., Zanoli, R.: Design and realization of a modular architecture for textual entailment. Natural Lang. Eng. **21**(2), 167–200 (2015)
20. Sen, A., Sinha, M., Mannarswamy, S., Roy, S.: Stance classification of multi-perspective consumer health information. In: Proceedings of the ACM India Joint Conference on Data Science and Management of Data (2018)
21. Sobhani, P., Inkpen, D., Zhu, X.: A dataset for multi-target stance detection. In: Proceedings of the Conference of the European Chapter of the Association for Computational Linguistics (2017)
22. Sobhani, P., Inkpen, D., Zhu, X.: Exploring deep neural networks for multitarget stance detection. Comput. Intell. **35**(1), 82–97 (2019)
23. Sulis, E., Farías, D.I.H., Rosso, P., Patti, V., Ruffo, G.: Figurative messages and affect in Twitter: differences between# irony,# sarcasm and# not. Knowl.-Based Syst. **108**, 132–143 (2016)
24. Taulé, M., et al.: Overview of the task on stance and gender detection in tweets on Catalan independence at IberEval 2017. In: Proceedings of the Workshop on Evaluation of Human Language Technologies for Iberian Languages (2017)
25. Wang, R., Zhou, D., Jiang, M., Si, J., Yang, Y.: A survey on opinion mining: from stance to product aspect. IEEE Access **7**, 41101–41124 (2019)
26. Wei, P., Lin, J., Mao, W.: Multi-target stance detection via a dynamic memory-augmented network. In: Proceedings of the ACM SIGIR Conference (2018)
27. Wei, W., Zhang, X., Liu, X., Chen, W., Wang, T.: pkudblab at semeval-2016 task 6: a specific convolutional neural network system for effective stance detection. In: SemEval@NAACL-HLT (2016)
28. Zarrella, G., Marsh, A.: MITRE at semeval-2016 task 6: transfer learning for stance detection. arXiv preprint arXiv:1606.03784 (2016)
29. Zubiaga, A., Aker, A., Bontcheva, K., Liakata, M., Procter, R.: Detection and resolution of rumours in social media: a survey. ACM Comput. Surv. (CSUR) **51**(2), 32 (2018)

TwitCID: A Collection of Data Sets for Studies on Information Diffusion on Social Networks

Thi Bich Ngoc Hoang[1,2](✉), Josiane Mothe[3], and Manon Baillon[4]

[1] UPS, Université de Toulouse, IRIT, UMR5505 CNRS, Toulouse, France
`thi-bich-ngoc.hoang@irit.fr`
[2] University of Economics, The University of Danang, Da Nang, Vietnam
[3] ESPE, UT2J, Université de Toulouse, IRIT, UMR5505 CNRS, Toulouse, France
`josiane.mothe@irit.fr`
[4] Université Capitole, Toulouse, France
`manon.baillon@ut-capitole.fr`

Abstract. Online social networks play a crucial role in spreading information at a very large scale. Modeling information propagation on social networks has been attracting a lot of attention from researchers. However, none of the data sets used in past works are made available to the research community, while they would be very useful for comparative studies. In this paper, we detail a collection of tweets composed of five data sets for a total of 18 million tweets that we release, and which is designed to evaluate methods on modeling the information spread, in the case of general information and brands marketing information. In addition to tweet IDs and a script to retrieve the whole tweet in JSON from the Twitter API, we release the values of the 29 extracted features for these data sets. These features consist of user based, content based and temporal based features. Finally, we provide the results of information diffusion prediction models (80% accuracy) which could serve as strong baselines for this research topic.

Keywords: Information diffusion · Evaluation collection ·
Tweet collection · Retweets · Social networks

1 Introduction

Predicting information diffusion is an important challenge for many tasks from marketing [6] to information check-worthiness [11]. It has attracted a lot of attention in social networks research community [1,5,12,18] and which is not yet solved. However, in past studies, the data sets used in the evaluation part of the studies are not made available while it is well acknowledge that benchmark collections are very useful for comparative studies.

In this paper, we introduce the TwitCID collection which consist of a set of five data sets of tweets. In total, there are more than 18 million of tweets in about

© Springer Nature Switzerland AG 2019
F. Crestani et al. (Eds.): CLEF 2019, LNCS 11696, pp. 88–100, 2019.
https://doi.org/10.1007/978-3-030-28577-7_5

"general" information (two data sets) and "brand marketing" information (three data sets), of which million tweets are forwarded hundreds to dozen thousand times. In addition, we include the description of features we extracted from these tweets and release their values for the five data sets. These features cover 29 characteristics related to the users who created the tweets, the content of the tweets and the time the tweets were created. Finally, we provide effectiveness results of two information diffusion prediction models defined respectively by Suh et al. [19] and Hoang et al. [7]. These models reach up to 80% accuracy and could serve as a strong baselines although there is still room for improving these results.

Other researchers can use our released material (data sets, extracted features, results of strong predictive models) to evaluate their method of predicting information diffusion. The TwitCID collection and the extracted feature values are provided at http://doi.org/10.5281/zenodo.3246705.

The rest of the paper is organized as follows: Sect. 2 presents the related work. Section 3 describes the TwitCID collection, the extracted features along with the descriptive analysis of the most peculiar features. In Sect. 4, we report the results of information diffusion prediction models on our collection which could serve as strong baseline for future studies. We conclude the paper in Sect. 5.

2   Related Work

While Twitter-based data sets are available for information extraction [2,14], name entity recognition evaluation [15,17], for sentiment analysis evaluation [13, 16,20] and information cascade modeling [3,22], there is no reference data sets to evaluate predicting information diffusion despite the growing interest in this domain [4,5,7,9,19,21].

In the area of predicting the information diffusion on social networks, various studies have been carried on and widely referenced. Guille et al. [5] developed a model to predict the temporal dynamics of information spreading on social networks based on machine learning algorithms and the inference of time dependent diffusion probabilities from a multidimensional individual behaviors analysis. They evaluated their method on a large data set which includes 467 million Twitter posts. Also using machine learning approach evaluated on a tweet data set, Varshney et al. [21] proposed a model to predict the information diffusion probabilities on social networks. They used a Bayesian network considering user interests and content similarity models. Dong et al. [4] used two data sets of around one million of tweets posted by Sina-Weibo to evaluate their approach on predicting the propagation of natural disaster information while Kafeza et al. [9] used 13,000 tweets related to the Malaysia airline flight 370 disappearance (#MH370) to evaluate their model on predicting the information spread patterns. However, none of these data sets have been made available to the research community.

Suh et al. [19] introduced several features that may affect the diffusion of a given message on social networks. Analysing a large scale data set of 74 million tweets, they showed that the number of followers and followees, the age of the user account and the number of favourites strongly correlate with the retweetability. Conversely, the total of the user's past tweets and the presence of hashtag/URL do not highly impact on the number of retweets. Hoang *et al.* proposed a model to predict whether a tweet is going to be diffused and the level of diffusion using machine learning algorithms. Their model is based on various features including Suh's that were shown effective for diffusion prediction evaluation. For this reason, we extract the features proposed in Suh and Hoang studies and release them to the community.

Two twitter-based data sets have been made available on information cascade. Domenico *et al.* [3] distributed a data set that includes about 450 thousand nodes and 15 million edges representing the spreading processes on Twitter, the relationships between friends and followers, between who retweets/replies/mentions from whom. Xie *et al.* [22] distributed a data set of 6 million URLs and 540 thousand hashtags extracted from a data flow of 32 millions tweets that they consider as identities of cascades. Each row in the released data set includes one URL/hashtag along with list of anonymized user-timestamp pairs. These two released data sets show which users interact with which users [3], or which users mentioned the same URLs/hashtags in their messages [22] but neither the tweet ID nor related information regarding the users' profile, the message contents or the time tweets were created which are main objects in a Tweet JSON and which are very crucial in predicting the diffusion of a message on social networks [9,10]. That make these data sets of limited use for information diffusion prediction evaluation.

In this paper we describe the TwitCID collection consisting of 5 Twitter data sets (around 18M tweets) that we make available for research purposes. It is designed to evaluate studies on predicting information diffusion on social networks. In addition, we provide a set of extracted features corresponding to data sets, along with results of predictive models of 80% accuracy which can be used as a baseline for other works in this area.

3   The TwitCID Collection

3.1   Data Sets on General and Brand Marketing Information

The TwitCID collection consists of five Twitter data sets which were extracted from the 1% of the tweets that Twitter agrees to be collected. The Firstweek and Secondweek data set were collected during the first week and second week of January 2017 while the Iphone, Gucci and Galaxy data sets were collected from 21 September 2015 to 31 May 2017 using the keywords "iphone", "gucci" and "galaxys" respectively. We designed the TwitCID collection so that it contains "general" information (Firstweek and Secondweek data sets) and more "marketing"-oriented information (the three other data sets). In that way, information diffusion can be studied in different scenario using the TwitCID collection.

Table 1 reports the number of tweets, the number of non-retweeted and the number of unique retweeted tweets for the five data sets. We can see that the

Table 1. The number of tweets and their distribution for our TwitCID collection.

	Firstweek	Secondweek	Iphone	Gucci	Galaxy
# of tweets	8,009,112	8,171,080	2,188,923	242,956	174,909
# of non-retweeted tweets	4,025,157	4,058,066	1,483,705	74,543	134,443
# of (unique) retweeted tweets	2,017,979	2,080,962	312,003	51,805	19,391

Table 2. The number of tweets and their distribution according to the level of retweets on the TwitCID collection. Class-0 corresponds to the tweets that are not retweeted, class-1 are retweeted less than 100 times, class-2 from 100 times to 10,000 times, and class-3 more than 10,000 times.

	Firstweek	Secondweek	Iphone	Gucci	Galaxy
Class-0	4,025,157	4,058,066	1,483,705	74,543	134,443
Class-1	1,675,859	1,727,666	271,147	41,752	17,446
Class-2	327,381	339,328	37,355	9,968	1,915
Class-3	14,739	13,905	501	85	30

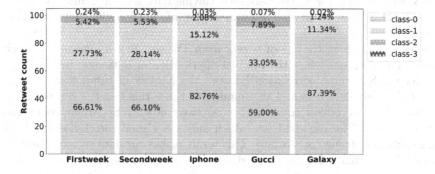

Fig. 1. Distributions of tweets in classes over our five data sets. Class-0 corresponds to the tweets that are not retweeted, class-1 are retweeted less than 100 times, class-2 from 100 times to 10,000 times, and class-3 more than 10,000 times.

proportion of tweets in each of these classes is about the same for the first and second week data sets, while they differ in the three other data sets.

Table 2 presents the distribution of tweets when we consider the level of retweets on the five data sets. In the Table 2, class-0 corresponds to the tweets that are not retweeted at all, class-1 are tweets that are retweeted less than 100 times, class-2 from 100 times to 10,000 times, and class-3 are tweets retweeted more than 10,000 times. To make the distribution more visual, we plot it in the Fig. 1. FirstWeek and SecondWeek data sets are very similar in terms of class distribution. Moreover, in general, the tweets that are not retweeted are the majority (from 59% to 87% depending on the data sets). The second most populated class is class-1, whatever the data set is and corresponds to from 11% to 33%. Class-2 is from 1% to 8%. Unsurprisingly, there are very few tweets in

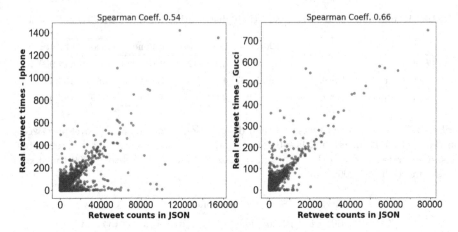

Fig. 2. Spear correlations between the number of times a tweet is retweeted in the data sets and retweet counts in the tweet objects.

class-3, less than 1% for all the data sets. Having data sets with different distributions is of interest to be able to evaluate the information diffusion prediction in different contexts.

Since we are using the 1% of tweets from Twitter, it is important to check whether our data sets keeps the original distribution of re-tweets. In Fig. 2, we consider the Spearman correlation between the number of times each tweet is retweeted in our data sets and the number of times this tweet is retweeted on Twitter (stored in retweet_count field of the tweet object). Spearman coefficient is from 0.5 to 0.7 for our data sets which indicate a good correlation (plots in Fig. 2 confirm a strong correlation). This result makes our data sets appropriate to evaluate information diffusion prediction for real world applications.

3.2 Tweet Features

In this section, we shortly describe the features representing a tweet that are released at the same time as the collection and that could be of use for research in the domain of microblog information diffusion. We also briefly present a descriptive analysis of the released data sets focusing on features that have been shown to be the most important to predict retweetability [7,19].

There are three categories of features: related to the tweets' authors (features F1 to F9), the tweet content (feature F14 to F29) and to the time when the tweet was created (features F10 to F13). Seven features come from [19] (features with a$^+$) and 24 features from [6,7]. Table 3 presents a short description of all the features.

Followers and Followees. In Twitter, followers are people who follow a user and followees are people whom a user follows. These two features have been shown to be important to predict retweetability: the higher the number of followers and followees, the higher the retweetability [19].

Table 3. The released features which are also used in the baselines for information diffusion prediction. Features with a [+] are from Suh *et al.* [19] while the others are from Hoang *et al.* [7]

Features	Features	Data Type
F1.Total_tweets[+]	Total of the user's past tweets	#Numeric
F2.Followers[+]	# of users who follow the author	#Numeric
F3.Followees[+]	# of users that the author is following	#Numeric
F4.Age_account[+]	# days since the account has been created	#Numeric
F5.Favourite[+]	# tweets that the author has liked	#Numeric
F6.Groups	# groups that the author is joining	#Numeric
F7.Aver_favourite	Average of tweets the author likes per day	#Numeric
F8.Aver_tweets	Average of tweets the author write per day	#Numeric
F9.Name_length	The length of the author's name	#Numeric
F10.Posted_holiday	The tweet is posted on a public holiday	Boolean
F11.Posted_noon	The tweet is posted at noon or not	Boolean
F12.Posted_eve	The tweet is posted in the evening or not	Boolean
F13.Posted_weeke	The tweet is posted at the weekend or not	Boolean
F14.Has_location	The tweet contains a location name or not	Boolean
F15.Has_org	The tweet contains an organization name	Boolean
F16.Has_tvshow	The tweet contains a TV show name or not	Boolean
F17.Sent_level	The tweet is positive, negative or neutral	P, N, Neu
F18.Has_video	The tweet contains a video or not	Boolean
F19.Has_Image	The tweet contains a picture not	Boolean
F20.Has_Uword	The tweet contains an upper word or not	Boolean
F21.Has_number	The tweet contains a number or not	Boolean
F22.Has_excl	The tweet contains an exclamation mark	Boolean
F23.Has_rt	The tweet contains the "RT" term or not	Boolean
F24.Has_username	The tweet mentions a user name or not	Boolean
F25.Has_suggest	The tweet contains a retweet suggestion	Boolean
F26.Has_URL[+]	The tweet contains an URL or not	Boolean
F27.Num_hashtag[+]	The number of hashtags contained in the tweet	#Numeric
F28.Opt_len	The tweet length is from 70 to 100 characters	Boolean
F29.Length_tweet	The length of the tweet content	#Numeric

In the rest of this section, we briefly present a descriptive analysis of our five data sets considering the most important features to predict retweetability according to [7,19]. Although other features could be developed by researchers in the future, this analysis provides some cues on the features that are related the most to retweetability.

In Fig. 3, we present the rate of tweets of which the authors have 1,000 followers or more (called F1000) for TwitCID. The diamond elements present the rate of F1000 tweets from class-0 and the circles present this rate from the

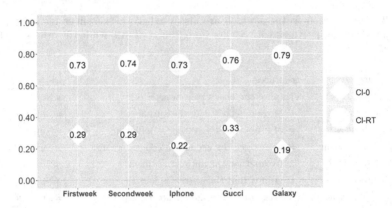

Fig. 3. Rate of tweets from authors who have 1,000 followers or more. Cl-0 represents for tweets that are not retweeted while Cl-RT represents tweets that are retweeted.

class-RT (the union of class-1, class-2 and class-3). As can be seen in this figure, a very large percentage of retweeted-tweets in these data sets are written by authors who have from 1,000 followers. This is shown by the fact that the rate of F1000 tweets from class-RT is very high in all data sets, from 73% to 79%. In addition, there is a low proportion of these F1000 tweets that are not retweeted. The rate of F1000 tweets from class-0 is 19% for the Galaxy data set and 22% for the Iphone data set.

Similarly, for the Followees feature, the rate of tweets created by authors who have 1,000 followees or more (called Fe1000) in class-RT is pretty high, about 34% to 38% depending on the data sets while this rate from class-0 is very low, around 18%. This means tweets created by users who are followed by many other users have a high possibility to be retweeted and low possibility to be non-retweeted.

Groups. Groups denote the number of lists or groups that a Twitter user is a member of. In our five data sets, the number of groups strongly correlate with retweet. We studied the rate of tweets created by authors who are members of at least 50 groups (called Gr50) in each class. This rate is low for class-0 but very high for other classes for all data sets, especially for class-3. For the Galaxy data set, there 34% Gr50 tweets from class-0 but 76% Gr50 tweets from class-2 and 93% from class-3 respectively. For other data sets, the percentage of Gr50 from class-0 is around 20% while this rate is from 39% to 83% for other classes. This result shows that the tweets of authors who join in at least 50 groups have high possibility to be retweeted and there is a high percentage of tweets that are retweeted more than 100 times belong to these users.

Image and Video. The image (resp. video) feature specifies whether a tweet contains an image (resp. video) or not. Figure 4 depicts the rate of tweets that contain either an image or a video (called ImVi). Each group of bars corresponds to a data set. Within a data set, each bar corresponds to a class of retweet level. From this figure, we can see that the trend is similar across the data sets. The

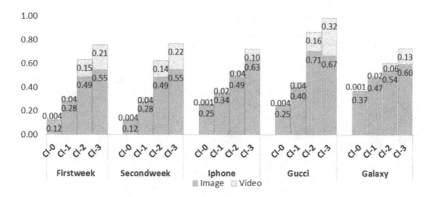

Fig. 4. Rate of tweets which contain either an image or a video (a very few contain both) for each data set and each retweet class.

rate of ImVi tweets increases with the class of retweet level; this holds even more for videos than for images. For example, the Firstweek, 12% tweets from class-0 contain a pictures while this percentage is much higher for class-1, class-2 and class-3: 28%, 49% and 55% respectively. The rate of tweets containing a video from class-0 is 0.4%, while this rate for class-1 is ten times more: 4%. This rate for class-2 and class-3 are significantly higher: 15% and 21%.

In Fig. 4, we can also observe that the rate of tweets containing an image or a video is generally higher in the "marketing" data sets (Iphone, Gucci and Galaxy) than in the "general" data sets (Firstweek and Secondweek).

Favourite. Favourite is the number of tweets that a user has liked in his timeline. In our collection, the rate of tweets of which the authors have at least 1,000 favourites (called Fav1000) is pretty high: around 50% for the Firstweek, Secondweek and Gucci data sets, and around 30% for the Iphone data set. For the Galaxy data set, although there is only 15% Fav1000 tweets in the whole data set, this rate on class-3 is 77%. The other data sets also have high rate of Fav1000 tweets in class-3: 77% for the Gucci data set and around 60% for the Iphone, Firstweek and Secondweek data sets. This result shows that tweets of authors who have likes at least 1,000 posts on their timeline are highly likely to be retweeted several times.

Age of Account. The Age of an account presents the number of days a user account is registered from.

We analyzed the relationship between the age of the author account and the retweet rate for the data sets of the TwitCID. We found that whatever the data set is, the age of account and retweet rate is linearly strongly correlated (see plot in Fig. 5).

Figure 5 presents the normalized retweet rate of different types of users. The junior users: who have registered their account less than 1,000 days, the intermediate users: from 1,000 days to 3,000 days and the senior users: greater than 3,000 days. In this figure, the retweet rate represents a normalized ratio of the

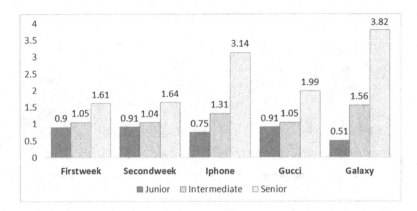

Fig. 5. Retweet rate vs Age of account on the five data sets. Junior are users who have created their account less than 1,000 days; Intermediate: from 1,000 days to 3,000 days; Senior: greater than 3,000 days.

number of retweeted tweets to the number of tweets. For example, the first bar in Fig. 5 presents the retweet rate of junior users' tweets for the Firstweek data set. We first divided the total of retweeted tweets of juniors (765,125 tweets) by the total of tweets of juniors (2,534,102 tweets). We then normalized this rate by a factor so that a value of 1.0 represents the average retweet rate. This normalization factor is calculated by the total of tweets (6,043,136) over the total of retweeted tweets in the whole data set (2,017,979).

Figure 5 shows a very strong relationship between the age of the account and the retweet rate for all data sets. Interestingly, the retweet rate of tweets from senior users for the "marketing" data sets is much higher than the one for the "general" data sets. For the Galaxy data set for example, the retweet rate for senior users is 3.82, for intermediate users it is 1.56 and for junior users it is 0.51 while this rate for senior, intermediate and junior for the Firstweek is 1.61, 1.05 and 0.9 respectively.

Our collection includes a large number of tweets in which million tweets are retweeted hundreds to dozen thousand times. In addition, this collection covers several important features regarding user profile, the content and the time the tweet is posted. Thus it is appropriate for studies on predicting information diffusion on social networks.

3.3 Released Data

Being compliant with Twitter developer agreement and policy[1], we publish our TwitCID collection on behalf of our academic institution IRIT [2] for the sole purpose of non commercial research, under the licence CC BY-NC-SA (Attribution -

---

[1] https://developer.twitter.com/en/developer-terms/agreement-and-policyid34.
[2] Institut de Recherche en Informatique de Toulouse, UMR5505 CNRS, France.

NonCommercial - ShareAlike). For each data set, we release all tweet IDs accompanied by a script so that researchers can retrieve the tweets in JSON from the Twitter API. We also provide extracted features described in the Table 3 corresponding to each data set in arff form. All these materials are available at http://doi.org/10.5281/zenodo.3246705

4   Baseline for Information Diffusion Prediction

In this section, we briefly describe a model for predicting information diffusion on social networks proposed in [7] evaluated on the TwitCID collection considering two sets of features as defined in [19] and [7]. Given a tweet, the model predicts whether this tweet is going to be diffused or not and the level of diffusion.

In [7], the authors considered the prediction of retweetability either as a binary classification problem or as a multi-class classification one like Hong *et al.* did [8]. For a binary problem, tweets are classified into two classes: class-0 and class-RT. For multi-class problem, tweets are categorized into the four classes as we presented before (class-0 for non retweeted, class-1 to -3 depending on the level of retweet).

The predictive model proposed by Hoang *et al.* [7] uses Random Forest (RF) implemented on Java Weka library[3]. The authors showed that RF consistently outperforms the other machine learning methods on this task; we thus report the results obtained by this model. The results of this model considering the features presented in the Table 3 We also report the result Hoang *et al.*'s model on Suh *et al.*'s features (features with a$^+$ in the Table 3).

Table 4. Averaged -measure over the sub-sets for each data set - Binary prediction on retweet on the TwitCID collections; * indicates statistically significant differences by Student's t-test with p-value < 0.05 between Suh and full feature set.

		Firstweek	Secondweek	Iphone	Gucci	Galaxy
Cl-0	Suh's	0.79	0.79	0.82	0.79	0.86
	Full set	0.83*	0.82*	0.85*	0.82*	0.88*
Cl-RT	Suh's	0.77	0.77	0.82	0.78	0.86
	Full set	0.81*	0.81*	0.85*	0.82*	0.87*
Aver.	Suh's	0.78	0.78	0.82	0.78	0.86
	Full set	0.82*	0.82*	0.85	0.82*	0.88*

Since the number of tweets in classes are highly different, the data was balanced during the classification process by: (a) each data set was divided into several subsets where the tweets from minor classes (class-1 to 3) are kept the same for all subsets and the tweets from major class (class-0) are divided into

---

[3] http://weka.sourceforge.net.

subsets so that the number of tweets from major class are approximated to the number of tweet from minor class. (b) SMOTE[4] technique is used the to synthetic minority over sampling.

From the Table 4, we can see that using the full set of features remarkably increases the F-measure on each class and on average compared to when using the reduced feature set for all the data sets both for binary classification.

On average, the complete model improves the F-measure by 4% (from 0.78 to 0.82) for the Firstweek, Secondweek and the Gucci data sets; by 3% (from 0.82 to 0.85) for the Iphone and by 2% (from 0.86 to 0.88) for the Galaxy data set compared to the reduced model. All these improvement are statistically significant. One interesting point is that the improvement on class-RT is equal or higher than on class-0 although the number of tweets in class-RT is smaller than the number of tweets in class-0. For the Gucci data set, F-measure is increased by 3% on class-0 while this increase is by 4% on class-RT. The complete model also achieved higher improvement on class-RT than on class-0 for the Galaxy data set that the reduced one (Table 4).

Table 5. F-measure of the model when predicting the level of retweet on the TwitCID collection. * indicates statistically significant differences when using Student's t-test with p-value < 0.05 when comparing the full set of features and the Suh's subset.

		Firstweek	Secondweek	Iphone	Gucci	Galaxy
Cl-0	Suh's	0.79	0.79	0.82	0.79	0.86
	Full set	0.82*	0.82*	0.85*	0.82*	0.88*
Cl-1	Suh's	0.64	0.65	0.72	0.65	0.77
	Full set	0.70*	0.74*	0.76*	0.68*	0.80
Cl-2	Suh's	0.73	0.73	0.59	0.62	0.58
	Full set	0.74*	0.74*	0.64*	0.62	0.61
Cl-3	Suh's	0.58	0.57	0.13	0.02	0.12
	Full set	0.57	0.57	0.10	0.05	0.12
Aver.	Suh's	0.72	0.72	0.75	0.71	0.80
	Full set	0.76*	0.76*	0.79*	0.74*	0.82*

Similarly to the case of binary classification, the complete model increases the F-measure on average and on every class compared to the reduced model for all the data sets for multi-class classification. On average, F-measure is increased by 4% for the Firstweek, Secondweek and Iphone data sets, by 3% for the Gucci data set and by 2% for the Galaxy data set compared to the reduced model. All these improvements are significantly different.

When considering each class, the complete model obtains higher F-measure on class-0, class-1 and class-2 but lower F-measure on class-3 compared to the

---

[4] This algorithm creates synthetic observations based upon the existing minority observations.

reduced model. The reason may be the number of tweets from class-3 which is extremely small compared to those from the other classes (see Table 2). For the Gucci data set, the complete model achieves 0.79, 0.65 and 0.62 (F-measure) on class-1, class-2 and class-3 respectively but only 0.02 on class-3. The highest F-measure is obtained on class-0 and class-1 for the Iphone data set which are 0.85 and 0.76 respectively.

5   Conclusions

In this paper, we introduced the TwitCID collection of 18 million tweets that is designed to evaluate studies on predicting information diffusion on social networks, both for 'general' information and 'marketing' information. We also provide extracted features corresponding to each data set regarding the user profile, tweet content and temporal information. In addition, we report results of information diffusion prediction models evaluated on our collection (around 80% accuracy) which could be strong baselines for comparative studies.

References

1. Bakshy, E., Rosenn, I., Marlow, C., Adamic, L.: The role of social networks in information diffusion. In: Conference on World Wide Web, pp. 519–528. ACM (2012)
2. Cano Basave, A.E., Varga, A., Rowe, M., Stankovic, M., Dadzie, A.-S.: Making sense of microposts (# MSM2013) concept extraction challenge. In: #MSM, pp. 1–15 (2013)
3. De Domenico, M., Lima, A., Mougel, P., Musolesi, M.: The Anatomy of a Scientific Rumor. (Nature Open Access) Scientific Reports 3, 2980 (2013)
4. Dong, R., Li, L., Zhang, Q., Cai, G.: Information diffusion on social media during natural disasters. IEEE Trans. Comput. Soc. Syst. 5(1), 265–276 (2018)
5. Guille, A., Hacid, H.: A predictive model for the temporal dynamics of information diffusion in online social networks. In: International Conference on World Wide Web, pp. 1145–1152 ACM (2012)
6. Hoang, T.B.N., Mothe, J.: Predicting the diffusion of brand's stories in social network. In: 19th Computational Linguistics and Intelligent Text Processing (2018)
7. Hoang, T.B.N., Mothe, J.: Predicting information diffusion on Twitter - analysis of predictive features. J. Comput. Sci. **28**, 257–264 (2018)
8. Hong, L., Dan, O., Davison, B.D.: Predicting popular messages in Twitter. In: International Conference on companion on World Wide Web, pp. 57–58. ACM (2011)
9. Kafeza, E., Kanavos, A., Makris, C., Vikatos, P.: Predicting information diffusion patterns in Twitter. In: Iliadis, L., Maglogiannis, I., Papadopoulos, H. (eds.) AIAI 2014. IAICT, vol. 436, pp. 79–89. Springer, Heidelberg (2014). https://doi.org/10.1007/978-3-662-44654-6_8
10. Lagnier, C., Denoyer, L., Gaussier, E., Gallinari, P.: Predicting information diffusion in social networks using content and user's profiles. In: Serdyukov, P., et al. (eds.) ECIR 2013. LNCS, vol. 7814, pp. 74–85. Springer, Heidelberg (2013). https://doi.org/10.1007/978-3-642-36973-5_7

11. Lespagnol, C., Mothe, J., Ullah, M.Z.: Information nutritional label and word embedding to estimate information check-worthiness. In: SIGIR. ACM (2019). https://doi.org/10.1145/3331184.3331298
12. Lu, R., Yang, Q.: Trend analysis of news topics on Twitter. Int. J. Mach. Learn. Comput. 2(3), 327–332 (2012)
13. Nakov, P., Kozareva, Z., Ritter, A., Rosenthal, S., Stoyanov, V., Wilson, T.: Semeval-2013 task 2: sentiment analysis in Twitter. In: International Workshop on Semantic Evaluation, pp. 1–18 (2013)
14. Ritter, A., Clark, S., Etzioni, O., et al.: Named entity recognition in tweets: an experimental study. In: Conference on Empirical Methods in Natural Language Processing, pp. 1524–1534. ACL (2011)
15. Röder, M., Usbeck, R., Hellmann, S., Gerber, D., Both, A.: N3-a collection of datasets for named entity recognition and disambiguation in the NLP interchange format. In: LREC, pp. 3529–3533 (2014)
16. Saif, H., Fernandez, M., He, Y., Alani, H.: Evaluation datasets for Twitter sentiment analysis: a survey and a new dataset, the STS-gold. In: 1st workshop on ESSEM at AIIA Conference (2013)
17. Sang, E.F.T.K., De Meulder, F.: Introduction to the CoNLL-2003 shared task: language-independent named entity recognition. In: Conference on Natural Language Learning at HLT-NAACL, pp. 142–147 (2003)
18. Speriosu, M., Sudan, N., Upadhyay, S., Baldridge, J.: Twitter polarity classification with label propagation over lexical links and the follower graph. In: Workshop on Unsupervised Learning in NLP, pp. 53–63. ACL (2011)
19. Suh, B., Hong, L., Pirolli, P., Chi, E.H.: Want to be retweeted? Large scale analytics on factors impacting retweet in Twitter network. In: IEEE International Conference on Social Computing, pp. 177–184. IEEE (2010)
20. Thelwall, M., Buckley, K., Paltoglou, G.: Sentiment strength detection for the social web. JASIST 63(1), 163–173 (2012)
21. Varshney, D., Kumar, S., Gupta, V.: Predicting information diffusion probabilities in social networks: a Bayesian networks based approach. Knowl.-Based Syst. 133, 66–76 (2017)
22. Xie, W., Zhu, F., Liu, S., Wang, K.: Modelling cascades over time in microblogs. In: IEEE International Congress on Big Data, pp. 677–686 (2015)

Sonny, Cerca! Evaluating the Impact of Using a Vocal Assistant to Search at School

Monica Landoni[1]([✉]), Davide Matteri[1], Emiliana Murgia[2], Theo Huibers[3], and Maria Soledad Pera[4]

[1] Università della Svizzera Italiana, Lugano, Switzerland
{monica.landoni,davide.matteri}@usi.ch
[2] Università degli Studi di Milano-Bicocca, Milan, Italy
emiliana.murgia@unimib.it
[3] University of Twente, Enschede, The Netherlands
t.w.c.huibers@utwente.nl
[4] People and Information Research Team, Boise State University, Boise, ID, USA
solepera@boisestate.edu

Abstract. Children struggle with translating their information needs into effective queries to initiate the search process. In this paper, we explore the degree to which the use of a Vocal Assistant (VA) as an intermediary between a child and a search engine can ease query formulation and foster completion of successful searches. We also examine the potential influence VA can have on the search process when compared to a traditional keyboard-driven approach. This comparison motivates the second contribution of our work, an evaluation framework that covers 4 dimensions: (1) a new *search strategy* (VA) for (2) a specific *user group* (children) given (3) a particular *task* (answering questions) in (4) a defined *environment* (school). The proposed framework can be adopted by the research community to conduct comprehensive assessments of search systems given new interaction methods, user groups, contexts, and tasks.

Keywords: Vocal assistant · Search · Schools · Evaluation

1 Introduction

Studies in information retrieval (IR) are categorized as experimental or theoretical [12]. In the past, the theoretical approach was quite common; a number of hypotheses were formulated on the basis of a well-defined IR-theory and then verified using a prototype. Each new theory could then be easily investigated and extended by other researchers. Developments in the field are now so fast-paced, and the possibilities for enhancements so diverse, that IR favors empirical studies [18]. Each new development requires new criteria for assessment. Yet, the added

F. Crestani et al. (Eds.): CLEF 2019, LNCS 11696, pp. 101–113, 2019.
https://doi.org/10.1007/978-3-030-28577-7_6

value of an empirical evaluation is in the *contextualization* of results, demonstrating the advantages of a strategy with respect to other relevant (academic) works, as well as the impact the strategy has on the community and users at large.

Evaluation of IR-related strategies (e.g., query suggestion or resource ranking) and systems (e.g., search engines) has been studied for decades. When focused on traditional audiences, TREC collections or CLEF labs enable appraisals based on comparisons with baselines and the state-of-the-art. Unfortunately, for non-traditional users, e.g., children, the lack of established benchmarks and frameworks prevent comprehensive assessments. Instead, evaluations are often carried out on a small scale, demonstrating that new solutions function well, but rarely involving comparisons across other solutions in exactly the same context. For example, consider the use of search engines (SEs) by children. How to determine if SE A fares better than SE B? Existing literature in this area is limited and tends to be fragmented: contributions come from different communities and findings obtained as a result of user studies or query log analysis cannot be replicated, as collected data cannot be shared often due to ethical and privacy concerns. The lack of standard procedures, criteria, and measures motivates the exploration for our work. We see it as a step towards the definition of a common ground for running user studies to help this area evolve across different research communities. Indeed, the European project PuppyIR made a giant leap forward in 2009–2011 by jointly investigating children's use of SEs. It provided a good basis [4], but this has not yet been translated into large-scale standardised evaluations.

In this paper, we focus our research efforts in setting foundation for the design of a framework that supports the study of children search, regardless of the context (e.g., at home or at school), purpose (e.g., leisure vs. learning), development stages (e.g., search habits of younger children differ from those of older ones), or interfaces (e.g., GUIs driven by text cues or novel multimedia-driven interactions). To control scope, we study children ages 9 to 11. While at this age children may not have the vocabulary and spelling skills to search well, they are developing analysis skills to identify sources that are trustworthy and of quality [7,15]. We restrict the search task to the classroom setting, regulating the breadth of topics we anticipate children being aware of. Lastly, there are many known challenges children face when interacting with SEs—the main being query formulation, which directly correlates with the types of resources retrieved and therefore the overall success of the search [17]. With that in mind, and based on the prevalent presence of speech-driven assistants like Alexa or Siri around children [25], we build on existing work regarding the use of vocal assistants (VAs) to aid searches [27]. In our case, we explicitly explore the influence VAs have on successful search completion.

Initial results from the user study we conducted with students in primary school grades in Lugano, Switzerland, evidence that a VA can facilitate search while keeping children focused. The results also reveal differences in search behaviour when using a keyboard-driven GUI vs. a VA. Preliminary insights can influence the design of interfaces so that they can help children search effectively in a formal context. Further, we expect our framework to serve as the basis for a protocol to compare and combine intrinsic user data (log files), with extrinsically captured and directly observed data (survey and observations)–an important step to help researchers deal with the complexity of involving children in evaluation.

The main outcomes of this work include: (a) detailed evaluation protocol that enables experiments regardless the strategy proposed, user group, task, or environment; (b) study based on the proposed protocol, as we fluctuate the type of interaction used to initiate the search process (text vs. speech), task (answering questions), context (education) and user group (children); (c) initial findings on the perceived satisfaction on the search process when the information discovery task is initiated via a VA or a more traditional interface; (d) lessons learned that can guide further iterations of VAs and GUIs targeting young users and how to assess and contextualize their performance.

2 Background and Related Work

Common patterns of behavior emerge at different levels of familiarity with technology and at different ages; causing **information seeking** behaviors to differ among children and adults. Marchionini's information seeking model [19] is comprised of 8 stages: problem recognition, problem understanding, choosing a search system, formulating a query, executing a search, examining results, extracting information, and reflecting/iterating/stopping. Wilson's model [26] instead describes 4 stages: problem recognition, problem definition, problem resolution, and solution statement. Neither model explicitly inspects differences in seeking behaviors across users of distinct age groups. We then turn to Nahl's ACS model [20] that associates user affective, cognitive and sensorimotor behaviors with information seeking on the Web. Nahl states that information needs (A) lead one to thoughts about solutions (C) that eventuate in some related overt action (S). According to Piaget's stages of cognitive development [11], children undertake 4 phases to develop cognitive abilities: sensorimotor, pre-operational, concrete, and formal operational. It is not till this last stage–around 12 years old–that children develop more complex cognitive structure involving abstraction and conceptual reasoning. This motivates our choice of target audience, as 9–11 year olds are yet to develop the ability to pursuit complex searches, leading us to explore their interactions with search interfaces to identify patterns that could inform IR systems that are highly supportive of their mental structures [21].

Various studies detail children's **challenges** interactions with SEs [1,5,13, 16]. They reveal that children (i) favor browsing, as it requires a lower amount of cognitive effort than searching, (ii) struggle with query formulation, as their limited vocabulary interferes with proper keyword selection, (iii) create natural language queries, as they lack familiarity with the more traditional keyword-based approach, (iv) exhibit a looping behavior (coming back to queries and

Table 1. Sample questions presented to participants.

Type	Example
Fact-based	What is the maximum speed of a tornado?
Open-ended	Briefly describe how a tornado develops and its effects
Multi-step	Where and when the "black monster" took place?

links), as they may find the required information but not realize it immediately, (v) focus on finding a concrete answer without trying to understand result content, as they have difficulty in understanding resources and judging relevance, which correlates with texts being above children's reading and cognitive processing level. The aforementioned characteristics translate into a longer time to execute a search; more than doubling the time required by an adult to complete the same task.

IR systems can aid children, as well as parents and educators, in finding online materials for learning and play that are not only of interest, but are also developmentally and educationally appropriate. Among **common IR systems**, we find general audience alternatives like Google, the most popular SE, and YouTube. Among the ones specifically designed for children, we find Youtube-Kids, Web for Classrooms, SuperAwesome, International Children's Digital Library, and ABCMouse, as well as academic counterparts that aim to address the challenges children face when trying to locate resources [8,17]. None of the existing child-friendly systems has emerged as the clear favorite. In addition, no exhaustive **assessment** have been conducted beyond high level reports on strengths and limitations [17] or comparisons across simple baselines [6,16]. This evidences the need for an evaluation protocol like the one we discuss in Sect. 3.

3   Our Evaluation Framework in Practice

We discuss the framework we designed for evaluating the use of a given set of *strategies* by a particular *user group, task*, and *context*. Along the way, we explain how we deploy it to conduct our comparative assessment.

3.1   Task and Context

When evaluating SEs, it is not always possible to conduct live experiments. Even then, results are limited to observations on systems under study and replication for comparison with other solutions might not be feasible. Mimicking the structure of known frameworks (e.g., TREC or CLEF), we designed a set of tasks that can be used to trigger interaction with SEs in the *classroom setting*.

Specifically, we selected *answering questions* related to school subjects (e.g., science, history, geography, and sports). We categorized these questions by type: **Fact-based** are straight-forward questions which require a very specific and quick answer; **Open-ended** are loose questions which require a short textual description and/or a drawing as an answer; and **Multi-step** are complex questions which require at least two queries to find an answer. (See Table 1 for sample questions.) Considering varied categories of inquiry tasks, allows participant observation when they are faced with challenges of increased complexity. By focusing on school subjects, we make it possible to outline new questions for future studies across different school grades and IR systems.

3.2   Search Strategy

To be of use, an evaluation framework should be applicable to different IR strategies. We describe below the two examples we consider in our study.

VA. We mimic a VA using a Wizard of Oz approach [24]. In this method, the researcher ("wizard") pretends to be an intelligent machine or computer application. The researcher and the testing subject are located in different rooms, so that the participant does not know he is, in fact, interacting with a human. Separating researchers from study participants enables us to observe kids' natural behaviour while they interact with the VA via Skype calls. According to recent discoveries [27], children prefer personified interfaces. This is why we use **Sonny**, a human-like VA that uses a strict protocol when interacting with children. Sonny has a limited number of functionalities[1], including reading titles and fragments of retrieved resources, processing question requests (i.e., queries) from users, and interrupt search session as per users' requests.

Traditional GUI. To mimic search environments children are familiar with (e.g., Google), we created a simple interface. As shown in Fig. 1, we rely on a traditional text-box where children could type a query, much like they would regularly do on popular SEs.

(a) Welcome page   (b) Search interface

Fig. 1. Environment used to conduct discovery tasks and archive query logs.

3.3   Data Gathering for Assessment

We gauge performance from task, system, and user perspectives.

---

[1] A detailed discussion of Sonny's functionalities can we found in [14].

Completion. Teachers provide a correct answer to each of the considered questions, which we use to determine if tasks have been terminated with a random answer, as opposed to *correctly completed* with a valid answer.

System. We leverage the query-log gathering framework in [16] and use collected data to compute statistics and metrics common in IR (e.g., number of queries per session and session duration). Using the same query-log gathering framework across evaluated strategies is essential for preventing inconsistencies that can otherwise occur due to different result sets retrieved in response to the same queries or ranking of the presented results.

Questionnaires. To identify user preferences and contextualize observations, we adapt the survey in [22]–inspired by the principles defined in [10]. The surveys presented to participants include the same questions, slightly rephrased, depending on the strategy a user interacted with during the study (see Fig. 2).

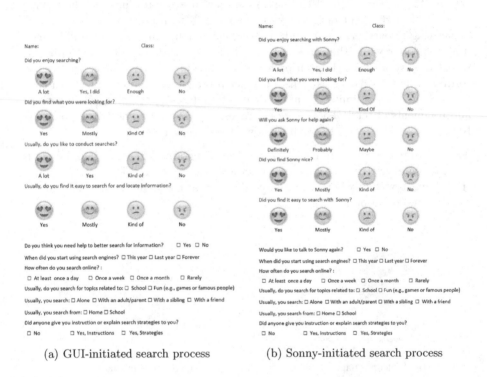

(a) GUI-initiated search process   (b) Sonny-initiated search process

Fig. 2. Questionnaire presented to study participants.

3.4 Participants

Upon agreement with the school principal and teachers, we recruited 42 students[2] from the 4th and 5th grades; aged 9–11, gender uniformly distributed (Table 2).

---

[2] Parents signed a consent form allowing children to take part of the study. Collected data was anonymized to ensure privacy of the population under study.

Due to time, space, and equipment constraints, children were grouped into teams of 2 or 3 members. The teams (a total of 14) were randomly created to avoid collaboration to play a role in the search process, and tasks were randomly assigned. More than half of children (24) interacted with both the VA and the GUI; working in new teams and picking fresh questions to work with each time.

As per responses to the aforementioned questionnaire, while children are very familiar with SEs (Fig. 4a), their interactions are not as frequent as one might expect (Fig. 4b), i.e., compared to teenagers/adults who use SEs daily [9].

Only 22 children stated needing help to conduct online inquiries; yet, as shown in Fig. 3, 45% of them have not been exposed to any form of search literacy. Children who received instructions or explicit information on how to search attributed the guidance to family members–parents and older siblings.

Table 2. Demographic distribution of study participants.

	Male	Female	Overall
9 yrs.	10	6	16
10 yrs.	7	14	21
11 yrs.	4	1	5
Overall	21	21	42

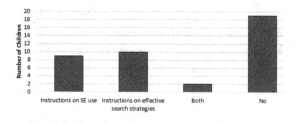

Fig. 3. Exposure to search instruction.

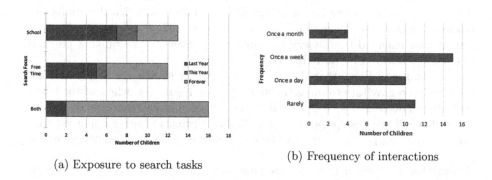

(a) Exposure to search tasks

(b) Frequency of interactions

Fig. 4. Insights on children and SEs.

3.5 Protocol

Children were asked to provide answers to a set of 4 questions that they could select from a pool of suitable ones for their age and expertise: (i) Two fact-based, which we deemed easier to answer and thus were presented first, (ii) one open-ended, as that increases task complexity, and (iii) one multi-step question.

In each session, children either used a traditional keyboard-driven (**GUI**) or **Sonny** to locate resources and then write answers to the 4 questions. Children were offered to interact with the GUI or VA in a random order, thus avoiding biases due to the training effect of using one consistently before the other. Upon session completion, children were asked to fill out a simple questionnaire.

4 Analysis and Discussion

Below we discuss the results of the study outlined in Sect. 3.

Inferences from Query Logs. For quantitative assessment, we use measurements that commonly showcase search ease. As reported in Table 3, search tasks completed with the aid of the VA resulted in a lower number of queries per session and a shorter session time[3].

Table 3. Query log analysis.

	Sonny	GUI
Avg. number of queries per session	3.8	6.6
Mean position of relevant resources	2.2	3.1
Avg. session duration (in minutes)	13.8	19.1

Retrieved resources deemed relevant by children consistently appeared higher in the ranking if the search task was initiated by Sonny as opposed to the GUI. In addition, both the average per session and overall number of resources visited during the search session using the GUI is more than twice the number of resources visited when using Sonny (4 vs. 8; 61 vs. 137, respectively). Another insight that emerged from query log interactions refers to the ranking position of resources selected by participants.

We can see in Fig. 5 that the distribution is very similar for Sonny and the GUI; children gravitate towards the first retrieved result, regardless of the interface used. This aligns with prior studies reporting that children usually do not search beyond the first page of results [3]. No selected resources appeared past the 10th ranking position; usually the last position of the first results page. We

---

[3] Query log data pertaining to session duration might be biased, e.g., problems with poor connection affect session length. Researcher observation, however, serve as another confirmation factor on shorter length for VA-initiated sessions.

did notice that children explored lower-ranked resources when using the GUI. With Sonny they did not explore pass the 6th result. This maybe due to pressing factors like having a synchronous interaction with another speaking entity. On their own, kids seemed more comfortable and relaxed and took time to explore. Moreover, when interacting with the GUI children had direct control on the result set and they could freely browse, as opposed to having to wait for Sonny to scan the results and read excerpts. This is a demanding process, as it requires children to keep track of the titles read and decide on whether these are relevant or not. This complexity could explain why children opted for exploring fewer results with Sonny than with the GUI.

While these results serve as indications of the benefit of using a VA to conduct search tasks in the classroom, they are not conclusive: they overlook the perception of completeness or user satisfaction with the search process itself. For this reason, we included in our framework other qualitative appreciations.

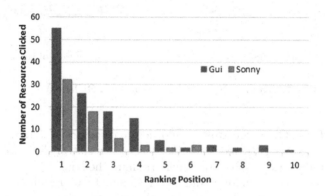

Fig. 5. Ranking position of selected results.

Inferences from Surveys. Regardless of the strategy used to initiate the search process, teams were able to provide answers to all of the fact-based tasks. For open-ended and multi-step tasks, teams fared better using the traditional GUI (see Fig. 6). We were also interested in exploring whether the answers provided to complete the prompted tasks were correct, i.e., if children extracted the required information from retrieved resources. Out of the responses provided, 46 were correct when the teams used the GUI, as opposed to the 41 when Sonny was guiding the search. In fact, on average, 3.3 out of 4 tasks were answered correctly by teams using the GUI; unlike the 2.9 using Sonny.

As illustrated in Fig. 7, regardless of the interfaced used, user preferences are fairly alike. While a few more children expressed that relying on Sonny made the search process easier (and, in fact, would use Sonny again), these numbers are not statistically significant.

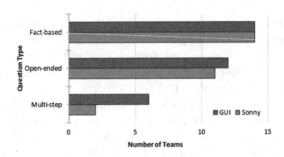

Fig. 6. Achieved search tasks, grouped by type.

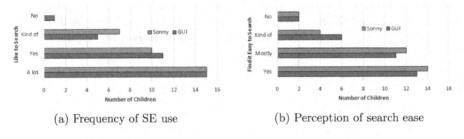

(a) Frequency of SE use   (b) Perception of search ease

Fig. 7. Overall search preferences using a GUI vs. a VA

Inferences from Observations. In addition to discoveries inferred from query logs and surveys, we gathered some insights as a result of direct observation, listening and notes taking, by researchers running the study.

For the most part, children did not reformulate or restructure requests. Instead, they submitted their queries exactly as they were written on the question sheets. This was most prominent when children interacted with Sonny, as children simply read the question they wanted to pose to the VA exactly as it was stated on the question sheet. When they did not get the expected answer from the VA, they got easily frustrated. Then they proceeded to repeat the query, speaking slower and aiming for a more clear pronunciation–emphasizing different words, but hardly ever changing the structure, composition, or the meaning of the request; aligning with reports on previous studies on speech interfaces [27] When using the GUI, children tended to formulate queries as they were drafted on the question sheet, in natural language, instead of using a keyword approach, typing only the most relevant terms. This is in accordance with the reports in [5]. Another interesting observation from VA interactions related to context. Sonny was not able to keep context of previous searches. Unfortunately, when performing sequential searches, children took for granted that Sonny would be able to keep the current context in memory for latter requests, as an attentive human being.

Even if children were familiar with the use of a GUI—unlike the use of a VA which was a novel experience for most of them—the number of correct responses identified with the help of the VA is just marginally lower than the counterpart generated with the use of the GUI. This contradicts our original assumption, in terms of easing the search process via the aid of a VA. This was unexpected, especially taking into account considerations related to task completion, which took less time with Sonny and required children to browse through less documents.

5   Conclusion and Future Work

We started our research journey questioning if, in the classroom, the use of a VA would ease the search process for children and thus translate to better overall performance; compared to a traditional keyboard-driven GUI. Faced with a lack of existing benchmarks that could support this exploration, we first designed an evaluation framework that would enable comparative analysis of diverse IR strategies when adopted by a given user group with the objective of completing a particular task in a certain environment. We then applied the framework to assess search systems driven by a VA and a traditional GUI; used by children ages 9 to 11 in a classroom in order to answer questions related to school subjects.

Results obtained via query logs, surveys, and researchers' observations revealed a complex picture with a number of factors contributing to the overall search experience. Based on interface used, we noticed different expectations in terms of helpfulness, trust, and levels of distraction. In addition, we observed that the number of correct answers found, levels of serendipity, and encouragement to browsing were also deeply influenced by the interface. Children's abilities played a crucial role too, as we expected children to understand the proposed tasks, interact with the system, find out how to formulate the right query, make sense of results to determine relevance, and finally complete the task.

We will consider how to support the aforementioned steps in future studies; starting from considerations on the role the VA and its desirable features, as discussed in [23]. We will also explore how to design a VA to support special educational needs (e.g., dyslexic students). In this case, tailoring the evaluation framework to account for users' different abilities—related to age and cognitive skills—will be our next step. Given the context of our work, we argue in favor of incorporating another perspective on our framework: impact of learning. In doing so, we will leverage research on search as learning [2], an emerging area in IR, and explore how children learn as result of a search, as the majority of the existing works currently focus on adults.

Acknowledgements. We would like to thank children in the after school program at the Leonardo da Vinci school in Lugano and Thomas Del Prete for helping us conduct the study. Work partially funded by NSF Award 1565937.

References

1. Bilal, D., Kirby, J.: Differences and similarities in information seeking: children and adults as web users. Inf. Process. Manag. **38**(5), 649–670 (2002)
2. Collins-Thompson, K., Rieh, S.Y., Haynes, C.C., Syed, R.: Assessing learning outcomes in web search: a comparison of tasks and query strategies. In: ACM CHIIR, pp. 163–172. ACM (2016)
3. Druin, A., et al.: How children search the internet with keyword interfaces. In: ACM IDC, pp. 89–96 (2009)
4. Duarte Torres, S.: Information retrieval for children: search behavior and solutions. Master's thesis, University of Twente (2014)
5. Duarte Torres, S., Hiemstra, D., Serdyukov, P.: Query log analysis in the context of information retrieval for children. In: ACM SIGIR, pp. 847–848. ACM (2010)
6. Eickhoff, C., Dekker, P., De Vries, A.P.: Supporting children's web search in school environments. In: IIiX Symposium, pp. 129–137. ACM (2012)
7. Farrall, M.L.: Reading Assessment: Linking Language, Literacy, and Cognition. Wiley, Hoboken (2012)
8. Gossen, T.: Search Engines for Children: Search User Interfaces Andinformation-Seeking Behaviour. Springer, Wiesbaden (2016). https://doi.org/10.1007/978-3-658-12069-6
9. Halavais, A.: Search Engine Society. Wiley, Hoboken (2017)
10. Hall, L., Hume, C., Tazzyman, S.: Five degrees of happiness: effective smiley face likert scales for evaluating with children. In: ACM IDC, pp. 311–321. ACM (2016)
11. Inhelder, B., Piaget, J.: The Psychology of the Child. Basic Books, New York (1969)
12. Jansen, B., Rieh, S.: The seventeen theoretical constructs of information searching and information retrieval. JASIST **61**(8), 1517–1534 (2010)
13. Jochmann-Mannak, H., Lentz, L., Huibers, T., Sanders, T.: How interface design and search strategy influence children's search performance and evaluation. In: Web Design and Development, pp. 1332–1379 (2016)
14. Landoni, M., Murgia, E., Huibers, T., Pera, M.S.: My name is sonny, how may i help you searching for information? In: KidRec Workshop at ACM IDC, p. 6 (2019)
15. Macedo-Rouet, M., Braasch, J.L., Britt, M.A., Rouet, J.F.: Teaching fourth and fifth graders to evaluate information sources during text comprehension. Cogn. Instr. **31**(2), 204–226 (2013)
16. Madrazo Azpiazu, I., Dragovic, N., Anuyah, O., Pera, M.S.: Looking for the movie seven or sven from the movie frozen?: A multi-perspective strategy for recommending queries for children. In: ACM CHIIR, pp. 92–101. ACM (2018)
17. Madrazo Azpiazu, I., Dragovic, N., Pera, M.S., Fails, J.A.: Online searching and learning: yum and other search tools for children and teachers. Inf. Retrieval J. **20**(5), 524–545 (2017)
18. Manning, C., Raghavan, P., Schütze, H.: Introduction to information retrieval. Natural Lang. Eng. **16**(1), 100–103 (2010)
19. Marchionini, G.: Information Seeking in Electronic Environments. Cambridge University Press, Cambridge (1997)
20. Nahl, D.: Information counseling inventory of affective and cognitive reactions while learning the internet. In: Internet Reference Services Quarterly, pp. 11–33 (1997)

21. Nahl, D., Bilal, D.: Information and Emotion: The Emergent Affective Paradigm in Information Behavior Research and Theory. Information Today, Inc., Medford (2007)
22. Van Mechelen, M., Høiseth, M., Baykal, G.E., Van Doorn, F., Vasalou, A., Schut, A.: Analyzing children's contributions and experiences in co-design activities: synthesizing productive practices. In: ACM IDC, pp. 769–772. ACM (2017)
23. Wang, I., Smith, J., Ruiz, J.: Exploring virtual agents for augmented reality. In: ACM CHI, p. 281. ACM (2019)
24. Weiss, A., Bernhaupt, R., Schwaiger, D., Altmaninger, M., Buchner, R., Tscheligi, M.: User experience evaluation with a wizard of oz approach: Technical and methodological considerations. In: IEEE RAS, pp. 303–308 (2009)
25. Wiederhold, B.K.: "Alexa, Are You My Mom?" The Role of Artificial Intelligence in Child Development (2018)
26. Wilson, T.D.: Human information behavior. Inf. Sci. Res. 3, 49–56 (2000)
27. Yarosh, S., et al.: Children asking questions: speech interface reformulations and personification preferences. In: ACM IDC, pp. 300–312. ACM (2018)

Generating Cross-Domain Text Classification Corpora from Social Media Comments

Benjamin Murauer[✉] and Günther Specht[✉]

Unitversität Innsbruck, Innsbruck, Austria
{benjamin.murauer,gunther.specht}@uibk.ac.at

Abstract. In natural language processing (NLP), cross-domain text classification problems like cross-topic, cross-genre or cross-language authorship attribution are characterized by having different contexts for training and testing data. That is, learning algorithms which are trained on the specific properties of the training data have to make predictions on test data which comprises substantially different properties. To this end, the corpora that are used for analyses in cross-domain problems are limited in size and variation, decreasing the expressive power and generalizability of the proposed solutions. In this paper, we present a methodological framework and toolset for dynamically creating cross-domain datasets by utilizing millions of Reddit comments. We show that different types of cross-domain datasets such as cross-topic or cross-lingual corpora can be constructed, and demonstrate a wide variety of use cases, including previously unfeasible analyses like cross-lingual authorship attribution on original, non-translated texts. Using state-of-the-art authorship attribution methods, we show the potential of a cross-topic corpus generated by our framework when compared to the corpora that were used in related approaches, and enable the advance of research previously limited by corpora availability.

1 Introduction

In natural language processing (NLP), a cross-domain scenario describes a setting where the data used for training and testing differs in a specific manner. For example, if a profiling software has to determine properties of an author of emails, but was trained on novels of potential authors, the different text genres (emails and novels) represent a domain shift which has to be met by the model.

The importance of such scenarios exceeds mere scientific significance, as for specific fields they represent realistic scenarios more closely than single-type text analyses, and extend potential use cases. For example, when determining the authorship of an incriminating letter, digital forensic researchers may have more text available for training their model if also other types (e.g., emails, tweets, blog entries or product reviews) can be used.

© Springer Nature Switzerland AG 2019
F. Crestani et al. (Eds.): CLEF 2019, LNCS 11696, pp. 114–125, 2019.
https://doi.org/10.1007/978-3-030-28577-7_7

However, differences in types of text also reflect on the performance of the models used. Stamatatos et al. [16] showed that a cross-topic authorship attribution (CTAA) problem is harder to solve than a comparable single-topic setting. Therefore, specific approaches for dealing with cross-domain settings have been developed. However, as is the case with every NLP model, the performance of the approaches greatly relies on the dataset used for developing them. Hence, in addition to cross-domain tasks themselves, an important aspect lies in creating datasets that are required for model development, which has been underinvestigated in recent research. Specifically, we point out three major problems that emerge:

Problem 1: For some cross-domain tasks, there are not enough corpora publicly available. In an overview study, Potthast et al. showed that many authorship attribution (AA) methods are not performing equally on different datasets, but are instead sensitive to different document sizes and candidate authors [13]. Although the selection of corpora tested in this study was limited to single-topic corpora, it still shows how important the type of corpus is for the development of classification models. Therefore, to develop more robust models, evaluation should ideally happen on multiple corpora. However, for cross-domain text analyses, the selection of publicly available, high-quality corpora is limited. Here, many studies rely on creating specific datasets for their respective research (e.g., [11]) or use different types of corpora for validation (e.g., [12]).

Additionally, many corpora frequently used in research are not publicly available, making the respective approaches hard to reproduce [13].

Problem 2: Many currently used datasets can be considered too small. As it has been shown that the minimal required length for reliable authorship attribution varies per author and—depending on the text type—exceeds several thousand words [2,6], some of these corpora are arguably on the edge of being too short to motivate more general models. For example, the *Guardian* dataset [16], which is frequently used in cross-topic and cross-domain NLP research [3,7,15], features an average of just over 1,000 words per document and 6.8 documents per author and topic. Moreover, it is used for only ten candidate authors in most of the studies.

Problem 3: For some cross-domain tasks, suitable corpora do not exist at all. For example, many studies which aim to research cross-lingual settings use translated corpora. That is, the evaluation part of the dataset is translated into a different language to artificially produce a test set [1,5]. While studies suggest that the process of translation is able to keep stylistic markers from the original authors [17], many aspects of the texts are shifted by this approach. For example, it is likely that real multilingual authors exhibit various differences in the languages used.

We tackle these problems by providing a framework which generates text classification corpora based on a large set of social media comments in a wide variety of categories. As data source, we rely on the discussion platform Reddit, which features a wide variety of different topics. Using this method, our contributions align with the previously stated problems and therefore is threefold:

1. **Our framework is able to generate many different corpora on demand.** For example, if a model for cross-topic analysis is developed, our framework can be used to generate different cross-topic corpora for validation and hence helps to decrease data-bias for those models.
2. **Our framework is able to create very large corpora for problems where usually small corpora have been used in the past.** By harnessing the large amount of data available by the Reddit community, the amount of data available for corpus construction allows us to use strict filters to create a wide variety of different corpora.
3. **Our framework is able to construct types of corpora which previously did not exist.** For example, a true cross-lingual corpus can be constructed for many different languages, where authors originally wrote in (at least) two different languages—which in turn can be used to further investigate whether the existing approaches using translation-based corpora perform equally on real, non-translated text.

Another important goal of the framework is to enable users to easily and reliably reproduce corpora. We fulfill this goal by designing the generation process so that a limited, well-defined set of parameters is sufficient for corpus reproduction. Therefore, our solution helps to increase the transparency and reproducibility of cross-domain NLP research.

2   Dataset

For our research, we rely on a freely available data dump from Reddit[1] which consists of user comments between December 2005 and March 2017. Dumps from current months are continuously added to this collection[2] using the same format, making this approach easy to refit to current data. The topic-related forums, which are called subreddits, are usually referred to including their URL prefix (i.e., */r/worldnews*), and are highly versatile. They are usually moderated by users to ensure that only content suitable for the respective subreddit is posted. Not only do they contain different topics for discussions, but also feature various types of texts. For example, in the subreddit */r/WritingPrompts*, users usually start a discussion by writing a fictional situation, and other users try to continue the storyline, while the subreddit */r/worldnews* mainly contains discussions about events of international relevance. Therefore, the data can be utilized to create cross-topic, cross-genre or cross-language corpora.

With authorship attribution as one of the main target problems, we focus on extracting original text written by users. Therefore, we need to exclude two main sources of unsuitable text: (1) text from other users, and (2) automatically generated content. While there is no reliable method to exclude *all* of these comments with certainty, we leverage two simple techniques to identify them.

---

[1] https://reddit.com/r/datasets/comments/64o7py/.
[2] https://files.pushshift.io/reddit/comments/.

Quotations can be identified by their markup notation, a line starting with '⌴>'. Automatically generated postings by bots are a prominent and in many cases desired feature of Reddit, but are often unwanted for NLP research. As the content produced by bots can vary greatly in style, we rely on a manually curated list[3] to filter posts from bots.

2.1 Preprocessing

We first perform preprocessing steps and subsequently select and group data according to a fixed set of parameters. All of the steps involved are implemented in Python scripts available online[4].

1. Markdown links are replaced by their textual label, and citations (lines starting with '⌴>') are removed.
2. URLs that were not marked as a markdown link are replaced by the term <URL>.
3. We perform language detection on all messages using the *langdetect*[5] library.

2.2 Filtering

Reddit comments contain many different types of text (e.g., ascii-art, tables, etc.), which may not be of interest for every NLP task. In this work, we focus on generating text corpora containing plain written text, suitable for NLP tasks like authorship attribution or topic detection. This means that comments containing non-plain text have to be excluded. We utilize simple textual features to filter out the following types of comments:

- When a user account is deleted on Reddit, the author field of messages by that user is set to [deleted], and no information about the specific user can be retrieved. We drop comments with such an author field, as they are of no use for many tasks such as authorship attribution.
- Comments which are less than t_c characters long are discarded. This increases the expressiveness of the content by dropping short and often meaningless messages, helps the language detection to work more accurately and reduces the file size of the dataset. This is a substantial benefit, as the entire dataset is over 2TB large and requires large amounts of time to process.
- After transforming the content to lower case, comments which have less than t_v distinct words are discarded. This helps to remove messages consisting of few words repeated over and over. The casing of the remaining messages is left untouched.

---

[3] Taken from https://www.reddit.com/r/autowikibot/wiki/redditbots.
[4] https://github.com/bmurauer/reddit_corpora.
[5] https://pypi.org/project/langdetect/.

- If a comment does not have at least t_w words remaining after removing all punctuation marks, it is excluded. Otherwise, it is kept with its original punctuation. This step helps to filter comments consisting of ascii-art or tables.
- The language detection tool which we use estimates the probability of multiple languages for a text. By setting a threshold of t_{lp}, we only keep messages which can be assigned a language with a high confidence.

While these methods are simple, they are quickly calculated, can be applied universally to comments of all languages and topics, and manual inspection of the resulting corpora presented in Sect. 4.2 show that no unwanted content is left in the generated corpora. For our experiments, we used values t_c=1,000, $t_v = 20$, $t_w = 50$, $t_{lp} = 0.99$. All of these steps are configurable in the provided scripts, enabling both customizable corpora as well as reliable reproduction of a generated corpus.

From the initial three billion messages, 50 million messages remain after these processing steps. The according statistics are shown in Table 1. The filtered version of the entire dataset is the starting point for generating all corpora described in the remainder of this paper.

Table 1. Global dataset statistics.

	Pre-filter	Post-filter
Comments	3,092,028,928	50,567,575
Authors	22,554,169	4,380,330
Subreddits	415,566	162,564

3   Corpus Generation

The comments in the dataset feature three categorical fields that can be used for text classification purposes: authorship, language and subreddit. The authorship and subreddit fields can be used as target y for classification tasks, enabling the generation of corpora for authorship attribution and topic detection, respectively. While generating language detection corpora ($y = $ language) is possible in theory, the language field is itself calculated and does therefore not provide a sufficiently solid ground truth.

3.1   Corpus Generation Parameters

Often, the large amount of comments may want to be limited to match custom requirements. By providing a minimal message length c as well as a minimal document amount m per target, corpora of different sizes can be created, ranging from two to thousands of target classes, which can be used by large-scale models [4,10]. Although such a limitation was already applied in the previous step, a more restrictive value may be chosen at this point, yielding longer texts.

Additionally, each of the three classification target fields can be restricted to specific values by setting the according limitations l_{auth}, l_{lang} and l_{sub}. Table 2 shows how these limitations lead to different corpora. When providing no such limitation, the values for the respective field will include different, *mixed* values. For example, by setting $y =$ author with no limitations, documents of different topics and languages are collected for each author, without grouping them. This notation of *mixed* does therefore not refer to any cross-domain division of the data, but rather states that the respective field contains different values, as no distinction between training and testing data is made at this point. While this is an undesired property for use cases, models using domain-independent features (e.g., [8]) are still able to use these corpora.

Table 2. Examples of limiting fields and resulting corpora.

y	l_{auth}	l_{lang}	l_{sub}	Resulting corpus
Author	—	—	—	Mixed language, mixed topic authorship attribution (AA)
Author	—	{en}	—	Single language, mixed topic AA
Author	—	{en}	{/r/ama}	Single language, single topic AA
Author	{u1,u2}	{en,de}	—	Mixed language, mixed topic AA for 2 specific users u1, u2
Subreddit	—	—	{/r/ama,/r/politics}	Mixed topic detection for 2 specific topics /r/ama, /r/politics

Cross–domain corpora can be created by specifying an additional grouping field f_g. Thereby, only those target values are included in the result set if they feature at least m comments for every possible value in the grouping field. For example, if $y =$ author, $f_g =$ language and $m = 5$, only those authors are kept who have written at least 5 comments in *every* language available. In most cases, this means that f_g must be limited by setting the respective limitation l_{f_g} to ensure that the intersection yields results. Examples for possible configurations and the resulting corpora are displayed in Table 3.

Table 3. Examples for different corpus types generated by selecting different values for f_g. All limitations from Table 2 can still be applied.

y	f_g	Example use-case
Author	—	Authorship attribution (AA)
Author	Subreddit	Cross-topic authorship attribution (CTAA), Cross-genre authorship attribution (CGAA)
Author	Language	Cross-language authorship attribution (CLAA)
Subreddit	—	Topic detection (TD)
Subreddit	Language	Cross-language topic detection (CLTD)

Furthermore, by tweaking the constraints c and m, different sizes of corpora can be created. Table 4a shows that by using small values for m, the dataset allows the generation of large single-domain corpora with tens of thousands of authors, and even cross-domain corpora (Table 4b) with thousands of authors.

Table 4. Effect of minimal comment length c and minimal document count m on generated corpus size in terms of number of resulting target classes, for $y =$ author, $l_{auth} = \{\}$ and $l_{lang} = \{en\}$.

(a) Single-Topic AA, $f_g = \emptyset$, $l_{sub} = \{/r/AskReddit\}$

m	c			
	1,000	2,000	4,000	6,000
10	61,251	7,543	467	87
30	13,323	1,085	54	12
50	5,970	382	23	3
70	3,391	195	14	1

(b) Cross-Topic AA, $f_g =$ subreddit, $l_{sub} = \{/r/worldnews, /r/AskReddit\}$

m	c		
	1,000	2,000	4,000
10	4,550	403	17
30	743	45	0
50	292	12	0
70	139	5	0

3.2 Cross-Topic Corpora

Grouping the comments by subreddit enables the generation of cross-topic corpora. It should be noted that while the authorship and language labels are clearly defined, the subreddit-field should be used more carefully, as some subreddits like */r/worldnews* mostly comprise coherent discussion about a single topic whereas other subreddits like */r/AskReddit* are more diverse. While this does not invalidate the respective target classes as a whole, it demonstrates that a certain amount of reddit-domain-knowledge is required to be able to compare results.

Existing corpora feature similar properties, where some target classes are more similar to others. For example, in the *Guardian*-dataset [16], which is a widely used cross-topic and cross-domain corpus, some topics (*Politics, World, UK*) are more similar to each other than others (*Books, Society*).

3.3 Cross-Language Corpora

Although many different types of corpora can be generated using our framework, we dedicate our attention in this section to the case of cross-language corpora, as these are underrepresented in literature and often only translated versions of the original texts are used. In this section, a brief qualitative analysis of the comments is performed to better understand which languages can be used for creating cross-language corpora. In Table 5, the global distribution of languages across all comments is shown. It confirms the intuition that English is by far the predominant language used on Reddit.

For the five most popular languages on Reddit (English, Spanish, German, French, Portuguese), we analyzed the distribution of these languages across

Table 5. Most common languages used in the comments.

English	49,964,620	98.808%
Spanish	81,162	0.160%
German	79,969	0.158%
French	74,333	0.147%
Portuguese	61,386	0.122%

Table 6. Top three subreddits with the most comments for selected languages. The last column describes the subreddit's fraction of all posts in the respective language.

Language	Subreddit	Count	Percentage
English	/r/AskReddit	3,787,110	7.6%
	/r/politics	1,234,722	2.5%
	/r/worldnews	738,144	1.5%
Spanish	/r/podemos	81,162	55.1%
	/r/argentina	28,200	19.2%
	/r/mexico	17,188	11.7%
German	/r/de	44,835	56.1%
	/r/rocketbeans	8,533	10.7%
	/r/Austria	5,408	6.7%
French	/r/france	49,520	66.6%
	/r/Quebec	14,947	20.4%
	/r/montreal	1,519	2.0%
Portuguese	/r/brasil	31,830	51.8%
	/r/portugal	22,063	35.9%
	/r/PremeiraLiga	980	1.6%

different subreddits, shown in Table 6. In many cases, the subreddit with the most comments relates to the nationality of that language. In cases where the respective language is the native language of multiple countries (e.g., Portuguese in Portugal and Brasil), the according distribution of subreddits shows related results.

This information can help to construct even finer-grained corpora based on subreddits. For example, given the subreddits from Table 6, two different types of cross-language corpora can be created by setting l_{sub} to $\{/r/brasil, /r/AskReddit\}$ or $\{/r/portugal, /r/AskReddit\}$, respectively. This way, nuances of the respective dialect can be analyzed easily.

Table 7 shows different cross-language corpora created by varying the l_{lang} limit. Interestingly, the sizes of the created corpora no longer correlate with the distribution of the languages in total. For the special case of Spanish, we explain this behaviour in the nature of the biggest Spanish subreddit in our dataset,

Table 7. Sizes of different CL-AA corpora created with y = author, f_g = language, $c = 1,000$, $m = 50$.

l_{lang}	Authors	Avg. docs/author
{en,es}	47	177
{en,de}	106	205
{en,fr}	106	208
{en,pt}	63	188

/r/podemos. In contrast to other languages, where the biggest subreddit typically is generic, */r/podemos* is the discussion board of a political movement with a rather narrow scope. Naturally, such deviations are dynamic and may change when taking more current comments into account.

4   Selected Corpora

In this section, we showcase several exemplary authorship attribution corpora of different characteristics which have been created with our framework. We encourage researchers to reuse and amend this collection. Additionally, we demonstrate the need for new corpora in the field of NLP by running previous CTAA solutions on two generated corpora.

4.1   Corpus Selection

By selecting the appropriate values for the parameters presented in Sect. 3, we created four different types of corpora which are listed in Table 8: single-topic (ST, ①+②), mixed topic (MT, ③), cross-topic (CT, ④ + ⑤), cross-genre (CG, ⑥) and cross-language (CL, ⑦ + ⑧) corpora. To ensure reusability, all presented corpora are available online[6].

4.2   CTAA Comparison

To compare the created corpora with existing studies, we selected CTAA approaches which use the *Guardian* dataset [16] and compare the performance of those models when applied to two subcorpora created by our framework, listed in Table 9. We rely on the information provided by the original authors, but the results of the experiments may deviate slightly as we did not have access to the author's original code.

As a widely used baseline, we perform authorship attribution using character n-grams [12,14] with a linear SVM classifier, which has also proven to be efficient in cross-genre settings [9]. In addition, we implemented an embedding approach similar to Gomez et al [3], where the features produced by POS-, character- and

---

[6] https://github.com/bmurauer/reddit_corpora.

Table 8. Parameters used for generating selected corpora for authorship attribution (y = author).

	Corpus	f_g	l_{lang}	l_{sub}	m	c	auth.s
①	R-ST1	—	en	/r/AskReddit	50	3k	69
②	R-ST2	—	en	/r/politics	50	3k	76
③	R-MT	—	en	—	50	4k	23
④	R-CT1	Subreddit	en	/r/worldnews, /r/politics	10	5k	10
⑤	R-CT2	Subreddit	en	/r/worldnews, /r/AskReddit	20	3k	18
⑥	R-CG	Subreddit	en	/r/AskReddit, /r/WritingPrompts	10	3k	47
⑦	R-CL1	Language	en, de	—	20	2k	37
⑧	R-CL2	Language	en, es	—	20	2k	20

Table 9. Characteristics of corpora used in the CTAA experiment. G_{PW} is part of the Guardian corpus [16] containing articles from the sections "Politics" and "World" for comparison.

Corpus	Train topic	Test topic	Authors	Docs/auth/topic	Chars/doc
R-CT1	/r/politics	/r/worldnews	10	30	6,678
R-CT2	/r/worldnews	/r/AskReddit	18	42.11	4,409
G_{PW}	Politics	World	13	6.83	6,379

word n-gram embedding are stacked to be used by the final linear SVM classifier. We used 5 epochs with 10 training cycles each, a window size of 5 and a vector size of 80. As sequences of tokens, we extracted all n-grams from size 1 to 4.

While many studies use accuracy as evaluation metric, we chose to use the F1 score for increased class-imbalance sensitivity. In Table 10, the performance of the character n-gram approach is shown on the original Guardian dataset when trained on *Politics* and tested on *World* (G_{PW}). The R-CT1 column contains the F1 score of the same model on a cross-topic corpus created by our system for two very similar topics (/r/Politics and /r/worldnews), which are subforums on Reddit. Finally, the R-CT2 column denotes a different, more distant topic combination (/r/worldnews and /r/AskReddit), whereby the latter is a general-purpose forum for asking questions.

The results of the character n-gram based solution show a constant behaviour across the similar sized corpora, while the performance of the embedding-approach differs substantially across the datasets. While one of the focus points of this experiment is to demonstrate how easily new datasets for validation can be created, the result itself underlines the observations of Potthast et al. [13] (i.e., the performance of methods differs greatly across corpora), and therefore, advocates the importance of a multi-corpora evaluation.

Table 10. Results for different datasets

Method	F1 (macro)		
	G_{PW}	R-CT1	R-CT2
Character n-grams	0.85	0.84	0.86
n-gram embeddings	0.87	0.93	0.95

5   Limitations and Future Work

As stated previously, the nature of the data source implies some limitations on the generated corpora, which consist of comments posted by users. While posts themselves are mostly subject to topical limitations imposed by moderators, the discussion in the comments following these posts can deviate from these topics. While this is a core property of social media text, it may be disadvantageous for tasks like topic detection. By creating a similar tooling for generating corpora based on reddit posts rather than comments, these topical variations may be circumvented.

Similarly, the rather simple preprocessing and filtering steps may be improved, as automatically created content by bots may still be present in the generated corpora.

6   Conclusion

In this paper, we present a framework for custom corpora generation based on Reddit user comments. Our solution is able to create a wide variety of different corpora, ranging from more generic single-topic, single-language corpora with tens of thousands of authors to highly specific cross-domain corpora, and the large amount of subreddits available from the entire dataset allows researchers to use previously unavailable data. Notably, our framework is able to generate original, untranslated cross-language corpora, which have been unavailable in the past.

We show that established NLP models perform differently on the constructed corpora, confirming previous suggestions that previous results may be too specific on the corpus used for training.

One important focus of this work is mitigating reproducibility problems by ensuring that a small, fixed set of parameters suffices to reliably reconstruct a corpus. Finally, we provide eight exemplary corpora for various cross-domain NLP settings and the parameters used for creating them, ensuring full transparency.

References

1. Bogdanova, D., Lazaridou, A.: Cross-language authorship attribution. In: Proceedings of the 9th International Conference on Language Resources and Evaluation, pp. 2015–2020 (2014)

2. Eder, M.: Does size matter? Authorship attribution, small samples, big problem. Digit. Sch. Hum. **30**(2), 167–182 (2013)
3. Gómez-Adorno, H., Posadas-Durán, J.P., Sidorov, G., Pinto, D.: Document embeddings learned on various types of n-grams for cross-topic authorship attribution. Computing **100**(7), 741–756 (2018).https://doi.org/10.1007/s00607-018-0587-8
4. Koppel, M., Schler, J., Argamon, S., Messeri, E.: Authorship attribution with thousands of candidate authors. In: Proceedings of the 29th Annual International ACM SIGIR Conference on Research and Development in Information Retrieval. ACM Press (2006). https://doi.org/10.1145/1148170.1148304
5. Llorens, M., Delany, S.J.: Deep level lexical features for cross-lingual authorship attribution. In: Proceedings of the First Workshop on Modeling, Learning and Mining for Cross/Multilinguality, pp. 16–25. Dublin Institute of Technology (2016)
6. Luyckx, K., Daelemans, W.: The effect of author set size and data size in authorship attribution. Literary Linguist. Comput. **26**(1), 35–55 (2011). https://doi.org/10.1093/llc/fqq013
7. Markov, I., Stamatatos, E., Sidorov, G.: Improving cross-topic authorship attribution: the role of pre-processing. In: Gelbukh, A. (ed.) CICLing 2017. LNCS, vol. 10762, pp. 289–302. Springer, Cham (2018). https://doi.org/10.1007/978-3-319-77116-8_21
8. Menon, R., Choi, Y.: Domain independent authorship attribution without domain adaptation. In: Proceedings of the International Conference Recent Advances in Natural Language Processing, pp. 309–315 (2011)
9. Murauer, B., Tschuggnall, M., Specht, G.: Dynamic parameter search for cross-domain authorship attribution. Working Notes of CLEF (2018)
10. Narayanan, A., et al.: On the feasibility of internet-scale author identification. In: 2012 IEEE Symposium on Security and Privacy. IEEE, May 2012. https://doi.org/10.1109/sp.2012.46
11. Overdorf, R., Greenstadt, R.: Blogs, Twitter feeds, and reddit comments: cross-domain authorship attribution. Proc. Privacy Enhancing Technol. **2016**(3), 155–171 (2016)
12. Posadas-Durán, J.P., Gómez-Adorno, H., Sidorov, G., Batyrshin, I., Pinto, D., Chanona-Hernández, L.: Application of the distributed document representation in the authorship attribution task for small corpora. Soft Computing **21**(3), 627–639 (2017). https://doi.org/10.1007/s00500-016-2446-x
13. Potthast, M., Hagen, M., Stein, B.: Author obfuscation: attacking the state of the art in authorship verification. In: Working Notes Papers of the CLEF 2016 Evaluation Labs. CEUR Workshop Proceedings, CLEF and CEUR-WS.org, September 2016
14. Sapkota, U., Bethard, S., Montes, M., Solorio, T.: Not all character n-grams are created equal: a study in authorship attribution. In: Proceedings of the 2015 Conference of the North American Chapter of the Association for Computational Linguistics: Human Language Technologies, pp. 93–102, June 2015
15. Sapkota, U., Solorio, T., y Gómez, M.M., Bethard, S., Rosso, P.: Cross-topic authorship attribution: will out-of-topic data help? In: Proceedings of the 25th International Conference on Computational Linguistics (COLING 2014), pp. 1228–1237, August 2014
16. Stamatatos, E.: On the robustness of authorship attribution based on character n-gram features. J. Law Policy **21**, 421–439 (2013)
17. Venuti, L.: The Translator's Invisibility: A History of Translation. Routledge, Abingdon (2017)

Efficient Answer-Annotation
for Frequent Questions

Markus Zlabinger[1]([✉]), Navid Rekabsaz[2], Stefan Zlabinger[1],
and Allan Hanbury[1]

[1] TU Wien, Vienna, Austria
{markus.zlabinger,stefan.zlabinger,allan.hanbury}@tuwien.ac.at
[2] Idiap Research Institute, Martigny, Switzerland
navid.rekabsaz@idiap.ch

Abstract. Ground truth is a crucial resource for the creation of effective question-answering (Q-A) systems. When no appropriate ground truth is available, as it is often the case in domain-specific Q-A systems (e.g. customer-support, tourism) or in languages other than English, new ground truth can be created by human annotation. The annotation process in which a human annotator looks up the corresponding answer label for each question from an answer catalog (SEQUENTIAL approach), however, is usually time-consuming and costly. In this paper, we propose a new approach, in which the annotator first manually groups questions that have the same intent as a candidate question, and then, labels the entire group in one step (GROUP-WISE approach). To retrieve same-intent questions effectively, we evaluate various unsupervised semantic similarity methods from recent literature, and implement the most effective one in our annotation approach. Afterwards, we compare the GROUP-WISE approach with the SEQUENTIAL approach with respect to answer look-ups, annotation time, and label-quality. We show based on 500 German customer-support questions that the GROUP-WISE approach requires 51% fewer answer look-ups, is 41% more time-efficient, and retains the same label-quality as the SEQUENTIAL approach. Note that the described approach is limited to Q-A systems where frequently asked questions occur.

Keywords: Question-answering ·
Unsupervised semantic text similarity · Data annotation

1 Introduction

Personal information services via phone, e-mail or live-chat are a major cost-factor for customer-oriented companies. To reduce these costs, companies implement question-answering (Q-A) systems so that users can obtain information autonomously. To determine the effectiveness of a deployed system, or to create a system based on supervised learning, ground truth data is a crucial resource. Despite the existence of publicly available ground truth, such as the Stanford

© Springer Nature Switzerland AG 2019
F. Crestani et al. (Eds.): CLEF 2019, LNCS 11696, pp. 126–137, 2019.
https://doi.org/10.1007/978-3-030-28577-7_8

Question Answering Dataset (SQuAD) [16] or the Microsoft MAchine Reading COmprehension Dataset (MS MARCO) [2], a lack still exists in domain-specific systems, and specially in the languages other than English.

A common property of many Q-A systems is that the number of questions is much larger than the number of available answers, such that many questions refer to the same information need provided by a corresponding answer. This scenario is common in various Q-A domains such as tourism [15], telecommunication [17], and medical [19], as well as in search engines [18]. To create a ground truth dataset in such cases, the common approach is to annotate the questions one-by-one and label each with the relevant answer. We refer to this approach as *Sequential Annotation* (SEQUENTIAL). Clearly, this approach is highly time-expensive, when considering that for each question the annotator has to look up the answer in an answer catalog, which could potentially contain hundreds of entries.

To approach this efficiency problem, we propose to first manually group the questions with the same information need, and then assign one answer to each group of questions. By doing so, only a single answer look-up is required for each group of questions. We refer to this approach as *Group-Wise Annotation* (GROUP-WISE), consisting of three steps: First, a candidate question is selected, and the most similar questions to it are provided to the annotator. Second, from the provided list, the annotator selects questions with the same information need (i.e. same intent) as the candidate question. Finally, the annotator labels the entire group, consisting of candidate question and selected same-intent questions, with an answer.

Using the GROUP-WISE approach for annotation raises two main research questions: (RQ1) What is the most effective text similarity method for retrieving the questions with same information needs? (RQ2) To what extent does the GROUP-WISE approach affect the efficiency as well as the annotation quality in comparison to the SEQUENTIAL approach?

In this paper, we study these questions in the context of question-answering annotation of the automatic customer-support system of a telecommunication company. The data provided from the system consists of 500 questions and a pre-defined set of answers, where each addresses a specific information need. The aim of the system is to map each question to its answer. All questions and answers are in German.

To explore the first research question, we first annotate 500 questions using the SEQUENTIAL approach. From the annotated questions, we create a text similarity benchmark, by considering the questions with the same answers as relevant questions. Based on the benchmark, we evaluate the performance of various unsupervised text similarity methods from recent literature, by comparing their effectiveness in retrieving relevant questions. In line with the results on the SemEval question-to-question similarity dataset [12], our experiments show the effectiveness of the *Smooth Inverse Frequency (SIF)* [1] method, such that this approach achieves on par or better than other text similarity methods, including methods based on word/sentence embeddings.

Based on the evaluation, we implement the SIF method in the GROUP-WISE approach, which we then use to re-annotate the 500 questions. By comparing the two annotation approaches with respect to number of answer look-ups, annotation time, and label-quality, we show that the GROUP-WISE approach requires 51% fewer answer look-ups, is 41% more time-efficient, and retains the same label-quality.

The contribution of this paper is two-fold:

- We evaluate and compare various unsupervised text similarity methods for the task of similar question retrieval.
- We propose a new annotation approach, and thoroughly examine its effects for the labeling of Q-A datasets from the perspectives of annotation time and label-quality.

The remainder of this paper is organized as follows: In Sect. 2, we review related work. In Sect. 3, we describe and explain unsupervised semantic text similarity methods from recent literature. Afterwards, we provide a definition of the GROUP-WISE approach in Sect. 4. In Sect. 5, we describe our experimental setup. Finally, in Sect. 6, we report our evaluation results, and discuss the effects of the annotation approaches.

2   Related Work

In this section, we review work from two related fields: similar question retrieval, and Q-A annotation.

2.1   Similar Question Retrieval

One part in our approach is the retrieval of same-intent questions with respect to a candidate question. The retrieval of similar questions is also an important topic in the area of Community Question Answering (CQA) where one research problem is the retrieval of duplicate questions [4,6,8,12,13].

A duplicate question retrieval task was part of the Semantic Evaluation workshop in 2017 [12] (task 3 subtask B). The objective in the task was to re-rank 10 related questions with respect to a candidate question. In the scope of the task, a competition was organized where various teams participated (first place [5], second place [7]). After the SemEval competition, the dataset was publicly released, and is now considered a standard benchmark for the evaluation of question-to-question similarity methods. The benchmark consists of training set, development set and test set.

Since the benchmark is accompanied by training data, the developed methods (e.g. [5,7,8]) are mostly based on supervised learning. To also get an idea how state-of-the-art unsupervised methods perform, we re-implement and compare various methods based on the SemEval benchmark dataset.

2.2 Q-A Annotation

We describe here the annotation procedures of widely known Q-A benchmark datasets. A commonly pursued approach is to use crowdsourcing. For example, the Stanford Question Answering Dataset (SQuAD) [16] dataset was created by asking crowdsourcing workers to formulate questions based on a shown Wikipedia article.

Another benchmark dataset is the Microsoft MAchine Reading COmprehension Dataset (MS MARCO) [2]. For the creation of the MS MARCO dataset, questions (sampled from the Bing search engine) and potential answer passages (retrieved from the Bing web index) were presented to the human annotators. From the presented passages, the annotators selected the passages that contain information for answering the question.

The main objective of the described related works was to create new benchmarks for the evaluation of scientific methodologies in the area of Q-A. In contrast for this paper, the focus is on how to create such benchmarks more efficiently.

3 Text Similarity Methods

In this section, we summarize unsupervised semantic text similarity methods. The methods used in this work can be divided into three categories: First, methods that are based on an aggregation (e.g. averaging) of individual word embeddings. Second, methods that directly compute an embedded representation for a given text (i.e. text embeddings), and third, traditional methods that are based on word counts. In the following, we first describe three methods from the first category, two methods from the second category, and finally, one method from the third category.

Average Embedding (AVG) [9]: A simple method to compute the similarity between two pieces of text is to first compute the average embedding vector and then, the cosine similarity between two texts' average vectors. The average embedding vector of a text t is computed as $avg(t) = \frac{1}{|t|} \sum_{w \in t} v_w$, where v_w is the embedding vector for word w, and $|t|$ is the number of words in t. The similarity between two texts t_i and t_j is computed as $\cos(avg(t_i), avg(t_j))$, where cos is the cosine similarity.

Weighted Average Embedding (WAVG) [9]: In the AVG method, each embedding vector is weighted equally, neglecting the degrees of importance of words. To incorporate the word importance, we can weight each word vector by its TFIDF value. The TFIDF weighting for a text t is defined as $wavg(t) = \frac{1}{|t|} \sum_{w \in t} v_w \times tfidf(t)$, where $tfidf(w)$ is the TFIDF weight for word w. The similarity between two texts t_i and t_j is computed as $\cos(wavg(t_i), wavg(t_j))$.

Smooth Inverse Frequency (SIF): Arora et al. [1] introduce another weighting scheme for averaging word embedding. In this method, the embedding for the text t is computed in two steps: First, a weighted average embedding vector is computed as $sif(t) = \frac{1}{|t|} \sum_{w \in t} \frac{a}{a+p(w)} v_w$, where a is a hyper-parameter, and $p(w) = \frac{tf(w)}{|W|}$ is the relative term frequency of word $w \in W$ across all texts $t \in T$. In the second step, the weighted average vectors for all $(t_1, \ldots, t_n) \in T$ are organized as a matrix $M = (sif(t_1), \ldots, sif(t_n))$. From M, the projection of the first principal component is removed resulting in the matrix M_{pca}^{-}. The principal component removal can be considered as a form of denoising [1]. The similarity between two texts t_i and t_j is the cosine similarity between the row vectors i and j of M_{pca}^{-}.

Doc2Vec [9]: This method directly calculates the embedding of a text such as a sentence, a paragraph, or a document. After training on a text corpus, the model can provides a vector representation for any given text. The similarity between two texts t_i and t_j is the cosine similarity computed based on the inferred vectors. Note that in the Doc2Vec method, words can only be used if they appeared during the model training phase. Words in the given text that did not appear in the training corpus, namely Out-Of-Vocabulary (OOV) words, are ignored.

Sent2Vec [14]: This method is the state-of-the-art of the short-text embeddings, calculated by incorporating word embeddings (word2vec [11]) and character n-gram embeddings (fastText [3]) in the model training process. The incorporation of fastText embeddings provides a solution for the OOV problem. After training, the model can be used to infer a vector representation for a given text. The similarity between two inferred texts is computed with the cosine similarity.

TFIDF: In this method, the similarity between weighted word vectors is computed with the cosine similarity. The word weight is based on the *term frequency* and the *inverse document frequency*.

4   Group-Wise Question-Answer Annotation

In this section, the proposed GROUP-WISE approach to create ground truth for question-answering tasks is explained. Given a set of unlabeled questions Q, and an answer set A, the GROUP-WISE approach is defined as follows:

1. A candidate question $c \in Q$ is presented to the annotator.
2. All questions in Q (except c) are ranked with respect to c, using an unsupervised semantic similarity method.
3. In the ranked list of similar questions, the annotator skims through the top ranked questions and manually selects the questions that have the same information intent as c.
4. For the selected questions as well as the candidate question c, the annotator looks up the corresponding answer label $a \in A$ and labels the questions. If no appropriate answer exists, a *no-answer* label is assigned.
5. Finally, the questions labeled in the previous step are removed from the question pool Q, and a new iteration is started at *step 1*, until all questions are labeled, namely when $Q = \{\}$.

5   Experiment Setup

In this section, we describe our experimental setup with regards to: the data used, the applied preprocessing steps, the initialization of the similarity methods, and the setup of the annotation process.

Datasets

Customer-Support Questions : This dataset consists of 500 customer-support questions of an automatic Q-A system of a telecommunication company. The questions were randomly sampled from a set of 113,394 questions that were asked from February 2016 to July 2016. The questions in the dataset are usually of two types: First, questions of customers who encounter technical problems, e.g., connection disturbance, forgotten credentials, or a locked phone. And second, questions of customers who look for general information about topics like contract, phone usage in a foreign country, or accessing webmail. The questions originate from a chat-bot system that maps questions to an answer set, namely a static set of Frequently Asked Questions (FAQ). In our experiments, the FAQ set, containing 373 entries, is used as the answer set. Both the questions and the FAQ database are in German. The average question length is 3.18 words, and the median length is 2 words (both computed when ignoring the stop words).

SemEval 2017 : The second dataset we use in our experiments is the benchmark dataset of the SemEval 2017 question-to-question similarity task (task 3 subtask B) [12]. The dataset consists of candidate questions, and 10 related questions per candidate. The goal in the task is to re-rank the related questions, which can be either relevant or irrelevant with respect to the candidate. For our experiments, we consider the test-set of the dataset (contains 88 candidate questions) and the *subject* text of the questions for the computation of the semantic similarity. The questions in the dataset stem from the Qatar Living CQA forum and are in English. The average length of the questions is 3.09 words and the median is 3 words.

Preprocessing. As preprocessing, for both datasets, we applied stemming via porter stemmer, removed non-alphanumeric characters, and removed stop words (based on a standard English and German stop word lists). For the SemEval dataset, we replaced URLs with the string *url_token* and images with *image_token*.

Model Preparation. For each of the two described datasets, we had a large amount of unlabeled text available that we used to train task-specific embedding models. More specifically, for the customer-support dataset we used the full set containing 113,394 questions to train our models, and for the SemEval 2017 dataset, we used a text corpus that was provided by the organizers of the

SemEval competition. For both sets of unlabeled text, we trained following task-specific models: fastText, Doc2Vec, Sent2Vec, and TF-IDF. Note that we used fastText rather than the word2vec model, since it is robust with respect to OOV words, which is an important aspect considering the characteristics of our scenario, namely using user-generated queries (e.g. misspellings), and the German language (e.g. compound words).

For the training of the models, we set following parameters: For the fastText model, we used the default parameters as described in [3]. For the Doc2Vec model, we set the vector size to 300 and the window size to 3. For the Sent2Vec model, we used the default parameters of the GitHub implementation[1]. For parameters that were not explicitly stated, we used the defaults of the Gensim (fastText, Doc2Vec), GitHub (Sent2Vec), or Scikit-learn (TF-IDF) implementations. In the SIF model, we set $a = 10^{-3}$ as proposed by Arora et al. [1].

Annotation Setup. We implemented the GROUP-WISE, and the SEQUENTIAL approach in the framework of an annotation tool. The annotators in our experiments are two university students with technical backgrounds. To get the annotators familiar with their task, we conducted a small-scale test-run before starting with the actual annotation runs.

6   Experiments and Results

To compare the GROUP-WISE annotation approach to the SEQUENTIAL annotation approach, we first annotate the 500 customer-support questions using the SEQUENTIAL approach. Based on the labeled questions, we evaluate the unsupervised text similarity methods, described in Sect. 6.1. The best-performing text similarity method is then used in the GROUP-WISE approach to re-annotate the customer-support questions. Given the results, we analyze and compare the annotation approaches.

To annotate the 500 customer-support questions using the SEQUENTIAL approach, the first annotator, namely $A1$, goes through the questions one-by-one and labels them with the answer, selected from the answer catalog. Questions that could not be answered—e.g., questions where no answer exists in the catalog, or questions without an actual information need (e.g. "Hello!", "what's the purpose of life")—were labeled with *no-answer*. The annotation took in total 508 min with an average time of 61 s per question (breaks excluded). From the possible 373 answer entries, 99 answers occurred (26.54%), and 211 questions were labeled with *no-answer*. Considering that we work with data that originate from a chat-bot, the high number of *no-answer* questions is not a surprise, since users often ask the chat-bot irrelevant questions (e.g. gender, or relationship status) or submit texts that are not actual questions (e.g. "Hi").

---

[1] https://github.com/epfml/sent2vec.

6.1 Evaluation of the Semantic Similarity Methods

In the previous experiment, 500 customer-support questions were labeled. We now use the labeled questions as well as the benchmark from the SemEval question similarity task, to identify the semantic similarity method that is best suited for our GROUP-WISE approach. We compare the following methods that were described earlier in this paper: AVG, WAVG, SIF, Doc2Vec, Sent2Vec, and TFIDF.

Experiment Preparation. Before we can use the labeled customer-support questions to evaluate the semantic similarity methods, we need to adapt the dataset (i.e. by transforming it into a similar question retrieval task). Therefore, we perform following adaption steps: First, the questions are grouped based on their answer label. Second, from each group that contains at least two questions, one question is randomly selected as query question, resulting in the set of queries Q. Finally, for each $q \in Q$, we use the similarity methods to rank the remaining 499 questions, consisting of relevant questions (same answer label as q) and irrelevant questions (different answer label than q).

Note that in the described adaption we assume that questions with the same answer are relevant to each other (i.e. same intent). This assumption, however, can be problematic for certain datasets; e.g., there might be an answer that describes two things: the extension of a contract, but also the termination of a contract. Now, two questions that are labeled with such an answer could be about either things, i.e., contract extension or termination. The answer catalog that we use in our experiments, however, is a FAQ database that consists of specific answers to specific questions; e.g., there is an answer about contract extension, but a separate answer about contract termination. Therefore, the assumption that two questions that have the same answer label also have the same intent is valid in our case.

Evaluation Results. Based on the adapted customer-support dataset and the SemEval 2017 dataset, we compared the semantic similarity methods by mean average precision (MAP). The results in Table 1 show that the SIF method outperforms the other methods. As a comparison to the supervised methods, the best performing system of the SemEval 2017 competition achieved a MAP of 0.472 [12] using a supervised approach. Based on the conducted evaluation, we use SIF in our GROUP-WISE annotation approach, discussed in the next section.

Qualitative Analysis. Our case-based error diagnosis show a substantial loss of MAP for long questions. For example, consider the question "My contract runs out for my iPhone how can I extend it?" A question this long often contains words that do not contribute to the actual information need of the question (e.g. the word "iPhone" in the mentioned question). Despite not contributing to the information need, the word "iPhone" could lead to the retrieval of false

Table 1. MAP of the semantic similarity methods on our dataset (Customer-Support) and on the SemEval 2017 question-to-question similarity task [12].

Model	DataSets	
	Customer-Support	SemEval
TFIDF	0.301	0.388
AVG	0.404	0.396
Doc2Vec	0.411	0.425
WAVG	0.434	0.427
Sent2Vec	0.460	0.420
SIF	**0.463**	**0.437**

positives, like "what case colors are available for the iPhone?".[2] We find this issue as an open challenge, specially when only using unsupervised approaches for text similarity.

6.2 Group-Wise Annotation Approach

In this section, we describe the annotation of the 500 customer-support questions using the GROUP-WISE approach, followed by a comparison with the SEQUENTIAL approach.

Annotating the customer-support questions took 209 min, with an average of 25 s per question. The annotator assigned labels to 242 question-groups, where some groups only contained a single question (e.g. questions with an unique intent). From the possible 373 answer entries, 79 answers occurred (21.18%), and 200 questions were labeled as *no-answer*. Particular to this annotation method, even some of the *no-answer* questions were annotated together; e.g., questions with greeting formulas ("Hello!", "hi.").

In the following, we compare the two approaches with respect to efficiency and label accuracy (label-quality). As mentioned before, the SEQUENTIAL approach is used by the first annotator ($A1$), and the GROUP-WISE approach by the second annotator ($A2$). The choice of two annotators, each assigned to a different annotation approach, enables the comparison of the approaches. However, the differences between the annotators could become a possible source of bias in our comparisons, as explained in more detail later.

Comparison of the Efficiency. The results with respect to number of answer look-ups is presented in Fig. 1a. The results show that by using the proposed tool, the number of look-ups to find relevant answers is reduced by 51%. Notice that to annotate the first 300 questions, less than 100 look-ups are performed in the GROUP-WISE approach. Furthermore, notice that from 300 questions

---

[2] Questions are translated from German.

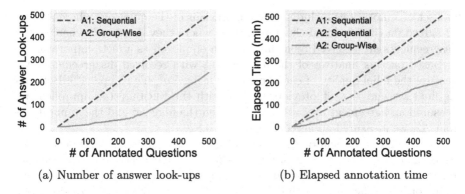

(a) Number of answer look-ups

(b) Elapsed annotation time

Fig. 1. Comparison between GROUP-WISE approach and SEQUENTIAL approach on the customer-support dataset

to 500 questions the number of answer look-ups grows similarly for both the GROUP-WISE and SEQUENTIAL approach. The reason for that is that in the end mostly unique questions remain, which cannot be annotated as a group with other questions.

While the reduction of answer look-ups is a positive indicator of efficiency, the GROUP-WISE approach also has the overhead of grouping the questions with the same information need. To also take this overhead into account, we compare the elapsed annotation time when using the GROUP-WISE approach with the elapsed time when using the SEQUENTIAL approach.

A specific consideration in this comparison is that the annotation speed can greatly depend on the speed of the annotator. To reduce this bias, we compute an estimation of the full annotation time of the annotator $A2$, when using the SEQUENTIAL approach. For that, $A2$ labels a set of 50 questions that are randomly sampled from the pool of the 500 questions. The annotation of these questions took on average 51 s per question. We use this estimation to compare the elapsed time of the annotation approaches.

The results of the comparison are presented in Fig. 1b. The plots for the SEQUENTIAL methods are based on the average annotation times of the annotator $A1$ and $A2$ ($A2$ based on the described estimation). The small bumps in Fig. 1b indicate the overhead of the GROUP-WISE approach, i.e., time elapses for the selection of same-intent questions and for the answer look-up.

Based on the experimental results, we observe that $A2$ is 41% faster when using the GROUP-WISE approach rather than the SEQUENTIAL approach. This finding suggest that the GROUP-WISE annotation approach is indeed more time-efficient than the SEQUENTIAL approach for the labeling of the customer-support dataset.

Comparison of the Annotation Quality. So far, we have analyzed the efficiency of the two approaches. Now we analyze if the GROUP-WISE approach has a negative impact on the quality of the annotation. Therefore, we first create a final set of annotations including the annotations of the questions where $A1$ and $A2$ agreed on the label and the annotations where they disagreed, whereas, the disagreements are resolved by a third person employed as a meta-annotator.

Based on this final set of the annotations with resolved disagreements, we measure the label-quality of each annotator using Cohen's Kappa [10]. Between the final set and the set provided by $A1$ with the SEQUENTIAL approach, we measured an agreement of $\kappa = 0.798$. Between the final set and the annotations from $A2$, we measured an agreement of $\kappa = 0.826$.

The similar agreement of $A1$ and $A2$ to the final set indicates that both annotators made a similar number of mistakes (or a similar degree of disagreements to the meta-annotator). We should note that a portion of this agreement might stem from the differences of the annotators. However, given the high similarity between the results of the approaches, we conclude that the label-quality is not affected (positively nor negatively) by using the GROUP-WISE approach for the annotation of the customer-support questions.

7   Conclusion

An annotation approach for the efficient creation of ground truth for Q-A datasets was proposed. In the approach, rather than labeling questions sequentially one-by-one, we propose to annotate groups of questions. Based on a dataset from the customer-support area, we compare the GROUP-WISE approach to the SEQUENTIAL approach. We show that the GROUP-WISE approach requires 51% fewer answer look-ups, is 41% faster, and retains the same label-quality as the SEQUENTIAL annotation approach. In future research, we plan to apply the GROUP-WISE approach for the creation of new datasets, to evaluate its generalization. Furthermore, the integration of the approach into a crowdsourcing platform and its evaluation in this setting presents another future research opportunity.

References

1. Arora, S., Liang, Y., Ma, T.: Simple but tough-to-beat baseline for sentence embeddings. In: International Conference on Learning Representations (2017)
2. Bajaj, P., et al.: MS MARCO: A Human Generated MAchine Reading COmprehension Dataset. arXiv:1611.09268 [cs], November 2016
3. Bojanowski, P., Grave, E., Joulin, A., Mikolov, T.: Enriching Word Vectors with Subword Information. arXiv:1607.04606 [cs], July 2016
4. Chahuara, P., Lampert, T., Gancarski, P.: Retrieving and Ranking Similar Questions from Question-Answer Archives Using Topic Modelling and Topic Distribution Regression. arXiv:1606.03783 [cs], June 2016
5. Charlet, D., Damnati, G.: SimBow at SemEval-2017 task 3: soft-cosine semantic similarity between questions for community question answering. In: Proceedings of the 11th International Workshop on Semantic Evaluation (SemEval-2017), pp. 315–319. Association for Computational Linguistics, Vancouver, August 2017

6. Franco-Salvador, M., Kar, S., Solorio, T., Rosso, P.: UH-PRHLT at SemEval-2016 task 3: combining lexical and semantic-based features for community question answering. In: Proceedings of the 10th International Workshop on Semantic Evaluation (SemEval-2016), pp. 814–821. Association for Computational Linguistics, San Diego, June 2016

7. Goyal, N.: LearningToQuestion at SemEval 2017 task 3: ranking similar questions by learning to rank using rich features. In: Proceedings of the 11th International Workshop on Semantic Evaluation (SemEval-2017), pp. 310–314 (2017)

8. Hazem, A., El Amal Boussaha, B., Hernandez, N.: MappSent: a textual mapping approach for question-to-question similarity. In: Recent Advances in Natural Language Processing Meet Deep Learning, RANLP 2017, pp. 291–300, November 2017

9. Le, Q., Mikolov, T.: Distributed representations of sentences and documents. In: International Conference on Machine Learning, pp. 1188–1196 (2014)

10. McHugh, M.L.: Interrater reliability: the kappa statistic. Biochemia Medica **22**(3), 276–282 (2012)

11. Mikolov, T., Sutskever, I., Chen, K., Corrado, G.S., Dean, J.: Distributed representations of words and phrases and their compositionality. In: Advances in Neural Information Processing Systems, pp. 3111–3119 (2013)

12. Nakov, P., et al.: SemEval-2017 task 3: community question answering. In: Proceedings of the 11th International Workshop on Semantic Evaluation (SemEval-2017), pp. 27–48. Association for Computational Linguistics, Vancouver, August 2017

13. Nakov, P., et al.: SemEval-2016 task 3: community question answering. In: Proceedings of the 10th International Workshop on Semantic Evaluation (SemEval-2016), pp. 525–545. Association for Computational Linguistics, San Diego, June 2016

14. Pagliardini, M., Gupta, P., Jaggi, M.: Unsupervised learning of sentence embeddings using compositional n-gram features. In: Conference of the North American Chapter of the Association for Computational Linguistics, NAACL 2018 (2018)

15. Pathak, S., Mishra, N.: Context aware restricted tourism domain question answering system. In: 2016 2nd International Conference on Next Generation Computing Technologies (NGCT), pp. 534–539, October 2016. https://doi.org/10.1109/NGCT.2016.7877473

16. Rajpurkar, P., Zhang, J., Lopyrev, K., Liang, P.: SQuAD: 100,000+ Questions for Machine Comprehension of Text. arXiv:1606.05250 [cs], June 2016

17. Wang, D.S.: A domain-specific question answering system based on ontology and question templates. In: 2010 11th ACIS International Conference on Software Engineering, Artificial Intelligence, Networking and Parallel/Distributed Computing, pp. 151–156, June 2010. https://doi.org/10.1109/SNPD.2010.31

18. Wen, J.R., Nie, J.Y., Zhang, H.J.: Query clustering using user logs. ACM Trans. Inf. Syst. **20**(1), 23 (2002)

19. Wu, C.H., Yeh, J.F., Chen, M.J.: Domain-specific FAQ retrieval using independent aspects. ACM Trans. Asian Lang. Inf. Process. **4**(1), 17 (2005)

Short Papers

Spare Pages

Improving Ranking for Systematic Reviews Using Query Adaptation

Amal Alharbi[1,2(✉)] and Mark Stevenson[1]

[1] University of Sheffield, Sheffield, UK
{ahalharbi1,mark.stevenson}@sheffield.ac.uk
[2] King Abdulaziz University, Jeddah, Saudi Arabia

Abstract. Identifying relevant studies for inclusion in systematic reviews requires significant effort from human experts who manually screen large numbers of studies. The problem is made more difficult by the growing volume of medical literature and Information Retrieval techniques have proved to be useful to reduce workload. Reviewers are often interested in particular types of evidence such as Diagnostic Test Accuracy studies. This paper explores the use of query adaption to identify particular types of evidence and thereby reduce the workload placed on reviewers. A simple retrieval system that ranks studies using TF.IDF weighted cosine similarity was implemented. The Log-Likelihood, Chi-Squared and Odds-Ratio lexical statistics and relevance feedback were used to generate sets of terms that indicate evidence relevant to Diagnostic Test Accuracy reviews. Experiments using a set of 80 systematic reviews from the CLEF2017 and CLEF2018 eHealth tasks demonstrate that the approach improves retrieval performance.

1 Introduction

Systematic reviews aim to identify and summarise all evidence available to answer a specific research question such as 'Is systemic inflammation present in stable chronic obstructive pulmonary disease?' [7]. Conducting a systematic review is a time-consuming and expensive process which can require up to 12 months of expert effort [5,10] and costs as much as a quarter of a million dollars [11]. The process of identifying relevant evidence for systematic reviews consists of several tasks: (1) *Boolean search* where the experts create a Boolean query that matches the criteria of a systematic review and apply the query to a medical database such as MEDLINE. (2) *Title and abstract screening* where reviewers screen the title and abstract of each retrieved study and exclude studies that are obviously not relevant to the systematic review. (3) *Content screening* where the reviewers screen the full studies identified as relevant from the previous step and decide their relevance to the systematic review [8]. A significant part of the experts' time is spent screening studies to identify those relevant to the review. Reviewers often manually screen a large number of irrelevant studies to identify the few relevant ones. Text mining techniques have been proven their

F. Crestani et al. (Eds.): CLEF 2019, LNCS 11696, pp. 141–148, 2019.
https://doi.org/10.1007/978-3-030-28577-7_9

effectiveness in reducing the workload and time needed to conduct systematic reviews [12,13,16].

In 2017 and 2018, the CLEF eHealth forum ran a task on systematic reviews that aimed to support the screening phase by (semi)automatically ranking the studies by relevance to the review [8,9]. Results from these exercises demonstrated that automating the screening stage of systematic review can be efficient in identifying most, if not all, relevant studies with less effort and time than manual screening.

Researchers are generally interested in a specific type of evidence (e.g. Randomised Control Trials). In this paper, we aim to exploit this fact by generating queries which aim to identify a particular type of evidence, Diagnostic Test Accuracy (DTA) studies. DTA reviews are considered to be challenging for text mining approaches [8]. This paper demonstrates that query adaptation methods can be used to identify the terms they are characteristic of studies likely to be relevant for DTA reviews. These terms are used to expand queries used for the CLEF2017 and CLEF2018 task where it is found that they lead to improved performance. These results show that incorporating information about the general type of review (e.g. DTA) improves performance when identifying relevant medical evidence. The code implementing the experiments described in this paper is available from https://github.com/Amal-Alharbi/Improving_ranking_for_systematic_reviews.git.

2   Query Adaptation

Query adaptation is the process of reformulating a given query with the aim of improving retrieval performance [4]. We hypothesised that there are terms which distinguish the studies that are likely to be included in DTA reviews from other literature. Expanding the Boolean query with those terms may help to find the most relevant studies. We aim to use several query adaption approaches to derive a list of key terms that indicate evidence relevant to DTA reviews. In this paper, we use lexical statistics in addition to relevance feedback.

2.1   Lexical Statistics

We use three lexical statistics: Log-Likelihood, Chi-Squared and Odds-Ratio. These statistics are widely applied in corpus linguistics where they are used to identify the key terms that are characteristic of a sub-corpus [6,14,15]. We treat the relevant documents as a sub-corpus and aim to identify the terms that characterise it so that they can be used to adapt the query.

Log-Likelihood is computed as

$$Log\text{-}Likelihood = 2 \times \left(O_{rel} \times \log \frac{O_{rel}}{E_{rel}} + O_{irrel} \times \log \frac{O_{irrel}}{E_{irrel}} \right) \quad (1)$$

where O_{rel} and O_{irrel} are the observed frequency of the term in different subsets of the collection (e.g. relevant and irrelevant documents). E_{rel} and E_{irrel} are the term's expected frequency calculated as

$$E_{rel} = N_{rel} \times \frac{O_{rel} + O_{irrel}}{N_{rel} + N_{irrel}}, \quad E_{irrel} = N_{irrel} \times \frac{O_{rel} + O_{irrel}}{N_{rel} + N_{irrel}} \quad (2)$$

where N_{rel} and N_{irrel} represent sub-corpus size (e.g. relevant and irrelevant documents). Terms are assigned high Log-Likelihood scores for a particular corpus when their observed frequency is (much) higher than the expected frequency.

Chi-Squared is calculated as

$$Chi\text{-}Squared = \frac{(O_{rel} - E_{rel})^2}{E_{rel}} + \frac{(O_{irrel} - E_{irrel})^2}{E_{irrel}} \quad (3)$$

where O_{rel} and O_{irrel} are the observed values and E_{rel} and E_{irrel} are expected values calculated using Eq. 2.

Odds-Ratio is most commonly applied for keyword analysis and terms identification [14]. The Odds-Ratio for each term calculated as

$$Odds\text{-}Ratio = \frac{O_{rel} \times (N_{irrel} - O_{irrel})}{O_{irrel} \times (N_{rel} - O_{rel})} \quad (4)$$

where O_{rel} and O_{irrel} are the frequency counts of the term in the relevant and irrelevant sub-corpus and N_{rel} and N_{irrel} are the total number of terms in each of those sub-corpus.

2.2   Relevance Feedback

This approach aims improve a query by taking account of feedback about the results it returned. Rocchio's algorithm [3] (Eq. 5) was used to reformulate the query by enriching it with additional terms weighted using information about the relevance of the documents it returned.

$$\vec{q}_m = \alpha\vec{q} + \frac{\beta}{N_{rel}} \sum_{\forall \vec{d}_j \in D_{rel}} \vec{d}_j - \frac{\gamma}{N_{irrel}} \sum_{\forall \vec{d}_j \in D_{irrel}} \vec{d}_j \quad (5)$$

where $\vec{q}$ is the original query vector, $\vec{d}_j$ is a weighted term vector associated with abstract j. D_{rel} is the set of relevant abstracts among the abstracts retrieved and N_{rel} is the number of abstracts in D_{rel}. D_{irrel} is the set of irrelevant abstracts among the abstracts retrieved and N_{irrel} is the number of abstracts in D_{irrel}. α, β and γ are weighting parameters.

3   Experiments

The experiments use reviews titles, Boolean queries, list of PubMed identifiers (PMIDs) and relevance judgements provided for the CLEF2017 and CLEF2018 tasks on Technology Assisted Reviews in Empirical Medicine [8,9]. The Boolean queries were manually constructed by experts and designed to match the criteria of each systematic review. The PMIDs refer to the documents retrieved from the Boolean queries. The relevance judgements files indicate which of the documents returned by the Boolean query were indicated as being relevant after the *Title and Abstract Screening* and *Content Screening* stages. All reviews are related to DTA studies. i.e. reviews which report the accuracy of a specific test for identifying a disease.

The CLEF2017 dataset contained 266,967 abstracts divided into training and test datasets containing 20 and 30 reviews, respectively. The CLEF2018 dataset contained 460,165 abstracts and divided into a training dataset consisting of 42 reviews and test dataset of 30 reviews. (Note that the training split of the CLEF2018 dataset is a subset of CLEF2017 dataset.)

3.1   Experiment 1: Lexical Statistics

The Log-Likelihood, Chi-Squared and Odds-Ratio statistics were used to derive lists of terms that indicate evidence relevant to DTA reviews as described in Sect. 2.1. The training sets from CLEF 2017 and CLEF 2018 were partitioned into relevant and irrelevant documents depending upon whether the study was included in the systematic review. Terms that occurred fewer than ten times were excluded since it is difficult to generate reliable statistics for these rare terms and, also, they are unlikely to be useful for identifying relevant studies. After computing the lexical statistics for each term in every review, the average for each statistic for each term across all the reviews in the training dataset was computed as

$$Avg\_statistic = \frac{\sum_{i=1}^{T} statistic_i}{T} \qquad (6)$$

where $statistic_i$ represent the statistic (Log-Likelihood, Chi-Squared or Odds-Ratio) for the term in review i and T is the total number of reviews in the training portion of the dataset (20 for the CLEF2017 dataset and 42 for the CLEF2018 dataset). For each lexical statistic, the terms with the highest scores are identified and added to the query for each review in the test portion of the dataset. The abstracts in the test dataset are ranked by matching terms from the expanded queries against those in the abstracts using a simple TF.IDF weighted cosine similarity measure.

The evaluation was carried out using software similar to trec_eval provided by CLEF2017 organisers[1]. The performance metrics reported here are average precision (AP) and work saved over sampling at 95% and 100% recall (WSS@95 and WSS@100). Table 1 shows the results of experiment 1. The baseline results

---

[1] https://github.com/leifos/tar.

Table 1. Lexical statistic results for CLEF2017 and CLEF2018 test datasets.

Lexical statistic	Terms	(a) CLEF2017 dataset			(b) CLEF2018 dataset		
		AP	WSS@100	WSS@95	AP	WSS@100	WSS@95
Baseline	-	0.218	0.385	0.493	0.224	0.377	0.506
Log-Likelihood	5	0.232	**0.389**	**0.507**	0.244	0.389	0.525
	10	0.227	0.380	0.497	0.251	0.407	0.535
	20	**0.233**	0.384	**0.507**	**0.259**	0.414	0.545
Chi-Squared	5	0.214	**0.389**	0.490	0.232	0.380	0.515
	10	**0.230**	**0.389**	0.507	0.242	0.396	0.530
	20	**0.230**	**0.389**	0.508	0.253	0.409	0.547
Odds-Ratio	5	0.214	**0.389**	0.490	0.221	0.377	0.505
	10	0.214	0.388	0.489	0.231	0.380	0.515
	20	**0.233**	**0.389**	0.506	0.252	0.398	0.541

were obtained without adding any additional terms to the query. The lower part of the table shows the results that were obtained when different numbers of terms with the highest scores were added to each query using different statistics (Log-Likelihood, Chi-Squared and Odds-Ratio). Retrieval performance improved when the additional terms are added to the queries, and this improvement is consistent across evaluation metrics for both dataset (CLEF2017 and CLEF2018). Enriching the query with more key terms generally improved performance. These results demonstrate that the additional terms, generated from an independent set of reviews, provide information about the types of studies that are likely to be relevant for DTA reviews, independently of their specific review.

Table 2. Ten terms with highest Log-Likelihood scores derived from CLEF2017 training dataset.

Term	Score	Term	Score
sensitivity	58.249	mtb rif	31.054
predictive	41.675	positive	30.308
gonadotropin	38.557	vulva	29.346
hcg	32.743	protein	28.686
false	31.090	fetoprotein	28.053

Table 2 shows the ten terms with the highest Log-Likelihood scores derived from the CLEF 2017 training dataset. We noticed that the top terms identified by the lexical statistic include ones that are highly indicative of the discussions that are found in DTA reviews, for example "sensitivity", "predictive" and "positive" are terms which describe the accuracy of a medical test. The presence of these terms is likely to indicate that the study will be relevant to a DTA review so adding them to the query improves performance. It is also interesting to note that several of the terms that appear in this list are also used in standard filters for DTA reviews that have been developed to support information professionals searching for relevant literature [1]. However, we also note that the list also includes terms that appear to be specific to particular DTA reviews (e.g. "gonadotropin"). The CLEF 2017 training dataset contains only 20 reviews, and if a particular term proves to be very important for a small set of reviews, then its overall score can be high enough for it to be included in this list.

3.2   Experiment 2: Relevance Feedback

In this experiment, abstracts in the test dataset were ranked using a simple TF.IDF weighted cosine similarity measure comparing each abstract with terms extracted from the Boolean query. Relevance judgement from the 10% top-ranked abstracts (up to a maximum of 1,000) were used to reformulate the query using Rocchio's algorithm and the remaining abstracts re-ranked using the updated query vector. A range of values for the weighting parameters were previously explored [2] and it was found that the best results were achieved by setting $\alpha = \beta = 1$ and $\gamma = 1.5$. In this experiment, we applied two approaches: (1) use all the terms of the modified query $\vec{q}_m$ and (2) exclude terms with weight less than or equal zero (i.e. terms with negative weight).

Results are shown in Table 3. Retrieval performance improves for most metrics when using relevance feedback (compared with the baseline and lexical statistics in Table 1). On the other hand, a higher AP score for the CLEF 2018 dataset is obtained using lexical statistics. Including only terms which Rocchio's algorithm weighted positively improves the AP score and saves more effort than using all terms.

Table 3. Relevance feedback results for CLEF2017 and CLEF2018 test datasets.

$\vec{q}_m$ terms	(a) CLEF2017 dataset			(b) CLEF2018 dataset		
	AP	WSS@100	WSS@95	AP	WSS@100	WSS@95
All	0.236	0.342	0.485	0.222	0.345	0.496
+ve	**0.243**	**0.432**	**0.557**	**0.238**	**0.420**	**0.608**

4   Conclusion and Future Work

Query adaption methods can be used to identify terms characteristic of studies likely to be relevant for DTA reviews. The experiments reported in this paper demonstrate that including general information about the type of publication that is likely to be of relevance for a systematic review can improve retrieval performance. The best performance was achieved using relevance feedback.

In the future, we would like to apply those methods to other types of systematic review (e.g. prognosis reviews and intervention reviews). In addition, we would like to explore alternative methods for identifying useful terms such as synonym-based query expansion that may overcome some of the limitations of approaches used in this study.

References

1. Search Filters for MEDLINE in Ovid Syntax and the PubMed Translation. https://hiru.mcmaster.ca/hiru/HIRU_Hedges_MEDLINE_Strategies.aspx. Accessed 18 Jan 2018
2. Alharbi, A., Briggs, W., Stevenson, M.: Retrieving and ranking studies for systematic reviews: University of Sheffield's approach to CLEF ehealth 2018 task 2. In: CLEF 2018 Evaluation Labs and Workshop: Online Working Notes. CEUR-WS, France (2018)
3. Baeza-Yates, R., Ribeiro-Neto, B.: Modern Information Retrieval: The Concepts and Technology Behind Search, 2nd edn. Addison-Wesley, Boston (2011)
4. Carpineto, C., Romano, G.: A survey of automatic query expansion in information retrieval. ACM Comput. Surv. **44**(1), 1–50 (2012)
5. Cohen, A.M., Ambert, K., McDonagh, M.: A prospective evaluation of an automated classification system to support evidence-based medicine and systematic review. In: AMIA Annual Symposium Proceedings, vol. 2010, pp. 121–125 (2010). http://www.ncbi.nlm.nih.gov/pubmed/21346953
6. Dunning, T.: Accurate methods for the statistics of surprise and coincidence. Comput. Linguist. **19**(1), 61–74 (1993)
7. Gan, W.Q., Man, S., Senthilselvan, A., Sin, D.: Association between chronic obstructive pulmonary disease and systemic inflammation: a systematic review and a meta-analysis. Thorax **59**(7), 574–580 (2004)
8. Kanoulas, E., Li, D., Azzopardi, L., Spijker, R.: CLEF technologically assisted reviews in empirical medicine overview. In: Working Notes of CLEF 2017 - Conference and Labs of the Evaluation Forum. CEUR Workshop Proceedings, Dublin, Ireland (2017). CEUR-WS.org
9. Kanoulas, E., Spijker, R., Li, D., Azzopardi, L.: CLEF 2018 technology assisted reviews in empirical medicine overview. In: CLEF 2018 Evaluation Labs and Workshop: Online Working Notes. CEUR-WS, France (2018)
10. Karimi, S., Pohl, S., Scholer, F., Cavedon, L., Zobel, J.: Boolean versus ranked querying for biomedical systematic reviews. BMC Med. Inform. Decis. Mak. **10**(1), 1–20 (2010)
11. McGowan, J., Sampson, M.: Systematic reviews need systematic searchers. J. Med. Libr. Assoc. **93**(1), 74–80 (2005)
12. O'Mara-Eves, A., Thomas, J., McNaught, J., Miwa, M., Ananiadou, S.: Using text mining for study identification in systematic reviews: a systematic review of current approaches. Syst. Rev. **4**(1), 5 (2015)
13. Paisley, S., Sevra, J., Stevenson, M., Archer, R., Preston, L., Chilcott, J.: Identifying potential early biomarkers of acute myocaridal infarction in the biomedical literature: a comparison of text mining and manual sifting techniques. In: Proceedings of the International Society for Pharmacoeconomics and Outcomes Research (ISPOR) 19th Annual European Congress, Vienna, Austria (2016)

14. Pojanapunya, P., Todd, R.W.: Log-likelihood and odds ratio: keyness statistics for different purposes of keyword analysis. Corpus Linguist. Linguist. Theory **14**(1), 133–167 (2018)

15. Rayson, P.: From key words to key semantic domains. Int. J. Corpus Linguist. **13**(4), 519–549 (2008)

16. Shemilt, I., Khan, N., Park, S., Thomas, J.: Use of cost-effectiveness analysis to compare the efficiency of study identification methods in systematic reviews. Syst. Rev. **5**(1), 140 (2016)

Analyzing the Adequacy of Readability Indicators to a Non-English Language

Hélder Antunes[1]([✉]) and Carla Teixeira Lopes[1,2]([✉]) [iD]

[1] Faculdade de Engenharia da Universidade do Porto, Porto, Portugal
{up201406163,ctl}@fe.up.pt
[2] INESC TEC, Porto, Portugal

Abstract. Readability is a linguistic feature that indicates how difficult it is to read a text. Traditional readability formulas were made for the English language. This study evaluates their adequacy to the Portuguese language. We applied the traditional formulas in 10 parallel corpora. We verified that the Portuguese language had higher grade scores (less readability) in the formulas that use the number of syllables per words or number of complex words per sentence. Formulas that use letters by words instead of syllables by words output similar grade scores. Considering this, we evaluated the correlation of the complex words in 65 Portuguese school books of 12 schooling years. We found out that the concept of complex word as a word with 4 or more syllables, instead of 3 or more syllables as originally used in traditional formulas applied to English texts, is more correlated with the grade of Portuguese school books. In the end, for each traditional readability formula, we adapted it to the Portuguese language performing a multiple linear regression in the same dataset of school books.

Keywords: Readability · Portuguese language · Text simplification · Natural language processing

1 Introduction

Readability refers to the difficulty in reading a particular text. Its automatic assessment is an important research topic nowadays. It is essential for efficient learning (it is important for a student to read texts that are appropriate to his level of education), evaluating automatic text simplification methods, etc. One way to evaluate readability is through formulas that consider lexical difficulty (word difficulty, for example, assessed by the average number of syllables per word) and syntactic difficulty (sentence length, for example, assessed by the average number of words per sentence). The classic formulas of readability were prepared for English, and there are no equivalent formulas for the Portuguese language. Any adaptation of these formulas to the Portuguese language will have to take into account the main differences between the two languages. For example, the number of syllables or characters per word is, on average, higher in the Portuguese language.

© Springer Nature Switzerland AG 2019
F. Crestani et al. (Eds.): CLEF 2019, LNCS 11696, pp. 149–155, 2019.
https://doi.org/10.1007/978-3-030-28577-7_10

This research is divided into two phases. In the first phase, we use English-Portuguese parallel corpora to compare the application of traditional formulas in the two languages. For this phase, we evaluate the main linguistic differences between the two languages. In the second phase, we discuss how the differences found can be applied to the Portuguese readability assessment, using a set of 65 Portuguese school books. In the end, we propose new readability formulas to the Portuguese language adapted from each English readability formula. In both phases, we consider five traditional readability formulas present in Table 1. All the formulas give the required grade level to understand a text.

Table 1. Traditional readability formulas used.

Metric	Formula
SMOG [11]	$1.043 \times \sqrt{CW \times 30 \div SE} + 3.1291$
Flesch Kincaid (FK) [8]	$0.39 \times WO \div SE + 11.8 \times SY \div WO - 15.59$
ARI [12]	$4.71 \times CH \div WO + 0.5 \times WO \div SE - 21.43$
Coleman Liau (CL) [2]	$5.88 \times CH \div WO - 29.6 \times SE \div WO - 15.8$
Gunning Fog (GF) [6]	$0.4 \times (WO \div SE + CW \div WO \times 100)$

CH - characters, CW - complex words, SY - syllables, WO - words, SE - sentences.

2 Background and Related Work

The possible use of traditional readability formulas in other languages is not new. These have already been applied to school texts in the Brazilian Portuguese language [10]. Martins et al. introduced a change of 42 points in the Flesch reading ease test, due to the higher number of syllables in the Portuguese words when compared to the English language. Authors found that the adaptation of the Flesch formula score (42 points decrease in readability) was more pronounced in the texts of the elementary school years.

A study carried out in 2012 [9] compared the readability of five books of translation courses in English and their translation into the Persian language. The used readability formulas were the Gunning Fog Index (GFI) and the Flesch New Reading Ease formula. Samples of texts were randomly chosen from each original book. The results showed that texts translated into the Persian language were less readable than the original English texts.

In addition to the Persian language, in 2014, a similar study was carried out comparing the readability between the Swedish and English languages [15]. Three algorithms were used: Coleman-Liau Index (CLI), Läsbarhetsindex (LIX) and Automated Readability Index (ARI). The texts used were a collection of Wikipedia articles, "On the Origin of Species" by Charles Darwin and the Bible and their respective translations. The tests showed that both ARI and LIX work for both Swedish and English on less readable texts. CLI, however, seems to perform less well on these more demanding texts but works better on the Bible. The conclusion was that ARI and LIX work on difficult and average to read texts in both English and Swedish and that CLI only works on accessible texts in both languages.

This work will solely focus on traditional measures of readability. These measures are.the most used, easy to compute and there is a lack of adapted formulas to non-English languages. Other approaches, like classification models using new features provided by natural language processing [3,4], or even the recent use of word embeddings [1,7] will be ignored.

3   Readability Comparison in EN-PT Parallel Corpora

We use multiple parallel corpora in English and Portuguese obtained from the OPUS website[1] [13,14], a collection of translated texts from the web. To cover different topics and different levels of readability, we analyze different linguistic corpora within the OPUS collection. Overall, we analysed 10 parallel corpora: PHP (PHP programming language documentation), Wikipedia (parallel sentences extracted from Wikipedia), ECB (documentation from the European Central Bank), Europarl (translated texts obtained from the European Parliament website), OpenSubtitles (Movie and TV series Subtitles in multiple languages), TED2013 (TED talks subtitles), EUconst (A parallel corpus collected from the European Constitution), ParaCrawl (Parallel corpora from Web Crawls), NewsCommentary11 (News Commentaries), and GlobalVoices (news from the Global Voices website). For each parallel corpus, we analyze a TMX file (Translation Memory eXchange - an XML specification for the exchange of translation data). For each TMX file, we calculate the readability of 10 randomly selected excerpts, where each excerpt is composed of 100 translation units. We used an open source Java library[2] to calculate the readability of extracts.

To analyze the differences between the scores obtained for the two languages, we performed a paired samples Wilcoxon test for each readability formula. We used the non-parametric Wilcoxon test because the Shapiro-Wilk's method showed that the distribution of data is significantly different from the normal distribution. The results of this test can be found in Table 2. It can be verified that the ARI and Coleman Liau metrics show smaller differences than the other readability metrics. The Coleman Liau metric does not show significant differences between the two languages (p-value > 0.05). The reason for this discrepancy between the metrics seems to lie in the inclusion/exclusion of the number of syllables of the words and of complex words (words with 3 or more syllables) in the respective formulas. In Table 1, we see that only the ARI and Coleman Liau metrics use the number of characters by word, instead of the number of syllables by word or complex words. Figure 1 shows the readability

---

[1] http://opus.nlpl.eu/index.php.
[2] https://github.com/ipeirotis/ReadabilityMetrics.

152   H. Antunes and C. T. Lopes

distribution for all metrics in both languages. Only the ARI and Coleman Liau metrics maintain similar scores across languages, unlike other metrics.

Table 2. Paired samples Wilcoxon test between English and Portuguese texts.

Metric	EN	PT	Difference	p-value
SMOG	13.938	17.888	−3.95	4.077e−18
Flesch Kincaid (FK)	12.332	17.666	−5.334	4.202e−18
ARI	12.381	13.444	−1.063	4.714e−08
Coleman Liau (CL)	10.657	10.962	−0.305	0.254
Gunning Fog (GF)	15.364	21.072	−5.708	8.404e−18

By this analysis, we see that existing the readability metrics initially formulated for the English language, need changes to be used in Portuguese texts, especially those that use the number of syllables or the amount of complex words. A simple method will be adding a constant to the original formulas. That constant would be the mean difference between the formula scores of the languages found in the parallel corpora. However, in the next section, we present another approach using Portuguese school books.

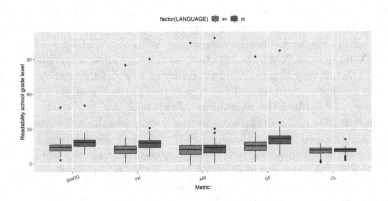

Fig. 1. Metrics score comparison between languages in all parallel corpora.

4   Readability Assessment of Portuguese School Books

We analyse linguistic features in a set of Portuguese school books from elementary through high school (through 1–12 grades). The books include Portuguese native learning, study of the environment, history, biology, geology, physics and chemistry courses of a well-known Portuguese publisher of school books. A total of 65 books were analyzed. Each page of a book is in the XHTML format, so we parsed it to clean the text. Finally, we used the previously mentioned Java library to parse the texts and extract related readability parameters.

The differences found in the parallel corpora points to a difference in the average number of syllables between the two languages. The concept of complex words used in the traditional readability formulas is defined as words with 3 or more syllables. We performed the Kendall correlation test between grade level and different types of complex words and found that the number of complex words per text with 4 or more syllables is more correlated with grade level ($r = 0.347$ for words with 4 or more syllables and $r = 0.310$ for words with 3 or more syllables). For the Portuguese language, given the higher number of syllables per word in comparison with the English language, it seems more correct to consider a word as difficult if it has 4 or more syllables.

We performed a multiple linear regression using the parameters of the original English readability formulas. For each original formula, we adjust it to the Portuguese language using the corresponding parameters. Based on the early finding about the complex words, SMOG and Gunning Fog measures for the Portuguese language consider a complex word a word with 4 or more syllables. We averaged the parameters used in the traditional formulas for each grade. We did this because we found out a large variance on the texts of a school year, and a linear regression using the simple features of the traditional formulas leads to bad results. Only the use of more complex features provided by natural language processing and machine learning could lead to better performances [5], and, as already mentioned, these approaches are ignored in this study. The final formulas to the Portuguese language are presented in Table 3. We apply these formulas to each year of schooling; the results are shown in Fig. 2.

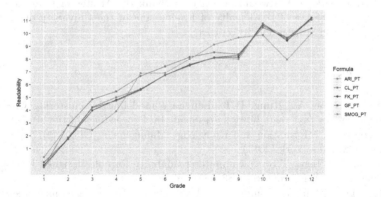

Fig. 2. Readability evolution along with the school grades using the Portuguese formulas.

Table 3. Adjusted Portuguese formulas.

	Formula	RSE	Error rate
SMOG	$16.830 \times \sqrt{CW \times 30 \div SE} - 23.809$	1.469	0.225
Flesch Kincaid	$0.883 \times WO \div SE + 17.347 \times SY \div WO - 41.239$	0.987	0.152
ARI	$6.286 \times CH \div WO + 0.927 \times WO \div SE - 36.551$	1.064	0.164
Coleman Liau	$5.730 \times CH \div WO - 171.365 \times SE \div WO - 6.662$	1.375	0.212
Gunning Fog	$0.760 \times WO \div SE + 58.600 \times CW \div WO - 12.166$	1.001	0.154

CH - characters, CW - complex words, SY - syllables, WO - words, SE - sentences, RSE - residual standard error.

5   Conclusions

In this work, we adjust the traditional readability metrics, formulated for the English, to Portuguese. Firstly, we analyze the grade score differences between the two languages using ten parallel corpora. The Portuguese language has, on average, a greater number of syllables per words. However, these differences are not as significant in the number of letters per word, since ARI and Coleman Liau metrics don't differ so much between the two languages.

Using 65 Portuguese school books, we found out that in the Portuguese language a complex word with 4 or more syllables, instead of 3 syllables or more, is more correlated with the readability. For each traditional English formula, we performed a multiple linear regression with the same corresponding parameters, leading to a new formula adjusted to the Portuguese language.

Acknowledgment. This work is financed by National Funds through the Portuguese funding agency, FCT - Fundação para a Ciência e a Tecnologia within the project: UID/EEA/50014/2019. We would also like to thank the Master in Informatics and Computing Engineering of the Faculty of Engineering of the University of Porto for supporting the registration and travel costs.

References

1. Cha, M., Gwon, Y., Kung, H.T.: Language modeling by clustering with word embeddings for text readability assessment. In: Proceedings of the 2017 ACM on Conference on Information and Knowledge Management, CIKM 2017, pp. 2003–2006. ACM, New York (2017)
2. Coleman, M., Liau, T.L.: A computer readability formula designed for machine scoring. J. Appl. Psychol. **60**, 283–284 (1975)
3. Collins-Thompson, K.: Computational assessment of text readability: a survey of current and future research. ITL - Int. J. Appl. Linguist **165**(2), 97–135 (2015)
4. Feng, L., Jansche, M., Huenerfauth, M., Elhadad, N.: A comparison of features for automatic readability assessment. In: COLING 2010 Proceedings of the 23rd International Conference on Computational Linguistics: Posters, pp. 276–284. Association for Computational Linguistics, Stroudsburg (2010)

5. François, T., Miltsakaki, E.: Do NLP and machine learning improve traditional readability formulas? In: Proceedings of the First Workshop on Predicting and Improving Text Readability for Target Reader Populations, PITR 2012, pp. 49–57. Association for Computational Linguistics, Stroudsburg (2012)
6. Gunning, R.: The Technique of Clear Writing. McGraw-Hill, New York (1952)
7. Jiang, Z., Gu, Q., Yin, Y., Chen, D.: Enriching word embeddings with domain knowledge for readability assessment. In: Proceedings of the 27th International Conference on Computational Linguistics, pp. 366–378. Association for Computational Linguistics, Santa Fe (2018)
8. Kincaid, J.: Derivation of new readability formulas: (automated readability index, fog count and Flesch reading ease formula) for navy enlisted personnel. Research Branch report, Chief of Naval Technical Training, Naval Air Station Memphis (1975)
9. Kolahi, S., Shirvani, E.: A comparative study of the readability of english textbooks of translation and their Persian translations. Int. J. Linguist. 4, 344–366 (2012)
10. Martins, T.B.F., Ghiraldelo, C.M., Nunes, M.D.G.V., Oliveira Junior, O.N.D.: Readability Formulas Applied to Textbooks in Brazilian Portuguese (1996)
11. McLaughlin, H.G.: SMOG grading - a new readability formula. J. Read. 12(8), 639–646 (1969)
12. Smith, E.A., Senter, R.: Automated readability index. In: AMRL-TR. Aerospace Medical Research Laboratories, pp. 1–14 (1967)
13. Tiedemann, J.: News from OPUS - a collection of multilingual parallel corpora with tools and interfaces. In: Nicolov, N., Bontcheva, K., Angelova, G., Mitkov, R. (eds.) Recent Advances in Natural Language Processing, vol. V, pp. 237–248. John Benjamins, Amsterdam (2009)
14. Tiedemann, J.: Parallel data, tools and interfaces in opus. In: Chair, N.C.C., et al. (eds.) Proceedings of the Eight International Conference on Language Resources and Evaluation (LREC 2012). European Language Resources Association (ELRA), Istanbul, Turkey, May 2012
15. Tillman, R., Hagberg, L.: Readability algorithms compability on multiple languages (2014)

How Many Labels? Determining the Number of Labels in Multi-Label Text Classification

Hosein Azarbonyad[1]([✉]) and Maarten Marx[2]

[1] KLM Royal Dutch Airlines, Amsterdam, The Netherlands
`hosein.azarbonyad@klm.com`
[2] University of Amsterdam, Amsterdam, The Netherlands
`maartenmarx@uva.nl`

Abstract. Multi-Label Text Classification (MLTC) is a supervised machine learning task in which the goal is to learn a classifier that assigns multiple labels to text documents. When all documents have the same number of labels, this task is very close to ordinary (single label) text classification. However, in case this number varies another classifier needs to determine, for each document, how many labels to assign. The topic of this paper is exactly this additional classifier. We compare several baselines to a system which learns a dynamic threshold for a given text classifier. The thresholding classifier receives the ranked list of scores for each label for a document as input and returns a threshold score. All labels with a score higher than this threshold will then be assigned to the document. Our results show that, first, this dynamic thresholding significantly improves recall but has the same precision as a static system which assigns the same (the mean) number of classes to each document, and second, that the accuracy of predicting the number of classes is positively related to the quality (measured by MAP) of the text classifier.

1 Introduction

Multi-Label Text Classification (MLTC) is a supervised machine learning task in which the goal is to learn a classifier that assigns multiple labels to text documents [9]. It has been shown that simple classification-based approaches such as SVM-based models fail when the number of classes is high [17]. The main reason is that these models need to create a separate classifier for each class. This puts an assumption of independence between classes which is not realistic. Moreover, this approach becomes computationally expensive as the number of classes grow.

A more effective and efficient alternative for classification-based MLTC approach is ranking-based models. A ranking based MLTC model receives a document as input and returns a ranked list of classes, inversely ordered by relevance to the document. Here relevance can be seen as the confidence or probability

© Springer Nature Switzerland AG 2019
F. Crestani et al. (Eds.): CLEF 2019, LNCS 11696, pp. 156–163, 2019.
https://doi.org/10.1007/978-3-030-28577-7_11

that the class is a true label of the document. This is both effective, as it can model the relations between classes, and efficient, as only one model is trained to classify all documents. Ranking-based MLTC is a two step process: to classify a document, first, classes are ranked based on the probability of assigning them to the given document. Then the *top k* classes in the ranked list are selected as labels of the document.

Selecting the k for each document is not trivial in case documents in the collection can have different number of classes. In many cases, we can expect the number of classes to be normally distributed. Then the difficulty of predicting this k depends on the variance of the distribution: the higher, the more mistakes an optimal fixed (in case of a normal distribution the median) k will make. Even with a perfect class ranker, a system with a fixed k cannot achieve a precision not recall of 1. To select k in a dynamic way, a common approach is dynamic thresholding in which the scores generated for each class are calibrated, a threshold is set on the scores, and classes with a higher score than the threshold are assigned to documents [17]. This paper is about this classifier which assigns a threshold to each document.

We compare several baselines to a system which learns a dynamic threshold for a given text classifier based on the work of Yang and Gopal [17] and Elisseeff and Weston [6]. Our experiments are performed on the JRC-Acquis dataset [14] labeled with EuroVoc concepts [7]. This set consists of legislative and political documents from the European Parliament and Commission, consists of 16K documents, labeled with 1639 different classes. The distribution of classes is slightly skewed to the right, with a mean number of classes of 5.4 and a median of 5.

Our results show that, first, this dynamic thresholding significantly improves recall but has the same precision as a static system which assigns the same (the median) number of classes to each document, and second, that the accuracy of predicting the number of classes is positively related to the quality (measured by MAP) of the text classifier.

2   Related Work

A well-known approach for MLTC is training a different classifier for each class and ranking and selecting the classes with regards to the probability of documents belonging to them [5,18]. It has been shown that simple classification approaches become computationally expensive when the number of classes is high [3]. Babbar and Schölkopf [1] propose a scalable approach for multi-label classification by training one-versus-rest classifiers.

The main characteristic of MLTC discriminating it from single-label text classification is that documents can have more than one label. Therefore, capturing the dependencies between classes and incorporating them in the classification process could be useful to improve the accuracy of classifiers [2,8,11,12]. To classify documents in MLTC, there is a need to first determine the number of classes to be assigned to documents. A common approach for choosing the number of classes in MLTC is calibrating the scores generated for each class, setting a threshold on the scores, and assigning classes with a score higher than the threshold to documents [10,18]. A static approach (fixing a threshold and using it for all documents) or dynamic approach (learning from training samples and having different threshold values for different documents) can be used for setting the threshold.

The dynamic threshold is set using a training set in which samples are a set of pairs of ranked lists with scores and, for each ranked list, an optimal threshold that minimizes a classification loss such as false positives or false negatives given the ranked list [6,17]. For samples in the training set, the optimal threshold can be determined, however, for test samples the threshold should be estimated. This is done by learning a mapping function based on training samples that takes a ranked list and maps it to a threshold. This strategy has been shown to be very effective for MLTC [6,17]. Similarly, instead of learning a mapping from ranked lists of document to a threshold, the mapping can be learned to map ranked lists to the number of classes directly [15].

3   Learning the Number of Classes

We describe the three different thresholding methods which are compared in this paper. The first is independent of a classifier. The last two assume a classifier $C(d)$, which given a document d, returns a score for each label.

Content-Based. This method predicts the number of classes for documents based on their content. We model this problem as a regression problem in which the input is a vector representation of the document and the output the number of classes for that document. We represent documents as TF-IDF weighted bag of words.

Generic Threshold: Learning a Generic Threshold on Scores. This model estimates, given a text classifier which returns scores for each label, an optimal generic threshold which is then applied to all documents. Classes that have a score higher than the threshold are assigned to the document. The optimal threshold given a classifier $C(.)$, is determined as follows: for each document in an evaluation set, we select the top 20 classes and normalize their scores to the $[0, 1]$ interval. Then we use a grid search to find the threshold θ that, when used uniformly on all documents with classifier C, minimizes the sum of false negatives and false positives.

Mapping-Based Method: Learning a Threshold for Documents. This method learns a mapping $\theta_C(d)$ which receives for each document d the scores assigned to all labels by the classifier C and returns a threshold score [6,17]. This document specific threshold is then used to assign the labels to d. The function is learned on the same training data D used for training the classifier C. As in [6], the classification loss is defined as the sum of false negatives and false positives. An optimal mapping is learned based on a linear-least-square-fit solution using the following equation:

$$\min_{w^*,b^*} \sum_{d \in D} ((w^* r_C(d) + b^*) - s(d))^2, \tag{1}$$

where $r_C(d)$ is the vector of scores assigned to all labels by the classifier C, and $s(d)$ is the optimal threshold for $r_C(d)$ determined by minimizing the classification loss. The goal of the linear-least-square-fit is to determine the parameters w^* and b^* of the linear mapping $\theta_C(.)$.

4   Experimental Setup

4.1   Datasets

We use the English version of the JRC-Acquis dataset [13] labled with EuroVoc concepts [7]. As in [4], we use the documents from 2002 to 2006. This subsection of dataset contains 16,824 documents. The mean, median, and standard deviation of the number of classes assigned to the documents are 5.4, 5, and 1.83, respectively. We use the same setup used by [4] to evaluate the performance of MLTC classifier. We used the 70% oldest documents to construct the representations of classes (to be used to rank classes given documents) and the remaining 30% of the collection for training and testing. We remove the classes from the documents that do not occur in the first part. As reported in [4], this leads to 1,639 different classes in our dataset. We do 5-fold cross validation on the newest part.

4.2   Ranking Model

We use three different rankers to rank classes given documents:

- **BM25.** For each class C a profile is created by concatenating the titles of documents labeled by C. Then we compute BM25 scores between profiles of classes and content of documents. We use titles as it has been shown that titles are more effective than the whole content of documents for MLTC on the JRC-Acquis dataset [4].
- **LTR.** We take the model created in [4] to rank classes given documents. This model is created using a learning to rank model (AdaRank [16]). To create the model, first for each class, different profiles are created each by concatenating a specific part (such as title or body text) of documents labeled by them. Then several features reflecting the similarity of classes and documents are defined based on the similarity of profiles of classes and the content of documents. The similarity is estimated using common IR measures such as BM25 scores or language model score. After creating feature vectors for document-class pairs in this way, the learning to rank model is trained on the document-class pairs in the training set.

– **JEX** is one of the state of the art systems developed for classifying JRC-Acquis documents [14]. This method first represents each class as a bag of keywords. The keywords are extracted using TF-IDF statistics. Similarly, documents are also represented as bags of keywords. Then, the similarity (cosine and BM25) of document and class representations are used to rank the classes with respect to the documents.

5 Results

We first answer our main research question: How effective are different thresholding methods for selecting the number of classes in MLTC? Table 1 shows the performance of different MLTC systems based on different thresholding methods. Neither the content based, nor the generic threshold method performs better than the classifier which assigns the same median number of classes to every document. The dynamic mapping based thresholder however significantly performs better and the improvement is obtained by increasing recall, while not lossing on precision. Overall, the results show that dynamic thresholding in general is more effective than a static threshold.

Table 1. Performance of JEX, BM25, and LTR for MLTC using different thresholding methods for selecting the number of classes. Static threshold is the method that assigns the median number of classes in the dataset to all documents. ▲ indicates significantly better performance (p-value < 0.05) compared to best performing baseline.

Ranker	Method	Precision	Recall	F1	MAP
JEX	Static threshold	**0.453**	0.486	0.437	0.483
	Content-based	0.445	0.489	0.465	0.480
	Generic threshold	0.441	0.473	0.456	0.462
	Mapping-based	0.442	**0.501▲**	**0.469**	**0.501▲**
BM25	Static threshold	0.479	0.506	0.492	0.551
	Content-based	0.483	0.510	0.496	0.571
	Generic threshold	0.480	0.508	0.493	0.559
	Mapping-based	**0.487**	**0.519▲**	0.503	**0.584▲**
LTR	Static threshold	0.521	0.547	0.536	0.610
	Content-based	**0.525**	0.561	0.542	0.618
	Generic threshold	0.519	0.550	0.534	0.613
	Mapping-based	**0.525**	**0.569▲**	0.546	**0.626▲**

Table 2 shows the root mean squared error (RMSE) and the mean absolute error (MAE) between the true number of classes and the estimated number of classes for different methods. The results are achieved using the LTR ranker. It also provides the accuracy for choosing the correct number of classes. The results clearly indicate the superiority of the Mapping-based method.

Table 2. RMSE, MAE and accuracy for deciding the correct number of classes based on the LTR method.

Method	RMSE	MAE	Accuracy
Static threshold	1.87	1.39	0.23
Content-based	1.58	1.02	0.28
Generic threshold	1.63	1.12	0.25
Mapping-based	1.33	0.83	0.34

We now consider our second research question: How does the quality of the underlying classifier affect the performance of the dynamic thresholding approach? The results show that that the accuracy of predicting the number of classes is positively related to the quality (measured by MAP) of the text classifier. This is as expected, because the optimal performance for the thresholding method will be achieved with a perfect classifier which ranks all true classes on top of the ranked list, as in this case the optimal threshold will correspond to the actual number of classes.

To conclude, we answer our third research question: What kind of documents benefit the most from dynamic thresholding? Figure 1 shows the distribution of number of classes for documents in the dataset. The distribution of classes is slightly skewed to the right. The distribution shows that there is more to gain in recall than in precision, and indeed that is what we saw. The Mapping-based method created using LTR increased the number of classes for 89% of the documents with more than 5 classes. For documents with less than 5 classes, only in 69% of times a number less than 5 is picked.

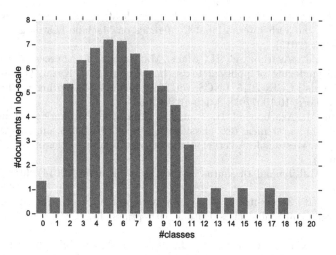

Fig. 1. The distribution of number of classes in documents. Y-axis is in log-scale.

Overall, our results suggest that thresholding has a big impact on the performance of classifiers in MLTC. When the underlying classifier has a good performance, the thresholding method which works based on scores estimated for classes using the classifier performs better.

6   Conclusions

Our results show that, first, this dynamic thresholding significantly improves recall but has the same precision as a static system which assigns the same (the mean) number of classes to each document, and second, that the accuracy of predicting the number of classes is positively related to the quality (measured by MAP) of the text classifier.

Clearly this is just a beginning, and further evidence of our findings should be obtained by considering other datasets and other dynamic thresholding methods. JRC-Acquis classes are assigned by professionals using a carefully constructed thesaurus (EuroVoc). It would be nice to replicate our experiments on "wilder" multi-class labeled documents, for instance stack overflow questions with tags, or scientific articles with keywords. The effect of the shape of the class size distribution and the effect of outliers needs to be further investigated too. The discussed setup trains the threshold function given a classifier. It would be interesting to see whether both can be trained simultaneously.

References

1. Babbar, R., Schölkopf, B.: Dismec: distributed sparse machines for extreme multi-label classification. In: WSDM 2017, pp. 721–729 (2017)
2. Bi, W., Kwok, J.T.: Multi-label classification on tree and dag-structured hierarchies. In: ICML 2011, pp. 17–24 (2011)
3. Bi, W., Kwok, J.T.: Efficient multi-label classification with many labels. In: Proceedings of the 30th International Conference on Machine Learning, ICML 2013, pp. 405–413 (2013)
4. Dehghani, M., Azarbonyad, H., Marx, M., Kamps, J.: Sources of evidence for automatic indexing of political texts. In: Hanbury, A., Kazai, G., Rauber, A., Fuhr, N. (eds.) ECIR 2015. LNCS, vol. 9022, pp. 568–573. Springer, Cham (2015). https://doi.org/10.1007/978-3-319-16354-3_63
5. Dehghani, M., Azarbonyad, H., Kamps, J., Marx, M.: On horizontal and vertical separation in hierarchical text classification. In: ICTIR 2016, pp. 185–194 (2016)
6. Elisseeff, A., Weston, J.: A kernel method for multi-labelled classification. In: NIPS 2001 (2001)
7. EuroVoc. Multilingual thesaurus of the European union (2014). http://eurovoc.europa.eu/
8. Hariharan, B., Zelnik-manor, L., Vishwanathan, S.V.N., Varma, M.: Large scale max-margin multi-label classification with priors. In: ICML 2010, pp. 423–430 (2010)
9. Herrera, F., Charte, F., Rivera, A.J., del Jesus, M.J.: Multilabel Classification. In: Herrera, F., Charte, F., Rivera, A.J., del Jesus, M.J. (eds.) Multilabel Classification: Problem Analysis, Metrics and Techniques, pp. 17–31. Springer, Cham (2016). https://doi.org/10.1007/978-3-319-41111-8_2

10. Ioannou, M., Sakkas, G., Tsoumakas, G., Vlahavas, I.: Obtaining bipartitions from score vectors for multi-label classification. In: ICTAI 2010, pp. 409–416 (2010)
11. Nam, J., Kim, J., Loza Mencía, E., Gurevych, I., Fürnkranz, J.: Large-scale multi-label text classification—revisiting neural networks. In: Calders, T., Esposito, F., Hüllermeier, E., Meo, R. (eds.) ECML PKDD 2014. LNCS (LNAI), vol. 8725, pp. 437–452. Springer, Heidelberg (2014). https://doi.org/10.1007/978-3-662-44851-9_28
12. Read, J., Pfahringer, B., Holmes, G., Frank, E.: Classifier chains for multi-label classification. Mach. Learn. **850**(3), 333–359 (2011)
13. Steinberger, R., Pouliquen, B., Widiger, A., Ignat, C., Erjavec, T., Tufis, D.: The JRC-Acquis: a multilingual aligned parallel corpus with 20+ languages. In: LREC 2006 (2006)
14. Steinberger, R., Ebrahim, M., Turchi, M.: JRC EuroVoc indexer JEX-A freely available multi-label categorisation tool. In: LREC 2012 (2012)
15. Tang, L., Rajan, S., Narayanan, V.K.: Large scale multi-label classification via metalabeler. In: WWW 2009, pp. 211–220 (2009)
16. Xu, J., Li, H.: Adarank: a boosting algorithm for information retrieval. In: SIGIR 2007, pp. 391–398 (2007)
17. Yang, Y., Gopal, S.: Multilabel classification with meta-level features in a learning-to-rank framework. Mach. Learn. **880**(1–2), 47–68 (2012)
18. Zhang, M.L., Zhou, Z.H.: A review on multi-label learning algorithms. IEEE Trans. Knowl. Data Eng. **260**(8), 1819–1837 (2014)

Using Audio Transformations to Improve Comprehension in Voice Question Answering

Aleksandr Chuklin[1]([✉]), Aliaksei Severyn[1], Johanne R. Trippas[2],
Enrique Alfonseca[1], Hanna Silen[3], and Damiano Spina[2]

[1] Google Research, Zürich, Switzerland
{chuklin,severyn,ealfonseca}@google.com
[2] RMIT University, Melbourne, Australia
{johanne.trippas,damiano.spina}@rmit.edu.au
[3] Google Research, London, UK
silen@google.com

Abstract. Many popular form factors of digital assistants—such as Amazon Echo or Google Home—enable users to converse with speech-based systems. The lack of screens presents unique challenges. To satisfy users' information needs, the presentation of answers has to be optimized for voice-only interactions. We evaluate the usefulness of audio transformations (i.e., prosodic modifications) for voice-only question answering. We introduce a crowdsourcing setup evaluating the quality of our proposed modifications along multiple dimensions corresponding to the informativeness, naturalness, and ability of users to identify key parts of the answer. We offer a set of prosodic modifications that highlight potentially important parts of the answer using various acoustic cues. Our experiments show that different modifications lead to better comprehension at the expense of slightly degraded naturalness of the audio.

Keywords: Speech generation · Question answering · Crowdsourcing

1 Introduction

Recent advances in technology have transformed the ways we access information. With the rise of voice-only digital assistant devices, such as Amazon Echo, Apple Homepod, or Google Home users can express information needs verbally and receive answers exclusively via voice. However, providing answers via voice in the absence of a screen is a challenging task which leads to different interaction strategies employed by both users and the system.

Searching is traditionally considered as a visual task since reading information-dense sections such as search snippets is already a cognitively demanding undertaking. Thus, screen-based systems typically provide visual

For extended version of this paper, please refer to Chuklin et al. [2].

© Springer Nature Switzerland AG 2019
F. Crestani et al. (Eds.): CLEF 2019, LNCS 11696, pp. 164–170, 2019.
https://doi.org/10.1007/978-3-030-28577-7_12

cues to *highlight* key parts of text responses (e.g., boldfacing key parts in passages) which helps to identify answers while skimming a results page. However, the serial nature of audio-only communication channels hampers "skimming" the information as can be done in a visual interface.

In this paper, we explore different prosody modifications—such as insertion of pauses, decreasing of speaking rate, and increase in pitch—to highlight key answer parts in audio responses. While these features of prosody in natural speech have been associated with positive effects, to our knowledge they have not been analysed empirically for presenting answers in voice-only channels. Moreover, it remains unclear which effects it would have when incorporated in a voice Question Answering (QA) system and how these effects can be evaluated at scale. We propose to address the problem by asking the following questions:

RQ1 Can we use crowdsourcing to quantify the utility of the prosody modifications for voice-only QA?

RQ2 Which effects do prosody modification techniques have on informativeness and perceived naturalness of the response?

Related Work. Most of the related work on QA systems with speech interfaces focuses on the problem of spoken language recognition and understanding of voice-based questions [5,6,14]. The scope of our work is to better understand how to *present* answers when delivered via the audio-channel.

In contrast to traditional desktop search, there are no commonly agreed task and evaluation guidelines for assessing *voice-only* QA. Filippova et al. [4] proposed to evaluate sentence compression techniques in terms of readability and informativeness using human raters. In contrast to that work, we propose an evaluation setup where raters are asked to *listen* and assess the voice answers across *multiple* dimensions, as well as to *extract* the key answer part, which we check for correctness.

The audio modifications presented in this paper alter the *prosody* of the spoken answer (i.e., the patterns of stress and intonation in speech). Prosody has an essential cognitive role in speech perception [13]. Sentence stress seems to ease comprehension of stressed words and has been shown to lower reaction time independent of a word's syntactic function [3]. Simultaneously, pauses in speech convey information about intonational boundaries [9].

2 Methodology

Assume that for a user's *question* we have an *answer sentence* where we identify the *answer key* (key answer part) with the help of some algorithm. Example:

- *Question*: Which guitarist inspired Queen?
- *Answer Sentence*: Queen drew artistic influence from British rock acts of the 60s and early 1970s [...] in addition to American guitarist **Jimi Hendrix**, with Mercury also inspired by the gospel singer Aretha Franklin.
- *Answer Key*: Jimi Hendrix

This pattern is used by commercial search engines, e.g., Google's featured snippets[1] or Bing Distill answers [7], where the most important parts of the answer are highlighted or called-out separately. Additionally, there are datasets available for researchers to study text-based QA, such as MS MARCO [8] or the Stanford Question-Answering Dataset (SQuAD) [11], which we use here.

We hypothesize that highlighting the key answer part by modifying the prosody during the audio generation step, makes it easier for the worker to understand the answer, potentially at the expense of naturalness of the audio.

The problem of identifying key parts is an active area of research in QA and is beyond the scope of the current work. Note that, unlike human-curated datasets mentioned above, the quality of the automatically extracted answer keys may not be high enough for them to be surfaced as stand-alone answers in a production system. Without the context of the entire sentence, the risk of misleading the user by a low-quality short answer is high. This potential risk motivates our work on how to *emphasize* the key part of the answer when presented via voice.

We propose to ask *crowd workers* to evaluate the prosody modifications. Given a *question* and verbalization of a corresponding *answer sentence*, crowd workers need to give feedback on the quality of the audio response as well as identify the phrase in the audio that corresponds to the answer key. The judgments were collected using the Figure Eight crowdsourcing platform.[2] Tasks were randomly assigned to paid workers residing in English-speaking countries. The dataset and crowd judgments can be accessed at https://github.com/rmit-ir/clef2019-prosody.

Prosody Modification. We perform four different prosody modifications in the Text-to-Speech (TTS) generation:

- **pause:** inserted before and after the key answer part;
- **rate:** the speaking rate of the key answer part is decreased;
- **pitch:** the key answer part is spoken in a higher pitch than the rest of the answer sentence;
- **emphasis:** the key answer part is spoken with prominence, which is typically implemented as a combination of prosody modifications such as speaking **rate** and **pitch**.

Evaluation. We study the following four explicit dimensions to evaluate the utility of highlighting via prosody modifications and naturalness of the audio response: *informativeness* (how satisfactorily the audio-response answers the user's question on the scale of 0 to 4), *elocution* (whether the words in the full answer sentence were pronounced correctly, 0 to 2), presence of unwarranted *interruptions* (0 or 1), appropriateness of the audio *length* (−1 to 1). These dimensions are based on the guidelines for evaluating speech in the Google Assistant.[3]

---

[1] https://blog.google/products/search/reintroduction-googles-featured-snippets.
[2] Experiments performed under Ethics Application BSEH 10–14 at RMIT University.
[3] https://ai.googleblog.com/2017/12/evaluation-of-speech-for-google.html.

Table 1. Prosody modification settings: `strength` parameter of the `<break>` SSML tag, `rate`/`pitch` parameters of `<prosody>`, and `level` parameter of `<emphasis>`.

TTS engine	Voice	pause	rate	pitch	emphasis
IBM	Lisa	strong	x-slow	x-high	n/a
Google	Wavenet-F	strong	slow	+2st	strong

In addition to collecting the aforementioned judgments, we also calculate one objective measure, the *correctness* of the workers' typed answer key. To compute correctness, we compare the answer key typed by the worker against the given short answer from the dataset (what we treat as the gold answer key for highlighting). We convert both into a Metaphone representation [10] to account for typos and misheard words, and then compute the difference using the Ratcliff-Obershelp algorithm [12]. The *correctness* value ranges from 0 to 1.

Quality Control. To detect whether a worker is reliable, we use two different types of *test questions*: (i) we ask the worker to type in the short answer after listening to the full audio and then compare the provided short answer against the ground-truth, and (ii) we include questions that are off-topic and do not contain an answer. In the first case, we filter out workers who achieve answer *correctness* below 0.5 while in the second case we expect the worker to give the lowest rating on the *informativeness* scale.

3 Experimental Setup

In our study, we use question/answer pairs from the widely used SQuAD [11]. In our experiments, whole SQuAD paragraph were fed to a TTS generating the audio response and the ground truth answers are used to highlight the key part of it. For our set of experiments, we used the first 300 Wikipedia articles and their corresponding question/audio pairs. We further split these articles into four groups of 75 question/audio pairs (one group per modification: pause, rate, pitch, and emphasis). Different articles were used for each prosody modification to reduce the chance that a crowd worker is exposed to the same question multiple times. We then generated the audio of the baseline (no modifications) and modified versions of the answer sentence. Three crowd workers rated each of the resulting question/audio pairs.

We use two TTS platforms in our experiments: IBM Watson (https:// ibm.com/watson/services/text-to-speech) and Google Wavenet (https://cloud. google.com/text-to-speech). The settings are summarized in Table 1.[4] Note that these settings are chosen ad-hoc based on the subjective perception and test runs. The perceived size of the effect depends on the TTS engine and voice used,

---

[4] The `emphasis` feature is currently only available in the Google TTS and the implementation details are not specified in the SSML standard nor the documentation.

as well as on the sentence being modified. We leave the optimization of these settings for future work.

After removing judgments used for quality control, we have 1,454 rows of judgments for the IBM engine from 99 workers for 450 question-audio pairs (75 for each of the three modifications (pause, rate, pitch), plus an equal number of baseline pairs); 1,820 rows of judgments for the Google TTS engine from 85 workers for 600 question-audio pairs (four modification plus baseline).

Agreement between crowd workers is rather low when measured by the Krippendorff's alpha. For *informativeness* and *length* the scores are low (ranging from 0.27 to 0.37 for the IBM engine, and from 0.06 to 0.43 for Google TTS), but are comparable with similar crowdsourcing judgment collections [1]. The agreement is even lower for *elocution* and *interruption* scores. When it comes to majority agreement (two out of three workers), however, it was substantially high across all dimensions/modifications/voices (above 0.79 for the lowest slice).

Judgments are treated as Likert scale and, in case of *length*, the absolute value is taken, making it binary ("OK" vs. "too short/too long"). We use the median to aggregate judgments per item. Wilcoxon signed-rank test on a per-item level was used to report statistical significance. We use * (**) to indicate statistical significance with $p < 0.05$ ($p < 0.01$ respectively). Equivalent results were obtained when the t-test and/or average instead of median was used.

4   Results and Discussion

Table 2 shows the result. We only report absolute difference in the score given by the raters to avoid a direct comparison between two commercial systems. Note also that the results are not comparable across two systems because the prosody modifications with the same name have a noticeably different effect on them.

Table 2. Absolute difference relative to the baseline. The higher the better for *inform.*, *correctness*, and *elocution* (↑); the lower the better for *interruption* and *length* (↓).

		inform.↑	correctness↑	elocution↑	interruption↓	length↓
IBM	pauses	−0.21	+0.04	−0.03	+0.37**	+0.08
	rate	+0.26	+0.02	−0.24**	+0.03	+0.03
	pitch	+0.02	−0.03	−0.11	+0.01	−0.03
Google	pauses	+0.21	+0.09	−0.04	+0.15**	+0.00
	rate	+0.22	+0.07	−0.18**	+0.18**	+0.03
	pitch	−0.03	+0.08	+0.08	+0.13**	+0.07
	emphasis	+0.87**	+0.28**	−0.07	+0.13**	−0.07

The main pattern that emerges from the data is an increase in informativeness and correctness, and a decrease in speech quality through naturalness, as captured by *elocution* or *interruption* ratings. Interestingly, only **rate** modification was deemed to significantly hurt elocution and no significant *length* change were reported. As expected, workers identified more unexpected *interruptions* when **pauses** are used to highlight the answer keys in both TTS engines. There were also *interruptions* reported for other modifications in the Google TTS engine, which is due to the peculiarity of that engine, which always adds sentence breaks—and therefore small pauses—around `<prosody>` and `<emphasis>` tags. We expect that once that issue is resolved, no interruptions will be reported.

We also observe that our prosody modifications either improve or leave the *correctness* score unchanged, and most of them—although not all—are perceived by workers as more useful for the job of identifying the answer (*informativeness*).

5 Conclusions

We investigate how prosody modifications can help users to identify answers from audio responses in a QA setting. To answer our first research question (**RQ1**) we conclude that, yes, the proposed crowdsourcing setup is viable and gives an actionable breakdown of quality dimensions. To our knowledge, this is the first experiment that validates the use of a crowdsourcing methodology to analyze prosody modification in voice-only QA.

Answering our second research question (**RQ2**), we show that emphasizing the answer—via lowering speaking rate and simultaneously increasing pitch—provides subjectively more informative responses and makes workers more effective in identifying the answers, at the expense of the naturalness in the audio (interruptions), which is an artefact of a particular TTS implementation.

The near future work includes further studies to find the optimal combination of prosody modification to highlight answers in a given audio response depending on the different answer features (and possibly on the user features). Another open question for future work is to better understand how modifying the prosody impacts the users' comprehension and satisfaction in a more general context, such as when users are not asked to extract answers and converse naturally.

References

1. Chuklin, A., de Rijke, M.: Incorporating clicks, attention and satisfaction into a search engine result page evaluation model. In: CIKM (2016)
2. Chuklin, A., Severyn, A., Trippas, J.R., Alfonseca, E., Silen, H., Spina, D.: Prosody modifications for question-answering in voice-only settings. CoRR abs/1806.03957 (2018). http://arxiv.org/abs/1806.03957
3. Cutler, A., Foss, D.J.: On the role of sentence stress in sentence processing. Lang. Speech **20**, 1–10 (1977)
4. Filippova, K., Alfonseca, E., Colmenares, C.A., Kaiser, L., Vinyals, O.: Sentence compression by deletion with LSTMs. In: EMNLP (2015)
5. Kumar, A.J., Schmidt, C., Köhler, J.: A knowledge graph-based speech interface for question answering systems. Speech Commun. **92**, 1–12 (2017)

6. Mishra, T., Bangalore, S.: Qme!: a speech-based question-answering system on mobile devices. In: Proceedings of NAACL 2010, pp. 55–63 (2010)
7. Mitra, B., Simon, G., Gao, J., Craswell, N., Deng, L.: A proposal for evaluating answer distillation from web data. In: Proceedings of the SIGIR 2016 WebQA Workshop (2016)
8. Nguyen, T., et al.: MS MARCO: a human generated machine reading comprehension dataset (2016)
9. Pannekamp, A., Toepel, U., Alter, K., Hahne, A., Friederici, A.D.: Prosody-driven sentence processing: an event-related brain potential study. J. Cogn. Neurosci. **17**, 407–421 (2005)
10. Philips, L.: The double metaphone search algorithm. C/C++ Users J. **18**(6), 38–43 (2000)
11. Rajpurkar, P., Zhang, J., Lopyrev, K., Liang, P.: SQuAD: 100,000+ questions for machine comprehension of text. In: EMNLP (2016)
12. Ratcliff, J.W., Metzener, D.E.: Pattern matching: the gestalt approach. Dr. Dobb's J. **13**(7), 46 (1988)
13. Sanderman, A.A., Collier, R.: Prosodic phrasing and comprehension. Lang. Speech **40**(4), 391–409 (1997)
14. Whittaker, E.W.D., Mrozinski, J., Furui, S.: Factoid question answering with web, mobile and speech interfaces. In: NAACL (2006)

A User Modeling Shared Challenge Proposal

Owen Conlan[1], Kieran Fraser[1], Liadh Kelly[2(✉)], and Bilal Yousuf[1]

[1] Adapt Centre, Trinity College Dublin, Dublin, Ireland
{owen.conlan,kieran.fraser,bilal.yousuf}@adaptcentre.ie
[2] Maynooth University, Kildare, Ireland
liadh.kelly@mu.ie

Abstract. Comparative evaluation in the areas of User Modeling, Adaptation and Personalization (UMAP) is significantly challenging. It has always been difficult to rigorously compare different approaches to personalization, as the function of the resulting systems is, by their nature, heavily influenced by the behavior of the users involved in trialing the systems. Developing comparative evaluations in this space would be a huge advancement as it would enable shared comparison across research. Here we present a proposal for a shared challenge generation in UMAP, focusing on user model generation using logged mobile phone data, with an assumed purpose of supporting mobile phone notification suggestion. The dataset, evaluation metrics, and challenge operation are described.

Keywords: Personalization · Evaluation · Shared task

1 Introduction

There is currently no established or standardized means for comparative evaluation of algorithms and systems developed by researchers in the User Modeling, Adaptation and Personalization (UMAP) space. The development of such methodologies has proven to be extremely difficult, but would be highly rewarding for the community. Privacy concerns, the challenges of working with interactive scenarios, and the individual differences in behavior between users all must be addressed in order to facilitate repeatable and comparable evaluation and to advance research in this domain. The EvalUMAP workshop series[1] [1,2] is a new concerted drive towards the establishment of shared challenges for comparative evaluation within the UMAP community. The first workshop in the series brought the community together to discuss challenges and potential solutions associated with generating shared evaluation challenges in the UMAP space.

---

[1] http://evalumap.adaptcentre.ie.

Authors listed alphabetically.

© Springer Nature Switzerland AG 2019
F. Crestani et al. (Eds.): CLEF 2019, LNCS 11696, pp. 171–177, 2019.
https://doi.org/10.1007/978-3-030-28577-7_13

Building on the success of the first edition of the workshop, the second edition made concrete steps towards identifying datasets and methods that could be exploited for shared UMAP evaluation challenges. It is intended that the third edition of the workshop, running at UMAP 2019, will further progress this move towards shared challenge generation. In this paper we present a proposed methodology for such a shared challenge in the community, including practical steps to implementation.

2   Related Work

Adaptive system evaluation has been a recurrent topic within the community over the years, for example [8,9,11]. However, a solution capable of delivering repeatable and comparable results that would become the standard method to evaluate UMAP research has yet to emerge.

Lessons can be learned here from progress in other domains in shared challenge generation. The nearest to our UMAP challenge being arguably that of the Information Retrieval (IR) community. In recent years the community has started to look more closely at bringing the user into the loop, exploring the creation of shared challenges that consider iterative search sessions (for example in initiatives such as [7]), providing profiles of individual users to aid search (for example, the new PIR-CLEF task[2]) and providing access to real users conducting real search tasks [6,10]. In working towards the possibility of shared challenges in the UMAP community we can learn from such initiatives. However, the types of algorithms and systems which the UMAP community seek to evaluate are of a distinct nature, and as such will require their own unique solution.

3   Proposed Shared Challenge Description

The use-case for the proposed challenge is personalized mobile phone notification generation with the intention of expanding to other use-cases and challenges in the future. Our previous work in this space [4] has explored intercepting incoming mobile notifications, mediating their delivery such that irrelevant or unnecessary notifications do not reach the end-user and generating synthetic notification datasets from real world usage data. The next step toward an improved notification experience is to generate personalised notifications in real-time, removing the need for interception and delivery mediation. Specifically, assuming individuals' interactions with their mobile phone have been logged, the challenge is to create an approach to generate personalized notifications on individuals' mobile phones, whereby such personalization would consist of deciding what events (SMS received, etc.) to show to the individual and when to show them. Given the number of steps associated with such personalization, the task proposed in this paper will focus on the first step in this process, that of user model generation using the logged mobile phone interactions. For this task a dataset consisting of several individuals' mobile phone interactions would be provided, described next.

---

[2] http://www.ir.disco.unimib.it/pir-clef2019/.

3.1   Challenge Dataset

The dataset associated with this proposed shared challenge is a simulated dataset that is based on mobile notifications gathered by the WeAreUs Android app. The dataset generation approach is described in [5]. The synthetic data provided in the challenge dataset is comprised of notification, engagement and contextual features. The notification features relate to the event: posting of notification to the user's device. The contextual features describe the user/device context at particular moments of interest such as when a notification is posted and when it is removed. The engagement features describe the reaction the user has to the notification. See Table 2 for an outline of the captured data features. Since this dataset consists of synthetic data, as opposed to real individuals data, the ethical and privacy concerns are negligible as the data cannot be combined or analysed to identify real individuals.

4   Challenge Operation

The challenge would operate with a campaign style format. Participants will be provided with a sample of data as described in the previous section, and will be required to create user models for the individuals described in the data.

As a means of steering user model creation toward a tangible goal, and hence toward evaluative metrics, two tasks in the domain of mobile notification management are proposed. Task 1 is an offline scenario where models are trained and then evaluated on a static test set. Task 2, in contrast, simulates a live interactive environment in which models must adapt on the fly. Participants can take part in one or both of these tasks to complete the challenge.

An OpenAI Gym environment, specifically Gym-push, is used for the challenge tasks. OpenAI Gym is an open source interface to reinforcement learning (RL) tasks. It provides environments for researchers to benchmark RL agents on simulations of real-world problems. Gym-push is a custom OpenAI Gym environment developed for this proposed challenge which simulates push-notifications arriving on a user's device, the context in which the user receives the notification and the subsequent reward received for engagements made by the user. Gym-push is the simulated environment which will be used to evaluate the performance of the challenge participants' user models. The participants will receive various context features from the environment which they can apply as input to their user models to generate personalized notifications. They can then pass these generated notifications to the environment for evaluation. Within the environment, an agent, acting as the user, will engage with the generated notifications and metrics measuring various facets of performance (discussed further in Sect. 5) which will be tracked. It is important therefore that the user models created conform to the requirements of the Gym-push environment to ensure evaluation can take place (implementation guidelines detailed in Sect. 4.3).

Following ACM's policy on *Artifact Review and Badging*[3] and to support best practice with regard to reproducibility [3], submitted participant models

---

[3] https://www.acm.org/publications/policies/artifact-review-badging.

will be stored in the Gym-push environment along with the version of data used to obtain their final performance results. Subsequently, the environment will be able to generate additional diverse notification datasets using these models. These additional datasets can also be utilised by other communities for various research purposes.

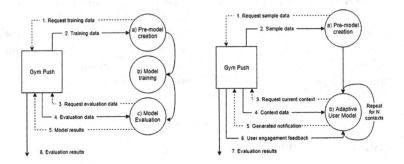

Fig. 1. Left: Task 1 operation flow; Right: Task 2 operation flow.

4.1   Task 1

Figure 1 (Left) illustrates the operation flow for participants partaking in Task 1. Participant can query Gym-push for 3 months of historical data, which takes a context (e.g. Time: 'morning', Place: 'airport', etc.) as input and outputs a personalized notification (e.g. App: 'news', Subject: 'weather', etc.) for the given context. Once the model is built, it can be evaluated, again using Gym-push. This is achieved by giving the participant an additional 3 months of contextual evaluation data with which to generate notifications. The resulting notifications are then returned to the environment where evaluation metrics are calculated.

4.2   Task 2

Figure 1 (Right) illustrates the differing operation flow for participants partaking in Task 2. Participants are asked to create a user model based on the same notification, context and engagement features but without historical notification data to train with (although, they can query the environment for sample data with which to create their model). In contrast to Task 1, this user model will need to query the Gym-push environment at each step to receive a current context feature and a previous user notification-engagement feature. As the environment steps through each context item and as engagement history becomes available, the user model can exploit this information to improve the generation of personalized notifications. The goal is to develop a model which adapts and learns how to generate personalized notifications in real-time, without prior history of the user (cold-start problem). Evaluation is continuous for this task and a summary of results is issued once all context features have been processed.

4.3 Model Guidelines

Task 1. The user model should take a context as input and produce a personalized notification as output. The context and notification should be strictly represented by the *Contextual* and *Notification* category features detailed in Table 2. More detail, including the set of values each feature can take, is available at the Gym-push repository.

Task 2. In addition to data available in Task 1, this model can also make use of notification-engagement data relating to a generated notification. The notification-engagements are represented by the *Engagement* category features noted in Table 2.

5   Evaluation Approach and Metrics

The Gym-push environment will evaluate the user models by deploying an agent to act as a user engaging with the generated personalized notifications. The agent will be trained on historical data of the user and decide, given the context, to open or dismiss the notification generated by the model. The following two metrics will be tracked in both Tasks 1 and 2:

Diversity - This metric will evaluate the diversity of generated personalized notifications which have been accepted by the agent over the 3 months. Notification sets which boast greater diversity will be scored higher.

Performance - This metric will track and compare engagements resulting from the generated personalized notifications with those of the actual notifications. Scenarios which improve end-user engagements are scored higher (see Table 1).

Table 1. Performance metric

For a given context		
Actual notification	Generated notification	Reward
Opened	Opened	+1
Dismissed	Dismissed	+0
Dismissed	Opened	+2
Opened	Dismissed	−1

Table 2. Dataset features

Category	Features
Notification	App, category, updates, subject, priority, ongoing, visibility
Contextual	Day, time, place, contact-significance, activity, noise, battery level, charging, headphones-in, light intensity, music-active, proximity, ringer-mode
Engagement	Time app last used, seen time, decision time, response time, action

Two additional metrics are tracked in Task 2:

Response Time - This metric evaluates the time it takes the user model to generate a notification once given the context by the environment. Shorter times are scored higher.

Learning Rate - This metric evaluates how quickly the performance metric (above) of the model improves over each time step (context item) of the environment.

6 Conclusions

While evaluation is an active topic of research within the UMAP community, to-date there are no shared evaluation challenges in the UMAP community which would allow comparison of developed systems in controlled environments similar to the evaluation labs offered in other research communities. Improved solutions for UMAP evaluation that have lower cost, are more repeatable, and more realistic are required. In this paper we propose one possible approach for shared challenge generation in the UMAP community, including use-case, data collection and evaluation methodology. This challenge focuses on user model generation using logged mobile phone data, with an assumed purpose of supporting mobile phone notification suggestion. It is not expected that this proposal is the only possible UMAP shared challenge, rather in putting forward this challenge proposal we seek to open further discussion and progress towards shared challenge generation for the UMAP community.

References

1. Conlan, O., Kelly, L., Koidl, K., Lawless, S., Levacher, K., Staikopoulos, A.: Eval-UMAP 2016: towards comparative evaluation in the user modelling, adaptation and personalization space workshop. In: UMAP 2016 (2016)
2. Conlan, O., Kelly, L., Koidl, K., Lawless, S., Staikopoulos, A.: EvalUMAP 2017: towards comparative evaluation in the user modelling, adaptation and personalization space workshop. In: UMAP 2017 (2017)
3. Fehr, J., Heiland, J., Himpe, C., Saak, J.: Best practices for replicability, reproducibility and reusability of computer-based experiments exemplified by model reduction software. arXiv preprint arXiv:1607.01191 (2016)
4. Fraser, K., Yousuf, B., Conlan, O.: Synthesis and evaluation of a mobile notification dataset. In: Adjunct Publication of UMAP 2017 (2017)
5. Fraser, K., Yousuf, B., Conlan, O.: Scrutable and persuasive push-notifications. In: Oinas-Kukkonen, H., Win, K.T., Karapanos, E., Karppinen, P., Kyza, E. (eds.) PERSUASIVE 2019. LNCS, vol. 11433, pp. 67–73. Springer, Cham (2019). https://doi.org/10.1007/978-3-030-17287-9_6
6. Hopfgartner, F., Kille, B., Lommatzsch, A., Plumbaum, T., Brodt, T., Heintz, T.: Benchmarking news recommendations in a living lab. In: Kanoulas, E., et al. (eds.) CLEF 2014. LNCS, vol. 8685, pp. 250–267. Springer, Cham (2014). https://doi.org/10.1007/978-3-319-11382-1_21

7. Hui Yang, G., Soboroff, I.: TREC 2016 dynamic domain track overview. In: TREC 2016 (2016)
8. Paramythis, A., Weibelzahl, S., Masthoff, J.: Layered evaluation of interactive adaptive systems: framework and formative methods. User Model. User-Adap. Interact. **20**(5), 383–453 (2010). https://doi.org/10.1007/s11257-010-9082-4
9. Park, K.S., Hwan Lim, C.: A structured methodology for comparative evaluation of user interface designs using usability criteria and measures. Int. J. Ind. Ergon. **23**(5–6), 379–389 (1999). https://doi.org/10.1016/S0169-8141(97)00059-0
10. Schuth, A., Balog, K., Kelly, L.: Overview of the Living Labs for Information Retrieval Evaluation (LL4IR) CLEF lab 2015. In: Mothe, J., et al. (eds.) CLEF 2015. LNCS, vol. 9283, pp. 484–496. Springer, Cham (2015). https://doi.org/10.1007/978-3-319-24027-5_47
11. Van Velsen, L., van der Geest, T., Klaassen, R., Steehouder, M.: User-centered evaluation of adaptive and adaptable systems: a literature review. Knowl. Eng. Rev. **23**(3), 261–281 (2008). https://doi.org/10.1017/S0269888908001379

How Lexical Gold Standards Have Effects on the Usefulness of Text Analysis Tools for Digital Scholarship

Jussi Karlgren[✉][iD]

KTH Royal Institute of Technology and Gavagai, Stockholm, Sweden
jussi@gavagai.io

Abstract. This paper describes how the current lexical similarity and analogy gold standards are built to conform to certain ideas about what the models they are designed to evaluate are used for. Topical relevance has always been the most important target notion for information access tools and related language technology technologies, and while this has proven a useful starting point for much of what information technology is used for, it does not always align well with other uses to which technologies are being put, most notably use cases from digital scholarship in the humanities or social sciences. This paper argues for more systematic formulation of requirements from the digital humanities and social sciences and more explicit description of the assumptions underlying model design.

Keywords: Gold standard · Lexical semantics · Digital scholarship

1 Text Analysis Is Mostly Based on Lexical Features

Text analysis technology is almost exclusively based on lexical features, i.e. on observing the presence and the frequency of occurrence of words in a text or a section of text of interest. These observations are used typically for classifying or scoring texts. Features are treated variously by algorithms ranging from simple observation of presence, to frequency calculations, or to non-linear combinations of items using e.g. neurally inspired models. In most cases, algorithms rely on background lexical models primed by observations made on large amounts of data to be able to discern what lexical features are of specific interest in the data set at hand. Evaluating the quality of such background models is made using semantic tests of some generality, intended to provide a reasonable sample of language to capture the general competence of a model.

Human linguistic behaviour rests on *predications*: a speaker or author indicates some referents of interest and formulates something of interest about them, relating them to each other or to preceding discourse. Prototypically, referents are realised in text as noun phrases; the relations among referents, between referents and the discourse itself, or between referents and the surrounding context

© Springer Nature Switzerland AG 2019
F. Crestani et al. (Eds.): CLEF 2019, LNCS 11696, pp. 178–184, 2019.
https://doi.org/10.1007/978-3-030-28577-7_14

are prototypically realised as verb phrases. This simplified model of how semantics and pragmatics work in functional discourse will serve to elucidate some challenges for evaluating lexical resources given below.

2   Referential Semantics and Topicality

Referentiality covers one of the more important aspects of language use: that of topicality, where language calls up items, concepts, notions of interest to discourse participants. In most computational text analysis tasks, topicality has been at the center of attention: what a text is *about* is the primary categorisation criterion. The general intuition is that topical terms appear in a tight bursty pattern to indicate that some matter of interest is under treatment, and that structural terms appear in a wider distribution. As an example, texts which contain terms *helicopter, rotor, airfield,* and *pilot* vs. texts which contain the terms *cow, milk, dairy,* and *barn* can with some ease be classified topically from bursty term occurrence alone. Terms such as *see, move, rotate,* or *yield* are not as useful for this purpose. Text analysis tools address coverage by including additional related terms, if some initial terms have been given. These may be synonyms or near synonyms (*autogiro, chopper, whirlybird*) or other related terms (*airfoil, camber, translational lift*).

Much of what is in a text does not directly contribute to its topicality. The text also organises the structure of the discourse into appropriately complex chunks, aids the listener or reader to achieve coherence in what is being communicated, indicates speaker or author attitude and stance, and communicates temporal and process qualities of the predication given. A text also evokes other texts and other usages through its stylistic and lexical choices, by adhering to conventions, by quoting, paraphrasing, or reformulating other works and other authors. Some such qualities of the text are highly rule-bound and conventionalised, others are free for the author or speaker to make explicit if they should so wish. Some such qualities are general over an entire discourse, with observable surface items sprinkled throughout the textual data and thus cannot be pinpointed to any single utterance or to the occurrence patterns of some small set of linguistic items. These functions cannot be crisply demarcated.

3   Close and Distant Reading

In recent years, research in the humanities has adopted the possibility of working with collections of documents rather than small focussed selected sets. The attendant methodological debate is frequently framed as a distinction between *close reading,* the traditional approach of the humanities to *engage* closely with cultural items—in this case, texts and their contexts—and *distant reading,* the potentially fruitful set of methods having to do with working on comprehensive data sets from e.g. a certain period, genre, or class of author, using computational tools, visualisation and graphing techniques, and overview analyses to find patterns which would not have been notable using traditional methods [13].

These new tools, new methods, and new results are not universally welcomed by scholars in the humanities. The debate over how to best use new technologies is lively and goes to the roots of what the ultimate research goals of the humanities and the social sciences are. The humanities and the social sciences do not only have different methods than engineering and the natural sciences do, but their goals and aims when they produce knowledge are different, and they approach information differently [4,5,7,18]. Debate notwithstanding, it is not difficult to compile a long and comprehensive list of research questions, most of which are only incidentally topical in nature: how authors and schools of thought spread and influence each other, how much or little knowledge of distant cultures there was at some time in some cultural area, how political institutions change over time, how argumentation influences decision making, how public sentiment affects financial indicators, how the well-being of individuals are manifested in their writing, how a scholarly field selects its focus topics, how language change is motivated by local prestige markers, how social change is reflected in literary work, how to determine who has authored a given work, and so forth [9,14, e.g.]. Many of these questions are related to large scale work on collections, and many of these questions have been touched upon or addressed directly in recent years in experimental work here at CLEF.

From the point of view of information access research, we can expect quite interesting new use cases to emerge for language technologists and information access researchers to work with once the methodological discussions in the humanities settle: the topical content of texts or text is only one of the objects of study, engagement in the material is the prime method, and future computational tools will be there to allow for new types of engagement in more extensive collections of material.

4   Target Notions for Text Analysis

Most tools built for information access are explicitly designed to optimise for topical relevance and for timelines. This goes together well with referential semantics. In view of the preceding discussion on referentiality this translates to observable and computable *burstiness* as an obvious evaluation metric to decide which items mentioned in a text are useful to characterise it [10].

For this reason, one of the very effective mechanisms in document processing is that of term weighting. The idea behind term weighting is selectivity: what makes a term valuable is whether it can pick any of the few relevant documents from the many non-relevant ones. Karen Spärck Jones defined what was to become the *idf* measure in 1972: "*... terms should be weighted according to collection frequency, so that matches on less frequent, more specific, terms are of greater value than matches on frequent terms*" [17] and this measure has been adopted—for good reason—in just about every term weighting mechanism in use today. This measure weights terms according to their topical specificity: how

well they distinguish documents from each other by way of referential content.[1]
This is a sensible approach if topical relevance is the target notion.

Table 1 gives some observed statistics, computed over a collection of two
years of news text, with 170 000 documents and more than 72 million words. As
expected, there are more noun occurrences than adjectives or verbs, and those
occurrences come from a much larger lexicon of nouns: 200 000 nouns occur more
than 24 000 000 times in the material as compared to 8 000 verbs occurring
7 000 000 times. Only a small proportion of the nouns occur in more than 100
or 1000 of the documents, and even less if only the number of documents they
occur more than twice in are counted; the distribution of verbs and adjectives is
very different. Interpreting these observations in terms of referential semantics,
we can posit that human language can refer to an unimaginably wide variety of
entities using noun phrases, and, using verbs, to a more constrained variety of
events or processes.

Table 1. Lexical categories and their occurrence frequencies in documents.

	Nouns	Adjectives	Verbs
Number of occurrences	24 000 000	5 000 000	7 000 000
Number of different items	200 000	25 000	8 000
>100 documents	6%	15%	28%
>200 documents	4%	9%	20%
>1000 documents	1%	3%	8%
More than twice in the same document			
>100 documents	2%	3%	6%
>200 documents	1%	2%	4%
>1000 documents	0.4%	0.5%	1.5%

There are several test sets that are used specifically for experimentation with
how choice of representation, algorithm, and training set jointly contribute to
the qualities of a semantic model. Most, as can be seen in Table 2, are focussed
on nouns and relations between nominals. This, given the discussion above, is
unsurprising. There several further experiment sets with a broader selection of
lexical classes, but they tend to be embedded into more specialised conceptual
models, such as semantic role labeling, word sense disambiguation, or other prag-
matic constraints, which raise the threshold for including them in a standard test.
These standard test sets have been proven to be quite useful tools to develop
lexical resources, as can be seen from their widespread adoption in various evaluation experiments. However, even if a tool built on top of them professes to be

---

[1] Spärck Jones argues that this should be understood in terms of occurrence statistics
rather than more elusive statistical notions. However, the target notion is a relevance-
oriented one.

Table 2. Some typical test sets for lexical similarity.

Test sets	*Size*	Nouns or NP	Adjectives	Verbs	Other	Reference	Year
RG	65	100%				[15]	1965
Chiarello et al.	144	100%				[3]	1990
TOEFL	80	21%	25%	21%	32%	[11]	1997
WordSimilarity	353	97%	1%	2%		[6]	2001
ConceptSim		100%				[16]	2011
BLESS	200	100%				[2]	2011
Entailment	15 992	100%				[1]	2012
Syntactic analogy	8 000	25%	37.5%	37.5%		[12]	2013
SIMLEX	999	67%	11%	22%		[8]	2016

general and use case independent, the background lexical resources will have to some extended tuned the tool to fit these ostentatively general gold standards, which in turn will have tool implicitly yield results optimised for topical analysis.

5   Lessons Learned and Paths Forward

In conclusion, it is crucial to understand that gold standards are not use case free, not even term lists, and that applying them to optimise technologies will have downstream effects. The effects of the implicit use cases in evaluation are of varying importance. The major risk is that technologies may obscure that what most interests its users in digital scholarship, which will first result in shoddy or uninteresting research, with an attendant backlash and skepticism to computational methods in general. Both of these effects are evident already.

Much of the intradisciplinary debate in the various fields of digital scholarship is based on a prejudicial view of what the aims of engineering and the natural sciences are: "the sciences simplify, where the humanities embrace complexity". These sort of statements are frequently accompanied by calls for engineers to study more humanities. While this is a worthy goal in general and might make engineers happier people, it would not necessarily improve the tools used in digital scholarship. More important is for those who use tools to examine what the tools are built to work with and to take responsibility of those assumptions when they draw conclusions from their output. If those assumptions fit poorly with the tasks they intend to address, they should request other tools.

Similarly, those who design, build, and evaluate tools must pay more attention to what underlying assumptions they bring with technology components and evaluation procedures, and to make them known to those who use the tools further on down the line.

For those of us who worry about systematic evaluation, we must make sure to engineer gold standards to ensure their coverage over a larger space of downstream use cases, and to document the underlying assumptions and observable distributional characteristics of the gold standard items in greater detail. This applies to simple lexical gold standards discussed in this paper, but also to more sophisticated sets of texts and utterances. We cannot expect the typical end user to be able to do so, since much of the feature space under consideration is opaque for engineers and humanities scholars or social scientists alike. Building a fair and reasonably representative gold standard for text will involve analysis of the character of textual material in general and the items under consideration specifically. This requires both an understanding of the feature space and an ability to describe it formally which in turn means that the construction of gold standards must systematically involve expertise in the feature space of the material the gold standard is fashioned from.

References

1. Baroni, M., Bernardi, R., Do, N.Q., Shan, C.C.: Entailment above the word level in distributional semantics. In: Proceedings of the Conference of the European Chapter of the Association for Computational Linguistics. ACL (2012)
2. Baroni, M., Lenci, A.: How we BLESSed distributional semantic evaluation. In: Proceedings of the GEMS 2011 Workshop on GEometrical Models of Natural Language Semantics. Association for Computational Linguistics (2011)
3. Chiarello, C., Burgess, C., Richards, L., Pollock, A.: Semantic and associative priming in the cerebral hemispheres: some words do, some words don't... sometimes, some places. Brain Lang. **38**(1), 75–104 (1990)
4. Da, N.Z.: The computational case against computational literary studies. Crit. Inq. **45**(3), 601–639 (2019)
5. Da, N.Z.: The digital humanities debacle—computational methods repeatedly come up short. The Chronicle of Higher Education (2019)
6. Finkelstein, L., et al.: Placing search in context: the concept revisited. In: Proceedings of the International Conference on World Wide Web. ACM (2001)
7. Fitzpatrick, K.: The humanities, done digitally. The Chronicle of Higher Education (2011)
8. Hill, F., Reichart, R., Korhonen, A.: Simlex-999: evaluating semantic models with (genuine) similarity estimation. Comput. Linguist. **41**, 665–695 (2016)
9. Jänicke, S., Franzini, G., Cheema, M.F., Scheuermann, G.: On close and distant reading in digital humanities: a survey and future challenges. In: Eurographics Conference on Visualization (EuroVis), vol. 2 (2015)
10. Katz, S.M.: Distribution of content words and phrases in text and language modelling. Nat. Lang. Eng. **2**(1), 15–59 (1996)
11. Landauer, T.K., Dumais, S.T.: A solution to Plato's problem: the latent semantic analysis theory of acquisition, induction, and representation of knowledge. Psychol. Rev. **104**(2), 211–240 (1997)
12. Mikolov, T., Yih, W., Zweig, G.: Linguistic regularities in continuous space word representations. In: Proceedings of the Conference of the North American Chapter of the Association for Computational Linguistics (2013)
13. Moretti, F.: Distant Reading. Verso Books, London (2013)
14. O'Connor, B., Bamman, D., Smith, N.A.: Computational text analysis for social science: model assumptions and complexity. In: Second Workshop on Computational Social Science and the Wisdom of Crowds (2011)

15. Rubenstein, H., Goodenough, J.B.: Contextual correlates of synonymy. Commun. ACM **8**(10), 627–633 (1965)
16. Schwartz, H.A., Gomez, F.: Evaluating semantic metrics on tasks of concept similarity. In: Proceedings of FLAIRS (2011)
17. Sparck Jones, K.: A statistical interpretation of term specificity and its application in retrieval. J. Doc. **28**(1), 11–21 (1972)
18. Underwood, T.: Dear Humanists: Fear Not the Digital Revolution. The Chronicle of Higher Education (2019)

Personality Facets Recognition from Text

Wesley Ramos dos Santos and Ivandré Paraboni[(⊠)]

School of Arts, Sciences and Humanities, University of São Paulo,
Av. Arlindo Bettio, 1000, São Paulo, Brazil
{wesley.ramos.santos,ivandre}@usp.br

Abstract. Fundamental Big Five personality traits (e.g., Extraversion) and their facets (e.g., Activity) are known to correlate with a broad range of linguistic features and, accordingly, the recognition of personality traits from text is a well-known Natural Language Processing task. Labelling text data with facets information, however, may require the use of lengthy personality inventories, and perhaps for that reason existing computational models of this kind are usually limited to the recognition of the fundamental traits. Based on these observations, this paper investigates the issue of personality facets recognition from text labelled only with information available from a shorter personality inventory. In doing so, we provide a low-cost model for the recognition of certain personality facets, and present reference results for further studies in this field.

Keywords: Personality recognition · Big Five · Facets

1 Introduction

The Big Five personality model [4] comprises five fundamental categories of personality - Extraversion, Agreeableness, Conscientiousness, Neuroticism, and Openness to experience - which are further divided into dozens of more specific *facets*. For instance, the Neuroticism category includes facets representing Anxiety, Depression etc. Big Five categories are strongly correlated to (and possibly defined by) language use and, as a result, the recognition of an individual's personality traits from text is a well-established task in the Natural Language Processing (NLP) field [14].

Models for the recognition of personality traits from text are usually based on supervised machine learning methods that take as an input a text corpus labelled with personality scores. These scores, in turn, are computed from a range of personality inventories (or questionnaires) such as the BFI-44 inventory [7]. The BFI-44 consists of a relatively short, 44 multiple-choice inventory conveying short items such as 'I see myself as someone who *is depressed, blue*'. Items are to be answered on a zero (disagree strongly) to five (agree strongly) scale.

Knowing the five fundamental categories of personality of an individual may be sufficient for a number of practical applications. For others, however, a more detailed assessment of personality facets may be called-for. Assessing personality

© Springer Nature Switzerland AG 2019
F. Crestani et al. (Eds.): CLEF 2019, LNCS 11696, pp. 185–190, 2019.
https://doi.org/10.1007/978-3-030-28577-7_15

facets usually involves the use of a more extensive personality inventory, such as the 260-item NEO-PI-R [8]. From a computational perspective, however, large or complex inventories of this kind may be impractical, which may explain why studies on personality recognition from text [9,11,14,17] are usually limited to the five main personality categories obtainable from short inventories such as the BFI-44.

Despite these difficulties, a compromise between convenience (as in the BFI-44) and expressiveness (as in NEO-PI-R) may still be possible. In particular, we notice that the work in [18] proved evidence that, although most facets cannot be explicitly captured by the BFI-44, a small subset of 10 facets (two from each of the main Big Five factors) are inferable from this short scale. Thus, it may be possible to obtain at least some of the facet labels available from NEO-PI-R at a much lower cost.

Based on these observations, the actual NLP question to be investigated in this paper is whether the 10 additional facets proposed in [18] may be automatically recognised from text labelled with BFI-44 information only. To this end, we developed a series of binary classifiers for Big Five facet recognition from a labelled corpus of Brazilian Facebook status updates, and we present reference results for further studies in this field. To the best of our knowledge, our work is the first attempt to learn personality facets in this way, and it is most likely the first of its kind to be devoted to the Brazilian Portuguese language.

2   Related Work

We are not aware of any large-scale work on Big Five facet recognition from text, but there is a wide range of studies focused on the more general task of recognising its main five personality categories. Given that the applicable methods are presumably similar, in what follows we briefly review a number of instances of the latter.

The work in [9] presents a comprehensive view of the personality recognition task from multiple computational perspectives (i.e., as classification, regression and ranking tasks), by comparing the use of written essays and speech corpus as input data, and by comparing the use of self-reported Big Five scores and those produced by specialists, among other issues. The study makes extensive use of psycholinguistic features provided by the LIWC [12] and MRC [3] databases, and results suggest that using ranking algorithms, speech as input data, and personality reports produced by specialists work best.

Contrary to the use of psycholinguistics-motivated features in [9] and others, the work in [11] makes use of n-gram models to classify extremes of personality using both Naive-Bayes and SVM models. Evaluation based on a corpus of personal blogs achieves maximum accuracy of 65%.

In the context of the PAN-CLEF shared task series [14], a number of supervised models of personality recognition based on Twitter data labelled with personality scores obtained from a 10-item Big Five inventory have been developed. These include the overall winner of the competition [1], which combines second order attributes with a LSA text representation; the work in [5], which makes use of char and POS n-gram models, and the work in [19], which makes use of TF-IDF counts and stylistic features. For details, we refer to [14].

3   Personality Facet Recognition

The present study aims to compare a number of models of personality facet recognition from text. More specifically, we consider the set of 10 personality facets that, according to the method discussed in [18], may be inferred from the BFI-44 inventory [7]: Assertiveness and Activity facets (under the main Extraversion category), Altruism and Compliance (under Agreeableness), Order and Self-discipline (under Conscientiousness), Anxiety and Depression (under Neuroticism), and Aesthetics and Ideas (under Openness to experience).

The method proposed in [18] consists of a series of theoretically-motivated calculations (in addition to those already performed to obtain the basic Big Five personality scores) over the set of 44 responses provided by the BFI-44 inventory. Thus, provided that the full set of BFI-44 responses about an individual is known, computing these 10 additional facet scores is straightforward.

For instance, according to [18], the Activity facet of the Big Five Extraversion category is defined as the simple average of two of the BFI-44 scores from which the main Extraversion score is obtained in the first place. In the present work, these facet scores are therefore taken as given, and we do not discuss the underlying method to obtain them. For details, see [18].

Following existing work on Big Five personality recognition for the English language and others [9,11], personality facet recognition is presently regarded as a set of independent binary classification tasks. To this end, a document is to be labelled as a positive instance of a given facet if the corresponding author shows an above-average score for that facet when considering the entire set of authors in the domain. Since personality facets are, by definition, independent from each other [4], each document is to be assigned ten individual labels corresponding to each facet, which are to be classified one at a time.

4   Experiment

4.1   Overview

We devised an experiment to compare three binary classifiers for personality facet recognition from text:

- BoW: bag-of-words features from the 3000 most frequent words in corpus
- skip: average word vectors obtained from a skip-gram-1000 model
- cbow: average word vectors obtained from a cbow-1000 model

The Bow model is built using Naive Bayes classification. Both skip and cbow models are built using logistic regression and pre-trained word embeddings computed from a 150-million Brazilian Twitter corpus using word2vec [10] with window size = 5 and min_count = 10. In addition to these three classifiers, we also consider a simple Majority class baseline system for illustration purposes.

4.2 Data

We use the 2.2 million-words *b5-post* corpus of Brazilian Facebook [13], conveying 194k status updates written by 1019 users, which are accompanied by self-reported BFI-44 [7] inventories filled-in by every user. The *b5-post* corpus has been previously taken as the input to a number of author profiling tasks [6], including personality recognition [17].

The text portion of the corpus was subject to basic spell checking and term substitution (e.g., laugh expressions such as 'haha' were replaced by a common $LAUGH$ symbol etc.) From the corpus inventories, 10 additional personality facets were inferred according to the method in [18]. This information constitutes the set of ten class labels for each document as discussed in the previous section.

4.3 Procedure

All models were built using 10-fold cross validation over the entire *b5-post* dataset. However, since that we now intend to learn ten (facet) classes, and not only five (main categories), and since many facets may be considerably more sparse than others (e.g., the Depression facet of Neuroticism may be naturally less common than, say, Self-consciousness), data imbalance is a major concern to our work. As a means to alleviate this, we resort to SMOTE minority sampling [2] with $k = 5$ neighbours.

5 Results

Table 1 shows reference results for the majority class baseline, and for the three models of interest. The first column represents mean F1 scores over the ten classification tasks, followed by the number of times (wins) in which each model was the overall winner, and the mean F1 measure for each individual class.

Table 1. 10-fold cross validation mean F1 scores.

Model	Overall	Wins	assert.	activ.	altr.	compl.	order	selfd.	ans.	depr.	aesth	ideas
Baseline	0.33	0	0.33	0.34	0.34	0.34	0.33	0.33	0.34	0.33	0.33	0.33
BoW	0.57	4	0.60	0.59	0.61	0.54	0.56	0.61	0.57	0.52	0.60	0.58
skip	0.58	4	0.60	0.58	0.62	0.52	0.55	0.62	0.59	0.54	0.62	0.58
cbow	0.58	7	0.60	0.59	0.60	0.54	0.55	0.60	0.59	0.55	0.63	0.60

Although all models present a considerable improvement over our admittedly simple baseline, the distinction among them is narrow, particularly between BoW and skip. A slight advantage of the cbow model over the others is however noticeable in the number of classes (wins) for which cbow was the overall winner (7 out of 10 classification tasks).

As it is usually the case in personality classification, some personality traits tend to be more evident from text than others. In the present setting, we notice that Compliance and Depression recognition were the most challenging tasks. However, it remains unclear whether these facets are less explicit in language use in general, or simply less explicit in our Facebook domain.

Finally, we notice that the present results are generally similar to those observed in Big Five personality classification in English [9] and other languages, and also along the lines of previous studies on the recognition of the main Big Five categories from the *b5-post* corpus [15,16].

6 Final Remarks

This paper presented a number of models of Big Five facet recognition from a Brazilian Portuguese Facebook corpus and corresponding BFI-44 information. Our study suggests that, not unlike basic Big Five categories, the ten facets proposed in [18] may be recognised from text with reasonable accuracy if compared to a simple baseline system. In other words, our experiments suggest that we may in principle develop supervised models of personality recognition at a level of abstraction more specific than those obtainable from existing work, and without resorting to larger or more complex inventories to provide the required text labels.

The current work provides only initial reference results for further studies in this field, and a number of possible improvements are left as future work. In particular, we envisage the use of larger word embedding models and alternative learning architectures for this task, and further evaluation work by directly comparing our results against text labelled with actual facet information.

Acknowledgements. This work received support by FAPESP grant 2017/06828-1 and 2016/14223-0.

References

1. Álvarez-Carmona, M., López-Monroy, A., Montes-y-Gómez, M., Villaseñor-Pineda, L., Escalante, H.: INAOE's participation at PAN'15: author profiling task. In: CLEF 2015 (2015)
2. Chawla, N.V., Bowyer, K.W., Hall, L.O., Kegelmeyer, W.P.: SMOTE: synthetic minority over-sampling technique. J. Artif. Intell. Res. **16**(1), 321–357 (2002)
3. Coltheart, M.: The MRC psycholinguistic database. Q. J. Exp. Psychol. Sect. A: Hum. Exp. Psychol. **33**(4), 497–505 (1981)
4. Goldberg, L.R.: An alternative description of personality: the Big-Five factor structure. J. Pers. Soc. Psychol. **59**, 1216–1229 (1990)
5. González-Gallardo, C., et al.: Tweets classification using corpus dependent tags, character and POS N-grams. In: CLEF 2015 (2015)
6. Hsieh, F.C., Dias, R.F.S., Paraboni, I.: Author profiling from Facebook corpora. In: 11th International Conference on Language Resources and Evaluation (LREC-2018), Miyazaki, Japan, pp. 2566–2570. ELRA (2018)
7. John, O.P., Naumann, L.P., Soto, C.J.: Paradigm Shift to the Integrative Big-Five Trait Taxonomy: History, Measurement, and Conceptual Issues, pp. 114–158. Guilford Press, New York (2008)

8. Costa Jr., P.T., McCrae, R.R.: Revised NEO Personality Inventory (Neo-PI-R) and NEO Five-Factor Inventory (NEO-FFI): Professional Manual. Psychological Assessment Resources, Odessa (1992)
9. Mairesse, F., Walker, M., Mehl, M., Moore, R.: Using linguistic cues for the automatic recognition of personality in conversation and text. J. Artif. Intell. Res. (JAIR) **30**, 457–500 (2007)
10. Mikolov, T., Yih, W., Zweig, G.: Linguistic regularities in continuous space word representations. In: Proceedings of NAACL-HLT-2013, Atlanta, USA, pp. 746–751. Association for Computational Linguistics (2013)
11. Nowson, S., Oberlander, J.: Identifying more bloggers: towards large scale personality classification of personal weblogs. In: Proceedings of the International Conference on Weblogs and Social Media, Boulder, Colorado, USA (2007)
12. Pennebaker, J.W., Francis, M.E., Booth, R.J.: Inquiry and Word Count: LIWC. Lawrence Erlbaum, Mahwah (2001)
13. Ramos, R.M.S., Neto, G.B.S., da Silva, B.B.C., Monteiro, D.S., Paraboni, I., Dias, R.F.S.: Building a corpus for personality-dependent natural language understanding and generation. In: 11th International Conference on Language Resources and Evaluation (LREC-2018), Miyazaki, Japan, pp. 1138–1145. ELRA (2018)
14. Rangel, F., Celli, F., Rosso, P., Potthast, M., Stein, B., Daelemans, W.: Overview of the 3rd author profiling task at PAN 2015. In: CLEF 2015 Evaluation Labs and Workshop, Toulouse, France (2015). CEUR-WS.org
15. dos Santos, V.G., Paraboni, I., da Silva, B.B.C.: Big five personality recognition from multiple text genres. In: Ekštein, K., Matoušek, V. (eds.) TSD 2017. LNCS (LNAI), vol. 10415, pp. 29–37. Springer, Cham (2017). https://doi.org/10.1007/978-3-319-64206-2_4
16. da Silva, B.B.C., Paraboni, I.: Learning personality traits from Facebook text. IEEE Latin Am. Trans. **16**(4), 1256–1262 (2018). https://doi.org/10.1109/TLA.2018.8362165
17. da Silva, B.B.C., Paraboni, I.: Personality recognition from Facebook text. In: Villavicencio, A., et al. (eds.) PROPOR 2018. LNCS (LNAI), vol. 11122, pp. 107–114. Springer, Cham (2018). https://doi.org/10.1007/978-3-319-99722-3_11
18. Soto, C.J., John, O.P.: Ten facet scales for the Big Five Inventory: convergence with NEO PI-R facets, self-peer agreement, and discriminant validity. J. Res. Pers. **43**(1), 84–90 (2009). https://doi.org/10.1016/j.jrp.2008.10.002
19. Şulea, O.M., Dichiu, D.: Automatic profiling of twitter users based on their tweets. In: CLEF 2015 (2015)

Unsupervised System Combination for Set-Based Retrieval with Expectation Maximization

Han-Chin Shing[2]([✉]), Joe Barrow[2], Petra Galuščáková[1],
Douglas W. Oard[1,3], and Philip Resnik[1,4]

[1] UMIACS, University of Maryland, College Park, USA
petra@umiacs.umd.edu, {oard,resnik}@umd.edu
[2] Department of Computer Science, University of Maryland, College Park, USA
{shing,jdbarrow}@cs.umd.edu
[3] iSchool, University of Maryland, College Park, USA
[4] Department of Linguistics, University of Maryland, College Park, USA

Abstract. System combination has been shown to improve overall performance on many rank-based retrieval tasks, often by combining results from multiple systems into a single ranked list. In contrast, set-based retrieval tasks call for a technique to combine results in ways that require decisions on whether each document is in or out of the result set. This paper presents a set-generating unsupervised system combination framework that draws inspiration from evaluation techniques in sparse data settings. It argues for the existence of a duality between evaluation and system combination, and then capitalizes on this duality to perform unsupervised system combination. To do this, the framework relies on the consensus of the systems to estimate latent "goodness" for each system. An implementation of this framework using data programming is compared to other unsupervised system combination approaches to demonstrate its effectiveness on CLEF and MATERIAL collections.

Keywords: Unsupervised system combination ·
Expectation-maximization

1 Introduction

System combination, or data fusion, has been shown to improve performance over individual systems across a variety of information retrieval (IR) tasks [1,8, 12,18]. Most of the literature focuses on rank-based retrieval, where the goal is to generate a merged and improved ranked list. Returning the entire ranked list, however, might not always be optimal. Set-based retrieval studies the situation in which returning a subset of the entire rank list can be beneficial, such as when the downstream application involves heavy computation (e.g, question answering, summarization, or machine translation).

This work has been supported in part by IARPA/AFRL contract FA8650-17-C-9117.

F. Crestani et al. (Eds.): CLEF 2019, LNCS 11696, pp. 191–197, 2019.
https://doi.org/10.1007/978-3-030-28577-7_16

System combination for set-based retrieval has not been as well studied as for rank-based retrieval. It is also important to note that our interest in a set as the final retrieval result does not, however, mean that it must be sets that we take as the input to the combination process: a set selection strategy (such as finding a cutoff or a threshold) can be applied after merging ranked retrieval systems. This leads to questions about whether it is best to do set selection before the combination, after the combination, or even both. Furthermore, set selection often requires training data or expert knowledge and can vary greatly depending on the query of interest.

In this paper, we present a fully unsupervised set-generating system combination technique. It yields competitive results with widely used rank-based system combination methods that require further tuning data for set selection. Our approach draws inspiration from a duality between evaluation and system combination: evaluation allows us to estimate how good an underlying system is, and system combination can benefit from estimating how good each system is. By using expectation-maximization (E-M), we can estimate latent relevance labels with which to evaluate the systems, and then combine the systems based on how good each system is estimated to be (if we treat those labels as correct).

2   Related Work

A duality between system combination and evaluation has been suggested in the evaluation literature. Soboroff et al. [19] show that if you randomly assign relevance judgements and use them to evaluate the systems in TREC, you can still get a ranking of systems that correlates fairly well with the official ranking. Nuray and Can [16] further show that using system combination results as pseudo-relevance judgements can increase this correlation. However, they do not report how well the pseudo-relevance judgements correlate with the truth.

E-M techniques for ranked-retrieval system combination have been explored by Klementiev et al. [10]. In their work on unsupervised rank aggregation, they used the extended Mallows model to estimate the quality of each ranker's output by comparing it to a "consensus ranking". Although Klementiev et al. developed a method for unsupervised rank aggregation, their method does not address set-based retrieval, which would require further tuning a threshold to cut off the merged rank list. Other unsupervised rank aggregation methods, such as Borda counts [2], reciprocal rank fusion [3], or CombMNZ [18], all require threshold tuning when sets are the goal.

Data Programming [17] introduces an alternative E-M framework for generating a large pseudo-gold collection by combining many simple rules constructed by experts. Its E-M framework estimates the goodness of each rule by considering credit assignment and evaluation jointly, though the focus is on constructing a labelled collection to train a representation learning model. In this paper, we adapt the model presented in the Data Programming work to a set-based retrieval setting. We show that the model naturally fits the problem of set-based retrieval and allows us to combine diverse rankers.

As our interest in set-based retrieval stems from reducing the load on computationally intensive downstream applications such as QA, missing a relevant document has a high cost. Two recall-oriented metrics are thus used: F_3, and *Actual Query Weighted Value* (AQWV) [13]. F_3 is the well known F-measure with a heavier weight placed on recall. AQWV is a measure that combines the recall, $P_{q,\text{recall}}$, and the probability of a false alarm, $P_{q,\text{false\_alarm}}$:

$$\text{AQWV} = Avg_{q \in Q_{rel}} P_{q,\text{recall}} - \zeta \cdot Avg_{q \in Q} P_{q,\text{false\_alarm}} \tag{1}$$

$Q_{rel} \subset Q$ is the set of queries that has any relevant document. Since we usually have many more irrelevant documents than relevant documents, $P_{q,\text{false\_alarm}}$ is usually quite small compared to $P_{q,\text{recall}}$. Thus, $\zeta \propto \frac{N_{\text{total}}}{N_{\text{relevant}}}$ is used to control the balance between $P_{q,\text{recall}}$ and $P_{q,\text{false\_alarm}}$.[1]

Keyword Specific Thresholding (KST) [9] is a set selection and score normalization method originally developed for the Spoken Term Detection task on a measure with a similar structure to AQWV [6]. KST is designed to find an optimal threshold for each query when performing set-based retrieval. By assuming that the score is the probability that the retrieval is correct, KST calculates a threshold for each query by balancing the risk of miss and false alarm using Bayes decision theory. For each query q, a threshold ρ_q is calculated as:

$$\rho_q = \frac{\zeta N_{q,relevant}}{\|D\| + (\zeta - 1)N_{q,relevant}} \tag{2}$$

However, as $N_{q,relevant}$ is unknown at test time, it is estimated by summing over all the scores of documents retrieved by a query, $N_{q,relevant} = \delta \sum_{d=1}^{D} s_{q,d}^{\gamma}$, where δ and γ are tunable parameters. We use $\delta = 1.5$ and $\gamma = 1$ as suggested by Wang and Metze [20].

3   System Combination Model

The proposed system combination model consists of two components: a method of set selection for the underlying rankers based on KST, and an E-M algorithm for combination. We are given a document collection, D, a set of queries, Q, and a set of rankers to combine, M. We then let the raw score assigned by ranker $m \in M$ to the pair (query $q \in Q$, document $d \in D$) be $s_{m,q,d}$. We use s_m as a shorthand for $s_{m,q,d}$ if the query and document can be inferred from context.

Set Selection. The threshold ρ_q calculated from KST (see Eq. 2) is used to partition the documents into three sets:

$$s'_{m,q,d} = \begin{cases} 1 & \text{if } s_{m,q,d} > \rho_q \\ -1 & \text{if } s_{m,q,d} \text{ not available (i.e., d is not retrieved)} \\ 0 & \text{otherwise} \end{cases} \tag{3}$$

---

[1] For the MATERIAL Somali and Swahili collections, $\zeta = 40$. For the CLEF French collection, $\zeta = 240$ to account for the fact that $\frac{N_{\text{total}}}{N_{\text{relevant}}}$ for CLEF French is 6 times more than that of MATERIAL Somali or Swahili. See Table 1.

where $s'_{m,q,d}$ is the normalized score. As a ranker might not fully assign scores to all documents, -1 is assigned to any document that is missing a score, whereas $s'_{m,q,d} = 0$ represents that ranker m retrieved the document, but is not confident about the results.

Table 1. Counts of queries, documents, and positive relevance judgments.

	MATERIAL				CLEF	
	Swahili		Somali		French	
	Dev	Eval	Dev	Eval	Dev	Eval
Query #	300	1,000	300	1,000	194	141
Doc #	666	14,745	695	15,377	87,191	90,261
Relevance #	434	20,198	540	17,247	3,413	3,185

Expectation-Maximization. Suppose a "goodness" measure for each ranker is provided a priori, then we would know something about how to combine results from the rankers. Conversely, if we use the system combination results as pseudo-gold labels to evaluate the rankers we wish to combine, we can estimate the "goodness" of each ranker, which we can further use to combine the rankers again. This formulation can be captured by E-M [5]. In this paper, we use Data Programming [17] to estimate two "goodness" measures: accuracy, α_m, and coverage, β_m. Coverage is the probability that a ranker will assign a **confident** label (i.e. $s'_m \in \{1, -1\}$). Accuracy is the probability that a ranker is **correct** given that it is **confident**. We can derive the following probability distribution:

$$\mu_{\alpha,\beta}(S', y) = \tfrac{1}{2} \prod_{m=1}^{M} \left(\alpha_m \beta_m \mathbb{I}_{[s'_m = y]} + (1 - \alpha_m)\beta_m \mathbb{I}_{[s'_m \neq y]} + (1 - \beta_m)\mathbb{I}_{[s'_m = 0]} \right) \quad (4)$$

where $S' = \left\{ s'_1, s'_2, \cdots, s'_{\|M\|} \right\}$ represents a collection of the rankers' normalized scores across a single document and query pair, y is the latent relevance of said document and query pair, and $\alpha = \{\alpha_1, \cdots, \alpha_{\|M\|}\}, \beta = \{\beta_1, \cdots, \beta_{\|M\|}\}$ are the collections of parameters from each ranker.

We wish to find $\hat{\alpha}$ and $\hat{\beta}$ such that they maximize:

$$\hat{\alpha}, \hat{\beta} = \arg\max_{\alpha,\beta} \sum_{d=i}^{D} \log \left(\sum_{y=\{-1,1\}} \mu_{\alpha,\beta}(S', y) \right) \quad (5)$$

Note that the latent relevance, y, is marginalized in the above equation, so both the E and M steps can be combined into Eq. 5. Also note that the above maximization sums over all the log probabilities of the documents over a single query, and thus our E-M combination is a per-query combination technique.

Finally, to obtain the probability of retrieval for each query/document pair, we can calculate:

$$p\left(y=1|\alpha,\beta,S'\right) = \frac{\mu_{\alpha,\beta}\left(S',y=1\right)}{\sum_{y'=\{-1,1\}}\mu_{\alpha,\beta}\left(S',y'\right)}. \tag{6}$$

If $p\left(y=1|\alpha,\beta,S'\right) > 0.5$, a (query, doc) pair is considered relevant.

4 Experimental Setup

We report results on the IARPA MATERIAL Swahili and Somali collections and the CLEF French collection [15], which are Cross-Language Information Retrieval (CLIR) collections. All three collections contain relevance judgments for English queries and documents in different languages, see Table 1. Each collection consists of two disjoint sets of sub-collections: a development collection and an evaluation collection.[2]

We choose four underlying CLIR rankers based on diversity: three Document Translation methods done with machine translation (two Neural MT [7,14], one Statistical MT [11]) and one Query Translation [4] method.

Baselines. We compare our results against three rank-based system combination methods: (1) RR sums the reciprocal rank (RR) of the documents across all rankers to re-rank the documents [3], (2) BORDA sums the $N-Rank$ of the document, where N is the maximum rank across rankers [2], and (3) COMBMNZ [18]. For CombNMZ, a standard score normalization technique is used before applying combination [12]: $CombMNZ_{d,q} = t \cdot \sum_{m=1}^{M} \frac{s_m - \min s_m}{\max s_m - \min s_m}$, where t is the number of times $s_{m,d,q}$ has a value across the rankers.

Scaled and Oracle: Note that although the baselines can generate a merged ranked list without supervision, they still require a set selection process that involves tuning on the collection, as our goal is set-based retrieval. We report two set selection approaches: (1) SCALED: tune rank cutoffs for each of the combination methods on the development collection, and project the cutoffs to the evaluation collection by multiplying by $\frac{\|D_{\text{EVAL}}\|}{\|D_{\text{DEV}}\|}$. (2) ORACLE: to remove the confounding error of selecting a cutoff and effectiveness of system combination, we also report results at the *oracle* rank cutoff tuned on the *evaluation* collections. In all cases, the same learned rank cutoff is applied for every query.

Expectation-Maximization. EM - as described in Sect. 3. Each ranker to be combined is first normalized by KST using Eq. 3 with the default parameters. Then the E-M combination is applied to combine the rankers.

---

[2] For MATERIAL Swahili and Somali, development and evaluation collections are provided by IARPA. For CLEF French, we selected query sets 2000–2003 with document sets ATS 94, Le Monde 94 as the development collection, and query sets 2004–2006 with document sets ATS 95, Le Monde 95 as the evaluation collection.

5   Results and Discussion

Table 2 shows the results of the three evaluation collections. Overall, EM performs well, achieving the best scores on Somali and French by either set-based measure. On Swahili, EM again achieves the highest F_3, and its AQWV is exceeded only by our ORACLE baseline. Notably, our EM method on Somali outperforms our ORACLE baselines with rank cutoffs unfairly (against ourselves) optimized on the *evaluation* collection. This is possible in part due to a score cutoff technique like KST calculating different thresholds for each query, whereas a tied rank cutoff is used in the ORACLE baselines. We also note that there are substantial differences between the performance of the SCALED and ORACLE baselines on Swahili and Somali; that likely results from scaling an integer cutoff on the small development set by a large factor ($\approx$ 22.13 in each case, see Table 1). More generally, this suggests that tuning on small development collections may be useful, but sometimes far from optimal. When the development and evaluation collections have similar size, as in French, the difference is not as evident. On the other hand, our EM method, without using training data, demonstrates robustness and competitiveness across different collections.

Table 2. Results on evaluation collections.

		Somali		Swahili		French	
		F_3	AQWV	F_3	AQWV	F_3	AQWV
	EM	**18.47**	**19.00**	**28.09**	29.54	**39.30**	**47.66**
Scaled	COMBMNZ	14.62	15.93	22.92	27.55	35.22	44.29
	RR	14.75	14.59	24.31	27.39	36.48	46.73
	BORDA	13.82	13.60	20.59	26.05	34.84	43.05
Oracle	COMBMNZ	17.98	16.73	26.28	30.04	35.58	45.09
	RR	17.85	16.18	26.44	**30.89**	36.92	**47.62**
	BORDA	17.22	13.94	24.44	26.68	35.03	43.51

6   Conclusion

We have presented an unsupervised set-generating system combination technique. Drawing inspiration from the evaluation literature, we reason that a duality exists between evaluation and system combination. We show that E-M combination, by jointly solving the problems of credit assignment and threshold selection, can be both effective and robust in a low resource setting where relevance judgments that can be used for development are limited or nonexistent. Finally, using two set-based retrieval measures, we compare with both scaled and oracle versions of the baselines and show that E-M combination achieves competitive results.

References

1. Belkin, N., et al.: Combining the evidence of multiple query representations for information retrieval. IP&M **31**(3), 431–448 (1995)
2. de Borda, J.C.: Mémoire sur les élections au scrutin (1781)
3. Cormack, G., et al.: Reciprocal rank fusion outperforms condorcet and individual rank learning methods. In: SIGIR, vol. 9, pp. 758–759 (2009)
4. Darwish, K., Oard, D.: Probabilistic structured query methods. In: SIGIR (2003)
5. Dempster, A., et al.: Maximum likelihood from incomplete data via the EM algorithm. J. Roy. Stat. Soc. **39**(1), 1–22 (1977)
6. Fiscus, J.G., Ajot, J., Garofolo, J.S., Doddingtion, G.: Results of the 2006 spoken term detection evaluation. In: SIGIR, vol. 7, pp. 51–57 (2007)
7. Haddow, B., et al.: The University of Edinburgh's submissions to the WMT18 news translation task. In: WMT, Belgium, Brussels, pp. 403–413, October 2018
8. Harman, D.: Overview of the third text retrieval conference. In: TREC (1995)
9. Karakos, D., et al.: Score normalization and system combination for improved keyword spotting. In: ASRU, pp. 210–215 (2013)
10. Klementiev, A., Roth, D., Small, K.: Unsupervised rank aggregation with distance-based models. In: ICML, pp. 472–479 (2008)
11. Koehn, P., et al.: Moses: open source toolkit for statistical machine translation. In: ACL, pp. 177–180 (2007)
12. Lee, J., et al.: Analyses of multiple evidence combination. In: SIGIR (1997)
13. NIST: The Official Original Derivation of AQWV (2017). https://www.nist.gov/sites/default/files/documents/2017/10/26/aqwv_derivation.pdf
14. Niu, X., et al.: Bi-directional differentiable input reconstruction for low-resource neural machine translation. CoRR abs/1811.01116 (2018)
15. Di Nunzio, G.M., Ferro, N., Mandl, T., Peters, C.: CLEF 2006: ad hoc track overview. In: Peters, C., et al. (eds.) CLEF 2006. LNCS, vol. 4730, pp. 21–34. Springer, Heidelberg (2007). https://doi.org/10.1007/978-3-540-74999-8_3
16. Nuray, R., Can, F.: Automatic ranking of information retrieval systems using data fusion. IP&M **42**(3), 595–614 (2006)
17. Ratner, A., et al.: Data programming: creating large training sets, quickly. In: NIPS, pp. 3567–3575 (2016)
18. Shaw, J., Fox, E.: Combination of multiple searches. In: TREC (1994)
19. Soboroff, I., et al.: Ranking retrieval systems without relevance judgments. In: SIGIR, pp. 66–73 (2001)
20. Wang, Y., Metze, F.: An in-depth comparison of keyword specific thresholding and sum-to-one score normalization. In: ISCA (2014)

Best of CLEF 2018 Labs

An Ensemble Approach to Cross-Domain Authorship Attribution

José Eleandro Custódio and Ivandré Paraboni[(✉)]

School of Arts, Sciences and Humanities (EACH), University of São Paulo (USP),
São Paulo, Brazil
{eleandro,ivandre}@usp.br

Abstract. This paper presents an ensemble approach to cross-domain authorship attribution that combines predictions made by three independent classifiers, namely, standard character n-grams, character n-grams with non-diacritic distortion and word n-grams. Our proposal relies on variable-length n-gram models and multinomial logistic regression to select the prediction of highest probability among the three models as the output for the task. The present approach is compared against a number of baseline systems, and we report results based on both the PAN-CLEF 2018 test data, and on a new corpus of song lyrics in English and Portuguese.

1 Introduction

Authorship attribution (AA) is the computational task of determining the author of a given document from a number of possible candidates [5]. Systems of this kind have a wide range of possible applications, from on-line fraud detection to plagiarism and/or copyright protection. AA is presently a well-established research field, and a recurrent topic in the PAN-CLEF shared task series [14,16].

At PAN-CLEF 2018, a cross-domain authorship attribution task applied to fan fiction text has been proposed. In this task, texts written by the same authors in multiple domains were put together, creating a cross-domain setting. The task consists of identifying the author of a given document based on text of a different domain.

The present work describes an ensemble approach to cross-domain authorship attribution that combines predictions made by three independent classifiers, namely, standard character n-grams, character n-grams with non-diacritic distortion and word n-grams. Our proposal relies on variable-length n-gram models and multinomial logistic regression to select the prediction of highest probability among the three models as the output for the task. This approach, which obtained the overall best results at the PAN-CLEF 2018 AA shared task [8], is presently compared against a number of baseline systems by reporting results based on both the PAN-CLEF 2018 test data, and on a new corpus of song lyrics in English and Portuguese.

© Springer Nature Switzerland AG 2019
F. Crestani et al. (Eds.): CLEF 2019, LNCS 11696, pp. 201–212, 2019.
https://doi.org/10.1007/978-3-030-28577-7_17

The rest of this paper is structured as follows. Section 2 briefly reviews a number of AA studies related to our current work. Section 3 describes our main AA approach. Section 4 describes an evaluation experiment based on the PAN-CLEF 2018 AA test data. Section 5 describes additional evaluation work using test data in the song lyrics domain. Finally, Sect. 6 discusses these results and suggests future work.

2   Related Work

The present work shares similarities with a number of AA studies. Some of these are briefly discussed below.

First, we notice that writing styles may change across topics and domains and, as a result, may cause the AA model to overfit. To alleviate this, a number of studies have resorted to some form of text distortion. In [19], for instance, frequent words are kept as in the original input text, and rare words are replaced by sequences of asterisks. The work makes use of SVM and compression methods, and concludes that function words were unsuitable to distortion, among other findings.

Another example of text distortion use in AA is illustrated by the work in [12]. In this case, text distortion is applied to digits, named entities and highly frequent words, and using SVM and multinomial Naive Bayes as learning methods.

Multiple knowledge sources may also help the AA task. The work in [1], for instance, makes use of Doc2vec embeddings [10] based on variable-length n-grams of words, characters and POS, which are taken as the input to a softmax logistic regression model.

Convolution Neural Networks (CNNs) are known for their ability to extract information from multiple levels of representation. Based on this observation, the work in [18] makes use of CNN models to perform AA on social media texts. A CNN is fed with embeddings of character n-grams of size 1 and 2, and pre-trained word embeddings. Results are compared with the use of character n-grams of size ranging from 2 to 4 using logistic regression and Long Short-Term Memory networks (LSTMs) with a character bigram model.

Finally, the work in [17] investigates the role of affixes in the AA task by using char n-gram models for the English language. Similarly, the work in [11] addresses the use of char n-grams models for the Portuguese language, and discusses the role of affix information in the AA task. This is in principle relevant to our current work since the Portuguese language shares a great deal of its structure with Spanish and Italian, which are two of the target languages for our experiment based on the PAN-CLEF 2018 AA data. In addition to that, Portuguese will be one of the target languages in our second experiment, focused on song lyrics AA.

3 An Ensemble Approach to Authorship Attribution

Central to our approach is the idea that the AA task may rely on the combination of different knowledge sources such as lexical preferences, morphological inflection, upper-case usage, and text structure, and that different kinds of knowledge may be obtained either from character-based or word-based text models. These issues are further discussed as follows.

Word or content-based models may encode semantic information [4], and may also indicate word usage preferences. In particular, function words [7] were found to be useful for AA due to their relation with subconscious language usage. Thus, in our current work we will consider the use of a standard word-based model for AA, hereby called *Std.wordN*.

Word models will however ignore multiword expressions as in, e.g., 'above all', 'on the other hand' etc., and will discard punctuation and spaces, all of which known to be valuable knowledge sources for AA. Character-based models, by contrast, are known for their ability to capture time and gender inflection as well as punctuation and spacing patterns, among others [15]. Moreover, features of this kind are usually language-independent, and may provide a kind of representation that is arguably more dense than those provided by word models alone [4]. Thus, in the present work we will also consider the use of a standard character-based model for AA, hereby called *Std.charN*.

Finally, we notice that standard word and character models will usually preprocess input texts by removing rare symbols such as diacritics, punctuation marks, consecutive spaces and others. In the present work, however, we will attempt the opposite as well, that is, we will consider a third model that focuses on symbols rather than letters. More specifically, we will consider a model in which all letters are replaced by '*'. This strategy, hereby called *Dist.charN*, may be seen as a form of text distortion [19], and it is motivated by the observation that, in languages that make use of diacritics, some authors may consistently use the correct spelling (as in 'é', which is Portuguese for 'is'), whereas others tend to ignore the need for diacritics by producing the incorrect spelling (e.g., 'e') for the same purpose. An example of text representation obtained by this strategy is illustrated in Fig. 1.

Original text	Transformed text
-¿Y cómo sabes que no lo	-¿* *ó** ***** *** ** **
ama? -Inglaterra se preguntó	***? -********** ** *******ó
a su vez si habría un muñeco	* ** *** ** ****í* ** **ñ***
del esposo también.	*** ****** *****é*.

Fig. 1. Example of text distortion.

Each of the three individual models - *Std.wordN*, *Std.charN* and *Dist.charN* - consists of variable-length n-grams, and makes use of multinomial logistic regression (or softmax classifier.) The use of variable-length n-grams is intended to capture different types of word and character sequences.

The outputs of the three models are probability vectors, which are presently concatenated and taken as learning features to an ensemble model - hereby called EACH-USP Ensemble - built using multinomial logistic regression. This architecture is illustrated in Fig. 2.

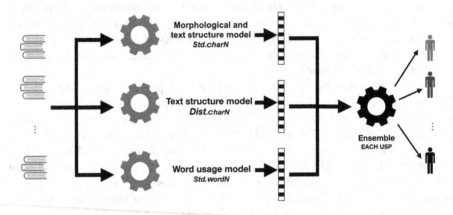

Fig. 2. Ensemble cross-domain AA architecture from [2].

4   Experiment 1: Authorship Attribution at PAN-CLEF 2018

The work in [2] reports results of the EACH-USP Ensemble method as submitted to the PAN-CLEF 2018 AA shared task based on development data. In what follows, we present a more comprehensive analysis of this method based on the PAN-CLEF 2018 evaluation corpus[1] instead.

4.1   Data

The PAN-CLEF 2018 evaluation corpus consists of twenty problems in five languages (English - En, French - Fr, Italian - It, Polish - Pl and Spanish - Sp) with 5, 10, 15 and 20 candidate authors per problem. Documents have, on average, 800 words each. Table 1 presents the corpus descriptive statistics.

We notice that Polish words are, on average, longer than in other languages, and that Polish texts use more non-alphanumeric characters, and fewer space and new line characters. English texts, by contrast, use less non-alphanumeric and more space characters than the other languages.

---

[1] https://pan.webis.de/clef18/pan18-web/author-identification.html.

Table 1. PAN-CLEF 2018 evaluation corpus statistics

Language	Words	Chars	Chars/Word	% symbols	% spaces
En	823	4,504	5.5	3.6	18.7
Fr	785	4,386	5.6	7.0	18.1
It	804	4,808	6.0	4.6	17.3
Pl	779	5,198	6.7	11.0	16.5
Sp	825	4,766	5.8	5.6	18.3

4.2 Evaluation

The models introduced in the previous section were built using scikit-learn [13] and had their parameters set by using the PAN-CLEF development dataset as follows. Features were scaled using MaxAbsScaler, and dimensionality was reduced using a standard PCA implementation. PCA also helps remove correlated features, which is useful in the present case since our models make use of variable length feature concatenation. The resulting feature sets were submitted to multinomial logistic regression by considering a range of values, as summarized in Table 2.

Table 2. Pipeline - model parameters

Module	Parameters	Possible values
Feature extraction	N-gram range	Start = (1 to 3) - End = (1 to 5) where End >= Start
	Min document frequency	[5, 0.01, 0.05, 0.1]
	Max document frequency	[0.25, 0.50, 0.90, 1.0]
	TF	Normal, sublinear, none
	IDF	Normal, smoothed, none
	Document normalisation	L1, L2
Transformation	Scaling	MaxAbsScaler
	PCA percentage of explained variance	[0.10, 0.25, 0.50, 0.75, 0.90, 0.99]
Classifier	Logistic regression	Multinomial-Softmax

Optimal values for the regression task were determined by making use of grid search and 5-fold cross validation using an ensemble method. The optimal values that were selected for training our actual models are illustrated in Table 3, in which Start/End values denote the range of subsequences that were concatenated, such that Star values are not greater than End values. For instance, $Start = 2$ and $End = 5$ represent the concatenation of subsequences $[(2,2),(2,3),\cdots,(4,3),(4,5)]$. The PCA value of 0.99 is to be interpreted as keeping the principal components that correspond to the reported percentage of explained variance.

Table 3. PAN2018 evaluation corpus - pipeline optimal values

Module	Parameters	Optimal values
Feature extraction	N-gram range	Std.charN $=$ (2,4)
		Dist.charN $=$ (2,5)
		Std.wordN $=$ (1,2)
	Min corpus frequency	5
	Max corpus frequency	1.0
	TF	sublinear
	IDF	smoothed
	Document normalisation	Std.charN $=$ L1
		Dist.charN $=$ L2
		Std.wordN $=$ L1
Transformation	PCA	0.99

In the choice of parameter values, we initially attempted to optimize the models for each language, but the results were generally very close to each other. In particular, due to the small size of the training data, Min and Max corpus frequency estimates were found to be inconclusive, and were kept as the most common values observed across all problems, datasets and languages for simplicity.

For evaluation purposes, the SVM baseline system provided by the PAN-CLEF 2018 AA shared task [8] was optimized by making use of 4-gram counts, a minimum document frequency of 5, and by using One-vs-Rest as the SVM multi-class strategy. Other parameters remained as in the original implementation, which makes use of a linear kernel.

4.3 Results

Table 4 presents macro F1 results obtained by the PAN-CLEF 2018 SVM baseline system, by our three individual classifiers, their pairwise combinations, and the EACH-USP Ensemble model based on the PAN-CLEF 2018 evaluation data. Best results are highlighted.

From these results, a number of observations are warranted. First, we notice that our ensemble model consistently outperformed the alternatives by using soft voting. Second, we notice that $Std.charN$ generally obtained the best results among the three individual classifiers, being worse than $Std.charN$ for English and French, and better for Polish and Spanish.

Table 5 shows the five most relevant features for the PAN-CLEF 2018 AA problem identified as Problem00004, comprising texts written in the English language by five authors each. In this representation, blank spaces were encoded as underscore symbols, and relevance is represented by the absolute value of the weights of multinomial logistic regression. These values were estimated by scaling the features to a mean value equal to 0, and to a standard deviation value equal to 1.

Table 4. Macro F1 results for the PAN-CLEF 2018 AA evaluation corpus (C = Std.charN, W = Std.wordN, and O = Dist.charN.) Best results are highlighted.

Problem info			Baseline	Channels			Ensembles			
#	Language	Authors	SVM	C	W	O	C+W	C+O	W+O	EACH-USP
01	En	20	0.61	**0.67**	0.47	0.58	0.64	0.65	0.58	0.65
02	En	15	0.61	0.69	0.53	0.63	0.63	0.64	0.61	**0.71**
03	En	10	0.68	0.72	0.60	0.71	0.72	0.76	0.71	**0.87**
04	En	5	0.79	0.88	0.78	0.68	0.83	0.76	0.73	**0.88**
05	Fr	20	0.56	0.56	0.42	0.48	0.55	0.54	0.52	**0.58**
06	Fr	15	0.55	0.54	0.48	0.51	0.54	0.51	0.54	**0.59**
07	Fr	10	0.53	0.63	0.43	0.61	0.61	0.68	**0.70**	0.68
08	Fr	5	**0.76**	0.71	0.65	0.56	0.73	0.58	0.58	0.66
09	It	20	0.62	0.60	0.48	0.66	0.64	0.68	0.66	**0.68**
10	It	15	0.56	0.63	0.46	0.69	0.62	0.67	0.69	**0.70**
11	It	10	0.76	0.77	0.51	0.78	0.75	0.78	0.78	**0.85**
12	It	5	**0.50**	0.45	0.39	0.44	0.42	0.48	0.46	0.49
13	Pl	20	0.47	0.51	0.33	0.54	0.47	0.60	0.59	**0.60**
14	Pl	15	0.53	0.55	0.30	0.49	0.43	0.51	0.53	**0.53**
15	Pl	10	0.40	0.39	0.44	0.47	0.40	0.47	0.47	**0.47**
16	Pl	5	0.49	0.40	0.42	0.50	0.46	**0.50**	0.48	0.47
17	Sp	20	0.58	0.63	0.48	0.68	0.63	0.75	0.74	**0.77**
18	Sp	15	0.65	0.67	0.60	0.79	0.70	0.84	0.83	**0.89**
19	Sp	10	0.74	0.72	0.66	0.80	0.72	0.85	0.91	**0.93**
20	Sp	5	0.73	0.73	0.63	**0.90**	0.73	0.88	0.91	0.88
Overall			0.61	0.62	0.50	0.62	0.61	0.66	0.65	**0.69**

Being a language-independent approach, information regarding function words was not explicitly taken into account, although this could have been helpful since function words usually play a prominent role in AA. Function words (and some collocations as well) were nevertheless captured by the *Std.wordN* model, and all models turned out to make explicit (at least to some extent) a number of individual preferences regarding word usage, punctuation and spacing. In particular, we notice that *Dist.charN* provided some evidence of the role of punctuation marks, spacing and hyphenation.

The present ensemble method was the overall best-performing participant system at the PAN-CLEF 2018 AA shared task [8]. For the original results obtained from the development corpus, we refer to [2].

Table 5. Most relevant features per candidate and model.

Candidate	001	002	003	004	005
Models					
Std.charN	n_but	_Jen	_"An	roper	ts_t
	der_h	Mish	don'	ele	eyes,
	ropp	ha'	Pe	_upon	ng_ov
	t_fel	t_M	s."	r_wit	ill_d
	!_	n's	"Th	ly_to	ble.
Dist.charN	.s‖*	"s***	**...	_***	"***
	*|	"***,	" **	" *	***?
	? **	*_"	"	*'**	**_"
	,*	***'	...	!"	?"
	! ***	'**	...?	*!"	****'
Std.wordN	sweet	he_needed	perhaps	upon	beneath_the
	me_and	chin	he_looked	full	back_of
	hips	with_his	and_you	which	darkness
	under	apart	leaned	of_that	sharp
	it_felt	needed	here	the_other	power
	up_against	to_make	something	stepped	isn

5   Experiment 2: Authorship Attribution of Song Lyrics

In addition to the evaluation work carried out in the context of the PAN-CLEF 2018 AA shared task, the proposed EACH-USP ensemble approach and its individual components were evaluated against a second dataset in the song lyrics domain. Our choice for this particular domain was motivated by the observation that song lyrics AA may be potentially more challenging than literary AA since, for instance, punctuation and spacing information are in principle not relevant.

5.1   Data

Song lyrics AA has been investigated in the case of Turkish [9] and Bengali [6] languages. For the present work we collected a corpus of song lyrics in English and Portuguese - hereby called the Lyrics corpus - in a cross-domain setting conveying 49 music genres, including country music, pop, rock, jazz, bossa nova and many others. The dataset was taken from a crowd-sourced repository[2] where users may upload lyrics written by their favourite artists or by themselves. In what follows we briefly describe how the corpus was built. Further details, and the possible corpus release, will be discussed elsewhere.

From an initial set of 150k songs performed by the 100 most played singers in the year 2018, we removed all songs without a single author identification, and also those whose length was below a 750-character minimum. Since the

---

[2] https://www.letras.mus.br/.

language in which each song was written was not available, a simple procedure for language detection was performed. This consisted in computing language-specific vocabularies from a 50-language stopwords corpus[3], and assigning each song lyrics to the closest language based on cosine similarity.

Duplicates (e.g., a short and an extended version of the same song) were removed by identifying document pairs with cosine similarity equal or greater than 0.6. This procedure removed less than 1% of the documents in the corpus.

From the selected corpus, we built a set of ten AA problems by following the same general structure of the PAN-CLEF AA tasks. As a means to create a cross-domain setting, only authors who wrote songs in three or more music genres were considered, and we ensured that every author-genre pair was present in both training and test datasets. Each problem combines a target language (English or Portuguese) and a number of authors (from 5 to 25 at 5 intervals) as summarized in Table 6.

Table 6. Lyrics corpus descriptive statistics (Pt = Portuguese En = English.)

#	Language	Authors	Genres	Words	Chars	Chars/Word	% Symbols	% Spaces
01	Pt	5	9	205	1,067	5.2	5.0	19.4
02	Pt	10	12	212	1,086	5.1	5.2	20.0
03	Pt	15	13	207	1,050	5.1	5.0	19.8
04	Pt	20	13	218	1,126	5.8	5.1	19.6
05	Pt	25	14	227	1,177	5.2	5.1	19.8
06	En	5	8	274	1,289	4.7	3.0	20.6
07	En	10	11	303	1,437	4.78	3.1	20.2
08	En	15	20	309	1,458	4.7	3.4	20.3
09	En	20	21	305	1,434	4.7	3.3	20.4
10	En	25	21	283	1,342	4.8	3.1	20.3

5.2 Evaluation

Similarly to the previous Experiment 1, evaluation was carried out by comparing EACH-USP against the PAN-CLEF 2018 SVM baseline, the individual channels *Std.charN*, *Std.wordN* and *Dist.charN*, and their pairwise combinations. Macro F1 scores were computed by making use of the PAN-CLEF 2018 evaluation script.

Although each problem was optimized individually, the best values obtained through cross validation largely intersected, with few clear-cut differences. For that reason, the final parameter values were selected due to their higher frequency, or simply for having a wider scope (e.g., the n-gram range (2,5) also includes (2,4) etc.) These values are summarized in Table 7.

---

[3] https://github.com/6/stopwords-json.

Table 7. Lyrics corpus - pipeline parameters optimal values

Module	Parameters	Optimal values
Feature extraction	N-gram range	Std.charN = (2,4)
		Dist.charN = (2,5)
		Std.wordN = (1,1)
	Min corpus frequency	5
	Max corpus frequency	1.0
	TF	Sublinear
	IDF	Smoothed
	Document normalisation	L2
Transformation	PCA	0.99

5.3 Results

Table 8 presents macro F1 results obtained by the EACH-USP ensemble method and the baseline alternatives. Best results are highlighted.

Table 8. Macro F1 results for the Lyrics corpus - C (Std.charN), W (Std.wordN), O (Dist.charN). Best results are highlighted.

#	Baseline	Channels			Ensembles			
	SVM	C	W	O	C+W	C+O	W+O	EACH-USP
01	0.55	0.72	0.67	0.39	**0.78**	0.53	0.46	0.59
02	0.48	**0.56**	0.46	0.32	0.55	0.46	0.41	0.52
03	0.37	**0.42**	0.33	0.16	0.41	0.30	0.26	0.35
04	0.23	**0.39**	0.31	0.19	0.38	0.31	0.25	0.33
05	0.27	**0.39**	0.29	0.17	0.38	0.27	0.21	0.31
06	0.56	**0.69**	0.55	0.42	0.65	0.63	0.56	0.63
07	0.47	**0.68**	0.57	0.39	0.65	0.60	0.55	0.64
08	0.41	**0.52**	**0.52**	0.29	0.49	0.49	0.48	**0.52**
09	0.45	0.50	0.48	0.27	**0.52**	0.46	0.41	0.51
10	0.32	0.41	0.36	0.22	0.41	0.39	0.32	**0.42**
Overall	0.41	**0.53**	0.45	0.28	0.52	0.45	0.39	0.48

As expected, results obtained by the EACH-USP ensemble approach for the Lyrics corpus are inferior to those obtained by the use of the character-based model *Std.charN* alone. This may be explained by the smaller size of the documents in this domain, and by the aforementioned observation that punctuation and spacing information do not play a significant role in song lyrics AA.

6   Final Remarks

This paper presented an ensemble approach to cross-domain authorship attribution that combines predictions made by a standard char n-gram model, a char n-gram model with non-diacritic distortion and a word n-gram model using variable-length n-gram models and multinomial logistic regression. Two evaluation experiments were carried out, namely, using the PAN-CLEF 2018 test dataset, and using a new corpus of song lyrics in English and Portuguese.

In the case of the PAN-CLEF 2018 domain, results were generally superior to those obtained by the baseline system introduced in the shared task. In addition to that, as reported in [8], the present results were on average superior to those obtained by the other participants in the shared task as well.

In the song lyrics domain, by contrast, results remained similar to those obtained by a standard character-based model. This outcome suggests that the ensemble approach is more suitable for AA tasks in which the use of special characters and spacing information are relevant, as in the case of literary domains, but less so for song lyrics AA.

As future work, we intend to investigate alternative text models and distortion methods for prefixes, suffixes and other text components. Among these, we intend to investigate the use of part-of-speech and word embedding models, and include a character ranking model as part of the present ensemble architecture. Some of these improvements are to appear in [3]. A public release of the Lyrics corpus for research purposes also remains to be finalized.

Acknowledgements. The second author received financial support from FAPESP grant nro. 2016/14223-0 and by the University of São Paulo. The authors also thank the PAN-CLEF AA shared task organisers, and the anonymous reviewers for their valuable input.

References

1. Adorno, H.G., Posadas-Durán, J.P., Sidorov, G., Pinto, D.: Document embeddings learned on various types of n-grams for cross-topic authorship attribution. Computing **100**, 741–756 (2018)
2. Custódio, J.E., Paraboni, I.: EACH-USP ensemble cross-domain authorship attribution: notebook for PAN at CLEF 2018. In: Cappellato, L., Ferro, N., Nie, J.Y., Soulier, L. (eds.) Working Notes Papers of the CLEF 2018 Evaluation Labs. CEUR Workshop Proceedings, CLEF and CEUR-WS.org, September 2018
3. Custódio, J.E., Paraboni, I.: Multi-channel open-set cross-domain authorship attribution. In: Working Notes Papers of the Conference and Labs of the Evaluation Forum (CLEF-2019), Lugano, Switzerland (2019, to appear)
4. Goldberg, Y.: Neural Network Methods in Natural Language Processing. Morgan & Claypool Publishers, San Rafael (2017)
5. Gollub, T., et al.: Recent trends in digital text forensics and its evaluation. In: Forner, P., Müller, H., Paredes, R., Rosso, P., Stein, B. (eds.) CLEF 2013. LNCS, vol. 8138, pp. 282–302. Springer, Heidelberg (2013). https://doi.org/10.1007/978-3-642-40802-1_28

6. Hossain, R., Al Marouf, A.: BanglaMusicStylo: a stylometric dataset of Bangla music lyrics. In: 2018 International Conference on Bangla Speech and Language Processing (ICBSLP), pp. 1–5, September 2018

7. Kestemont, M.: Function words in authorship attribution from black magic to theory? In: 3rd Workshop on Computational Linguistics for Literature (CLFL 2014), pp. 59–66 (2014)

8. Kestemont, M., et al.: Overview of the author identification task at PAN-2018: cross-domain authorship attribution and style change detection. In: Cappellato, L., Ferro, N., Nie, J.Y., Soulier, L. (eds.) Working Notes Papers of the CLEF 2018 Evaluation Labs. CEUR Workshop Proceedings, CLEF and CEUR-WS.org, September 2018

9. Kırmacı, B., Oğul, H.: Evaluating text features for lyrics-based songwriter prediction. In: 2015 IEEE 19th International Conference on Intelligent Engineering Systems (INES), pp. 405–409, September 2015

10. Le, Q., Mikolov, T.: Distributed representations of sentences and documents. In: Proceedings of Machine Learning Research, vol. 32, no. 2, pp. 1188–1196. PMLR, Beijing (2014)

11. Markov, I., Baptista, J., Lagunas, O.P.: Authorship attribution in portuguese using character N-grams. Acta Polytechnica Hungarica **14**(3), 59–78 (2017)

12. Markov, I., Stamatatos, E., Sidorov, G.: Improving cross-topic authorship attribution: the role of pre-processing. In: Gelbukh, A. (ed.) CICLing 2017. LNCS, vol. 10762, pp. 289–302. Springer, Cham (2018). https://doi.org/10.1007/978-3-319-77116-8_21

13. Pedregosa, F., et al.: Scikit-learn: machine learning in python. J. Mach. Learn. Res. **12**, 2825–2830 (2011)

14. Potthast, M., Rangel, F., Tschuggnall, M., Stamatatos, E., Rosso, P., Stein, B.: Overview of PAN'17. In: Jones, G.J.F., et al. (eds.) CLEF 2017. LNCS, vol. 10456, pp. 275–290. Springer, Cham (2017). https://doi.org/10.1007/978-3-319-65813-1_25

15. Rocha, A., et al.: Authorship attribution for social media forensics. IEEE Trans. Inf. Forensics Secur. **12**(1), 5–33 (2017)

16. Rosso, P., Rangel, F., Potthast, M., Stamatatos, E., Tschuggnall, M., Stein, B.: Overview of PAN'16. In: Fuhr, N., et al. (eds.) CLEF 2016. LNCS, vol. 9822, pp. 332–350. Springer, Cham (2016). https://doi.org/10.1007/978-3-319-44564-9_28

17. Sapkota, U., Bethard, S., Montes-y-Gómez, M., Solorio, T.: Not all character n-grams are created equal: a study in authorship attribution. In: NAACL HLT 2015, The 2015 Conference of the North American Chapter of the Association for Computational Linguistics: Human Language Technologies, Denver, Colorado, USA, pp. 93–102 (2015)

18. Shrestha, P., Sierra, S., Gonzalez, F., Rosso, P., Montes-Y-Gomez, M., Solorio, T.: Convolutional neural networks for authorship attribution of short texts. In: Proceedings of the 15th Conference of the European Chapter of the Association for Computational Linguistics, vol. 2, pp. 669–674. Association for Computational Linguistics (ACL) (2017)

19. Stamatatos, E.: Authorship attribution using text distortion. In: Proceedings of the Conference of the European Chapter of the Association for Computational Linguistics (EACL-2017). Association for Computational Linguistics, Valencia (2017)

Evaluation of Deep Species Distribution Models Using Environment and Co-occurrences

Benjamin Deneu[1(✉)], Maximilien Servajean[2],
Christophe Botella[3], and Alexis Joly[1]

[1] Inria, LIRMM, Montpellier, France
{benjamin.deneu,alexis.joly}@inria.fr
[2] AMIS, Université Paul Valéry Montpellier LIRMM UMR 5506, CNRS,
University of Montpellier, Montpellier, France
maximilien.servajean@lirmm.fr
[3] INRA, Inria, AMAP, LIRMM, Montpellier, France
christophe.botella@inria.fr

Abstract. This paper presents an evaluation of several approaches of plants species distribution modeling based on spatial, environmental and co-occurrences data using machine learning methods. In particular, we re-evaluate the environmental convolutional neural network model that obtained the best performance of the GeoLifeCLEF 2018 challenge but on a revised dataset that fixes some of the issues of the previous one. We also go deeper in the analysis of co-occurrences information by evaluating a new model that jointly takes environmental variables and co-occurrences as inputs of an end-to-end network. Results show that the environmental models are the best performing methods and that there is a significant amount of complementary information between co-occurrences and environment. Indeed, the model learned on both inputs allows a significant performance gain compared to the environmental model alone.

1 Introduction

Automatically predicting the list of species that are the most likely to be observed at a given location is useful for many scenarios in biodiversity informatics. First of all, it could improve species identification processes and tools by reducing the list of candidate species that are observable at a given location (be they automated, semi-automated or based on classical field guides or flora). More generally, it could facilitate biodiversity inventories through the development of location-based recommendation services (typically on mobile phones) as well as the involvement of non-expert nature observers. Last but not least, it might serve educational purposes thanks to biodiversity discovery applications providing innovative features such as contextualized educational pathways.

This problem is known as Species Distribution Modeling (SDM) in ecology. SDM have become increasingly important in the last few decades for the study of

© Springer Nature Switzerland AG 2019
F. Crestani et al. (Eds.): CLEF 2019, LNCS 11696, pp. 213–225, 2019.
https://doi.org/10.1007/978-3-030-28577-7_18

biodiversity, macro ecology, community ecology and the ecology of conservation. An accurate knowledge of the spatial distribution of species is actually of crucial importance for many concrete scenarios including landscape management, preservation of rare and/or endangered species, surveillance of alien invasive species, measurement of human impact or climate change on species, etc. Concretely, the goal of SDM is to infer the spatial distribution of a given species, and they are often based on a set of geo-localized occurrences of that species (collected by naturalists, field ecologists, nature observers, citizen sciences project, etc.). However, it is usually not reliable to learn that distribution directly from the spatial positions of the input occurrences. The two major problems are the limited number of occurrences and the bias of the sampling effort compared to the real underlying distribution. In a real-world dataset, the raw spatial distribution of the occurrences is actually highly influenced by the accessibility of the sites and the preferences and habits of the observers. Another difficulty is that an occurrence means a punctual presence of the species, while no occurrences doesn't mean the species is absent, which makes us very uncertain about regions without observed specimens.

For all these reasons, SDM is usually achieved through *environmental niche modeling* approaches, *i.e.* by predicting the distribution in the geographic space on the basis of a representation in the environmental space [1,2,7–9,11,15]. This environmental space is in most cases represented by climate data (such as temperature, and precipitation), but also by other variables such as soil type, land cover, distance to water, etc. Then, the objective is to learn a function that takes the environmental feature vector of a given location as input and outputs an estimate of the abundance of the species. The main underlying hypothesis is that the abundance function is related to the *fundamental ecological niche* of the species. That means that in theory, a given species is likely to live in a privileged ecological niche, characterized by an hypervolume in the environmental space. However, this volume can have a very irregular shape and, in addition, many phenomena can actually affect the distribution of the species relative to its so called *abiotic* preferences. The real distribution of the species is called *realized ecological niche* it can differ from the *fundamental ecological niche* by environmental perturbations, geographical constraints, or interactions with other living organisms (including humans) that might have encourage specimens of that species to live in a different environment. As a consequence, the *realized ecological niche* of a species can be much more diverse and complex than its hypothetical fundamental niche.

Very recently, SDM based on deep neural networks have started to appear [4]. These first experiments showed that they can have a good predictive power, potentially better than the models used conventionally in ecology. Actually, deep neural networks are able to learn complex nonlinear transformations in a wide variety of domains. In addition, they make it possible to learn an area of environmental representation common to a large number of species, which stabilizes predictions from one species to another and improves them globally [16]. Finally, spatial patterns in environmental variables often contain useful information for species distribution but are generally not considered in conventional models. Conversely, convolutional neural networks effectively use this information and improve prediction performance.

In this paper, we report an evaluation study of four main kinds of plants SDM:

1. A convolutional neural network aimed at learning the ecological preferences of species thanks to environmental image patches provided as inputs (temperature, soil type, etc.).
2. Two purely spatial models, one based on a random forest fitted on the spatial coordinates of the occurrences of each species. The other named closest-locations classifier is close to a nearest neighbours classifier.
3. A species co-occurrence model aiming at predicting the likelihood of presence of a given species thanks to the knowledge of the presence of other species.
4. We finally introduce a new neural network that jointly learn on environment and co-occurrences and compare it to the two separated models to study the joint information between the environment and co-occurrences. And in parallel to it, a model consisting of a late merging of the outputs of the co-occurrences model and the environmental CNN.

This paper is an extended and revised version of the working note that we wrote beforehand in the context of our participation to the GeoLifeCLEF 2018 challenge [6]. It improves it two main ways. First we re-evaluate the environmental convolutional neural network models that obtained the best performance during the GeoLifeCLEF 2018 challenge but on a revised dataset that fixes some of the issues of the previous one (that were discovered after the end of the challenge). We also go deeper in the analysis of co-occurrences information by evaluating a new model that jointly takes environmental variables and co-occurrences as inputs of an end-to-end network. Section 2 gives an overview of the data and evaluation methodology. Sections 3 and 4 provide the detailed description of the evaluated models. Section 5 presents the results of the experiments and their analysis.

2   Data and Evaluation Methodology

A detailed description of the protocol used to build the GeoLifeCLEF2018 dataset is provided in [3,13]. In a nutshell, the dataset was built from occurrence data of the Global Biodiversity Information Facility (GBIF), the world's largest open data infrastructure in this domain, funded by governments. It is composed of $291,392$ occurrences of $N = 3,336$ plant species observed on the French territory between 1835 and 2017. This dataset was split in 3/4 for training and 1/4 for testing with the constraints that: (i) for each species in the test set, there is at least one observation of it in the train set and (ii), an observation of a species in the test set is distant of more than 100 m from all observations of this species in the train set.

Concerning the environmental images used to learn CNN models, those given during the 2018 session of the challenge were found to be erroneous and enabled the models to actually overfit a part of the test set (mostly the occurrences that overlapped the sea). To resolve this problem, new environmental images of each occurrence were extracted using the patch extractor from GeoLife-CLEF2019[1]. The environmental data is composed of 33 environmental rasters. Each raster encodes an environmental variable on the French territory. They were constructed from various open datasets including Chelsea Climate, ESDB soil pedology data, Corine Land Cover 2012 soil occupation data, CGIAR-CSI evapotranspiration data, USGS Elevation data (Data available from the U.S. Geological Survey.) and BD Carthage hydrologic data. To construct the input tensor we extract for each occurrence a matrix of 64×64 pixels from each raster centered of the location of the occurrence. Most of the environmental variables are continuous variables such as the average temperature, the altitude or the distance to water. Thus, the corresponding 64×64 pixel matrices can be processed as classical image channels provided as input of the CNN. Some of the variables are rather of ordinal type (such as ESDB v2). However, they still can be considered as additional channels of the CNN in the sense that the order of the pixel values remains meaningful. This is not true, however, for categorical variables such as the Corine Land Cover variable. This variable take up to 45 different categorical values but the order of these values does not have any meaning. Consequently, this patch is unstacked into 45 different binary patches. We finally obtain a tensor of size $64 \times 64 \times (32 + 45 = 77)$ for each occurrence.

In the following, we usually denote as $x \in X$ a particular occurrence, each x being associated to a spatial position $p(x)$ in the spatial domain D, a species label $y(x)$ and an environmental tensor $\mathbf{g}(x)$ of size $64 \times 64 \times 77$. We denote as P the set of all spatial positions p covered by X. It is important to note that a given spatial position $p \in P$ usually corresponds to several occurrences $x_j \in X, p(x_j) = p$ observed at that location (18 000 spatial locations over a total of 60 000, because of quantized GPS coordinates or Names-to-GPS transforms). In the training set, up to several hundreds of occurrences can be located at the same place (be they of the same species or not). The occurrences in the test set might also occur at identical locations but, by construction, the occurrence of a given species does never occur at a location closer than 100 m from the occurrences of the same species in the training set.

The used evaluation metric is the Mean Reciprocal Rank (MRR). The MRR is a statistic measure for evaluating any process that produces a list of possible responses ordered by probability of correctness. It is well adapted to assess the scenario targeted by the GeoLifeCLEF challenge, *i.e.* providing a short-list of species that are the most likely to be observed at a given location to users of field applications. The reciprocal rank of a query response is the multiplicative inverse of the rank of the first correct answer. The MRR is the average of the reciprocal ranks for the whole test set:

[1] https://github.com/maximiliense/GLC19.

$$MRR = \frac{1}{Q} \sum_{q=1}^{Q} \frac{1}{\text{rank}_q} \tag{1}$$

where Q is the total number of query occurrences x_q in the test set and $rank_q$ is the rank of the correct species $y(x_q)$ in the ranked list of species predicted by the evaluated method for x_q.

3 Evaluated SDM Models in GeoLifeCLEF2018

3.1 Convolutional Neural Network

It has been previously shown in [4] that Convolutional Neural Networks (CNN) may reach better predictive performance than classical models used in ecology. Our approach builds upon this idea but differs from the one of Botella *et al.* in two important points:

- **Softmax loss:** whereas the CNN of Botella *et al.* [4] was aimed at predicting species abundances thanks to a Poisson regression on the learned environmental features, our model rather attempts to predict the most likely species to be observed according to the learned environmental features. In practice, this is simply done by using a softmax layer and a categorical loss instead of the Poisson loss layer used in [4].
- **Model architecture:** we also used a different architecture of the convolutional layers compared to the one of Botella *et al.* and the one submitted during our participation in the challenge [6]. We used the inception v3 architecture [17] but with the three following modifications: (i) we change the classifier size to 3336 (number of classes), (ii) we add a dropout layer between the last fully-connected layer and the classifier, and (iii), we change the input size from 3 channels (classical images classification) to 77 channels according to the size of the input environmental tensors.

Learning Set Up and Parameters: All our experiments were conducted using PyTorch deep learning framework[2] and were run on a single computing node equipped with 4 Nvidia GTX 1080 ti GPU. We used the Stochastic Gradient Descent optimization algorithm with a learning rate of 0.1 (divided by 10 at epoch 90, 130, 150 and 170), a momentum of 0.9, a mini-batch size of 128 and a dropout of 0.7. We perform a validation every 10 epochs and the final model is chosen as the one with the highest validation score.

3.2 Spatial Models

For this category of models, we rely solely on the spatial positions $p(x)$ to model the species distribution (*i.e.* we do not use the environmental information at all). We did evaluate two different classifiers based on such spatial data:

---

[2] https://pytorch.org/.

1. **Closest-location classifier:** For any occurrence x_q in the test set and its associated spatial position $p(x_q)$, we return the labels of the species observed at the closest location p_{NN} in P_{train} (except $p(x_q)$ itself if $p(x_q) \in P_{train}$). The species are then ranked by their frequency of appearance at location p_{NN}. Note that $p(x_q)$ is excluded from the set of potential closest locations because of the construction protocol of the test. Indeed, as mentioned earlier, it was enforced that the occurrence of a given species in the test set does never occur at a location closer than 100 m from the occurrences of the same species in the training set. As a consequence, if we took $p_{NN} = p(x_q)$, the right species would never belong to the predicted set of species.
   One of the problem of the above method is that it returns only a subset of species for a given query occurrence x_q (*i.e.* the ones located at p_{NN}). Returning a ranked list of all species in the training set would be more profitable with regard to the used evaluation metric (Mean Reciprocal Rank). Thus, to improve the overall performance, we extended the list of the closest species by the list of the most frequent species in the training set (up to reaching the authorized number of 100 predictions for each test item).

2. **Random forest classifier:** Random forests are known to provide good performance on a large variety of tasks, including in ecology [5,10], and are likely to outperform the naive closest-location based classifier described above. In particular we used the random forest algorithm implemented within the scikit-learn framework[3]. We used only the spatial positions $p(x)$ as input variables and the species labels $y(x)$ as targets. For any occurrence x_q in the test set, the random forest classifier predicts a ranked list of the most likely species according to $p(x_q)$. Concerning the hyper-parametrization of the method, we conducted a few validation tests on the training data and finally used 50 trees of depth 8 for the final runs submitted to the GeoLifeCLEF challenge.

3.3   Co-occurrence Model

Species co-occurrence is an important information in that it may capture interdependencies between species that are not explained by the observed environment. For instance, some species live in a community because they share preferences for a kind of environment that we do not observe (communities of weeds are often specialized to fine scale agronomic practices that are not reported in our environmental data), they use the available resources in a complementary way, or they favor one another by affecting the local environment (leguminous and graminaceous plants in permanent grasslands). On the opposite, some species are not likely to be observed jointly because they live in different environments, they compete for resources or negatively affect the environment for others (allelopathy, etc.).

To capture this co-occurrence information, it is required to train a model aimed at predicting the likelihood of presence of a given species thanks to the

---

[3] http://scikit-learn.org/stable/.

knowledge of the presence of other species (without using the environmental information or the explicit spatial positions). Therefore, we did train a feed-forward neural network taking species *abundance vectors* as input data and species labels as targets. The abundance vectors were built in a similar way than the closest-location classifier described in Sect. 3.2. For any spatial position $q \in D$, we first aggregate all the occurrences located at the closest location p_{NN} in P_{train} (except q itself). Then, we count the number of occurrences of each species in the aggregated set. More formally, we define the *abundance vector* $\mathbf{z}(q) \in \mathbb{R}^N$ of any spatial position $q \in D$ as:

$$\forall i, \forall x, z_i(q) = \sum_{p(x)=p_{NN}} \mathbb{1}(y(x) = i) \tag{2}$$

where $\mathbb{1}()$ is an indicator function equals to 1 if the condition in parenthesis is true and 0 otherwise and $z_i(q)$ is the component of $\mathbf{z}(q)$ corresponding to the abundance of the i-th species at position q.

Architecture Description: The neural network we used to predict the most likely species based on a given abundance vector is a simple Multi-Layered Perceptron (MLP) with one hidden layer of 256 fully connected neurons. We used ReLU activation functions [14] and Batch Normalization [12] for the hidden layer, and a softmax loss function as output of the network.

Learning set up and parameters: This model was implemented and trained within PyTorch deep learning framework (See footnote 2) and were run on a single computing node equipped with 4 Nvidia GTX 1080 ti GPU. We used the Stochastic Gradient Descent optimization algorithm with a learning rate of 0.001, a momentum of 0.9, a mini-batch size of 32. We perform a validation every epochs and the final model is chosen as the one with the highest validation score.

3.4   Late Fusion of Previous Models

We also produced an other model corresponding to a late fusion of the environmental CNN and the co-occurrence model. Indeed, the two base models being trained on different kinds of input data, we expect that their fusion may benefit from their complementarity. We process the late fusion by averaging the prediction probabilities of the two models and then we re-sort the predictions.

4   New Model Using Jointly Environment and Co-occurrences in an End-to-End Network

The previous neural networks allow to capture in one case information contained in plant co-occurrences and in the other case environmental information from patches. However, co-occurrences can also be seen as a complementary environmental information. Indeed, the species close to a plant are directly part of its environment. Thus, species interact with each other and with the physical environment. To capture the interdependencies between co-occurrences and the environment we have developed a model that uses both inputs: environmental tensors and vector of co-occurrences.

Architecture Description: the environmental tensors are exactly the same as the CNN model and are described in Sect. 2. The co-occurrences inputs remains the same as the co-occurrences model of the previous section, *i.e.* the *abundance vector* describe in Sect. 3.3. This model is a deep neural network that is partly convolutional. The architecture is describe in Table 1. It is first composed of two separate branches. One branch of the network is identical to the environmental CNN with the inception v3 architecture without the dropout layer. The other branch of the network is a small neural network like the co-occurrence model consisting in two fully-connected layer of size 32 with a batch normalization after the first one. Instead of making two classifiers, the tensors from the last layers of the two branches are concatenated and, followed by a batch normalization and a dropout layer, and finally a single classifier on this final tensor. The role of this additional layer is to learn a common representation space that captures the potential interdependencies between the environment and the co-occurrences.

Learning Set Up and Parameters: This model is learned with the same setup, parameters and process than the environmental CNN (see Sect. 3.1) but with dropout of 0.8 instead of 0.7.

Table 1. Architecture of the fusion environmental and co-occurrences model

environmental tensors	co-occurrences vector
size: 64x64x77	size: 3336
inception v3	fully-connected (32) + batch normalization + fully-connected (32)
size: 2048	size: 32
concatenation + batch normalisation + dropout	
size: 2080	
classifier	
size: 3336	
prediction	

5   Experiments and Results

5.1   Evaluated Models Synthesis

In summary, we evaluate the six following models:

Spa-CC: the spatial closest-location classifier model (see Sect. 3.2).
Spa-RF: the spatial random forest classifier (see Sect. 3.2).
Cooc-NN: the co-occurrence model (see Sect. 3.3).
Env-CNN: the environmental CNN (see Sect. 3.1).
Env-Cooc-LF: late fusion of the probabilities given by the **Env-CNN** and the **Cooc-NN** models (see Sect. 3.4).
Env-Cooc-JNN: joint neural network on environment and co-occurrences (see Sect. 4).

The 3 first ones (**Spa-CC**, **Spa-RF** and **Cooc-NN**) are exactly the same than submitted in our participation in the challenge (see **FLO_1**, **FLO_4** and **FLO_2** in [6]). **Env-CNN** is the new CNN architecture (see Sect. 3.1) that was trained on the revised GeoLifeCLEF patches. **Env-Cooc-LF** is the same fusion model than **FLO_5** in [6] but with the new environmental CNN predictions. Finally, **Env-Cooc-JNN** is our new model no submitted in our participation.

5.2   Model Selection and Validation Experiments

We conducted a first set of experiments to evaluate the performances of our models in the case of an independently and identically distributed validation set. Therefore, we extracted a part of the training set (10% occurrences selected at random) and used it as a validation set. For neural networks we extracted an additional 10% of remaining train occurrences to have a pre-validation set. We choose two cross-validation protocols:

- For the three neural network models (*i.e.* co-occurrences neural network, environmental CNN and environmental and co-occurrences fusion model) we choose to fix the split between training set, validation set and pre-validation set (Holdout cross-validation). As, the neural networks took around one day to be learned completely, it was not workable to repeat split and learning many times. Thus, we worked with a single validation set to calibrate all our neural networks models. By fixing the split we assume to introduce a bias, but this bias is then constant between the experiments which allows us to compare the performance obtained on a single learning.
- For the two spatial models, that require a lower computation time, we choose to not fix the train-validation split but to learn the model on twenty random train-validation splits (Monte Carlo cross-validation). The performance of a model is defined by the average performance of the model on the twenty different splits. Like this we don't introduce a bias as for the neural networks but we keep the possibility to compare two models. Note that for the random forest classifier of scikit-learn we need to have at least one occurrence of each species in the training set and one occurrence of each species in the test set. However, some species are present only once in the data, so we had to remove them for validation experiments of this model.

5.3   Results

Table 2. Results of our models on validation set and official test set.

Model	Validation MRR	Official test set MRR
Spa-CC (run FLO_1 of [6])	0.0640	0.0199
Spa-RF (run FLO_4 of [6])	0.0781	0.0329
Cooc-NN (run FLO_2 of [6])	0.0669	0.0274
Env-CNN	0.0916	0.0458
Env-Cooc-LF	0.0908	0.0457
Env-Cooc-JNN	0.0927	0.0479

The performance of each model is given in Table 2. In validation, the best models are those based on environmental and co-occurrences data. The **Env-CNN** achieves a pretty good MRR of 0.0916 knowing that the ideal MRR cannot exceed 0.409 (due to the fact that several outputs exist for the same entry). On average, it returns the correct species in the first position with a success rate of 1/30 (0.0330) (knowing that there is 3336 species in the training set). Concerning the two fusion models, if the late fusion did not result in a performance gain, the joint model (**Env-Cooc-JNN**) give a better score than the environmental model alone (0.0927 vs. 0.0916) and is the best model evaluated here.

Nevertheless, the other models achieve good results too, all are over 0.06 of MRR and the random forest (**Spa-RF**) reaches almost 0.08. They return the good species label between 1 time out of 40 and 1 time out of 30. These results show that some fairly simple models can capture a strong information. For all models, the score on the official GeoLifeCLEF 2018 test set is much lower than the one obtained in validation. However, the order of performance of the models is maintained. The **Env-Cooc-JNN** model remains the best on the official test set, not far but significantly ahead of the **Env-CNN** model alone (0.0479 vs. 0.0458).

These results allow us to draw the following conclusions:

- **official test set results vs. validation test set results**: overall, the MRR values achieved by our models on the blind test set of GeoLifeCLEF are much lower than the ones obtained within our validation experiments (see Table 2). We believe that this performance loss is mainly due to the construction of the blind test set, *i.e.* to the fact that the occurrence of a given species in the test set does never occur at a location closer than 100 meters from the occurrences of the same species in the training set. This rule was not taken into account during our cross-validation experiments on the training set. An other point is that, for the official evaluation, the prediction size is limited at 100 ranked species for each test occurrences. We observe that this have also an impact on the MRR score.

- **Supremacy of environmental models**: the results show that our models based on environmental data are the best performing ones. The environmental CNN model (**Env-CNN**) is ahead from co-occurrences and spatial models. The late fusion model on environment and co-occurrences (**Env-Cooc-LF**) obtained similar scores to the **Env-CNN** alone and the **Env-Cooc-JNN** outperform all other models on the two evaluation process. After the environmental models the spatial classifier based on random forest (**Spa-RF**) obtains a very fair performance considering that it only uses the spatial positions of the occurrences (which makes it very easy to implement in a real-world system). The co-occurrence model (**Cooc-NN**) obtains significantly lower performance, while the closest-location classifier, which uses only the nearest point species data, is the worst model (**Spa-CC**).
- **The new environmental and co-occurrences model**: the joint environmental and co-occurrences model (**Env-Cooc-JNN**) is the best performing one. It allows a significant gain compared to the environmental model alone. This result indicates that there is a complementary information between co-occurrences and the environment. It also indicates that taking into account co-occurrences makes it possible to better characterize the ecological niche of the species compared to abiotic-only models.
- **Score with new patches vs. old patches**: as discussed in Sect. 2, in this paper, we used a new set of environmental patches since a part of them was corrupted in the initial GeoLifeCLEF 2018 dataset. However, the results of this new study are still in accordance from the one reported in the context of the challenge ([6]). In particular, the performance achieved by the environmental CNN on the new dataset confirms its superior predictive power over other proposed methods during the challenge. After patch correction, it remains the best model of the challenge, even better than the model learned on old environmental patches with a score of 0.0458 against 0.0435 (see **FLO_3** in [6]).
- **Species community**: the co-occurrence model (**Cooc-NN**) seems to generalize better than the closest-location classifier (**Spa-CC**), though both methods used almost the same input information which is the species of the neighborhood. It is likely that the neural network detect the signature of a community from its input co-occurrences. For example, the network is able to predict a common Mediterranean species when it gets a rare Mediterranean species as entry. Indeed, the probability of observing this same rare species near its known observation is very small, but the closest location classifier would do the error.
- **Non-performing late fusion**: the late fusion between the environmental model and the co-occurrence model (**Env-Cooc-LF**) did not result in a performance gain. However the **Env-Cooc-JNN** shows that there is some complementary information between co-occurrences and environment. This information seems to be therefore at the intersection of the environment and co-occurrences and requires joint learning to be effectively captured.

6   Conclusion and Perspectives

This paper compared four main types of models aimed at predicting species distribution: (i) a convolutional neural network trained on environmental variables extracted around the location of interest, (ii) a purely spatial model trained with a random forest, (iii) a co-occurrence based model aimed at predicting the likelihood of presence of a given species thanks to the knowledge of the presence of other species, and (iv), two fusions models between the environmental CNN and the co-occurrences model, one late fusion of predictions and one learned jointly on the to inputs. Our study shows that the convolutional neural network model maintains a high score with unbiased environmental patches. Indeed, it achieved the best performance over the others GeoLifeCLEF 2018 submitted models. However the main contribution of our study is the new joint model on environment and co-occurrences that achieve good results, significantly better than the environmental CNN. This shows that there is useful information in co-occurrences and that this information is at least partly complementary to environmental information. Few studies currently use this co-occurrences information. It would be interesting, in future work, to study more about how useful is the information in co-occurrences and how its complementarity with the environment can be explained.

References

1. Antoine, G., Wilfried, T.: Predicting species distribution: offering more than simple habitat models. Ecol. Lett. **8**(9), 993–1009 (2005). https://doi.org/10.1111/j.1461-0248.2005.00792.x
2. Araujo, M.B., Guisan, A.: Five (or so) challenges for species distribution modelling. J. Biogeogr. **33**(10), 1677–1688 (2006). https://doi.org/10.1111/j.1365-2699.2006.01584.x
3. Botella, C., Bonnet, P., Joly, A.: Overview of GeoLifeCLEF 2018: location-based species recommendation. In: CLEF working notes 2018 (2018)
4. Botella, C., Joly, A., Bonnet, P., Monestiez, P., Munoz, F.: A deep learning approach to species distribution modelling. In: Joly, A., Vrochidis, S., Karatzas, K., Karppinen, A., Bonnet, P. (eds.) Multimedia Technologies for Environmental and Biodiversity Informatics, pp. 169–199. Springer, Heidelberg (2018). https://doi.org/10.1007/978-3-319-76445-0_10
5. Cutler, D.R., et al.: Random forests for classification in ecology. Ecology**88**(11), 2783–2792 (2007). https://doi.org/10.1890/07-0539.1
6. Deneu, B., Servajean, M., Botella, C., Joly, A.: Location-based species recommendation using co-occurrences and environment- GeoLifeCLEF 2018 challenge. In: CLEF Working Notes 2018 (2018)
7. Elith, J., et al.: Novel methods improve prediction of species' distributions from occurrence data. Ecography **29**(2), 129–151 (2006). http://www.jstor.org/stable/3683475
8. Ferrarini, A., Alsafran, M.H.S.A., Dai, J., Alatalo, J.M.: Improving niche projections of plant species under climate change: silene acaulis on the british isles as a case study. Clim. Dyn. **52**(3), 1413–1423 (2019). https://doi.org/10.1007/s00382-018-4200-9

9. Franklin, J.: Mapping Species Distributions: Spatial Inference and Prediction. Cambridge University Press, Cambridge (2010)
10. Gobeyn, S., Mouton, A.M., Cord, A.F., Kaim, A., Volk, M., Goethals, P.L.: Evolutionary algorithms for species distribution modelling: a review in the context of machine learning. Ecol. Model. **392**, 179–195 (2019). https://doi.org/10.1016/j.ecolmodel.2018.11.013, http://www.sciencedirect.com/science/article/pii/S0304380018304010
11. Guisan, A., Zimmermann, N.E.: Predictive habitat distribution models in ecology. Ecol. Model. **135**(2), 147–186 (2000). https://doi.org/10.1016/S0304-3800(00)00354-9, http://www.sciencedirect.com/science/article/pii/S0304380000003549
12. Ioffe, S., Szegedy, C.: Batch normalization: accelerating deep network training by reducing internal covariate shift. In: International Conference on Machine Learning, pp. 448–456 (2015)
13. Joly, A., et al.: Overview of LifeCLEF 2018: a large-scale evaluation of species identification and recommendation algorithms in the era of AI. In: Bellot, P., et al. (eds.) CLEF 2018. LNCS, vol. 11018, pp. 247–266. Springer, Cham (2018). https://doi.org/10.1007/978-3-319-98932-7_24
14. Nair, V., Hinton, G.E.: Rectified linear units improve restricted Boltzmann machines. In: Proceedings of the 27th International Conference on Machine Learning (ICML 2010), pp. 807–814 (2010)
15. Peterson, A.T.: Ecological Niches and Geographic Distributions. Princeton University Press, Princeton (2011)
16. Pollock, L.J., et al.: Understanding co-occurrence by modelling species simultaneously with a joint species distribution model (JSDM). Methods Ecol. Evol. **5**(5), 397–406 (2014). https://doi.org/10.1111/2041-210X.12180
17. Szegedy, C., Vanhoucke, V., Ioffe, S., Shlens, J., Wojna, Z.: Rethinking the inception architecture for computer vision. CoRR abs/1512.00567 (2015). http://arxiv.org/abs/1512.00567

Interactive Learning-Based Retrieval Technique for Visual Lifelogging

Ergina Kavallieratou[1]([✉]), Carlos R. del-Blanco[2], Carlos Cuevas[2],
and Narciso García[2]

[1] Department of Information and Communication Systems Engineering,
University of the Aegean, 83200 Samos, Greece
`kavallieratou@aegean.gr`
[2] Grupo de Tratamiento de Imágenes, Information Processing and
Telecommunications Center (IPTC) and ETSI Telecomunicacioìn,
Universidad Politécnica de Madrid, 28040 Madrid, Spain

Abstract. Currently, there is a plethora of video wearable devices that can easily collect data from daily user life. This fact has promoted the development of lifelogging applications for security, healthcare, and leisure. However, the retrieval of not-pre-defined events is still a challenge due to the impossibility of having a potentially unlimited number of fully annotated databases covering all possible events. This work proposes an interactive and weakly supervised learning approach that is able of retrieving any kinds of events using general and weakly annotated databases. The proposed system has been evaluated with the database provided by the Lifelog Moment Retrieval (LMRT) challenge of ImageCLEF (Lifelog2018), where it reached the first position in the final ranking.

Keywords: Lifelogging · Deep learning · Interactive · Weakly annotated · Event detection

1 Introduction

Wearable video cameras are omnipresent in the current consumer market, which has been steadily growing in recent years. Market studies predict that the number of sales will reach 30 million units by 2020 [1]. One of the main keys has been the affordability of wearable cameras, which allow users to continuously record large amounts of unconstrained video data from a first-person point of view, without compromising their mobility or the use of the hands. These facts have promoted video lifelogging, where a user continuously records his everyday experiences by wearing a camera over a long period of time. The acquired images can be exploited to get very useful information about how people live, opening new opportunities for a wide range of applications, such as security, healthcare, and leisure [2–5].

However, the huge amount of image and video data may cause the user never revisits most of those recorded visual memories. Even more, the few relevant events for the user can be extremely difficult to find among long uninteresting segments and repetitive images. Therefore, wearable video devices, and more specifically visual

F. Crestani et al. (Eds.): CLEF 2019, LNCS 11696, pp. 226–237, 2019.
https://doi.org/10.1007/978-3-030-28577-7_19

lifelogging, require the development of advanced analysis techniques to identify and locate those meaningful and interesting events and memories. And thus, allowing a fast and efficient data browsing and retrieval.

As a result, the number of research articles and events have increased in the last years to find solutions to the previous demands, such as LifeLog [6], MyLifeBits [7, 8], NTCIR Lifelog Task [9], and the several editions of ImageCLEF Lifelog [10–12]. Most of the existing techniques for video segmentation, summarization, retrieval, and browsing are oriented to Third Person View (TPV) recordings, instead of First Person View (FPV) ones. The analysis of TPV recordings benefits from the existence of constraints imposed by the application domain (sports, news, movies, TV dramas, music videos, etc.) [13, 14]. For example, they rely on flash lights or "score" cuts, background music, shot duration and silences, text captions in broadcast news and shows, etc. [15]. However, these cues are absent in FPV video [16, 17]. Even more, the lack of an intentional structure in the FPV recordings is a source of additional challenges: long streams of data with subtle temporal and spatial boundaries, low quality of the recordings, unknown and diverse context, large number of non-informative images (such as walls or the sky), etc. Consequently, applying TPV analysis techniques to FPV videos is far for providing satisfactory results, even they can perform worse than uniform sampling in some cases [18].

There are also additional challenges in visual lifelogging that restrict the type of visual analysis techniques that can be applied. Some of them makes unreliable the use of computer vision techniques based on temporal coherence and motion estimation, such as the free motion of the camera, the abrupt changes in lighting conditions, and the repetitive image content. Other problems affect the recognition capability of objects in the video, such as occluded objects, blurring, and light saturation [19]. Moreover, the huge volume of data generated by these wearable cameras, along with the current increasing rate of available devices, requires of efficient methods to extract and locate relevant content [20].

Several articles have been proposed in the literature to face the previous challenges for event retrieval and content search in visual lifelogging. Aghazadeh et al. [21] retrieve relevant scenes and actions using a previously acquired egocentric dataset. For this purpose, a query sequence is aligned with sequences in the dataset through dynamic time warping. In [22], visual lifelog data is split into segments, extracting time data, low visual features, and audio features per segment. Then, the user provides a time reference and a query image to extract representative clips per segment by using a clustering approach. Finally, the user can provide additional query images to refine the search and improve the results. Other research proposes to use a more semantic representation, instead of low visual features. In this line, Wang and Smeaton 23 proposed to reason on semantic networks using a density-based approach to extract the most appropriate concepts for event representation. In 2425, a dataset of egocentric images is represented by a graph, adding connections between nodes when the underlying images have a similar Bag-of-Words representation. Finally, a local graph-clustering strategy is applied to retrieve the desired information. Instead of providing a query image, Radeva et al. [26] proposed to measure the similarity between daily visual data, combining dynamic time warping and the Swain's distance. Penna et al. [27] proposed a generative model to capture the feature distribution in video data using deep features. Then,

Markov [28] walks are applied over a model that captures the spatial interdependence of the image features. This allows to classify scenes with few labeled training examples.

In this paper, a strategy to retrieve events not previously pre-defined from a huge lifelogging dataset without ground truth is presented. The proposal is based on an interactive and weakly supervised learning approach, where a few query images are required (between 6 and 12). By using semantic image representations based on deep features, a set of related images to the query ones is obtained from the lifelogging database. The user, then, interactively selects the images closest to his original queries. Automatically, the learning-based engine is re-trained, making new predictions that provide the final retrieval results. This procedure is user-friendly, avoiding the requirement of experts to prepare the retrieval system for obtaining new events. This approach has been evaluated in the LMRT challenge of imageCLEF 2018, reaching the first place (out of a total of 29 strategies proposed by 6 different teams).

The rest of the paper is organized as follows. Section 2 describes in brief the LMRT challenge. In Sect. 3 the developed challenge winning strategies are introduced. Sections 4, 5, and 6 describes the database preprocessing, the main methodology after the proposed strategies, and the postprocessing, respectively. Section 7 presents the experimental results. Finally, conclusions are drawn in Sect. 8.

Table 1. Topics considered in the LMRT challenge.

Topic ID	Topic title
LST001	Preparing salad
LST002	VR experiments
LST003	My presentations
LST004	Interviewed by a TV presenter
LST005	Dinner at home
LST006	Assembling furniture
LST007	Taking a coach/bus in foreign countries
LST008	Costa coffee with friends
LST009	Using mobile phone or tablets in a vehicle
LST010	Graveyard

2 Lifelog Moment Retrieval (LMRT) Challenge

The aim of the LMRT challenge is to retrieve specific moments in a lifelogger's life for the 10 topics shown in Table 1. Such moments are defined as semantic events or activities that happened throughout the day.

The provided lifelogging dataset is composed by 50 days of data from a lifelogger. The data can be divided into images, visual concepts, and semantic content. The image data consists of 1500–2500 images per day, acquired from a wearable camera. Visual concepts are automatically extracted with varying rates of accuracy. Regarding semantic content, it is composed by locations, activities, and biometrics information (heart rate, galvanic skin response, calorie burn, steps, etc.), obtained with different sensors and devices. Finally, it must be noted that the dataset does not include specific ground truth related to the specific topics.

3 Proposed Strategies

Three different strategies have been developed for addressing the LMRT challenge. All of them have in common the adoption of a Deep Neural Network-based classification approach that uses an interactive transfer learning method. On the other hand, they differ in the number of simultaneous considered classes (i.e. topics).

The first strategy, called two-class strategy, considers every topic independently, and it requires a trained deep neural network (DNN) per each topic with two outputs: Correct/Wrong. Therefore, since each DNN considers only one topic, each of them will lead to a binary output that represents the topic event or its absence.

The second strategy, called ten-class strategy, considers all the topics simultaneously. Consequently, in this case, only one trained DNN with ten outputs is considered (one output per topic).

Finally, the third strategy, called eleven-class strategy, is an evolution of the previous one with an additional output to consider events that do not belong to any of the 10 topics.

The details concerning each of the three above described strategies are provided throughout the following sections. In addition, the offline pre-processing and post-processing stages that are applied for all the strategies are also detailed.

Table 2. Corresponding images per topic, as they have been described in Table 1.

Topic ID	Category	#images
LST001	Location	27,880
LST002	Activity	66,506
LST003	Activity	66,506
LST004	Location	27,880
LST005	Location	8,986
LST006	Activity	66,506
LST007	Activity	8,800
LST008	Location	601
LST009	Activity	10,754
LST010	Location	26,393

4 Off-Line Preprocessing

According to the types of metadata associated to the images in the dataset, they are first classified into two classes (Activity and Location), and then in several subcategories. For the case of Activity category, the subcategories are: transport, airplane, walking, and no-activity (all the images with no activity information). Regarding the Location category, 96 subcategories are considered, 95 are associated to specific geographical locations, and the last one to images without geographical position information.

This preprocessing will help the user to select images related to specific moments. Moreover, since the process is offline, there is no impact in the computational cost of the proposed strategies.

Table 2 shows how the categories have been assigned to each of the above challenge topics. In addition, the amount of frames conforming each topic is shown.

5 Methodology

The proposed retrieval strategies are based on a six-stage methodology, in which the user must adjusts a pre-trained DNN in an interactive, easy, and fast way to recover the required information of the events. The six stages in the proposed methodology, which are illustrated in Fig. 1, are described below.

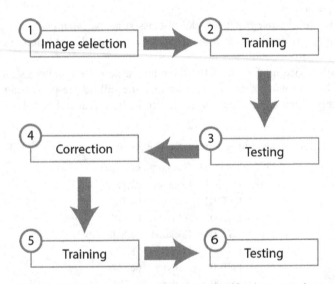

Fig. 1. Block diagram of the proposed classification strategies.

1-Image Selection: First, helped by the classifications performed in the pre-processing stage, the user manually selects sets of images corresponding to each of the topics to be retrieved (true samples). Additionally, for each topic, a second set of images not related to it is also manually created (false samples). Table 3 summarizes the number of positive and negative samples manually selected to address each of the topics. It can be observed that different amounts of true and false samples have been chosen in each topic. To prove that this manual step is not critical, and it can be done easily and quickly, for each topic, the true images have been chosen from a unique event (i.e. same day and same place). In the case of false samples, they have been just selected from the true images corresponding to other topics. Consequently, as it is shown in the table, some topics contain large amounts of true/false samples (e.g. LST003), whereas other ones include much less samples (e.g. LST008). However, it will be proven that the obtained results are successful independently of this large variety of sample set sizes. Consequently, their manual selection can be performed very easily.

2-Training: Once Positive and Negative sets of samples have been manually chosen, the pre-trained Convolution Neural Networks (CNNs) AlexNet [29] and GoogleNet [30] are retrained using such sets.

3-Testing. For each topic, both CNNs are used to automatically classify the images selected in the previous stage as belonging to a topic or not. Depending on the applied strategy (two-class, ten-class, or eleven-class), this stage is performed considering different number of classes. More details are provided later.

Table 3. Number of initial positive and negative samples per topic.

Topic ID	Positive	Negative
LST001	12	400
LST002	22	431
LST003	26	1201
LST004	10	431
LST005	10	2044
LST006	24	26
LST007	10	26
LST008	9	78
LST009	10	102
LST010	8	691

4-Correction: The results obtained for each topic are supervised and, if necessary, manually corrected. In most topics such results were very successful. So, few minutes were necessary to correct the classification results. However, in some topics (e.g. 006), in which the image selection step was problematic, and the final set of true samples was small, the number of misclassified images was significantly higher. Therefore, much more than a couple of minutes would be necessary to correct such misclassifications. However, to prove that the proposed strategy does not require so hard manual inter-actions, a maximum time of five minutes has been established to perform this correction step in each category. Obtained results have proven that even if all the results initially obtained have not been corrected, the subsequent stages will be able to correctly reclassify the images.

5-Training: Again, once the results previously obtained have been re-classified, both CNNs are retrained using the new sets of true and false sets of images for each topic.

6-Testing: Each CNN is finally used to classify the full set of original images (i.e. all the 80,439 images, without having made any previous classification among them).

In the case of the two-class strategy, the six described stages are applied independently for each topic. That is, for each topic, two classes are considered: images belonging to the topic (true samples) and images not belonging to it (false samples). Therefore, each CNN is used individually for each topic. The initial true samples are set as those manually classified (stage 1) as positive for the corresponding topic, whereas the initial false positives are those belonging to the remaining ones.

Regarding the ten-class strategy, in contrast to the previous one, the CNNs are used to classify the images simultaneously among ten classes, each of them corresponding to each of the topics. Therefore, in this case, in the initial manual classification the samples corresponding to each class are those set as positive (in the corresponding topic) in the pre-processing stage.

Finally, the eleven-class strategy also considers the ten topics simultaneously. However, in contrast to the ten-class strategy, an eleventh class is considered, which includes images not belonging to any of the topics. The samples for this class results from the union of all the groups of negative samples that have been obtained in the pre-processing stage, but discarding those samples belonging to other events.

6   Postprocessing

Once the final classifications have been performed, according to the LMRT rules, a set of 50 images representing each of the topics must be provided. Therefore, a final post-processing stage is necessary to select such 50 images from the set of images classified as belonging to each of the topics.

The used CNNs not only provide a final classification but also a confidence score for each analyzed image. Consequently, to select the 50 most representative images of each class, all the images have been ranked according to such score and those with the highest 50 values have been finally selected.

7   Experimental Results

The proposed system has been evaluated with the databases provided by the Lifelog Moment Retrieval (LMRT) challenge of ImageCLEF (Lifelog2018), where it reached the first position in the final ranking. At the competition, the organizers proposed the classic metrics for retrieval, specifically:

- Cluster Recall at X (CR@X) - a metric that assesses how many different clusters from the ground truth are represented among the top X results;

- Precision at X (P@X) - measures the number of relevant photos among the top X results;
- F1-measure at X (F1@X) - the harmonic mean of the previous two.

Table 4. Indicative results of F1@10 for the proposed strategies. subm#0 has not been submitted to the challenge.

Submission ID	Strategy	CNN	F1@10
subm#1	Two-class	AlexNet	0.504
subm#2	**Two-class**	**GoogleNet**	**0.545**
subm#3	Two-class	Average	0.477
subm#4	Ten-class	AlexNet	0.536
subm#5	Ten-class	GoogleNet	0.477
subm#6	Eleven-class	AlexNet	0.480
subm#0	Eleven-class	GoogleNet	0.542

Table 5. All the results of the competition. DCU was given as reference by the organizers.

Group Name	F1@10	Rank F1@10
AILabGTi	**0.545**	**1**
HCMUS	0.479	2
Regim_Lab	0.424	3
NLP-lab	0.395	4
CAMPUS-UPB	0.216	5
DCU*	0.131	0

All the presented results have been performed using Matlab along with a computer provided with multi-CPU system at 2.80 GHz and a GPU. The mentioned results were also provided by the organizers, off competition.

Official ranking metrics this year is considered the F1-measure@10, which gives equal importance to diversity (via CR@10) and relevance (via P@10). In Table 4, indicative results of F1@10 are given for all the submissions (subm#1-6), plus the not-submitted trial of the third strategy (subm#0). Thus, formally the best strategy proved to be the two-class strategy with the GoogleNet pretrained network. In Table 5, the formal best result of the subtask for every team is presented. Please notice that the runs of DCU* are not ranked since they are the organizing team.

In Table 6, F1@X for various cut off points are considered, with X = 5, 10, 20, 30, 40, 50, for all the submissions.

In Fig. 2, the resulted F1@X are presented in chart per submission. As it is apparent, in most submission the result is not significantly changing by checking more data. As only exception, at subm#1: two-class Alexnet, considering more data improves significantly the result, and it reaches to be much better than the other submissions.

In Fig. 3, the F1@10 is presented per topic. Here, more conclusions can be extracted:

- For the topics LST003, LST004 and LST006, the results do not change by the different techniques. More obvious is the case of LST006, where it is always 0, since the initially selected images were wrong examples.
- It seems that in subm4: ten-classes Alexnet, most of the queries present a peak, except of LST002 that presents low.
- It is interesting that LST004: Interviewed by a TV presenter, gives almost perfect results. Since there were many images in different places, and just few were selected at first, could it be that the presence of the camera is enough to distinguish the moments?

Table 6. Results for all the trials of F1@X for X = 5, 10, 20, 30, 40, 50. subm#0 has not been submitted to the challenge.

Trial	F1@5	F1@10	F1@20	F1@30	F1@40	F1@50
sub#1	0.395	0.504	0.571	0.604	0.606	0.594
sub#2	**0.520**	**0.545**	**0.562**	**0.547**	**0.523**	**0.522**
sub#3	0.452	0.477	0.445	0.438	0.465	0.473
sub#4	0.543	0.536	0.543	0.552	0.562	0.556
sub#5	0.452	0.477	0.459	0.438	0.465	0.473
sub#6	0.480	0.480	0.495	0.521	0.528	0.549
sub#0	0.507	0.542	0.525	0.534	0.508	0.532

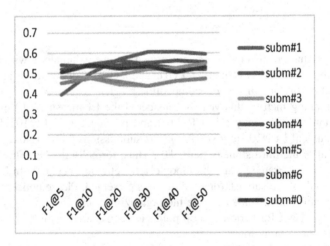

Fig. 2. F1@X per submission.

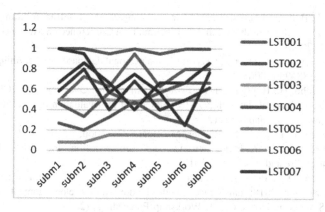

Fig. 3. F1@10 per topic.

8 Conclusions

This paper describes an interactive and weakly supervised learning system that is able of retrieving any kinds of events using general and weakly annotated databases. It was evaluated in the framework of the Lifelog Moment Retrieval (LMRT) challenge of ImageCLEF Lifelog2018, that it came first in the final ranking [31]. The competition was quite challenging as it required to handle a huge number of images for retrieving moments for ten specific topics. We proposed 3 different strategies to respond to the topics, all using deep learning-based algorithms and specifically AlexNet and GoogleNet.

References

1. Wearable Cameras: Global Market Analysis and Forecasts, Tractica, Boulder, CO, USA, (2015)
2. Jalal, A., Uddin, M.Z., Kim, T.S.: Depth video-based human activity recognition system using translation and scaling invariant features for life logging at smart home. IEEE Trans. Consum. Electron. **58**(3), 863–871 (2012)
3. Doherty, A.R., et al.: Experiences of aiding autobio- graphical memory using the sensecam. Hum.-Comput. Interact. **27**(1–2), 151–174 (2012)
4. Hodges, S., et al.: SenseCam: a retrospective memory aid. In: Dourish, P., Friday, A. (eds.) UbiComp 2006. LNCS, vol. 4206, pp. 177–193. Springer, Heidelberg (2006). https://doi.org/10.1007/11853565_11
5. Lee, M.L., Dey, A.K.: Lifelogging memory appliance for people with episodic memory impairment. In: Proceedings of the 10th International Conference on Ubiquitous Computing, pp. 44–53. ACM (2008)
6. Magazine, G.: LifeLog: DARPA looking to record lives of interested parties (2013). https://www.geek.com/news/lifelog-darpa-looking-torecord-lives-of-interested-parties-552879/. Accessed 28 May 2018

7. Gemmell, J., Bell, G., Lueder, R., Drucker, S., Wong, C.: MyLifeBits: fulfilling the Memex vision. In: Proceedings of the Tenth ACM International Conference on Multimedia, pp. 235–238. ACM (2002)

8. Gemmell, J., Bell, G., Lueder, R.: MyLifeBits: a personal database for everything. Commun. ACM **49**(1), 88–95 (2006)

9. Gurrin, C., Joho, H., Hopfgartner, F., Zhou, L., Albatal, R.: Overview of NTCIR-12 lifelog task. In: Proceedings of the 12th NTCIR Conference on Evaluation of Information Access Technologies, Tokyo, Japan (2012)

10. Dang-Nguyen, D.T., Piras, L., Riegler, M., Boato, G., Zhou, L., Gurrin, C.: Overview of ImageCLEFlifelog 2017: lifelog retrieval and summarization. In: CLEF2017 Working Notes, Dublin, Ireland, vol. 1866 (2017)

11. Dang-Nguyen, D.T., Piras, L., Riegler, M., Zhou, L., Lux, M., Gurrin, C.: Overview of ImageCLEFlifelog 2018: daily living understanding and lifelog moment retrieval. In: CLEF2018 Working Notes. CEUR Workshop Proceedings (2018)

12. Ionescu, B., et al.: Overview of ImageCLEF 2018: challenges, datasets and evaluation. In: Bellot, P., et al. (eds.) CLEF 2018. LNCS, vol. 11018, pp. 309–334. Springer, Cham (2018). https://doi.org/10.1007/978-3-319-98932-7_28

13. Gygli, M., Grabner, H., Van Gool, L.: Video summarization by learning submodular mixtures of objectives. In: Proceedings of the IEEE Conference on Computer Vision and Pattern Recognition, pp. 3090–3098 (2015)

14. Lin, Y.-L., Morariu, V., Hsu, W.: Summarizing while recording: context-based highlight detection for egocentric videos. In: Proceedings of the IEEE International Conference on Computer Vision Workshops, pp. 51–59 (2015)

15. Money, A.G., Agius, H.: Video summarisation: a conceptual frame- work and survey of the state of the art. J. Vis. Commun. Image Represent. **19**(2), 121–143 (2008)

16. Bolanos, M., Dimiccoli, M., Radeva, P.: Towards storytelling from visual lifelogging: an overview, arXiv preprint arXiv:1507.06120 (2015)

17. Betancourt, A., Morerio, P., Regazzoni, C.S., Rauterberg, M.: The evolution of first person vision methods: a survey. IEEE Trans. Circ. Syst. Video Technol. **25**(5), 744–760 (2015)

18. Lee, Y.J., Grauman, K.: Predicting important objects for egocentric summarization. Int. J. Comput. Vis. **114**, 38–55 (2015)

19. Tan, C., Goh, H., Chandrasekhar, V., Li, L., Lim, J.H.: Understanding the nature of first-person videos: characterization and classification using low-level features. In: IEEE Conference on Computer Vision and Pattern Recognition Workshops, pp. 549–556. IEEE (2014)

20. Bolanos, M., Dimiccoli, M., Radeva, P.: Toward storytelling from visual lifelogging: an overview. IEEE Trans. Hum.-Mach. Syst. **47**(1), 77–90 (2017)

21. Aghazadeh, O., Sullivan, J., Carlsson, S.: Novelty detection from an ego-centric perspective. In: IEEE Conference on Computer Vision and Pattern Recognition, pp. 3297–3304 (2011)

22. Wang, Z., Hoffman, M.D., Cook, P.R., Li, K.: Vferret: content-based similarity search tool for continuous archived video. In: ACM Workshop on Continuous Archival and Retrieval of Personal Experiences, pp. 19–26 (2006)

23. Wang, P., Smeaton, A.F.: Semantics-based selection of everyday concepts in visual lifelogging. Int. J. Multimedia Inf. Retrieval **1**(2), 87–101 (2012)

24. Min, W., Li, X., Tan, C., Mandal, B., Li, L., Lim, J.H.: Efficient retrieval from large-scale egocentric visual data using a sparse graph representation. In: IEEE Conference on Computer Vision and Pattern Recognition Workshops, pp. 541–548 (2014)

25. Chandrasekhar, V., Tan, C., Min, W., Liyuan, L., Xiaoli, L., Hwee, L.J.: Incremental graph clustering for efficient retrieval from streaming egocentric video data. In: IEEE International Conference on Pattern Recognition, pp. 2631–2636 (2014)

26. Radeva, P., Aksasse, B., Ouanan, M.: Using content-based image retrieval to automatically assess day similarity in visual lifelogs. In: 2017 Intelligent Systems and Computer Vision (ISCV). IEEE (2017)
27. Penna, A., Mohammadi, S., Jojic, N., Murino, V.: Summarization and classification of wearable camera streams by learning the distributions over deep features of out-of-sample image sequences. In: IEEE International Conference on Computer Vision (ICCV), Venice, pp. 4336–4344 (2017)
28. Rabiner, L.R.: A tutorial on hidden Markov models and selected applications in speech recognition. Proc. IEEE **77**(2), 257–286 (1989)
29. Krizhevsky, A., Sutskever, I., Hinton, G.E.: Imagenet classification with deep convolutional neural networks. In: Advances in Neural Information Processing Systems, pp. 1097–1105 (2012)
30. Szegedy, C., et al.: Going deeper with convolutions. In: Proceedings of the IEEE Conference on Computer Vision and Pattern Recognition, pp. 1–9 (2015)
31. http://imageclef.org/2018/lifelog. Accessed 25 Aug 2018

An Effective Deep Transfer Learning and Information Fusion Framework for Medical Visual Question Answering

Feifan Liu[1]([✉]), Yalei Peng[2], and Max P. Rosen[1]

[1] University of Massachusetts Medical School, Worcester, MA 01655, USA
feifan.liu@umassmed.edu, max.rosen@umassmemorial.org
[2] Worcester Polytechnic Institute, Worcester, MA 01609, USA
ypeng5@wpi.edu

Abstract. Medical visual question answering (Med-VQA) is very important for better clinical decision support and enhanced patient engagement in patient-centered medical care. Compared with open domain VQA tasks, VQA in medical domain becomes more challenging due to limited training resources as well as unique characteristics on medical images and domain vocabularies. In this paper, we propose and develop a novel deep transfer learning model, ETM-Trans, which exploits embedding topic modeling (ETM) on textual questions to derive topic labels to pair with associated medical images for finetuning the pretrained ImageNet model. We also explore and implement a co-attention mechanism where residual networks is used to extract visual features from image interacting with the long-short term memory (LSTM) based question representation providing fine-grained contextual information for answer derivation. To efficiently integrate visual features from the image and textual features from the question, we employ Multimodal Factorized Bilinear (MFB) pooling as well as Multimodal Factorized High-order (MFH) pooling. The ETM-Trans model won the international Med-VQA 2018 challenge, achieving the best WBSS score of 0.186.

Keywords: Visual question answering · Attention mechanism · LSTM · Residual nets · Multimodal fusion · Topic analysis

1 Introduction

Visual question answering (VQA) [1] aims to infer the correct answer to a question based on the information content of an image. It is a very challenging artificial intelligence (AI) task that combines computer vision with natural language processing (NLP) and has received increasing attention in both academia and industry. Various approaches including joint embedding approaches, attention mechanisms and compositional models, have been proposed on this task promoted by a series of VQA challenges[1]. Meanwhile, data sets for learning

---

[1] https://visualqa.org/challenge.html.

© Springer Nature Switzerland AG 2019
F. Crestani et al. (Eds.): CLEF 2019, LNCS 11696, pp. 238–247, 2019.
https://doi.org/10.1007/978-3-030-28577-7_20

VQA have also been evolving from simple image-QA datasets like COCO [2] to knowledge base-enhanced datasets like Visual Genome [3].

However, the study of VQA so far is mainly in the general domain. Little work has been done for VQA in the medical domain. With the surging interests in applying artificial intelligence (AI) on different clinical applications, Med-VQA has emerged as a prominent multi-discipline research topic since the launching of the inaugural edition of Med-VQA challenge [5] by ImageCLEF 2018 [4]. Given a clinically relevant question in natural language and a medical image, Med-VQA is expected to unlock the semantics of both image and question and generate the best answer automatic reasoning on multimodal information. Such a system would be very helpful in patient-centered medical care through which more patient engagement activities are facilitated as they can better understand their conditions by accessing their health care data available in the patient portal, including clinical notes and medical images. On the other hand, a reliable Med-VQA system can enhance clinicians' confidence, by providing a second opinion, in interpreting complex medical images, leading to optimal treatment decisions and improved outcomes.

Deep neural networks in the last few years have made dramatic impact in computer vision [6] and natural language processing [7] fields. Different visual attention-based deep learning models have been successful in open domain VQA. However, data dependence is one of the most serious problems in deep learning, as it needs a large amount of data to understand the latent patterns of data. It poses more challenges for developing an efficient VQA system in the medical domain because it is very difficult to construct a large-scale well-annotated dataset (such as ImageNet [10]) due to the expense of data acquisition and costly annotation. Transfer learning has been widely applied to overcome this problem through knowledge transfer from the source domain (with sufficient data) to the target domain (with limited data) and led to successes across all applications of machine learning [11].

In this paper, we explore deep transfer learning in an effective co-attention-based information fusion framework for Med-VQA. A novel deep transfer learning approach, ETM-Trans, is proposed to effectively extract meaningful features from the medical images. ETM-Trans derives the topic label for each image through topic analysis of the textual question associated with that image, and the derived topic labels paired with images are used to train an image classifier to finetune the pre-trained ImageNet model. We leverage the state-of-the-art embedding topic modeling (ETM) [15] method because it is specifically designed for short text topic analysis. Our main contributions are as follows:

- We propose ETM-Trans for transfer learning to improve the feature extraction on the image channel.
- We adapt and implement the co-attention mechanism integrated with cutting-edge multimodal information fusion techniques: Multimodal Factorized Bilinear Pooling (MFB) and Multimodal Factorized High-order Pooling (MFH).

2   Related Work

Research on VQA has been showing increased interest due to methodological advances in both computer vision and NLP, as well as the availability of relevant large-scale datasets. The straightforward solution to VQA is the joint embedding method (e.g. [14]), where image and question are represented as global features which are merged to predict the answers. The limitation for this approach is that an image could contain more information than needed to answer a question, which may add noises to the classification model, making it difficult to answer questions pertaining to a specific part of the image. Therefore recent work on VQA explored attention mechanisms (e.g. [8]) to improve the performance by steering the model to specific sections of the input (an image and/or a question). The main idea is to replace the global image features with fine-grained spatial feature maps so that feature maps can interact with the given question to derive salient features for answer prediction.

Another line of work in VQA focuses on efficient ways for multimodal feature fusion. A simple approach that has been widely used is a linear fusion model, where visual features from the image and textual features from question are concatenated or element-wise added. Due to the largely different distributions of two feature sets, the expressive power of the resulting fused representation is limited in terms of facilitating the final answer prediction. To address this issue, several approaches were proposed, such as Multimodal Compact Bilinear (MCB) [13], Multimodal Low-rank Bilinear (MLB) [9], and Multimodal Factorized Bilinear pooling (MFB) [12]. In our medical VQA system, we integrated the MFB approach for multimodal feature fusion which was shown to outperform both MCB and MLB in general domain VQA datasets.

3   Methods

Our Med-VQA system consists of four main components: Feature fusion, Co-attention Mechanism, Transfer Learning, and Answer Prediction, which are shown in Fig. 1. Specifically, visual context is extracted from the image facilitated by transfer learning, then fused with textual context from the question using co-attention mechanism and feature fusion techniques. Finally, the answer is predicted based on the fused multimodal contextual information.

3.1   Feature Fusion with Multimodal Factorized Bilinear Pooling

We used the MFB pooling method to merge the visual features from the image and textual features from the question, as it was shown to have dual benefits of compact output features of MLB and robust expressive capacity of MCB. For comparison, we also integrated multimodal factorized high-order (MFH) pooling which consists of N MFB modules (N is a hyper-parameter).

Each MFB block contains two stages: expand and squeeze. In the expand stage, the textual context and the visual context are transformed into the same

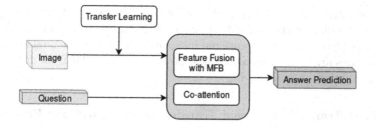

Fig. 1. The system architecture of our Med-VQA system.

dimension by a fully-connected layer respectively for the next element-wise multiplication. Additionally, a dropout layer is next to the element-wise multiplication unit. Then, the fused context is further transformed in squeeze stage which contains sum pooling, power normalization and L2-normalization.

In the MFH module, the output from the dropout layer of the previous MFB block is fed into the next MFB block as additional input as shown in Fig. 2, and the output from multiple MFB blocks are merged together as a final fused feature representation.

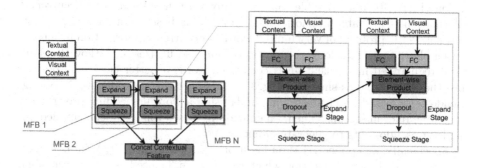

Fig. 2. The high-order MFH model which consists of N MFB blocks [12]

3.2   Co-attention with MFB

Similar to [12], we also implemented Co-attention mechanism for Med-VQA. The pre-trained ResNet152 model of ImageNet (excluding the last 3 layers) is used as an image feature extractor, and an LSTM layer is used to encode the question into textual feature vectors. A pre-trained word-embedding (dimension of 200) on Wikipedia, Pubmed articles, and Pittsburgh clinical notes are used as embedding input layer. MFB was used to fuse the multimodal features, followed by some feature transformations (e.g., 1 ∗ 1 convolution and ReLU activation) and softmax normalization to predict the attention weight for each grid location. Based on the attention map, the attentional image features are obtained by the weighted sum of the spatial grid vectors. Multiple attention maps are generated to enhance the learned attention map, and these attention maps are concatenated to output the attentional image features. Next, the final attentional image features are merged with the question features using MFB for downstream answer prediction.

3.3   ETM-Trans: ETM-based Transfer Learning to Tune Pre-trained ResNet

ImageNet data are very different from medical images in Med-VQA task, which motivates us to employ transfer learning to adapted a pre-trained model to this task. Instead of fine tuning the pre-trained model during the end-to-end training process, we employed an off-line transfer learning method which can do the full model finetuning while not increasing the end-to-end training efficiency.

We proposed a new transfer learning approach, ETM-Trans, which explored ETM topic analysis to derive a semantic label for each image to enable finetuning-based transfer learning. The assumption is that the semantics of the question text should match the corresponding image. However, the question text is typically short which is challenging for traditional topic analysis approaches, such as probabilistic latent semantic analysis (PLSA) and latent Dirichlet allocation (LDA), to infer reliable topics as only very limited word co-occurrence information is available in short texts. Embedding-based topic model [15] not only solves the problem of very limited word co-occurrence information by aggregating short texts into long pseudo-texts, but also utilizes a Markov Random Field regularized model that gives correlated words a better chance to be put into the same topic as shown in Fig. 3. First, short texts are merged into long pseudo-texts based on clustering methods using a word embedding pre-trained on a large relevant corpus. Then, an embedding-based topic model is applied on the long pseudo-texts to generate latent topics.

Specifically, we applied ETM on question texts of the Med-VQA data, assigning a topic label to each question which can, in turn, be used as a semantic label for its corresponding image. We then performed transfer learning in a context of image classification, where the parameters of pre-trained residual nets were tuned with the goal of correctly classifying all the images to their corresponding topic labels. The fine-tuned network (removing the last convolution block, fully-connected layer, and softmax layer) was used as the static feature extractor in our system architecture.

3.4   Answer Prediction

The input to answer prediction is the attentional image features from Co-attention, fused with the LSTM-based question representational features through MFB. Here we employed a simple multi-label classification method where each unique word in the answer sentence is considered an answer label for the corresponding image-question pair. Based on the distribution of all the answer labels, the final answer is generated using the sampling method.

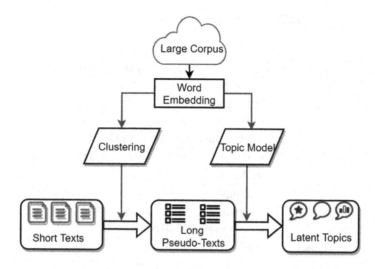

Fig. 3. Embedding based topic model for short texts [15].

4   Experiments

4.1   Data

Statistics of Med-VQA dataset is shown in Table 1. The training, validation and test data splits have 5413, 500 and 500 instances respectively. Both questions and answers are on average longer than those in VQA datasets in general domain. The word-embedding (dimension of 200), which was pre-trained on Wikipedia, Pubmed articles and Pittsburgh clinical notes, has good coverage (roughly over 95%) on both question and answer words of each data split. Also, note that the number of images is less than the number of question-answer pairs, which means several question-answer pairs may share a common image. Especially in training dataset shown in Table 1, there are 2278 images which are less than half of the number of question-answer pairs (5413).

4.2   Pre-processing

Question-Answer Pair. Pre-processing on question-answer pairs includes tokenization and lower casing so that each word can be mapped to its dense representation by looking up pre-trained word embeddings.

Image. Although the original pre-processing procedure is recommended to better facilitate the transfer learning, we notice that lots of images in medical VQA data set are long shape consisting 2–5 sub-images. When original pre-processing is directly applied, a lot of areas would be cut off, and features would be resized to be too small and blur. Therefore, we reshape the long images into approximate squares by re-arranging the order of sub-images. Then, the original pre-processing when pre-training the ImageNet ResNet is applied.

Table 1. Statistics of Med-VQA datasets

		Train	Valid	Test
Question	Num	5413	500	500
	Max_length	28	15	14
	Min_length	3	4	4
	Avg_length	9.63	7.38	6.968
	Emd_Coverage	94.99%	96.93%	95.52%
Answer	Num	5413	500	500
	Max_length	26	14	\
	Min_length	1	1	\
	Avg_length	6.03	4.06	\
	Emd_Coverage	95.05%	96.54%	\
Image	Num	2278	324	264

4.3   Validation Runs

We experimented with the three co-attention systems with variant settings
on feature fusion and transfer learning: (1) ResNet152+MFB which uses
MFB for feature fusion and the pre-trained ResNet152 is directly used; (2)
ResNet152+MFH which uses MFH for feature fusion and the pre-trained
ResNet152 is directly used; (3) ResNet152+ETM+MFH which uses MFH for feature fusion, and the pre-trained ResNet152 is tuned through ETM-Trans transfer
learning approach. In Fig. 4, we show the performance curves of 3 systems on

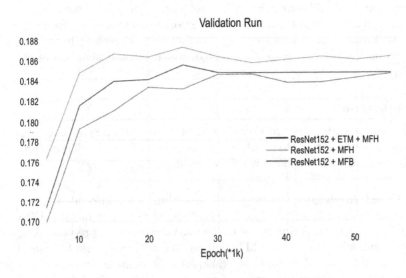

Fig. 4. Validation runs of 3 architectures

the validation dataset. We can see the MFH based feature fusion constantly out-performs the MFB based method. For the ETM model, we experimented with 10, 15 and 20 topics and found 15 is optimal based on the system performance on the validation data.

4.4   Official Test Runs in ImageCLEF 2018

We submitted 3 valid runs based on the aforementioned system architectures, and the run from "ResNet152+ETM+MFH" achieved the best WBSS score of 0.186, and the run from "ResNet152+MFH" obtained the best BLEU score of 0.162 as shown in Table 2.

Table 2. Summary of submissions in ImageCLEF 2018

Run	Models	WBSS	BLEU	CBSS
6069	ResNet152 + ETM + MFH	0.18616	0.15833	0.02295
6113	ResNet152 + MFH	0.18455	0.16159	0.01649
5980	ResNet152 + MFB	0.18445	0.15966	0.02053

5   Error Analysis

We conducted error analysis on the results of our Med-VQA system on the validation data, and identified three types of dominating errors as shown in Fig. 5.

- The question is very general (e.g. "What does ... show?") such that the system has difficulty to focus on a specific area to generate a matched answer. In case 1, the system identified "lesion" correctly, but failed on other details.
- The question involves organs or body parts. As shown in case 2, the system recognized the correct laterality but didn't recognize the "lung".
- The answer is too detailed overwhelming the system. In case 3, the answer describes the location in such a detailed manner, which is a formidable challenge even for a human expert.

Question:
What does the axial section of
the CT of the neck show?

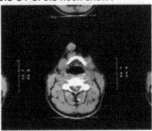

Prediction: right anterior lesion
Ground Truth: well defined soft
tissue lesion

Case 1

Question:
Where is the pleural effusion located?

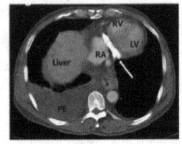

Prediction: right
Ground Truth: right lung

Case 2

Question:
where are the lesions in the MRI located?

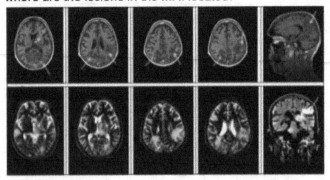

Prediction: left
Ground Truth: left thalamus internal capsule right side pons basal ganglion

Case 3

Fig. 5. Examples from our Med-VQA system

6   Conclusions

We proposed a deep learning framework integrating a proposed ETM-Trans
based model finetuning method with MFB-enhanced co-attention mechanism for
visual question answering in the medical domain. Our system achieved promising results in the Med-VQA 2018 challenge, demonstrating the effectiveness of
the ETM-trans strategy for transfer learning. Error analysis shows that general
questions or question involving specific organs are more challenging for the system to infer the correct answer. In the future, we will explore integrating domain
knowledge and a larger amount of unlabeled medical data to overcome the data

scarcity challenge. We will also add sequential modeling capacity in the answer prediction component to generate more natural and readable answers.

Acknowledgements. We gratefully acknowledge the support of NVIDIA Corporation with the donation of the Titan Xp GPU used for this research.

References

1. Gupta, A.K.: Survey of visual question answering: datasets and techniques. arXiv:1705.03865 [cs] (2017)
2. Lin, T.-Y., et al.: Microsoft COCO: common objects in context. arXiv:1405.0312 [cs] (2014)
3. Krishna, R., et al.: Visual genome: connecting language and vision using crowd-sourced dense image annotations. arXiv:1602.07332 [cs] (2016)
4. Ionescu, B., et al.: Overview of ImageCLEF 2018: challenges, datasets and evaluation. In: Bellot, P., et al. (eds.) CLEF 2018. LNCS, vol. 11018, pp. 309–334. Springer, Cham (2018). https://doi.org/10.1007/978-3-319-98932-7_28
5. Hasan, S.A., Ling, Y., Farri, O., Liu, J., Lungren, M., Müller, H.: Overview of the ImageCLEF 2018 medical domain visual question answering task. In: CLEF2018 Working Notes, Avignon, France (2018). http://ceur-ws.org/
6. Ren, S., He, K., Girshick, R., Sun, J.: Faster R-CNN: towards real-time object detection with region proposal networks. arXiv:1506.01497 [cs] (2015)
7. Collobert, R., Weston, J.: A unified architecture for natural language processing: deep neural networks with multitask learning (2008)
8. Ilievski, I., Yan, S., Feng, J.: A focused dynamic attention model for visual question answering. arXiv:1604.01485 [cs] (2016)
9. Kim, J.-H., On, K.-W., Lim, W., Kim, J., Ha, J.-W., Zhang, B.-T.: Hadamard product for low-rank bilinear pooling. arXiv:1610.04325 [cs] (2016)
10. Krizhevsky, A., Sutskever, I., Hinton, G.E.: Imagenet classification with deep convolutional neural networks. In: Advances in Neural Information Processing Systems, pp. 1097–1105 (2012)
11. Tan, C., Sun, F., Kong, T., Zhang, W., Yang, C., Liu, C.: A survey on deep transfer learning. arXiv:1808.01974 [cs, stat] (2018)
12. Yu, Z., Yu, J., Fan, J., Tao, D.: Multi-modal factorized bilinear pooling with co-attention learning for visual question answering. arXiv:1708.01471 [cs] (2017)
13. Fukui, A., Park, D.H., Yang, D., Rohrbach, A., Darrell, T., Rohrbach, M.: Multimodal compact bilinear pooling for visual question answering and visual grounding. In: Proceedings of the 2016 Conference on Empirical Methods in Natural Language Processing, pp. 457–468. Association for Computational Linguistics, Austin (2016)
14. Kim, J.-H., et al.: Multimodal residual learning for visual QA. arXiv:1606.01455 [cs] (2016)
15. Qiang, J., Chen, P., Wang, T., Wu, X.: Topic modeling over short texts by incorporating word embeddings. arXiv:1609.08496 [cs] (2016)

Language Modeling in Temporal Mood Variation Models for Early Risk Detection on the Internet

Waleed Ragheb[1,2]($\boxtimes$), Jérôme Azé[1,2], Sandra Bringay[1,3],
and Maximilien Servajean[1,3]

[1] LIRMM UMR 5506, CNRS, University of Montpellier, Montpellier, France
{waleed.ragheb,jerome.aze,sandra.bringay,maximilien.servajean}@lirmm.fr
[2] IUT de Béziers, University of Montpellier, Béziers, France
[3] AMIS, Paule Valery University - Montpellier 3, Montpellier, France

Abstract. Early risk detection can be useful in different areas, particularly those related to health and safety. Two tasks are proposed at CLEF eRisk-2018 for predicting mental disorder using users posts on Reddit. Depression and anorexia disorders must be detected as early as possible. In this paper, we extend the participation of LIRMM (Laboratoire d'Informatique, de Robotique et de Microélectronique de Montpellier) in both tasks. The proposed model addresses this problem by modeling the temporal mood variation detected from user posts. The proposed architectures use only textual information without any hand-crafted features or dictionaries. The basic architecture uses two learning phases through exploration of state-of-the-art text vectorizations and deep language models. The proposed models perform comparably to other contributions while further experiments shows that attentive based deep language models outperformed the shallow learning text vectorizations.

Keywords: Classification · Word2vec · Doc2vec · LSTM · Attention · Temporal variation · Depression · Anorexia

1 Introduction

Depression is a common mental disorder. Globally, more than 300 million people of all age stages suffer from depression [7]. It has a direct and indirect effect on the economic growth because of its major impact on the productivity. Depression also has dramatic consequences not only for those affected but also for their families and their social and work related environments [18]. It may be the psycho-physiological basis for panic and anxiety symptoms. At its worst consequences, depression is one of the major causes of suicide [2]. Another common mental disorder is Anorexia which is described as an eating disorder. It is characterized by low weight, worry of gaining weight, and a powerful need to be skinny, leading to food restriction. Individuals with eating disorders have also been shown to have lower employment rates, in addition to an overall loss of

F. Crestani et al. (Eds.): CLEF 2019, LNCS 11696, pp. 248–259, 2019.
https://doi.org/10.1007/978-3-030-28577-7_21

earnings. According to the National Eating Disorder Association (NEDA), up to 70 million people worldwide suffer from eating disorders [1].

Social media is becoming increasingly used not only by adults but also at different age stages. Mental disordered patients also turn to online social media and web forums for information on specific conditions and emotional support. Even though social media can be used as a very helpful tool in changing a person's life, it may cause such conflicts that can have a negative impact. This puts responsibilities for content and community management for monitoring and moderation. With the increasing number of users and their contents, these operations turn out to be extremely difficult. Previous researches on social media have established the relationship between an individual's psychological state and his\her linguistic and conversational patterns [14,15]. This motivate the task organizers to initiate the pilot task for detecting depression from user posts on Reddit[1] in eRisk-2017 [8]. In eRisk-2018 the extension of the study was planned to include detection of anorexia. The main idea is to detect such problems from users posts as early as possible.

In this paper, we revised our new proposed model for early detection of signs of depression and anorexia in eRisk-2018 [16] and examining possible improvements based on language models and attention mechanisms. The originality of our approach is to perform the detection through two main learning phases using text vectorizations and state-of-the-art language modeling. The first phase is to construct a time series representing temporal mood variation through users posts. The second phase is to build variable length time series classification model to obtain the proper decision. The main idea is to give a decision once the time series prove clear signs of mental disorder from current and previous mood extracted from the content.

The rest of the paper is organized as follows. In Sect. 2, the related work is introduced. Then in Sect. 3, the problem definition of early risk detection and used datasets are presented. Section 4 presents the proposed model architecture and its variants. In Sect. 5, the evaluation results are presented. We conclude the study and experiments in Sect. 6.

2 Related Work

Recent psychological studies showed the correlation between person's mental status and mood variation over time [8]. It is also evident that some mental disordered may have chronic week-to-week mood instability. It is a common presenting symptom for people with a wide variety of mental disorders, with as many as 8 of 10 patients reporting some degree of mood instability during assessment. These studies suggest that clinicians should screen for temporal mood variation across most common mental health disorders.

---

[1] Reddit is an open-source platform where community members (red-ditors) can submit content (posts, comments, or direct links), vote submissions, and the content entries are organized by areas of interests (subreddits).

Concerning text representation, traditional Natural Language Processing (NLP) modules starts with feature extraction from text such as the count or frequency of specific words, predefined patterns, Part-of-Speech tagging, etc. These hand-crafted features should be selected carefully and sometimes with an expert view. However these features are interesting [19], sometimes they loose the sense of generalization. Another recent trend is the use of words and documents vectorization methods. These strategies that convert either words, sentences or even overall documents into vectors take into account all the text not just parts of it. There are many ways to transform a text to high-dimensional space such as term frequency and inverse document frequency (TF-IDF), Latent Semantic Analysis (LSA), Latent Dirichlet Allocation (LDA), etc [10]. This direction was revolutionized by Mikolov et al. [12,13] who proposed the Continuous Bag Of Words (CBOW) and skip-gram models known as Word2vec. It is a probabilistic based model that makes use of a two layered neural network architecture to compute the conditional probability of a word given its context. Based on this work Le et al. [6] propose Paragraph Vector model. The algorithm which is also known as Doc2vec learns fixed-length feature representations from variable-length pieces of texts, such as sentences, paragraphs, and documents. Both words vectors and documents vectors are trained using stochastic gradient descent and back-propagation shallow neural network language models. The development of Universal Language Model Fine Tuning (ULMFiT) can be considered as moving from shallow to deep contextual pre-training word representation [5]. This idea has been proved to achieve Computer Vision (CV)-like transfer learning for many NLP task. ULMFiT make use of the state-of-the art language model AWD-LSTM (Average stochastic gradient descent - Weighted Dropout LSTM) proposed by Merity et al. [11]. The same 3-layer LSTM recurrent architecture with the same hyperparameters and no additions other than tuned dropout hyperparameters are used. The classifier layers above the base LM encoder is simply a pooling layer (maximum and average pool) followed by two fully-connected linear layers. The overall models significantly outperforms the state-of-the-art on six text classification tasks including three tasks for sentiment analysis [5]. In this paper, we will use these techniques for text representations.

Attention mechanism is considered as one of the recent trends in NLP models [3]. It can be described as mapping a query and a set of key-value pairs to an output, where the query, keys, values and output are all vectors. The output is computed as a weighted sum of the values, where the weight assigned to each value is computed by a compatibility function of the query with the corresponding key. This can be seen as take a collection of vectors, whether it be a sequence of vectors representing a sequence of words, or an unordered collections of vectors representing a collection of attributes and summarize them into a single vector. This summarization is done by scoring each input sequence with a probability-like scores obtained from the attention. This helps the model to pay close attention to the sequence items with higher attention scores. In this paper, we will evaluate the effect of attention mechanisms on the model.

Other interesting work on text distributed representation is the bayesian inversion proposed by Taddy in [17]. Bayesian inversion will not always outperform other classification methods. It rather provides simple, scalable, interpretable and effective option for classification whenever distributed representations are used. In this paper, we will use bayesian inversion in addition to deep attention based classifier to construct a time series representing temporal mood variation.

3   Problem Definition

In CLEF eRisk 2018, two tasks are presented [9]. Both tasks are considered as a binary classification problem. The first task is to discriminate between depressed and non-depressed users while the second one is between users diagnosed with anorexia and non-anorexia. The datasets are a dated textual data of user posts and comments -posts without titles- on Reddit. The training and testing datasets are divided into 10 chunks in chronological order. Each chunk contains 10% of the user's posts. A brief summary and statistics for these datasets are provided in Tables 1 and 2. The goal is not only to perform classification but also to do it as early as possible using minimum amount of data or chunks for each user. The decision corresponding to each user data chunk could be one of the classes or could be postponed for future chunks. At the end of the 10th chunk, all classification propositions must have been submitted.

For evaluation, the classical classification performance measures (Precision, recall and F1) are computed for each run. In addition error measures called Early Risk Detection Error ($ERDE_{5,50}$) are computed. It takes into account the correctness of the (binary) decision and the delay taken by the system to make the decision [8]. The classification ground truth (golden truth) is given or expected to be predicted on user level.

Table 1. Summary on Task.1-depression datasets

	Training dataset	Testing dataset
No. of users (depressed/non-depressed)	886 (135/752)	820 (79/741)
No. of submissions	531,394	544,447
Avg. no. of submissions/user	608.04	663.95
No. of sentences	1,157,230	1,336,379
Avg. no. of sentences per submission	2.29	2.45
Avg. sentence size (words)	14.31	14.26
Vocabulary size	234,181	222,201

Table 2. Summary on Task.2-Anorexia datasets

	Training dataset	Testing dataset
No. of users (anorexia/non-anorexia)	152 (20/132)	320 (41/279)
No. of submissions	84,834	168,507
Avg. no. of submissions/user	558.12	526.58
No. of sentences	193,026	370,281
Avg. no. of sentences per submission	2.28	2.12
Avg. sentence size (words)	14.74	14.30
Vocabulary size	81,497	103,380

4   Proposed Model Architecture

The temporal aspects of the eRisk-2018 tasks inspired us to model the temporal mood variation trough user's text content. The average number of days ranging from the first submission to the last submission is approximately 600 days. So, determining the way in which user's posts and comments vary from positive to negative and vice versa through time is worth inspecting. In the proposed models, time aspects are given as chunks. The main idea is to process user submissions for each chunk and determine the probability of how positive or negative the chunk is. A detailed description of our model can be found in the corresponding working notes paper [16]. The proposed architecture of our models comes in three main steps.

Step 1 - Text Vectorization Module: It is considered as language modeling step. The input of this step is the textual chunk training datasets and the output is text vectorization model.

Step 2 - Mood Evaluation Module: This step is considered as the first supervised learning phase. Assign each chunk a probability like score representing how positive (risky) the chunk is. The output of this step is a time series representing the mood variability over time.

Step 3 - Temporal Modeling Module: Another learning phase is to build machine learning models to learn some patterns from these time series to come up with the final classification model. These time series will be the training set of the second learning phase.

We tried also to encapsulate text vectorization and mood evaluation modules and proposed Deep Mood Evaluation Module (DMEM). This module are based on ULMFiT architecture [5] and the idea of transfer learning for language modeling in addition to using attention layers for classifications.

4.1   Deep Mood Evaluation Module (DMEM)

We propose a modification of the basic architecture of the ULMFiT mainly by adding attention to the model. The proposed architecture will help the model to focus on the important parts of the text that influence the network decision. Figure 1 shows the proposed model and the separation between encoder layers (text vectorization module) and classifier layers (mood evaluation module).

The input sequence is passed to the embedding layer then the three Bi-LSTM layers to form the output of the encoder. The encoder output has the form of $X_i = \{x_1^i, x_2^i, x_3^i, \ldots, x_N^i\}$ where N is the sequence length. The attention layer takes the encoded input sequence and compute the attention scores S^i. The attention layer can be viewed as a linear layer without bias.

$$\alpha^i = \{W^i . X^i\} \tag{1}$$

$$S^i = log[\frac{exp(\alpha^i)}{\sum_{j=1}^{N} exp(\alpha_j^i)}]$$

Where W^i is the weight of the attention layer of the ith sequence. The attention scores S^i is used to compute the scored sequence $O^i = \{o_1^i, o_2^i, o_3^i, \ldots, o_N^i\}$ which has the same length as the input sequence.

$$O^i = S^i \odot X^i \tag{2}$$

Where $\odot$ is the element-wise multiplication. Since the input sequence to the attention layer (encoder output) resulted from Bi-LSTM layers, the last element in the scored output S_N^i can be used for representing the whole sequence. But as we used attention scores, the whole sequence is represented by the weighted sum of all output sequences $\bar{O}^i$. This is done by:

$$\bar{O}^i = \sum_{<N>} S^i \odot X^i \tag{3}$$

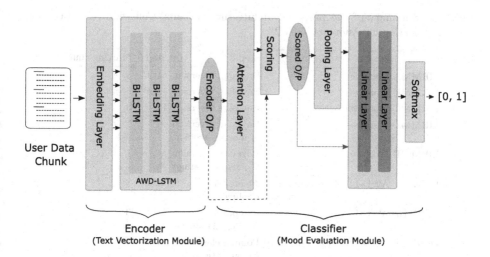

Fig. 1. Deep Mood Evaluation Module (DMEM)

We tried this scoring strategy in addition to the base model which skip the attention layer and move the output of the encoder directly to the classifier layers. For classification layers, a simple concatenation between the maximum and average pooling in addition to the scored output is inputted to a group of two different sizes fully connected linear layers. The output of the last linear layer is passed to the Softmax to form the network decision.

Training the over whole models comes into three main steps proposed in [5].

1. The LM is initialized by training the encoder on a general-domain corpus (Wikitext-103 dataset [21]). This helps to capture general features of the language. preserve low-level representations and adapt high-level ones
2. The pre-trained LM is fine-tuned using the training datasets for both tasks.
3. The classifier and the encoder is fine-tuned on the target task using different strategies for each layer group.

The training of the architecture is done using slanted triangular learning rates (STLR), discriminative fine-tuning (Discr) and layers gradual unfreezing proposed for ULMFiT with the same hyperparameters settings [5]. We train the model on the forward language models for both the general-domain and task specific datasets. Training the attention layer uses the same learning rates and cycles used in the classification layers group.

4.2 The Proposed Architecture Variants

Table 3 summarizes the main steps of our proposed system variants for both tasks and the starting chunk number for each run to make the first positive decisions.

Table 3. Summary of the proposed architecture variants. Cells with (*) stand for different selection for Anorexia Task-2

	Step 1	Step 2	Step 3	Starting chunk
LIRMMA	Doc2vec	Bayesian inversion	MLP	8
LIRMMB	Word2vec*	Bayesian inversion	MLP	5*
LIRMMC	Word2vec	Bayesian inversion	RF	3
LIRMMD	Word2vec	Bayesian inversion + moving average	———	1
LIRMME	Word2vec	Bayesian inversion + moving average	———	1
DMEM$_A$	AWD-LSTM (pre-trained)	Attention + pooling classifier	MLP	3
DMEM$_B$	AWD-LSTM	Attention + pooling classifier	MLP	3
DMEM$_C$	AWD-LSTM (pre-trained)	Pooling classifier (no attention)	MLP	3

For document vectorization (Doc2vec), the resultant vectors had 200 dimensions. The model used a context window of 10 words and a minimum of two for word counts. It used a negative sampling loss with DBOW version and trained for 20 training epochs. In the word level vectorization, the vector size of a word had a dimension of 200 with context window size of five words. Hierarchical softmax was used and a minimum count of two words was considered. In the second learning phase and for temporal modeling, the used architecture of the Multi-layered perceptron (MLP) had two hidden layers with ten neurons each. Concerning the Random Forest (RF) classifier, ten estimators were used.

For LIRMMB in annorexia task, we used Doc2vec rather than Word2vec and it starts to detect positive user in eighth chunk. We expected that Doc2vec could give better results especially for small size datasets. Hence we proposed LIRMMD and LIRMME to give a decision from the first chunk, we substitute the second learning phase with a window moving average from the output of the bayesian inversion technique. For LIRMMD, we assumed the positive users will have risky mood in the first chunks than the lasts. Two varying thresholds were used; one for the number of sentences and the other for the positive probability threshold. The size of averaging window is three and the probability changing from 0.6 with number of sentences higher than 100 to 0.8 and zero for sentences count threshold. For LIRMME, the difference comes from the assumptions that higher probability threshold was given to last chunks than the first chunks with the same sentences thresholds. The risk probability starts with 0.8 in the first chunk to 0.6 in the last chunk.

For $DMEM_A$ variant, we use the same set of hyperparameter of AWD-LSTM proposed by [11] replacing the LSTM with Bi-LSTM and keep the same embedding size of 400 and 1150 hidden activations. We used weighted dropout of 0.2 and 0.25 as the input embedding dropout and the learning rate is 0.004. We fine-tuned the LM by training datasets provided in Tables 1 and 2. We train the LM for 14 epochs using batch size of 128 and limit the number of vocabulary to all token that appear more than twice. For classifier, we used masked self-attention layers and concatenation of maximum and average pooling. For the linear block, we used hidden linear layer of size 100 and apply dropout of 0.4. We used Adam optimizer [4] with $\beta_1 = 0.8$ and $\beta_2 = 0.99$. The base learning rate is 0.01. We used the same batch size used in training LMs. For training the classifier, we create each batch using weighted random sampling to handle the problem of imbalance in the datasets. We train the classifier on training set for 30 epochs and select the best model on validation set to get the final model. We tried two other variants of the DMEM. The first one ($DMEM_B$) use the AWD-LSTM encoders without pre-training step while the other one ($DMEM_C$) skip the attention layer for the classification to use only concatenation pooling layer. The three variants of DMEM will give a good ablation analysis of the model.

5   Results

5.1   Evaluation Results

Upon the submission of the last chunk, the evaluation process started for all runs results. As mentioned in Sect. 3, the tasks organizers use the two versions of

ERDE in addition to the classical classification measures: Precision (P), Recall (R) and F1-Measure (F1). Tables 4 and 5 show the evaluation results of all proposed variants for both tasks.

Table 4. Results of proposed runs for Depression Task-1

	$ERDE_5$	$ERDE_{50}$	F1	P	R
LIRMMA	**10.66%**	9.16%	**0.49**	**0.38**	0.68
LIRMMB	11.81%	9.20%	0.36	0.24	**0.73**
LIRMMC	11.78%	9.02%	0.35	0.23	0.71
LIRMMD	11.32%	**8.08%**	0.32	0.22	0.57
LIRMME	10.71%	8.38%	0.37	0.29	0.52
$DMEM_A$	**9.50%**	**6.60%**	**0.61**	**0.52**	0.72
$DMEM_B$	10.12%	7.79%	0.54	0.47	0.63
$DMEM_C$	9.88%	6.82%	0.56	0.62	0.51

Table 5. Results of proposed runs for Anorexia Task-2

	$ERDE_5$	$ERDE_{50}$	F1	P	R
LIRMMA	**13.65%**	13.04%	**0.54**	**0.52**	0.56
LIRMMB	14.45%	12.62%	0.52	0.41	0.71
LIRMMC	16.06%	15.02%	0.42	0.28	**0.78**
LIRMMD	17.14%	14.31%	0.34	0.22	0.76
LIRMME	14.89%	**12.69%**	0.41	0.32	0.59
$DMEM_A$	**12.90%**	**8.16%**	**0.8**	**0.73**	**0.88**
$DMEM_B$	14.66%	10.33%	0.75	0.79	0.73
$DMEM_C$	13.46%	9.02%	0.78	0.72	0.84

5.2   Discussions

From the first look of the results, It is clear that the DMEM models outperform all other variants of the temporal mood variation models. The use of deep AWD-LSTM language modeling rather than the shallow Word2vec and Doc2vec is very useful. The effect of transfer learning is obvious for $DMEM_A$ and $DMEM_C$. The main reason is that the language model encoder is pre-trained by general-purpose text data before being used in the model. This improvement is more remarkable for the anorexia task with much less training data. The attention layer in the classification stage ($DMEM_A$) of the model helps to focus on the most important parts in long text chunk for active users. The use of MLP in the temporal modeling -second learning phase of the model- from the third chunk helps in early detection of risky users. In contrast with all runs using Doc2vec (LIRMMA for task-1 and LIRMMA & LIRMMB for task-2) that started giving decisions later (eighth chunck).

Comparing word and document level vectorization, it is clear that Doc2vec behaves better than Word2vec in terms of classical classification measures. The runs with higher recall use word level vectorization with either MLP or RF as the second learning phase. In mood evaluation step, fake stories were misleading and made a lot of false positive predictions. In addition, our models do not discriminate between user posts and comments (posts without titles) which could be beneficial for evaluating user mood.

For some at-risk users, first chunks posts don't have any proof of depression or anorexia and suddenly users started to express their status late. For the second learning phase, the model classify the overall mood time series and late signs of disorders could not be predicted earlier by our models. So, in some runs (for both tasks) some moderation on the proposed assumptions (classification probability thresholds) are needed. Tables 6 and 7 show some statistics of all submitted runs compared to the proposed models. The ranking of our official participation best run and proposed DMEM runs for each evaluation metric is also included. The statistics of the depression task are for 45 runs of 11 teams. The anorexia task statistics on results are for 34 runs of 9 teams. Most of the teams have participated in both tasks with at least one run for each. All the variants of our models behaves comparably with all other participants runs. The improvement of the results of using DMEM especially for anorexia task is clear on the ranking for each evaluation measure.

The ERDE-score has been discussed critically as for the 2017 and 2018 chunk based settings [20]. The study and experiments show that it is not a meaningful metric for the described shared tasks. Only the correct prediction of few positive samples has an effect on this score and the best results can therefore often be obtained by only minimizing false positives.

Table 6. Statistics on 45 participating runs results and our ranks for Depression Task-1

	$ERDE_5$	$ERDE_{50}$	F1	P	R
Average	10.33%	8.23%	0.42	0.37	0.55
Standard deviation	1.13%	1.09%	0.12	0.15	0.16
Max	15.79%	11.95%	0.64	0.67	0.95
Min	8.78%	6.44%	0.18	0.1	0.15
Official runs rank	31	22	13	15	3
DMEM runs rank	8	3	2	10	4

Table 7. Statistics on 34 participating runs results and our ranks for Anorexia Task-2

	$ERDE_5$	$ERDE_{50}$	F1	P	R
Average	13.31%	10.89%	0.56	0.63	0.58
Standard deviation	1.62%	2.69%	0.19	0.22	0.2
Max	19.90%	19.27%	0.85	0.91	0.88
Min	11.40%	5.96%	0.17	0.15	0.1
Official runs rank	28	27	20	24	4
DMEM runs rank	15	8	4	19	1

6   Conclusion

In this paper, we present a revised participation of LIRMM in the two CLEF eRisk-2018 tasks. Both tasks are for early detection of signs of depression and anorexia from users posts on Reddit. We proposed a new modification to the temporal mood variation architecture. The proposed model combined the text vectorization and mood evaluation modules into DMEM. We proposed three variants of the model and the results outperform the official five runs. Also, these results are comparable to other contributions. The proposed framework architecture used the text without any handcrafted features. It performs the classification through two phases of supervised learning using state-of-the-art deep language modeling. The first learning phase builds a time series representing the mood variation using attention-based transfer learning classification model. The second learning phase is a classification model that learns patterns from these time series to detect early signs of such mental disorders.

Acknowledgments. We would like to acknowledge La Région Occitanie and l'Agglomération Béziers Méditerranée which finance the thesis of Waleed Ragheb as well as INSERM and CNRS for their financial support of CONTROV project.

References

1. The national eating disorders association (NEDA): Envisioning a world without eating disorders. In: The newsletter of the National Eating Disorders Association. Issue 22 (2009)
2. World Health Organization: Depression and other common mental disorders: global health estimates. In: World Health Organization (2017). http://www.who.int/iris/handle/10665/254610
3. Bahdanau, D., Cho, K., Bengio, Y.: Neural machine translation by jointly learning to align and translate. In: International Conference on Learning Representations (ICLR), vol. abs/1409.0473, September 2014
4. Dozat, T., Manning, C.D.: Deep biaffine attention for neural dependency parsing. In: ICLR-2017 (2017)
5. Howard, J., Ruder, S.: Universal language model fine-tuning for text classification. In: Proceedings of the 56th Annual Meeting of the Association for Computational Linguistics (Volume 1: Long Papers), pp. 328–339 (2018)

6. Le, Q.V., Mikolov, T.: Distributed representations of sentences and documents. In: ICML. JMLR Workshop and Conference Proceedings, vol. 32, pp. 1188–1196. JMLR.org (2014)
7. Leite Barroso, M., Lucena Grangeiro Maranhão, T., Melo teixeira batista, H., Pereira de Brito Neves, F., Farias de Oliveira, G.: Social panic disorder and its impacts. Amadeus Int. Multidisciplinary J. **2**, 1–17 (2018)
8. Losada, D.E., Crestani, F., Parapar, J.: eRISK 2017: CLEF lab on early risk prediction on the internet: experimental foundations. In: Jones, G.J.F., et al. (eds.) CLEF 2017. LNCS, vol. 10456, pp. 346–360. Springer, Cham (2017). https://doi.org/10.1007/978-3-319-65813-1_30
9. Losada, D.E., Crestani, F., Parapar, J.: Overview of eRisk: early risk prediction on the internet. In: Bellot, P., et al. (eds.) CLEF 2018. LNCS, vol. 11018, pp. 343–361. Springer, Cham (2018). https://doi.org/10.1007/978-3-319-98932-7_30
10. Maas, A.L., Daly, R.E., Pham, P.T., Huang, D., Ng, A.Y., Potts, C.: Learning word vectors for sentiment analysis. In: Proceedings of the 49th Annual Meeting of the Association for Computational Linguistics: Human Language Technologies, HLT 2011, vol. 1, pp. 142–150 (2011)
11. Merity, S., Keskar, N.S., Socher, R.: Regularizing and optimizing LSTM language models. In: International Conference on Learning Representations (2018)
12. Mikolov, T., Sutskever, I., Chen, K., Corrado, G.S., Dean, J.: Distributed representations of words and phrases and their compositionality. In: Advances in Neural Information Processing Systems, vol. 26, pp. 3111–3119. Curran Associates, Inc. (2013)
13. Mikolov, T., Yih, S.W.T., Zweig, G.: Linguistic regularities in continuous space word representations. In: (NAACL-HLT-2013) (2013)
14. Moulahi, B., Azé, J., Bringay, S.: DARE to care: a context-aware framework to track suicidal ideation on social media. In: Bouguettaya, A., et al. (eds.) WISE 2017. LNCS, vol. 10570, pp. 346–353. Springer, Cham (2017). https://doi.org/10.1007/978-3-319-68786-5_28
15. Paul, M.J., Dredze, M.: You are what you tweet: analyzing Twitter for public health. In: ICWSM (2011)
16. Ragheb, W., Moulahi, B., Azé, J., Bringay, S., Servajean, M.: Temporal mood variation: at the CLEF erisk-2018 tasks for early risk detection on the internet. In: Working Notes of CLEF 2018 - Conference and Labs of the Evaluation Forum, 10–14 September 2018, Avignon, France (2018)
17. Taddy, M.: Document classification by inversion of distributed language representations. In: CoRR. vol. abs/1504.07295 (2015)
18. Trautmann, S., Rehm, J., Wittchen, H.: The economic costs of mental disorders: Do our societies react appropriately to the burden of mental disorders? In: EMBO (2016)
19. Trotzek, M., Koitka, S., Friedrich, C.: Linguistic metadata augmented classifiers at the CLEF 2017 task for early detection of depression. In: Working Notes of CLEF 2017 - Conference and Labs of the Evaluation Forum, vol. CEUR-WS 1866 (2017)
20. Trotzek, M., Koitka, S., Friedrich, C.: Utilizing neural networks and linguistic metadata for early detection of depression indications in text sequences. IEEE Trans. Knowl. Data Eng. (2018)
21. Wang, H., Keskar, N.S., Xiong, C., Socher, R.: Identifying generalization properties in neural networks. In: ICLR (2019)

Medical Image Labelling and Semantic Understanding for Clinical Applications

Xuwen Wang, Zhen Guo, Yu Zhang, and Jiao Li[✉]

Institute of Medical Information/Medical Library,
Chinese Academy of Medical Sciences and Peking Union Medical College,
Beijing 100020, China
li.jiao@imicams.ac.cn

Abstract. Semantic concept detection contributes to machine understanding and learning from medical images; it also plays an important role in image reading and image-assisted diagnosis. In this study, the problem of detecting high-frequency concepts from medical images was transformed into a multi-label classification task. The transfer learning method based on convolutional neural networks (CNNs) was used to recognize high-frequency medical concepts. The image retrieval-based topic modelling method was used to obtain the semantically related concepts from images similar to the given medical images. Our group participated in the concept detection subtasks that were launched by ImageCLEFcaption 2018 and ImageCLEFmed Caption 2019. In the 2018 task, the CNN-based transfer learning method achieved an F1 score of 0.0928, while the retrieval-based topic model achieved an F1 score of 0.0907. Although the latter method recalled some low-frequency concepts, it heavily depended on the image retrieval results. For the latter 2019 task, we proposed body part-based pre-classification strategies and achieved an F1 score of 0.2235. The results indicated that the transfer learning-based multi-label classification method was more robust in high-frequency concept detection across different data sets, but there is still much room for improvement in large-scale open semantic concept detection research.

Keywords: Concept detection · Transfer learning · Multi-label classification · Pre-classification · Medical image retrieval

1 Introduction

Medical images, such as ultrasound images, X-ray photographs, computed tomography images (CT) and pathological images, have become the key evidence for clinical decision making. Automatically detecting concepts or semantic labels from large-scale medical images allows doctors to obtain useful multimodal information, and it plays an important role in medical image reading and computer-aided diagnosis.

The ImageCLEF task [1] is focused on developing machine learning methods for medical image interpretation, starting from visual content and textual descriptor alignment. The concept detection subtask of the ImageCLEFcaption session aims to identify the UMLS [2] Concept Unique Identifiers (CUIs) for a given medical image from the biomedical literature. Our Image Semantics group (ImageSem) participated in

F. Crestani et al. (Eds.): CLEF 2019, LNCS 11696, pp. 260–270, 2019.
https://doi.org/10.1007/978-3-030-28577-7_22

the concept detection subtask of ImageCLEFcaption 2018 [3] and ImageCLEFmed Caption 2019 [4]. In the ImageCLEFcaption 2018 tasks, we proposed a transfer learning-based multi-label classification method for high-frequency concept detection and an information retrieval-based topic modelling method for concept detection from visually similar images [5]. Convolutional neural networks (CNNs) were applied for multi-label classification [6]. The LIRE search engine was employed as the information retrieval approach [7] and the Latent Dirichlet Allocation (LDA) was used to model the concept topics [8] of retrieved images.

This paper is organized as follows. Section 2 introduces the related work on medical image understanding. Section 3 describes the concept detection datasets that we used. Section 4 details the concept detection methods that we employed in ImageCLEFcaption 2018 and briefly introduces the improved strategy that we employed in ImageCLEFmed Caption 2019. Section 5 illustrates the experimental results from different concept detection datasets. Section 6 makes a brief conclusion.

2 Related Work

With the significant progress of artificial intelligence, the interdisciplinary research of medical imaging and advanced intelligence technology has become the focus of the field of international medical imaging [9]. In the world, approximately 1 billion chest and breast X-rays are produced annually, which is an average of 120 medical images per second [10]. Along with the rapid growth of digital medical image data, researchers in the field of biomedical and information sciences have applied advanced technologies (such as computer vision, natural language understanding, deep learning, etc.) to medical imaging related issues, and these technologies have had excellent performance in medical image processing and analysis, medical image classification and recognition, positioning and detection, organ and lesion segmentation, etc.

A corpus of annotated medical images, as well as the interpretation and summarization of the insights of the images, is important for understanding medical images. For example, the ImageCLEFcaption 2018 task derived an experimental corpus from scholarly biomedical articles on PMC [3]. Clinical and radiological images and their corresponding captions were extracted from the PMC literature. By using automatic classification and noise removal [11], the collection comprised 232,305 image-caption pairs, and a large number of unique UMLS concepts were extracted from the training set using the QuickUMLS library [12]. The ImageCLEFmed Caption 2019 task also provides a concept detection collection from the Radiology Objects in COntext (ROCO) dataset containing 70,786 image-concept pairs [13].

With these valuable multimodal corpora, researchers are able to apply image annotation techniques to determine the semantics of medical images. Traditionally, structured or semi-structured medical concepts are used as the semantic labels (such as diseases, locations, lesions, organs, etc.), and supervised learning is applied to manually labelled data to automatically annotate medical images [14]. Esteva et al. classify images of skin lesions as benign lesions or malignant skin cancers and achieve the same accuracy as board-certified dermatologists [15]. The participating teams in the

ImageCLEFcaption evaluation tasks generally applied deep learning methods to identify useful semantic concepts [1, 3].

However, the research on understanding and explaining medical images is still far from what is desired. Generating clinically explainable and understandable interpretations for medical images may enrich medical knowledge systems and facilitate the human-machine interactive diagnosis practice.

3   Data Sets

3.1   Concept Detection Dataset of ImageCLEFcaption 2018

In the concept detection subtask of ImageCLEFcaption 2018, the training and test datasets contain 222,305 and 10,000 biomedical images, respectively, which were extracted from PubMed Central (PMC) articles [16]. Each medical image in the training set is assigned multiple UMLS concepts as semantic labels. However, due to automatic labelling and unknown expansion strategies, the training set contains a total of 111,155 concepts that are mixed with a great amount of noise or irrelevant concepts. This noise makes it is difficult to analyse the semantic associations between concepts and medical images.

3.2   Concept Detection Dataset Processed by ImageSem

To reduce the influence of uneven noisy data and interpret medical images with more useful concepts, we reconstructed the concept detection dataset based on the image-caption pairs from the ImageCLEFcaption 2018 collection and named it the ImageSem collection [17].

The ImageSem collection contains a training set (Rec-training) and a test set (Rec-test) containing 222,314 and 9,938 medical images, respectively. We used MetaMap [18] to recognize the concepts in image captions and chose the strict strategy to guarantee the quality of concepts. Images in the Rec-training set are annotated with 76,938 non-repetitive concepts (CUIs). Compared with the concepts annotated by the ImageCLEFcaption 2018 task, the concepts from the ImageSem collection are more loyal to the image caption and concise enough for interpreting the given image.

3.3   Concept Detection Dataset of ImageCLEFmed Caption 2019

The ImageCLEFmed Caption 2019 task uses a subset of the Radiology Objects in COntext (ROCO) dataset [13]. To focus on radiology images and non-compound figures, automatic filtering and manual revisions were applied, reducing the dataset to 70,786 radiology images of several medical imaging modalities and totalling 5,528 annotated concepts. Table 1 shows the statistics of the three concept detection datasets we used. It can be seen that the amount of concepts used for labelling medical images decreased significantly.

Table 1. Statistics of different concept detection datasets.

Data set	Source	# Training set Image	# Training set Concept	# Test set Image
ImageCLEFcaption 2018	PMC literature	222,305	111,155	10000
ImageSem collection	PMC literature	222,314	76,938	9,938
ImageCLEFmed Caption 2019	ROCO	70,786	5,528	10000

4 Method

In the ImageCLEFcaption 2018 task, we employed two methods to identify multiple CUIs for a specific image, including the transfer learning-based multi-label classification method and the retrieval-based topic modelling method.

4.1 Transfer Learning-Based Multi-label Classification

In recent years, convolutional neural networks (CNNs) and recurrent neural networks (RNN) have made great progress in large-scale image processing, image content recognition, and image caption generation, especially in the medical domain. In this study, the problem of detecting high-frequency concepts from medical images was viewed as a multi-label classification task, and the CNN model was used to assign one or multiple predefined CUIs to a given medical image.

We applied Inception-V3 [19], which is a CNN model that was released by Google, to perform multi-label classification. Benefitting from improvements in the factorization of convolution kernel, the Inception-V3 model can decompose a 7×7 convolution kernel into two one-dimensional convolution kernels (a 1×7 kernel and a 7×1 kernel), which accelerates the calculations and increases the network depth. The Inception-V3 model was pre-trained using the ImageNet datasets including 1.2 million images with more than 1,000 common object classes [20]. Specifically, all the parameters of the previous layers were kept constant and the last softmax layer was replaced with a fully connected layer and a sigmoid layer. During the re-training step, only the last two new layers were trained to map medical images to concept CUIs, which costs a very short amount of time.

By observing the ImageCLEFcaption 2018 data set, we noticed that the large amount of low frequency CUIs may not suitable for multi-label classification. Therefore, we selected the high-frequency CUIs that appear in more than 1000 training images, which results in a total of 1,312 CUIs for training the multi-label classification model. We also noticed that a number of CUIs co-occur in some similar medical images. To make use of this characteristic, we cluster the CUIs according to the similar scores of CUIs' co-occurrence. The formula for calculating the similar scores between CUIs is shown as follows:

$$\text{Sim}(A, B) = \frac{Images_A \cap Images_B}{Images_A \cup Images_B} \quad (1)$$

Here, $\text{Sim}(A, B)$ denotes the similarity score between CUI_A and CUI_B. $Images_A$ and $Images_B$ respectively represent the sets of medical images in which CUI_A and CUI_B appear. CUIs with similarity scores above 0.8 are clustered into the same group. Accordingly, 1,312 CUIs are clustered into 459 semantic groups and the first CUI in each group is selected as the "representative CUI". The count of the representative CUI is equal to the occurrence of all the CUIs in its group. Only the 459 representative CUIs are fed into the multi-label classification model, while all the medical images that contain at least one of the 1,312 CUIs are selected for training. For the training images, we re-build the annotated CUIs set by retaining the CUIs that belong to the 1,312 high frequency CUIs and mapping them to the representative CUIs of their corresponding groups. Finally, 208,595 medical images with 459 representative CUIs are used to train the transfer learning-based multi-label classification model. After testing the transfer learning model, we collect the predicted results for the test set and then extend the results by replacing the representative CUIs with all the CUIs in the corresponding groups.

With respect to the ImageSem data set, we separately selected 332 CUIs that appeared in more than 1,000 medical images and 725 CUIs that appeared in more than 500 images in the Rec-training set, which were named the F1000 and F500 subsets. Then, we extracted all the medical images containing high-frequency CUIs from the Rec-training set, which resulted in a total of 192,478 medical images for the F1000 subset and 200,662 medical images for the F500 subset. For each medical image, we filtered out the low-frequency CUIs. Since the medical images in the ImageSem collection vary greatly from the ImageNet dataset, we retrained more layers of the CNN model and fine-tuned the weights layer by layer, which may incur longer training time, and we named this process global fine-tuned transfer learning.

With respect to the ImageCLEFmed Caption 2019 data set, we selected 87 CUIs that appeared in more than 1,000 medical images as the high-frequency labels and collected the corresponding medical images from the training set. We also retrained the CNN model and fine-tuned the weights layer by layer.

4.2   Retrieval-Based Topic Modelling Method

To recall the lower frequency CUIs, we used LIRE [7] to retrieve the most similar images from the training set of the ImageCLEFcaption 2018 dataset, and then we used LDA model to analyse the topic distribution of the concept CUIs from the retrieved similar images.

LIRE is an open source Java library that provides a simple way to retrieve images and photos based on colour and texture characteristics. We used LIRE to create a Lucene index of the image features of the whole training set for content-based image retrieval. We submitted each query image from the test set to LIRE and selected the top 50 visually similar images from the training set. Then, we combined the related CUIs of similar images as candidate concepts.

On the basis of the retrieved similar images and candidate CUIs, we employed the topic modelling method to select the most relevant concept for a given test image. LDA is a widely used generative statistical topic model in natural language processing. In this subtask, we assume that the concepts that are related to each image are collected into documents such that each document is a mixture of a number of topics and each concept is attributable to one of the document's topics. We applied Gensim [21], which is a topic modelling Python package, to model the topic distribution of the retrieved similar images and candidate CUIs. For a given test image with its retrieved 50 similar images, we collected 50 documents of CUIs as the input of the LDA model. According to the topic distribution θ of the current document set, we pick the topic with the highest probability as the candidate topic and further select the CUIs from the candidate topic that have probabilities above the default threshold.

4.3   Improved Strategies in ImageCLEFmed Caption 2019

In the ImageCLEFmed Caption 2019 task, we paid more attention to the distinction of the labels between images of different body parts. By observing the radiological images of the ROCO dataset from the ImageCLEFmed Caption 2019 task and analysing the semantic types of the concept CUIs, we were inspired to cluster the images into different groups based on the body parts.

First, we defined four classes of body parts based on the UMLS semantic types, including "abdomen", "chest", "head and neck" and "skeletal muscle". Some training concepts with body part semantic types were assigned to the corresponding classes. Second, we employed AlexNet [22] to perform the pre-classification work, and automatically classified the medical images in the training set according to the semantic type of annotated concepts. In this step, we manually double check the images that are being assigned to different body part classes. The subsets of the image-concepts pairs based on four body parts were then created. Third, we trained a multi-label classification model by using the different categories of medical images. More technical details can be found in our working notes from ImageCLEFmed caption 2019 [4, 23].

5   Results and Discussion

Experiments were performed on different datasets to verify the performance of the concept detection methods. The performance evaluation follows the ImageCLEFcaption 2018 task [3]. The balanced precision and recall trade-off were measured in terms of the F1 scores, which were computed by using Python's scikit-learn library.

Table 2 shows our concept detection results for the ImageCLEFcaption 2018 collection. It can be seen that the transfer learning-based multi-label classification model achieved an F1 score of 0.0928 (run10-TL), which was ranked 4th overall. The retrieval-based method achieved an F1 score of 0.0907 (run4_RT), which ranked 6th overall. It can be observed that the deep transfer learning methods are good at predicting finite high-frequency concepts, but they cannot recognize low-frequency concepts or out of vocabulary concepts. The image retrieval-based topic models can reveal the high-frequency concepts and low-frequency concepts simultaneously, but they depend heavily on the quality of the retrieved images. The higher the similarity between the query image and the retrieved images is, the greater the number of related concepts that can be recalled. However, the LIRE search engine often retrieves images that are similar to the query images in the lower level, including similarities in colour, greyscale, contour and texture, which may introduce a number of irrelevant images and many noisy concepts.

Table 2. Concept detection performance of the top 3 teams for ImageCLEFcaption 2018.

Team	Run	Micro F1
UA.PT Bioinformatics	aae-500-o0-2018-04-30 1217	**0.1102**
	aae-2500-merge-2018-04-30 1812	0.1082
	lin-orb-500-o0-2018-04-30 1142	0.0978
ImageSem	**run10_TL**	**0.0928**
	run02_TL	0.0909
	run4_RT	**0.0907**
	run01_RT	0.0894
	run05_TL	0.0828
	run06_TL	0.0662
IPL	DET_IPL_CLEF2018_w_300_annot_70_gboc_200	0.0509

Table 3 shows our experimental results on the ImageSem collection [17]. The baseline result combined the concepts of the top 10 similar images that were retrieved for a given image. "TL_500" and "TL_1000" respectively denote the results of the transfer learning models that are trained on the F500 subset and F1000 subset, while "TL_500_fine" and "TL_1000_fine" denote the results of the global fine-tuned transfer learning models. "RT" represents the best results of the image retrieval-based topic model.

Table 3. Experimental results of the ImageSem Lab on the ImageSem collection.

Method	P	R	Micro F1
TL_500	0.0918	0.0978	0.0874
TL_500_fine	0.1313	0.1413	0.1245
TL_1000	0.0931	0.0991	0.0885
TL_1000_fine	0.1365	0.1486	**0.1298**
RT	0.0411	0.0906	0.0515
Baseline	0.0209	0.1867	0.0363

It can be observed that the global fine-tuned transfer learning model "TL_1000_fine" is robust and achieved the best F1 score of 0.1298, which verified the robustness of transfer learning methods across different datasets. The image retrieval-based models achieved a recall of 0.0906, which was similar to normal transfer learning methods. However, the low precision indicated that noisy concepts account for a large proportion in results, and the F1 score declined to 0.0515.

Figure 1 shows an example of concept detection from ImageCLEFcaption 2018 task. We can learn from the image caption that the figure is an echocardiographic image. It is observed that the ground truth (GT) medical concepts varied with respect to their frequency distribution in the training set. Concepts with higher frequency, such as "C1704254 Medical Image", are more likely to be detected, especially by the transfer learning-based multi-label classification model. However, as mentioned in Sect. 3.1, that the unknown expansion strategies of automatic concept labelling introduced a number of redundancy concepts, e.g., synonyms such as "Medical Image", "image-dosage form", "Image", "Image (foundation metadata concept)" etc., are assigned to the same image repeatedly. Therefore we cluster similar high-frequency concepts to semantic groups before multi-label classification. The image retrieval-based topic model shows the ability of identifying high-frequency concepts and low-frequency concepts at the same time, in this case, "C0013516 Echocardiography" and "C0175723 Bands", which are more suitable for interpreting the given medical image.

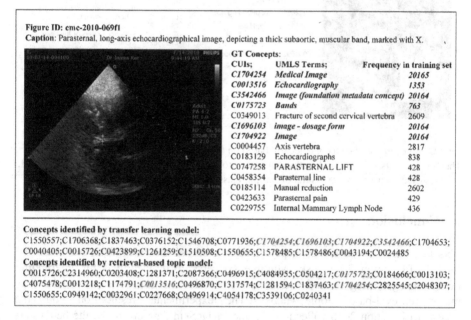

Figure ID: cmc-2010-069f1

Caption: Parasternal, long-axis echocardiographical image, depicting a thick subaortic, muscular band, marked with X.

GT Concepts:

CUIs;	UMLS Terms;	Frequency in training set
C1704254	Medical Image	20165
C0013516	Echocardiography	1353
C3542466	Image (foundation metadata concept)	20164
C0175723	Bands	763
C0349013	Fracture of second cervical vertebra	2609
C1696103	image - dosage form	20164
C1704922	Image	20164
C0004457	Axis vertebra	2817
C0183129	Echocardiographs	838
C0747258	PARASTERNAL LIFT	428
C0458354	Parasternal line	428
C0185114	Manual reduction	2602
C0423633	Parasternal pain	429
C0229755	Internal Mammary Lymph Node	436

Concepts identified by transfer learning model:
C1550557;C1706368;C1837463;C0376152;C1546708;C0771936;*C1704254;C1696103;C1704922;C3542466*;C1704653; C0040405;C0015726;C0423899;C1261259;C1510508;C1550655;C1578485;C1578486;C0043194;C0024485

Concepts identified by retrieval-based topic model:
C0015726;C2314960;C0203408;C1281371;C2087366;C0496915;C4084955;C0504217;*C0175723*;C0184666;C0013103; C4075478;C0013218;C1174791;*C0013516*;C0496870;C1317574;C1281594;C1837463;*C1704254*;C2825545;C2048307; C1550655;C0949142;C0032961;C0227668;C0496914;C4054178;C3539106;C0240341

Fig. 1. An example of concept detection from the training set of ImageCLEFcaption 2018 collection. The GT concepts were ground truths that were provided by the concept detection subtask organizers. We backtracked UMLS terms for each CUI to facilitate analysis. The concepts identified by the transfer learning model and the retrieval-based topic model are listed in the lower half, in which CUIs matched with GT are marked in red. (Color figure online)

It is worth mentioning that on the ImageCLEFmed Caption 2019 dataset, we applied a transfer learning model plus a pre-classification strategy and achieved an F1 score of 0.2235. The reason for the improvement may be due to the better data quality, as well as the predefined classification of body parts, which made the model concentrate on the semantic labels of "nearby parts" images. Figure 2 shows an example (an echocardiography similar to Fig. 1) of concept detection from the ImageCLEFmed Caption 2019 collection. It is observed that the GT concepts provided by organizers, such as "Ventricular", are more relevant to clinical issues. Although the predicted concepts matched only one label (C0018827 Ventricular) with the ground truth concepts, other unmatched concepts were still meaningful for the given image; e.g., the image was identified as an "echocardiograph" (C0183129) that was also identified by the concept "ultrasound on heart" (C0013516); the body parts were the "atria" (C0524422) and "ventricle" (C2355267), and the lesion may concern a "valva" (C1186983) or "valve" (C0184252).

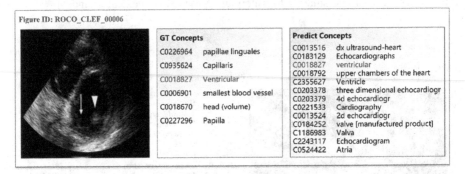

Fig. 2. An example of concept detection based on the ImageCLEFmed Caption 2019 collection. The GT concepts were ground truths that were provided by ImageCLEF task organizers, while the Predicted Concepts were results of the pre-classification-based transfer learning method.

6   Conclusion

This paper introduced the concept detection work of the ImageSem Group on the ImageCLEFcaption 2018 task. Multiple concepts were identified for interpreting medical images using a transfer learning-based multi-label classification model and an image retrieval-based topic model. The experimental results on both the ImageCLEFcaption 2018 collection and the ImageSem data illustrated the better performance of deep transfer learning models for predicting high-frequency concepts. The image retrieval-based topic model depended heavily on the retrieval results, and the F1 score declined significantly across different data sets. Therefore, we continued to use the deep transfer learning based multi-classification model on the ImageCLEFmed Caption 2019 collection, and we further introduced a pre-classification strategy based on different body parts and improved the overall performance.

However, due to the variety and diversity of the medical images and the massive quantity of medical concepts, the work on the semantic concept detection of large-scale open medical images still requires further research and improvement. In future work, we will try to seek more useful semantic clues from high quality externally labelled data.

Acknowledgments. This study was supported by the Non-profit Central Research Institute Fund of Chinese Academy of Medical Sciences (Grant No. 2018-I2 M-AI-016, Grant No. 2017PT63010 and Grant No. 2018PT33024); the National Natural Science Foundation of China (Grant No. 81601573) and the Fundamental Research Funds for the Central Universities (Grant No. 3332018153).

References

1. Eickhoff, C., Schwall, I., García Seco de Herrera, A., Müller, H.: Overview of ImageCLEFcaption 2017 - the image caption prediction and concept extraction tasks to understand biomedical images. In: CLEF 2017 Working Notes, CEUR Workshop Proceedings. CEUR-WS.org, Dublin (2017). http://ceur-ws.org
2. Bodenreider, O.: The unified medical language system (UMLS): integrating biomedical terminology. Nucleic Acids Res. **32**(90001), 267–270 (2004)
3. García Seco de Herrera, A., Eickhoff, C., Andrearczyk, V., Müller, H.: Overview of the ImageCLEF 2018 caption prediction tasks. In: CLEF 2018 Working Notes, CEUR Workshop Proceedings. CEUR-WS.org, Avignon (2018). http://ceur-ws.org
4. Pelka, O., Friedrich, C.M., García Seco de Herrera, A., Müller, H.: Overview of the ImageCLEFmed 2019 concept detection task. In: CLEF 2019 Working Notes, CEUR Workshop Proceedings, CEUR-WS.org, Lugano (2019). http://ceur-ws.org
5. Zhang, Y., Wang, X., Guo, Z., Li, J.: ImageSem at ImageCLEF 2018 caption task: image retrieval and transfer learning. In: CLEF 2018 Working Notes. CEUR Workshop Proceedings, CEUR-WS.org, Avignon (2018). http://ceur-ws.org
6. Razavian, A.S., Azizpour, H., Sullivan, J., Carlsson, S.: CNN features off the shelf: an astounding baseline for recognition. In: Proceedings of the IEEE Conference on Computer Vision and Pattern Recognition Workshops, pp. 806–813 (2014)
7. Lux, M., Chatzichristofis, S.A.: Lire: lucene image retrieval: an extensible java CBIR library. In: Proceedings of the 16th ACM International Conference on Multimedia. British Columbia, Canada (2008)
8. Blei, D.M., Ng, A.Y., Jordan, M.I.: Latent dirichlet allocation. J Mach. Learn. Res. Arch. **3**, 993–1022 (2003)
9. Interagency Working Group on Medical Imaging Committee on Science. National Science and Technology Coucil, Roadmap for medical imaging research and development (2017)
10. Krupinski, E.A.: Current perspectives in medical image perception. Attent. Percept. Psychophys. **72**(5), 1205–1217 (2010)
11. Andrearczyk, V., Müller, H.: Deep multimodal classification of image types in biomedical journal figures. In: Bellot, P., Trabelsi, C., et al. (eds.) CLEF 2018. LNCS, vol. 11018, pp. 3–14. Springer, Cham (2018). https://doi.org/10.1007/978-3-319-98932-7_1
12. Soldaini, L., Goharian, N.: QuickUMLS: a fast, unsupervised approach for medical concept extraction. In: Proceedings of the Medical Information Retrieval (MedIR) Workshop at SIGIR, Pisa, Italy (2016)

13. Pelka, O., Koitka, S., Rückert, J., Nensa, F., Friedrich, Christoph M.: Radiology objects in COntext (ROCO): a multimodal image dataset. In: Stoyanov, D., et al. (eds.) LABELS/CVII/STENT -2018. LNCS, vol. 11043, pp. 180–189. Springer, Cham (2018). https://doi.org/10.1007/978-3-030-01364-6_20

14. Shin, H.C., Roberts, K., Lu, L., Demner-Fushman, D., Yao, J., Summers, R.M.: Learning to read chest X-rays: recurrent neural cascade model for automated image annotation. In: Proceedings of the 2016 IEEE Conference on Computer Vision and Pattern Recognition, pp. 2497–2506 (2016)

15. Esteva, A., et al.: Dermatologist-level classification of skin cancer with deep neural networks. Nature 542(7639), 115–118 (2017)

16. Gamble, A.: PubMed Central (PMC). Charleston Advisor 19(2), 48–54 (2017)

17. Wang, X., Zhang, Y., Guo, Z., Li, J.: Identifying concepts from medical images via transfer learning and image retrieval. Math. Biosci. Eng. 16(4), 1978–1991 (2019)

18. Aronson, A.R.: Effective mapping of biomedical text to the UMLs metathesaurus: the metamap program. In: Proceedings, AMIA Symposium, pp. 17–21 (2001)

19. Szegedy, C., Vanhoucke, V., Ioffe, S., Shlens, J., Wojna, Z.: Rethinking the inception architecture for computer vision. In: Proceedings of the 2016 IEEE Conference on Computer Vision and Pattern Recognition, pp. 2818–2826 (2016)

20. Russakovsky, O., et al.: Imagenet large scale visual recognition challenge. Int. J. Comput. Vis. 115(3), 211–252 (2015)

21. Řehůřek, R., Sojka, P.: Software framework for topic modelling with large corpora. In Proceedings of LREC 2010 Workshop New Challenges for NLP Frameworks, Malta, University of Malta, Valletta, Malta, pp. 46–50 (2010)

22. Ding, L., Li, H., Hu, C., Zhang, W., Wang, S.: ALEXNET feature extraction and multi-kernel learning for object oriented classification. J. ISPRS – Int. Arch. Photogram. Remote Sens. Spat. Inf. Sci. 277–281 (2018)

23. Guo, Z., Wang, X., Zhang, Y., Li, J.: ImageSem at ImageCLEFmed caption 2019 task: a two-stage medical concept detection strategy. In: CLEF 2019 Working Notes, CEUR Workshop Proceedings. CEUR-WS.org, Lugano (2019). http://ceur-ws.org

To Check or Not to Check: Syntax, Semantics, and Context in the Language of Check-Worthy Claims

Chaoyuan Zuo[1](✉), Ayla Ida Karakas[2], and Ritwik Banerjee[1]

[1] Department of Computer Science, Stony Brook University,
Stony Brook, New York 11794, USA
{chzuo,rbanerjee}@cs.stonybrook.edu
[2] Department of Linguistics, Stony Brook University,
Stony Brook, New York 11794, USA
ayla.karakas@stonybrook.edu

Abstract. As the spread of information has received a compelling boost due to pervasive use of social media, so has the spread of misinformation. The sheer volume of data has rendered the traditional methods of expert-driven manual fact-checking largely infeasible. As a result, computational linguistics and data-driven algorithms have been explored in recent years. Despite this progress, identifying and prioritizing *what* needs to be checked has received little attention. Given that expert-driven manual intervention is likely to remain an important component of fact-checking, especially in specific domains (e.g., politics, environmental science), this identification and prioritization is critical. A successful algorithmic ranking of "check-worthy" claims can help an expert-in-the-loop fact-checking system, thereby reducing the expert's workload while still tackling the most salient bits of misinformation. In this work, we explore how linguistic syntax, semantics, and the contextual meaning of words play a role in determining the check-worthiness of claims. Our preliminary experiments used explicit stylometric features and simple word embeddings on the English language dataset in the Check-worthiness task of the CLEF-2018 Fact-Checking Lab, where our primary solution outperformed the other systems in terms of the mean average precision, R-precision, reciprocal rank, and precision at k for multiple values k. Here, we present an extension of this approach with more sophisticated word embeddings and report further improvements in this task.

Keywords: Check-worthiness · Multi-layer perceptron · SVM · Word embedding · Context · Syntax · Semantics

1 Introduction

We live in an age where a significant part of our lives may be infused with the information we see on the web and social media platforms, and most Internet

© Springer Nature Switzerland AG 2019
F. Crestani et al. (Eds.): CLEF 2019, LNCS 11696, pp. 271–283, 2019.
https://doi.org/10.1007/978-3-030-28577-7_23

The World Health Organization recently classified obses-
sive video-gaming as an addiction. I bet it will not be
long until "gaming disorder"
is joined in the WHO's International Classification of
Diseases by another modern,
screen-based malady: "Netflix disorder".

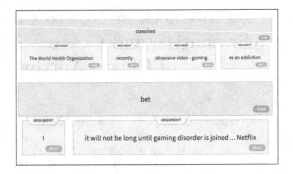

Fig. 1. A two-sentence excerpt from an article about Netflix addiction and the main pieces of information extracted by Open IE [34]. A pipeline of such tools is ill-suited for fact-checking since there is no distinction between check-worthy and other events. Here, only the first sentence is worth verifying, and there is no need to fact-check the author's bet. Source: https://www.theguardian.com/commentisfree/2018/jun/20/netflix-addiction-is-real-we-are-entertaining-ourselves-to-death (accessed May 27, 2019).

users readily acquire the power of civilian commentary [2,13]. Thus, any information available on the web has the potential to be disseminated with unprecedented speed and scope. As a result, the ordinary web or social media user is often subjected to information overload [33]. Given how onerous the task of fact-checking can become under vast amounts of information, users often resort to confirmation bias when it comes to selection and retention of information [22]. Such a confluence of information overload and bias can create a society where unverified claims can easily masquerade as facts. We may not be able to overcome individual biases purely with technology. We can, however, mitigate the ill-effects of misinformation by identifying and prioritizing *what* needs to be verified. For small snippets, this is obvious to the human reader but beyond the scope of existing tools, as illustrated by the excerpt in Fig. 1. Prior work on automatic fact-checking cannot, however, make this distinction, and need to extract statements to be fact-checked before the actual verification process can begin [4,5,17,36,38].

An evident benefit of prioritizing check-worthy statements is that the ranked list can then be provided to journalists and users to help them focus on verifying the most important statements without information overload. Moreover, accurate identification of check-worthy statements will clearly benefit any subsequent fact-checking processes. With this as our motivation, we focus on the task of identifying and ranking statements based on their check-worthiness, as defined by the CLEF 2018 Fact Checking Lab [1]. Here, we present our work using the data and evaluation framework provided by the CLEF 2018 Lab on Automatic Identification and Verification of Claims in Political Debates [27], and present a solution that significantly outperforms other systems in terms of several performance measures.

The remainder of this paper is organized into a discussion of related work in Sect. 2, a description of our methodology in Sect. 3, followed by the experiments and their evaluation in Sect. 4. Then in Sect. 5 we provide a detailed analysis of our results before finally concluding with some possible directions for future work in Sect. 6.

2 Related Work

The importance of accurate information has been widely appreciated in many distinct but increasingly interconnected fields, from journalism to social psychology to computational linguistics. Computational approaches to fact-checking are intended to overcome the hurdle of verifying large amounts of information, and have become a fundamental component of computational journalism due to its critical role in upholding the accuracy and verifiability of information [5,7,10].

Very recently, some work has also been done on the extraction of numerical and statistical claims to identify whether or not a statement is worth verifying [3]. This, however, is orthogonal to our exploration of check-worthiness based on linguistic constructs, where early research focused on general misinformation such as rumors and hoaxes [23,31], and soon, several automatic fact-checking systems were developed for the verification of political news [17,36]. The preliminary step of identifying *what* is worth checking, however, received little attention until 2015 (ClaimBuster [16]), and it was not until its later incarnation that the identification of check-worthiness was incorporated into a fact-checking system [17].

Initially, ClaimBuster modeled the identification of check-worthy statements as a three-class supervised classification task where each sentence had one of three possible labels: check-worthy factual, unimportant factual, and non-factual. They used a dataset of political debates by U.S. presidential candidates, and crowdsourced the sentence labels. A small set of lexical (words and sentence length), shallow syntactic (part-of-speech tags), and semantic (sentiment and entity types) features were extracted and filtered through a random forest classifier for selection. Later, each sentence was assigned a score based on a classification and scoring model, with similar features as before [17]. Another notable work on check-worthiness treated it as a ranking task [11] using a richer set of features. This work also released the CW-USPD-2016 dataset [11], which comprises four political debates. Soon, a larger dataset was built with fifteen additional political debates [29], and a multi-classifier named TATHYA was designed to identify the check-worthy statements in this dataset. This generated a topic probability distribution together with the use of lexical and shallow syntactic features, and provided a comparison against ClaimBuster on the test set. Both systems, however, reported relatively low F1-scores of 0.179 and 0.214, respectively.

Evidently, there is scope for improvement in identifying and ranking check-worthy statements. With the above-mentioned body of work as the foundation, and based on observations regarding the extent of overlap between lexical and shallow syntactic features [11,24], we use a significantly richer set of features including clause and phrase structures and word embeddings to account for syntax, semantics, and linguistic context.

3   Methodology

In this section we begin with a description of the data and then proceed to describe the feature selection and the use of algorithmic heuristics. At this point, we would like to underscore that our long-term goal is to aid fact-checking in a domain-independent manner. Thus, we have chosen to work purely with linguistic constructs, without explicit external domain knowledge.

3.1   Data

We use the English language political debate dataset provided as part of the CLEF 2018 Check-Worthiness task [1]. The training data consists of three political debates, where each sentence is associated with its speaker and expert-annotated as check-worthy or not. It is a highly imbalanced dataset where out of the total 3,989 sentences, only 94 (2.36%) are labeled check-worthy.

The test data consists of two debates and five speeches with 2,815 and 2,064 sentences, respectively[1]. In this dataset, a speaker is associated with every sentence, but they are not normalized. For example, it includes "HILLARY CLINTON (D-NY)", "FORMER SECRETARY OF STATE, PRESIDENTIAL CANDIDATE", and simply "CLINTON". Since these are all referring to the same speaker, we map these variations to a single entity. The training set comprises only debates where multiple entities frequently engage in a conversation. The test set, however, contains speeches by each presidential candidate. The rhetorical structure of a debate, of course, is very different from a speech. We thus extract all the sentences attributed to a particular entity and create entity-specific sub-datasets, which serve to train models to identify check-worthy sentences from speeches. For debates, on the other hand, we use the original training data to train the models.

3.2   Feature Design and Selection

For lexical features, we remove function words and stem the content words using the Snowball stemmer [30]. The remaining set of features we explore can be broadly grouped into (a) syntactic or stylometric, (b) semantic, and (c) contextual.

Syntactic Features. This category may further be divided into shallow and deep syntactic features. Following Gencheva et al. [11], we extract the following shallow syntactic features from a sentence: part-of-speech tags, total number of tokens in a sentence, number of negations, and number of tokens in the past, present, and future tenses. The more complex patterns of language and how they may serve as cues to deceptive statements cannot, however, be understood based on these features [8]. To this end, we generate the constituency parse tree for every sentence, and extract the clause-level and phrase-level tags.

---

[1] The dataset does not provide this categorization, but we treat them differently since a *debate*, unlike a *speech*, has interactive discourse between multiple speakers.

Semantic Features. We use the Stanford named entity recognition system [9] to extract the number of named entities in each sentence. We also distinguish between mentions of people and other entity types by appending an extra feature for entities recognized as the type PERSON. To capture even more meaning from each sentence, we also extract "affect" (direct sentiment as well as connotation). For sentiment scoring, we use the TextBlob [25] library to train a naïve Bayes classifier on the well known movie review corpus [28]. To extract the use of more subtle semantics, we use markers for connotation, subjectivity, bias, and opinion. While the last three have been used in earlier work [11], our approach is the first to incorporate connotation features for check-worthiness. We use Connotation WordNet [20] to obtain a score for each word, and for a sentence, we compute the mean of the connotation scores of its words. For subjectivity and bias, we use lexicons to obtain information about the extent to which each word is used to (a) voice a subjective notion [37], (b) make biased statements [32], and (c) share positive or negative opinions [19]. For each sentence, we thus have four new features beyond overt sentiment – connotation, subjectivity, bias, and opinion – with each feature's value simply being the total score in the corresponding lexicon of all the words in that sentence.

Contextual Features. When incorporating context, we resort to explicit feature extraction as well as word embeddings.

The explicit features comprise metadata and discourse. We use three binary metadata features, indicating whether or not (i) the speaker is the anchor/host, (ii) the speaker's opponent is mentioned in the sentence, and (iii) the sentence is immediately followed by an intense reaction from the audience, which is encoded in the training data as a 'system' reaction. All the features described so far make no distinction between speeches and debates. However, since debates have an interactive discourse structure, we identify every "segment" in the data, defined to be a maximal set of consecutive sentences by the same speaker [11]. As discourse features, we use the relative position of a sentence within its segment, and also the number of sentences in the previous, current, and the following segments.

Beyond explicit features, we use word and sentence embeddings to model context. Traditional vector space modeling associates each dimension with a word, which does not account for the distributional hypothesis in linguistics: words occurring in similar contexts tend to have similar meanings [15]. In contrast, recent work has shown that using the embedding of a word in a latent semantic space often leads to better results in various tasks [6,26] since such embeddings try to account for the word's context in various ways. Inspired by this approach to capturing context, we use word embeddings such that a whole sentence is represented by a vector in a low-dimensional space where similar meanings are closer together. Since this is a topic of extensive research in its own right, we make use of readily available embeddings.

The first approach is to use the 300-dimensional pre-trained Google News word embeddings developed by Mikolov et al. [26], and take the arithmetic mean of all the word vectors to obtain a representation for the entire sentence. The second is to use the state-of-the-art BERT [6] embeddings to obtain sentence-level encoding through their service API [39].

Feature Selection. All the above features result in a very high-dimensional feature space, which is known to decrease the predictive power of models [35]. Especially in this work, the extreme class imbalance (see Sect. 3.1) could mean that features indicative of the minority label get ignored by the classifier. Therefore, we apply a two-stage dimensionality reduction process for the combination of all the features described earlier, except for BERT embeddings. This two-stage feature selection together with the sampling process is novel for this task.

First, we perform univariate feature selection using the χ^2-test and retain the 2,000 best features. Second, we exploit the property that linear predictive models with L1 loss lead to sparse solutions and encourage the vanishing coefficients for weakly correlated features. We do this first for the entire training data, and then with repeated undersampling for the majority class. This way, after each iteration we obtain a small but balanced training set. For every sample generated in this manner, we train a L1-regularized support vector machine (SVM) classifier and discard the features with vanishing coefficients. At the end of this, we are left with a space of 2,655 and 2,404 features for debates and speeches, respectively.

For BERT sentence embeddings, which are provided as pre-trained continuous space language models for text representation, we avoid the χ^2-test because BERT was designed to capture contextual linguistic information and the individual dimensions do not represent separate variables in the traditional sense. Its training process captures deep bidirectional representations from enormous amounts of text in an unsupervised fashion. allowing the embedding to implicitly capture both the left and right context of words in a sentence. We do however, use SVM with L1 regularization as above, resulting in 306 and 260 features for debates and speeches, respectively.

3.3   Classification Models

We use two supervised learning algorithms, SVM and multilayer perceptrons (MLP). Here, we describe these models along with their training processes.

As discussed in Sect. 3.2, we use SVM with L1 regularization for feature selection. However, since the L1 loss function suffers from a tendency to miss optimal solutions, we use L2 loss to build the final model after feature selection. Our MLP uses two hidden layers with 100 units and 8 units, respectively. We use the hyperbolic tangent (tanh) as the activation function, as it achieved better results when compared to rectified linear units (ReLU). Stochastic optimization is done with Adam [21]. Finally, to avoid overfitting, we use L2-regularization in both SVM and MLP. The regularization parameter of SVM is set to 0.02 for debates and 0.01 for speeches. For both learners, the extreme class imbalance was an obstacle, and we use the adaptive synthetic sampling algorithm ADASYN [18] to overcome it. Additionally, we also build an ensemble model combining the SVM and MLP with equal weights. In this model, we provide the final score for each sentence as a normalization by standard deviation of the results of SVM and MLP followed by computing the average.

We use 3-fold cross-validation to select the final model for debates, using two files for training and the remaining one for testing, performance evaluation, and parameter tuning. For speeches, we split the training samples into two halves (one file in each) for 2-fold cross-validation.

Algorithm 1 Heuristics for assigning the check-worthiness score $w(\cdot)$ to sentences. The minimum token count constants were experimentally chosen by measuring the cross-validation performance on the training data.

Require: category $\in$ {SPEECH, DEBATE}, strict_mode $\in$ {**true, false**}, sentence S.

MIN_TOKEN_COUNT $\leftarrow 0$
if category is SPEECH **then**
  if strict_mode **then**
    MIN_TOKEN_COUNT $\leftarrow 10$
  else
    MIN_TOKEN_COUNT $\leftarrow 8$
  end if
else
  if strict_mode **then**
    MIN_TOKEN_COUNT $\leftarrow 7$
  else
    MIN_TOKEN_COUNT $\leftarrow 5$
  end if
end if

if S_{SPEAKER} is SYSTEM **then**
  $w(S) \leftarrow 10^{-8}$
end if
if $S_{\text{NUMBER OF TOKENS}} <$ MIN_TOKEN_COUNT **then**
  $w(S) \leftarrow 10^{-8}$
end if
if S contains "thank you" **then**
  $w(S) \leftarrow 10^{-8}$
end if
if $S_{\text{NUMBER OF SUBJECTS}} < 1$ **then**
  if category is SPEECH **then**
    $w(S) \leftarrow 10^{-8}$
  else if S contains "?" **then**
    $w(S) \leftarrow 10^{-8}$
  end if
end if

3.4 Heuristics

As a final step of our approach, we introduce a few simple rules to override the scores assigned by the MLP models. These (specified in Algorithm 1) differ slightly based on (i) the category, i.e., speech or debate, and (ii) whether or not 'strict' (a flag to control the threshold sentence size) heuristics are being used – when active, it tends to discard more sentences. One rule requires the identification of nominal subjects in a sentence. To extract this, we generate dependency parse trees of the sentence and count the number of times any of the following dependency labels appear: nsubj, csubj, nsubjpass, csubjpass, or xsubj. The first four indicate nominal and clausal subjects in active and passive clauses, respectively, and the last label denotes a controlling subject, which relates an open clausal complement to its external clause.

4   Experiments and Results

The primary evaluation measure in the CLEF 2018 task was the mean average precision (MAP), where average precision is defined in terms of the number of check-worthy sentences n_{chk}, the total number of sentences n, the precision $\text{Prec}(k)$ at cut-off k in the ranked list of sentences, and the indicator function $\delta(k)$ equaling 1 if the sentence at rank k is check-worthy, and 0 otherwise:

$$AP = \frac{1}{n_{chk}} \sum_{k=1}^{n} \text{Prec}(k) \cdot \delta(k).$$

Table 1. Primary submission results of the top three teams, based on mean average precision (MAP). The mean reciprocal rank (MRR), mean R-precision, and mean precision at rank k (MP@k) evaluation measures are also shown.

TEAM	MAP	MRR	MRP	MP@1	MP@3	MP@5	MP@10	MP@20	MP@50
Zuo *et al.* [40]*	**0.1332**	**0.4965**	**0.1352**	**0.4286**	**0.2857**	0.2000	0.1429	**0.1571**	0.1200
Hansen *et al.* [14]	0.1152	0.3159	0.1100	0.1429	0.1429	0.1143	0.1286	0.1286	**0.1257**
Ghanem *et al.* [12]	0.1130	0.4615	0.1315	0.2857	0.2381	**0.3143**	**0.2286**	0.1214	0.0866

As part of the CLEF 2018 Check-Worthiness task, we submitted the MLP model without the strict heuristics as our primary run. The results of the top three teams and their primary runs are shown in Table 1, where our model [40] achieved the best performance with respect to multiple evaluation criteria. In particular, our approach performed the best in terms of the primary evaluation measure MAP, with a score of 0.1332. Our primary submission also had the best performance with regard to placing the most check-worthy statements at the very top of the ranked list, as shown by the mean precision at lower ranks, MP@1 and MP@3. We submitted two contrastive runs as well, one with the strict heuristics and another with the ensemble model where the MLP component was without the strict heuristics. Additionally, we also tested the MLP model with no heuristics at all. For all these models, we used the hand-crafted linguistic features described in Sect. 3.2 and the Google News word embeddings. Our experiments with BERT embeddings were driven to test whether or not they already capture contextual information better than the hand-crafted features. To explore this, we used both MLP and SVM with and without (a) the handcrafted linguistic features, and (b) the feature selection steps.

The performance of these models on the test set are shown in Table 2. For the sake of brevity, we have omitted a few other combinations of feature selection and heuristics. One of our contrastive runs, MLP$_{\neg str}$, performed even better on the test set than the primary submission. The overall best performance is achieved by SVM with BERT embeddings where feature selection (from the sentence embedding vectors) is done using L1 regularization, but no hand-crafted features are used. For this model, we also report our results on the speeches and debates separately in Table 3.

5 Error Analysis and Conjectures

Identifying and prioritizing check-worthy sentences is clearly a difficult task, with even the best model suffering from a rather large number of incorrect

Table 2. Model performance on the test set. *With Google News word embeddings*: MLP*, MLP$_{\neg str}$, and MLP$_{none}$ (strict, non-strict, and no heuristics); ENS (ensemble model). MLP* was our primary submission, and MLP$_{\neg str}$ and ENS were the two contrastive submissions in the CLEF 2018 Lab task. *With BERT embeddings*: the subscript $\pm\mathcal{L}$ denotes whether or not the handcrafted linguistic features are used, and the superscript (†) denotes that feature selection was not performed.

	MAP	MRR	MRP	MP@1	MP@3	MP@5	MP@10	MP@20	MP@50
With Google News embeddings:									
MLP*	0.1332	0.4965	0.1352	0.4286	0.2857	0.2000	0.1429	0.1571	0.1200
MLP$_{\neg str}$	0.1366	0.5246	0.1475	0.4286	0.2857	0.2286	0.1571	0.1714	0.1229
MLP$_{none}$	0.1086	0.4767	0.1037	0.2857	0.2857	0.2000	0.1286	0.1071	0.1000
ENS	0.1317	0.4139	0.1523	0.2857	0.1905	0.1714	0.1571	0.1571	0.1429
With BERT embeddings:									
MLP$_{-\mathcal{L}}$	0.1499	0.4931	0.1601	0.2857	0.3333	0.2571	0.1571	0.1857	0.1314
SVM$_{+\mathcal{L}}^{(\dagger)}$	0.1648	0.3967	0.2170	0.1429	0.2381	0.2286	0.2714	0.20171	0.1600
SVM$_{-\mathcal{L}}^{(\dagger)}$	0.1770	0.5276	0.2002	0.2857	0.2381	0.2286	0.2286	0.2643	0.1486
SVM$_{+\mathcal{L}}$	0.1760	0.4396	0.2157	0.1429	0.2857	0.2571	0.2429	2071	0.1742
SVM$_{-\mathcal{L}}$	**0.1974**	**0.7508**	**0.2201**	**0.7143**	**0.3333**	**0.2857**	**0.2286**	**0.2571**	**0.1657**

classifications. In this section, we analyze the models explored, and present our conjectures regarding why they may be failing to handle many sentences.

First, we observe that tense plays a logically consistent role in check-worthiness – future actions cannot be verified, of course. POS tagging, however, often confuses the future tense with political promises made using the present continuous (e.g., "We're cutting taxes."). We also observe that anecdotes are often wrongly prioritized as check-worthy. These sentences are usually complex, with a lot of content, which makes it easy for the model to conflate them with other complex sentences about check-worthy real events. The dataset contains a few duplicate sentences as well as very similar sentences with different labels, which could be amplifying errors or discarding potentially useful features.

Rhetoric, too, plays a critical role. They often break the structures associated with standard sentence formation. Several incorrect predictions were due to constructs such as *scesis onomaton*, where words or phrases with nearly equivalent meaning are repeated. This could make the model falsely believe that there is more informational content in the sentence. This is even harder to handle with multiple speakers in debates. The conversational aspect also causes another problem: quite a few sentences are short, and in isolation, would not be check-worthy. However, as a response to things mentioned earlier in the debate, they are. A related issue is the use of sentence fragments. This is sparingly used in the literature to intentionally create dramatic effect, but was seen frequently in the debates due to the prevalence of ill-formed or partly-formed sentences stopping and giving way to another sentence. The fragments are verbal repetitions, *e.g.*, "Ambassador Stevens – Ambassador Stevens sent 600 requests for help." In light of such error examples, we believe that our features are better suited for formal written language than speech or debate transcripts.

It is worth noting that the BERT embeddings, too, fail on such examples. Ill-formed or partly-formed sentences are also used much more frequently in debates, due to the conversational nature. This is a major cause of the relatively poor performance on debates of the best performing model, $SVM_{-\mathcal{L}}$ (shown in Table 3). For example, BERT labels this incorrectly: "Now, in fact – in fact, there is an effort, Patty Murray has introduced legislation for \$12 minimum wage."

Table 3. Performance of the best performing model $SVM_{-\mathcal{L}}$ (SVM with BERT embeddings and no hand-crafted features) on debates and speeches from the test set.

	MAP	MRR	MRP	MP@1	MP@3	MP@5	MP@10	MP@20	MP@50
Debates	0.1185	0.5278	0.1234	0.5000	0.3333	**0.3000**	**0.3000**	**0.2750**	**0.1500**
Speeches	**0.2290**	**0.8400**	**0.2588**	**0.8000**	**0.3333**	0.2800	0.1400	0.1600	0.1040

Overall, the SVM model using only BERT embeddings achieved the best performance. This may seem somewhat surprising, but consider that the deep bidirectional network implicitly captures a lot of contextual information (unlike older methods like the Google News embeddings). It is worth noting, however, that feature selection played an important role across all models. With BERT embeddings, we observe that while it performs significantly better on many sentences, if often continues to fail in the presence of complex syntactic structures and frequent use of named entities. This is quite possibly because the context captured by these embeddings regard a sentence as a flat structure, which works reasonably well until the parse trees become deeper. Another potential reason for failure could be that the pre-trained embeddings are derived from vast amounts of data where the named entities (*e.g.*, Iraq, Donald, ISIS) are, indeed, correlated with check-worthy statements whereas in the data used in this work, these entities also frequently appear in sentences that are not worth checking.

6   Conclusion and Future Work

We described several models to detect check-worthy sentences in political debates and speeches. Some models combine a few rules with supervised learning using linguistic features, whereas others use contextual embeddings. This work opens up several possibilities for future research in the field of fact-checking. First, we would like to perform ablation tests to confirm some of the conjectures made on the basis of manual error analysis. Next, we would also like to study in greater detail the linguistic forms of *informational* content. This has been done qualitatively in sociolinguistics, and some work has even looked into deep syntactic features, but it has not yet been applied to identifying check-worthy sentences.

The use of BERT embeddings show that even with deep learning, there is significant scope for improvement in terms of modeling context in word and sentence representations, especially for context to be explored in conjunction with deep syntactic structures. For this line of research to create social impact, there is also a need for complementary thrusts in related areas such as social network analysis, information source identification, and trustworthy crowdsourcing.

Acknowledgment. This work was supported in part by the U.S. National Science Foundation (NSF) under the award SES-1834597.

References

1. Atanasova, P., et al.: Overview of the CLEF-2018 CheckThat! Lab on automatic identification and verification of political claims, task 1: check-worthiness. In: Cappellato, L., Ferro, N., Nie, J.Y., Soulier, L. (eds.) CLEF 2018 Working Notes (2018)
2. Bruns, A., Highfield, T.: Blogs, Twitter, and breaking news: the produsage of citizen journalism. In: Produsing Theory in a Digital World: The Intersection of Audiences and Production in Contemporary Theory, vol. 80, pp. 15–32. Peter Lang (2012)
3. Cao, T.D., Manolescu, I., Tannier, X.: Extracting statistical mentions from textual claims to provide trusted content. In: Métais, E., Meziane, F., Vadera, S., Sugumaran, V., Saraee, M. (eds.) NLDB 2019. LNCS, vol. 11608, pp. 402–408. Springer, Cham (2019). https://doi.org/10.1007/978-3-030-23281-8_36
4. Cazalens, S., Lamarre, P., Leblay, J., Manolescu, I., Tannier, X.: A content management perspective on fact-checking. In: Journalism, Misinformation and Fact Checking Alternate Paper Track of The Web Conference (2018)
5. Cohen, S., Li, C., Yang, J., Yu, C.: Computational journalism: a call to arms to database researchers. In: Conference on Innovative Data Systems Research, CIDR 2011, ACM, Asilomar (2011)
6. Devlin, J., Chang, M., Lee, K., Toutanova, K.: BERT: pre-training of deep bidirectional transformers for language understanding. CoRR abs/1810.04805 (2018)
7. Diakopoulos, N.: A functional roadmap for innovation in computational journalism. Rutgers University, Technical report (2011)
8. Feng, S., Banerjee, R., Choi, Y.: Syntactic stylometry for deception detection. In: ACL, no. 2, pp. 171–175 (2012)
9. Finkel, J.R., Grenager, T., Manning, C.: Incorporating non-local information into information extraction systems by Gibbs sampling. In: ACL, pp. 363–370 (2005)
10. Flew, T., Spurgeon, C., Daniel, A., Swift, A.: The promise of computational journalism. Journal. Pract. **6**(2), 157–171 (2012)
11. Gencheva, P., Nakov, P., Màrquez, L., Barrón-Cedeño, A., Koychev, I.: A context-aware approach for detecting worth-checking claims in political debates. In: RANLP 2017, pp. 267–276 (2017)
12. Ghanem, B., Montes-y Gómez, M., Rangel, F., Rosso, P.: UPV-INAOE-Autoritas-Check that: preliminary approach for checking worthiness of claims. In: CLEF Working Notes (2018)
13. Goode, L.: Social news, citizen journalism and democracy. New Media Soc. **11**(8), 1287–1305 (2009)

14. Hansen, C., Hansen, C., Simonsen, J.G., Lioma, C.: The Copenhagen team participation in the check-worthiness task of the competition of automatic identification and verification of claims in political debates of the CLEF-2018 CheckThat! Lab. In: CLEF Working Notes (2018)

15. Harris, Z.S.: Distributional Structure. Word **10**(2–3), 146–162 (1954)

16. Hassan, N., Li, C., Tremayne, M.: Detecting check-worthy factual claims in presidential debates. In: CIKM, pp. 1835–1838. CIKM (2015)

17. Hassan, N., et al.: ClaimBuster: the first-ever end-to-end fact-checking system. Proc. VLDB Endow. **10**(12), 1945–1948 (2017)

18. He, H., Bai, Y., Garcia, E.A., Li, S.: ADASYN: adaptive synthetic sampling approach for imbalanced learning. In: Proceedings of the IEEE Joint Conference on Neural Networks (IJCNN), pp. 1322–1328. IEEE (2008)

19. Hu, M., Liu, B.: Mining and summarizing customer reviews. In: ACM SIGKDD, pp. 168–177. ACM (2004)

20. Kang, J.S., Feng, S., Akoglu, L., Choi, Y.: ConnotationWordNet: learning connotation over the word+sense network. In: ACL, pp. 1544–1554. Association for Computational Linguistics, June 2014

21. Kingma, D.P., Ba, J.: Adam: a method for stochastic optimization. arXiv preprint arXiv:1412.6980 (2014)

22. Klayman, J.: Varieties of confirmation bias. In: Psychology of Learning and Motivation, vol. 32, pp. 385–418. Elsevier (1995)

23. Kumar, S., West, R., Leskovec, J.: Disinformation on the web: impact, characteristics, and detection of wikipedia hoaxes. In: Proceedings of 25th International Conference on World Wide Web, pp. 591–602. International WWWW Conference Committee (IW3C2) (2016)

24. Le, D.T., Vu, N.T., Blessing, A.: Towards a text analysis system for political debates. In: Proceedings of the 10th SIGHUM Workshop on Language Technology for Cultural Heritage, Social Sciences, and Humanities, pp. 134–139 (2016)

25. Loria, S.: TextBlob: simplified text processing (2014). http://textblob.readthedocs.org/en/dev/

26. Mikolov, T., Chen, K., Corrado, G., Dean, J.: Efficient estimation of word representations in vector space. arXiv preprint arXiv:1301.3781 (2013)

27. Nakov, P., et al.: Overview of the CLEF-2018 lab on automatic identification and verification of claims in political debates. In: Working Notes of CLEF 2018 - Conference and Labs of the Evaluation Forum, CLEF 2018, Avignon, France, September 2018

28. Pang, B., Lee, L., Vaithyanathan, S.: Thumbs up?: sentiment classification using machine learning techniques. In: EMNLP, pp. 79–86 (2002)

29. Patwari, A., Goldwasser, D., Bagchi, S.: TATHYA: a multi-classifier system for detecting check-worthy statements in political debates. In: CIKM, pp. 1–4 (2017)

30. Porter, M.F.: Snowball: a language for stemming algorithms (2001). http://snowball.tartarus.org/texts/introduction.html

31. Qazvinian, V., Rosengren, E., Radev, D., Mei, Q.: Rumor has it: identifying misinformation in microblogs. In: EMNLP, pp. 1589–1599. ACL (2011)

32. Recasens, M., Danescu-Niculescu-Mizil, C., Jurafsky, D.: Linguistic models for analyzing and detecting biased language. In: ACL, vol. 1, pp. 1650–1659 (2013)

33. Rodriguez, M.G., Gummadi, K., Schoelkopf, B.: Quantifying information overload in social media and its impact on social contagions. In: ICWSM (2014)

34. Stanovsky, G., Michael, J., Zettlemoyer, L., Dagan, I.: Supervised open information extraction. In: NAACL-HLT, vol. 1 (Long Papers), pp. 885–895 (2018)

35. Trunk, G.V.: A problem of dimensionality: a simple example. IEEE Trans. Pattern Anal. Mach. Intell. **1**(3), 306–307 (1979)
36. Vlachos, A., Riedel, S.: Fact checking: task definition and dataset construction. In: Proceedings of the ACL 2014 Workshop on Language Technologies and Computational Social Science, pp. 18–22 (2014)
37. Wilson, T., Wiebe, J., Hoffmann, P.: Recognizing contextual polarity in phrase-level sentiment analysis. In: EMNLP, pp. 347–354 (2005)
38. Wu, Y., Agarwal, P.K., Li, C., Yang, J., Yu, C.: Toward computational fact-checking. Proc. VLDB Endow. **7**(7), 589–600 (2014)
39. Xiao, H.: bert-as-service (2018). https://github.com/hanxiao/bert-as-service
40. Zuo, C., Karakas, A., Banerjee, R.: A hybrid recognition system for check-worthy claims using heuristics and supervised learning. In: Cappellato, L., Ferro, N., Nie, J.Y., Soulier, L. (eds.) CLEF 2018 Working Notes (2018)

CLEF 2019 Lab Overviews

Overview of CENTRE@CLEF 2019: Sequel in the Systematic Reproducibility Realm

Nicola Ferro[1(✉)], Norbert Fuhr[2], Maria Maistro[1,3(✉)],
Tetsuya Sakai[4], and Ian Soboroff[5]

[1] University of Padua, Padua, Italy
{ferro,maistro}@dei.unipd.it
[2] University of Duisburg-Essen, Duisburg, Germany
norbert.fuhr@uni-due.de
[3] University of Copenhagen, Copenhagen, Denmark
mm@di.ku.dk
[4] Waseda University, Tokyo, Japan
tetsuyasakai@acm.org
[5] National Institute of Standards and Technology (NIST), Gaithersburg, USA
ian.soboroff@nist.gov

Abstract. Reproducibility has become increasingly important for many research areas, among those IR is not an exception and has started to be concerned with reproducibility and its impact on research results. This paper describes our second attempt to propose a lab on reproducibility named CENTRE, held during CLEF 2019. The aim of CENTRE is to run both a replicability and reproducibility challenge across all the major IR evaluation campaigns and to provide the IR community with a venue where previous research results can be explored and discussed. This paper reports the participant results and preliminary considerations on the second edition of CENTRE@CLEF 2019.

1 Introduction

Reproducibility is becoming a primary concern in many areas of science [18,26] as well as in computer science, as also witnessed by the recent ACM policy on result and artefact review and badging.

Also in *Information Retrieval (IR)* replicability and reproducibility of the experimental results are becoming a more and more central discussion items in the research community [4,13,19,25,30]. We now commonly find questions about the extent of reproducibility of the reported experiments in the review forms of all the major IR conferences, such as SIGIR, CHIIR, ICTIR and ECIR, as well as journals, such as ACM TOIS. We also witness to the raise of new activities aimed at verifying the reproducibility of the results: for example, the "Reproducibility Track" at ECIR since 2015 hosts papers which replicate, reproduce and/or generalize previous research results.

© Springer Nature Switzerland AG 2019
F. Crestani et al. (Eds.): CLEF 2019, LNCS 11696, pp. 287–300, 2019.
https://doi.org/10.1007/978-3-030-28577-7_24

Nevertheless, it has been repeatedly shown that best TREC systems still outperform off-the-shelf open source systems [4–6,24,25]. This is due to many different factors, among which lack of tuning on a specific collection when using default configuration, but it is also caused by the lack of the specific and advanced components and resources adopted by the best systems.

It has been also shown that additivity is an issue, since adding a component on top of a weak or strong base does not produce the same level of gain [6,24]. This poses a serious challenge when off-the-shelf open source systems are used as stepping stone to test a new component on top of them, because the gain might appear bigger starting from a weak baseline.

Moreover, besides the problems encountered in replicating/reproducing research, we lack any well established measure to assess and quantify the extent to which something has been replicated/reproduced. In other terms, even if a later researcher can manage to replicate or reproduce an experiment, to which extent can we claim that the experiment is successfully replicated or reproduced? For the replicability task we can compare the original measure score with the score of the replicated run, as done in [16,17]. However, this can not be done for reproducibility, since the reproduced system is obtained on a different data set and it is not directly comparable with the original system in terms of measure scores.

Finally, both a Dagstuhl Perspectives Workshop [12] and the recent SWIRL III strategic workshop [1] have put on the IR research agenda the need to develop both better explanatory models of IR system performance and new predictive models, able to anticipate the performance of IR systems in new operational conditions.

Overall, the above considerations stress the need and urgency for a systematic approach to reproducibility and generalizability in IR. Therefore, the goal of *CLEF, NTCIR, TREC REproducibility (CENTRE)* at CLEF 2019 is to run a joint CLEF/NTCIR/TREC task on challenging participants:

- to replicate and reproduce best results of best/most interesting systems in previous editions of CLEF/NTCIR/TREC by using standard open source IR systems;
- to contribute back to the community the additional components and resources developed to reproduce the results in order to improve existing open source systems;
- to start exploring the generalizability of our findings and the possibility of predicting IR system performance;
- to investigate possible measures for replicability and reproducibility in IR.

The paper is organized as follows: Sect. 2 introduces the setup of the lab; Sect. 3 discusses the participation and the experimental outcomes; and, Sect. 4 draws some conclusions and outlooks possible future works.

2   Evaluation Lab Setup

2.1   Tasks

Similarly to its previous edition, CENTRE@CLEF 2019 offered the following two tasks:

- *Task 1 - Replicability*: the task focuses on the replicability of selected methods on the same experimental collections;
- *Task 2 - Reproducibility*: the task focuses on the reproducibility of selected methods on different experimental collections;

For *Replicability* and *Reproducibility* we refer to the ACM Artifact Review and Badging definitions[1]:

- *Replicability* (different team, same experimental setup): the measurement can be obtained with stated precision by a different team using the same measurement procedure, the same measuring system, under the same operating conditions, in the same or a different location on multiple trials. For computational experiments, this means that an independent group can obtain the same result using the author's own artifacts. In CENTRE@CLEF 2019 this meant to use the same collections, topics and ground-truth on which the methods and solutions have been developed and evaluated.
- *Reproducibility* (different team, different experimental setup): The measurement can be obtained with stated precision by a different team, a different measuring system, in a different location on multiple trials. For computational experiments, this means that an independent group can obtain the same result using artifacts which they develop completely independently. In CENTRE@CLEF 2019 this meant to use a different experimental collection, but in the same domain, from those used to originally develop and evaluate a solution.

For Task 1 and Task 2, CENTRE@CLEF 2019 teams up with the *Open-Source IR Replicability Challenge (OSIRRC)* [11] at SIGIR 2019. Therefore, participating groups could consider to submit their runs both to CENTRE@CLEF 2019 and OSIRRC 2019, where the second venue requires to submit the runs as Docker images.

Besides Task 1 and Task 2, CENTRE@CLEF 2019 offered also a new pilot task:

- *Task 3 - Generalizability*: the task focuses on collection performance prediction and the goal is to rank (sub-)collections on the basis of the expected performance over them.

---

[1] https://www.acm.org/publications/policies/artifact-review-badging.

In details, Task 3 was instantiated as follows:

- *Training*: participants need to run plain BM25 and, if they wish, also their own system on the test collection used for TREC 2004 Robust Track (they are allowed to use the corpus, topics and qrels). Participants need to identify features of the corpus and topics that allow them to predict the system score with respect to *Average Precision (AP)*.
- *Validation*: participants can use the test collection used for TREC 2017 Common Core Track (corpus, topics and qrels) to validate their method and determine which set of features represent the best choice for predicting AP score for each system. Note that the TREC 2017 Common Core Track topics are an updated version of the TREC 2004 Robust track topics.
- *Test* (submission): participants need to use the test collection used for TREC 2018 Common Core Track (only corpus and topics). Note that the TREC 2018 Common Core Track topics are a mix of "old" and "new" topics, where old topics were used in TREC 2017 Common Core track. Participants will submit a run for each system (BM25 and their own system) and an additional file (one for each system) including the AP score predicted for each topic. The score predicted can be a single value or a value with the corresponding confidence interval.

2.2 Replicability and Reproducibility Targets

For the previous edition of CENTRE@CLEF 2018 [16,17] we selected the target runs for replicability and reproducibility among the Ad Hoc tasks in previous editions of CLEF, TREC, and NTCIR. However, even though CENTRE@CLEF 2018 had 17 enrolled teams, eventually only one team managed to submit a run. One of the main issues reported by the participating team is the lack of the external resources exploited in the original paper, which are no longer available [21]. Therefore, for CENTRE@CLEF 2019 we decided to focus on more recent papers submitted at TREC Common Core Track in 2017 and 2018.

Below we list the runs selected as targets of replicability and reproducibility among which the participants can choose. For each run, we specify the corresponding collection for replicability and for reproducibility. For more information, the list also provides references to the papers describing those runs as well as the overviews describing the overall task and collections.

- **Runs**: WCrobust04 and WCrobust0405 [20]
  - **Task Type**: TREC 2017 Common Core Track [2]
  - **Replicability**: New York Times Annotated Corpus, with TREC 2017 Common Core Topics
  - **Reproducibility**: TREC Washington Post Corpus, with TREC 2018 Common Core Topics
- **Runs**: RMITFDA4 and RMITEXTGIGADA5 [7]
  - **Task Type**: TREC 2018 Common Core Track [3]
  - **Replicability**: TREC Washington Post Corpus, with TREC 2018 Common Core Topics

- **Reproducibility**: New York Times Annotated Corpus, with TREC 2017 Common Core Topics

Since these runs were not originally thought for being used as targets of a replicability/reproducibility exercise, we contacted the authors of the papers to inform them and ask their consent to use the runs.

2.3 Evaluation Measures

Task 1 - Replicability: As done in the previous edition of CENTRE [16,17], the quality of the replicability runs has been evaluated from two points of view:

- *Effectiveness*: how close are the performance scores of the replicated systems to those of the original ones. This is measured using the *Root Mean Square Error (RMSE)* [23] between the new and original measures scores $M(\cdot)$:

$$\text{RMSE} = \sqrt{\frac{1}{T}\sum_{i=1}^{T}\left(M_{orig,i} - M_{replica,i}\right)^2} \tag{1}$$

where T is the total number of topics, $M_{orig,i}$ is the measure score of the original target run on topic t_i and $M_{replica,i}$ is the measure score of the replicated run on topic t. Equation (1) is instantiated with AP, *Normalized Discounted Cumulated Gain (nDCG)* and *Expected Reciprocal Rank (ERR)*.
- *Ranked result lists*: since different result lists may produce the same effectiveness score, we also measure how close are the ranked results list of the replicated systems to those of the original ones. This is measured using Kendall's τ correlation coefficient [22] among the list of retrieved documents for each topic, averaged across all the topics. The Kendall's τ correlation coefficient on a single topic is given by:

$$\tau_i\left(orig, replica\right) = \frac{P - Q}{\sqrt{\left(P + Q + U\right)\left(P + Q + V\right)}}$$
$$\bar{\tau}\left(orig, replica\right) = \frac{1}{T}\sum_{i=1}^{T}\tau_i(orig, replica) \tag{2}$$

where T is the total number of topics, P is the total number of concordant pairs (document pairs that are ranked in the same order in both vectors) Q the total number of discordant pairs (document pairs that are ranked in opposite order in the two vectors), U and V are the number of ties, respectively, in the first and in the second ranking.

Note that the definition of Kendall's τ in Eq. (2) is originally proposed for permutations of the same set of items, therefore it is not applicable whenever two rankings do not contain the same set of documents. However, for real rankings of systems it is highly likely that two lists do not contain the same set of items, thus we performed some pre-processing with the runs before computing Kendall's τ in Eq. (2).

In details, consider a fixed topic t, the original ranking $r_{t,orig}$ and the replicated ranking $r_{t,replica}$. If one of the rankings contains a document that is not retrieved by the other ranking, we define the rank position of that document as zero. For example, if for a document d, $d \in r_{t,orig}$, but $d \notin r_{t,replica}$, then the rank position of d in $r_{t,replica}$ is zero. Whenever the two rankings contains the same set of documents, Eq. (2) is not affected by this pre-processing step and the computation of Kendall's tau is performed as usual. Furthermore, if two rankings retrieves different documents and place them in the same rank positions, Kendall's tau will still be equal to 1, and the comparison is performed just with respect to the relative order of the documents retrieved by both the rankings.

Task 2 - Reproducibility: Since for the reproducibility runs we do not have an already existing run to compare against, we compare the reproduced run score with respect to a baseline run, to see whether the improvement over the baseline is comparable between the original collection C and the new collection D. In particular we compute the *Effect Ratio (ER)*, which is also exploited in CENTRE@NTCIR 14 [27].

In details, given two runs, we refer to the A-run, as the advanced run, and B-run, as the baseline run, where the A-run has been reported to outperform the B-run on the original test collection C. The intuition behind ER is to evaluate to which extent the improvement on the original collection C is reproduced on a new collection D. For any evaluation measure M, let $M_i^C(A)$ and $M_i^C(B)$ denote the score of the A-run and that of the B-run for the i-th topic of collection C ($1 \leq i \leq T_C$). Similarly, let $M_i^D(A')$ and $M_i^D(B')$ denote the scores for the reproduced A-run and B-run respectively, on the new collection D. Then, ER is computed as follows:

$$\mathrm{ER}(\Delta M_{reproduced}^D, \Delta M_{orig}^C) = \frac{\frac{1}{T_D}\sum_{i=1}^{T_D} \Delta M_{i,reproduced}^D}{\frac{1}{T_C}\sum_{i=1}^{T_C} \Delta M_{i,orig}^C} \quad (3)$$

where $\Delta M_{i,orig}^C = M_i^C(A) - M_i^C(B)$ is the per-topic improvement of the original advanced and baseline runs for the i-th topic on C. Similarly $\Delta M_{i,reproduced}^D = M_i^C(A') - M_i^C(B')$ is the per-topic improvement of the reproduced advanced and baseline runs for the i-th topic on D. Note that the per-topic improvement can be negative, for those topics where the advanced run fails to outperform the baseline run.

If ER ≤ 0, that means that the replicated A-run failed to outperform the replicated B-run: the replication is a complete failure. If $0 <$ ER < 1, the replication is somewhat successful, but the effect is smaller compared to the original experiment. If ER $= 1$, the replication is perfect in the sense that the original effect has been recovered as is. If ER > 1, the replication is successful, and the effect is actually larger compared to the original experiment.

Finally, ER in Eq. (3) is instantiated with respect to AP, nDCG and ERR.

Table 1. Path to the submitted runs files in the online repository with their description and the number of assessed topics included in each run.

Run Path	Description	# Topics
official/task1/irc_task1_WCrobust04_001	official run, replicating WCrobust04	50
official/task1/irc_task1_WCrobust0405_001	official run, replicating WCrobst0405	33
official/task2/irc_task2_WCrobust04_001	official run, reproducing WCrobust05	25
official/task2/irc_task2_WCrobust0405_001	official run, reproducing WCrobust0405	15
unofficial/complete_topics/task1/irc_task1_WCrobust04_001	unofficial run, replicating WCrobust04	50
unofficial/complete_topics/task1/irc_task2_WCrobust04_001	unofficial run, replicating WCrobust0405	50
unofficial/complete_topics/task2/irc_task2_WCrobust04_001	unofficial run, reproducing WCrobust05	25
unofficial/complete_topics/task2/irc_task2_WCrobust0405_001	unofficial run, reproducing WCrobust0405	25

Task 3 - Generalizability: For the generalizability task we planned to compare the predicted run score with the original run score. This is measured with Mean Absolute Error and RMSE between the predicted and original measures scores, with respect to AP, nDCG and ERR. However, we did not receive any run for the generalizability task, so we did not put in practice this part of the evaluation task.

3 Participation and Outcomes

19 groups registered for participating in CENTRE@CLEF2019, but unfortunately only one group succeeded in submitting two replicability runs and two reproducibility runs. No runs were submitted for the generalizability task.

The team from the University of Applied Science TH Köln [8] replicated and reproduced the runs by Grossman and Cormack [20], i.e. WCrobust04 and WCrobust0405. They could not replicate the runs by Benham et al. [7] since they do not have access to the Gigaworld dataset[2], which is publicly available upon payment of a fee. The dataset is necessary to perform the external query expansion exploited by the selected runs from [7].

Eventually, the participating team submitted four official runs and four unofficial runs described in Table 1. The runs and all the code is publicly available online[3].

The paper by Grossman and Cormack [20] exploits the principle of automatic routing runs: first, a logistic regression model is trained with the relevance judgments from one or more collections for each topic, then the model is used to predict relevance assessments of documents from a different collection. Both the training and the prediction phases are done on a topic-wise basis.

The routing process represented a challenge for the participating team, which initially submitted a set of four official runs, where some of the topics were missing. For example, the official run irc_task1_WCrobust0405_001 contains only 33 topics, while the corresponding original run WCrobust0405 contains

---

[2] https://catalog.ldc.upenn.edu/LDC2012T21.

[3] https://bitbucket.org/centre_eval/c2019_irc/src/master/.

Table 2. Evaluation of the replicability task for the unofficial `WCrobust04` (50 topics): measures scores averaged across the topics and RMSE.

	Original Run `WCrobust04`	Replicated Run `irc_task1_WCrobust04_001`	RMSE
AP@10	0.0506	0.0564	0.0224
AP@100	0.2252	0.1862	0.0868
AP@1000	0.3821	0.2963	0.1371
nDCG@10	0.1442	0.1503	0.0567
nDCG@100	0.3883	0.3421	0.1110
nDCG@1000	0.6299	0.5418	0.1374
ERR@10	0.5340	0.5663	0.2463
ERR@100	0.5341	0.5693	0.2437
ERR@1000	0.5663	0.5695	0.2436

all the 50 topics. The participating team could not understand how to derive document rankings for those topics such that no training topics were available for the logistic regression model. For example, when they were attempting to replicate `WCrobust0405`, they exploited as training set the intersection between the topics from TREC 2004 Robust and TREC 2005 Robust. Then, for the prediction phase, only 33 topics from TREC 2017 Common Core were contained in the training set, and no prediction could be performed for the remaining topics. Due to similar issues, the official `irc_task2_WCrobust04_001` and `irc_task2_WCrobust0405_001` contain 25 and 15 topics respectively.

Afterwards, the participating team contacted the authors of the original paper, Grossman and Cormack [20], to understand how to derive rankings even when there are no training topics available. The authors clarified that for `WCrobust0405` the training set contains both the topics from TREC 2004 Robust and TREC 2005 Robust, and when a topic is not contained in TREC 2005 Robust, they used just the TREC 2004 Robust collection as training set. Therefore, the authors submitted four additional unofficial runs, where both `irc_task1_WCrobust04_001` and `irc_task1_WCrobust0405_001` contain all the 50 topics, while the reproduced runs `irc_task2_WCrobust04_001` and `irc_task-2_WCrobust04_001` contain 25 topics. Note that some of the topics are missing for the reproduced runs, since no training data is available for 25 out of the 50 topics of TREC 2018 Common Core.

In the following we report the evaluation results for the replicability and reproducibility tasks, just for the unofficial submissions, which contain more topics than the official submission. The complete results for all the submitted runs can be found in [14].

Tables 2 and 3 report AP, nDCG and ERR scores for the unofficial replicated runs. As shown by RMSE, the replication task was fairly successful with respect to AP and nDCG, while when ERR is considered, RMSE is greater than 0.2, showing that it is harder to replicate ERR than the other evaluation measures. Indeed, it is well known that ERR is highly sensitive to the position of relevant documents at the very beginning of the ranking, thus even the misplacement of a single relevant documents may cause a significant drop in ERR score.

Table 3. Evaluation of the replicability task for the unofficial `WCrobust0405` (50 topics): measures scores averaged across the topics and RMSE.

	Original Run WCrobust0405	Replicated Run irc_task1_WCrobust0405_001	RMSE
AP@10	0.0584	0.0604	0.0209
AP@100	0.2699	0.2244	0.0798
AP@1000	0.4378	0.3534	0.1227
nDCG@10	0.1675	0.1698	0.0484
nDCG@100	0.4480	0.3994	0.1024
nDCG@1000	0.6878	0.6064	0.1279
ERR@10	0.6330	0.6572	0.2106
ERR@100	0.6359	0.6593	0.2095
ERR@1000	0.6360	0.6593	0.2095

Table 4. Kendall's τ between the original and replicated runs.

Replicated Run	Original Run	τ@10	τ@100	τ@1000
irc_task1_WCrobust04_001	WCrobust04	-0.0222	0.0073	0.0021
irc_task1_WCrobust0405_001	WCrobust0405	-0.0107	0.0199	0.0029

Furthermore, as the cut-off increases, even RMSE for AP and nDCG increases, showing that the replication is less accurate at lower cut-off levels. On the other side, RMSE for ERR is almost constant when the cut-off increases, showing once more that ERR focuses on the top rank positions rather than considering the whole ranking.

Table 4 reports the Kendall's τ correlation between the original and replicated runs, for the unofficial runs. We computed Kendall's τ at different cut-off levels, where we first trimmed the runs at the specified cut-off and subsequently computed Kendall's τ between the trimmed runs.

Table 4 shows that the replication was not successful for any of the runs in terms of Kendall's τ. This means that even if the considered replicated runs were similar to the original runs in terms of placement of relevant and non relevant documents, they actually retrieves different documents.

Figures 1 and 2 shows the first 10 rank positions for `WCrobust04` and its replicated version `irc_task1_WCrobust04_001`, for topic 307 from TREC 2017

Common Core Track. We can observe that even if the runs retrieves a similar set of documents, the relative position of each document is different. For example, document 309412 is at rank position 1 for the original run, but at rank position 2 for the replicated run, similarly document 733642 is at rank position 1 for the replicated run and at rank position 5 for the original run. Moreover, document 241240 is at rank position 3 for the replicated run, but it does not apper on the first 10 positions for the original run.

```
307 Q0  309412  1   -1  WCrobust04
307 Q0  582044  2   -2  WCrobust04
307 Q0  672305  3   -3  WCrobust04
307 Q0  1438673 4   -4  WCrobust04
307 Q0  733642  5   -5  WCrobust04
307 Q0  377253  6   -6  WCrobust04
307 Q0  284810  7   -7  WCrobust04
307 Q0  1248807 8   -8  WCrobust04
307 Q0  1241952 9   -9  WCrobust04
307 Q0  587044  10  -10 WCrobust04
```

```
307 Q0  733642   1  0.8666604108653863  IRC
307 Q0  309412   2  0.8367380559490579  IRC
307 Q0  241240   3  0.8262481009460336  IRC
307 Q0  1248807  4  0.7941459503093672  IRC
307 Q0  125806   5  0.7714647940416018  IRC
307 Q0  617046   6  0.7704302957730799  IRC
307 Q0  672305   7  0.7682124713790986  IRC
307 Q0  1677923  8  0.7614708545584544  IRC
307 Q0  566174   9  0.7530631567740554  IRC
307 Q0  1620713 10  0.7422523019156065  IRC
```

Fig. 1. First 10 rank positions for WCrobust04 for topic 307 form TREC 2017 Common Core Track.

Fig. 2. First 10 rank positions for irc_ task1_WCrobust04_001 for topic 307 form TREC 2017 Common Core Track.

Table 5. Evaluation of the reproducibility task with mean per-topic improvement and *Effect Ratio (ER)* for the unofficial runs (50 topics for original runs and 25 topics for the reproduced runs).

	ΔM^C_{orig}	$\Delta M^D_{reproduced}$	ER
AP@10	0.0078	0.0065	0.8333
AP@100	0.0446	0.0241	0.5404
AP@1000	0.0556	0.0336	0.6043
nDCG@10	0.0233	0.0155	0.6652
nDCG@100	0.0597	0.0426	0.7136
nDCG@1000	0.0578	0.0509	0.8806
ERR@10	0.1042	0.0004	0.0038
ERR@100	0.1019	0.0033	0.0324
ERR@1000	0.1019	0.0029	0.0285

Table 4, Figs. 1 and 2 highlights how hard is to replicate the exact ranking of documents. Therefore, whenever a replicability task is considered, comparing the evaluation scores with RMSE or ER might not be enough, since these approaches consider just the position of relevant and not relevant documents, and overlook the actual ranking of documents.

Finally, Table 5 reports the mean per-topic improvement and ER for the unofficial runs from the reproducibility task. We considered WCrobust0405 as advanced run and WCrobust04 as baseline run, on the test collection from

TREC 2017 Common Core Track. Analougsly, the reproduced advanced run is irc_task2_WCrobust0405_001 and the reproduced baseline run is irc_task2-_WCrobust04_001, on the test collection from TREC 2018 Common Core Track. Both the reproduced unofficial runs contain the same 25 topics, therefore the per-topic improvement is computed as irc_task2_WCrobust0405_001 scores minus irc_task2_WCrobust04_001 scores for each topic.

Table 5 shows that the reproducibility task is fairly successful with respect to AP@10 and nDCG@1000, thus the effect of the advanced run over the baseline run is better reproduced at the beginning of the ranking for AP, and when the whole ranked list is considered, for nDCG. Similarly to the replicability task, ERR is the hardest measure to be reproduced, indeed it has the lowest ER score for each cut-off level.

Furthermore, when the cut-off increases, the accuracy of the reproducibility exercise increases for nDCG, while it decreases for AP, and increases for ERR even if it remains very low. Therefore, the effect of the advanced run over the baseline run is better reproduced at the beginning of the ranking for AP and with respect to the whole ranking for nDCG.

4   Conclusions and Future Work

This paper reports the results on the second edition of CENTRE@CLEF2019. A total of 19 participants enrolled in the lab, however just one group managed to submit two replicability runs and two reproducibility runs. As reported in Sect. 3, the participating team could not reproduce the runs from Benham et al. [7], due to the lack of the Gigaworld dataset, but they managed to replicate and reproduce the runs from Grossman and Cormack [20]. More details regarding the implementation are described in their paper [8].

The experimental results show that the replicated runs are fairly successful with respect to AP and nDCG, while the lowest replicability results are obtained with respect to ERR. As ERR mainly focuses on the beginning of the ranking, misplacing even a single relevant document can deteriorate ERR score and have a great impact on the replicability evaluation scores.

Moreover, whenever replicability is considered, RMSE and ER are not enough to evaluate the replicated runs. Indeed, they only account for the position of relevant and not relevant documents by considering the similarity between the original scores and the replicated scores, and they overlook the actual ranking of documents. When the runs are evaluated with Kendall's τ to account for the actual position of the documents in the ranking, the experiments show that the replicability is not successful at all, with Kendall's τ values close to 0. This confirms that, even if it is possible to achieve similar scores in terms of IR evaluation measures, it is challenging to replicate the same documents ranking.

When it comes to reproducibility, there are no well-established evaluation measures to determine to which extent a system can be reproduced. Therefore, we compute ER, firstly exploited in [27], which focuses on the reproduction of the improvement of an advanced run over a baseline run. The experiments show that reproducibility was fairly successful in terms of AP@10 and nDCG@1000, while, similarly to the replicability task, ERR is the hardest measure in terms of reproducibility success.

Finally, as reported in [16,17], the lack of participation is a signal that the IR community is somehow overlooking replicability and reproducibility issues. As it also emerged from a recent survey within the SIGIR community [15], while there is a very positive attitude towards reproducibility and it is considered very important from a scientific point of view, there are many obstacles to it such as the effort required to put it into practice, the lack of rewards for achieving it, the possible barriers for new and inexperienced groups, and, last but not least, the (somehow optimistic) researcher's perception that their own research is already reproducible.

For the next edition of the lab we are planning to propose some changes in the lab organization to increase the interest and participation of the research community. First, we will target for more popular systems to be replicated and reproduced, moreover we will consider other tasks than the AdHoc, as for example the medical or other popular domains.

References

1. Allan, J., et al.: Research frontiers in information retrieval – report from the third strategic workshop on information retrieval in Lorne (SWIRL 2018). In: SIGIR Forum, vol. 52, no. 1, June 2018
2. Allan, J., Harman, D.K., Kanoulas, E., Li, D., Van Gysel, C., Voorhees, E.M.: TREC 2017 common core track overview. In: Voorhees and Ellis [28]
3. Allan, J., Harman, D.K., Kanoulas, E., Li, D., Van Gysel, C., Voorhees, E.M.: TREC 2018 common core track overview. In: Voorhees and Ellis [29]
4. Arguello, J., Crane, M., Diaz, F., Lin, J., Trotman, A.: Report on the SIGIR 2015 workshop on reproducibility, inexplicability, and generalizability of results (RIGOR). In: SIGIR Forum, vol. 49, no. 2, pp. 107–116 (2015)
5. Armstrong, T.G., Moffat, A., Webber, W., Zobel, J.: Has adhoc retrieval improved since 1994? In: Allan, J., Aslam, J.A., Sanderson, M., Zhai, C., Zobel, J. (eds.) Proceedings of 32nd Annual International ACM SIGIR Conference on Research and Development in Information Retrieval (SIGIR 2009), pp. 692–693. ACM Press, New York (2009)
6. Armstrong, T.G., Moffat, A., Webber, W., Zobel, J.: Improvements that don't add up: ad-hoc retrieval results since 1998. In: Cheung, D.W.L., Song, I.Y., Chu, W.W., Hu, X., Lin, J.J. (eds.) Proceedings of 18th International Conference on Information and Knowledge Management (CIKM 2009), pp. 601–610. ACM Press, New York (2009)
7. Benham, R., et al.: RMIT at the 2018 TREC CORE Track. In: Voorhees and Ellis [29]
8. Breuer, T., Schaer, P.: Replicability and reproducibility of automatic routing runs. In: Cappellato et al. [9]
9. Cappellato, L., Ferro, N., Losada, D., Müller, H. (eds.): CLEF 2019 Working Notes, CEUR Workshop Proceedings. CEUR-WS.org (2019)

10. Cappellato, L., Ferro, N., Nie, J.Y., Soulier, L. (eds.): CLEF 2018 Working Notes, CEUR Workshop Proceedings. CEUR-WS.org, ISSN 1613–0073 (2018)
11. Clancy, R., Ferro, N., Hauff, C., Lin, J., Sakai, T., Wu, Z.Z.: The SIGIR 2019 open-source IR replicability challenge (OSIRRC 2019). In: Chevalier, M., Gaussier, É., Piwowarski, B., Maarek, Y., Nie, J.Y., Scholer, F. (eds.) Proceedings of 42nd Annual International ACM SIGIR Conference on Research and Development in Information Retrieval (SIGIR 2019) (2019)
12. Ferro, N., et al.: The Dagstuhl perspectives workshop on performance modeling and prediction. In: SIGIR Forum, vol. 52, no. 1, June 2018
13. Ferro, N., Fuhr, N., Järvelin, K., Kando, N., Lippold, M., Zobel, J.: Increasing reproducibility in IR: findings from the Dagstuhl seminar on "reproducibility of data-oriented experiments in e-science". In: SIGIR Forum, vol. 50, no. 1, pp. 68–82 (2016)
14. Ferro, N., Fuhr, N., Maistro, M., Sakai, T., Soboroff, I.: CENTRE@CLEF2019: overview of the replicability and reproducibility tasks. In: Cappellato et al. [9]
15. Ferro, N., Kelly, D.: SIGIR initiative to implement ACM artifact review and badging. In: SIGIR Forum, vol. 52, no. 1, June 2018
16. Ferro, N., Maistro, M., Sakai, T., Soboroff, I.: CENTRE@CLEF2018: overview of the replicability task. In: Cappellato et al. [10]
17. Ferro, N., Maistro, M., Sakai, T., Soboroff, I.: Overview of CENTRE@CLEF 2018: a first tale in the systematic reproducibility realm. In: Bellot, P., et al. (eds.) CLEF 2018. LNCS, vol. 11018, pp. 239–246. Springer, Cham (2018). https://doi.org/10.1007/978-3-319-98932-7_23
18. Freire, J., Fuhr, N., Rauber, A. (eds.): Report from Dagstuhl Seminar 16041: Reproducibility of Data-Oriented Experiments in e-Science. Dagstuhl Reports, vol. 6, no. 1. Schloss Dagstuhl-Leibniz-Zentrum für Informatik, Germany (2016)
19. Fuhr, N.: Some common mistakes in IR evaluation, and how they can be avoided. In: SIGIR Forum vol. 51, no. 3, pp. 32–41 (2017)
20. Grossman, M.R., Cormack, G.V.: MRG_UWaterloo and WaterlooCormack participation in the TREC 2017 common core track. In: Voorhees and Ellis [28]
21. Jungwirth, M., Hanbury, A.: Replicating an experiment in cross-lingual information retrieval with explicit semantic analysis. In: Cappellato et al. [10]
22. Kendall, M.G.: Rank Correlation Methods. Griffin, Oxford (1948)
23. Kenney, J.F., Keeping, E.S.: Mathematics of Statistics - Part One, 3rd edn. D. Van Nostrand Company, Princeton (1954)
24. Kharazmi, S., Scholer, F., Vallet, D., Sanderson, M.: Examining additivity and weak baselines. ACM Trans. Inf. Syst. (TOIS) **34**(4), 23:1–23:18 (2016)
25. Lin, J., et al.: Toward reproducible baselines: the open-source IR reproducibility challenge. In: Ferro, N., et al. (eds.) ECIR 2016. LNCS, vol. 9626, pp. 408–420. Springer, Cham (2016). https://doi.org/10.1007/978-3-319-30671-1_30
26. Munafò, M.R., et al.: A manifesto for reproducible science. Nat. Hum. Behav. **1**, 0021:1–0021:9 (2017)
27. Sakai, T., Ferro, N., Soboroff, I., Zeng, Z., Xiao, P., Maistro, M.: Overview of the NTCIR-14 CENTRE task. In: Ishita, E., Kando, N., Kato, M.P., Liu, Y. (eds.) Proceedings of 14th NTCIR Conference on Evaluation of Information Access Technologies, pp. 494–509. National Institute of Informatics, Tokyo (2019)
28. Voorhees, E.M., Ellis, A. (eds.): The Twenty-Sixth Text REtrieval Conference Proceedings (TREC 2017). National Institute of Standards and Technology (NIST), Special Publication 500–324, Washington, USA (2018)

29. Voorhees, E.M., Ellis, A. (eds.): The Twenty-Seventh Text REtrieval Conference Proceedings (TREC 2018). National Institute of Standards and Technology (NIST), Washington, USA (2019)
30. Zobel, J., Webber, W., Sanderson, M., Moffat, A.: Principles for robust evaluation infrastructure. In: Agosti, M., Ferro, N., Thanos, C. (eds.) Proceedings of Workshop on Data infrastructurEs for Supporting Information Retrieval Evaluation (DESIRE 2011), pp. 3–6. ACM Press, New York (2011)

Overview of the CLEF-2019 CheckThat! Lab: Automatic Identification and Verification of Claims

Tamer Elsayed[1], Preslav Nakov[2], Alberto Barrón-Cedeño[3],
Maram Hasanain[1(✉)], Reem Suwaileh[1], Giovanni Da San Martino[2],
and Pepa Atanasova[4]

[1] Computer Science and Engineering Department, Qatar University, Doha, Qatar
{telsayed,maram.hasanain,rs081123}@qu.edu.qa
[2] Qatar Computing Research Institute, HBKU, Doha, Qatar
{pnakov,gmartino}@qf.org.qa
[3] DIT, Università di Bologna, Forlì, Italy
a.barron@unibo.it
[4] Department of Computer Science, University of Copenhagen,
Copenhagen, Denmark
pepa@di.ku.dk

Abstract. We present an overview of the second edition of the CheckThat! Lab at CLEF 2019. The lab featured two tasks in two different languages: English and Arabic. Task 1 (English) challenged the participating systems to predict which claims in a political debate or speech should be prioritized for fact-checking. Task 2 (Arabic) asked to (A) rank a given set of Web pages with respect to a check-worthy claim based on their usefulness for fact-checking that claim, (B) classify these same Web pages according to their degree of usefulness for fact-checking the target claim, (C) identify useful passages from these pages, and (D) use the useful pages to predict the claim's factuality. CheckThat! provided a full evaluation framework, consisting of data in English (derived from fact-checking sources) and Arabic (gathered and annotated from scratch) and evaluation based on mean average precision (MAP) and normalized discounted cumulative gain (nDCG) for ranking, and F_1 for classification. A total of 47 teams registered to participate in this lab, and fourteen of them actually submitted runs (compared to nine last year). The evaluation results show that the most successful approaches to Task 1 used various neural networks and logistic regression. As for Task 2, learning-to-rank was used by the highest scoring runs for subtask A, while different classifiers were used in the other subtasks. We release to the research community all datasets from the lab as well as the evaluation scripts, which should enable further research in the important tasks of check-worthiness estimation and automatic claim verification.

Keywords: Check-worthiness estimation · Fact-checking · Veracity · Evidence-based verification · Fake news detection · Computational journalism

© Springer Nature Switzerland AG 2019
F. Crestani et al. (Eds.): CLEF 2019, LNCS 11696, pp. 301–321, 2019.
https://doi.org/10.1007/978-3-030-28577-7_25

1   Introduction

With the rise of "fake news," which spread in all types of online media, the need arose for systems that could detect them automatically [38]. The problem has various aspects [39], but here we are interested in predicting which claims are worth fact-checking, what information is useful for fact-checking, and finally predicting the factuality of a given claim [5,22,35,37,41,44]. Evidence-based fake news detection systems can serve fact-checking in two ways: (i) by facilitating the job of a human fact-checker, but not replacing her, and (ii) by increasing her trust in a system's decision [34,37,41]. We focus on the problem of checking the factuality of a claim, which has been studied before but rarely in the context of evidence-based fake news detection systems [3,4,7,19,24–26,28,29,32,36,43,47].

There are several challenges that make the development of automatic fake news detection systems difficult:

1. A fact-checking system is effective if it is able to identify a false claim before it reaches a large number of people. Thus, the current speed at which claims spread on the Internet and social media imposes strict efficiency constraints on fact-checking systems.
2. The problem is difficult to the extent that, in some cases, even humans can hardly distinguish between fake and true news [39].
3. There are very few *large-scale* benchmark datasets that could be used to test and improve fake news detection systems [39,41].

Thus, in 2018 we started the `CheckThat!` lab on Automatic Identification and Verification of Political Claims [2,6,33]. Given the success of the lab, we organized a second edition of the lab in 2019 [11], which aims at providing a full evaluation framework along with large-scale evaluation datasets. The lab this year is organized around two different tasks, which correspond to the main blocks in the verification pipeline, as depicted in Fig. 1.

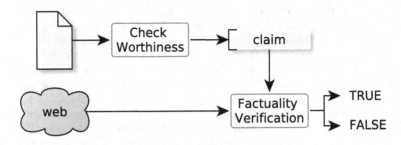

Fig. 1. Information verification pipeline with the two tasks in the `CheckThat!` lab: check-worthiness estimation and factuality verification.

Task 1: Check-worthiness Estimation. The task asks the participating systems to propose which claims in a text should be prioritized for fact-checking.

Whereas we focus on transcribed political debates and speeches, the task can be applied to other texts, such as news articles, blog entries, or interview transcriptions. Task 1 addresses a problem that is not as well studied as other steps in the fact-checking pipeline [2, 14, 20].

Task 2: Evidence and Factuality. This task focuses on extracting evidence from the Web to support the making of a veracity judgment for a given target claim. We divide Task 2 into the following four subtasks: (A) ranking Web pages with respect to a check-worthy claim based on their potential usefulness for fact-checking that claim; (B) classifying Web pages according to their degree of usefulness for fact-checking the target claim; (C) extracting passages from these Web pages that would be useful for fact-checking the target claim; and (D) using these useful pages to verify whether the target claim is factually true or not.

Whereas a practical system should be able to address all these tasks, we propose each of them independently in order to ease participation, to have focused evaluation for each task, and to enable more meaningful comparisons between the participating systems.

The dataset for Task 1 is an extension of the CT-CWC-18 dataset [2], which we used in the 2018 edition of the CheckThat! lab. We added annotations from three press conferences, six public speeches, six debates, and one post, all fact-checked by human experts on factcheck.org. We further manually refined the annotations to make sure they contain only sentences that were part of the fact-checked claim, and to include all occurrences of a claim. For Task 2, we built a new dataset from scratch by manually curating claims, retrieving Web pages through a commercial search engine, and then hiring both in-house and crowd annotators to collect judgments for the four subtasks. As a result of our efforts, we release two datasets. CT19-T1 includes English claims and judgments for Task 1. CT19-T2 includes Arabic claims and retrieved Web pages along with three sets of annotations for the four subtasks.

A total of fourteen teams participated in this year's lab, which represents about 55% increase in participation with respect to the 2018 edition [33]. In both tasks, the most successful systems relied on supervised machine learning models for both ranking and classification. We believe that there is still large room for improvement, and thus we release the annotated corpora and the evaluation scripts, which should enable further research on check-worthiness estimation and automatic claim verification.[1]

The remainder of this paper is organized as follows. Sections 2 and 3 discuss Task 1 and Task 2, respectively, covering the task definitions, the evaluation framework, an overview of the participants' approaches, and the official results. Then, Sect. 4 draws some conclusions and points to possible directions for future work.

---

[1] http://sites.google.com/view/clef2019-checkthat/datasets-tools.

H. Clinton:	I think my husband did a pretty good job in the 1990s.	
H. Clinton:	I think a lot about what worked and how we can make it work again...	
D. Trump:	Well, he approved NAFTA...	⊘

(a) Fragment from the First 2016 US Presidential Debate.

| H. Clinton: | He provided a good middle-class life for us, but the people he worked for, he expected the bargain to be kept on both sides. | |
| H. Clinton: | And when we talk about your business, you've taken business bankruptcy six times. | ⊘ |

(b) Another fragment from the First 2016 US Presidential Debate.

D. Trump:	It's a lot of murders, but it's not close to 2,000 murders right on the other side of the wall, in Mexico.	⊘
D. Trump:	So everyone knows that walls work.	⊘
D. Trump:	And there are better examples than El Paso, frankly.	

(c) Fragment from Trump's National Emergency Remarks in February 2019.

Fig. 2. English debate fragments: check-worthy sentences are marked with ⊘.

2 Overview of Task 1: Check-Worthiness

Task 1 aims at helping fact-checkers prioritize their efforts. In particular, it asks participants to build systems that can mimic the selection strategies of a particular fact-checking organization: factcheck.org. The task is defined as follows:

> Given a political debate, interview, or speech, transcribed and seg-
> mented into sentences, rank the sentences with respect to the priority
> with which they should be fact-checked.

This is a ranking task and the participating systems are asked to produce one score per sentence, according to which the sentences are to be ranked. This year, Task 1 was offered for English only (it was also offered in Arabic in 2018 [2]). Figure 2 shows examples of annotated debate fragments. In Fig. 2a, Hillary Clinton discusses the performance of her husband Bill Clinton as US president. Donald Trump fires back with a claim that is worth fact-checking, namely that Bill Clinton approved NAFTA. In Fig. 2b, Donald Trump is accused of having filed for bankruptcy six times, which is also a claim that is worth fact-checking. In Fig. 2c, Donald Trump claims that border walls work. In a real-world scenario, the intervention by Donald Trump in Fig. 2a, the second one by Hillary Clinton in Fig. 2b, and the first two by Donald Trump in Fig. 2c should be ranked on top of the ranked list in order to get the attention of the fact-checker.

Table 1. Total number of sentences and number of check-worthy ones in the CT19-T1 corpus.

Type	Partition	Sentences	Check-worthy
Debates	Train	10,648	256
	Test	4,584	46
Speeches	Train	2,718	282
	Test	1,883	50
Press conferences	Train	3,011	36
	Test	612	14
Posts	Train	44	8
Total	Train	**16,421**	**433**
	Test	**7,079**	**110**

2.1 Dataset

The dataset for Task 1 is an extension of the CT-CWC-18 dataset [2]. The full English part of CT-CWC-18 (training and test) has become the training data this year. For the new test set, we have produced labeled data from three press conferences, six public speeches, six debates, and one post.

As in last year, the annotations for the new instances have been derived from the publicly available analysis carried out by factcheck.org. We considered those claims whose factuality was challenged by the fact-checkers as check-worthy and we made them positive instances in CT19-T1. Note that our annotation is at the sentence level. Therefore, if only part of a sentence was fact-checked, we annotated the entire sentence as a positive instance. If a claim spanned more than one sentence, we annotated all these sentences as positive. Moreover, in some cases, the same claim was made multiple times in a debate/speech, and thus we annotated all these sentences that referred to it rather than only the one that was fact-checked. Finally, we manually refined the annotations by moving them to a neighboring sentence (e.g., in case of argument) or by adding/excluding some annotations. Table 1 shows some statistics about the CT19-T1 corpus.

2.2 Overview of the Approaches

Eleven teams took part in Task 1. The most successful approaches relied on training supervised classification models to assign a check-worthiness score to each of the sentences. Some participants tried to model the context of each sentence, e.g., by considering the neighbouring sentences to represent an instance [12,16]. Yet, the most successful systems considered each sentence in isolation. Table 2 shows an overview of the approaches. Whereas many approaches opted for embedding representations, feature engineering was also popular in this year's submissions.

The most popular features were bag-of-words representations, part-of-speech (PoS) tags, named entities (NEs), sentiment analysis, and statistics about word use, to mention just a few. Two of the systems also made use of co-reference resolution. The most popular classifiers included SVM, linear regression, Naïve Bayes, decision trees, and neural networks.

Team **Copenhagen** achieved the best overall performance by building upon their approach from 2018 [16,17]. Their system learned dual token embeddings—domain-specific word embeddings and syntactic dependencies—, and used them in an LSTM recurrent neural network. They further pre-trained this network with previous Trump and Clinton debates, and then supervised it weakly with the ClaimBuster system.[2] In their primary submission, they further used a contrastive ranking loss, which was excluded from their contrastive1 submission. For their contrastive2 submission, they concatenated the sentence representations for the current and for the previous sentence.

Team **TheEarthIsFlat** [12] trained a feed-forward neural network with two hidden layers, which takes as input Standard Universal Sentence Encoder (SUSE) embeddings [8] for the current sentence as well as for the two previous sentences as a context. In their contrastive1 run, they replaced the embeddings with the Large Universal Sentence Encoder's ones, and in their constrastive2 run, they trained the model for 1,350 epochs rather than for 1,500 epochs.

Team **IPPAN** first extracted various features about the claims, including bag-of-words n-grams, word2vec vector representations [30], named entity types, part-of-speech tags, sentiment scores, and features from statistical analysis of the sentences [13]. Then, they used these features in an L1-regularized logistic regression to predict the check-worthiness of the sentences.

Team **Terrier** represented the sentences using bag of words and named entities [40]. They used co-reference resolution to substitute the pronouns by the referring entity/person name. They further computed entity similarity [45] and entity relatedness [46]. For prediction, they used an SVM classifier.

Team **UAICS** used a Naïve Bayes classifier with bag-of-words features [9]. In their contrastive submissions, they used other models, e.g., logistic regression.

Team **Factify** used the pre-trained ULMFiT model [21] and fine-tuned it on the training set. They further over-sampled the minority class by replacing words randomly with similar words based on word2vec similarity. They also used data augmentation based on back-translation, where each sentence was translated to French, Arabic and Japanese and then back to English.

Team **JUNLP** extracted various features, including syntactic n-grams, sentiment polarity, text subjectivity, and LIX readability score, and used them to train a logistic regression classifier with high recall [10]. Then, they trained an LSTM model fed with word representations from GloVe and part-of-speech tags. The sentence representations from the LSTM model were concatenated with the extracted features and used for prediction by a fully connected layer, which had high precision. Finally, they averaged the posterior probabilities from both models in order to come up with the final check-worthiness score for the sentence.

---

[2] http://idir.uta.edu/claimbuster/.

Table 2. Overview of the approaches to Task 1: check-worthiness. The learning model and the representations for the best system [17] are highlighted.

Learning Models [1][9][10][12][13][17][31][40]	[1]	[9]	[10]	[12]	[13]	[17]	[31]	[40]
Neural Networks								
LSTM					☑	☑		
Feed-forward				☑				
SVM							☑	
Naïve Bayes		☑						
Logistic regressor			☑					
Regression trees	☑							

Represent.	[1]	[9]	[10]	[12]	[13]	[17]	[31]	[40]
Embeddings								
PoS		☑						
word		☑				☑	☑	
syntactic dep.						☑		
SUSE			☑					
Bag of ...								
words	☑				☑			☑
n-grams	☑							
NEs	☑				☑			☑
PoS	☑				☑			
Readability				☑				
Synt. n-grams		☑						
Sentiment		☑	☑					
Subjectivity		☑						
Sent. context		☑						
Topics	☑							

Teams

[1] TOBB ETU   [31] é proibido cochilar
[9] UAICS   [40] Terrier
[10] JUNLP   [–] IIT (ISM) Dhanbad
[12] TheEarthIsFlat   [–] Factify
[13] IPIPAN   [–] nlpir01
[17] Copenhagen

Team **nlpir01** extracted features such as tf-idf word vectors, tf-idf PoS vectors, word, character, and PoS tag counts. Then, they used these features in a multi-layer perceptron regressor with two hidden layers, each of size 2,000. For their contrastive1 run, they oversampled the minority class, and for their contrastive2 run, they reduced the number of units in each layer to 480.

Team **TOBB ETU** used linguistic features such as named entities, topics extracted with IBM Watson's NLP tools, PoS tags, bigram counts and indicators of the type of sentence to train a multiple additive regression tree [1]. They further decreased the ranks of some sentences using hand-crafted rules. In their contrastive1 run, they added the speaker as a feature, while in their contrastive2 run they used logistic regression.

Team **IIT (ISM) Dhanbad** trained an LSTM-based recurrent neural network. They fed the network with word2vec embeddings and features extracted from constituency parse trees as well as features based on named entities and sentiment analysis.

Team **é proibido cochilar** trained an SVM model on bag-of-words representations of the sentences, after performing co-reference resolution and removing all digits [31]. They further used an additional corpus of labeled claims, which they extracted from fact-checking websites, aiming at having a more balanced training corpus and potentially better generalizations.[3]

---

[3] Their claim crawling tool: http://github.comx/vwoloszyn/fake_news_extractor.

2.3   Evaluation

Evaluation Measures. Task 1 is shaped as an information retrieval problem, in which check-worthy instances should be ranked at the top of the list. Hence, we use mean average precision (MAP) as the official evaluation measure, which is defined as follows:

$$MAP = \frac{\sum_{d=1}^{D} AveP(d)}{D} \tag{1}$$

where $d \in D$ is one of the debates/speeches, and $AveP$ is the average precision, which in turn is defined as follows:

$$AveP = \frac{\sum_{k=1}^{K} (P(k) \times \delta(k))}{\# \text{ check-worthy claims}} \tag{2}$$

where $P(k)$ refers to the value of precision at rank k and $\delta(k) = 1$ iff the claim at that position is actually check-worthy.

As in the 2018 edition of the task [2], following [14] we further report some other measures: (i) mean reciprocal rank (MRR), (ii) mean R-Precision (MR-P), and (iii) mean precision@k (P@k). Here *mean* refers to macro-averaging over the testing debates/speeches.

Results. The participants were allowed to submit one primary and up to two contrastive runs in order to test variations of their primary models or entirely different alternative models. Only the primary runs were considered for the official ranking. A total of eleven teams submitted 21 runs. Table 3 shows the results.

The best-performing system was the one by team **Copenhagen**. They achieved a strong MAP score using a ranking loss based on contrastive sampling. Indeed, this is the only team that modeled the task as a ranking one and the decrease in the performance without the ranking loss (see their contrastive1 run) shows the importance of using this loss.

Two teams made use of external datasets: team **Copenhagen** used a weakly supervised dataset for pretraining, and team **é proibido cochilar** included claims scraped from several fact-checking Web sites. In order to address the class imbalance in the training dataset, team **nlpir01** used oversampling in their contrastive1 run, but could not gain any improvements. Oversampling and augmenting with additional data points did not help team **é proibido cochilar** either.

Many systems used pretrained sentence or word embedding models. Team **TheEarthIsFlat**, which is the second-best performing system, used the Standard Universal Sentence Embeddings, which performed well on the task. The best MAP score overall was obtained by the second contrastive run by this team: the only difference with respect to their primary submission was the number of training epochs. Some teams also used fine-tuning, e.g., team **Factify** fine-tuned the ULMFiT model on the training dataset.

Table 3. Results for Task 1: Check-worthiness. The results for the primary submission appear next to the team's identifier, followed by the contrastive submissions (if any). The subscript numbers indicate the rank of each primary submission with respect to the corresponding evaluation measure.

	Team	MAP	RR	R-P	P@1	P@3	P@5	P@10	P@20	P@50
[17]	Copenhagen	**.1660**$_1$	.4176$_3$	.1387$_4$	.2857$_2$	**.2381**$_1$	**.2571**$_1$	.2286$_2$	.1571$_2$	.1229$_2$
	contr.-1	.1496	.3098	.1297	.1429	.2381	.2000	.2000	.1429	.1143
	contr.-2	.1580	.2740	.1622	.1429	.1905	.2286	.2429	.1786	.1200
[12]	**TheEarthIsFlat**	.1597$_2$	.1953$_{11}$	**.2052**$_1$	.0000$_4$	.0952$_3$	.2286$_2$	.2143$_3$	**.1857**$_1$	**.1457**$_1$
	contr.-1	.1453	.3158	.1101	.2857	.2381	.1429	.1429	.1357	.1171
	contr.-2	.1821	.4187	.1937	.2857	.2381	.2286	.2286	.2143	.1400
[13]	**IPIPAN**	.1332$_3$	.2864$_6$	.1481$_2$	.1429$_3$	.0952$_3$	.1429$_5$	.1714$_5$	.1500$_3$	.1171$_3$
[40]	**Terrier**	.1263$_4$	.3253$_5$	.1088$_8$	.2857$_2$	**.2381**$_1$	.2000$_3$	.2000$_4$	.1286$_6$	.0914$_7$
[9]	**UAICS**	.1234$_5$	**.4650**$_1$	.1460$_3$	**.4286**$_1$	**.2381**$_1$	.2286$_2$	**.2429**$_1$	.1429$_4$	.0943$_6$
	contr.-1	.0649	.2817	.0655	.1429	.2381	.1429	.1143	.0786	.0343
	contr.-2	.0726	.4492	.0547	.4286	.2857	.1714	.1143	.0643	.0257
	Factify	.1210$_6$	.2285$_8$	.1292$_5$	.1429$_3$	.0952$_3$	.1143$_6$	.1429$_6$	.1429$_4$	.1086$_4$
[10]	**JUNLP**	.1162$_7$	.4419$_2$	.1128$_7$	.2857$_2$	.1905$_2$	.1714$_4$	.1714$_5$	.1286$_6$	.1000$_5$
	contr.-1	.0976	.3054	.0814	.1429	.2381	.1429	.0857	.0786	.0771
	contr.-2	.1226	.4465	.1357	.2857	.2381	.2000	.1571	.1286	.0886
	nlpir01	.1000$_8$	.2840$_7$	.1063$_9$	.1429$_3$	**.2381**$_1$	.1714$_4$	.1000$_8$	.1214$_7$	.0943$_6$
	contr.-1	.0966	.3797	.0849	.2857	.1905	.2286	.1429	.1071	.0886
	contr.-2	.0965	.3391	.1129	.1429	.2381	.2286	.1571	.1286	.0943
[1]	**TOBB ETU**	.0884$_9$	.2028$_{10}$	.1150$_6$	.0000$_4$	.0952$_3$	.1429$_5$	.1286$_7$	.1357$_5$	.0829$_8$
	contr.-1	.0898	.2013	.1150	.0000	.1429	.1143	.1286	.1429	.0829
	contr.-2	.0913	.3427	.1007	.1429	.1429	.1143	.0714	.1214	.0829
	IIT (ISM) Dhanbad	.0835$_{10}$	.2238$_9$	.0714$_{11}$	.0000$_4$	.1905$_2$	.1143$_6$	.0857$_9$	.0857$_9$	.0771$_9$
[31]	**é proibido cochilar**	.0796$_{11}$	.3514$_4$	.0886$_{10}$	.1429$_3$	**.2381**$_1$	.1429$_5$	.1286$_7$	.1071$_8$	.0714$_{10}$
	contr.-1	.1357	.5414	.1595	.4286	.2381	.2571	.2714	.1643	.1200

3   Overview of Task 2: Evidence and Factuality

Task 2 focuses on building tools to verify the factuality of a given check-worthy claim. This is the first-ever version of this task, and we run it in Arabic.[4] The task is formally defined as follows:

> *Given a check-worthy claim c associated with a set of Web pages P (that constitute the retrieved results of Web search in response to a search query that represents the claim), identify which of the Web pages (and passages A of those Web pages) can be useful for assisting a human in fact-checking the claim. Finally, determine the factuality of the claim according to the supporting information in the useful pages and passages.*

---

[4] In 2018, we had a different fact-checking task, where no retrieved Web pages were provided [6].

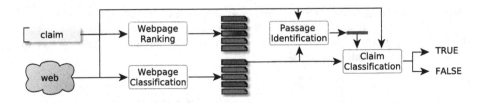

Fig. 3. A zoom into the four subtasks in Task 2.

As Fig. 3 shows, the task is divided into four subtasks that target different aspects of the problem:

Subtask A, Rerank search results: *Rank the Web pages P based on how useful they are for verifying the target claim.* The systems are required to produce a score for each page, based on which the pages would be ranked. See the definition of "useful" pages below.

Subtask B, Classify search results: *Classify each of the Web pages P as "very useful for verification", "useful", "not useful", or "not relevant."* A page is considered *very useful* for verification if it is *relevant* with respect to the claim (i.e., on-topic and discussing the claim) and it *provides sufficient evidence* to verify the veracity of the claim, such that there is no need for another document to be considered for verifying this claim. A page is *useful* for verification if it is relevant to the claim and provides some valid evidence, but it is *not solely sufficient* to determine the claim's veracity on its own. The evidence can be a source, some statistics, a quote, etc. However, a particular piece of evidence is considered not valid if the source cannot be verified or is ambiguous (e.g., expressing that "experts say that..." without mentioning who those experts are), or it is just an opinion of a person/expert instead of an objective analysis.

Notice that this is different from *stance detection*, as a page might agree with a claim, but it might still lack evidence to verify it.

Subtask C, Classify passages from useful/very useful pages: *Find passages within those Web pages that are **useful** for claim verification.* Again, notice that this is different from stance detection.

Subtask D, Verify the claim: *Classify the claim's factuality as "true" or "false."* The claim is considered true if it is accurate as stated (or there is sufficient reliable evidence supporting it), otherwise it is considered false.

Figure 4 shows an example. For the sake of readability, the example is given in English, but this year the task was offered only in Arabic. The example shows a Web page that is considered useful for verifying the given claim, since it has evidence showing the claim to be true and as the page itself is an official United Kingdom page on national statistics. The useful passage in the page is the one reporting the supporting statistics.

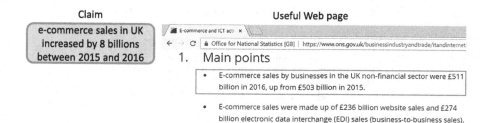

Fig. 4. A claim, a useful Web page, and a useful passage (in the box).

3.1 Dataset

Collecting Claims. Subtasks A, B, and C are all new to the lab this year. As a result, we built a new evaluation dataset to support all subtasks—the CT19-T2 corpus. We selected 69 claims from multiple sources including a pre-existing set of Arabic claims [5], a survey in which we asked the public to provide examples of claims they have heard of, and some headlines from six Arabic news agencies that we rewrote into claims. The news agencies selected are well-known in the Arab world: Al Jazeera, BBC Arabic, CNN Arabic, Al Youm Al Sabea, Al Arabiya, and RT Arabic. We made sure the claims span different topical domains, e.g., health or sports, besides politics. Ten claims were released for training and the rest were used for testing.

Labelling Claims. We acquired the veracity labels for the claims in two steps. First, two of the lab organizers labelled each of the 69 claims independently. Then, they met to resolve any disagreements, and thus reach consensus on the veracity labels for all claims.

Labelling Pages and Passages. For each claim, we formulated a query representing the claim, and we issued it against the Google search engine in order to extract the top 100 Web pages returned as a result. We used a language detection tool to filter out non-Arabic pages, and we eventually used the top-50 of the remaining pages. The labelling pipeline was carried out as follows:

1. **Relevance.** We first identified relevant pages, since we assume that non-relevant pages cannot be useful for claim verification, and thus should be filtered out from any further labelling. In order to speedup the relevance labelling process, we hired two types of annotators: crowd-workers, through Amazon Mechanical Turk, and in-house annotators. Each page was labelled by *three* annotators, and the majority label was used as the final page label.
2. **Usefulness as a whole.** Relevant pages were then given to in-house annotators to be labelled for usefulness using a two-way classification scheme: *useful* (including *very useful*, but not distinguishing between the two) and *not useful*. Similar to relevance labelling, each page was labelled by three annotators, and the final page label was the majority label.

Table 4. Statistics about the CT19-T2 corpus for Task 2.

Set	Claims		Pages		Passages	
	Total	True	Total	Useful	Total	Useful
Training	10	5	395	32	167	54
Test	59	30	2,641	575	1,722	578

3. **Useful vs. very useful.** One of the lab organizers went over the useful pages (from the previous step) and further classified them into *useful* and *very useful*. We opted for this design since we found through pilot studies that the annotators found it difficult to differentiate between *useful* and *very useful* pages.
4. **Splitting into passages.** We further manually split the *useful* and the *very useful* pages into passages, as we found that the automatic techniques for splitting pages into passages were not accurate enough.
5. **Useful passages.** Finally, one of the lab organizers labelled each passage for usefulness. Due to time constraints, we could not split the pages and label the resulting passages for all the claims in the *testing set*. Thus, we only release labels for passages of pages corresponding to 33 out of the 59 testing claims. Note that this only affects subtask C.

Table 4 summarizes the statistics about the training and the test data for Task 2. Note that the passages in the test set are for 33 claims only (see above).

3.2 Subtask A

Runs. Three teams participated in this subtask submitting a total of seven runs [12,18,42]. There were two kinds of approaches. In the first kind, token-level BERT embeddings were used with text classification to rank pages [12]. In the second kind, runs used a learning-to-rank model based on different classifiers, including Naïve Bayes and Random Forest, with a variety of features for ranking [18]. In one run, external data was used to train the text classifier [12], while all other runs represent systems trained on the provided labelled data only.

Evaluation Measures. Subtask A was modelled as a ranking problem, in which *very useful* and *useful* pages should be ranked at the top. Since this is a graded usefulness problem, we evaluate it using the mean of Normalized Discounted Cumulative Gain (nDCG) [23,27]. In particular, we consider nDCG@10 (i.e., nDCG computed at cutoff 10) as the official evaluation measure for this subtask, but we report nDCG at cutoffs 5, 15, and 20 as well.

We also report precision at cutoffs 5, 10, 15, and 20, in addition to Mean Average Precision (MAP). For precision-based measures, we consolidate the labels into two labels instead of four: we combined the *very useful* and the *useful* pages under the *useful* label, and we considered the rest as *not useful*. In all measures, we used macro-averaging over the testing claims.

Table 5. Results for Subtask 2.A, ordered by nDCG@10 score. The runs that used external data are marked with a *.

Team	Run	nDCG@5	nDCG@10	nDCG@15	nDCG@20
Baseline		**0.52**	**0.55**	**0.58**	**0.61**
bigIR	1	0.47	0.50	0.54	0.55
bigIR	3	0.41	0.47	0.50	0.52
EvolutionTeam	1	0.40	0.45	0.48	0.51
bigIR	4	0.39	0.45	0.48	0.51
bigIR	2	0.38	0.41	0.45	0.47
TheEarthIsFlat2A	1	0.08	0.10	0.12	0.14
TheEarthIsFlat2A*	2	0.05	0.07	0.10	0.12

Results. Table 5 shows the results for all seven runs. It also includes the results of a simple baseline: the original ranking in the search result list. We can see that the baseline surprisingly performs the best. This is due to the fact that in our definition of usefulness, useful pages must be relevant, and Google, as an effective search engine, has managed to rank relevant pages (and consequently, many of the *useful* pages) first. This result indicates that the task of ranking pages by usefulness is not easy and systems need to be further developed in order to differentiate between relevance and usefulness, while also benefiting from the relevance-based rank of a page.

3.3 Subtask B

Runs. Four teams participated in this subtask, submitting a total of eight runs [12,15,18,42]. All runs used supervised text classification models, such as Random Forest and Gradient Boosting [18]. In terms of representation, two teams opted for using embedding-based language representation, with one team using word embeddings [15], and the other one opting for BERT-based token-level embeddings for all their runs [12]. In one run, external data was used to train the model [12], while all the remaining runs were trained on the provided labelled training data only.

Evaluation Measures. Similar to Subtask A, Subtask B also aims at identifying useful pages for claim verification, but it is modeled as a *classification* problem, while Subtask A was a ranking problem. Thus, for evaluation we use standard evaluation measures for text classification: Precision, Recall, F_1, and Accuracy, with F_1 being the official score for the task.

Results. Table 6 shows the results. Table 6a reports the results for 2-way classification—*useful/very useful* vs. *not useful/not relevant*—, reporting results for predicting the *useful* class. Table 6b shows the results for 4-way classification—*very useful* vs. *useful* vs. *not useful* vs. *not relevant*—, reporting macro-averaged scores over the four classes, for each of the evaluation measures.

Table 6. Results for Subtask 2.B for 2-way and 4-way classification. The runs are ranked by F_1 score. Runs tagged with a * used external data.

(a) 2-way classification

Team	Run	F_1	P	R	Acc
Baseline		**0.42**	**0.30**	**0.72**	**0.57**
UPV-UMA	1	0.38	0.26	0.73	0.49
bigIR	1	0.08	0.40	0.04	0.78
bigIR	3	0.07	0.39	0.04	0.78
bigIR	4	0.07	0.57	0.04	0.78
bigIR	2	0.04	0.22	0.02	0.77
TheEarthIsFlat	1	0.00	0.00	0.00	0.78
TheEarthIsFlat*	2	0.00	0.00	0.00	0.78
EvolutionTeam	1	0.00	0.00	0.00	0.78

(b) 4-way classification

Team	Run	F_1	P	R	Acc
TheEarthIsFlat	1	0.31	0.28	0.36	0.59
bigIR	3	0.31	0.37	0.33	0.58
TheEarthIsFlat*	2	0.30	0.27	0.35	0.60
bigIR	4	0.30	0.41	0.32	0.57
EvolutionTeam	1	0.29	0.26	0.33	0.58
Baseline		**0.28**	**0.32**	**0.32**	**0.30**
UPV-UMA	1	0.23	0.30	0.29	0.24
bigIR	1	0.16	0.25	0.23	0.26
bigIR	2	0.16	0.25	0.22	0.25

We also included a baseline, which is based on the original ranking in the search results list. The baseline assumes the top-50% of the results to be *useful* and the rest *not useful* for the 2-way classification. For the 4-way classification, the baseline assumes the top-25% to be *very useful*, the next 25% to be *useful*, the third 25% to be *not useful*, and the rest to be *not relevant*.

Table 6a shows that almost all systems struggled to retrieve any *useful* pages at all. Team UPV-UMA is the only one that managed to achieve high recall. This is probably due to the *useful* class being under-represented in the training dataset, while being much more frequent in the test dataset: we can see in Table 4 that it covers just 8% of the training examples, but 22% of the testing ones. Training the models with a limited number of *useful* pages might have caused them to learn to underpedict this class. Similar to Subtask A, the simple baseline that assumes the top-ranked pages to be more useful is most effective. This again can be due to the correlation between usefulness and relevance.

Comparing the results in Table 6a to those in Table 6b, we notice a very different performance ranking; runs that had the worst performance at finding *useful* pages, are actually among the best runs in the 4-way classification. These runs were able to effectively detect the *not relevant* and *not useful* pages as compared to *useful* ones. The baseline, which was effective at identifying *useful* pages, is not as effective at identifying pages in the other classes. This might indicate that *not useful* and *not relevant* pages are not always at the bottom of the ranked list as this baseline assumes, which sheds some light on the importance of usefulness estimation to aid fact-checking. One additional factor that might have caused such varied ranking of runs is our own observation on the difficulty and subjectivity of differentiating between *useful* and *very useful* pages. At annotation time, we observed that annotators and even lab organizers were not able to easily distinguish between these two types of pages.

Table 7. Performance of the models when predicting useful passages for Subtask 2.C. The runs are ranked by F_1.

Team	Run	F_1	P	R	Acc
TheEarthIsFlat2Cnoext	1	0.56	0.40	0.94	0.51
TheEarthIsFlat2Cnoext	2	0.55	0.41	0.87	0.53
bigIR	2	0.40	0.39	0.42	0.58
bigIR	1	0.39	0.38	0.41	0.58
bigIR	4	0.37	0.37	0.38	0.57
Baseline		**0.37**	**0.42**	**0.39**	**0.57**
bigIR	3	0.19	0.33	0.14	0.61

3.4   Subtask C

Runs. Two teams participated in this task [12,18], submitting a total of seven runs. One of the teams used text classifiers including Naïve Bayes and SVM with a variety of features such as bag-of-words and named entities [18]. All runs also considered using the similarity between the claim and the passages as a feature in their models.

Evaluation Measures. Subtask C aims at identifying useful passages for claim verification and we modelled it as a classification problem. As in typical classification problems, we evaluated it using Precision, Recall, F_1, and Accuracy, with F_1 being the official evaluation measure for the task.

Results. Table 7 shows the evaluation results. The scores for precsion, recall and F_1 are calculated with respect to the positive class, i.e., *useful*. The table also shows the evaluation results for a simple baseline that assumes the first passage in a page to be *not useful*, the next two passages to be *useful*, and the remaining passages to be *not useful*. This baseline is motivated by our observation that *useful* passages are typically located at the heart of the document following some introductory passage(s).

We can see that team TheEarthIsFlat managed to identify most of the *useful* passages, thus achieving very high recall (0.94 for its run 1), while also having relatively similar precision to the other runs and the baseline. Further analysis of the performance of that system is needed in order to understand how it managed to achieve such a high recall. Note that in all the runs by the bigIR system, as well as in the baseline system, the precision and the recall are fairly balanced. We can see that the baseline performed almost as well as the four runs by bigIR. This indicates that considering the position of the passage in a page might be a useful feature when predicting the passage usefulness, and thus it should be considered when addressing that problem.

316   T. Elsayed et al.

Table 8. Results for Subtask 2.D for both cycles 1 and 2. The runs are ranked by F_1 score. The runs tagged with a * used external data.

(a) Cycle 1, where the usefulness of the Web pages was unknown.

(b) Cycle 2, where the the usefulness of the Web pages was known.

Team	F_1	P	R	Acc
EvolutionTeam	0.48	0.55	0.53	0.53
Baseline	**0.34**	**0.25**	**0.50**	**0.51**

Team	Run	F_1	P	R	Acc
UPV-UMA*	21	0.62	0.63	0.63	0.63
UPV-UMA*	11	0.55	0.56	0.56	0.56
UPV-UMA*	22	0.54	0.60	0.57	0.58
bigIR	1	0.53	0.55	0.55	0.54
bigIR	3	0.53	0.55	0.54	0.54
bigIR	2	0.51	0.53	0.53	0.53
bigIR	4	0.51	0.53	0.53	0.53
UPV-UMA*	12	0.51	0.65	0.57	0.58
EvolutionTeam	1	0.43	0.45	0.46	0.46
Baseline		**0.34**	**0.25**	**0.50**	**0.51**

3.5 Subtask D

The main aim of Task 2 was to study the effect of using identified *useful* and *very useful* pages for claim verification. Thus, we had two evaluation cycles for Subtask D. In the first cycle, the teams were asked to fact-check claims using the given Web pages, without knowing which of the Web pages were *useful/very useful*. In the second cycle, the usefulness labels were released in order to allow the systems to fact-check the claims when knowing which of the Web pages are *useful/very useful*.

Runs. Two teams participated in cycle 1, submitting one run each [18,42], but one of the runs was invalid, and thus there is only one official run. Cycle 2 attracted more participation: three teams with nine runs [15,18,42]. Thus, we will focus our discussion on cycle 2. One team opted for using textual entailment with embedding-based representations for classification [15]. Another team used text classifiers such as Gradient Boosting and Random Forests [18]. External data was used to train the textual entailment component of the system in four runs, whereas the remaining runs were trained on the provided data only.

Evaluation Measures. Subtask D aims at predicting a claim's veracity. It is a classification task, and thus we evaluate it using Precision, Recall, F_1, and Accuracy, with F_1 being the official measure for the task.

Results. Table 8 shows the results for cycles 1 and 2, where we macro-average precision, recall, and F_1 over the two classes. We show the results for a simple majority-class baseline, which all runs manage to beat for both cycles.

Due to the low participation in cycle 1, it is difficult to draw conclusions about whether providing systems with useful pages helps to improve their performance.

4   Conclusion and Future Work

We have presented an overview of the CLEF–2019 CheckThat! Lab on Auto-matic Identification and Verification of Claims, which is the second edition of the lab. CheckThat! proposed two complementary tasks. Task 1 asked the partici-pating systems to predict which claims in a political debate should be prioritized for fact-checking. Task 2 was designed to aid a human who is fact-checking a claim. It asked the systems (A) to rank Web pages with respect to a check-worthy claim based on their usefulness for fact-checking that claim, (B) to classify the Web pages according to their degree of usefulness, (C) to identify useful pas-sages from these pages, and (D) to use the useful pages to predict a claim's factuality. As part of CheckThat!, we release datasets in English (derived from fact-checking sources) and Arabic in order to enable further research in check-worthiness estimation and in automatic claim verification.

A total of 14 teams participated in the lab (compared to 9 in 2018) sub-mitting a total of 57 runs. The evaluation results show that the most successful approaches to Task 1 used various neural networks and logistic regression. As for Task 2, learning-to-rank was used by the highest-scoring runs for subtask A, while different classifiers were used in the other subtasks.

Regarding the task of selecting check-worthy claims, we consider expanding the dataset with more annotations. This will pave the way for the development of various neural architectures and it will also likely boost the accuracy of the final systems. We also plan to include more sources of annotations. As noted in [14], the agreement between different media sources on the task was low, meaning that there is a certain bias in the selection of the claims for each of the media outlets. Aggregating the annotations from multiple sources would potentially decrease this selection bias.

Although one of the aims of the lab was to study the effect of using *useful* pages for claim verification, the low participation in the first cycle of Subtask D of Task 2 has hindered carrying such a study. In the future, we plan to setup this subtask, so that teams must participate in both cycles in order for their runs to be considered valid. We also plan to extend the dataset for Task 2 to include claims in at least one other language than Arabic.

Acknowledgments. This work was made possible in part by NPRP grant# NPRP 7-1330-2-483 from the Qatar National Research Fund (a member of Qatar Foundation). The statements made herein are solely the responsibility of the authors.

This research is also part of the Tanbih project,[5] which aims to limit the effect of "fake news", propaganda and media bias by making users aware of what they are read-ing. The project is developed in collaboration between the Qatar Computing Research Institute (QCRI), HBKU and the MIT Computer Science and Artificial Intelligence Laboratory (CSAIL).

---

[5] http://tanbih.qcri.org/.

References

1. Altun, B., Kutlu, M.: TOBB-ETU at CLEF 2019: prioritizing claims based on check-worthiness. In: CLEF 2019 Working Notes. Working Notes of CLEF 2019 - Conference and Labs of the Evaluation Forum. CEUR Workshop Proceedings, CEUR-WS.org, Lugano (2019)
2. Atanasova, P., et al.: Overview of the CLEF-2018 CheckThat! Lab on automatic identification and verification of political claims, Task 1: Check-worthiness. In: Cappellato, L., Ferro, N., Nie, J.Y., Soulier, L. (eds.) CLEF 2018 Working Notes. Working Notes of CLEF 2018 - Conference and Labs of the Evaluation Forum. CEUR Workshop Proceedings, CEUR-WS.org, Avignon (2018)
3. Atanasova, P., et al.: Automatic fact-checking using context and discourse information. J. Data Inf. Qual. **11**(3), 12:1–12:27 (2019)
4. Ba, M.L., Berti-Equille, L., Shah, K., Hammady, H.M.: VERA: a platform for veracity estimation over web data. In: Proceedings of the 25th International Conference Companion on World Wide Web, WWW 2016, pp. 159–162 (2016)
5. Baly, R., Mohtarami, M., Glass, J., Màrquez, L., Moschitti, A., Nakov, P.: Integrating stance detection and fact checking in a unified corpus. In: Proceedings of the 2018 Conference of the North American Chapter of the Association for Computational Linguistics: Human Language Technologies, NAACL-HLT 2018, New Orleans, Louisiana, USA, pp. 21–27 (2018)
6. Barrón-Cedeño, A., et al.: Overview of the CLEF-2018 CheckThat! Lab on automatic identification and verification of political claims, task 2: factuality. In: Cappellato, L., Ferro, N., Nie, J.Y., Soulier, L. (eds.) CLEF 2018 Working Notes. Working Notes of CLEF 2018 - Conference and Labs of the Evaluation Forum. CEUR Workshop Proceedings. CEUR-WS.org, Avignon (2018)
7. Castillo, C., Mendoza, M., Poblete, B.: Information credibility on Twitter. In: Proceedings of the 20th International Conference on World Wide Web, WWW 2011, Hyderabad, India, pp. 675–684 (2011)
8. Cer, D., et al.: Universal sentence encoder. arXiv preprint arXiv:1803.11175 (2018)
9. Coca, L., Cusmuliuc, C.G., Iftene, A.: CheckThat! 2019 UAICS. In: CLEF 2019 Working Notes. Working Notes of CLEF 2019 - Conference and Labs of the Evaluation Forum, CEUR Workshop Proceedings. CEUR-WS.org, Lugano (2019)
10. Dhar, R., Dutta, S., Das, D.: A hybrid model to rank sentences for check-worthiness. In: CLEF 2019 Working Notes. Working Notes of CLEF 2019 - Conference and Labs of the Evaluation Forum, CEUR Workshop Proceedings. CEUR-WS.org, Lugano (2019)
11. Elsayed, T., et al.: CheckThat! at CLEF 2019: automatic identification and verification of claims. In: Azzopardi, L., Stein, B., Fuhr, N., Mayr, P., Hauff, C., Hiemstra, D. (eds.) ECIR 2019. LNCS, vol. 11438, pp. 309–315. Springer, Cham (2019). https://doi.org/10.1007/978-3-030-15719-7_41
12. Favano, L., Carman, M., Lanzi, P.: TheEarthIsFlat's submission to CLEF'19 CheckThat! challenge. In: CLEF 2019 Working Notes. Working Notes of CLEF 2019 - Conference and Labs of the Evaluation Forum, CEUR Workshop Proceedings. CEUR-WS.org, Lugano (2019)
13. Gasior, J., Przybyła, P.: The IPIPAN team participation in the check-worthiness task of the CLEF2019 CheckThat! Lab. In: CLEF 2019 Working Notes. Working Notes of CLEF 2019 - Conference and Labs of the Evaluation Forum, CEUR Workshop Proceedings. CEUR-WS.org, Lugano (2019)

14. Gencheva, P., Nakov, P., Màrquez, L., Barrón-Cedeño, A., Koychev, I.: A context-aware approach for detecting worth-checking claims in political debates. In: Proceedings of the International Conference Recent Advances in Natural Language Processing, RANLP 2017, Varna, Bulgaria, pp. 267–276 (2017)

15. Ghanem, B., Glavaš, G., Giachanou, A., Ponzetto, S., Rosso, P., Rangel, F.: UPV-UMA at CheckThat! lab: verifying arabic claims using cross lingual approach. In: CLEF 2019 Working Notes. Working Notes of CLEF 2019 - Conference and Labs of the Evaluation Forum, CEUR Workshop Proceedings, CEUR-WS.org, Lugano (2019)

16. Hansen, C., Hansen, C., Alstrup, S., Grue Simonsen, J., Lioma, C.: Neural check-worthiness ranking with weak supervision: finding sentences for fact-checking. In: Companion Proceedings of the 2019 World Wide Web Conference, WWW 2019, San Francisco, USA, pp. 994–1000 (2019)

17. Hansen, C., Hansen, C., Simonsen, J., Lioma, C.: Neural weakly supervised fact check-worthiness detection with contrastive sampling-based ranking loss. In: CLEF 2019 Working Notes. Working Notes of CLEF 2019 - Conference and Labs of the Evaluation Forum, CEUR Workshop Proceedings. CEUR-WS.org, Lugano (2019)

18. Haouari, F., Ali, Z., Elsayed, T.: bigIR at CLEF 2019: automatic verification of Arabic claims over the web. In: CLEF 2019 Working Notes. Working Notes of CLEF 2019 - Conference and Labs of the Evaluation Forum, CEUR Workshop Proceedings. CEUR-WS.org, Lugano (2019)

19. Hardalov, M., Koychev, I., Nakov, P.: In search of credible news. In: Dichev, C., Agre, G. (eds.) AIMSA 2016. LNCS (LNAI), vol. 9883, pp. 172–180. Springer, Cham (2016). https://doi.org/10.1007/978-3-319-44748-3_17

20. Hassan, N., Li, C., Tremayne, M.: Detecting check-worthy factual claims in presidential debates. In: Proceedings of the 24th ACM International Conference on Information and Knowledge Management, CIKM 2015, Melbourne, Australia, pp. 1835–1838 (2015)

21. Howard, J., Ruder, S.: Universal language model fine-tuning for text classification. arXiv preprint arXiv:1801.06146 (2018)

22. Jaradat, I., Gencheva, P., Barrón-Cedeño, A., Màrquez, L., Nakov, P.: ClaimRank: detecting check-worthy claims in Arabic and English. In: Proceedings of the 16th Annual Conference of the North American Chapter of the Association for Computational Linguistics, NAACL-HLT 2018, New Orleans, Louisiana, USA, pp. 26–30 (2018)

23. Järvelin, K., Kekäläinen, J.: Cumulated gain-based evaluation of IR techniques. ACM Trans. Inf. Syst. (TOIS) 20(4), 422–446 (2002)

24. Karadzhov, G., Gencheva, P., Nakov, P., Koychev, I.: We built a fake news & click-bait filter: what happened next will blow your mind! In: Proceedings of the 2017 International Conference on Recent Advances in Natural Language Processing, RANLP 2017, Varna, Bulgaria, pp. 334–343 (2017)

25. Karadzhov, G., Nakov, P., Màrquez, L., Barrón-Cedeño, A., Koychev, I.: Fully automated fact checking using external sources. In: Proceedings of the International Conference on Recent Advances in Natural Language Processing, RANLP 2017, Varna, Bulgaria, pp. 344–353 (2017)

26. Ma, J., et al.: Detecting rumors from microblogs with recurrent neural networks. In: Proceedings of the 25th International Joint Conference on Artificial Intelligence, IJCAI 2016, New York, New York, USA, pp. 3818–3824 (2016)

27. Manning, C.D., Raghavan, P., Schütze, H.: Introduction to Information Retrieval. Cambridge University Press, New York (2008)

28. Mihaylova, T., Karadzhov, G., Atanasova, P., Baly, R., Mohtarami, M., Nakov, P.: SemEval-2019 task 8: fact checking in community question answering forums. In: Proceedings of the 13th International Workshop on Semantic Evaluation, SemEval 2019, Minneapolis, Minnesota, USA, pp. 860–869 (2019)

29. Mihaylova, T., et al.: Fact checking in community forums. In: Proceedings of the 33rd AAAI Conference on Artificial Intelligence, AAAI 2018, New Orleans, Louisiana, USA, pp. 5309–5316 (2018)

30. Mikolov, T., Yih, W.T., Zweig, G.: Linguistic regularities in continuous space word representations. In: Proceedings of the 2013 Conference of the North American Chapter of the Association for Computational Linguistics: Human Language Technologies, NAACL-HLT 2013, Atlanta, Georgia, USA, pp. 746–751 (2013)

31. Mohtaj, S., Himmelsbach, T., Woloszyn, V., Möller, S.: The TU-Berlin team participation in the check-worthiness task of the CLEF-2019 CheckThat! Lab. In: CLEF 2019 Working Notes. Working Notes of CLEF 2019 - Conference and Labs of the Evaluation Forum, CEUR Workshop Proceedings. CEUR-WS.org, Lugano (2019)

32. Mukherjee, S., Weikum, G.: Leveraging joint interactions for credibility analysis in news communities. In: Proceedings of the 24th ACM International on Conference on Information and Knowledge Management, CIKM 2015, Melbourne, Australia, pp. 353–362 (2015)

33. Nakov, P., et al.: Overview of the CLEF-2018 CheckThat! lab on automatic identification and verification of political claims. In: Bellot, P., et al. (eds.) CLEF 2018. LNCS, vol. 11018, pp. 372–387. Springer, Cham (2018). https://doi.org/10.1007/978-3-319-98932-7_32

34. Nguyen, A.T., Kharosekar, A., Lease, M., Wallace, B.: An interpretable joint graphical model for fact-checking from crowds. In: Proceedings of the 32nd AAAI Conference on Artificial Intelligence, AAAI 2018, New Orleans, LA, USA, pp. 1511–1518 (2018)

35. Nie, Y., Chen, H., Bansal, M.: Combining fact extraction and verification with neural semantic matching networks. In: Proceedings of the 33rd AAAI Conference on Artificial Intelligence, AAAI 2019, Honolulu, Hawaii, USA (2019)

36. Popat, K., Mukherjee, S., Strötgen, J., Weikum, G.: Credibility assessment of textual claims on the web. In: Proceedings of the 25th ACM International Conference on Information and Knowledge Management. CIKM 2016, Indianapolis, Indiana, USA, pp. 2173–2178 (2016)

37. Popat, K., Mukherjee, S., Yates, A., Weikum, G.: DeClarE: debunking fake news and false claims using evidence-aware deep learning. In: Proceedings of the 2018 Conference on Empirical Methods in Natural Language Processing, EMNLP 2018, Brussels, Belgium, pp. 22–32 (2018)

38. Rubin, V.L., Chen, Y., Conroy, N.J.: Deception detection for news: three types of fakes. In: Proceedings of the 78th ASIS&T Annual Meeting: Information Science with Impact: Research in and for the Community, p. 83. American Society for Information Science (2015)

39. Shu, K., Sliva, A., Wang, S., Tang, J., Liu, H.: Fake news detection on social media: a data mining perspective. ACM SIGKDD Explor. Newsl. **19**(1), 22–36 (2017)

40. Su, T., Macdonald, C., Ounis, I.: Entity detection for check-worthiness prediction: Glasgow Terrier at CLEF CheckThat! 2019. In: CLEF 2019 Working Notes. Working Notes of CLEF 2019 - Conference and Labs of the Evaluation Forum, CEUR Workshop Proceedings. CEUR-WS.org, Lugano, Switzerland (2019)

41. Thorne, J., Vlachos, A., Christodoulopoulos, C., Mittal, A.: FEVER: a large-scale dataset for Fact Extraction and VERification. In: Proceedings of the 2018 Conference of the North American Chapter of the Association for Computational Linguistics: Human Language Technologies, NAACL-HLT 2018, New Orleans, LA, USA, pp. 809–819 (2018)
42. Touahri, I., Mazroui, A.: Automatic identification and verification of political claims. In: CLEF 2019 Working Notes. Working Notes of CLEF 2019 - Conference and Labs of the Evaluation Forum, CEUR Workshop Proceedings. CEUR-WS.org, Lugano, Switzerland (2019)
43. Yasser, K., Kutlu, M., Elsayed, T.: Re-ranking web search results for better fact-checking: a preliminary study. In: Proceedings of 27th ACM International Conference on Information and Knowledge Management, CIKM 2019, Turin, Italy, pp. 1783–1786 (2018)
44. Yoneda, T., Mitchell, J., Welbl, J., Stenetorp, P., Riedel, S.: UCL machine reading group: four factor framework for fact finding (HexaF). In: Proceedings of the First Workshop on Fact Extraction and VERification, FEVER 2018, Brussels, Belgium, pp. 97–102 (2018)
45. Zhu, G., Iglesias, C.A.: Computing semantic similarity of concepts in knowledge graphs. IEEE Trans. Knowl. Data Eng. **29**(1), 72–85 (2016)
46. Zhu, G., Iglesias Fernandez, C.A.: Sematch: semantic entity search from knowledge graph. In: Joint Proceedings of the 1st International Workshop on Summarizing and Presenting Entities and Ontologies and the 3rd International Workshop on Human Semantic Web Interfaces, SumPre-HSWI@ESWC 2015, Portorož, Slovenia (2015)
47. Zubiaga, A., Liakata, M., Procter, R., Hoi, G.W.S., Tolmie, P.: Analysing how people orient to and spread rumours in social media by looking at conversational threads. PloS One **11**(3), e0150989 (2016)

Overview of the CLEF eHealth
Evaluation Lab 2019

Liadh Kelly[1]([✉]), Hanna Suominen[2,3], Lorraine Goeuriot[4], Mariana Neves[5],
Evangelos Kanoulas[6], Dan Li[6], Leif Azzopardi[7], Rene Spijker[8], Guido Zuccon[9],
Harrisen Scells[9], and João Palotti[10]

[1] Maynooth University, Kildare, Ireland
liadh.kelly@mu.ie
[2] The Australian National University,
Data61/Commonwealth Scientific and Industrial Research Organisation,
University of Canberra, Canberra, ACT, Australia
hanna.suominen@anu.edu.au
[3] University of Turku, Turku, Finland
[4] Univ. Grenoble Alpes, CNRS, Grenoble INP, LIG, 38000 Grenoble, France
Lorraine.Goeuriot@imag.fr
[5] German Centre for the Protection of Laboratory Animals (Bf3R),
German Federal Institute for Risk Assessment (BfR), Berlin, Germany
mariana.lara-neves@bfr.bund.de
[6] Informatics Institute, University of Amsterdam, Amsterdam, Netherlands
{E.Kanoulas,D.Li}@uva.nl
[7] Computer and Information Sciences, University of Strathclyde, Glasgow, UK
leif.azzopardi@strath.ac.uk
[8] Cochrane Netherlands and UMC Utrecht,
Julius Center for Health Sciences and Primary Care, Utrecht, Netherlands
R.Spijker-2@umcutrecht.nl
[9] University of Queensland, Brisbane, Australia
{g.zuccon,h.scells}@uq.edu.au
[10] Qatar Computing Research Institute (QCRI), HBKU, Doha, Qatar
jpalotti@hbku.edu.qa

Abstract. In this paper, we provide an overview of the seventh annual edition of the CLEF eHealth evaluation lab. CLEF eHealth 2019 continues our evaluation resource building efforts around the easing and support of patients, their next-of-kins, clinical staff, and health scientists in understanding, accessing, and authoring electronic health information in a multilingual setting. This year's lab advertised three tasks: Task 1 on indexing non-technical summaries of German animal experiments with International Classification of Diseases, Version 10 codes; Task 2 on technology assisted reviews in empirical medicine building on 2017 and 2018 tasks in English; and Task 3 on consumer health search in mono- and multilingual settings that builds on the 2013–18 Information Retrieval tasks. In total nine teams took part in these tasks (six in Task 1 and three

---

LK, HSu & LG co-chaired the lab. MN; EK, DL, LA & RS; and GZ, HSc & JP led Tasks 1–3, respectively.

in Task 2). Herein, we describe the resources created for these tasks and evaluation methodology adopted. We also provide a brief summary of participants of this year's challenges and results obtained. As in previous years, the organizers have made data and tools associated with the lab tasks available for future research and development.

Keywords: Evaluation · Entity linking · Information retrieval · Health records · High recall · Information extraction · Medical informatics · Self-diagnosis · Systematic reviews · Test-set generation · Text classification · Text segmentation

1   Introduction

Retrieving, digesting, and summarising valid and relevant information to make health-centered decisions has become increasingly difficult in today's information overloaded society. More and more *electronic health* (eHealth) content is becoming available in a variety of forms ranging from scientific papers and health-related websites through patient records and medical dossiers to medical-related topics shared across social networks [27]. Laypeople, clinicians, and policy makers need bespoke systems to retrieve relevant and reliable contents and access them in a clear and concise way to easily judge and make sense of them to support their decision making.

Information retrieval (IR) systems have been commonly used as a means to access health information available online. To illustrate the immense worldwide popularity of going online to consume and produce health information, five years ago, in Australia, 40 per cent of searches were to fulfill health information needs; in Europe, nearly half of the population consider the Internet as a significant source of health information; and in the USA, nearly 70 per cent of people using web search engines want information about diseases, health conditions, or other medical disorders [1]. Based on the "Household Use of Information Technology" survey for 2016–2017 by the *Australian Bureau of Statistics* (ABS)[1], this popularity has grown and stabilised itself to almost 90 per cent of Australian households having access to the Internet (up to 97% for those households that have children aged under 15 years), and approximately 50 per cent of Australians are using it to meet their health or healthcare information needs. However, the information seekers find it difficult to express their health information needs as search queries that find the right information, and also the quality, reliability, and suitability of the information for the target audience varies greatly while high recall or coverage—that is, finding all relevant information about a topic— is often as important as (if not more important than) high precision [24].

CLEF eHealth[2], established as a lab workshop in 2012 as part of the *Conference and Labs of the Evaluation Forum* (CLEF), has offered evaluation labs

---

[1] Statistics extracted from the ABS pages at https://www.abs.gov.au/AUSSTATS/ abs@.nsf/Lookup/8146.0Main+Features12016-17?OpenDocument, titled "8146.0 – Household Use of Information Technology, Australia, 2016–17", on 28 May 2019.

[2] http://clef-ehealth.org/ (last accessed on 28 May 2019).

since 2013 in the fields of layperson and professional health information extraction, management, and retrieval with the aims of bringing together researchers working on related information access topics and providing them with data sets to work with and validate the outcomes. More specifically, these labs and their subsequent workshops target (1) developing processing methods and resources in a multilingual setting to enrich difficult-to-understand eHealth texts and provide personalized reliable access to medical information, and provide valuable documentation; (2) developing an evaluation setting and releasing evaluation results for these methods and resources; and (3) contributing to the participants and organizers' professional networks and interaction with all interdisciplinary actors of the ecosystem for producing, processing, and consuming eHealth information.

The CLEF eHealth labs are open for everybody. We particularly welcome academic and industrial researchers, scientists, engineers, and graduate students in natural language processing, machine learning, and biomedical/health informatics to participate. We also encourage participation by multi-disciplinary teams that combine technological skills with biomedical expertise.

This, the seventh year of the evaluation lab (and eight year of the workshop), aiming to build upon the resource development and evaluation approaches by the previous six or seven years of CLEF eHealth [8,9,14,16,26,28,29], offered the following two tasks [15]:

- *Task 1.* Multilingual Information Extraction: *International Classification of Diseases, Version 10* (ICD-10) coding of *non-technical summaries* (NTSs) of animal experiments in German [22] and
- *Task 2. Technology Assisted Reviews* (TAR) in Empirical Medicine in English [13].

In addition, Task 3. Consumer Health Search in Mono- and Multilingual Settings was initially advertised, but unfortunately, due to unforeseen circumstances, it had to be postponed[3].

The *Multilingual Information Extraction* task challenged participants to index German NTSs of animal experiments with the ICD-10 terminology of diseases. A detailed analysis based on the diseases addressed by the NTSs allows more transparency of the animal experiments being carried out by researchers [2]. It could be treated as a text classification or cascaded named entity recognition and normalization task. Even though we only addressed one language (German), we encouraged participants to explore multilingual approaches. The results of high performing systems could be used within the workflow of institutes mandated by the *European Union* (EU) to publish the NTSs approved in their states. The 2019 Task 1 built upon the 2016–2018 information extraction tasks [19–21], which already addressed the ICD-10 terminology to code causes of death from a corpus of death reports in French (2016, 2017, and 2018), English (2017), Hungarian (2018), and Italian (2018). Prior to this, the CLEF eHealth tasks considered *Unified Medical Language System* (UMLS) and *Systematized*

---

[3] The organizers apologize to the teams that registered their interest in the task for any inconvenience caused by this delay.

Nomenclature of Medicine—Clinical Terms (SNoMed-CT) codification of clinical reports in English in 2013, and UMLS named entity recognition of clinical reports in French in 2015, among others [27].

The *TAR* task was a high-recall IR task in English that aimed at evaluating search algorithms that seek to identify all studies relevant for conducting a systematic review in empirical medicine. The results of the explored approaches in the submitted systems towards generating a clear overview of the current scientific consensus could be informing health care and its policy making in the future. This automated generator might release scientists and policy advisors' time from the currently laborious iterative process of conducting publication searches and revising them in order to retrieve all the documents that are relevant for the purposes of writing reliable systematic reviews; this hard challenge is known in the IR domain as the total recall problem and with the number of published medical papers expanding rapidly, the need for automation in this process becomes of utmost importance.

This year's Task 2, differed from the past two years [11,12] by diversifying the focus across different type of reviews including *Diagnostic Test Accuracy* (DTA), *Intervention, Prognosis*, and *Qualitative* reviews. Even though search in the area of DTA reviews is generally considered the hardest [18], this year we wanted to investigate how the technology that has been developed over the past two years would extend to other types of reviews. The typical process of searching for scientific publications to conduct a systematic review consists of three stages: (a) specifying a number of inclusion criteria that characterize the articles relevant to the review and constructing a complex Boolean Query to express them, (b) screening the abstracts and titles that result from the Boolean query, and (c) reading and screening the full documents that passed the Abstract and Title Screening. Building on the 2017 task, which focused on the second stage of the process, that is, Abstract and Title Screening, and same as the 2018 task, the 2019 task focused both on the first stage (*subtask 1*) and second stage (*subtask 2*) of the process, that is, Boolean Search and Abstract and Title Screening.

More precisely, these subtasks of Task 2 were defined as follows:

– *Subtask 1.* Prior to constructing a Boolean Query researchers have to design and write a search protocol that in written and in detail defines what constitutes a relevant study for their review. For the challenge associated with the first stage of the process, participants were provided with the relevant pieces of a protocol, in an attempt to complete search effectively and efficiently bypassing the construction of the Boolean query.
– *Subtask 2.* Given the results of the Boolean Search from stage 1 as the starting point, participants were required to rank the set of *abstracts* (A). The task had the following two goals: (i) to produce an efficient ordering of the documents, such that all of the relevant abstracts are retrieved as early as possible, and (ii) to identify a subset of A which contains all or as many of the relevant abstracts for the least effort (i.e., total number of abstracts to be assessed).

The *Consumer Health Search* task was advertised as a continuation of the previous CLEF eHealth IR tasks that ran every year since the onset of

CLEF eHealth evaluation labs in 2013 [5–7, 10, 23, 25, 30], and embraced the *Text REtrieval Conference* (TREC) -style evaluation process, with a shared collection of searchable documents and their search queries, the contribution of runs from participants, and the subsequent formation of relevance assessments and evaluation of these participants' submissions. For the first time, the search queries (and their variants) were intended to not only be in written format but also in spoken format, with automatic speech-to-text transcripts provided. The new document collection introduced in the 2018 Task 3, consisting of over 5 million pages from the *World Wide Web* (WWW) was to be used for this task. This was a compilation of Web pages of selected domains acquired from the CommonCrawl[4]. User stories for search query and query variant generation were those, using the discharge summaries and forum posts, we used in previous years of the task.

The remainder of this overview paper is structured as follows: First, in Sect. 2, we detail for each task its text documents; human annotations, queries, and relevance assessments; and evaluation methods. After this, in Sect. 3, we describe the task submissions and results of the CLEF eHealth 2019 evaluation lab. Finally, in Sect. 4 we conclude the study.

2   Materials and Methods

In this section, we describe the materials and methods used in the two tasks of the CLEF eHealth evaluation lab 2019. After specifying our text documents to process in Sect. 2.1, we address their human annotations, queries, and relevance assessments in Sect. 2.2. Finally, in Sect. 2.3 we introduce our evaluation methods. We also include in Sects. 2.1 and 2.2 a brief description of the document set and its intended query set for Task 3.

2.1   Text Documents

Task 1. The multilingual information extraction task challenged its participants with the fully automated semantic indexing of NTSs of animal experiments using codes from the German version of the ICD-10. The NTPs were short publicly-available summaries[5] written as part of the approval procedure for animal experiments in Germany. The database currently contains more than 10, 000 NTPs (as of May/2019).

Task 2. The technologically assisted reviews in empirical medicine task used the PubMed document collection for its Boolean Search challenge and a subset of PubMed documents for its challenge to make Abstract and Title Screening more effective. More specifically, for the Abstract and Title Screening subtask the *PubMed Document Identifiers* (PMIDs) of potentially relevant

---

[4] http://commoncrawl.org/ (last accessed on 28 May 2019).
[5] The *AnimalTestInfo* database was publicly available at https://www.animaltestinfo. de when the task was launched.

PubMed Document abstracts were provided for each training and test topic. The PMIDs were collected by the task coordinators by re-running the MEDLINE Boolean query used in the original systematic reviews conducted by Cochrane to search PubMed.

Task 3. The document corpus is the same as the corpus used in 2018. It consists of web pages acquired from the CommonCrawl. An initial list of websites was identified for acquisition. The list was built by submitting the CLEF 2018 queries to the Microsoft Bing Apis (through the Azure Cognitive Services) repeatedly over a period of a few weeks, and acquiring the URLs of the retrieved results. The domains of the URLs were then included in the list, except some domains that were excluded for decency reasons. The list was further augmented by including a number of known reliable health websites and other known unreliable health websites, from lists previously compiled by health institutions and agencies.

2.2   Human Annotations, Queries, and Relevance Assessments

Task 1. The task consisted of assigning codes with respect to chapters or groups of the 2016 German Modification of ICD-10[6]. The training and development data set[7] contained a total of 8,386 NTSs of animal experiments recently carried out in Germany (as of September 2018). It was split into training and development sets with 7,544 and 842 NTSs, respectively. For the test set, we released 407 NTSs[8] for which participants should predict the ICD-10 codes. In all data sets, each NTS contained a title, benefits (goals) of the experiments, possible harms caused to the animals, and comments related to the *replacement, reduction and refinement* (3R) principles. All documents were in the German language. The data set included the ICD-10 codes manually assigned by experts. However, some NTSs had no ICD-10 codes assigned to them, since the codes were not applicable to the benefits described in the NTS.

Task 2. In Task 2 Subtask 1, for the No-Boolean-Search challenge as input for each topic participants were provided with

1. a Topic-ID,
2. the title of the review, written by Cochrane experts,

---

[6] Available at https://www.dimdi.de/static/de/klassifikationen/icd/icd-10-gm/kode-suche/htmlgm2016/.

[7] Publicly available on 24 January 2019 at https://www.openagrar.de/receive/openagrar_mods_00046540?lang=en under the *Creative Commons, Attribution-NonCommercial-NoDerivatives 4.0 International* (CC BY-NC-ND 4.0) license as DOI https://doi.org/10.17590/20190118-134645-0.

[8] Publicly available on 6 May 2019 https://www.openagrar.de/receive/openagrar_mods_00049062?lang=en under the *Creative Commons, Attribution-NonCommercial-NoDerivatives 4.0 International* (CC BY-NC-ND 4.0) license.

3. the most important parts of the protocol, written by Cochrane experts, and
4. the entire PubMED database (which was available for downloaded directly from PubMED, through ftp://ftp.ncbi.nlm.nih.gov/pubmed/baseline).

In Task 2 Subtask 2, focusing on title and abstract screening, topics consisted of the Boolean Search from the first step of the systematic review process. Specifically, for each topic the following information was provided.

1. a Topic-ID,
2. the title of the review, written by Cochrane experts,
3. the Boolean query, manually constructed by Cochrane experts, and
4. the set of PMIDs returned by running the query in MEDLINE.

Participants were provided with eight topics of DTA reviews, 20 topics of Intervention reviews, one topic of Prognosis, and two of Qualitative reviews, as a test set for both subtasks. The 72 DTA topics (which excludes topics that were reviewed and found unreliable) considered in CLEF 2017 and 2018 TAR tasks were used as training set. Further, we developed 20 Intervention topics that were also provided as training set to participants.

The original systematic reviews written by Cochrane experts included a reference section that listed Included, Excluded, and Additional references to medical studies. The union of Included and Excluded references are the studies that were screened at a Title and Abstract level and were considered for further examination at a full content level. These constituted the relevant documents at the abstract level, while the Included references constituted the relevant documents at the full content level. References in the original systematic reviews were collected from a variety of resources, not only MEDLINE. Therefore, studies that were cited but did not appear in the results of the Boolean query were excluded from the label set for both Subtask 1 and Subtask 2.

Regarding Subtask 2, that is, the Title and Abstract Screening, relevance was assessed at two levels, at abstract level, which expresses the potential of the article to be relevant and included in the review, and hence need to be read in full, and at full content level, after the full article has been read and decided whether to be included or excluded from the study. The following numbers present for each type of study the percentage of relevant document (abstract or content level) in the development set and in the test set, so that the reader can get an idea of the difficulty of the task, the differences across different types of reviews if any, and any changes in the relevance distribution between training and test sets.

Hence, the percentage of relevant document (1) for the DTA studies, (1a) at abstract level, in the training set was 1.7% and in the test set 1.4% of the total number of PMIDs released, while (1b) at content level it was 0.3% in the training set, and 0.8% in the test set. (2) For the Intervention studies, the percentage of relevant documents (2a) at abstract level in the training set was 1.7% and in the test set 0.9%, while at the content level the average percentage was 2.2% in the training set, and 1.2% in the test set. For the Prognosis and Qualitative reviews no training data was provided. (3) In the test set for the Prognosis, (3a) the percentage of relevant documents is 5.7% at the abstract level and (3b) 2.7% at the content level, while (4) for the Qualitative, (4a) the percentage of relevant documents is 1.7% at the abstract level and(4b) 0.4% at the content level.

All the released data for the 2017 – 2019 CLEF eHealth TAR tasks can be found at https://github.com/CLEF-TAR.

Task 3. With the aim to acquire more relevance assessments and increase the collection reusability, the intent this year was to reuse the same set of 50 query narratives developed in 2018's Task 3 [10]. In 2018, query creators devised 7 query variants from each query narrative. This was accomplished by asking laypeople and medical experts to generate written queries based on the textual narratives. In 2019, in order to increase the variability of generated queries, written narratives were converted into spoken audio. After hearing the narratives, a set of query creators were to generate spoken query variants by speaking their queries aloud. Our intention was to make the generated original spoken queries as well as the output of a speech-recognition software available to the participants.

2.3   Evaluation Methods

Task 1. The training and development sets were released on 24 January 2019, and the test set on 6 May 2019. Teams could submit by 13 May 2019 up to three runs/solutions for the test data set. We evaluated the runs based on the usual metrics of the precision, recall, and F-measure using a publicly-available Python script[9].

Task 2. Teams could submit an unlimited number of runs per task. In addition, participants were also encouraged to submit any number of runs that result from their 2017 and 2018 frozen systems. System performance was assessed using the same evaluation approach as that used for the 2018 TAR challenge [12]. Specifically, (i) similarly to the previous year, runs were evaluated on the basis of identifying the studies to be included (relevant documents), (ii) different from previous years, runs were evaluated on the basis of not only finding the studies to be included, but also finding high quality included studies before low quality included studies.

The assumption behind this evaluation approach (i) was the following: The user of your system is the researcher that performs the abstract and title screening of the retrieved articles. Every time an abstract is returned (i.e., ranked) there is an incurred cost/effort, while the abstract is either irrelevant (in which case no further action will be taken) or relevant (and hence passed to the next stage of document screening) to the topic under review.

---

[9] https://github.com/mariananeves/clef19ehealth-task1.

Evaluation measures were as follows: Area under the recall-precision curve (i.e., Average Precision); Minimum number of documents returned to retrieve all relevant documents; Work Saved over Sampling at different Recall levels; Area under the cumulative recall curve normalized by the optimal area; Recall @ 0% to 100% of documents shown; a number of newly constructed cost-based measures; and reliability [3].

Evaluation approach (ii) considered not only the relevance but the quality of the articles as well, taking into account indicators such as the risk-of-bias, and the sample size of the trials reported of the studies. This second evaluation approach depended on assessments Cochrane reviewers made manually on aspects of the included studies. Obtaining these assessments turned out to be a difficult task therefore this second evaluation approached was postponed for the future.

The training data set was released at the end of March 2019 and the test data set on 14 May 2019. The relevance labels on the testing data (required by active learning techniques) were provided to participants on 14 May 2019 as well, while the submission deadline was set to 21 May 2019 so that participants could not tune their systems towards the actual labels.

More details on the evaluation are provided in the Task 2 overview paper [13].

3   Results

The number of people who registered their interest in CLEF eHealth tasks was 31 in Task 1 and 36 in Task 2. In total, nine teams submitted to the two shared tasks.

Task 1 received considerable interest with the submission of 14 runs from six teams. We had two teams from Germany (MLT-DFKI and WBI), one from India (SSN_NLP), one from Italy (IMS_UNIPD), one as a collaboration between Spain and UK (TALP_UPC) and one from Turkey (DEMIR). Table 1 summarizes the results obtained by each team.

Participants relied on a diverse range of approaches. WBI utilized the multilingual version of the BERT-Base model [4] and made use of additional resources, such as the *German Clinical Trials Register* (DRKS)[10]. MLT-DFKI utilized Google Translate to convert documents into English and then relied on pre-trained BioBERT [17] to perform the prediction of ICD-10 codes. DEMIR utilized ElasticSearch for searching for similar NTSs and selected top documents (NTSs) based on *k-nearest neighbors* (KNN) and on threshold-based methods. SSN_NLP relied on a seq2seq mapping model based on bidirectional *long short-term memory* (LSTM) and experimented with the Normed_Bahdanau and the Scaled Luong attention mechanisms. IMS-UNIPD tried three Naïve Bayes classifiers (Bernoulli, Multinomial and Poisson) based on a 2D representation of the probabilities.

---

[10] See https://www.drks.de/drks_web/setLocale_EN.do.

Task 2 attracted the interest of 3 teams submitting runs, all from Europe, including one team from The Netherlands (UvA), one team from the UK (Sheffield), and one team from Italy (UNIPD). For Subtask 1, we received no runs. For Subtask 2, we received 36 runs from the three teams. The results on a selected subset of metrics on DTA, Intervention, Prognosis, and Qualitative studies are shown in Tables 2, 3, 4, and 5, respectively. The three teams used a variety of ranking methods including traditional BM25, interactive BM25, continuous active learning, relevance feedback, as well as a variety of stopping criteria to provide a threshold on the ranking.

Table 1. System performance for ICD-10 coding on the test set for German NTSs in terms of Precision (P), recall (R) and F-measure (F). The results are ordered in decreasing order of the scores for F-Measure. We highlight in **bold** the highest scores for P, R, and F.

Team	P	R	FM
WBI-run1	0.83	0.77	**0.80**
WBI-run2	**0.84**	0.74	0.79
WBI-run3	0.80	0.78	0.79
MLT-DFKI	0.64	**0.86**	0.73
DEMIR-run1	0.46	0.50	0.48
DEMIR-run3	0.46	0.49	0.48
DEMIR-run2	0.49	0.44	0.46
TALP_UPC	0.37	0.35	0.36
SSN_NLP-run2	0.19	0.27	0.23
SSN_NLP-run1	0.19	0.27	0.22
SSN_NLP-run3	0.13	0.34	0.19
IMS_UNIPD-run3	0.10	0.05	0.07
IMS_UNIPD-run2	0.009	0.50	0.017
IMS_UNIPD-run1	0	0	0

Table 2. DTA studies with abstract-level QRELs

Run	L-Rel	MAP	R@5%	R@10%	R@20%	R@30%	WSS95	WSS100	Rely	R@k	k
ILPS/DTA/abs-hh-ratio-ilps@uva.out	2420	0.493	0.589	0.682	0.789	0.834	0.406	0.304	0.189	0.815	1132
ILPS/DTA/abs-th-ratio-ilps@uva.out	2676	0.399	0.418	0.536	0.661	0.734	0.312	0.253	0.273	0.744	1558
Padua/DTA/2018_stem_original-p10_t400.out	1190	0.229	0.448	0.634	0.818	0.895	0.662	0.512	0.136	0.963	605
Padua/DTA/distributed_effort-p10_t1500.out	1111	0.229	0.445	0.63	0.814	0.895	0.652	0.513	0.204	0.963	2453
Padua/DTA/2018_stem_original-p10_t1000.out	1141	0.229	0.445	0.63	0.814	0.893	0.658	0.509	0.19	0.986	1195
Padua/DTA/2018_stem_original-p10_t200.out	1282	0.229	0.445	0.634	0.823	0.891	0.66	0.507	0.115	0.877	336
Padua/DTA/2018_stem_original-p10_t500.out	1200	0.229	0.445	0.634	0.818	0.893	0.662	0.509	0.147	0.97	719
Padua/DTA/2018_stem_original-p10_t300.out	1280	0.229	0.452	0.627	0.816	0.893	0.66	0.5	0.113	0.936	477
Padua/DTA/2018_stem_original-p10_t1500.out	1126	0.229	0.445	0.63	0.814	0.895	0.657	0.514	0.228	0.995	1524
Padua/DTA/distributed_effort-p10_t1000.out	1109	0.229	0.445	0.63	0.814	0.895	0.649	0.514	0.129	0.93	1776
Padua/DTA/2018_stem_original-p10_t100.out	2024	0.221	0.418	0.609	0.791	0.868	0.525	0.399	0.291	0.604	180
Padua/DTA/baseline_bm25_t500.out	2470	0.119	0.236	0.402	0.548	0.65	0.39	0.252	0.342	0.638	451
Padua/DTA/distributed_effort-p10_t300.out	1111	0.232	0.445	0.63	0.814	0.886	0.649	0.528	0.117	0.818	802
Padua/DTA/2018_stem_original-p50_t1000.out	1127	0.229	0.445	0.63	0.811	0.893	0.652	0.528	0.235	0.995	1473
Padua/DTA/distributed_effort-p10_t100.out	1271	0.204	0.439	0.614	0.77	0.839	0.61	0.468	0.308	0.572	284
Padua/DTA/2018_stem_original-p50_t200.out	1291	0.229	0.445	0.634	0.82	0.898	0.66	0.499	0.141	0.89	364
Padua/DTA/baseline_bm25_t1000.out	2395	0.119	0.236	0.389	0.543	0.659	0.396	0.26	0.274	0.761	826
Padua/DTA/distributed_effort-p10_t500.out	1116	0.229	0.445	0.63	0.814	0.891	0.634	0.521	0.096	0.874	1083
Padua/DTA/baseline_bm25_t300.out	2493	0.119	0.239	0.405	0.541	0.652	0.391	0.244	0.415	0.499	280
Padua/DTA/baseline_bm25_t100.out	2130	0.12	0.239	0.414	0.564	0.659	0.394	0.295	0.683	0.241	101
Padua/DTA/2018_stem_original-p50_t400.out	1189	0.229	0.448	0.634	0.816	0.891	0.654	0.527	0.154	0.965	672
Padua/DTA/2018_stem_original-p50_t300.out	1272	0.229	0.452	0.627	0.814	0.893	0.656	0.518	0.146	0.945	522
Padua/DTA/2018_stem_original-p50_t100.out	2027	0.222	0.418	0.609	0.786	0.868	0.549	0.394	0.308	0.618	189
Padua/DTA/distributed_effort-p10_t200.out	1194	0.225	0.445	0.632	0.811	0.877	0.663	0.509	0.17	0.735	566
Padua/DTA/baseline_bm25_t400.out	2492	0.119	0.239	0.405	0.539	0.65	0.386	0.246	0.355	0.596	367
Padua/DTA/2018_stem_original-p50_t1500.out	1056	0.229	0.445	0.63	0.814	0.898	0.651	0.537	0.31	1.0	2018
Padua/DTA/2018_stem_original-p50_t500.out	1200	0.229	0.445	0.634	0.809	0.889	0.649	0.524	0.169	0.97	820
Padua/DTA/baseline_bm25_t1500.out	2476	0.119	0.236	0.389	0.541	0.652	0.364	0.254	0.256	0.853	1171
Padua/DTA/baseline_bm25_t200.out	2253	0.12	0.234	0.405	0.55	0.652	0.409	0.278	0.504	0.407	192
Padua/DTA/distributed_effort-p10_t400.out	1116	0.231	0.445	0.63	0.814	0.886	0.634	0.528	0.1	0.856	942
Sheffield/DTA/DTA_sheffield-Chi-Squared.out	1964	0.222	0.305	0.45	0.641	0.73	0.475	0.375	0.479	1.0	3815
Sheffield/DTA/DTA_sheffield-baseline.out	2250	0.175	0.22	0.336	0.525	0.675	0.451	0.338	0.479	1.0	3815
Sheffield/DTA/DTA_sheffield-Odds_Ratio.out	2184	0.248	0.382	0.561	0.707	0.805	0.49	0.347	0.479	1.0	3815
Sheffield/DTA/DTA_sheffield-Log_Likelihood.out	1972	0.234	0.35	0.527	0.668	0.759	0.487	0.381	0.479	1.0	3815

Table 3. Intervention studies with abstract-level QRELs

Run	L_Rel	MAP	R@5%	R@10%	R@20%	R@30%	WSS95	WSS100	Rely	R@k	k
ILPS/Int/abs-hh-ratio-ilps@uva.out	958	0.567	0.518	0.628	0.736	0.813	0.526	0.48	0.213	0.915	773
ILPS/Int/abs-th-ratio-ilps@uva.out	986	0.556	0.478	0.576	0.692	0.774	0.535	0.45	0.197	0.868	555
Padua/Int/2018_stem_original_p10_t400.out	985	0.28	0.307	0.502	0.663	0.744	0.632	0.511	0.334	0.941	487
Padua/Int/distributed_effort_p10_t1500.out	981	0.28	0.306	0.499	0.664	0.745	0.633	0.517	0.247	0.968	1349
Padua/Int/2018_stem_original_p10_t1000.out	977	0.28	0.306	0.499	0.664	0.745	0.63	0.51	0.415	0.973	870
Padua/Int/2018_stem_original_p10_t200.out	1180	0.28	0.312	0.501	0.671	0.775	0.617	0.488	0.267	0.901	301
Padua/Int/2018_stem_original_p10_t500.out	975	0.28	0.306	0.502	0.662	0.742	0.63	0.514	0.353	0.946	560
Padua/Int/2018_stem_original_p10_t300.out	1141	0.28	0.313	0.496	0.665	0.771	0.617	0.494	0.322	0.922	405
Padua/Int/2018_stem_original_p10_t1500.out	952	0.28	0.306	0.499	0.664	0.745	0.63	0.522	0.474	0.984	1117
Padua/Int/distributed_effort_p10_t1000.out	992	0.279	0.306	0.499	0.664	0.745	0.62	0.492	0.157	0.921	975
Padua/Int/2018_stem_original_p10_t100.out	1153	0.274	0.306	0.483	0.639	0.737	0.54	0.474	0.292	0.711	164
Padua/Int/baseline_bm25_t500.out	1233	0.222	0.191	0.282	0.41	0.515	0.435	0.394	0.481	0.741	402
Padua/Int/distributed_effort_p10_t300.out	974	0.276	0.306	0.499	0.664	0.733	0.592	0.481	0.122	0.794	441
Padua/Int/2018_stem_original_p50_t1000.out	836	0.29	0.306	0.498	0.688	0.795	0.643	0.542	0.493	0.988	1139
Padua/Int/distributed_effort_p10_t100.out	1114	0.248	0.315	0.444	0.604	0.704	0.458	0.372	0.402	0.45	156
Padua/Int/2018_stem_original_p50_t200.out	1185	0.29	0.312	0.499	0.693	0.792	0.63	0.481	0.331	0.911	334
Padua/Int/baseline_bm25_t1000.out	1241	0.222	0.191	0.282	0.408	0.524	0.446	0.392	0.471	0.827	682
Padua/Int/distributed_effort_p10_t500.out	991	0.278	0.306	0.499	0.664	0.743	0.606	0.483	0.115	0.842	594
Padua/Int/baseline_bm25_t300.out	1262	0.222	0.187	0.286	0.41	0.523	0.44	0.398	0.506	0.664	270
Padua/Int/baseline_bm25_t100.out	1397	0.223	0.186	0.291	0.429	0.557	0.414	0.368	0.485	0.507	99
Padua/Int/2018_stem_original_p50_t400.out	985	0.29	0.307	0.501	0.685	0.767	0.646	0.514	0.374	0.949	572
Padua/Int/2018_stem_original_p50_t300.out	1144	0.29	0.313	0.495	0.682	0.788	0.639	0.497	0.355	0.933	462
Padua/Int/2018_stem_original_p50_t100.out	1150	0.284	0.306	0.483	0.653	0.752	0.556	0.481	0.362	0.728	188
Padua/Int/distributed_effort_p10_t200.out	965	0.271	0.306	0.482	0.651	0.752	0.56	0.445	0.165	0.714	312
Padua/Int/baseline_bm25_t400.out	1242	0.222	0.191	0.286	0.412	0.523	0.434	0.393	0.485	0.713	337
Padua/Int/2018_stem_original_p50_t1500.out	796	0.29	0.306	0.498	0.688	0.785	0.642	0.553	0.541	0.999	1425
Padua/Int/2018_stem_original_p50_t500.out	1001	0.29	0.306	0.501	0.691	0.779	0.65	0.505	0.395	0.961	677
Padua/Int/baseline_bm25_t1500.out	1203	0.222	0.191	0.282	0.411	0.533	0.453	0.399	0.461	0.933	932
Padua/Int/baseline_bm25_t200.out	1263	0.222	0.189	0.284	0.417	0.535	0.438	0.396	0.466	0.624	191
Padua/Int/distributed_effort_p10_t400.out	981	0.277	0.306	0.499	0.663	0.734	0.595	0.483	0.116	0.822	518
Sheffield/Int/Int_sheffield-Log_likelihood.out	1132	0.293	0.258	0.378	0.583	0.695	0.458	0.381	0.599	1	2100
Sheffield/Int/Int_sheffield-Odds_Ratio.out	1070	0.261	0.267	0.404	0.569	0.7	0.462	0.384	0.599	1	2100
Sheffield/Int/Int_sheffield-baseline.out	1276	0.245	0.22	0.334	0.507	0.653	0.47	0.386	0.599	1	2100
Sheffield/Int/Int_sheffield-Chi_Squared.out	1149	0.262	0.238	0.36	0.537	0.687	0.469	0.415	0.599	1	2100

Table 4. Prognosis studies with abstract-level QRELs

Run	L_Rel	MAP	R@5%	R@10%	R@20%	R@30%	WSS95	WSS100	Rely	R@k	k
ILPS/Pro/abs/abs-hh-ratio-ilps@uva	2885	0.673	0.562	0.714	0.875	0.911	0.591	0.143	0.018	0.948	1221
ILPS/Pro/abs/abs-th-ratio-ilps@uva	2537	0.628	0.521	0.682	0.818	0.927	0.566	0.247	0.014	0.922	867
Padua/Pro/abs/2018_stem_original_p10_t400	2967	0.235	0.214	0.484	0.812	0.901	0.567	0.119	0.035	0.828	735
Padua/Pro/abs/distributed_effort_p10_t1500	2594	0.235	0.214	0.484	0.812	0.896	0.554	0.23	0.049	0.99	2165
Padua/Pro/abs/2018_stem_original_p10_t1000	2644	0.235	0.214	0.484	0.812	0.896	0.554	0.215	0.022	0.943	1332
Padua/Pro/abs/2018_stem_original_p10_t200	2911	0.242	0.214	0.536	0.812	0.901	0.53	0.135	0.162	0.599	398
Padua/Pro/abs/2018_stem_original_p10_t500	2920	0.235	0.214	0.484	0.812	0.891	0.56	0.133	0.027	0.859	832
Padua/Pro/abs/2018_stem_original_p10_t300	2955	0.239	0.214	0.547	0.818	0.891	0.556	0.122	0.054	0.776	597
Padua/Pro/abs/2018_stem_original_p10_t1500	2578	0.235	0.214	0.484	0.812	0.896	0.554	0.234	0.035	0.984	1831
Padua/Pro/abs/distributed_effort_p10_t1000	2563	0.235	0.214	0.484	0.812	0.896	0.554	0.239	0.026	0.974	1566
Padua/Pro/abs/2018_stem_original_p10_t100	2802	0.259	0.286	0.562	0.797	0.891	0.6	0.168	0.411	0.359	198
Padua/Pro/abs/baseline_bm25_t500	3343	0.071	0.057	0.13	0.281	0.422	0.084	0.007	0.621	0.214	501
Padua/Pro/abs/distributed_effort_p10_t300	2964	0.235	0.214	0.484	0.812	0.906	0.567	0.12	0.038	0.818	709
Padua/Pro/abs/2018_stem_original_p50_t1000	2556	0.221	0.214	0.484	0.74	0.87	0.571	0.241	0.041	0.995	1981
Padua/Pro/abs/distributed_effort_p10_t100	2789	0.252	0.25	0.568	0.786	0.875	0.594	0.172	0.288	0.464	248
Padua/Pro/abs/2018_stem_original_p50_t200	2911	0.242	0.214	0.536	0.812	0.901	0.53	0.135	0.162	0.599	398
Padua/Pro/abs/baseline_bm25_t1000	3346	0.07	0.057	0.13	0.276	0.396	0.057	0.006	0.382	0.391	1001
Padua/Pro/abs/distributed_effort_p10_t500	2708	0.235	0.214	0.484	0.812	0.891	0.566	0.196	0.026	0.87	955
Padua/Pro/abs/baseline_bm25_t300	3350	0.071	0.057	0.135	0.276	0.385	0.104	0.005	0.794	0.109	301
Padua/Pro/abs/baseline_bm25_t100	3350	0.066	0.047	0.13	0.255	0.365	0.059	0.005	0.939	0.031	101
Padua/Pro/abs/2018_stem_original_p50_t400	2955	0.231	0.214	0.484	0.807	0.896	0.556	0.122	0.033	0.839	798
Padua/Pro/abs/2018_stem_original_p50_t300	2955	0.239	0.214	0.547	0.818	0.891	0.556	0.122	0.054	0.776	597
Padua/Pro/abs/2018_stem_original_p50_t100	2802	0.259	0.286	0.562	0.797	0.891	0.6	0.168	0.411	0.359	198
Padua/Pro/abs/distributed_effort_p10_t200	2968	0.24	0.214	0.542	0.807	0.906	0.548	0.119	0.079	0.724	501
Padua/Pro/abs/baseline_bm25_t400	3347	0.071	0.057	0.13	0.281	0.417	0.109	0.006	0.696	0.167	401
Padua/Pro/abs/2018_stem_original_p50_t1500	1975	0.219	0.214	0.484	0.74	0.828	0.5	0.413	0.091	1	2966
Padua/Pro/abs/2018_stem_original_p50_t500	2660	0.228	0.214	0.484	0.807	0.891	0.576	0.21	0.022	0.891	993
Padua/Pro/abs/baseline_bm25_t1500	3346	0.07	0.057	0.13	0.276	0.396	0.05	0.006	0.258	0.516	1501
Padua/Pro/abs/baseline_bm25_t200	3350	0.069	0.057	0.125	0.266	0.385	0.111	0.005	0.86	0.073	201
Padua/Pro/abs/distributed_effort_p10_t400	2920	0.235	0.214	0.484	0.812	0.891	0.56	0.133	0.028	0.854	830
Sheffield/Pro/abs/Pro_sheffield-baseline	2990	0.126	0.146	0.255	0.448	0.594	0.247	0.112	0.117	1	3367
Sheffield/Pro/abs/Pro_sheffield-relevence-feedback	2775	0.141	0.151	0.307	0.484	0.646	0.305	0.176	0.117	1	3367

Table 5. Qualitative studies with abstract-level QRELs

Run	L_Rel	MAP	R@5%	R@10%	R@20%	R@30%	WSS95	WSS100	Rely	R@k	k
ILPS/Qual/abs/abs-hh-ratio-ilps@uva.out	1796	0.204	0.478	0.655	0.876	0.929	0.417	0.397	0.326	0.919	1247
ILPS/Qual/abs/abs-th-ratio-ilps@uva.out	2564	0.187	0.487	0.628	0.805	0.92	0.398	0.215	0.341	0.878	1158
Padua/Qual/abs/2018_stem_original_p10_t400.out	2547	0.109	0.496	0.717	0.779	0.894	0.302	0.183	0.568	0.387	704
Padua/Qual/abs/distributed_effort_p10_t1500.out	2544	0.109	0.496	0.743	0.77	0.885	0.268	0.168	0.37	0.745	2098
Padua/Qual/abs/2018_stem_original_p10_t1000.out	2662	0.109	0.496	0.743	0.77	0.885	0.273	0.141	0.29	0.714	1320
Padua/Qual/abs/2018_stem_original_p10_t200.out	2934	0.089	0.478	0.522	0.699	0.805	0.216	0.101	0.627	0.266	397
Padua/Qual/abs/2018_stem_original_p10_t500.out	2535	0.109	0.496	0.743	0.77	0.894	0.301	0.185	0.578	0.396	820
Padua/Qual/abs/2018_stem_original_p10_t300.out	2660	0.103	0.496	0.655	0.752	0.858	0.303	0.159	0.582	0.338	554
Padua/Qual/abs/2018_stem_original_p10_t1500.out	2534	0.109	0.496	0.743	0.77	0.885	0.268	0.17	0.447	0.732	1819
Padua/Qual/abs/distributed_effort_p10_t1000.out	2469	0.109	0.496	0.743	0.77	0.885	0.295	0.199	0.628	0.491	1515
Padua/Qual/abs/2018_stem_original_p10_t100.out	2996	0.071	0.327	0.416	0.637	0.796	0.186	0.09	0.726	0.167	198
Padua/Qual/abs/baseline_bm25_t500.out	2700	0.051	0.274	0.425	0.469	0.611	0.412	0.256	0.683	0.221	501
Padua/Qual/abs/distributed_effort_p10_t300.out	2518	0.109	0.496	0.743	0.77	0.894	0.309	0.193	0.547	0.396	684
Padua/Qual/abs/2018_stem_original_p50_t1000.out	2438	0.116	0.496	0.743	0.92	0.947	0.357	0.194	0.545	0.745	1977
Padua/Qual/abs/distributed_effort_p10_t100.out	2920	0.083	0.416	0.469	0.681	0.814	0.258	0.106	0.659	0.221	244
Padua/Qual/abs/2018_stem_original_p50_t200.out	2934	0.089	0.478	0.522	0.699	0.805	0.216	0.101	0.627	0.266	397
Padua/Qual/abs/baseline_bm25_t1000.out	3040	0.055	0.274	0.425	0.496	0.788	0.239	0.101	0.278	0.601	1001
Padua/Qual/abs/distributed_effort_p10_t500.out	2641	0.109	0.496	0.743	0.77	0.894	0.295	0.162	0.553	0.446	924
Padua/Qual/abs/baseline_bm25_t300.out	2697	0.049	0.274	0.372	0.451	0.628	0.294	0.257	0.726	0.171	301
Padua/Qual/abs/baseline_bm25_t100.out	2700	0.056	0.301	0.389	0.637	0.743	0.399	0.256	0.845	0.086	101
Padua/Qual/abs/2018_stem_original_p50_t400.out	2566	0.109	0.496	0.717	0.779	0.894	0.293	0.174	0.594	0.387	795
Padua/Qual/abs/2018_stem_original_p50_t300.out	2687	0.103	0.496	0.655	0.752	0.858	0.29	0.147	0.591	0.338	595
Padua/Qual/abs/2018_stem_original_p50_t100.out	2996	0.071	0.327	0.416	0.637	0.796	0.186	0.09	0.726	0.167	198
Padua/Qual/abs/distributed_effort_p10_t200.out	2762	0.104	0.496	0.673	0.761	0.867	0.303	0.135	0.56	0.347	486
Padua/Qual/abs/baseline_bm25_t400.out	2700	0.052	0.274	0.434	0.469	0.619	0.417	0.256	0.694	0.203	401
Padua/Qual/abs/2018_stem_original_p50_t1500.out	1970	0.116	0.496	0.743	0.92	0.965	0.356	0.301	0.532	1	2568
Padua/Qual/abs/2018_stem_original_p50_t500.out	2576	0.11	0.496	0.743	0.788	0.894	0.283	0.168	0.624	0.405	991
Padua/Qual/abs/baseline_bm25_t1500.out	3039	0.055	0.274	0.425	0.496	0.779	0.24	0.101	0.382	0.669	1501
Padua/Qual/abs/baseline_bm25_t200.out	2698	0.053	0.274	0.381	0.619	0.726	0.395	0.256	0.764	0.14	201
Padua/Qual/abs/distributed_effort_p10_t400.out	2636	0.109	0.496	0.743	0.77	0.894	0.301	0.165	0.545	0.432	804
Sheffield/Qual/abs/Qual_sheffield-relevance-feedback.out	2940	0.06	0.274	0.549	0.717	0.832	0.185	0.103	0.593	1	3268
Sheffield/Qual/abs/Qual_sheffield-baseline	3031	0.051	0.265	0.451	0.619	0.743	0.135	0.082	0.593	1	3268

4   Conclusions

This paper provided an overview of the CLEF eHealth 2019 evaluation lab. The CLEF eHealth series began its life as a scientific workshop in 2012 with an aim of establishing an evaluation lab [26]. This ambition was realised in 2013, with the running of the first annual CLEF eHealth evaluation lab. Since 2013, this annual lab has run two or more preceding shared tasks each year, in other words, the CLEF eHealth 2013–2019 evaluation labs [8,9,14,16,28,29]. During these past eight years, the CLEF eHealth series has offered a recurring contribution to the creation and dissemination of text analytics resources, methods, test collections, and evaluation benchmarks in order to ease and support patients, their next-of-kins, clinical staff, and health scientists in understanding, accessing, and authoring eHealth information in a multilingual setting.

The CLEF eHealth 2019 lab ran two shared tasks: Task 1 on multilingual information extraction to extend the 2018 task on French, Hungarian, and Italian corpora to German; and Task 2 on technologically assisted reviews in empirical medicine building on the 2018 task in English. In addition, a Task 3 on consumer health search in mono- and multilingual settings was initially advertised, but unfortunately, due to unforeseen circumstances, this task had to be postponed.

Test collections generated by this year's CLEF eHealth 2019 lab offered a specific task definition, implemented in a data set distributed together with an implementation of relevant evaluation metrics to allow for direct comparability of the results reported by systems evaluated on the collections. The CLEF eHealth information extraction task (Task 1) used a traditional shared task model for evaluation in which a community-wide evaluation is executed in a controlled setting: independent training and test data sets are used and all participants gain access to the test data at the same time, following which no further updates to systems are allowed. Shortly after releasing the test data (without labels or other solutions), the participating teams are to submit their outputs from the frozen systems to the task organizers, who are to evaluate these results and report the resulting benchmarks to the community. The CLEF technologically assisted reviews task (Task 2) also followed the same setting with independent training and test data sets and all participants gaining access to the test data at the same time; however, labels on the test data were provided to participants to allow for the development of interactive retrieval systems.

Given the significance of the CLEF eHealth tasks over the years, all problem specifications, test collections, and text analytics resources associated with the 2019 and previous years' lab tasks have been made available to the wider research community. They can be found on our CLEF eHealth website[11].

Acknowledgements. We gratefully acknowledge the contribution of the people and organizations involved in the CLEF eHealth 2019 evaluation lab as participants or organizers. The lab has been supported in part by (in alphabetical order) The Australian National University, College of Engineering and Computer Science, Research School

---

[11] http://clef-ehealth.org (last accessed on 24 May 2019).

of Computer Science; the CLEF Initiative; and Data61/Commonwealth Scientific and Industrial Research Organisation. We thank Dr Benjamin Lecouteux (LIG, Université Grenoble Alpes) for his help in Task 3. We are also thankful to the people involved in the task preparation, data annotation, query creation, and relevance assessment exercise. Last but not least, we gratefully acknowledge the participating teams' hard work. We thank them for their submissions and interest in the lab.

References

1. Adnan, M., Warren, J., Suominen, H.: Patient empowerment via technologies for patient-friendly personalized language. In: Grando, A.M., Rozenblum, R., Bates, D. (eds.) Engaging Patients with Health Information Technology, pp. 147–158. De Gruyter, Berlin (2015)
2. Bert, B., et al.: Rethinking 3R strategies: digging deeper into animaltestinfo promotes transparency in in vivo biomedical research. PLOS Biol. **15**(12), 1–20 (2017). https://doi.org/10.1371/journal.pbio.2003217
3. Cormack, G.V., Grossman, M.R.: Engineering quality and reliability in technology-assisted review. In: Proceedings of the 39th International ACM SIGIR Conference on Research and Development in Information Retrieval, SIGIR 2016, pp. 75–84. ACM, New York (2016). https://doi.org/10.1145/2911451.2911510
4. Devlin, J., Chang, M., Lee, K., Toutanova, K.: BERT: pre-training of deep bidirectional transformers for language understanding. CoRR abs/1810.04805 (2018). http://arxiv.org/abs/1810.04805
5. Goeuriot, L., et al.: ShARe/CLEF eHealth Evaluation Lab 2013, Task 3: Information retrieval to address patients' questions when reading clinical reports. CLEF 2013 Online Working Notes 8138 (2013)
6. Goeuriot, L., et al.: An analysis of evaluation campaigns in ad-hoc medical information retrieval: CLEF eHealth 2013 and 2014. Inf. Retrieval J. **21**, 507–540 (2018)
7. Goeuriot, L., et al.: ShARe/CLEF eHealth Evaluation Lab 2014, Task 3: user-centred health information retrieval. In: CLEF 2014 Evaluation Labs and Workshop, Sheffield, UK, Online Working Notes (2014)
8. Goeuriot, L., et al.: Overview of the CLEF eHealth evaluation lab 2015. In: Mothe, J., et al. (eds.) CLEF 2015. LNCS, vol. 9283, pp. 429–443. Springer, Cham (2015). https://doi.org/10.1007/978-3-319-24027-5_44
9. Goeuriot, L., et al.: CLEF 2017 eHealth evaluation lab overview. In: Jones, G.J.F., et al. (eds.) CLEF 2017. LNCS, vol. 10456, pp. 291–303. Springer, Cham (2017). https://doi.org/10.1007/978-3-319-65813-1_26
10. Jimmy, Z.G., Palotti, J.: Overview of the clef 2018 consumer health search task. In: Working Notes of Conference and Labs of the Evaluation (CLEF) Forum, CEUR Workshop Proceedings (2018)
11. Kanoulas, E., Li, D., Azzopardi, L., Spijker, R.: CLEF 2017 technologically assisted reviews in empirical medicine overview. In: Working Notes of Conference and Labs of the Evaluation (CLEF) Forum, CEUR Workshop Proceedings (2017)
12. Kanoulas, E., Li, D., Azzopardi, L., Spijker, R.: CLEF 2018 technologically assisted reviews in empirical medicine overview. In: Working Notes of Conference and Labs of the Evaluation (CLEF) Forum, CEUR Workshop Proceedings (2018)
13. Kanoulas, E., Li, D., Azzopardi, L., Spijker, R.: CLEF 2019 technology assisted reviews in empirical medicine overview. In: Working Notes of Conference and Labs of the Evaluation (CLEF) Forum, CEUR Workshop Proceedings (2019)

14. Kelly, L., Goeuriot, L., Suominen, H., Névéol, A., Palotti, J., Zuccon, G.: Overview of the CLEF eHealth evaluation lab 2016. In: Fuhr, N., et al. (eds.) CLEF 2016. LNCS, vol. 9822, pp. 255–266. Springer, Cham (2016). https://doi.org/10.1007/978-3-319-44564-9_24

15. Kelly, L., et al.: CLEF ehealth 2019 evaluation lab. In: Azzopardi, L., Stein, B., Fuhr, N., Mayr, P., Hauff, C., Hiemstra, D. (eds.) ECIR 2019. LNCS, vol. 11438, pp. 267–274. Springer, Heidelberg (2019). https://doi.org/10.1007/978-3-030-15719-7_36

16. Kelly, L., et al.: Overview of the ShARe/CLEF eHealth evaluation lab 2014. In: Kanoulas, E., et al. (eds.) CLEF 2014. LNCS, vol. 8685, pp. 172–191. Springer, Cham (2014). https://doi.org/10.1007/978-3-319-11382-1_17

17. Lee, J., et al.: BioBERT: a pre-trained biomedical language representation model for biomedical text mining. CoRR abs/1901.08746 (2019). http://arxiv.org/abs/1901.08746

18. Leeflang, M.M., Deeks, J.J., Takwoingi, Y., Macaskill, P.: Cochrane diagnostic test accuracy reviews. Syst. Rev. **2**(1), 82 (2013)

19. Névéol, A., et al.: Clinical information extraction at the CLEF eHealth evaluation lab 2016. In: Balog, K., Cappellato, L., Ferro, N., Macdonald, C. (eds.) CLEF 2016 Working Notes, CEUR Workshop Proceedings. CEUR-WS.org, ISSN 1613–0073 (2016). http://ceur-ws.org/Vol-1609/

20. Névéol, A., et al.: CLEF eHealth 2017 multilingual information extraction task overview: ICD10 coding of death certificates in English and French. In: CLEF 2017 Online Working Notes. CEUR-WS (2017)

21. Névéol, A., et al.: CLEF eHealth 2018 multilingual information extraction task overview: ICD10 coding of death certificates in French, Hungarian and Italian. In: CLEF 2018 Online Working Notes. CEUR-WS (2018)

22. Neves, M., et al.: Overview of task 1 in CLEF eHealth 2019: indexing German non-technical summaries of animal experiments. In: CLEF 2019 Online Working Notes. CEUR-WS (2019)

23. Palotti, J., et al.: CLEF eHealth evaluation lab 2015, Task 2: retrieving information about medical symptoms. In: CLEF 2015 Online Working Notes. CEUR-WS (2015)

24. Palotti, J., Zuccon, G., Hanbury, A.: Consumer health search on the web: study of web page understandability and its integration in ranking algorithms. J. Med. Internet Res. **21**(1), e10986 (2019). https://doi.org/10.2196/10986

25. Palotti, J., et al.: CLEF 2017 task overview: the IR task at the ehealth evaluation lab. In: Working Notes of Conference and Labs of the Evaluation (CLEF) Forum, CEUR Workshop Proceedings (2017)

26. Suominen, H.: CLEFeHealth2012 – The CLEF 2012 workshop on cross-language evaluation of methods, applications, and resources for eHealth document analysis. In: Forner, P., Karlgren, J., Womser-Hacker, C., Ferro, N. (eds.) CLEF 2012 Working Notes. CEUR Workshop Proceedings. CEUR-WS.org, ISSN 1613–0073 (2012). http://ceur-ws.org/Vol-1178/

27. Suominen, H., Kelly, L., Goeuriot, L.: Scholarly influence of the conference and labs of the evaluation forum eHealth initiative: review and bibliometric study of the 2012 to 2017 outcomes. JMIR Res. Protoc. **7**(7), e10961 (2018)

28. Suominen, H., et al.: Overview of the CLEF eHealth evaluation lab 2018. In: Bellot, P., et al. (eds.) Experimental IR Meets Multilinguality, Multimodality, and Interaction. LNCS, vol. 11018, pp. 286–301. Springer, Cham (2018). https://doi.org/10.1007/978-3-319-98932-7_26

29. Suominen, H., et al.: Overview of the ShARe/CLEF eHealth evaluation lab 2013. In: Forner, P., Müller, H., Paredes, R., Rosso, P., Stein, B. (eds.) CLEF 2013. LNCS, vol. 8138, pp. 212–231. Springer, Heidelberg (2013). https://doi.org/10.1007/978-3-642-40802-1_24
30. Zuccon, G., et al.: The IR task at the CLEF eHealth evaluation lab 2016: user-centred health information retrieval. In: CLEF 2016 Evaluation Labs and Workshop: Online Working Notes. CEUR-WS, September 2016

Overview of eRisk 2019 Early Risk Prediction on the Internet

David E. Losada[1(✉)], Fabio Crestani[2], and Javier Parapar[3]

[1] Centro Singular de Investigación en Tecnoloxías da Información (CiTIUS),
Universidade de Santiago de Compostela, Santiago, Spain
david.losada@usc.es
[2] Faculty of Informatics, Universitá della Svizzera italiana (USI),
Lugano, Switzerland
fabio.crestani@usi.ch
[3] Information Retrieval Lab,
Centro de Investigación en Tecnologías de la Información y las Comunicaciones,
Universidade da Coruña, Coruña, Spain
javierparapar@udc.es

Abstract. This paper provides an overview of eRisk 2019, the third edition of this lab under the CLEF conference. The main purpose of eRisk is to explore issues of evaluation methodology, effectiveness metrics and other processes related to early risk detection. Early detection technologies can be employed in different areas, particularly those related to health and safety. This edition of eRisk had three tasks. Two of them shared the same format and focused on early detecting signs of depression (T1) or self-harm (T2). The third task focused on an innovative challenge related to automatically filling a depression questionnaire based on user interactions in social media.

1 Introduction

The main purpose of eRisk is to explore issues of evaluation methodologies, performance metrics and other aspects related to building test collections and defining challenges for early risk detection. Early detection technologies are potentially useful in different areas, particularly those related to safety and health. For example, early alerts could be sent when a person starts showing signs of a mental disorder, when a sexual predator starts interacting with a child, or when a potential offender starts publishing antisocial threats on the Internet.

Although the evaluation methodology (strategies to build new test collections, novel evaluation metrics, etc) can be applied on multiple domains, eRisk has so far focused on psychological problems (essentially, depression, self-harm and eating disorders). In 2017 [4], we ran an exploratory task on early detection of depression. This pilot task was based on the evaluation methodology and test collection presented in [3]. In 2018 [5], we ran a continuation of the task on early detection of signs of depression together with a new task on early detection of signs of anorexia. Over these years, we have been able to compare a number of

© Springer Nature Switzerland AG 2019
F. Crestani et al. (Eds.): CLEF 2019, LNCS 11696, pp. 340–357, 2019.
https://doi.org/10.1007/978-3-030-28577-7_27

solutions that employ multiple technologies and models (e.g. Natural Language Processing, Machine Learning, or Information Retrieval). We learned that the interaction between psychological problems and language use is challenging and, in general, the effectiveness of most contributing systems is modest. For example, in terms of detecting signs of depression, the highest F1 was about 65%. This suggests that this kind of early prediction tasks require further research and the solutions proposed so far still have much room from improvement.

In 2019, the lab had three campaign-style tasks. Two of them had the same orientation of previous eRisk tasks but we changed the way in which data was released and, additionally, we expanded the set of evaluation measures. These two tasks were oriented to early detection of signs of anorexia and self-harm, respectively. The third task, which was completely new, was oriented to analyzing a user's history of posts and extracting useful evidence for estimating the user's depression level. More specifically, the participants had to process the user's posts and, next, estimate the user's answers to a standard depression questionnaire. These three tasks are described in the next sections of this overview paper.

2 Task 1: Early Detection of Signs of Anorexia

This is a continuation of eRisk 2018's T2 task. The challenge consists of sequentially processing pieces of evidence and detect early traces of anorexia as soon as possible. The task is mainly concerned about evaluating Text Mining solutions and, thus, it concentrates on texts written in Social Media. Texts had to be processed in the order they were created. In this way, systems that effectively perform this task could be applied to sequentially monitor user interactions in blogs, social networks, or other types of online media.

The test collection was built using the same methodology and sources as the collection described in [3]. It is a collection of writings (posts or comments) from a set of Social Media users. There are two categories of users, anorexia and non-anorexia, and, for each user, the collection contains a sequence of writings (in chronological order). The positive set is composed of users who explicitly mentioned that they were diagnosed with anorexia[1], while the negative set is mainly composed of random users from the same social media platform. To make the collection realistic, we also included in the negative group users who often post about anorexia (e.g. individuals who actively participate in the anorexia threads because they have a close relative suffering from this eating disorder). For every user, we collected all his submissions (up to 1000 posts+1000 comments, which is the limit imposed by the platform), and organized them in chronological order.

The task was organized into two different stages:

- **Training stage.** Initially, the teams that participated in this task had access to some training data. In this stage, the organizers of the task released the

---

[1] However, following the extraction method suggested by Coppersmith and colleagues [2], the post discussing the diagnosis was removed from the collection.

Table 1. Task1 (anorexia). Main statistics of the train and test collections

	Train		Test	
	Anorexia	Control	Anorexia	Control
Num. subjects	61	411	73	742
Num. submissions (posts & comments)	24,874	228,878	17,619	552,890
Avg num. of submissions per subject	407.8	556.9	241.4	745.1
Avg num. of days from first to last submission	≈ 800	≈ 650	≈ 510	≈ 930
Avg num. words per submission	37.3	20.9	37.2	21.7

entire history of submissions done by a set of training users. In 2019, the training data consisted of 2018's T2 data (2018 training split + 2018 test split). The participants could therefore tune their systems with the training data and build up from 2018's results. The training dataset was released on Nov 30th, 2018.

- **Test stage.** In 2019, we moved from a chunk-based release of test data (used in 2017 and 2018) to a item-by-item release of test data. We set up a server that iteratively gave user writings to the participating teams[2]. In this way, each participant had the opportunity to stop and make an alert at any point of the user chronology. After reading each user post, the teams had to choose between: (i) emitting an alert on the user, or (ii) making no alert on the user. Alerts were considered as final (further decisions about this individual were ignored), while *no alerts* were considered as non-final (i.e. the participants could later submit an alert for this user if they detected the appearance of signs of risk). This choice had to be made for each user in the test split. The systems were evaluated based on the accuracy of the decisions and the number of user writings required to take the decisions (see below). A REST server was built to support the test stage. The server iteratively gave user writings to the participants and waited for their responses (no new user data provided until the system said alert/no alert). This server was running from March 3rd, 2019 to April 10th, 2019.

Table 1 reports the main statistics of the train and test collections used for T1. In 2019, we also decided to expand the toolkit of evaluation measures. This is discussed next.

2.1 Decision-Based Evaluation

This form of evaluation revolves around the (binary) decisions taken for each user by the participating systems. Besides standard classification measures (Precision, Recall and F1 computed with respect to the positive class), we computed $ERDE$, the early risk detection error used in the previous editions of the lab. A full

---

[2] More information about the server can be found on the lab website http://early.irlab.org/server.html.

description of $ERDE$ can be found in [3]. Essentially, $ERDE$ is an error measure that introduces a penalty for correct alerts (true positives). The penalty grows with the delay in emitting the alert, and the delay is measured here as the number of user posts that had to be processed before making the alert.

In 2019, we complemented the evaluation report with additional decision-based metrics that try to capture additional aspects of the problem. These metrics try to overcome some limitations of $ERDE$, namely:

- the penalty associated to true positives goes quickly to 1. This is the case because of the functional form of the cost function (sigmoid).
- a perfect system, which detects the true positive case right after the first round of messages (first chunk), does not get error equal to 0.
- with a method based on releasing data in a chunk-based way (as it was done in 2017 and 2018) the contribution of each user to the performance evaluation has a large variance (users with few writings per chunk vs users with many writings per chunk).
- $ERDE$ is not interpretable.

Some research teams have analysed these issues and proposed alternative ways for evaluation. Trotzek and colleagues [7] proposed $ERDE_o^\%$. This is a variant of ERDE that does not depend on the number of user writings seen before the alert but, instead, it depends on the *percentage* of user writings seen before the alert. In this way, user's contributions to the evaluation are normalized (now, all users weight the same). However, there is an important limitation of $ERDE_o^\%$. In real life applications, the overall number of user writings is not known in advance. Social Media users post contents online and screening tools have to make predictions with the evidence seen. In practice, you do not know when (and if) a user's thread of message is exhausted. Thus, the performance metric should not depend on knowledge about the total number of user writings.

Another proposal of an alternative evaluation metric for early risk prediction was done by Sadeque and colleagues [6]. They proposed $F_{latency}$, which fits better with our purposes. This measure is described next.

Imagine a user $u \in U$ and an early risk detection system that iteratively analyzes u's writings (e.g. in chronological order, as they appear in Social Media) and, after analyzing k_u user writings ($k_u \geq 1$), takes a binary decision $d_u \in \{0,1\}$, which represents the estimation of the system about the user being a risk case. By $g_u \in \{0,1\}$, we refer to the user's golden truth label. A key component of an early risk evaluation should be the delay on detecting true positives (we do not want systems that detect these cases too late). Therefore, a first and intuitive measure of delay can be defined as follows[3]:

$$\text{latency}_{TP} = \text{median}\{k_u : u \in U, d_u = g_u = 1\} \qquad (1)$$

---

[3] Observe that Sadeque et al. (see [6], p. 497) computed the latency for all users such that $g_u = 1$. We argue that latency should be computed only for the true positives. The false negatives ($g_u = 1$, $d_u = 0$) are not detected by the system and, therefore, they would not generate an alert.

This measure of latency goes over the true positives detected by the system and assesses the system's delay based on the median number of writings that the system had to process to detect such positive cases. This measure can be included in the experimental report together with standard measures such as Precision (P), Recall (R) and the F-measure (F):

$$P = \frac{|u \in U : d_u = g_u = 1|}{|u \in U : d_u = 1|} \tag{2}$$

$$R = \frac{|u \in U : d_u = g_u = 1|}{|u \in U : g_u = 1|} \tag{3}$$

$$F = \frac{2 \cdot P \cdot R}{P + R} \tag{4}$$

Furthermore, Sadeque et al. proposed a measure, $F_{latency}$, which combines the effectiveness of the decision (estimated with the F measure) and the delay[4]. This is based on multiplying F by a penalty factor based on the median delay. More specifically, each individual (true positive) decision, taken after reading k_u writings, is assigned the following penalty:

$$penalty(k_u) = -1 + \frac{2}{1 + \exp^{-p \cdot (k_u - 1)}} \tag{5}$$

p is a parameter that determines how quickly the penalty should increase. In [6], p was set such that the penalty equals 0.5 at the median number of posts of a user[5]. Observe that a decision right after the first writing has no penalty ($penalty(1) = 0$). Figure 1 plots how the latency penalty increases with the number of observed writings.

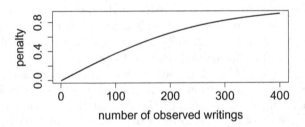

Fig. 1. Latency penalty increases with the number of observed writings (k_u)

The system's overall speed factor is computed as:

$$speed = (1 - \text{median}\{penalty(k_u) : u \in U, d_u = g_u = 1\}) \tag{6}$$

---

[4] Again, we adopt Sadeque et al.'s proposal but we estimate latency only over the true positives.

[5] In the eRisk 2017 collection this led to setting p to 0.0078.

Speed equals 1 for a system whose true positives are detected right at the first writing. A slow system, which detects true positives after hundreds of writings, will be assigned a speed score near 0.

Finally, the *latency-weighted* F score is simply:

$$F_{latency} = F \cdot speed \tag{7}$$

In 2019, user's data was processed by the participants in a writing by writing basis (i.e. we avoided a chunk-based release of data). Under these conditions, the evaluation approach has the following nice properties:

– smooth grow of penalties.
– a perfect system gets $F_{latency} = 1$.
– for each user u the system can opt to stop at any point k_u and, therefore, we do not have now the effect of an imbalanced importance of users.
– $F_{latency}$ is more interpretable than $ERDE$.

2.2 Ranking-Based Evaluation

This section discusses an alternative form of evaluation, which was used as a complement of the evaluation described above. After each release of data (new user writing) the participants had to send back the following information (for each user in the collection): (i) a decision for the user (alert/no alert), which was used to compute the decision-based metrics discussed above, and (ii) a score that represents the user's level of risk (estimated from the evidence seen so far). We used these scores to build a ranking of users in decreasing estimation of risk. For each participating system, we have one ranking at each point (ranking after 1 writing, ranking after 2 writings, etc.). This simulates a continuous re-ranking approach based on the evidence seen so far. In a real life application, this ranking would be presented to an expert user who could take decisions (e.g. by inspecting the rankings).

Each ranking can be scored with standard IR metrics, such as P@10 or NDCG. We therefore report the ranking-based performance of the systems after seeing k writings (with varying k).

2.3 Task 1: Results

Table 2 shows the participating teams, the number of runs submitted and the approximate lapse of time from the first response to the last response. This lapse of time is indicative of the degree of automation of each team's algorithms. Most of the submitted runs processed the entire thread of messages (around 2000 iterations), but a few variants opted for stopping earlier. Only a few teams (HULAT, BiTeM, BioInfo@UAVR and UNSL) processed the thread of messages in a reasonably fast way (less than a day for processing the entire history of user messages). The rest of the teams took several days to run the whole process. This suggests that they incorporated some form of offline processing.

Table 2. Task 1. Participating teams: number of runs, number of user writings processed by the team, and lapse of time taken for the whole process.

Team	#runs	#user writings processed	Lapse of time (from 1st to last response)
UppsalaNLP	5	2000	2 days + 7 h
BioInfo@UAVR	1	2000	14 h
BiTeM	5	11	4 h
lirmm	5	2024	8 days + 15 h
CLaC	5	109	11 days + 16 h
SINAI	3	317	10 days + 7 h
HULAT	5	83	18 h
UDE	5	2000	5 days + 3 h
SSN-NLP	5	9	6 days + 22 h
Fazl	3	2001	21 days + 15 h
UNSL	5	2000	23 h
LTL-INAOE	2	2001	17 days + 23 h
INAOE-CIMAT	5	2000	8 days + 2 h

Table 3 reports the decision-based performance achieved by the participating teams. In terms of $F1$ and latency-weighted $F1$, the best performing run was sent by the ClaC team. The runs submitted by this team suggest that you can get to effectiveness of about 70% based on a few user writings. As a matter of fact, the best performing run had a median of 7 user writings analyzed for the true positives detected. Other teams submitted quicker decisions ($latency_{TP}$ and $speed$ equal to 1) but the associated effectiveness was poor. This is not surprising because decisions based on a single user post are likely premature.

In terms of precision, the lirmm team sent a run with 77% performance. This variant, which also had reasonable figures for recall and $F1$, looks promising and its true positive decisions were fast (about 20 user posts processed). Some teams submitted runs with very high values of recall but the associated precision and other metrics were very low.

In terms of $ERDE$, the two best performing runs were sent by UNSL. As argued above, this measure sets a strong penalty on late decisions and this teams opted to send true positive decisions after seeing a couple of user writings.

Overall, these results suggest that with a few dozen user writings some systems led to reasonably high effectiveness. The best predictive algorithms could be used to support expert humans in early detecting signs of anorexia.

Table 4 reports the ranking-based performance achieved by the participating teams. Many teams only processed a few dozens of user writings and, thus, we could only compute their rankings of users for the initial points. Other teams (e.g., UppsalaNLP or BioInfo@UAVR) have the same ranking-based effectiveness

Table 3. Task 1. Decision-based evaluation

team	run	P	R	$F1$	$ERDE_5$	$ERDE_{50}$	$latency_{TP}$	speed	latency-weighted $F1$
UppsalaNLP	0	.32	.44	.37	5.83%	5.77%	1	1	.37
UppsalaNLP	1	.36	.39	.37	6.13%	6.07%	1	1	.37
UppsalaNLP	2	.34	.42	.38	5.88%	5.81%	1	1	.38
UppsalaNLP	3	.39	.30	.34	6.68%	6.63%	1	1	.34
UppsalaNLP	4	.40	.42	.41	5.73%	5.66%	1	1	.41
BioInfo@UAVR	0	.32	.44	.37	5.84%	5.77%	1	1	.37
BiTeM	0	.42	.07	.12	8.58%	8.42%	1	1	.12
BiTeM	1	.44	.70	.54	5.89%	3.40%	3	.99	.54
BiTeM	2	.73	.11	.19	8.42%	8.01%	3	.99	.19
BiTeM	3	1	.01	.03	8.84%	8.83%	1	1	.03
BiTeM	4	0	0	0	-	-	-	-	-
lirmm	0	.74	.63	.68	9.13%	5.14%	21	.92	.63
lirmm	1	**.77**	.60	.68	9.10%	5.51%	21	.92	.62
lirmm	2	.66	.70	.68	9.24%	5.81%	31	.88	.60
lirmm	3	.74	.42	.54	9.08%	6.62%	31	.88	.48
lirmm	4	.57	.75	.65	9.41%	7.32%	2023	$3e^{-7}$	$2e^{-7}$
CLaC	0	.45	.74	.56	6.72%	3.93%	7	.98	.54
CLaC	1	.61	.82	.70	5.73%	3.13%	4	.99	.69
CLaC	2	.60	.81	.69	6.02%	3.13%	6	.98	.68
CLaC	3	.63	.76	.69	6.27%	3.55%	7	.98	.68
CLaC	4	.64	.79	**.71**	6.25%	3.43%	7	.98	**.69**
SINAI	0	.12	.97	.21	10.58%	6.59%	5	.98	.21
SINAI	1	.11	.99	.20	10.80%	6.76%	5	.98	.20
SINAI	2	.18	.95	.30	9.04%	4.89%	8	.97	.30
HULAT	0	.11	.30	.17	10.84%	8.14%	16.5	.94	.16
HULAT	1	.11	.30	.17	10.84%	8.14%	16.5	.94	.16
HULAT	2	.11	.30	.17	10.84%	8.14%	16.5	.94	.16
HULAT	3	.11	.30	.17	10.84%	8.14%	16.5	.94	.16
HULAT	4	.11	.30	.17	10.84%	8.14%	16.5	.94	.16
UDE	0	.51	.74	.61	8.48%	3.87%	11	.96	.58
UDE	1	.44	.73	.55	7.48%	3.94%	9	.97	.53
UDE	2	.13	.68	.22	12.52%	8.21%	35	.87	.19
UDE	3	0	0	0	-	-	-	-	-
UDE	4	0	0	0	-	-	-	-	-
SSN-NLP	0	.32	.16	.22	8.24%	7.76%	2	1	.22
SSN-NLP	1	.30	.22	.25	7.90%	7.41%	1	1	.25
SSN-NLP	2	.47	.22	.30	7.80%	7.19%	2	1	.30
SSN-NLP	3	.48	.26	.34	7.61%	6.86%	2	1	.33
SSN-NLP	4	.32	.15	.21	8.08%	7.86%	1	1	.21
Fazl	0	.09	1	.16	17.11%	13.91%	97	.64	.11
Fazl	1	.09	1	.16	17.11%	13.79%	88	.67	.11
Fazl	2	.09	1	.16	17.11%	11.22%	34	.87	.14
UNSL	0	.42	.78	.55	**5.54%**	3.92%	2	1	.55
UNSL	1	.43	.75	.55	5.68%	4.10%	2	1	.55
UNSL	2	.36	.86	.51	5.56%	3.34%	2	1	.50
UNSL	3	.35	.85	.50	5.59%	3.49%	2	1	.49
UNSL	4	.31	.92	.47	6.14%	**2.97%**	3	.99	.46
LTL-INAOE	0	.45	.75	.57	7.78%	4.23%	11	.96	.54
LTL-INAOE	1	.47	.75	.58	7.74%	4.20%	11	.96	.55
INAOE-CIMAT	0	.56	.78	.66	9.30%	3.98%	15	.95	.62
INAOE-CIMAT	1	0	0	0	-	-	-	-	-
INAOE-CIMAT	2	.58	.77	.66	9.28%	9.16%	65	.76	.50
INAOE-CIMAT	3	.67	.68	.68	9.17%	4.75%	20	.93	.63
INAOE-CIMAT	4	.69	.63	.66	9.13%	5.08%	20	.93	.61

over multiple points (after 1 writing, after 100 writings, and so forth). This suggests that these teams did not change the risk scores estimated from the initial stages.

Other participants (ClaC, UDE, Fazl, UNSL and LTL-INAOE) show the expected behaviour: the rankings of estimated risk get better as they are built from more user evidence. Notably, some UNSL and UDE variants led to almost perfect $P@10$ and $NDCG@10$ performance after analyzing more than 100 writings. This suggests that, with enough pieces of evidence, the methods implemented by these teams are highly effective at prioritizing at-risk users.

Table 4. Task 1. Ranking-based evaluation

team	run	1 writing			100 writings			500 writings			1000 writings		
		$P@10$	$NDCG$ @10	$NDCG$ @100	$P@10$	$NDCG$ @10	$NDCG@100$	$P@10$	$NDCG$ @10	$NDCG$ @100	$P@10$	$NDCG$ @10	$NDCG$ @100
UppsalaNLP	0	.6	.59	.47	.6	.59	.47	.6	.59	.47	.6	.59	.47
UppsalaNLP	1	.4	.31	.40	.4	.31	.40	.4	.31	.40	.4	.31	.40
UppsalaNLP	2	.5	.38	.42	.5	.38	.42	.5	.38	.42	.5	.38	.42
UppsalaNLP	3	.7	.65	.45	.7	.65	.45	.7	.65	.45	.7	.65	.45
UppsalaNLP	4	.8	.75	.52	.8	.75	.52	.8	.75	.52	.8	.75	.52
BioInfo@UAVR	0	.6	.59	.47	.6	.59	.47	.6	.59	.47	.6	.59	.47
BiTeM	0	.6	.44	.52	-	-	-	-	-	-	-	-	-
BiTeM	1	.8	.75	.47	-	-	-	-	-	-	-	-	-
BiTeM	2	.8	.71	.46	-	-	-	-	-	-	-	-	-
BiTeM	3	.8	.71	.48	-	-	-	-	-	-	-	-	-
BiTeM	4	.8	.71	.48	-	-	-	-	-	-	-	-	-
lirmm	0	-	-	-	-	-	-	-	-	-	-	-	-
lirmm	1	-	-	-	-	-	-	-	-	-	-	-	-
lirmm	2	-	-	-	-	-	-	-	-	-	-	-	-
lirmm	3	-	-	-	-	-	-	-	-	-	-	-	-
lirmm	4	-	-	-	-	-	-	-	-	-	-	-	-
CLaC	0	.1	.10	.05	.8	.86	.28	-	-	-	-	-	-
CLaC	1	.1	.10	.04	.3	.45	.16	-	-	-	-	-	-
CLaC	2	-	-	-	-	-	-	-	-	-	-	-	-
CLaC	3	-	-	-	-	-	-	-	-	-	-	-	-
CLaC	4	-	-	-	-	-	-	-	-	-	-	-	-
SINAI	0	.2	.12	.11	-	-	-	-	-	-	-	-	-
SINAI	1	.2	.12	.11	-	-	-	-	-	-	-	-	-
SINAI	2	.2	.12	.11	-	-	-	-	-	-	-	-	-
HULAT	0	.3	.33	.18	-	-	-	-	-	-	-	-	-
HULAT	1	.3	.33	.18	-	-	-	-	-	-	-	-	-
HULAT	2	.3	.33	.18	-	-	-	-	-	-	-	-	-
HULAT	3	.3	.33	.18	-	-	-	-	-	-	-	-	-
HULAT	4	.3	.33	.18	-	-	-	-	-	-	-	-	-
UDE	0	.2	.12	.11	.9	.92	.81	.9	.93	.85	.9	.94	.86
UDE	1	.6	.75	.54	.9	.94	.81	1	1	.87	1	1	.88
UDE	2	.7	.76	.49	.9	.94	.60	.9	.94	.64	.8	.88	.64
UDE	3	-	-	-	-	-	-	-	-	-	-	-	-
UDE	4	.0	.0	.11	.0	.0	.08	.0	.0	.06	.0	.0	.07
SSN-NLP	0	.6	.64	.29	-	-	-	-	-	-	-	-	-
SSN-NLP	1	.3	.28	.15	-	-	-	-	-	-	-	-	-
SSN-NLP	2	.5	.48	.29	-	-	-	-	-	-	-	-	-
SSN-NLP	3	.6	.64	.30	-	-	-	-	-	-	-	-	-
SSN-NLP	4	.3	.33	.15	-	-	-	-	-	-	-	-	-
Fazl	0	.2	.12	.11	.1	.10	.26	.0	.0	.35	.1	.06	.39
Fazl	1	.3	.29	.26	.6	.60	.59	.7	.78	.67	.7	.78	.68
Fazl	2	.2	.12	.11	.8	.82	.46	.9	.94	.62	1	1	.66
UNSL	0	.8	.82	.54	1	1	.77	1	1	.79	1	1	.79
UNSL	1	.8	.82	.54	1	1	.77	1	1	.79	1	1	.79
UNSL	2	.8	.82	.55	1	1	.83	1	1	.83	1	1	.84
UNSL	3	.8	.82	.53	1	1	.83	1	1	.84	1	1	.84
UNSL	4	.8	.82	.52	.9	.94	.85	1	1	.85	.9	.94	.84
LTL-INAOE	0	.8	.75	.34	1	1	.76	.9	.92	.73	.7	.78	.65
LTL-INAOE	1	.8	.75	.34	1	1	.76	.9	.92	.73	.7	.78	.66
INAOE-CIMAT	0	-	-	-	-	-	-	-	-	-	-	-	-
INAOE-CIMAT	1	-	-	-	-	-	-	-	-	-	-	-	-
INAOE-CIMAT	2	-	-	-	-	-	-	-	-	-	-	-	-
INAOE-CIMAT	3	-	-	-	-	-	-	-	-	-	-	-	-
INAOE-CIMAT	4	-	-	-	-	-	-	-	-	-	-	-	-

3   Task 2: Early Detection of Signs of Self-harm

This task is new in 2019. T2 has a similar organization as T1, but T2 provided no training data. The challenge consists of sequentially processing pieces of evidence and detect early traces of self-harm as soon as possible. There are two categories of users, self-harm and non-self-harm, and, for each user, the collection contains a sequence of writings (in chronological order). T2 had only a test stage (no training stage) and, therefore, we encouraged participants to design their own unsupervised (e.g. search-based) strategies to detect possible cases of self-harm. Similar to T1, the test stage consisted of a period of time where the participants had to connect to our server and iteratively get user writings and send responses.

Table 5. Task2 (self-harm). Main statistics of the collection

	Self-Harm	Control
Num. subjects	41	299
Num. submissions (posts & comments)	6,927	163,506
Avg num. of submissions per subject	169.0	546.8
Avg num. of days from first to last submission	≈ 495	≈ 500
Avg num. words per submission	24.8	18.8

Table 5 reports the main statistics of the T2 dataset. The self-harm group is composed of users who were active on the self-harm Reddit community and explicitly said that they had committed self-harm (e.g., cuts or injuries). We wanted to further instigate the creation of algorithms that act as early as possible. To meet this aim, for each individual, the algorithms were given only the history of the postings *before* the individual entered into the self-harm community (all posts before the first entry in the self-harm communities). An individual who is active on self-harm forums perhaps has already done some sort of self-harm to his body. We want algorithms that detect the cases earlier on (and not when the cases are explicit and the individual is already engaging in a support forum). As a consequence, the participants were only given the texts posted by the affected individuals before they first engaged in the self-harm community. Similar to T1, the systems had an item-by-item access to the user's history of posts.

We expected that effectiveness was lower compared to T1. First, because T2 provided no training data. Second, because user history consisted solely on the postings before entering the self-harm community (and, thus, signals related to self-harm might not be that explicit).

The evaluation approach employed for T2 was exactly the same used for T1 (see Sect. 2).

3.1 Task 2: Results

Table 6 shows the participating teams, the number of runs submitted, and the approximate lapse of time from the first response to the last response. Most of the submitted runs processed the entire thread of postings (around 2000 iterations), but one participant (BiTeM) opted for stopping earlier. Compared with T1, the teams were quicker at processing the entire thread of user writings but there were still some teams that took more than a day for running the whole estimation process. Again, this suggests that some participants incorporated some form of offline processing.

Table 6. Task 2 (Self-harm). Participating teams: number of runs, number of user writings processed by the team, and lapse of time taken for the whole process.

Team	#runs	#user writings processed	Lapse of time (from 1st to last response)
BiTeM	5	8	3 min
BioInfo@UAVR	1	1992	4 h
Fazl	3	1993	18 days + 21 h
UNSL	5	1992	13 h
UDE	5	1992	1 day + 2 h
LTL-INAOE	4	1993	17 h
lirmm	5	2004	2 days + 22 h
CAMH	5	1992	1 day + 19 h

Table 7 reports the decision-based metrics. Not surprisingly, effectiveness scores are lower than those achieved for T1. $F1$ and its latency-weighted version are barely higher than 50% for the best performing runs. The best performing run, from UNSL, was extremely fast at making decisions (the median number of postings analyzed before making a true positive decision was about 2) but the effectiveness of its decisions was rather modest. A few runs deeply analyzed the entire user history (e.g., some runs from lirmm) but this did not lead to better decisions. Overall, these results suggest that it is unclear that early traces of self-harm can be detected from the user interactions in Social Media prior to their first entry in the self-harm community. In the future, it would be interesting to study how much benefit these algorithms can take from training data.

The corresponding ranking-based scores are reported in Table 8. The *initial* ranking-based performance (rankings based on a single writing) is low for most of the participants. However, some runs (particularly some UNSL runs) managed to produce effective rankings after analyzing 100 or more user posts. This suggests that the tendency to make early alerts (as indicated by the latency and speed statistics shown in Table 7) was detrimental to the identification of at-risk individuals.

Table 7. Task 2 (Self-harm). Decision-based evaluation

team	run	P	R	F1	$ERDE_5$	$ERDE_{50}$	$latency_{TP}$	speed	latency-weighted $F1$
BiTeM	0	.52	.41	.46	9.73%	7.63%	3	.99	.46
BiTeM	1	1	.05	.09	11.84%	11.47%	6.5	.98	.09
BiTeM	2	0	0	0	-	-	-	-	-
BiTeM	3	0	0	0	-	-	-	-	-
BiTeM	4	0	0	0	-	-	-	-	-
BioInfo@UAVR	0	.55	.39	.46	10.79%	8.11%	6	.98	.45
Fazl	0	.12	1	.22	22.66%	16.71%	51	.81	.17
Fazl	1	.12	1	.22	22.66%	16.42%	47	.82	.18
Fazl	2	.12	1	.22	22.66%	13.24%	35	.87	.19
UNSL	0	.71	.41	.52	9.01%	7.31%	2	1	.52
UNSL	1	.70	.39	.50	9.03%	7.60%	2.5	.99	.50
UNSL	2	.20	.90	.32	9.20%	6.86%	2	1	.32
UNSL	3	.31	.85	.45	8.79%	5.44%	3	.99	.45
UNSL	4	.31	.88	.46	8.21%	4.93%	3	.99	.45
UDE	0	.50	.07	.13	12.02%	11.28%	13	.95	.12
UDE	1	.45	.22	.30	11.27%	9.80%	7	.98	.29
UDE	2	.18	.68	.29	13.75%	9.56%	13.5	.95	.28
UDE	3	.06	.34	.10	20.04%	20.02%	73.5	.72	.07
UDE	4	0	0	0	-	-	-	-	-
LTL-INAOE	0	.12	1	.22	12.53%	10.60%	1	1	.22
LTL-INAOE	1	.12	1	.22	13.15%	10.90%	2	1	.21
LTL-INAOE	2	.12	1	.22	16.64%	10.90%	4	.99	.21
LTL-INAOE	3	.12	1	.22	17.15%	10.90%	5	.98	.21
lirmm	0	.57	.29	.39	12.22%	10.02%	28.5	.89	.35
lirmm	1	.53	.22	.31	12.18%	10.58%	21	.92	.29
lirmm	2	.48	.49	.48	12.84%	11.67%	2004	$3e^{-7}$	$1e^{-7}$
lirmm	3	.47	.44	.46	12.77%	11.89%	2004	$3e^{-7}$	$1e^{-7}$
lirmm	4	.52	.41	.46	12.63%	11.74%	2004	$3e^{-7}$	$1e^{-7}$
CAMH	0	.12	.95	.22	16.67%	10.60%	7	.98	.22
CAMH	1	.12	.93	.22	16.81%	10.98%	7	.98	.21
CAMH	2	.12	.90	.22	17.41%	11.49%	8	.97	.21
CAMH	3	.12	.98	.22	15.70%	10.70%1	3.5	.99	.22
CAMH	4	.12	1	.22	14.84%	10.32%	4	.99	.22

4 Task 3: Measuring the Severity of the Signs of Depression

This is a new task in 2019. The task consisted of estimating the level of depression from a thread of user submissions. For each user, the participants were given its full history of postings (single release of data) and the participants had to fill a standard depression questionnaire (based on the evidence found in the history of postings).

The questionnaires are defined from Beck's Depression Inventory (BDI) [1], which assesses the presence of feelings like sadness, pessimism, loss of energy, etc. The questionnaire contains 21 questions (see Figs. 2 and 3).

Instructions:

This questionnaire consists of 21 groups of statements. Please read each group of statements carefully, and then pick out the one statement in each group that best describes the way you feel. If several statements in the group seem to apply equally well, choose the highest number for that group.

1. Sadness
0. I do not feel sad.
1. I feel sad much of the time.
2. I am sad all the time.
3. I am so sad or unhappy that I can't stand it.

2. Pessimism
0. I am not discouraged about my future.
1. I feel more discouraged about my future than I used to be.
2. I do not expect things to work out for me.
3. I feel my future is hopeless and will only get worse.

3. Past Failure
0. I do not feel like a failure.
1. I have failed more than I should have.
2. As I look back, I see a lot of failures.
3. I feel I am a total failure as a person.

4. Loss of Pleasure
0. I get as much pleasure as I ever did from the things I enjoy.
1. I don't enjoy things as much as I used to.
2. I get very little pleasure from the things I used to enjoy.
3. I can't get any pleasure from the things I used to enjoy.

5. Guilty Feelings
0. I don't feel particularly guilty.
1. I feel guilty over many things I have done or should have done.
2. I feel quite guilty most of the time.
3. I feel guilty all of the time.

6. Punishment Feelings
0. I don't feel I am being punished.
1. I feel I may be punished.
2. I expect to be punished.
3. I feel I am being punished.

7. Self-Dislike
0. I feel the same about myself as ever.
1. I have lost confidence in myself.
2. I am disappointed in myself.
3. I dislike myself.

8. Self-Criticalness
0. I don't criticize or blame myself more than usual.
1. I am more critical of myself than I used to be.
2. I criticize myself for all of my faults.
3. I blame myself for everything bad that happens.

9. Suicidal Thoughts or Wishes
0. I don't have any thoughts of killing myself.
1. I have thoughts of killing myself, but I would not carry them out.
2. I would like to kill myself.
3. I would kill myself if I had the chance.

10. Crying
0. I don't cry anymore than I used to.
1. I cry more than I used to.
2. I cry over every little thing.
3. I feel like crying, but I can't.

11. Agitation
0. I am no more restless or wound up than usual.
1. I feel more restless or wound up than usual.
2. I am so restless or agitated that it's hard to stay still.
3. I am so restless or agitated that I have to keep moving or doing something.

12. Loss of Interest
0. I have not lost interest in other people or activities.
1. I am less interested in other people or things than before.
2. I have lost most of my interest in other people or things.
3. It's hard to get interested in anything.

13. Indecisiveness
0. I make decisions about as well as ever.
1. I find it more difficult to make decisions than usual.
2. I have much greater difficulty in making decisions than I used to.
3. I have trouble making any decisions.

14. Worthlessness
0. I do not feel I am worthless.
1. I don't consider myself as worthwhile and useful as I used to.
2. I feel more worthless as compared to other people.
3. I feel utterly worthless.

15. Loss of Energy
0. I have as much energy as ever.
1. I have less energy than I used to have.
2. I don't have enough energy to do very much.
3. I don't have enough energy to do anything.

Fig. 2. Beck's Depression Inventory (part 1)

Table 8. Task 2 (Self-harm). Ranking-based evaluation

team	run	1 writing P@10	NDCG @10	NDCG @100	100 writings P@10	NDCG @10	NDCG @100	500 writings P@10	NDCG @10	NDCG @100	1000 writings P@10	NDCG @10	NDCG @100
BiTeM	0	.3	.35	.53	-	-	-	-	-	-	-	-	-
BiTeM	1	.4	.47	.39	-	-	-	-	-	-	-	-	-
BiTeM	2	.5	.48	.44	-	-	-	-	-	-	-	-	-
BiTeM	3	.2	.38	.41	-	-	-	-	-	-	-	-	-
BiTeM	4	.4	.56	.50	-	-	-	-	-	-	-	-	-
BioInfo@UAVR	0	-	-	-	-	-	-	-	-	-	-	-	-
Fazl	0	.1	.12	.30	.1	.06	.42	.1	.06	.41	.6	.40	.59
Fazl	1	.2	.27	.36	.9	.94	.83	.9	.94	.84	.9	.94	.84
Fazl	2	0	0	.13	.6	.73	.73	.7	.68	.71	.7	.68	.74
UNSL	0	.7	.79	.48	.9	.94	.61	.9	.94	.66	.9	.94	.66
UNSL	1	.6	.74	.48	.9	.94	.60	.9	.94	.65	.9	.94	.65
UNSL	2	.9	.88	.62	.8	.75	.75	.5	.59	.74	.6	.64	.74
UNSL	3	1	1	.67	.9	.94	.84	.7	.63	.75	.7	.63	.75
UNSL	4	1	1	.64	.9	.93	.86	.7	.67	.79	.8	.74	.78
UDE	0	0	0	.09	.7	.77	.69	.7	.67	.69	.7	.67	.70
UDE	1	.7	.56	.52	.7	.66	.69	.8	.75	.74	.8	.75	.74
UDE	2	.5	.63	.53	.5	.56	.64	.6	.66	.68	.6	.65	.67
UDE	3	.2	.19	.21	0	0	.11	.2	.16	.14	.1	.07	.15
UDE	4	.2	.25	.30	.1	.07	.20	.1	.07	.15	.1	.08	.17
LTL-INAOE	0	.5	.50	.45	.4	.41	.55	.2	.19	.25	.1	.19	.37
LTL-INAOE	1	.6	.73	.56	.1	.19	.17	.1	.06	.07	0	0	.04
LTL-INAOE	2	.4	.42	.32	.1	.07	.43	.2	.19	.25	.1	.19	.37
LTL-INAOE	3	.7	.72	.44	.1	.19	.27	.1	.06	.19	0	0	.29
lirmm	0	.1	.19	.15	0	0	.01	-	-	-	-	-	-
lirmm	1	.1	.19	.15	0	0	.01	-	-	-	-	-	-
lirmm	2	.1	.19	.15	0	0	.01	-	-	-	-	-	-
lirmm	3	.1	.19	.15	0	0	.01	-	-	-	-	-	-
lirmm	4	.1	.19	.15	0	0	.01	-	-	-	-	-	-
CAMH	0	.3	.37	.47	.6	.71	.49	.7	.72	.50	.6	.66	.48
CAMH	1	.4	.41	.43	.6	.65	.42	.7	.72	.49	.6	.66	.47
CAMH	2	.3	.41	.51	.5	.62	.39	.7	.72	.45	.6	.66	.44
CAMH	3	.3	.25	.42	.5	.55	.32	.7	.72	.37	.6	.66	.37
CAMH	4	.5	.48	.50	.6	.59	.34	.6	.66	.43	.6	.66	.39

```
16. Changes in Sleeping Pattern
0. I have not experienced any change in my sleeping pattern.
1a. I sleep somewhat more than usual.
1b. I sleep somewhat less than usual.
2a. I sleep a lot more than usual.
2b. I sleep a lot less than usual.
3a. I sleep most of the day.
3b. I wake up 1-2 hours early and can't get back to sleep.

17. Irritability
0. I am no more irritable than usual.
1. I am more irritable than usual.
2. I am much more irritable than usual.
3. I am irritable all the time.

18. Changes in Appetite
0. I have not experienced any change in my appetite.
1a. My appetite is somewhat less than usual.
1b. My appetite is somewhat greater than usual.
2a. My appetite is much less than before.
2b. My appetite is much greater than usual.
3a. I have no appetite at all.
3b. I crave food all the time.

19. Concentration Difficulty
0. I can concentrate as well as ever.
1. I can't concentrate as well as usual.
2. It's hard to keep my mind on anything for very long.
3. I find I can't concentrate on anything.

20. Tiredness or Fatigue
0. I am no more tired or fatigued than usual.
1. I get more tired or fatigued more easily than usual.
2. I am too tired or fatigued to do a lot of the things I used to do.
3. I am too tired or fatigued to do most of the things I used to do.

21. Loss of Interest in Sex
0. I have not noticed any recent change in my interest in sex.
1. I am less interested in sex than I used to be.
2. I am much less interested in sex now.
3. I have lost interest in sex completely
```

Fig. 3. Beck's Depression Inventory (part 2)

The task aims at exploring the viability of automatically estimating the severity of multiple symptoms associated with depression. Given the user's history of writings, the algorithms had to estimate the user's response to each individual question. We collected questionnaires filled by Social Media users together with their history of writings (we extracted each history of writings right after the user provided us with the filled questionnaire). The questionnaires filled by the users (ground truth) were used to assess the quality of the responses provided by the participating systems.

The participants were given a dataset with 20 users and they were asked to produce a file with the following structure:

```
username1 answer1 answer2 .... answer21
username2 ....
....
```

Each line has a user identifier and 21 values. These values correspond with the responses to the questions of the depression questionnaire (the possible values are 0, 1a, 1b, 2a, 2b, 3a, 3b -for questions 16 and 18- and 0, 1, 2, 3 -for the rest of the questions-).

4.1 Task 3: Evaluation Metrics

We considered a number of metrics in order to assess the quality of a questionnaire filled by a system when compared to the real questionnaire filled by actual Social Media user:

- Hit Rate (HR). This is a stringent measure that computes the ratio of cases where the automatic questionnaire has exactly the same answer as the real questionnaire. For example, an automatic questionnaire with 5 matches gets HR equal to 5/21 (because there are 21 questions in the form).
  Average Hit Rate (AHR): HR averaged over all users.
- Closeness Rate (CR). This measure takes into account that the answers of the depression questionnaire represent an ordinal scale. For example, consider the #17 question:

```
17. Irritability
0. I am no more irritable than usual.
1. I am more irritable than usual.
2. I am much more irritable than usual.
3. I am irritable all the time.
```

Imagine that the real user answered "0". A system S1 whose answer is "3" should be penalised more than a system S2 whose answer is "1".
For each question, CR computes the absolute difference (ad) between the real and the automated answer (e.g. ad=3 and ad=1 for S1 and S2, respectively) and, next, this absolute difference is transformed into an effectiveness score as follows: $CR = (mad - ad)/mad$, where mad is the maximum absolute

difference, which is equal to the number of possible answers minus one.

Average Closeness Rate (ACR): CR averaged over all users.

NOTE: in the two questions (#16 and #18) that have seven possible answers $\{0, 1a, 1b, 2a, 2b, 3a, 3b\}$ the pairs $(1a, 1b)$, $(2a, 2b)$, $(3a, 3b)$ are considered equivalent because they reflect the same depression level. As a consequence, the difference from $3b$ to 0 is equal to 3 (and the difference from $1a$ to $1b$ is equal to 0).

- Difference between overall depression levels ($DODL$).

  The previous measures assess the systems' ability to answer each question in the form. This measure, instead, does not look at question-level hits or differences but computes the overall depression level (sum of all the answers) for the real and automated questionnaire and, next, the absolute difference ($ad\_overall$) between the real and the automated score is computed.

  Depression levels are integers between 0 and 63 and, thus, $DODL$ is normalised into [0,1] as follows: $DODL = (63 - ad\_overall)/63$.

  average DODL (ADODL): $DODL$ averaged over all users.

- in the psychological domain, it is customary to associate depression levels with the following categories:

```
minimal depression (depression levels 0-9)
mild depression (depression levels 10-18)
moderate depression (depression levels 19-29)
severe depression (depression levels 30-63)
```

The last effectiveness measure consists of computing the fraction of cases where the automated questionnaire led to a depression category that is equivalent to the depression category obtained from the real questionnaire. This measure will be referred to as **DCHR (DEPRESSION CATEGORY HIT RATE)**.

4.2   Task 3: Results

Table 9 presents the results achieved by the participants in this task. In terms of AHR, the best performing run (ANSLC) shows that it is possible to get more than 40% of the answers right. The distance-based variant (ACR) shows also promising figures (e.g. greater than 70% for UNSLE). Observe that most of the questions have four possible answers and, thus, a random algorithm would get AHR near 25%[6]. This suggests that the analysis of the user posts is useful at extracting some signals or symptoms related to depression. However, ADODL and, particularly, DCHR show that the participants, although effective at answering some depression-related questions, do not fare well at estimating the overall level of depression of the individuals. For example, the best performing run gets the depression category right for only 45% of the individuals.

---

[6] Slightly less than 25% because a couple of questions have more than four possible answers.

Table 9. Task 3. Performance results

Run	AHR	ACR	ADODL	DCHR
BioInfo@UAVR	34.05%	66.43%	77.70%	25.00%
BiTeM	32.14%	62.62%	72.62%	25.00%
CAMH_GPT_nearest_unsupervised	23.81%	57.06%	**81.03%**	**45.00%**
CAMH_GPT_supervised.181_features.58hr	35.47%	68.33%	75.63%	20.00%
CAMH_GPT_supervised.769_features.55hr	36.43%	67.22%	72.30%	20.00%
CAMH_GPT_supervised.949_features.75hr	36.91%	69.13%	75.63%	15.00%
CAMH_LIWC_supervised_SVM	35.95%	66.59%	75.48%	25.00%
Fazl	22.38%	56.27%	72.78%	5.00%
Illinois	22.62%	56.19%	66.35%	40.00%
ISIKol_multiSimilarity-5000-Dtac-Qtac	29.76%	57.94%	74.13%	25.00%
ISIKol-bm25-1.2-0.75-5000-Dtac-Qtac	29.76%	57.06%	72.78%	25.00%
ISIKol-lm-d-1.0-5000-Dtac-Qtac	30.00%	57.94%	73.02%	15.00%
Kimberly	38.33%	64.44%	66.19%	20.00%
UNSLA	37.38%	67.94%	72.86%	30.00%
UNSLB	36.93%	70.16%	76.83%	30.00%
UNSLC	**41.43%**	69.13%	78.02%	40.00%
UNSLD	38.10%	67.22%	78.02%	30.00%
UNSLE	40.71%	**71.27%**	80.48%	35.00%

Overall, these experiments indicate that it is possible to automatically extract some depression-related evidence from social media activity but we are still far from a really effective depression screening tool. In the near future, it will be interesting to further analyze the participants' estimations in order to investigate which particular BDI questions are easier or harder to automatically answer based on Social Media activity.

5 Conclusions

This paper provided an overview of eRisk 2019. This was the third edition of this lab and the lab's activities concentrated on two different types of tasks: early detection of signs of anorexia or self-harm (where the participants had a sequential access to the user's social media posts and they had to send alerts about at-risk individuals), and measuring the severity of the signs of depression (given the full user history the participants had to automatically estimate the user's responses to a standard depression questionnaire).

Overall, the proposed tasks received 105 variants or runs. Although the effectiveness of the proposed solutions is still modest, the experiments suggest that evidence extracted from Social Media is valuable and automatic or semi-automatic screening tools could be designed to early detect at-risk individuals.

This promising result encourages us to further explore the creation of benchmarks for text-based screening of signs of risk.

Acknowledgements. We thank the support obtained from the Swiss National Science Foundation (SNSF) under the project "Early risk prediction on the Internet: an evaluation corpus", 2015.

We also thank the financial support obtained from the (i) "Ministerio de Ciencia, Innovación y Universidades" of the Government of Spain (research grants RTI2018-093336-B-C21 and RTI2018-093336-B-C22), (ii) "Consellería de Educación, Universidade e Formación Profesional", Xunta de Galicia (grants ED431C 2018/29, ED431G/08 and ED431G/01 − "Centro singular de investigación de Galicia" −). All grants were co-funded by the European Regional Development Fund (ERDF/FEDER program).

References

1. Beck, A.T., Ward, C.H., Mendelson, M., Mock, J., Erbaugh, J.: An inventory for measuring depression. JAMA Psychiatry **4**(6), 561–571 (1961). https://doi.org/10.1001/archpsyc.1961.01710120031004
2. Coppersmith, G., Dredze, M., Harman, C.: Quantifying mental health signals in Twitter. In: ACL Workshop on Computational Linguistics and Clinical Psychology (2014)
3. Losada, D.E., Crestani, F.: A test collection for research on depression and language use. In: Fuhr, N., et al. (eds.) CLEF 2016. LNCS, vol. 9822, pp. 28–39. Springer, Cham (2016). https://doi.org/10.1007/978-3-319-44564-9_3
4. Losada, D.E., Crestani, F., Parapar, J.: eRISK 2017: CLEF lab on early risk prediction on the internet: experimental foundations. In: Jones, G.J.F., et al. (eds.) CLEF 2017. LNCS, vol. 10456, pp. 346–360. Springer, Cham (2017). https://doi.org/10.1007/978-3-319-65813-1_30
5. Losada, D.E., Crestani, F., Parapar, J.: Overview of eRisk: early risk prediction on the internet. In: Bellot, P., et al. (eds.) CLEF 2018. LNCS, vol. 11018, pp. 343–361. Springer, Cham (2018). https://doi.org/10.1007/978-3-319-98932-7_30
6. Sadeque, F., Xu, D., Bethard, S.: Measuring the latency of depression detection in social media. In: WSDM, pp. 495–503. ACM (2018)
7. Trotzek, M., Koitka, S., Friedrich, C.M.: Utilizing neural networks and linguistic metadata for early detection of depression indications in text sequences. CoRR abs/1804.07000 (2018)

ImageCLEF 2019: Multimedia Retrieval in Medicine, Lifelogging, Security and Nature

Bogdan Ionescu[1(✉)], Henning Müller[2], Renaud Péteri[3], Yashin Dicente Cid[2],
Vitali Liauchuk[9], Vassili Kovalev[9], Dzmitri Klimuk[17], Aleh Tarasau[17],
Asma Ben Abacha[11], Sadid A. Hasan[10], Vivek Datla[10], Joey Liu[10],
Dina Demner-Fushman[11], Duc-Tien Dang-Nguyen[16], Luca Piras[5],
Michael Riegler[6], Minh-Triet Tran[7], Mathias Lux[8], Cathal Gurrin[4],
Obioma Pelka[12], Christoph M. Friedrich[12], Alba Garcìa Seco de Herrera[13],
Narciso Garcia[14], Ergina Kavallieratou[15], Carlos Roberto del Blanco[14],
Carlos Cuevas[14], Nikos Vasillopoulos[15], Konstantinos Karampidis[15],
Jon Chamberlain[13], Adrian Clark[13], and Antonio Campello[13,18]

[1] University Politehnica of Bucharest, Bucharest, Romania
bogdan.ionescu@upb.ro
[2] University of Applied Sciences Western Switzerland (HES-SO),
Sierre, Switzerland
[3] La Rochelle University, La Rochelle, France
[4] Dublin City University, Dublin, Ireland
[5] Pluribus One & University of Cagliari, Cagliari, Italy
[6] University of Oslo, Oslo, Norway
[7] University of Science, Ho Chi Minh City, Vietnam
[8] Klagenfurt University, Klagenfurt, Austria
[9] Institute for Informatics, Minsk, Belarus
[10] Philips Research Cambridge, Cambridge, USA
[11] National Library of Medicine, Bethesda, USA
[12] University of Applied Sciences and Arts Dortmund,
Dortmund, Germany
[13] University of Essex, Colchester, UK
[14] E.T.S. Ingenieros Telecomunicación, Madrid, Spain
[15] University of the Aegean, Mitilini, Greece
[16] University of Bergen, Bergen, Norway
[17] Republican Research and Practical Centre for Pulmonology and TB,
Minsk, Belarus
[18] Filament, London, UK

Abstract. This paper presents an overview of the ImageCLEF 2019 lab, organized as part of the Conference and Labs of the Evaluation Forum - CLEF Labs 2019. ImageCLEF is an ongoing evaluation initiative (started in 2003) that promotes the evaluation of technologies for annotation, indexing and retrieval of visual data with the aim of providing information access to large collections of images in various usage scenarios and domains. In 2019, the 17th edition of ImageCLEF runs four main tasks: (i) a *medical* task that groups three previous tasks (caption

F. Crestani et al. (Eds.): CLEF 2019, LNCS 11696, pp. 358–386, 2019.
https://doi.org/10.1007/978-3-030-28577-7_28

analysis, tuberculosis prediction, and medical visual question answering) with new data, (ii) a *lifelog* task (videos, images and other sources) about daily activities understanding, retrieval and summarization, (iii) a new *security* task addressing the problems of automatically identifying forged content and retrieve hidden information, and (iv) a new *coral* task about segmenting and labeling collections of coral images for 3D modeling. The strong participation, with 235 research groups registering, and 63 submitting over 359 runs, shows an important interest in this benchmark campaign.

Keywords: Medical retrieval ·
Life logging retrieval and summarization · File Forgery Detection ·
Coral image segmentation and classification ·
ImageCLEF benchmarking · Annotated data sets

1   Introduction

ImageCLEF[1] is the image retrieval and classification lab of the CLEF (Conference and Labs of the Evaluation Forum) conference. ImageCLEF has started in 2003 with only four participants [9]. It increased its impact with the addition of medical tasks in 2004 [8], attracting over 20 participants already in the second year. An overview of ten years of the medical tasks can be found in [25]. It continued the ascending trend, reaching over 200 participants in 2019.

The tasks have changed much over the years but the general objective has always been the same, to combine text and visual data to retrieve and classify visual information. Tasks have evolved from more general object classification and retrieval to many specific application domains, e.g., nature, security, medical. A detailed analysis of several tasks and the creation of the data sets can be found in [29]. ImageCLEF has shown to have an important impact over the years, already detailed in 2010 [41, 42].

2   Overview of Tasks and Participation

ImageCLEF 2019 consists of four main tasks with the objective of covering a *diverse range* of multimedia retrieval applications, namely: *medicine, lifelogging, security,* and *nature*. Compared to 2018 [24], 2019 focused on a diversity of tasks [2,7,10,14,26,32]. The visual question answering, caption and tuberculosis tasks from 2018 had a sequel and were organized as a specific medical track to foster collaboration. The life logging task also had a follow-up. New in 2019 are the coral and security tasks. Therefore, the 2019 tasks are presented as follows:

– **ImageCLEFmedical.** Medical tasks have been part of ImageCLEF every year since 2004. In 2018, all but one task were medical, but little interaction

---

[1] http://www.imageclef.org/.

happened between the medical tasks. For this reason, the medical tasks were focused towards one specific problem but combined as a single task with several subtasks. This allows exploring synergies between the domains:

- *Tuberculosis*: This is the third edition of the task. The main objective is to provide an automatic CT-based evaluation of tuberculosis (TB) patients. This is done by detecting visual TB-related findings and by assessing a TB severity score based on the automatic analysis of lung CT scans and clinically relevant meta-data. Being able to generate this automatic analysis from the image data allows to limit laboratory analyses to determine the TB stage. This can lead to quicker decisions on the best treatment strategy, reduced use of antibiotics and lower impact on the patient;

- *Visual Question Answering*: This is the second edition of the task. With the increasing interest in artificial intelligence (AI) to support clinical decision making and improve patient engagement, opportunities to generate and leverage algorithms for automated medical image interpretation are currently being explored. The clinicians' confidence in interpreting complex medical images can be enhanced by a "second opinion" provided by an automated system. Since patients may now access structured and unstructured data related to their health via patient portals, such access motivates the need to help them better understand their conditions regarding their available data, including medical images. In view of this and inspired by the success of visual question answering in the general domain[2] and with ImageCLEF [2,20], we propose an enhanced and nicely curated enlarged data set. Like last year, given a medical image accompanied with a clinically relevant question, participating systems are tasked with answering the question based on the visual content;

- *Caption*: This is the third edition of the task in this format, however, it is based on previous medical tasks. The proposed task is the first step towards automatic medical image captioning. Relevant UMLS (Unified Medical Language System®) concepts, that serve as building blocks from which captions can be composed, are to be automatically predicted. There is a considerable need for automatic mapping of visual information to textual content, as the interpretation of knowledge from medical images is time-consuming. In view of better-structured medical reports, the more information and image characteristics known, the more efficient are the radiologist regarding interpretation. Based on the lessons learned in previous years [13,21,22], this year [32] the task focus on detecting UMLS® concepts in radiology images.

- **ImageCLEFlifelog**. This is the third edition of the task. It is now possible to record, capture, photograph and make a video almost in every moment of our life. Wearable devices have further expanded these possibilities and are able to keep track of all our vital functions: heart rate, burned calories, blood sugar and so on. All these data must be indexed, categorized and it must be possible to retrieve them easily for such applications to become

---

[2] https://visualqa.org/.

usable. Hence, this task addresses the problems of lifelog data understanding, summarizing and retrieval.

- **ImageCLEFsecurity**. This is the first edition of the task. File Forgery Detection (FFD) is a serious problem concerning digital forensics examiners. Fraud or counterfeits are common causes for altering files. It is also common that anyone who wants to hide any kind of information in plain sight without being perceived to use steganography. The objective of the specific task is first to examine if an image was forged, then if it could also hide a text message, and last to retrieve the potential hidden message from the forged stego images.
- **ImageCLEFcoral**. This is the first edition of the task. The increasing use of structure-from-motion photogrammetry for modelling large-scale environments from action cameras attached to drones has driven the next generation of visualisation techniques that can be used in augmented and virtual reality headsets. Advances in automatically annotating images for complexity and benthic composition have been promising. The task [7] aims to automatically identify areas of interest and to label them for monitoring coral reefs.

Table 1. Key figures regarding participation in ImageCLEF 2019.

Task	Completed registrations	Groups that subm. results	Submitted runs	Submitted working notes
Tuberculosis	38	13	89	12
VQ Answering	60	17	80	12
Caption	49	11	60	8
Lifelog	17	10	67	10
Security	58	7	43	4
Coral	13	5	20	4
Overall	235	63	359	50

In order to participate in the evaluation campaign, the research groups had to register by following the instructions on the ImageCLEF 2019 web page[3]. To ease the overall management of the campaign, in 2019 the challenge was again organized through the crowdAI platform[4]. To actually get access to the data sets, the participants were required to submit a signed End User Agreement (EUA). Exception was the security task, for which no data usage agreement was required. Table 1 summarizes the participation in ImageCLEF 2019, including the number of completed registrations, indicated both per task and for the overall lab. The table also shows the number of groups that submitted runs and the ones that

---

[3] https://www.imageclef.org/2019.
[4] https://www.crowdai.org/.

submitted a working notes paper describing the techniques used. Teams were allowed to register for participating in several different tasks.

After a decrease in participation in 2016, the participation increased in 2017 and 2018, and increased again in 2019. In 2018, 31 teams completed the tasks and 28 working notes papers were received. In 2019, 63 teams completed the tasks and 50 working notes papers were retrieved. This is almost twice as many papers as in 2018. This is due to several factors: (i) in 2019 there were more tasks and sub-tasks and also a diversity of applications, attracting several different communities; (ii) the crowdAI platform facilitates an online registration which is easier than the previous registration system and much more accessible. It provides visibility to a benchmark community outside of the classical CLEF, and ImageCLEF; (iii) the lab was promoted much more intensively, especially with online communities on social platforms such as Linkedin[5] and Facebook[6]. Overall, the success ratio, i.e., the number of teams completing the tasks reported to the number of teams completing the registration is more or less in the same range as in the previous editions, 27% for 2019 compared to 23% for 2018.

The following sections are dedicated to each of the tasks. Only a short overview is reported, including general objectives, description of the tasks and data sets, and a short summary of the results. A detailed review of the received submissions for each task is provided with the task overview working notes [2,7,10,14,26,32].

3   The Tuberculosis Task

Tuberculosis (TB) is a bacterial infection discovered about 130 years ago. The bacteria usually attack the lungs and the disease remains a persistent threat and an important cause of death worldwide [46]. Generally, TB can be cured with antibiotics. However, the different types of TB require different treatments and therefore the detection of the TB type and the evaluation of the severity stage are two important tasks. In the first and second editions of this task [13,15] participants had to detect Multi-drug resistant patients (MDR subtask) and to classify the TB type (TBT subtask) both based only on the CT image. After the two editions it was concluded that the detection of MDR TB was not possible based in good quality only using the image. In the TBT subtask, there was a slight improvement in 2018 with respect to 2017 on the classification results. However, this was not strong considering the amount of additional data provided in the 2018 edition, both in terms of new images and meta-data. Most of the participants obtained good results in the severity scoring (SVR) subtask introduced in 2018. From a medical point of view, the 3 subtasks proposed previously had a limited utility. The MDR subtask was finally not feasible, and the TBT and SVR subtasks are tasks that expert radiologists can perform in a relatively short time. This encouraged us to add a new subtask based on providing an

---

[5] https://www.linkedin.com/.
[6] https://www.facebook.com/.

automatic report of the patient, an outcome that can have a major impact in the clinical routine.

3.1 Task Setup

Two subtasks were proposed in the ImageCLEF 2019 tuberculosis task [14]: (i) Severity score assessment (SVR subtask), (ii) Automatic CT report generation (CTR subtask).

The SVR subtask aims at assessing the TB severity score. The Severity score is a cumulative score of severity of a TB case assigned by a medical doctor (MD). Originally, the score varied from 1 ("critical/very bad") to 5 ("very good"). In the process of scoring, the MDs consider many factors like pattern of lesions, results of microbiological tests, duration of treatment, patient age and other data. The goal of this subtask is to assess the severity based on the CT image and additional meta-data, including disability, relapse, co-morbidity, bacillary and smoking history and a few more data items. The original severity score is included as training meta-data but the final score that participants have to assess is reduced to a binary category: "low" (scores 4 and 5) and "high" (scores 1, 2 and 3). In the case of the CTR subtask, the participants had to generate an automatic report based on the CT image. This report needed to include the following information in binary form (0 or 1): Left lung affected, right lung affected, presence of calcifications, presence of caverns, pleurisy, lung capacity decrease.

3.2 Data Set

Both subtasks (SVR and CTR) used the same data set containing 335 chest CT scans of TB patients along with a set of clinically relevant meta-data, divided into 218 patients for training and 117 for testing. The selected meta-data include the following binary measures: disability, relapse, symptoms of TB, comorbidity, bacillary, drug resistance, higher education, ex-prisoner, alcoholic, smoking history, and severity. For all patients we provided 3D CT images with an image size per slice of 512×512 pixels and number of slices varying from 50 to 400. For all patients we provided automatically extracted masks of the lungs obtained using the method described in [12].

3.3 Participating Groups and Submitted Runs

In 2019, 13 groups from 11 countries submitted at least one run to one of the two subtasks. There were 11 groups participating in the SVR subtask and 10 groups participating in the CTR subtask. Similar to previous editions, each group could submit up to 10 runs. 54 runs were submitted to the SVR subtask and 35 to the CTR subtask.

Similar to the previous edition, deep learning had a high presence in the submissions with 10 out of the 12 groups using convolutional neural networks

Table 2. Results obtained by the participants in the SVR subtask. Only the best run of each participant is reported here.

Group name	Run	AUC	Accuracy	Rank
UIIP_BioMed	SRV_run1_linear.txt	**0.7877**	0.7179	1
UIIP	subm_SVR_Severity	0.7754	0.7179	2
HHU	SVR_HHU_DBS2_run01.txt	0.7695	0.6923	3
CompElecEngCU	SVR_mlp-text.txt	0.7629	0.6581	6
SD VA HCS/UCSD	SVR_From_Meta_Report1c.csv	0.7214	0.6838	7
MedGIFT	SVR_SVM.txt	0.7196	0.6410	9
UniversityAlicante	SVR-SVM-axis-mode-4.txt	0.7013	0.7009	12
MostaganemFSEI	SVR_FSEI_run3_resnet_50_55.csv	0.6510	0.6154	22
SSN CoE	SVRtest-model1.txt	0.6264	0.6068	29
UoAP	SVRfree-text.txt	0.6111	0.6154	32
FIIAugt	SVRab.txt	0.5692	0.5556	38

Table 3. Results obtained by the participants in the CTR subtask. Only the best run of each participant is reported here.

Group name	Run	Mean AUC	Min AUC	Rank
UIIP_BioMed	CTR_run3_pleurisy_as_SegmDiff.txt	**0.7968**	**0.6860**	1
CompElecEngCU	CTRcnn.txt	0.7066	0.5739	4
MedGIFT	CTR_SVM.txt	0.6795	0.5626	5
SD VA HCS/UCSD	CTR_Cor_32_montage.txt	0.6631	0.5541	6
HHU	CTR_HHU_DBS2_run01.txt	0.6591	0.5159	7
UIIP	subm_CT_Report	0.6464	0.4099	10
MostaganemFSEI	CTR_FSEI_run1_lungnet_50_10slices.csv	0.6273	0.4877	14
UniversityAlicante	svm_axis_svm.txt	0.6190	0.5366	15
PwC	CTR_results_meta.txt	0.6002	0.4724	19
LIST	predictionCTReportSVC.txt	0.5523	0.4317	25

(CNNs), at least in one of their attempts, for feature extraction or directly for patient classification. Five groups used 2D CNNs with pre-processed CT slices and four groups used 3D CNNs (three of them used partial CT volumes and only one used the entire CT scan). The remaining group used 2D CNN to classify feature maps derived from a graph model of the lungs. Despite the general use of CNNs, all these approaches differ in the pre-processing steps, using many techniques such as 2D projections, resizing, slice filtering or concatenations of multiple projections. In addition, one group considered the CT scans as a time sequence and applied optical flow. Another group modeled each CT scan with a set of random pixels and applied decision trees and weak classifiers. Finally, a group applied a handcrafted technique for each CT finding in the CTR subtask based on image binarization and morphology.

3.4   Results

The SVR subtask was evaluated as a binary classification problem, including measures such as Area Under the ROC Curve (AUC) and accuracy. The ranking of the techniques is first based on the AUC and then on the accuracy. Similarly, the CTR subtask was considered a multi-binary classification problem (6 binary findings). Measures again include AUC and accuracy to evaluate the subtask. The ranking of this task is done first by average AUC and then by min AUC (both over the 6 CT findings). Tables 2 and 3 show the final results for each best run and its rank. More detailed results, including other performance measures, can be found in the overview article of the TB task [14].

3.5   Lessons Learned and Next Steps

The results obtained in the SVR subtask improved with respect to the 2018 edition. UIIP_BioMed obtained the highest rank in both editions, passing from 0.70 to 0.79 AUC. Most of the groups that participated in both editions present similar improvements. According to their reports, this improvement is mainly due to the integration of the new meta-data into their algorithms. In the case of the CTR subtask, also won by UIIP_BioMed, the results of this first edition are very promising with a mean AUC of 0.80. Most of the groups developed a single approach and applied it to detect each of the CT-findings in a multi-binary classification setup. However, UIIP_BioMed and a few other groups applied differing techniques for each finding, obtaining impressive results with somewhat trivial techniques in some of them, e.g., comparing the mask size of the right and left lungs to detect lung capacity decrease. This suggests that a delicate analysis of the images before applying any computer vision approach is essential. Thanks to the large amount of new meta-data offered it was possible to use a single data set for both subtasks. Having larger data sets without this information does not seem optimal and in future editions it is planned to focus on increasing the data set without reducing the amount of meta-data provided.

4   The Visual Question Answering Task

Visual Question Answering is an exciting problem that combines natural language processing and computer vision techniques. With the increasing interest in artificial intelligence (AI) to support clinical decision making and improve patient engagement, opportunities to generate and leverage algorithms for automated medical image interpretation are currently being explored. Inspired by the success of visual question answering in the general domain, we conducted a pilot task (VQA-Med 2018) in ImageCLEF 2018 to focus on visual question answering in the medical domain [20]. Based on the success of the initial edition and the huge interest from both computer vision and medical informatics communities, we continued the task this year (VQA-Med 2019) [2] with enhanced focus on a well curated enlarged data set.

Table 4. Participating groups in the VQA-Med 2019 task.

Team	Institution	# Runs
abhishekthanki	Manipal Institute of Technology (India)	8
AIOZ	AIOZ Pte Ltd (Singapore)	6
ChandanReddy	Virginia Tech (USA)	4
Dear stranger	School of Information Science and Engineering, Kunming (China)	6
deepak.gupta651	Indian Institute of Technology Patna (India)	1
Hanlin	Zhejiang University (China)	5
IBM Research AI	IBM Research, Almaden (USA)	4
IITISM@CLEF	Indian Institute of Technology Dhanbad (India)	3
JUST19	(Jordan) University of Science and Technology & University of Manchester (UK)	4
LIST	Faculty of Sciences and Technologies, Tangier (Morocco)	7
minhvu	Umeå University (Sweden) & University of Bern (Switzerland)	10
Team_Pwc_Med	Pricewaterhouse Coopers US Advisory (India)	5
Techno	Faculty of Technology Tlemcen (Algeria)	2
TUA1	Tokushima University (Japan)	1
Turner.JCE	Azrieli College of Engineering Jerusalem (Israel)	10
UMMS	Worcester Polytechnic Institute & University of Massachusetts Medical School (USA)	3
yan	Zhejiang University (China) & National Institute of Informatics (Japan)	1

4.1 Task Setup

In the same way as in 2018, given a medical image accompanied by a clinically relevant question, participating systems in VQA-Med 2019 are tasked with answering the question based on the visual image content. In VQA-Med 2019, we specifically focused on radiology images and four main categories of questions: modality, plane, organ system, and abnormality. We mainly considered medical questions asking about one element only (e.g., "what is the organ principally shown in this MRI?", "in what plane is this mammograph taken?", "is this a t1 weighted, t2 weighted, or flair image?", "what is most alarming about this ultrasound?"), which can be answered from the image content without requiring additional medical knowledge or domain-specific inference.

4.2 Data Set

We automatically constructed the training, validation, and test sets by: (i) applying several filters to select relevant images and associated annotations, and, (ii) creating patterns to generate the questions and their answers. We selected relevant medical images from the MedPix[7] database with filters based on their captions, modalities, planes, localities, categories, and diagnosis methods. We selected only the cases where the diagnosis was made based on the image. Examples of the selected diagnosis methods include: CT/MRI imaging, angiography, characteristic imaging appearance, radiographs, imaging features, ultrasound, and diagnostic radiology. Finally, we considered the most frequent question categories: Modality, Plane, Organ System, and Abnormality to create the data set, which included a training set of 3,200 medical images with 12,792 Question-Answer (QA) pairs (having 3 to 4 questions per image), a validation set of 500 medical images with 2,000 QA pairs, and a test set of 500 medical images with 500 questions. To further ensure the quality of the data, the test set was manually validated by two medical doctors. For more details, please refer to the task overview paper [2].

4.3   Participating Groups and Submitted Runs

Out of 104 online registrations, 61 participants submitted signed end user agreement forms. Finally, 17 groups submitted a total of 90 runs, indicating a notable interest in the VQA-Med 2019 task. Table 4 gives an overview of all participants and the number of submitted runs[8].

4.4   Results

The evaluation of the participant systems of the VQA-Med 2019 task was conducted based on two primary metrics: accuracy and BLEU [2]. We use an adapted version of accuracy from the general domain VQA[9] task that strictly considers exact matching of a participant provided answer and the ground truth answer. We calculate the overall accuracy as well as the scores for each question category. To compensate for the strictness of the accuracy metric, BLEU [31] is used to capture the word overlap-based similarity between a system-generated answer and the ground truth answer. The overall methodology and resources for the BLEU metric are essentially similar to last year's task [20]. The overall results of the participating systems are presented in Tables 5 and 6 for the two metrics in a descending order of the scores (the higher the better).

---

[7] https://medpix.nlm.nih.gov.

[8] There was a limit of maximum 10 run submissions per team. The table includes only the valid runs that were graded (total# 80 out of 90 submissions).

[9] https://visualqa.org/evaluation.html.

Table 5. Accuracy for several query aspects.

Team	Run ID	Modality	Plane	Organ	Abnormality	Overall
Hanlin	26889	0.202	0.192	0.184	0.046	0.624
Hanlin	26891	0.202	0.192	0.184	0.042	0.620
yan	26853	0.202	0.192	0.184	0.042	0.620
minhvu	26881	0.210	0.194	0.190	0.022	0.616
minhvu	27195	0.212	0.190	0.192	0.022	0.616
Hanlin	26890	0.202	0.192	0.184	0.038	0.616
minhvu	26862	0.206	0.192	0.194	0.022	0.614
minhvu	26863	0.208	0.194	0.188	0.024	0.614
minhvu	26879	0.206	0.194	0.192	0.022	0.614
minhvu	27197	0.204	0.194	0.194	0.022	0.614
Hanlin	26917	0.202	0.192	0.184	0.036	0.614
minhvu	26880	0.208	0.194	0.188	0.022	0.612
minhvu	27196	0.208	0.194	0.194	0.016	0.612
minhvu	27198	0.202	0.192	0.192	0.022	0.608
minhvu	26843	0.208	0.192	0.188	0.018	0.606
TUA1	26822	0.186	0.204	0.198	0.018	0.606
Hanlin	26922	0.202	0.192	0.184	0.020	0.598
UMMS	27306	0.168	0.190	0.184	0.024	0.566
AIOZ	26873	0.182	0.180	0.182	0.020	0.564
AIOZ	26833	0.188	0.174	0.182	0.018	0.562
IBM Research AI	27199	0.160	0.196	0.192	0.010	0.558
LIST	26908	0.180	0.184	0.178	0.014	0.556
IBM Research AI	27340	0.156	0.192	0.192	0.012	0.552
LIST	26906	0.166	0.178	0.182	0.012	0.538
Turner.JCE	26913	0.164	0.176	0.182	0.014	0.536
JUST19	27142	0.160	0.182	0.176	0.016	0.534
Turner.JCE	26882	0.174	0.176	0.170	0.014	0.534
Turner.JCE	26939	0.164	0.174	0.182	0.014	0.534
Turner.JCE	27187	0.176	0.174	0.164	0.016	0.530
JUST19	26870	0.160	0.182	0.176	0.010	0.528
JUST19	27143	0.160	0.182	0.176	0.010	0.528
JUST19	27293	0.160	0.182	0.176	0.010	0.528
AIOZ	26783	0.178	0.174	0.162	0.014	0.528
LIST	26900	0.156	0.178	0.180	0.012	0.526
IBM Research AI	27335	0.130	0.190	0.186	0.018	0.524
Turner.JCE	27083	0.176	0.174	0.164	0.010	0.524
AIOZ	26818	0.168	0.170	0.160	0.026	0.524

(continued)

Table 5. (*continued*)

Team	Run ID	Modality	Plane	Organ	Abnormality	Overall
Turner.JCE	27001	0.152	0.174	0.182	0.014	0.522
AIOZ	26814	0.172	0.170	0.162	0.016	0.520
AIOZ	26819	0.172	0.170	0.162	0.016	0.520
Turner.JCE	26940	0.152	0.174	0.182	0.010	0.518
Turner.JCE	27002	0.152	0.174	0.164	0.014	0.504
Turner.JCE	26883	0.174	0.144	0.166	0.014	0.498
Turner.JCE	26781	0.156	0.176	0.164	0	0.496
Team_Pwc_Med	26941	0.148	0.150	0.168	0.022	0.488
Team_Pwc_Med	26955	0.148	0.150	0.168	0.022	0.488
Team_Pwc_Med	27295	0.148	0.150	0.168	0.018	0.484
Team_Pwc_Med	27296	0.148	0.150	0.168	0.018	0.484
UMMS	26931	0.156	0.168	0.152	0.004	0.480
Team_Pwc_Med	27297	0.148	0.150	0.168	0.010	0.476
IBM Research AI	26937	0.094	0.194	0.186	0	0.474
LIST	26829	0.154	0.162	0.138	0.012	0.466
Techno	27079	0.082	0.184	0.170	0.026	0.462
Techno	27100	0.082	0.184	0.170	0.026	0.462
LIST	26828	0.160	0.148	0.144	0.010	0.462
LIST	26831	0.142	0.148	0.138	0.010	0.438
LIST	26832	0.138	0.148	0.138	0.010	0.434
deepak.gupta651@gmail.com	27232	0.096	0.140	0.124	0.006	0.366
ChandanReddy	26884	0.094	0.126	0.064	0.010	0.294
ChandanReddy	26946	0.102	0.122	0.048	0.014	0.286
ChandanReddy	26947	0.094	0.126	0.058	0.008	0.286
Dear stranger	26895	0.062	0.140	0	0.008	0.210
Dear stranger	26894	0.078	0.114	0.002	0.006	0.200
Dear stranger	26919	0.076	0.086	0.004	0.012	0.178
Dear stranger	26920	0.076	0.086	0.004	0.012	0.178
abhishekthanki	27307	0.122	0	0.028	0.010	0.160
abhishekthanki	27298	0.122	0	0.026	0.010	0.158
abhishekthanki	26824	0.112	0	0.026	0.012	0.150
abhishekthanki	27315	0.114	0	0.026	0.010	0.150
abhishekthanki	27317	0.112	0	0.026	0.012	0.150
abhishekthanki	26936	0.104	0	0.024	0.014	0.142
abhishekthanki	26935	0.096	0	0.020	0.010	0.126
abhishekthanki	27316	0.086	0	0	0.012	0.098
IITISM@CLEF	26905	0.052	0.004	0.026	0.006	0.088

(continued)

Table 5. (*continued*)

Team	Run ID	Modality	Plane	Organ	Abnormality	Overall
IITISM@CLEF	26953	0.052	0.004	0.026	0.006	0.088
Dear stranger	26927	0.054	0	0	0.010	0.064
Dear stranger	26928	0.054	0	0	0.010	0.064
ChandanReddy	26945	0	0.030	0.008	0	0.038
UMMS	26903	0.010	0	0	0.008	0.018
IITISM@CLEF	27304	0	0	0	0	0

Table 6. Results of the VQA task in terms of BLEU scores.

Team	Run ID	BLEU	Team	Run ID	BLEU
Hanlin	26889	0.644	Turner.JCE	27002	0.538
Hanlin	26891	0.640	Team_Pwc_Med	26955	0.534
yan	26853	0.640	Team_Pwc_Med	27295	0.531
Hanlin	26890	0.636	Team_Pwc_Med	27296	0.531
minhvu	26881	0.634	Team_Pwc_Med	26941	0.530
minhvu	27195	0.634	AIOZ	26814	0.529
Hanlin	26917	0.634	AIOZ	26819	0.529
minhvu	26862	0.633	Team_Pwc_Med	27297	0.521
minhvu	26863	0.633	Turner.JCE	26883	0.512
TUA1	26822	0.633	UMMS	26931	0.509
minhvu	26879	0.632	LIST	26828	0.495
minhvu	27196	0.632	LIST	26829	0.493
minhvu	27197	0.632	IBM Research AI	26937	0.486
minhvu	26880	0.631	Techno	27079	0.486
minhvu	26843	0.623	Techno	27100	0.486
minhvu	27198	0.622	abhishekthanki	26824	0.462
Hanlin	26922	0.615	abhishekthanki	27317	0.462
UMMS	27306	0.593	LIST	26831	0.459
JUST19	27142	0.591	abhishekthanki	27298	0.455
LIST	26908	0.583	abhishekthanki	26936	0.453
IBM Research AI	27199	0.582	abhishekthanki	27307	0.453
AIOZ	26833	0.579	LIST	26832	0.451
AIOZ	26873	0.576	abhishekthanki	27315	0.447
Turner.JCE	26940	0.572	abhishekthanki	26935	0.433
IBM Research AI	27340	0.569	Dear stranger	26895	0.393
Turner.JCE	26781	0.561	deepak.gupta651@gmail.com	27232	0.389
Turner.JCE	27187	0.558	ChandanReddy	26946	0.323
LIST	26906	0.556	ChandanReddy	26884	0.318
Turner.JCE	26939	0.554	Dear stranger	26894	0.310
Turner.JCE	27083	0.554	ChandanReddy	26947	0.307
JUST19	26870	0.553	abhishekthanki	27316	0.301
Turner.JCE	26913	0.552	Dear stranger	26919	0.270
Turner.JCE	27001	0.552	Dear stranger	26920	0.270
JUST19	27143	0.550	ChandanReddy	26945	0.126
JUST19	27293	0.550	IITISM@CLEF	26905	0.096
Turner.JCE	26882	0.547	IITISM@CLEF	26953	0.096
LIST	26900	0.546	Dear stranger	26927	0.064
IBM Research AI	27335	0.542	Dear stranger	26928	0.064
AIOZ	26783	0.542	UMMS	26903	0.039
AIOZ	26818	0.540	IITISM@CLEF	27304	0.025

4.5 Lessons Learned and Next Steps

Similar to last year, participants mainly used deep learning techniques to build their VQA-Med systems [2]. In particular, the best-performing systems leveraged deep convolutional neural networks (CNNs) like VGGNet or ResNet with a variety of pooling strategies e.g., global average pooling to encode image features and transformer-based architectures like BERT or recurrent neural networks (RNN) to extract question features. Then, various types of attention mechanisms are used coupled with different pooling strategies such as multimodal factorized bilinear (MFB) pooling or multi-modal factorized high-order pooling (MFH) in order to combine multimodal features followed by bilinear transformations to finally predict the possible answers. Analyses of the question category-wise[10] accuracy in Table 5 suggest that in general, participating systems performed well to answer modality questions, followed by plane and organ questions because the possible types of answers for each of these question categories were finite [2]. However, for the abnormality type questions, systems did not perform good in terms of accuracy because of the underlying complexity of open-ended questions and possibly due to the strictness of the accuracy metric. To compensate for the strictness of the accuracy, we computed the BLEU scores to understand the similarity of the system generated answers and the ground-truth answers. The higher BLEU scores of the systems this year (0.631 best BLEU vs. 0.162 in 2018) further verify the effectiveness of the proposed deep learning-based models for the visual question answering task. Overall, the results obtained this year clearly denote the robustness of the provided data set compared to last year's task.

In this second edition of the VQA challenge, we focused on designing goal-oriented VQA data sets and therefore systems by selecting radiology images and clinically relevant questions and categories. We also targeted medical questions that can be answered from the image content without requiring additional medical knowledge or domain-specific inference. For example, we did not consider questions such as: "Is this modality safe for pregnant women?", "What is located immediately inferior to the right hemidiaphragm?", "What can be typically visualized in this plane?", "How would you measure the length of the kidneys?". We would consider providing such kind of questions in the future editions of the challenge as well as context-sensitive questions, given the important role of context and background knowledge in medicine.

5 The Caption Task

The caption task was first proposed as part of the ImageCLEFmedical [22] in 2016. In 2017 and 2018 [13,21] the ImageCLEFcaption task comprised two subtasks: concept detection and caption prediction. In 2019 [32], the task concentrates on extracting Unified Medical Language System® (UMLS) Concept

---

[10] Note that the question category-wise accuracy scores are normalized (each divided by a factor of 4) so that the summation is equal to the overall accuracy.

Unique Identifiers (CUIs) [4] from radiology images. These automatically predicted concepts enable perceivable order for unlabeled and unstructured radiology images and for data sets lacking text information, as multi-modal approaches prove to obtain better results regarding image classification [34].

5.1 Task Setup

The ImageCLEFmed Caption 2019 [32] follows the format of the concept detection subtask running as part of the ImageCLEFcaption task in 2017 [13] and 2018 [21]. As in the previous two editions, given a medical image, the participating teams are tasked with predicting concepts based on the visual image representation. In 2019, the focus is solely on radiology images. However, no single specific disease or anatomic structure is targeted, but several medical imaging modalities are addressed.

The balanced precision and recall trade-off in terms of F1-scores was measured per image and averaged across all test images and computed with the default implementation of the Python scikit-learn (v0.17.1-2) library.

5.2 Data Set

The training and validation sets distributed are a subset of the Radiology Objects in COntext (ROCO) data set [33]. The training set include 56,629 images with 5,216 associated concepts. The number of related concepts to the validation set is 3,233 and contains 14,157 images. All images distributed are from biomedical journal articles extracted from the PubMed Central® (PMC)[11] repository [36].

For the concept detection evaluation, a test set containing 10,000 radiology images was distributed. The test set is not part of the ROCO data set but was extracted using the same procedures applied for the creation of ROCO. The maximum number of concepts per image varies between 34, 72 and 77 for the test, training and validation sets, respectively. All concepts in the ground truth, that were used for evaluation, are associated either to the training or validation.

5.3 Participating Groups and Submitted Runs

In the third edition of the concept detection task [32], 49 teams signed the EUA out of 99 who downloaded it. 60 graded runs were submitted for evaluation by 11 teams from 7 countries. Each group was allowed 10 graded runs and 7 faulty runs altogether. 17 submitted runs were graded as faulty.

Three teams had taken part in the previous editions, while the majority were new to the task. As deep learning techniques have improved accuracy rates in many medical visual classification tasks in the past years [47], most submitted runs were based on these techniques. To optimize input for the predicting systems, several methods were used: image normalization, pre-classification

---

[11] https://www.ncbi.nlm.nih.gov/pmc/.

Table 7. Performance of the participating teams in the ImageCLEF 2019 Concept Detection Task. The best run per team is selected. Teams with previous participation in 2018 are marked with an asterix.

Team	Institution	F1 score
AUEB NLP Group	Department of Informatics Athens University of Economics and Business	0.2823094
damo	Beihang University, Beijing, China	0.2655099
ImageSem*	Institute of Medical Information Chinese Academy of Medical Sciences	0.2235690
UA.PT_Bioinformatics*	Biomedical Informatics Research Group Universidade de Aveiro, Portugal	0.2058640
richard_ycli	The Hong Kong University of Science and Technology, Kowloon Hong Kong	0.1952310
Sam Maksoud	The University of Queensland Brisbane, Australia	0.1749349
AI600	University of International Business and Economics, Beijing, China	0.1656261
MacUni-CSIRO	Macquarie University, North Ryde Sydney, Australia	0.1435435
pri2si17	Mentor Graphics LibreHealth Uttar Pradesh, India	0.0496821
AILAB*	University of the Aegean Samos, Greece	0.0202243
LIST	Faculty of Sciences and Techniques Abdelmalek Essaâdi University, Morocco	0.0013269

based on body-parts, data augmentation regarding class imbalance, concept filtering and re-division. Transfer learning-based multi-label classification models and convolutional neural network (CNN) image encoders, as well as ensembles of adversarial auto-encoders and long short-term memory (LSTM) recurrent neural networks were the most frequently applied approaches.

5.4 Results

The binary ground truth vector is compared to the predicted UMLS CUIs. To get a better overview of the submitted runs, the best results for each team was selected and is listed in Table 7. The complete list of submissions is presented in [32].

5.5 Lessons Learned and Next Steps

The results improved with respect to both previous editions, from 0.1583 in ImageCLEF 2017 and 0.1108 in ImageCLEF 2018 to 0.2823 this year in terms of

F1-score. Three teams participated in the three editions. However, the majority were new to this task. The AUEB NLP Group [27] from Athens University of Economics and Business, who participated for the 1st time, achieved the highest ranked F1-score.

The decision to focus solely on radiology images proved to go into the right direction. Noisy concepts from a wide diversity of medical images were removed, reducing the number of concepts from 111,155 in the previous editions to 5,528 in ImageCLEF 2019, so an amount that is manageable. However, there is still an imbalance in the concept distribution over the images, which showed to be challenging for all teams.

The number of registered teams and submitted runs has increased over the three editions, showing the interest in this challenging task. In future work, better domain knowledge regarding the clinical relevance of the concepts in the development data should be explored. This will assist in creating efficient systems for automated medical data analysis.

6 The Lifelog Task

An increasingly wide range of personal devices, such as smartphones, video cameras as well as wearable devices that allow capturing pictures, videos, and audio clips for every moment of our lives are becoming available. Considering the huge volume of data created, there is a need for systems that can automatically analyse the data in order to categorize, summarize and also query to retrieve the information the user may need.

Despite the increasing number of successful related workshops and panels, lifelogging has seldom been the subject of a rigorous comparative benchmarking exercise. In this edition of this task we aim to bring the attention of lifelogging to an as wide as possible audience and to promote research into some of the key challenges of the coming years.

6.1 Task Setup

In 2019, the ImageCLEFlifelog task consists two sub-tasks: *Lifelog moment retrieval (LMRT)* This is the task used in 2018 with different topics. The participants are required to retrieve specific moments in a lifelogger's life. We define moments as semantic events, or activities that happened throughout the day. For example, they should return the relevant moments for the query "Find the moment(s) when the user1 is cooking in the kitchen." Particular attention needs to be paid to the diversification of the selected moments with respect to the target scenario. The ground truth for this subtask was created using manual annotation; *Solve my life puzzle (Puzzle)* Given a set of lifelog images with associated metadata (e.g., biometrics, location, etc.), but no timestamps, the participants need to analyse these images and rearrange them in chronological order and predict the correct day (Monday or Sunday) and part of the day (morning, afternoon, or evening). The data set is arranged into 75% training and 25% test data (Table 8).

Table 8. Statistics of the ImageCLEFlifelog 2019 data

Characters	Size
Number of lifeloggers	2
Number of days	43 days
Size of the collection	14 GB
Number of images	81,474 images
Number of locations	61 semantic locations
Number of puzzle queries	20 queries
Number of LMRT queries	20 queries

6.2 Data Set

The data consists of a medium-sized collection of multimodal lifelog data over 42 days by the two lifeloggers. The data consists of: *Multimedia Content*—Wearable camera images captured at a rate of about two images per minute and worn from breakfast to sleep. Accompanying this image data was a time-stamped record of music listening activities sourced from `Last.FM`[12] and an archive of all conventional (active-capture) digital photos taken by the lifelogger; *Biometrics Data*—Using the FitBit fitness trackers[13], the lifeloggers gathered 24×7 heart rate, calorie burn and steps. In addition, continuous blood glucose monitoring captured readings every 15 min using the Freestyle Libre wearable sensor[14]; *Human Activity Data*—The daily activities of the lifeloggers were captured in terms of the semantic locations visited, physical activities (e.g., walking, running, standing) from the Moves app[15], along with a time-stamped diet-log of all food and drink consumed; *Enhancements to the Data*—The wearable camera images were annotated with the outputs of a visual concept detector, which provided three types of outputs (Attributes, Categories and Concepts).

6.3 Participating Groups and Submitted Runs

In 2019, we received in total 50 valid submissions (46 official and 4 additional) for LMRT and 21 (all are official) for Puzzle, from 10 teams from 10 countries. Their submissions and the results are summarised in Tables 9 and 10.

---

[12] Last.FM Music Tracker and Recommender - https://www.last.fm/.
[13] Fitbit Fitness Tracker (FitBit Versa) - https://www.fitbit.com.
[14] Freestyle Libre wearable glucose monitor - https://www.freestylelibre.ie/.
[15] Moves App for Android and iOS - http://www.moves-app.com/.

Table 9. Official results of the ImageCLEFlifelog 2019 LMRT task.

Team	Run	P@10	CR@10	F1@10	Team	Run	P@10	CR@10	F1@10
Organiser [30]	RUN1*	0.41	0.31	0.29	UATP [35]	RUN1	0.03	0.01	0.02
	RUN2*	0.33	0.26	0.24		RUN2	0.08	0.02	0.03
ATS [40]	RUN1	0.10	0.08	0.08		RUN3	0.09	0.02	0.03
	RUN2	0.03	0.06	0.04		RUN4	0.1	0.02	0.03
	RUN3	0.03	0.04	0.04		RUN5	0.1	0.02	0.04
	RUN4	0.06	0.13	0.08		RUN6	0.06	0.06	0.06
	RUN5	0.07	0.06	0.05	UPB [16]	RUN1	0.17	0.22	0.13
	RUN6	0.07	0.13	0.08	ZJUTCVR	RUN1	**0.71**	0.38	0.44
	RUN7	0.08	0.19	0.1	[48]	RUN2†	0.74	0.34	0.43
	RUN8	0.05	0.11	0.07		RUN3†	0.41	0.31	0.33
	RUN9	0.10	0.14	0.10		RUN4†	0.48	0.35	0.36
	RUN11	0.14	0.16	0.12		RUN5†	0.59	0.5	0.48
	RUN12	0.35	0.36	0.25	TUC_MI	RUN1	0.02	0.10	0.03
BIDAL [11]	RUN1	0.69	0.29	0.37	[39]	RUN2	0.04	0.08	0.04
	RUN2	0.69	0.29	0.37		RUN3	0.03	0.06	0.03
	RUN3	0.53	0.29	0.35		RUN4	0.10	0.11	0.09
HCMUS [28]	RUN1	0.70	0.56	0.60		RUN5	0.08	0.13	0.09
	RUN2	0.70	**0.57**	**0.61**		RUN6	0.00	0.00	0.00
REGIM [1]	RUN1	0.28	0.16	0.19		RUN7	0.04	0.06	0.05
	RUN2	0.25	0.14	0.17		RUN8	0.04	0.01	0.02
	RUN3	0.25	0.10	0.14		RUN9	0.02	0.01	0.01
	RUN4	0.09	0.05	0.06		RUN10	0.15	0.15	0.12
	RUN5	0.07	0.09	0.06		RUN11	0.03	0.07	0.04
	RUN6	0.07	0.08	0.06		RUN12	0.06	0.11	0.06
						RUN13	0.01	0.01	0.01
						RUN14	0.06	0.21	0.09

Notes: * submissions from the organizer teams are just for reference.
† submissions submitted after the official competition.

6.4 Lessons Learned and Next Steps

We learned that all approaches are exploiting multi-modal instead of using only visual information. This trend was established from last year and now it is confirmed. We also confirmed the importance of deep neural networks in solving these challenges: all ten participants are using deep networks or exploiting the semantic concepts extracted by using some deep learning methods. Different from last year, we received more semi-automatic approaches, which combine human knowledge with state-of-the-art multi-modal information retrieval. Regarding the number of the signed-up teams and the submitted runs, the task keeps growing, with the highest number of registrations and participated teams. It is also a great success that team retention rate is high with two thirds of non-organiser teams from 2018 keeping participating in 2019. This confirms how interesting and challenging lifelogging is. As next steps, we do not plan to enrich the data set but rather provide richer and better concepts, improve the quality of the queries and narrow down the application of the challenges.

Table 10. Official Results of the ImageCLEFlifelog 2019 Puzzle Task.

Team	Run	Kendall's tau	Part of day	Final score
Organiser [30]	RUN1*	0.06	0.31	0.18
	RUN2*	0.03	0.35	0.19
	RUN3*	0.03	0.34	0.18
	RUN4*	0.05	0.49	0.27
BIDAL [11]	RUN1	0.12	0.30	0.21
	RUN2	0.08	0.31	0.20
	RUN3	0.06	0.28	0.17
	RUN4	0.12	0.38	0.25
	RUN5	0.10	0.30	0.20
	RUN6	0.09	0.29	0.19
	RUN7	0.15	0.26	0.21
	RUN8	0.07	0.30	0.19
	RUN9	0.19	0.55	0.37
	RUN10	0.17	0.50	0.33
	RUN11	0.10	0.49	0.29
DAMILAB [23]	RUN6	0.02	0.40	0.21
	RUN7	0.02	0.47	0.25
HCMUS [28]	RUN03ME	**0.40**	**0.70**	**0.55**
	RUN3	**0.40**	0.66	0.53
	RUN04ME	**0.40**	**0.70**	**0.55**
	RUN4	**0.40**	0.66	0.53

Notes: * submissions from the organizer teams are just for reference.

7 The Security Task

File Forgery Detection (FFD) is a serious problem concerning digital forensics examiners. Fraud or counterfeits are common causes for altering files. Another example is a child predator who hides porn images by altering the image extension and in some cases by changing the image signature. Many proposals have been made to solve this problem and the most promising ones concentrate on the image content. It is also common that anyone who wants to hide any kind of information in plain sight without being perceived to use steganography. Steganography is the practice of concealing a file, message, image or video within another file, message, image, or video. The word steganography combines the Greek words steganos, meaning "covered" and graphein meaning "writing". The most usual cover medium for hiding data are images.

7.1 Task Setup

The objective of the specific task is first to examine if an image was forged, then if it could also hide a text message and finally to retrieve the potential hidden message from the forged stego images:

Table 11. Number of files in the data set

	Task 1	Task 2	Task 3
Training set	2400	1000	1000
Test set	1000	500	500

Table 12. Results of task 1 of the security task: identification of forged images

Participant	runID	F-measure	Precision	Recall	Rank
UA.PT_Bioinformatics	26850	1.000	1.000	1.000	1
nattochaduke	26738	1.000	1.000	1.000	2
agentili	26735	1.000	1.000	1.000	4
abcrowdai	26994	0.748	0.798	0.703	5

Table 13. Results of task 2 of the security task: identification of stego images

Participant	runID	F-measure	Precision	Recall	Rank
UA.PT_Bioinformatics	26934	1.000	1.000	1.000	1
agentili	26816	0.888	0.908	0.868	9
nattochaduke	26830	0.660	0.508	0.944	10
Yasser	26844	0.626	0.524	0.776	11
abcrowdai	26910	0.525	0.467	0.600	24
cen_amrita	27454	0.438	0.422	0.456	25

Table 14. Results of task 3 of the security task: retrieval of the messages.

Participant	runID	Edit distance	Rank
UA.PT_Bioinformatics	27447	0.597828610	1
João Rafael Almeida	26896	0.563379028	7

Competition Scenario. You are a professional digital forensic examiner collaborating with the police, who suspects that there is an ongoing fraud in the Central

Bank. After obtaining a court order, police gain access to a suspect's computer in the bank with the purpose to look for images proving the suspect guilty. However, police suspects that he has managed to change extension and signature of some images, so that they look like pdf files. Additionally, it is highly probable that the suspect has used steganography software to hide messages within some images that could reveal valuable information of his collaborators. Police authorities asks you to: *Task 1: Identify Forged Images*—Perform detection of altered (forged) images (both extension and signature) and predict the actual type of the forged file; *Task 2: Identify Stego Images*—Identify the altered images that hide steganographic content; *Task 3: Retrieve the Message*—Retrieve the hidden messages (text) from the stego images.

7.2   Data Set

The data set contains 6,400 image and pdf files, divided into 3 sets. Each set is used for a specific task and the number of files contained in each one is shown in Table 11. All participants have access to the training data sets along with their respective ground truth. The test sets are distributed without the ground truth.

7.3   Participating Groups and Submitted Runs

Seven participating groups submitted at least one run to at least one of the tasks. Out of these 7 groups: 4 groups submitted 6 runs to the first task, 6 groups submitted 26 runs to the second task and 2 groups submitted 11 runs to the third task.

7.4   Results

Tables 12, 13 and 14 summarize the evaluation scores per run and participant for tasks 1–3, refereeing just the best submission per participant. The runs of the first two tasks were compared according to their F-measure, precision and recall, while the ranking of the third task's runs was based on the Lenenshtein edit distance.

7.5   Lessons Learned and Next Steps

The security task was a new task in ImageCLEF 2019. The number of the registered teams/individuals and the submitted runs show that the security challenges receive much attention and can be interesting and challenging. Almost every participant signed to all three tasks although this was not mandatory. This highlights the importance of each task. The majority of the approaches exploits and combines deep learning techniques, achieving very good results. The most difficult task proved to be the third one, in which the participants had to retrieve hidden messages from the images. The third task results also show that there is room for improvement, as more advanced techniques need to be used for better results. The analysis of the specific task results indicates that the training set was small for the specific problem i.e., the extraction of the hidden messages. To leverage the power of advanced deep learning algorithms towards improving the state-of-the-art in steganalysis, we plan to increase the data set. We also plan to narrow down the application of the challenges, e.g., focus in steganalysis, probably in another domain.

8   The Coral Task

Although they represent only a small percentage of the sea floor, coral reefs are extremely important because they are the most bio-diverse marine environments—yet most coral reefs are in danger of being lost within the next 30 years, and with them the ecosystems they support [3]. This catastrophe will see the extinction of many marine species, such as shellfish, corals and many micro-organisms in the ocean. It also reduces reef fishery production, which is an important source of income and food [5,37]. By monitoring changes in the structural complexity and composition of coral reefs we can help prioritize conservation efforts.

Autonomous Underwater Vehicles (AUV) can collect data for many hours at a time. However, the complexity of the images makes it impossible for human annotators to assess the contents of images on a large scale [6]. Advances in automatically annotating images for complexity and benthic composition have been promising [19,38]; however, the type of images being collected using action cameras present a particular challenge. Following the success of the ImageCLEF annotation task running between 2012 and 2016 [17,18,43–45], the first edition of the ImageCLEFcoral task [7] aims to automatically annotate images with benthic substrates for monitoring coral reefs.

8.1   Task Setup

In the first edition of the ImageCLEFcoral task, the following two subtasks were proposed: *Coral reef image annotation and localisation*—This task is similar to the classic ImageCLEF annotation task. This subtask requires the participants to label the images with types of benthic substrate together with their bounding box; *Coral reef image pixel-wise parsing task*—This subtask requires the participants to label the images with types of benthic substrate together with a more detailed polygon bounding each substrate the images.

8.2   Data Set

The images used in the ImageCLEFcoral task originates from a growing, large-scale collection of images taken from coral reefs around the world as part of a coral reef monitoring project with the Marine Technology Research Unit (MTRU) at the University of Essex. In particular, the data in the 2019 Image-CLEFcoral task was collected from several locations in the Wakatobi Marine

Reserve in Sulawesi, Indonesia in July 2018. The images are part of a monitoring collection and therefore most have a tape measure running through a portion of the image.

The distributed collection data set comprises several sets of overlapping images taken in an area of underwater terrain. Each image was then labelled by experts with the following 13 types of benthic substrates: Hard Coral – Branching, Hard Coral – Submassive, Hard Coral – Boulder, Hard Coral – Encrusting, Hard Coral – Table, Hard Coral – Foliose, Hard Coral – Mushroom, Soft Coral, Soft Coral – Gorgonian, Sponge, Sponge – Barrel, Fire Coral – Millepora and Algae - Macro or Leaves. The same set and annotations was provided for both subtasks. The training set contains 240 images with 6,670 substrates annotated and the test set contains 200 images with 5,370 substrates annotated.

8.3 Participating Groups and Submitted Runs

In the first edition of the ImageCLEFcoral task, there were 13 teams registered and 5 teams from 4 countries submitted 20 runs. Teams were limited to submit 10 runs per task.

Table 15. Coral reef image annotation and localisation performance in terms of $MAP0.5IoU$, $R0.5IoU$, and $MAP0IoU$. The best run per team in terms of $MAP0.5IoU$ is selected.

Run id	team	$MAP0.5IoU$	$R0.5IoU$	$MAP0IoU$
27417	HHUD	0.2427	0.1309	0.4877
27349	VIT	0.14	0.0682	0.431
27497	ISEC	0.0006	0.0006	0.0006

Table 16. Pixel-wise coral reef parsing performance in terms of $MAP0.5IoU$, $R0.5IoU$, and $MAP0IoU$. The best run per team in terms of $MAP0.5IoU$ is selected.

Run id	team	$MAP0.5IoU$	$R0.5IoU$	$MAP0IoU$
27500	MTRU	0.0419	0.049	0.2398
27343	SOTON	0.0004	0.0015	0.0484
27505	HHUD	0.0	0.0	0.0

8.4 Results

The task was evaluated using the PASCAL VOC style metric of intersection over union (IoU). The evaluation was carried out using the following 3 measures: $MAP0.5IoU$ the localised mean average precision (MAP) for each submitted method for using the performance measure of IoU $\geq$ 0.5 of the ground truth; $R0.5IoU$ the localised mean recall for each submitted method for using the performance measure of IoU ≥ 0.5 of the ground truth; $MAP0IoU$ the image annotation average for each method with success if the concept is simply detected in the image without any localisation. Tables 15 and 16 present the best runs per team in terms of $MAP0.5IoU$. The complete overview of the results can be found in [7], including the accuracy per benthic substrate type.

8.5 Lessons Learned and Next Steps

In the first edition of the ImageCLEF coral task there were 5 groups participating in the 2 tasks, only one group participated in both tasks. The teams explored a variety of machine learning and deep learning approaches. The best run achieved 0.24 in terms of MAP50 score in the coral reef image annotation and localisation subtask and 0.05 in the coral reef image pixel-wise parsing subtask. Poor results were achieved in the coral reef image pixel-wise parsing subtask probably due to the submission of many self-intersecting polygons which were not taken into account in the evaluation.

This is a difficult task due to the complexity of the images including the morphology of the benthic organisms and the similarity between the growth forms. In 2020, we are planning to increase the amount of images provided and limited the submission of self-intersecting polygons.

9   Conclusions

This paper presents a general overview of the activities and outcomes of the ImageCLEF 2019 evaluation campaign. Four tasks were organised, covering challenges in the medical domain (caption analysis, tuberculosis prediction, and medical visual question answering), life logging (daily activities understanding, retrieval and summarization), security (automatically identifying forged content and retrieve hidden information), and nature (segmenting and labeling collections of coral images).

The participation increased in an important way with the diversification of the application domains, reaching more than 235 registrations and 63 teams submitting over 359 runs. Whereas several of the participants had participated in the past, there was also a large number of groups totally new to ImageCLEF and also collaborations of research groups in several tasks.

Most of the proposed solutions evolved around state-of-the-art deep neural networks architectures, also for the medical domain. In the tuberculosis task, results improved over last year and this improvement seems to be driven by the integration of the new meta-data. In the visual question answering task, deep learning techniques were predominant. Attention mechanisms proved to be very useful in improving the performance. In the caption task, results also improved compared to the previous editions. The use of radiology images for the decision, proved to be the best choice, as it focused the task. In the lifelog task, all approaches now exploited multi-modal techniques. Again, deep learning proved to be the state-of-the-art. Notably, semi-automatic approaches became more popular. In the security task, deep learning prevailed as well. Retrieving hidden messages from the images was the most difficult task. Results show that a larger amount of training data is desirable. Finally, the coral task was explored using general machine learning and also deep learning. The task seemed difficult and the lowest results were achieved in the coral reef image pixel-wise parsing.

ImageCLEF 2019 again brought together an interesting mix of tasks and approaches and we are looking forward to the fruitful discussions at the workshop.

Acknowledgements. The work of Bogdan Ionescu was partially supported by the Ministry of Innovation and Research, UEFISCDI, project SPIA-VA, agreement 2SOL/2017, grant PNIII-P2-2.1-SOL-2016-02-0002.

The data collection of the ImageCLEFcoral task was funded by an IAA grant with support from Professor David Smith and Operation Wallacea. The work of Antonio Campello was supported by Innovate UK, Knowledge Transfer Partnership project KTP010993, and hosted at Filament Consultancy Group Limited.

References

1. Abdallah, F.B., Feki, G., Ammar, A.B., Amar, C.B.: Big data for lifelog moments retrieval improvement. In: CLEF2019 Working Notes. CEUR Workshop Proceedings, 09–12 September 2019, Lugano, Switzerland. CEUR-WS.org (2019). http://ceur-ws.org

2. Abacha, A.B., Hasan, S.A., Datla, V.V., Liu, J., Demner-Fushman, D., Müller, H.: VQA-Med: overview of the medical visual question answering task at ImageCLEF 2019. In: CLEF2019 Working Notes. CEUR Workshop Proceedings, 09–12 September 2019, Lugano, Switzerland. CEUR-WS.org (2019). http://ceur-ws.org

3. Birkeland, C.: Global status of coral reefs: in combination, disturbances and stressors become ratchets. In: World Seas: An Environmental Evaluation, pp. 35–56. Elsevier (2019)

4. Bodenreider, O.: The unified medical language system (UMLS): integrating biomedical terminology. Nucleic Acids Res. **32**(Database–Issue), 267–270 (2004). https://doi.org/10.1093/nar/gkh061

5. Brander, L.M., Rehdanz, K., Tol, R.S., Van Beukering, P.J.: The economic impact of ocean acidification on coral reefs. Climate Change Econ. **3**(01), 1250002 (2012)

6. Bullimore, R.D., Foster, N.L., Howell, K.L.: Coral-characterized benthic assemblages of the deep northeast atlantic: defining "coral gardens" to support future habitat mapping efforts. ICES J. Mar. Sci. **70**(3), 511–522 (2013)

7. Chamberlain, J., Campello, A., Wright, J.P., Clift, L.G., Clark, A., de Herrera, A.G.S.: Overview of ImageCLEFcoral 2019 task. In: CLEF2019 Working Notes. CEUR Workshop Proceedings. CEUR-WS.org (2019)

8. Clough, P., Müller, H., Sanderson, M.: The CLEF 2004 cross-language image retrieval track. In: Peters, C., Clough, P., Gonzalo, J., Jones, G.J.F., Kluck, M., Magnini, B. (eds.) CLEF 2004. LNCS, vol. 3491, pp. 597–613. Springer, Heidelberg (2005). https://doi.org/10.1007/11519645_59

9. Clough, P., Sanderson, M.: The CLEF 2003 cross language image retrieval track. In: Peters, C., Gonzalo, J., Braschler, M., Kluck, M. (eds.) CLEF 2003. LNCS, vol. 3237, pp. 581–593. Springer, Heidelberg (2004). https://doi.org/10.1007/978-3-540-30222-3_56

10. Dang-Nguyen, D.T., Piras, L., Riegler, M., Tran, M.T., Zhou, L., Lux, M., Le, T.K., Ninh, V.T., Gurrin, C.: Overview of ImageCLEFlifelog 2019: solve my life puzzle and lifelog moment retrieval. In: CLEF2019 Working Notes. CEUR Workshop Proceedings, 09–12 September 2019, Lugano, Switzerland. CEUR-WS.org (2019)

11. Dao, M.S., Vo, A.K., Phan, T.D., Zettsu, K.: BIDAL@imageCLEFlifelog2019: the role of content and context of daily activities in insights from lifelogs. In: CLEF2019 Working Notes. CEUR Workshop Proceedings, 09–12 September 2019, Lugano, Switzerland. CEUR-WS.org (2019). http://ceur-ws.org

12. Cid, Y.D., Jimenez-del-Toro, O., Depeursinge, A., Müller, H.: Efficient and fully automatic segmentation of the lungs in CT volumes. In: Goksel, O., Jimenez-del-Toro, O., Foncubierta-Rodriguez, A., Müller, H. (eds.) Proceedings of the VISCERAL Challenge at ISBI, pp. 31–35. No. 1390 in CEUR Workshop Proceedings, April 2015

13. Cid, Y.D., Kalinovsky, A., Liauchuk, V., Kovalev, V., Müller, H.: Overview of ImageCLEFtuberculosis 2017 - predicting tuberculosis type and drug resistances. In: CLEF2017 Working Notes. CEUR Workshop Proceedings, 11–14 September 2017, Dublin, Ireland. CEUR-WS.org (2017). http://ceur-ws.org

14. Cid, Y.D., Liauchuk, V., Klimuk, D., Tarasau, A., Kovalev, V., Müller, H.: Overview of ImageCLEFtuberculosis 2019 - automatic CT-based report generation and tuberculosis severity assessment. In: CLEF2019 Working Notes. CEUR Workshop Proceedings, 09–12 September 2019, Lugano, Switzerland. CEUR-WS.org (2019). http://ceur-ws.org

15. Cid, Y.D., Liauchuk, V., Kovalev, V., Müller, H.: Overview of ImageCLEFtuberculosis 2018 - detecting multi-drug resistance, classifying tuberculosis type, and assessing severity score. In: CLEF2018 Working Notes. CEUR Workshop Proceedings, 10–14 September 2018, Avignon, France. CEUR-WS.org (2019). http://ceur-ws.org

16. Dogariu, M., Ionescu, B.: Multimedia lab @ ImageCLEF 2019 lifelog moment retrieval task. In: CLEF2019 Working Notes. CEUR Workshop Proceedings, 09–12 September 2019, Lugano, Switzerland. CEUR-WS.org (2019). http://ceur-ws.org

17. Gilbert, A., et al.: Overview of the ImageCLEF 2015 scalable image annotation, localization and sentence generation task. In: CLEF Working Notes (2015)

18. Gilbert, A., et al.: Overview of the ImageCLEF 2016 scalable concept image annotation task. In: CLEF Working Notes, pp. 254–278 (2016)

19. Gonzalez-Rivero, M., et al.: The catlin seaview survey-kilometre-scale seascape assessment, and monitoring of coral reef ecosystems. Aquat. Conserv.: Mar. Freshw. Ecosyst. **24**, 184–198 (2014)

20. Hasan, S.A., Ling, Y., Farri, O., Liu, J., Lungren, M., Müller, H.: Overview of the ImageCLEF 2018 medical domain visual question answering task. In: CLEF2018 Working Notes. CEUR Workshop Proceedings, 10–14 September 2018, Avignon, France. CEUR-WS.org (2018). http://ceur-ws.org

21. de Herrera, A.G.S., Eickhoff, C., Andrearczyk, V., Müller, H.: Overview of the ImageCLEF 2018 caption prediction tasks. In: CLEF2018 Working Notes. CEUR Workshop Proceedings, 10–14 September 2018, Avignon, France. CEUR-WS.org (2018). http://ceur-ws.org

22. de Herrera, A.G.S., Schaer, R., Bromuri, S., Müller, H.: Overview of the ImageCLEF 2016 medical task. In: Working Notes of CLEF 2016 (Cross Language Evaluation Forum), September 2016

23. Hoang, T.H., Tran, M.K., Nguyen, V.T., Tran, M.T.: Solving life puzzle with visual context-based clustering and habit reference. In: CLEF2019 Working Notes. CEUR Workshop Proceedings, 09–12-2019, Lugano, Switzerland. CEUR-WS.org (2019). http://ceur-ws.org

24. Ionescu, B., et al.: Overview of ImageCLEF 2018: challenges, datasets and evaluation. In: Bellot, P., et al. (eds.) CLEF 2018. LNCS, vol. 11018, pp. 309–334. Springer, Cham (2018). https://doi.org/10.1007/978-3-319-98932-7_28

25. Kalpathy-Cramer, J., de Herrera, A.G.S., Demner-Fushman, D., Antani, S., Bedrick, S., Müller, H.: Evaluating performance of biomedical image retrieval systems: overview of the medical image retrieval task at ImageCLEF 2004–2014. Comput. Med. Imaging Graphics **39**, 55–61 (2015)

26. Karampidis, K., Vasillopoulos, N., Cuevas Rodríguez, C., del Blanco, C.R., Kavallieratou, E., Garcia, N.: Overview of the ImageCLEFsecurity 2019 task. In: CLEF2019 Working Notes. CEUR Workshop Proceedings, 09–12 September 2019, Lugano, Switzerland. CEUR-WS.org (2019)

27. Kougia, V., Pavlopoulos, J., Androusopoulos, I.: AUEB NLP group at Image-CLEFmed Caption 2019. In: CLEF2019 Working Notes. CEUR Workshop Proceedings, 09–12 September 2019, Lugano, Switzerland. CEUR-WS.org (2019). http://ceur-ws.org

28. Le, N.K., Nguyen, D.H., Nguyen, V.T., Tran, M.T.: Lifelog moment retrieval with advanced semantic extraction and flexible moment visualization for exploration. In: CLEF2019 Working Notes. CEUR Workshop Proceedings, 9–12 September 2019, Lugano, Switzerland. CEUR-WS.org (2019). http://ceur-ws.org

29. Müller, H., Clough, P., Deselaers, T., Caputo, B. (eds.): ImageCLEF - Experimental Evaluation in Visual Information Retrieval. The Springer International Series On Information Retrieval, vol. 32. Springer, Berlin (2010). https://doi.org/10.1007/978-3-642-15181-1

30. Ninh, V.T., et al.: LIFER 2.0: discover personal lifelog insight by interactive lifelog retrieval system. In: CLEF2019 Working Notes. CEUR Workshop Proceedings, 09–12 September 2019, Lugano, Switzerland. CEUR-WS.org (2019). http://ceur-ws.org

31. Papineni, K., Roukos, S., Ward, T., Zhu, W.J.: BLEU: a method for automatic evaluation of machine translation. In: Proceedings of the 40th Annual Meeting on Association for Computational Linguistics, pp. 311–318. Association for Computational Linguistics (2002)

32. Pelka, O., Friedrich, C.M., de Herrera, A.G.S., Müller, H.: Overview of the Image-CLEFmed 2019 concept prediction task. In: CLEF2019 Working Notes. CEUR Workshop Proceedings, 09–12 September 2019, Lugano, Switzerland. CEUR-WS.org (2019). http://ceur-ws.org

33. Pelka, O., Koitka, S., Rückert, J., Nensa, F., Friedrich, C.M.: Radiology Objects in COntext (ROCO): a multimodal image dataset. In: Stoyanov, D., et al. (eds.) LABELS/CVII/STENT 2018. LNCS, vol. 11043, pp. 180–189. Springer, Cham (2018). https://doi.org/10.1007/978-3-030-01364-6_20

34. Pelka, O., Nensa, F., Friedrich, C.M.: Adopting semantic information of grayscale radiographs for image classification and retrieval. In: Proceedings of the 11th International Joint Conference on Biomedical Engineering Systems and Technologies (BIOSTEC 2018) - Volume 2: BIOIMAGING, 19–21 January 2018, Funchal, Madeira, Portugal, pp. 179–187 (2018). https://doi.org/10.5220/0006732301790187

35. Ribeiro, R., Neves, A.J.R., Oliveira, J.L.: UAPTBioinformatics working notes at ImageCLEF 2019 lifelog moment retrieval (LMRT) task. In: CLEF2019 Working Notes. CEUR Workshop Proceedings, 09–12 September 2019, Lugano, Switzerland. CEUR-WS.org (2019). http://ceur-ws.org
36. Roberts, R.J.: PubMed central: the GenBank of the published literature. Proc. Nat. Acad. Sci. U.S.A. **98**(2), 381–382 (2001). https://doi.org/10.1073/pnas.98.2.381
37. Speers, A.E., Besedin, E.Y., Palardy, J.E., Moore, C.: Impacts of climate change and ocean acidification on coral reef fisheries: an integrated ecological-economic model. Ecol. Econ. **128**, 33–43 (2016)
38. Stokes, M., Deane, G.: Automated processing of coral reef benthic images. Limnol. Oceanogr. Methods **7**, 157–168 (2009)
39. Taubert, S., Kahl, S.: Automated lifelog moment retrieval based on image segmentation and similarity scores. In: CLEF2019 Working Notes. CEUR Workshop Proceedings, 09–12 September 2019, Lugano, Switzerland. CEUR-WS.org (2019). http://ceur-ws.org
40. Tournadre, M., Dupont, G., Pauwels, V., Cheikh, B., Lmami, M., Ginsca, A.L.: A multimedia modular approach to lifelog moment retrieval. In: CLEF2019 Working Notes. CEUR Workshop Proceedings, 09–12 September 2019, Lugano, Switzerland. CEUR-WS.org (2019). http://ceur-ws.org
41. Tsikrika, T., de Herrera, A.G.S., Müller, H.: Assessing the scholarly impact of ImageCLEF. In: Forner, P., Gonzalo, J., Kekäläinen, J., Lalmas, M., de Rijke, M. (eds.) CLEF 2011. LNCS, vol. 6941, pp. 95–106. Springer, Heidelberg (2011). https://doi.org/10.1007/978-3-642-23708-9_12
42. Tsikrika, T., Larsen, B., Müller, H., Endrullis, S., Rahm, E.: The scholarly impact of CLEF (2000–2009). In: Forner, P., Müller, H., Paredes, R., Rosso, P., Stein, B. (eds.) CLEF 2013. LNCS, vol. 8138, pp. 1–12. Springer, Heidelberg (2013). https://doi.org/10.1007/978-3-642-40802-1_1
43. Villegas, M., Paredes, R.: Overview of the ImageCLEF 2012 scalable web image annotation task. In: CLEF Working Notes (2012)
44. Villegas, M., Paredes, R.: Overview of the ImageCLEF 2014 scalable concept image annotation task. In: CLEF Working Notes, pp. 308–328. Citeseer (2014)
45. Villegas, M., Paredes, R., Thomee, B.: Overview of the ImageCLEF 2013 scalable concept image annotation subtask. In: CLEF Working Notes (2012)
46. World Health Organization, et al.: Global tuberculosis report 2016 (2016)
47. Xu, Y., Mo, T., Feng, Q., Zhong, P., Lai, M., Chang, E.I.: Deep learning of feature representation with multiple instance learning for medical image analysis. In: IEEE International Conference on Acoustics, Speech and Signal Processing, ICASSP 2014, 4–9 May 2014, Florence, Italy, pp. 1626–1630 (2014). https://doi.org/10.1109/ICASSP.2014.6853873
48. Zhou, P., Bai, C., Xia, J.: ZJUTCVR team at ImageCLEFlifelog2019 lifelog moment retrieval task. In: CLEF2019 Working Notes. CEUR Workshop Proceedings, 09–12 September 2019, Lugano, Switzerland. CEUR-WS.org (2019) http://ceur-ws.org

Overview of LifeCLEF 2019: Identification of Amazonian Plants, South & North American Birds, and Niche Prediction

Alexis Joly[1]([✉]), Hervé Goëau[2], Christophe Botella[1,3], Stefan Kahl[7],
Maximillien Servajean[8], Hervé Glotin[4], Pierre Bonnet[2], Robert Planqué[5],
Fabian Robert-Stöter[1,2,3,4,5,6,7,8], Willem-Pier Vellinga[5], and Henning Müller[6]

[1] Inria, LIRMM, Montpellier, France
`alexis.joly@inria.fr`
[2] CIRAD, UMR AMAP, Montpellier, France
[3] INRA, UMR AMAP, Montpellier, France
[4] Univ. Toulon, Aix Marseille Univ., CNRS, LIS, DYNI SABIOD,
Marseille, France
[5] Xeno-canto Foundation, Vlieland, The Netherlands
[6] HES-SO, Sierre, Switzerland
[7] Chemnitz University of Technology, Chemnitz, Germany
[8] LIRMM, Université Paul Valéry, University of Montpellier, CNRS,
Montpellier, France

Abstract. Building accurate knowledge of the identity, the geographic distribution and the evolution of living species is essential for a sustainable development of humanity, as well as for biodiversity conservation. Unfortunately, such basic information is often only partially available for professional stakeholders, teachers, scientists and citizens, and often incomplete for ecosystems that possess the highest diversity. In this context, an ultimate ambition is to set up innovative information systems relying on the automated identification and understanding of living organisms as a means to engage massive crowds of observers and boost the production of biodiversity and agro-biodiversity data. The Life-CLEF 2019 initiative proposes three data-oriented challenges related to this vision, in the continuity of the previous editions but with several consistent novelties intended to push the boundaries of the state-of-the-art in several research directions. This paper describes the methodology of the conducted evaluations as well as the synthesis of the main results and lessons learned.

1 LifeCLEF Lab Overview

Identifying organisms is a key for accessing information related to the uses and ecology of species. This is an essential step in recording any specimen on earth to be used in ecological studies. Unfortunately, this is difficult to achieve due to the level of expertise necessary to correctly record and identify living organisms (for instance plants are one of the most difficult groups to identify with an

© Springer Nature Switzerland AG 2019
F. Crestani et al. (Eds.): CLEF 2019, LNCS 11696, pp. 387–401, 2019.
https://doi.org/10.1007/978-3-030-28577-7_29

estimated number of 400,000 species). This *taxonomic gap* has been recognized since the Rio Conference of 1992, as one of the major obstacles to the global implementation of the Convention on Biological Diversity. Among the diversity of methods used for species identification, Gaston and O'Neill [10] discussed in 2004 the potential of automated approaches typically based on machine learning and multimedia data analysis. They suggested that, if the scientific community is able to (i) overcome the production of large training datasets, (ii) more precisely identify and evaluate the error rates, (iii) scale up automated approaches, and (iv) detect novel species, it will then be possible to initiate the development of a generic automated species identification system that could open up vistas of new opportunities for theoretical and applied work in biological and related fields.

Since the question raised by Gaston and O'Neill [10], *automated species identification: why not?*, a lot of work has been done on the topic (*e.g.* [5,12,22,27,31,34,35]) and it is still attracting much research today, in particular in deep learning [11,13,28]. In order to measure the progress made in a sustainable and repeatable way, the LifeCLEF[1] research platform was created in 2014 as a continuation of the plant identification task [20] that was run within the ImageCLEF lab[2] the three years before [17–19]. LifeCLEF enlarged the evaluated challenge by considering animals in addition to plants, and audio and video contents in addition to images. In 2018, a new challenge dedicated to the location-based prediction of species was finally introduced (GeoLifeCLEF). The main novelties of the 2019 edition of LifeCLEF compared to the previous year are the following:

1. **PlantCLEF focus on tropical flora**: The main novelty of the 2019 edition of PlantCLEF is to focus the challenge on the flora of *data deficient* tropical regions, *i.e.* regions having the richest biodiversity but for which data availability is much lower than northern countries.
2. **Big soundscape data for BirdCLEF**: The main novelty of the 2019 edition of BirdCLEF is the introduction of a very large dataset of 350 h of manually annotated soundscape recordings in addition to the historical mono-species recordings provided by the Xeno-canto community.
3. **New data and evaluation metric for GeoLifeCLEF**: The 2019 edition of the GeoLifeCLEF challenge tackles some of the methodological weaknesses that were revealed by the pilot 2018 edition and introduces a new big dataset fixing some issues of the previous one.

About 250 researchers or students registered to at least one of the three challenges of the lab and 16 of them finally crossed the finish line by completing runs and participating in the collaborative evaluation. In the following sections, we provide a synthesis of the methodology and main results of each of the three challenges of LifeCLEF2019. More details can be found in the overview reports of each challenge and the individual reports of the participants (references provided below).

---

[1] http://www.lifeclef.org/.
[2] http://www.imageclef.org/.

2   Task1: PlantCLEF

A detailed description of the task and a more complete discussion of the results can be found in the dedicated working note [16].

2.1   Methodology

The PlantCLEF challenge considers the problem of classifying plant observations based on several images of the same individual plant rather than considering a classical single-image classification task. Indeed, it is usually required to observe several organs of a plant to identify it accurately (e.g. the flower, the leaf, the fruit, the stem, etc.). As a consequence, the same individual plant is often photographed several times by the same observer resulting in contextually similar pictures and/or near-duplicates. To avoid bias, it is crucial to consider such image sets as a single plant observation that should not be split across the training and the test set. In addition to the raw pictures, plant observations are usually associated with contextual and social data. This includes geo-tags or location names, time information, author names, collaborative ratings, vernacular names (common names), picture type tags, etc. Within all PlantCLEF challenges, the use of this additional information was considered as part of the problem because it was judged as potentially useful for a real-world usage scenario.

In 2018, a novelty of the challenge was to involve expert botanists in the evaluation in order to evaluate how fare automated systems are from their expertise. In particular, 9 of the best expert botanists of the French flora accepted to compete with AI algorithms on a difficult subset of the whole test set. The results confirmed that identifying plants from images is a difficult task, even for some of the highly skilled specialists who accepted to participate in the experiment. The results showed that there is still a margin of progression but that it is becoming tighter and tighter. The best system was able to correctly classify 84% of the test samples, better than 5 of the 9 experts. The main novelty of the 2019 edition of PlantCLEF is to transpose this methodology to the flora of tropical regions, that is expected to be much more challenging because of the much lower amount of available training data for that species. Indeed, tropical regions are the richest in terms of biodiversity but unfortunately also the poorest in terms of data.

2.2   Dataset and Evaluation Protocol

We provided a new training data set of 10K species mainly focused on the Guiana shield and the Amazon rain forest, known to be the largest collection of living plants and animal species in the world (see Fig. 1). As for the previous two years, this training data was mainly aggregated by querying popular image search engines with the binomial Latin name of the targeted species. We actually did show in previous editions of LifeCLEF that training deep learning models on such noisy big data is as effective as training models on cleaner but smaller expert data [14,15]. The average number of images per species in that new data set is much lower than the data set used in the previous editions of PlantCLEF (about 1 vs. 3). Many species contain only a few images and some of them might even contain only 1 image, making a much more challenging task. Moreover, in this context of lack of data, image search engines very often return the same image several times for different species. This typically happens when an image is displayed in a web page that contains a text list of several species, for example a web page of a genus in Wikipedia: if the species in the list are quite rare and poorly illustrated on the web, an image search engine will return the same image for most species on the list. The training data were organized into sub-directories (one for each species), but each image was named according to its content with an MD5 like hash technique, in order to facilitate the detection of "duplicated" images.

For the test set, on the other hand, we relied on highly trusted expert data (with a presumably very low error rate). The test set contains 742 plant observations that all had to be classified by the participating systems. However, only a small part was used for the comparison with the 5 human experts who participated to the evaluation (actually 117 observations).

Participants were allowed to use complementary training data (e.g. for pre-training purposes) but at the condition that (i) the experiment is entirely reproducible, i.e. that the used external resource is clearly referenced and accessible to any other research group in the world, (ii) the use of external training data or not is mentioned for each run, and (iii) the additional resource does not contain any of the test observations. The main evaluation measure for the challenge was the top-1 accuracy in order to be comparable with the latter's task concerning flora in temperate regions. Mean Reciprocal Rank and the top-3 accuracy have also been used as complementary measures to allow a fair comparison with the human experts since they have been allowed to make up to three species proposals.

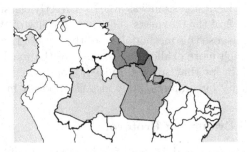

Fig. 1. Regions of origin of the 10k species selected for PlantCLEF 2019: French Guiana, Suriname, Guyana, Brazil (states of Amapa, Para, Amazonas)

2.3   Participants and Results

167 participants registered for the PlantCLEF challenge 2019 and downloaded the data set, but only 6 research groups succeeded in submitting runs, *i.e.* files

containing the predictions of the system(s) they ran. Details of the methods and systems used in the runs are synthesized in the overview working note paper of the task [16] and further developed in the individual working notes of most of the participants (Holmes [7], CMP [32], MRIM-LIG [9]). We report in Fig. 2 the performance achieved by the 26 collected runs and the 5 participating human experts, while Fig. 3 reports the results on the whole test data set.

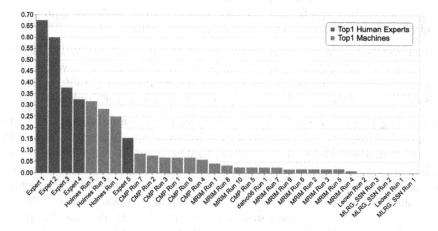

Fig. 2. Scores between experts and machine

The Tropical Flora Is Much More Difficult to Identify. Results are significantly lower than last year both for machines and human experts with an equivalent number of species of 10k, confirming the assumption that a tropical flora is inherently more difficult than the more generalist flora. The best of the experts, actually recognized by peers as the most expert in the world of the Guyanese flora, reached a top1 of 0.675 (against 0.96 for the best expert during ExpertCLEF 2018 [15]). Comparison of medians (0.376 vs 0.8) and minimums (0.154 vs 0.613) over the two years further highlights theses difficulties.

Deep Learning Algorithms Were Defeated from Far by the Best Experts. The best automated system is half as good as the best expert with a gap of 0.365, whereas last year the gap was only 0.12. Moreover, there is a strong disparity in results between participants despite the use of popular and recent Convolutional Neural Networks (DensetNet, ResNet, Inception-ResNet-V2, Inception-V4), while during the last four PlantCLEF editions a homogenization of high results forming a "skyline" has often been observed. These differences in accuracy can be explained in part by the way participants managed the training set. Although previous investigations have shown the unreasonable effectiveness of noisy data for fine-grained recognition [14,24], several teams considered that the training dataset was too noisy and too imbalanced. They made consistent efforts for removing duplicates pictures (Holmes), for removing non

plant pictures (Holmes, CMP), for adding new pictures (CMP), or for reducing the classes imbalance with smoothed re-sampling and other data sampling
schemes (MRIM).

Removing Duplicate Images Seems to be Effective. Even if it reduces
dramatically the training dataset to 230k pictures and from 8,263 species, and
even if it may remove images for valuable for poorly illustrated species, the
Holmes team reported in their preliminary tests that removing all the duplicate
pictures allowed to significantly increase the top1 from 43,7% to 47,97% on a
validation set of 20k images extracted from the training set [7].

Removing Non Plant Images Would Not Really Be Useful. The Holmes
team reported that if 29k non-plant images are automatically removed in addition to duplicates, it actually slightly decrease the top1 from 47.97% to 47.76%.
It is as if most of the non-plant noise is finally carried by the duplicate images.

Extending the Training Data Set Improve the Performances. The CMP
team did not remove duplicate images but automatically eliminated about 20k
non-plant images. Above all, they considerably extended the training set by
adding more than 238k images from the GBIF, exploiting finally more than 666k
images. At first glance, their best method obtained a top1 of 8.5%, far behind
the Holmes team which reached 31.6% with considerably fewer images (250k vs
666k) and a system based on same architectures (InceptionV4 and Inception-
ResNet-V2). However, the CMP team reported a bug in their submission files,
and the real best top-1 accuracy that they should have achieved was actually at
best 41%, 10 points more than the winning Holmes run file. It is worth noting
that this out-of-competition run could made better predictions than the third
human expert.

Open Questions. Could the CMP team have obtained even better accuracy if
they had massively eliminated duplicate images like the Holmes team? To what
extent the 238k additional images from GBIF are noisy? If the GBIF website
showed that there are few non plant pictures like faces and drawings, there is
actually a high proportion of herbarium images for rare species, and it is difficult
to evaluate how much pictures are duplicated in several species or/and incorrectly identified. Therefore, the management of different types of noise (duplicates, identification errors, non-plants, different domains like herbariums, ...) in
a data deficient context require further investigations.

3   Task2: BirdCLEF

A detailed description of the task and a more complete discussion of the results
can be found in the dedicated overview paper [23].

3.1   Methodology

The bird identification challenge of LifeCLEF, initiated in 2014 in collaboration
with Xeno-Canto, considerably increased the scale of the seminal challenges. The

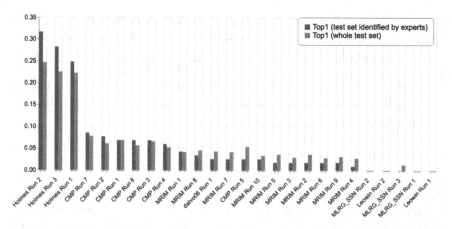

Fig. 3. Scores achieved by all systems evaluated within the plant identification task of LifeCLEF 2019

first bird challenge ICML4B [12] initiated in 2012 by DYNI/SABIOD, contained only 35 species, but received 400 runs. The next at MLSP only included 15 species, the third (NIPS4B [31] in 2013 by SABIOD) had 80 species. The community platform Xeno-canto launched in 2005 and hosts bird sounds from all continents and daily receives new recordings from some of the remotest places on Earth. The Xeno-canto archive currently consists of more than 460,000 recordings covering over 10,000 species of birds, making it one of the most comprehensive collections of bird sound recordings worldwide, and certainly the most comprehensive collection shared under Creative Commons licenses. The first BirdCLEF challenge in 2014 however, solely focused on recordings originating from the Amazonian rain forest. This region can be considered one of the richest in the world in terms of biodiversity, but also one of the most endangered. The geographical extent and the number of species were progressively increased over the years and reached 1,000 species in 2015/2016, and 1,500 in 2017/2018. One of the signature characteristics of the Xeno-Canto data—and therefore the BirdCLEF subset—are the weakly labeled samples with varying recording quality and (most notably) a massive class imbalance. For instance, the 2017/2018 dataset contained 48,843 recordings in total, with a minimum of four recordings for *Laniocera rufescens* and a maximum of 160 recordings for *Henicorhina leucophrys*.

In 2016, the BirdCLEF challenge was extended and also featured complex *soundscape* recordings in addition to the classical *mono-species* Xeno-Canto recordings. This enables research for more passive monitoring scenarios such as setting up a network of mobile recorders that would continuously capture the surrounding sound environment. One of the limitations of this new content, however, was that the vocalizing birds were not localized in the recordings. Thus, to allow a more accurate evaluation, new *time-coded soundscapes* were introduced within the BirdCLEF 2017 and 2018 challenges. In total, 6.5 h of recordings were collected in the Amazonian forests and were manually annotated by two experts including a native of the Amazon forest, in the form of time-coded segments with associated species name. Unfortunately, past editions of BirdCLEF showed no significant improvements in that domain, despite excellent scores for mono-species recordings. Therefore, the 2019 edition of the BirdCLEF challenge mainly focused on this soundscape scenario but extended it to North American bird species for which the available data is considerably bigger.

3.2   Dataset and Evaluation Protocol

The new data includes about 350 h of manually annotated soundscapes from past editions and soundscapes that were recorded using 30 field recorders between January and June of 2017 in Ithaca, NY, USA. This dataset was split into a validation set with labels provided to the participants (about 10%) and a test set to be processed by the evaluated systems. As for training data, we provided an newly composed Xeno-Canto subset covering 659 species from South and North America. Additionally, eBird.org frequency lists were provided to enable participants to decide which species are plausible for a given time, date and location.

The goal of the task was to localize and identify all audible birds within the provided soundscape test set. Each soundscape was divided into segments of 5 s, and a list of species associated to probability scores had to be returned for each segment. The used evaluation metric was the classification mean Average Precision ($cmAP$), considering each class c of the ground truth as a query. This means that for each class c, all predictions with $ClassId = c$ are extracted from the run file and ranked by decreasing probability in order to compute the average precision for that class. The mean across all classes is computed as the main evaluation metric. More formally:

$$cmAP = \frac{\sum_{c=1}^{C} AveP(c)}{C}$$

where C is the number of classes (species) in the ground truth and $AveP(c)$ is the average precision for a given species c computed as:

$$AveP(c) = \frac{\sum_{k=1}^{n_c} P(k) \times rel(k)}{n_{rel}(c)}.$$

where k is the rank of an item in the list of the predicted segments containing c, n_c is the total number of predicted segments containing c, $P(k)$ is the precision at cut-off k in the list, $rel(k)$ is an indicator function equaling 1 if the segment at rank k is a relevant one (i.e. is labeled as containing c in the ground truth) and $n_{rel}(c)$ is the total number of relevant segments for class c.

3.3   Participants and Results

103 participants registered for the BirdCLEF 2019 challenge and downloaded the dataset. Five of them succeeded in submitting runs. Details of the methods and

systems used in the runs are synthesized in the overview working notes paper of the task [23] and further developed in the individual working notes of the participants (MfN [26], ASAS [6], NWPU [21], MIHAI [8]). In Fig. 4 we report the performance achieved by the 25 collected runs.

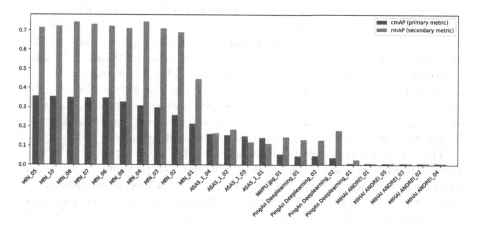

Fig. 4. Scores achieved by all systems evaluated within the bird identification task of LifeCLEF 2019

In this edition, participants built on established systems from previous years, all submitted runs featured a CNN classifier trained on spectrograms—very deep networks once again performed best. Participants were able to significantly improve the detection performance. In fact, we saw an increase of more than 180% for the best performing runs (2018: 0.193–2019: 0.356). This result is probably largely due to the high number of North American soundscapes that are less complex than their South American counterparts. However, the recognition performance for South American soundscapes also increased significantly compared to 2018 with a cmAP of 0.293 in 2019 over 0.222 from last year. Participants were allowed to use any publicly available metadata and even the provided validation data to improve the performance of their systems. Although expert annotations are not an adequate (or even easy-to-acquire) addition for the training of a recognition system for unseen habitats, the increase in overall performance is considerable. The highest scoring run submitted by MfN achieved a sample-wise mean average precision (our secondary metric) of 0.446 without the use of validation samples and 0.745 when validation data was used for training. These scores imply that domain adaption to new acoustic environments (and recorder characteristics) plays a crucial role and should be subject of investigation in future editions.

4   Task3: GeoLifeCLEF

A detailed description of the task and a more complete discussion of the results can be found in the dedicated working note [4].

4.1   Methodology

Predicting the shortlist of species that are likely to be observed at a given geographical location should significantly help to reduce the candidate set of species to be identified. However, none of the attempt to do so within previous Life-CLEF editions successfully used this information. The GeoLifeCLEF challenge was specifically created in 2018 to tackle this problem through a standalone task. More generally, automatically predicting the list of species that are likely to be observed at a given location might be useful for many other scenarios in biodiversity informatics. It could facilitate biodiversity inventories through the development of location-based recommendation services (typically on mobile phones) as well as the involvement of non-expert nature observers. It might also serve educational purposes thanks to biodiversity discovery applications providing functionalities such as contextualized educational pathways.

The aim of the challenge is to predict the list of species that are the most likely to be observed at a given location. Therefore, we provide a large training set of species occurrences, each occurrence being associated to a multi-channel image characterizing the local environment. Indeed, it is usually not possible to learn a species distribution model directly from spatial positions because of the limited number of occurrences and the sampling bias. What is usually done in ecology is to predict the distribution on the basis of a representation in the environmental space, typically a feature vector composed of climatic variables (average temperature at that location, precipitation, etc.) and other variables such as soil type, land cover, distance to water, etc. The originality of GeoLifeCLEF is to generalize such niche modeling approach to the use of an image-based environmental representation space. Instead of learning a model from environmental feature vectors, the goal of the task will be to learn a model from k-dimensional image patches, each patch representing the value of an environmental variable in the neighborhood of the occurrence. As last year, the task consists of predicting plant species from location, but we added a very large and newly published dataset of plant occurrences from a citizen science project. We also proposed to participants to use an even bigger dataset of non-plant species that might interact with plants.

4.2   Data Set and Evaluation Protocol

Training Set - The training data provided for the task included three distinct occurrences data sets:

- **Pl@ntNetFranceRaw**: 2,367,145 occurrences of plants that were collected via the Pl@ntNet application and automatically identified (using a convolutional neural network). These original data is described and permanently hosted in [3].
- **Pl@ntNetFranceTrusted**: a subset of Pl@ntNetFranceRaw including only the occurrences for which the prediction score (softmax output of the CNN) was higher than a threshold equal to 0.98.

- **GBIFPlantFrance**: 291,392 occurrences of 3,336 plant species collected by experts on the French territory between 1835 and 2017 (coming from the GBIF database[3].
- **GBIFAllFrance**: 10,618,839 occurrences of species from other kingdoms than plants including mammals, birds, amphibians, insects and fungus (also coming from the GBIF database).

Environmental Data - We provided 33 geographic rasters of various spatial resolutions containing containing bioclimatic, pedologic, topologic, hydrographic and land cover variables suited for modeling plant species distributions. The original data compilation is freely downloadable and described in details at [2]. We also provided a python tool allowing to extract the automatically environmental patches: A 3 dimensions array where each layer is the is a window matrix cropped into one raster, and centered at the specified location.

Test Set - We used 25,000 plant occurrences of high location accuracy (inferior to 50 m) and identification certainty collected by the Mediterranean National Botanical Conservatory (CBNmed) and their partners over the French Mediterranean region. They have been selected to insure that spatial coverage is uniform and that locally each present species have an equivalent number of occurrences.

Evaluation - Several tens of plant species coexist in some square meters. Thus, we have chosen to evaluate the ability of algorithms to predict the true species label of an occurrence among the predicted 30 highest ranked species. We thus used the top30 accuracy as primary metric:

$$\text{Top30}(L_1, ..., L_{\text{n\_occ}}) = \frac{\sum_{i=1}^{\text{n\_occ}} \mathbb{1}_{\{s_i \in L_i\}}}{\text{n\_occ}} \qquad (1)$$

where s_i is the species label of occurrence i and L_i is the list of the 30 species labels predicted with highest probability for occurrence i by the algorithm.

4.3   Participants and Results

61 participants registered for the GeoLifeCLEF 2019 challenge and downloaded the dataset. Five of them succeeded in submitting 44 runs in total. Details of the methods and systems used in the runs are synthesized in the overview working note paper of the task [4] and further developed in the individual working notes of the participants (**LIRMM** [30], **SaraSi** [33], **SSN_CSE** [25], **sergiu_atodiresei** [1] and **Lot_of_Lof** [29]). In Fig. 5 we report the performance achieved by the 44 collected runs.

The 5 best runs of this challenge all used Convolutional Neural Network models applied to environmental patches, which confirms results of last year edition. This performance gap might be also due to the fact that those models training included both **Pl@ntNetFranceRaw** and **GBIFPlantFrance** plant

---

[3] www.gbif.org.

occurrences, whereas non-CNN methods only used Pl@ntNet occurrences. The best run included non plant occurrences (corresponding species labels were added to the model output) along with plants occurrences. It had sharp performance improvement compared to the similar architecture learnt without including this data by the same participant (see run 27006). This strongly suggests that the model takes advantages of the correlations existing between plant species and other groups to reconstruct a more faithful biotic context that helps the prediction of plants species.

There may be significant room for improvement for the implementation of the best run. Indeed, the architecture or learning process employed by **LIRMM** for the CNN may be limiting as we can see the same method learnt on plants only (run 27006) achieved lower performance than **SaraSi** CNN implementations (runs 27086, 27087, 27088). More generally, further investigations should build on this approach of using a wide range of species in learning models. Also it would be important to compare **Pl@ntNetFranceRaw** and **GBIFPlantFrance** data sets and their fusion, to deal for example with observers preferences bias towards species.

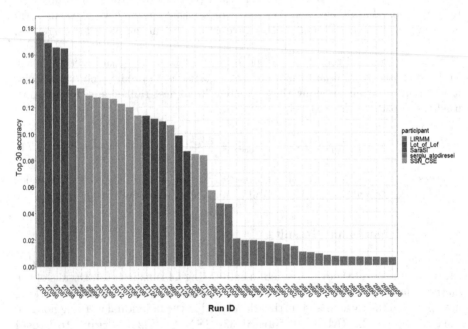

Fig. 5. Top30 metric per run and participant on GeoLifeCLEF 2019 task

5   Conclusions and Perspectives

The main outcome of this collaborative evaluation is a new snapshot of the performance of state-of-the-art computer vision, bio-acoustic and machine learning techniques towards building real-world biodiversity monitoring systems. This study shows that recent deep learning techniques still allow some consistent progress for most of the evaluated tasks. The results of GeoLifeCLEF, in particular, revealed for the first time that deep neural networks are able to transfer knowledge from a kingdom to another one in a very effective way. However, our study also shows that data availability is a major issue to be resolved if we want to transpose the best results obtained to any habitat on earth. The results of BirdCLEF have once again shown significant progress on a difficult task based on soundscapes even if the newly introduced North American soundscapes seems to be less complex than their South American counterparts. Domain adaption to new acoustic environments (and recorder characteristics) played a crucial role and should be subject of investigation in future editions. The results of Plant-CLEF, in particular, reveal that the identification performance on Amazonian plants is considerably lower than the one obtained on temperate plants of Europe and North America. The analysis of the results showed that the management of different types of noise (duplicates, errors, non-plants), of different type of domains (in the field vs herbarium), and of different data sampling schema (for reducing the imbalance) in a such data deficient context require further investigations.

Acknowledgements. We would like to thank very warmly Julien Engel, Rémi Girault, Jean-François Molino and the two other expert botanists who agreed to participate in the task on plant identification. We also we would like to thank the University of Montpellier and the Floris'Tic project (ANRU) who contributed to the funding of the 2019-th edition of LifeCLEF.

References

1. Atodiresei, C.S., Iftene, A.: Location-based species recommendation - GeoLife-CLEF 2019 challenge. In: CLEF Working Notes 2019 (2019)
2. Botella, C.: A compilation of environmental geographic rasters for SDM covering France (version 1) (data set). Zenodo (2019). https://doi.org/10.5281/zenodo.2635501
3. Botella, C., Bonnet, P., Joly, A., Lombardo, J.C., Affouard, A.: Pl@ntnet queries 2017–2018 in France. Zenodo (2019). https://doi.org/10.5281/zenodo.2634137
4. Botella, C., Servajean, M., Bonnet, P., Joly, A.: Overview of GeoLifeCLEF 2019: plant species prediction using environment and animal occurrences. In: CLEF Working Notes 2019 (2019)
5. Cai, J., Ee, D., Pham, B., Roe, P., Zhang, J.: Sensor network for the monitoring of ecosystem: bird species recognition. In: 2007 3rd International Conference on Intelligent Sensors, Sensor Networks and Information. ISSNIP 2007 (2007)
6. Koh, C.-Y., Chang, J.-Y., C.L.T.D.Y.H., Hsieh, H.H.: Bird sound classification using convolutional neural networks. In: CLEF Working Notes 2019 (2019)
7. Chulif, S., Jing Heng, K., Wei Chan, T., Al Monnaf, M.A., Chang, Y.L.: Plant identification on Amazonian and Guiana shield flora: neuon submission to LifeCLEF 2019 plant. In: CLEF (Working Notes) (2019)
8. Costandache, M.A.: Bird species identification using neural networks. In: CLEF Working Notes 2019 (2019)

9. Dat Nguyen Thanh, G.Q., Goeuriot, L.: Non-local DenseNet for plant CLEF 2019 contest. In: CLEF (Working Notes) (2019)

10. Gaston, K.J., O'Neill, M.A.: Automated species identification: why not? Philos. Trans. R. Soc. Lond. B Biol. Sci. **359**(1444), 655–667 (2004)

11. Ghazi, M.M., Yanikoglu, B., Aptoula, E.: Plant identification using deep neural networks via optimization of transfer learning parameters. Neurocomputing **235**, 228–235 (2017)

12. Glotin, H., Clark, C., LeCun, Y., Dugan, P., Halkias, X., Sueur, J.: Proceedings of 1st workshop on Machine Learning for Bioacoustics - ICML4B. ICML, Atlanta USA (2013). http://sabiod.org/ICML4B2013_book.pdf

13. Goëau, H., Bonnet, P., Joly, A.: Plant identification based on noisy web data: the amazing performance of deep learning (LifeCLEF 2017). In: CLEF 2017-Conference and Labs of the Evaluation Forum, pp. 1–13 (2017)

14. Goëau, H., Bonnet, P., Joly, A.: Plant identification based on noisy web data: the amazing performance of deep learning (LifeCLEF 2017). In: Working Notes of CLEF 2017 (Cross Language Evaluation Forum) (2017)

15. Goëau, H., Bonnet, P., Joly, A.: Overview of ExpertLifeCLEF 2018: how far automated identification systems are from the best experts? In: CLEF Working Notes 2018 (2018)

16. Goëau, H., Bonnet, P., Joly, A.: Overview of LifeCLEF plant identification task 2019: diving into data deficient tropical countries. In: Working Notes of CLEF 2019 (Cross Language Evaluation Forum) (2019)

17. Goëau, H., et al.: The imageclef 2013 plant identification task. In: CLEF 2013, Valencia (2013)

18. Goëau, H., et al.: The ImageCLEF 2011 plant images classification task. In: CLEF 2011 (2011)

19. Goëau, H., et al.: ImageCLEF 2012 plant images identification task. In: CLEF 2012, Rome (2012)

20. Goëau, H., et al.: The ImageCLEF plant identification task 2013. In: Proceedings of the 2nd ACM International Workshop on Multimedia Analysis for Ecological Data, pp. 23–28. ACM (2013)

21. Bai, J., Wang, B., Chen, C., Fu, Z.-H., Chen, J.: Inception-V3 based method of LifeCLEF 2019 bird recognition. In: CLEF Working Notes 2019 (2019)

22. Joly, A., et al.: Interactive plant identification based on social image data. Ecol. Inform. **23**, 22–34 (2014)

23. Kahl, S., Stöter, F.R., Glotin, H., Planqué, R., Vellinga, W.P., Joly, A.: Overview of BirdCLEF 2019: large-scale bird recognition in Soundscapes. In: CLEF (Working Notes) (2019)

24. Krause, J., et al.: The unreasonable effectiveness of noisy data for fine-grained recognition. In: Leibe, B., Matas, J., Sebe, N., Welling, M. (eds.) ECCV 2016. LNCS, vol. 9907, pp. 301–320. Springer, Cham (2016). https://doi.org/10.1007/978-3-319-46487-9_19

25. Krishna, N., Kumar, P., Kaushik, R.R., Mirunalini, P., Chandrabose, A., Jaisakthi, S.M.: Species recommendation using machine learning - GeoLifeCLEF2019. In: CLEF Working Notes 2019 (2019)

26. Lasseck, M.: Bird species identification in Soundscapes. In: CLEF Working Notes 2019 (2019)

27. Lee, D.J., Schoenberger, R.B., Shiozawa, D., Xu, X., Zhan, P.: Contour matching for a fish recognition and migration-monitoring system. In: Optics East, pp. 37–48. International Society for Optics and Photonics (2004)

28. Lee, S.H., Chan, C.S., Remagnino, P.: Multi-organ plant classification based on convolutional and recurrent neural networks. IEEE Trans. Image Process. **27**(9), 4287–4301 (2018)
29. Monestiez, P., Botella, C.: Species recommendation using intensity models and sampling bias correction (GeoLifeCLEF 2019: Lof_of_lof team). In: CLEF Working Notes 2019 (2019)
30. Negri, M., Servajean, M., Joly, A.: Plant prediction from CNN model trained with other kingdom species (GeoLifeCLEF 2019: LIRMM team). In: CLEF Working Notes 2019 (2019)
31. NIPS International Conference: Proceedings of Neural Information Processing Scaled for Bioacoustics, from Neurons to Big Data (2013). http://sabiod.org/nips4b
32. Picek, L.,Šulc, M., Matas, J.: Recognition of the Amazonian flora by inception networks with test-time class prior estimation. In: CLEF (Working Notes) (2019)
33. Si-Moussi, S., Hedde, M., Daufresne, T.: Species recommendation using environment and biotic associations. In: CLEF Working Notes 2019 (2019)
34. Towsey, M., Planitz, B., Nantes, A., Wimmer, J., Roe, P.: A toolbox for animal call recognition. Bioacoustics **21**(2), 107–125 (2012)
35. Trifa, V.M., Kirschel, A.N., Taylor, C.E., Vallejo, E.E.: Automated species recognition of antbirds in a Mexican rainforest using hidden Markov models. J. Acoust. Soc. Am. **123**, 2424 (2008)

Overview of PAN 2019: Bots and Gender Profiling, Celebrity Profiling, Cross-Domain Authorship Attribution and Style Change Detection

Walter Daelemans[1], Mike Kestemont[1], Enrique Manjavacas[1],
Martin Potthast[2(✉)], Francisco Rangel[3], Paolo Rosso[4], Günther Specht[5],
Efstathios Stamatatos[6], Benno Stein[7], Michael Tschuggnall[5],
Matti Wiegmann[7], and Eva Zangerle[5]

[1] University of Antwerp, Antwerp, Belgium
[2] Leipzig University, Leipzig, Germany
`martin.potthast@uni-leipzig.de`
[3] Autoritas Consulting, Valencia, Spain
[4] Universitat Politècnica de València, Valencia, Spain
[5] University of Innsbruck, Innsbruck, Austria
[6] University of the Aegean, Samos, Greece
[7] Bauhaus-Universität Weimar, Weimar, Germany
`http://pan.webis.de`

Abstract. We briefly report on the four shared tasks organized as part of the PAN 2019 evaluation lab on digital text forensics and authorship analysis. Each task is introduced, motivated, and the results obtained are presented. Altogether, the four tasks attracted 373 registrations, yielding 72 successful submissions. This, and the fact that we continue to invite the submission of software rather than its run output using the TIRA experimentation platform, demarcates a good start into the second decade of PAN evaluations labs.

1 Introduction

The PAN 2019 evaluation lab organized four shared tasks related to authorship analysis, i.e., the analysis of authors based on their writing style. Two of the tasks addressed the profiling of authors with respect to traditional demographics as well as new ones from two perspectives: (1) whether they are bots or humans, and, (2) studying the public personas of celebrities in particular. Another task tackled the most traditional task of authorship analysis, authorship attribution, but from the new angle of attributing authors across different writing domains (i.e., topics). The fourth task addressed the important, yet exceedingly difficult task of handling multi-author documents and the detection of style changes within a given text written by more than one author.

Authors are listed in alphabetical order.

F. Crestani et al. (Eds.): CLEF 2019, LNCS 11696, pp. 402–416, 2019.
https://doi.org/10.1007/978-3-030-28577-7_30

The four tasks continue the series of shared tasks, which has been organized for more than a decade now starting with PAN 2009 [19], preceded only by two PAN workshops at ECAI 2008 and SIGIR 2007, which laid the foundation for what was to come. Focusing on tasks from the areas digital text forensics, text reuse, and judging the trustworthiness and ethicality of texts, we have assembled new benchmarks for more than a dozen different tasks now, many of which continue to be used for evaluations throughout the research community. In this paper, each of the following sections gives a brief, condensed overview of the four aforementioned tasks, including their motivation and the results obtained.

2 Bots and Gender Profiling

Author profiling aims at classifying authors depending on how language is shared by groups of people. This may allow to identify demographics such as age and gender, and it can be of high interest from a marketing, security and foren-sics perspective. The research community has shown an increasing interest in the author profiling shared task throughout the past years, as evidenced by the growing number of participants.[1] Having addressed several aspects of author profiling in social media from 2013 to 2018, the author profiling shared task of 2019 aims at investigating whether the author of a Twitter feed is a bot or a human. Furthermore, in case of a human it was asked to profile the gender of the author. As in previous years, we have proposed the task from a multi-lingual perspective, covering English and Spanish languages. One of our main objectives was to demonstrate the feasibility of automatically identifying bots as well as demonstrating the difficulty of identifying more elaborate bots than basic information spreaders.

2.1 Evaluation Framework

To build the PAN-AP-2019 corpus,[2] we have combined Twitter accounts iden-tified as bots in existing datasets with newly discovered ones on the basis of specific search queries. In both cases, a minimum of three annotators agreed with the annotation, or else the Twitter user was discarded. To annotate gen-der, we followed the same methodology as in previous editions of the shared task. In Table 1, some corpus statistics are shown. The corpus is balanced per type (bot/human), and in case of human, it is also balanced per gender. Each author is composed of exactly 100 tweets.

---

[1] In the past seven editions of the author profiling shared task at PAN, we have had 21 (2013 [26]), 10 (2014 [23]), 22 (2015 [20]), 22 (2016 [28]), 22 (2017 [27]), 23 (2018 [25]), and 55 (2019 [22]) participating teams, respectively.

[2] We should highlight that we are aware of the legal and ethical issues related to collecting, analyzing, and profiling social media data [21], and that we are committed to legal and ethical compliance in our scientific research and its outcomes.

Table 1. Number of authors per language. The corpus is balanced regarding bots vs. humans, and regarding gender in case of humans, and it contains 100 tweets per author.

Dataset	English (EN)	Spanish (ES)
Training	4,120	3,000
Test	2,640	1,800

The participants were asked to send two predictions per author: (1) whether the author is a bot or a human, and in case of a human (2) whether the author is male or female. The participants were allowed to approach the task also in one instead of all of the languages, and to address only one subproblems (bots or gender). Classification accuracy has been employed for evaluation. For each language, we obtain the accuracy for both problems in both languages separately and average them to obtain the final ranking.

2.2   Results

This year, 55 teams participated in the shared task. In Table 2, the overall performance per language and participant's ranking are shown. The best results have been obtained for both identification (95.95% in English vs. 93.33% in Spanish) and gender profiling (84.17% in English vs. 81.72% in Spanish). As can be seen, results for bot identification are higher than 90% in some cases, revealing the relative ease of this task. A more in-depth analysis is presented in the overview paper [22] where we show that certain types of bots are not as easy to detect as others, and the risks this entails.

In Table 2, the best results per language and problem are highlighted in bold font. The overall best result (88.05%) has been obtained by the author in [16]. They have approached the task with a Support Vector Machine with character and word n-grams as features. It is worth mentioning the high performance obtained by the word and character n-grams baselines, even greater than that of word embeddings [12,13] and Low Dimensionality Statistical Embedding (LDSE) [24].

3   Celebrity Profiling

Celebrities are a highly prolific population of Twitter users. They influence public opinion, are role models to their fans and follower, and sometimes they are the voices of the disenfranchised. For these reasons, the "rich and famous" have been studied in the social sciences and economics as a matter of course, especially with regard to their presence on social media. Our recent seminal work on celebrity profiling [34], and this task at PAN 2019 introduce this particular group of people to computational linguistics. This task focuses on determining four demographics of celebrities based on their Twitter timelines:

Table 2. Accuracy per subtask and language, and global ranking as average.

Ranking	Team	Bots vs. Human		Gender		Average
		EN	ES	EN	ES	
1	Pizarro	0.9360	0.9333	0.8356	0.8172	0.8805
2	Srinivasarao & Manu	0.9371	0.9061	0.8398	0.7967	0.8699
3	Bacciu et al.	0.9432	0.9078	0.8417	0.7761	0.8672
4	Jimenez-Villar et al.	0.9114	0.9211	0.8212	0.8100	0.8659
5	Fernquist	0.9496	0.9061	0.8273	0.7667	0.8624
6	Mahmood	0.9121	0.9167	0.8163	0.7950	0.8600
7	Ipsas & Popescu	0.9345	0.8950	0.8265	0.7822	0.8596
8	Vogel & Jiang	0.9201	0.9056	0.8167	0.7756	0.8545
9	Johansson & Isbister	0.9595	0.8817	0.8379	0.7278	0.8517
10	Goubin et al.	0.9034	0.8678	0.8333	0.7917	0.8491
11	Polignano & de Pinto	0.9182	0.9156	0.7973	0.7417	0.8432
12	Valencia et al.	0.9061	0.8606	0.8432	0.7539	0.8410
13	Kosmajac & Keselj	0.9216	0.8956	0.7928	0.7494	0.8399
14	Fagni & Tesconi	0.9148	0.9144	0.7670	0.7589	0.8388
	char nGrams	0.9360	0.8972	0.7920	0.7289	0.8385
15	Glocker	0.9091	0.8767	0.8114	0.7467	0.8360
	word nGrams	0.9356	0.8833	0.7989	0.7244	0.8356
16	Martinc et al.	0.8939	0.8744	0.7989	0.7572	0.8311
17	Sanchis & Velez	0.9129	0.8756	0.8061	0.7233	0.8295
18	Halvani & Marquardt	0.9159	0.8239	0.8273	0.7378	0.8262
19	Ashraf et al.	0.9227	0.8839	0.7583	0.7261	0.8228
20	Gishamer	0.9352	0.7922	0.8402	0.7122	0.8200
21	Petrik & Chuda	0.9008	0.8689	0.7758	0.7250	0.8176
22	Oliveira et al.	0.9057	0.8767	0.7686	0.7150	0.8165
	W2V	0.9030	0.8444	0.7879	0.7156	0.8127
23	De La Peña & Prieto	0.9045	0.8578	0.7898	0.6967	0.8122
24	López Santillán et al.	0.8867	0.8544	0.7773	0.7100	0.8071
	LDSE	0.9054	0.8372	0.7800	0.6900	0.8032
25	Bolonyai et al.	0.9136	0.8389	0.7572	0.6956	0.8013
26	Moryossef	0.8909	0.8378	0.7871	0.6894	0.8013
27	Zhechev	0.8652	0.8706	0.7360	0.7178	0.7974
28	Giachanou & Ghanem	0.9057	0.8556	0.7731	0.6478	0.7956
29	Espinosa et al.	0.8413	0.7683	0.8413	0.7178	0.7922
30	Rahgouy et al.	0.8621	0.8378	0.7636	0.7022	0.7914
31	Onose et al.	0.8943	0.8483	0.7485	0.6711	0.7906
32	Przybyla	0.9155	0.8844	0.6898	0.6533	0.7858
33	Puertas et al.	0.8807	0.8061	0.7610	0.6944	0.7856
34	Van Halteren	0.8962	0.8283	0.7420	0.6728	0.7848
35	Gamallo & Almatarneh	0.8148	0.8767	0.7220	0.7056	0.7798
36	Bryan & Philipp	0.8689	0.7883	0.6455	0.6056	0.7271
37	Dias & Paraboni	0.8409	0.8211	0.5807	0.6467	0.7224
38	Oliva & Masanet	0.9114	0.9111	0.4462	0.4589	0.6819
39	Hacohen-Kerner et al.	0.4163	0.4744	0.7489	0.7378	0.5944
40	Kloppenburg	0.5830	0.5389	0.4678	0.4483	0.5095
	MAJORITY	0.5000	0.5000	0.5000	0.5000	0.5000
	RANDOM	0.4905	0.4861	0.3716	0.3700	0.4296
41	Bounaama & Amine	0.5008	0.5050	0.2511	0.2567	0.3784
42	Joo & Hwang	0.9333	-	0.8360	-	0.4423
43	Staykovski	0.9186	-	0.8174	-	0.4340
44	Cimino & Dell'Orletta	0.9083	-	0.7898	-	0.4245
45	Ikae et al.	0.9125	-	0.7371	-	0.4124
46	Jeanneau	0.8924	-	0.7451	-	0.4094
47	Zhang	0.8977	-	0.7197	-	0.4044
48	Fahim et al.	0.8629	-	0.6837	-	0.3867
49	Saborit	-	0.8100	-	0.6567	0.3667
50	Saeed & Shirazi	0.7951	-	0.5655	-	0.3402
51	Radarapu	0.7242	-	0.4951	-	0.3048
52	Bennani-Smires	0.9159	-	-	-	0.2290
53	Gupta	0.5007	-	0.4044	-	0.2263
54	Qurdina	0.9034	-	-	-	0.2259
55	Aroyehun	0.5000	-	-	-	0.1250

- Their **gender**, as male, female, or, for the first time, non-binary.
- Their precise **birth year** within a novel, variable-bucket evaluation scheme.
- Their degree of **fame**, as rising, star, or superstar.
- Their **occupation**, as in "claim to fame", categorized as sports, performer, creator, politics, manager, science, professional, or religious.

This is the first installment of celebrity profiling at PAN, with 92 registrations, 12 active participants and seven submitted solutions.

Table 3. Results on both test datasets for the celebrity profiling task.

Team	Test dataset 1					Test dataset 2				
	cRank	gender	age	fame	occup	cRank	gender	age	fame	occup
radivchev	**0.593**	**0.726**	**0.618**	0.551	**0.515**	**0.559**	**0.609**	**0.657**	**0.548**	0.461
morenosandoval	0.541	0.644	0.518	**0.563**	0.469	0.497	0.561	0.516	0.518	0.418
martinc	0.462	0.580	0.361	0.517	0.449	0.465	0.594	0.347	0.507	**0.486**
fernquist	0.424	0.447	0.339	0.493	0.449	0.413	0.465	0.467	0.482	0.300
petrik	0.377	0.595	0.255	0.480	0.340	0.441	0.555	0.360	0.526	0.385
asif	–	–	–	–	–	0.402	0.588	0.254	0.504	0.427
bryan	–	–	–	–	–	0.231	0.335	0.207	0.289	0.165
baseline-rand	0.223	0.344	0.123	0.341	0.125	–	–	–	–	–
baseline-uniform	0.138	0.266	0.117	0.099	0.152	–	–	–	–	–
baseline-mv	0.136	0.278	0.071	0.285	0.121	–	–	–	–	–

3.1 Datasets

The complete dataset for this task contained the Twitter timelines of 48,335 celebrity accounts, annotated with the four social variables gender, birth year, fame, and occupation. We constructed the dataset by matching all verified Twitter accounts to their respective Wikidata entries [34], omitting all memorial and business accounts. This method yielded 71,706 entries for verified, notable, and living humans with an estimated error rate of 0.6%. From these, we sampled all accounts which had Wikidata entries indicating gender, year of birth, and occupation and which had English as their main language marked in their Twitter profile, leaving 48,335 authors, each with an average 2,181 tweets. The training dataset comprised 33,836 authors and the test dataset 14,499 authors; 956 authors were sampled from the latter as small-scale test dataset. To label them, gender and year of birth were extracted from their respective Wikidata items; the 1,379 listed different occupations were grouped into eight categories. Fame was determined based on their number of followers: rising (below 1000), star, and superstar (>100,000). These boundaries reflect the standard deviation of a Gaussian distribution overlaid on the logarithm of the follower distribution across all datasets.

3.2 Evaluation Framework

The performance measure for this task is *cRank*, the harmonic mean of the measures employed for each individual demographic:

$$\text{cRank} = \frac{4}{\frac{1}{F_{1,\text{fame}}} + \frac{1}{F_{1,\text{occupation}}} + \frac{1}{F_{1,\text{gender}}} + \frac{1}{F_{1,\text{birth year}}}}.$$

For gender, fame, and occupation, performance is estimated as multi-class F_1. Since the dataset features a realistic distribution of the social variables, we favored micro- over macro-averaged F_1. For age, we chose a lenient approach: Instead of grouping the year of birth into fixed age buckets, participants were asked to determine a precise year, whereas we applied a variable-bucket strategy during evaluation. Here, the predicted year of birth of an author is correct if it is within an ε-environment of the truth. The threshold ε is between 2 and 9 years, increasing linearly with the true age of the author.

3.3 Results

Altogether, seven participants successfully submitted software to the celebrity profiling task. Table 3 lists the performance of their methods for cRank and the individual measures. A notable observation is that performance is more varied on the more difficult test dataset 1, where leading approaches perform better on the more difficult dataset while others perform weaker. Additionally, while the ordering of participants by cRank is the same for both datasets, it differs for individual demographics. We provide more insights into participants' performance and the analysis of the results in the extended task overview [35].

4 Cross-Domain Authorship Attribution

Authorship attribution [5,9,31] continues to be an important problem in information retrieval and computational linguistics, but also in applied areas such as law and journalism, where knowing the author of a document (such as a ransom note) may enable, e.g., law enforcement to save lives. The most common framework for testing candidate algorithms is the closed-set attribution task: given a sample of reference documents from a restricted and finite set of candidate authors, the task is to determine the most likely author of a previously unseen document of unknown authorship. This task may be quite challenging in cross-domain conditions, when documents of known and unknown authorship come from different domains (e.g., thematic area, genre). In addition, it is often more realistic to assume that the true author of a disputed document is not necessarily included in the list of candidates [10].

This year, we again focus on the attribution task in the context of transformative literature, more colloquially know as 'fanfiction'. Fanfiction refers to a rapidly expanding body of fictional narratives typically produced by non-professional authors who self-identity as 'fans' of a particular oeuvre or individual work [4]. When sharing their texts, fanfiction writers explicitly acknowledge taking inspiration from one (or more) literary domains that are known as 'fandoms'. From the perspective of writing style, fanfiction offers valuable benchmark data: the writings are unmediated and unedited before publication, meaning that they should accurately reflect an individual author's writing style. In the previous edition, this task dealt with authorship attribution in fanfiction, and specifically attribution across different domains or fandoms. This year, we have further increased the difficulty of the task, by focusing on *open-set* attribution conditions, meaning that the true author of a test text is not necessarily included in the list of candidate authors. More formally, an open cross-domain authorship attribution problem can be expressed as a tuple (A, K, U), with A as the set of candidate authors, K as the set of reference (known authorship) texts, and U as the set of unknown authorship texts. For each candidate author $a \in A$, we are given $K_a \subset K$, a set of texts unquestionably written by a. Each text in U should be assigned to exactly one $a \in A$ or the system should refrain from an attribution, if the target author of a text in U is not in A. From a text categorization point of view, K is the training corpus and U is the test corpus. Let D_K be the set of fandoms of texts in K. Then, all texts in U belong to a single (target) fandom $d_U \notin D_K$.

4.1 Datasets

This year's shared task worked with datasets in four major Indo-European languages: English ("en"), French ("fr"), Italian ("it"), and Spanish ("sp"). For each language, 10 "problems" were constructed on the basis of a larger dataset obtained from archiveofourown.org in 2017. Per language, five problems were released as a development set to the participants, in order to calibrate their systems. The final evaluation of the submitted systems was carried out on the five remaining problems (which were not publicly released before the final results were communicated). Each problem had to be solved fully independently from the other problems by a system. Importantly, the development material could not be treated as mere training material for supervised learning approaches, because the sets of candidate authors of the development and the evaluation corpora are not overlapping. Therefore, approaches should not be designed to particularly handle the candidate authors of the development corpus but should focus on their scalability to other author sets.

One "problem" corresponds to a single open-set attribution task, where we distinguish between the "source" and "target" material. The "source" material in each problem contains exactly 7 training texts for exactly 9 candidate authors. In the "target" material, these 9 authors are represented by at least one test text (but potentially more). Additionally, the target material also contains so-called "adversaries", which were not written by one of the candidate authors (indicated by the author label "<UNK>"). The proportion of the number of target texts written by the candidate authors in problems, as opposed to <UNK> documents, was varied across the problems in the development dataset, in order to discourage systems from opportunistic guessing.

Let U_K be the subset of U that includes all test documents actually written by the candidate authors while U_U is the subset of U containing the rest of test documents not written by any candidate author. Then, the *adversary ratio* $a = |U_U|/|U_K|$ determines the likelihood of a test document to belong to one of the candidates. If $a = 0$ (or close to 0), then it is essentially a closed-set attribution scenario, since all test documents belong to the candidate authors (or very few are actually written by adversaries). If $a = 1$, then it is equally probable for a test document to be written by a candidate author or by another author. If $a > 1$, then it is more likely for a test document to be written by an adversary not included in the list of candidates.

In this edition of the authorship attribution task, we examine cases where a ranges from 0.2 to 1.0. In more detail, as can be seen in Table 4, the development dataset comprises 5 problems per language that correspond to $a = [0.2, 0.4, 0.6, 0.8, 1.0]$. This dataset was released in order for the participants to develop and calibrate their submissions. The final evaluation dataset also includes 5 problems per language but with fixed $a = 1$. Thus, the participants are guided to develop generic approaches (varying likelihood a test document is written by a candidate or an adversary). In addition, it is possible to estimate the effectiveness of submitted methods when $a < 1$ by ignoring their answers for specific subsets of U_U in the evaluation dataset.

Table 4. Details about the fanfiction datasets built for the cross-domain authorship attribution task. $|A|$ refer to the size of candidates list, $|K_a|$ is the amount of training documents per author, $|U|$ is the amount of test documents, a is the adversary ratio, and $|d|$ denotes the average length (in words) of documents.

	Language	Problems	$|A|$	$|K_a|$	$|U|$	a	$|d|$
Development	English	5	9	7	137-561	0.2-1.0	804
	French	5	9	7	38-430	0.2-1.0	790
	Italian	5	9	7	46-196	0.2-1.0	814
	Spanish	5	9	7	112-450	0.2-1.0	846
Evaluation	English	5	9	7	98-180	1.0	817
	French	5	9	7	48-290	1.0	790
	Italian	5	9	7	34-302	1.0	821
	Spanish	5	9	7	172-588	1.0	838

4.2 Evaluation Framework

The submissions were separately evaluated in each attribution problem based on their open-set macro-averaged F_1 score (calculated over the training classes, i.e., when <UNK> is excluded) [11]. Participants were ranked according to their average open-set macro-F_1 across all attribution problems of the evaluation corpus. A reference implementation was made available to the participants. As customary, we provide the implementation of three baseline methods that offered an estimation of the overall difficulty of the problem given the state of the art in the field. These implementations were in Python (2.7+) and relied heavily on Scikit-learn and its base packages [14,15] as well as NLTK [1]:

1. BASELINE-SVM: a language-independent authorship attribution approach that frames attribution as a conventional text classification problem [30]. It is based on a character 3-gram representation and a linear SVM classifier with a reject option. It estimates the probabilities of output classes and assigns an unknown document to the <UNK> class when the difference of the top two candidates is less than a threshold.
2. BASELINE-COMPRESSOR: a language-independent approach that uses text compression to estimate the distance of an unknown document to each of the candidate authors (originally proposed by [32] and reproduced by [17]). It assigns an unknown document to the <UNK> class when the difference between the two most likely candidates is lower than a threshold.
3. BASELINE-IMPOSTERS: an implementation of the language-independent "imposters" approach for authorship verification [7,10], based on character tetragram features. During a bootstrapped procedure, the technique iteratively compares an unknown text to each candidate author's stylistic profile, as well as to a set of imposter documents, on the basis of a random feature set. If the highest ranking candidate author does not pass a fixed similarity threshold after this procedure, the document is assigned to the <UNK> class and left unattributed. We included a set of 5,000 problem-external documents per language written by "imposter" authors (the authorship of these texts is also encoded as "<UNK>".)

4.3   Evaluation Results

In total, 12 methods were submitted to the task. The task overview paper contains a more comprehensive overview and discussion of the submitted methods [6]. Table 5 shows an overview of the evaluation results of participants and their ranking according to their macro-F_1 (averaged across all attribution problems of the dataset). As can be seen, all but one submission surpass the three baseline methods. In general, the submitted methods and the baselines achieve better macro-recall than macro-precision. The two top-performing submissions obtain very similar macro-F_1 score. However, the winning approach of Muttenthaler et al. has better macro-precision while Neri et al. achieve better macro-recall. The winning approach also proved to be runtime-efficient.

Table 5. The final evaluation results of the cross-domain authorship attribution task. Participants and baselines are ranked according to macro-F$_1$.

Submission	Macro-Precision	Macro-Recall	Macro-F$_1$	Runtime
Muttenthaler et al.	**0.716**	0.742	**0.690**	00:33:17
Bacciu et al.	0.688	**0.768**	0.680	01:06:08
Custódio et al.	0.664	0.717	0.65	01:21:13
Bartelds & de Vries	0.657	0.719	0.644	11:19:32
Rodríguez et al.	0.651	0.713	0.642	01:59:17
Isbister	0.629	0.706	0.622	01:05:32
Johansson	0.593	0.734	0.616	01:05:30
Basile	0.616	0.692	0.613	00:17:08
Van Halteren	0.590	0.734	0.598	37:05:47
Rahgouy et al.	0.601	0.633	0.580	02:52:03
Gagala	0.689	0.593	0.576	08:22:33
baseline-svm	0.552	0.635	0.545	
baseline-compressor	0.561	0.629	0.533	
baseline-impostors	0.428	0.580	0.395	
Kipnis	0.270	0.409	0.259	20:20:21

5 Style Change Detection

Style change detection tasks at previous PAN editions [8,29,33] aimed to analyze multi-authored documents. In 2016, the task was to identify and group text fragments of individual authors [29], whereas, in 2017, the goal was to determine whether a given document is multi-authored, and if this is the case, to find the borders where authors switch [33]. These tasks showed that accurately identifying individual authors and their contributions within a single document is a complex task. Hence, last year, we substantially relaxed the problem by transforming it into a binary classification task that predicts whether a given document is single- or multi-authored [8]. Considering the promising results achieved by the submitted approaches, we continue last year's task and additionally ask participants to predict the number of involved authors. Hence, this year's style change detection task was defined as follows: given a document, (1) is the document written by one or more authors (i.e., are there style changes or not?), and, (2) if the document is multi-authored, how many authors have collaborated?

5.1 Evaluation Dataset

The datasets provided for training, validation, and testing of the approaches were curated based on data of the StackExchange Q&A platform.[3] We extract user questions and answers from 15 heterogeneous sites, which cover topics ranging from cooking to philosophy. The datasets are assembled by varying the following parameters:

- number of style changes (including 0 for single-authored documents)
- number of collaborating authors (1–5)
- document length (300–1500 tokens)
- allowing changes only at the end or within paragraphs
- uniform or random distribution of changes with respect to segment lengths

The split between training, validation, and test was performed by employing approximate 50/25/25% stratified random sampling. An overview of the datasets is depicted in Table 6, where we list the number of documents for the different number of authors (absolute numbers and relative share in the respective dataset) and the average number of tokens per document for single- and multi-authored documents.

Table 6. Overview style change detection datasets, where SA and MA refer to single-authored and multi-authored documents, respectively, and text length is measured by the average number of tokens per document.

Dataset	Docs	Authors					Text Length	
		1	2	3	4	5	SA	MA
training	2,546	1,273 50.00%	325 12.76%	313 12.29%	328 12.88%	307 12.06%	977	1,604
validation	1,272	636 50.00%	179 14.07%	152 11.95%	160 12.58%	145 11.40%	957	1,582
test	1,210	605 50.00%	147 12.15%	144 11.90%	159 13.15%	155 12.81%	950	1,627

5.2 Performance Measures

The style change detection task comprises answering two questions individually: distinguishing single- from multi-author documents and predicting the number of authors in case of a multi-authored document. Hence, the performance measure employed to assess the quality of the participant's approaches naturally incorporates the performance of the two sub-tasks. Particularly, we employ *accuracy*

---

[3] https://stackexchange.com/.

for the binary classification task of distinguishing between single-authored from multi-authored documents. For measuring the prediction performance regarding the actual number of authors, we reason that in this classification task, we are not only interested in measuring the number of correctly classified documents, but also aim to incorporate the extent to which the prediction differed from the actual class. As our classes employed are integers (the number of authors), we incorporate the distance between the predicted and the actual class in the performance measure. Hence, we employ the *Ordinal Classification Index (OCI)* [3] as an error measure for ordinal data in classification tasks. This index is based on the confusion matrices resulting from the classification task employed and yields a value between 0 and 1, with 0 being the best value (perfect prediction). Besides measuring accuracy and the ordinal classification index individually, we also combine those two measures into a single rank measure:

$$\text{score} = \frac{\text{accuracy} + (1 - \text{OCI})}{2}$$

5.3 Results

The style change detection task received two software submissions, which were evaluated on the TIRA experimentation platform. We depict the participant's results in Table 7, where we list accuracy, the ordinal classification index and the proposed overall rank measure. As can be seen, Nath achieves higher scores for both sub-tasks and hence, also in the combined rank measure. More details on the approaches taken can be found in the task overview [36].

Table 7. Overall results for the style change detection task

Participant	Accuracy	OCI	Rank
Zuo	0.6041	0.8086	0.3978
Nath	0.8479	0.8652	0.4913

6 Summary and Outlook

This year's PAN lab has been quite a success in terms of establishing new tasks for the coming years, community interest and scale, and quality of the newly developed benchmarking resources. While not every task attracted a large number of participants, we hope to continue to develop each one by introducing the new concept of an ongoing online task. Based on the TIRA evaluation platform [18], it becomes manageable to basically keep a task running, accepting new participants with little to no overhead on our part, while giving those who did not find the time to participate ahead of the submission deadline for PAN 2019 to do so afterwards, thereby making an early contribution for PAN 2020. If such a routine could be established, the development of new shared tasks would become more disentangled from a rigid timeline of deadlines. Rather, the only deadline remaining would be a cut-off date for the next PAN workshop that participants who want their submissions published have to meet, whereas they can plan and pursue their submission in their own time throughout the year. Still, many demand deadlines, so that a regular engagement of participants by organizers will continue to be an important part of organizing a shared task. We hope that, using the concept of ongoing online tasks, even tasks that did not attracts lots attention in terms of participants, but that are still of general interest and importance, will get a chance of being promoted. That said, we still plan to nurture our large tasks and to grow them even further, if possible.

Acknowledgments. The work of Paolo Rosso was partially funded by the Spanish MICINN under the research project MISMIS-FAKEnHATE on Misinformation and Miscommunication in social media: FAKE news and HATE speech (PGC2018-096212-B-C31). Our special thanks goes to all PAN participants for providing high-quality submission, to Symanto (https://www.symanto.net) for sponsoring the PAN Lab 2019 and to The Logic Value (https://thelogicvalue.com) for sponsoring the author profiling shared task award.

References

1. Bird, S., Klein, E., Loper, E.: Natural Language Processing with Python. O'Reilly Media, Sebastopol (2009)
2. Cappellato, L., Ferro, N., Losada, D., Müller, H. (eds.): CLEF 2019 Labs and Workshops, Notebook Papers. CEUR Workshop Proceedings. CEUR-WS.org, September 2019
3. Cardoso, J., Sousa, R.: Measuring the performance of ordinal classification. Int. J. Pattern Recognit Artif Intell. **25**(08), 1173–1195 (2011)
4. Hellekson, K., Busse, K. (eds.): The Fan Fiction Studies Reader. University of Iowa Press, Iowa City (2014)
5. Juola, P.: Authorship attribution. Found. Trends Inf. Retrieval **1**(3), 233–334 (2006)
6. Kestemont, M., Stamatatos, E., Manjavacas, E., Daelemans, W., Potthast, M., Stein, B.: Overview of the cross-domain authorship attribution task at PAN 2019. In: Cappellato et al. [2]
7. Kestemont, M., Stover, J.A., Koppel, M., Karsdorp, F., Daelemans, W.: Authenticating the writings of Julius Caesar. Expert Syst. Appl. **63**, 86–96 (2016). https://doi.org/10.1016/j.eswa.2016.06.029
8. Kestemont, M., et al.: Overview of the author identification task at PAN-2018: cross-domain authorship attribution and style change detection. In: Cappellato, L. et al. (eds.) Working Notes Papers of the CLEF 2018 Evaluation Labs, Avignon, France, 10–14 September 2018, pp. 1–25 (2018)
9. Koppel, M., Schler, J., Argamon, S.: Computational methods in authorship attribution. J. Am. Soc. Inf. Sci. Technol. **60**(1), 9–26 (2009)
10. Koppel, M., Winter, Y.: Determining if two documents are written by the same author. J. Assoc. Inf. Sci. Technol. **65**(1), 178–187 (2014)

11. Júnior, P.R.M., et al.: Nearest neighbors distance ratio open-set classifier. Mach. Learn. **106**(3), 359–386 (2017)

12. Mikolov, T., Chen, K., Corrado, G., Dean, J.: Efficient estimation of word representations in vector space. In: Proceedings of Workshop at International Conference on Learning Representations (ICLR 2013) (2013)

13. Mikolov, T., Sutskever, I., Chen, K., Corrado, G.S., Dean, J.: Distributed representations of words and phrases and their compositionality. In: Advances in Neural Information Processing Systems, pp. 3111–3119 (2013)

14. Oliphant, T.: NumPy: A Guide to NumPy. Trelgol Publishing (2006). http://www.numpy.org/

15. Pedregos, F., et al.: Scikit-learn: machine learning in Python. J. Mach. Learn. Res. **12**, 2825–2830 (2011)

16. Pizarro, J.: Using n-grams to detect bots on Twitter: notebook for PAN at CLEF 2019. In: Cappellato et al. [2]

17. Potthast, M., et al.: Who wrote the web? Revisiting influential author identification research applicable to information retrieval. In: Ferro, N., et al. (eds.) ECIR 2016. LNCS, vol. 9626, pp. 393–407. Springer, Cham (2016). https://doi.org/10.1007/978-3-319-30671-1_29

18. Potthast, M., Gollub, T., Wiegmann, M., Stein, B.: TIRA integrated research architecture. In: Ferro, N., Peters, C. (eds.) Information Retrieval Evaluation in a Changing World - Lessons Learned from 20 Years of CLEF. Springer, Heidelberg (2019)

19. Potthast, M., Rosso, P., Stamatatos, E., Stein, B.: A decade of shared tasks in digital text forensics at PAN. In: Azzopardi, L., Stein, B., Fuhr, N., Mayr, P., Hauff, C., Hiemstra, D. (eds.) ECIR 2019. LNCS, vol. 11438, pp. 291–300. Springer, Cham (2019). https://doi.org/10.1007/978-3-030-15719-7_39

20. Rangel, F., Celli, F., Rosso, P., Potthast, M., Stein, B., Daelemans, W.: Overview of the 3rd author profiling task at PAN 2015. In: Cappellato, L., Ferro, N., Jones, G., San Juan, E. (eds.) CLEF 2015 Evaluation Labs and Workshop - Working Notes Papers, 8–11 September, Toulouse, France. CEUR-WS.org (2015)

21. Rangel, F., Rosso, P.: On the implications of the general data protection regulation on the organisation of evaluation tasks. Lang. Law= Linguagem e Direito **5**(2), 95–117 (2018)

22. Rangel, F., Rosso, P.: Overview of the 7th author profiling task at PAN 2019: bots and gender profiling. In: Cappellato et al. [2]

23. Rangel, F., et al.: Overview of the 2nd author profiling task at PAN 2014. In: Cappellato, L., Ferro, N., Halvey, M., Kraaij, W. (eds.) CLEF 2014 Evaluation Labs and Workshop - Working Notes Papers, 15–18 September, Sheffield, UK. CEUR-WS.org (2014)

24. Rangel, F., Franco-Salvador, M., Rosso, P.: A low dimensionality representation for language variety identification. In: Gelbukh, A. (ed.) CICLing 2016. LNCS, vol. 9624, pp. 156–169. Springer, Cham (2018). https://doi.org/10.1007/978-3-319-75487-1_13

25. Rangel, F., Rosso, P., G'omez, M.M., Potthast, M., Stein, B.: Overview of the 6th author profiling task at PAN 2018: multimodal gender identification in Twitter. In: CLEF 2018 Labs and Workshops, Notebook Papers. CEUR Workshop Proceedings. CEUR-WS.org (2017)

26. Rangel, F., Rosso, P., Koppel, M., Stamatatos, E., Inches, G.: Overview of the author profiling task at PAN 2013. In: Forner, P., Navigli, R., Tufis, D. (eds.) CLEF 2013 Evaluation Labs and Workshop - Working Notes Papers, 23–26 September, Valencia, Spain, September 2013

27. Rangel, F., Rosso, P., Potthast, M., Stein, B.: Overview of the 5th author profiling task at PAN 2017: gender and language variety identification in Twitter. In: Cappellato, L., Ferro, N., Goeuriot, L., Mandl, T. (eds.) Working Notes Papers of the CLEF 2017 Evaluation Labs. CEUR Workshop Proceedings, CLEF and CEUR-WS.org, September 2017

28. Rangel, F., Rosso, P., Verhoeven, B., Daelemans, W., Potthast, M., Stein, B.: Overview of the 4th author profiling task at PAN 2016: cross-genre evaluations. In: Balog, K., Cappellato, L., Ferro, N., Macdonald, C. (eds.) CLEF 2016 Labs and Workshops, Notebook Papers. CEUR Workshop Proceedings. CEUR-WS.org., September 2016

29. Rosso, P., Rangel, F., Potthast, M., Stamatatos, E., Tschuggnall, M., Stein, B.: Overview of PAN'16: new challenges for authorship analysis: cross-genre profiling, clustering, diarization, and obfuscation. In: Fuhr, N., et al. (eds.) CLEF 2016. LNCS, vol. 9822, pp. 332–350. Springer, Cham (2016). https://doi.org/10.1007/978-3-319-44564-9_28

30. Sebastiani, F.: Machine learning in automated text categorization. ACM Comput. Surv. **34**(1), 1–47 (2002)

31. Stamatatos, E.: A survey of modern authorship attribution methods. J. Am. Soc. Inf. Sci. Technol. **60**, 538–556 (2009)

32. Teahan, W.J., Harper, D.J.: Using compression-based language models for text categorization. In: Croft, W.B., Lafferty, J. (eds.) Language Modeling for Information Retrieval. INRE, vol. 13, pp. 141–165. Springer, Dordrecht (2003). https://doi.org/10.1007/978-94-017-0171-6_7

33. Tschuggnall, M., et al.: Overview of the author identification task at PAN-2017: style breach detection and author clustering. In: Cappellato, L. et al. (eds.) Working Notes Papers of the CLEF 2017 Evaluation Labs, pp. 1–22 (2017)

34. Wiegmann, M., Stein, B., Potthast, M.: Celebrity profiling. In: 57th Annual Meeting of the Association for Computational Linguistics (ACL 2019). Association for Computational Linguistics, July 2019

35. Wiegmann, M., Stein, B., Potthast, M.: Overview of the celebrity profiling task at PAN 2019. In: Cappellato et al. [2]

36. Zangerle, E., Tschuggnall, M., Specht, G., Potthast, M., Stein, B.: Overview of the style change detection task at PAN 2019. In: Cappellato et al. [2]

Overview of the CLEF 2019 Personalised Information Retrieval Lab (PIR-CLEF 2019)

Gabriella Pasi[1], Gareth J. F. Jones[2], Lorraine Goeuriot[3], Liadh Kelly[4], Stefania Marrara[5(✉)], and Camilla Sanvitto[1]

[1] University of Milano Bicocca, Milan, Italy
[2] Dublin City University, Dublin, Ireland
[3] Universit Grenoble Alpes, Grenoble, France
[4] Maynooth University, Maynooth, Ireland
[5] Consorzio C2T, Milan, Italy
stefania.marrara@consorzioc2t.it

Abstract. The Personalised Information Retrieval Lab (PIR-CLEF 2019) lab is an initiative aimed at both providing and critically analysing the evaluation of Personalization in Information Retrieval (PIR) applications. PIR-CLEF 2019 is the second edition of the Lab after the successful Pilot lab organised at CLEF 2017 and the first edition of the Lab at CLEF 2018. PIR-CLEF 2019 provided registered participants with two tracks: the Web Search Task and the Medical Search Task. The Web Search Task continues the activities introduced in the previous editions of the PIR-CLEF Lab, while the Medical Search Track focuses on personalisation within an ad hoc search task introduced in previous editions of the CLEF eHealth Lab.

1 Introduction

The PIR-CLEF Lab at CLEF 2019 provides a framework for the evaluation of Personalised Information Retrieval (PIR). The application of personalisation in IR seeks to enhance traditional IR systems to better satisfy the information needs of individual users. PIR systems are intended to provide search results that are not only relevant to the query in general, but more specifically to the specific interests of the user who submitted the query. In order to provide a personalised service, a PIR system can leverage various types of information about the current user and their preferences and interests. These can be stated directly by the user, or may be inferred through a variety of interactions of the user with the system. This information is then represented in some form of user model, which can be employed in the search process with the objective of improving the search results for this user. This typically operates either by seeking to improve the user's query or by re-ranking a set of retrieved results so that documents more relevant to the user are presented in the top positions of a retrieval list.

F. Crestani et al. (Eds.): CLEF 2019, LNCS 11696, pp. 417–424, 2019.
https://doi.org/10.1007/978-3-030-28577-7_31

Evaluating the effectiveness of personalised approaches to search has been investigated for many years within studies of interactive IR In this work, the notion of relevance has been user centered with potential variation during a search session, depending both on the task at hand and on the user's interactions with the search system. This work has mostly been based on user studies; this approach involves real users undertaking search tasks in a supervised environment. By placing the user at the centre of the evaluation activity these studies have produced valuable insights and feedback. However, while this methodology has the advantage of enabling the detailed study of the activities of real users, it has the significant drawback of not being easily reproducible. This greatly limits the scope for algorithmic exploration of technologies for search personalisation. Among some previous attempts to define PIR benchmark tasks based on the Cranfield paradigm, the closest experiment to the PIR Lab is the TREC Session track[1] conducted annually between 2010 and 2014. This track focused on stand-alone search sessions, where a "session" is a continuous sequence of query reformulations on the same topic, along with any user interaction with the retrieved results in service of satisfying a specific information need; however no details of the searcher undertaking the task have been made available. Thus, the TREC Session track did not exploit any user model to personalise the search experience, nor did it allow user actions over multiple search sessions to be taken into consideration in the ranking of the search output.

The PIR-CLEF 2019 Lab had 29 registrations, and offered two distinct tasks: the Web Search Task and the Medical Search Task to evaluate personalised search.

The Web Search Task aimed to explore personalisation in Web search sessions based on user profiles and activity with the current and previous search sessions by this user [1]. Task participants were provided with user profile data and logs of search activity with the objective of improving search effectiveness over that achieved in the logged search sessions. In particular, the participants were provided with a test dataset and with a training dataset, delivered in two stages. This task was a direct extension of the tasks offered in PIR-CLEF at CLEF 2017 [2] and CLEF 2018 [3].

The Medical Search Task addresed medical search, which is one of the most common interests of users of search engines. For this year's pilot task, the challenge offered to participants was to work on the task of generating PIR techniques for queries posed by patients on viewing their discharge summaries, where the discharge summaries are used in this personalisation process. Optionally additional resources (ontologies) could also be used in their IR techniques. Participants were invited to submit any type of run they wanted to, so long as it was personalised in some way. This pilot challenge used test collections originating from CLEF eHealth 2013 and 2014 IR challenges [4,5].

The remainder of this paper is organised as follows: Sect. 2 outlines existing related work, Sect. 3 provides an overview of the PIR-CLEF 2019 tasks, and Sect. 4 concludes the paper.

---

[1] http://trec.nist.gov/data/session.html.

2   Related Work

Recent years have seen increasing attention in the study of context in search. Of particular interest here is the personalisation of search by incorporating knowledge of user preferences into the search process [6]. This focus on the incorporation of the individual user into the search process has raised the related issue of how to properly evaluate the effectiveness of personalised search in a scenario where relevance is strongly dependent on the interpretation of the individual user. To this end, several user-based evaluation frameworks have been developed, as discussed in [7].

A first category of approaches aimed at evaluating Personalised Information Retrieval Systems (PIRS) which focus on performing user-centered evaluation by providing a kind of extension to the laboratory based evaluation paradigm. The TREC Interactive track [8] and the TREC HARD track [9] are examples of this kind of evaluation framework. These aimed at involving users in interactive tasks to get additional information about them and the query context. The evaluation was done by comparing a baseline run ignoring the user/topic metadata with another run in which it is considered.

The more recent TREC Contextual Suggestion track [10] was proposed with the purpose of investigating search techniques for complex information needs that are highly dependent on both context and the user's interests. Participants in the track were given, as input, a set of geographical contexts and a set of user profiles containing a list of attractions that the user had previously rated. The task was to produce a list of ranked suggestions for each profile-context pair by exploiting the given contextual information. However, despite these extensions, the overall evaluation was still system controlled and only a few contextual features were available in the process.

TREC also introduced a Session track [11], the focus of which was to exploit user interactions during a query session to incrementally improve the results within that session. The novelty of this task was the evaluation of system performance over entire sessions instead of a single query.

The above tasks have various limitations in their injection of user behaviour into the evaluation process; for this reason the problem of defining a standard approach to the evaluation of personalised search is a hot research topic, which needs effective solutions.

A first attempt to create a collection satisfactorily accounting for the user behaviour in search was done in the FIRE Conference held in 2011. The Personalised and Collaborative Information Retrieval track [12] was organised with the aim of extending a standard IR ad-hoc test collection by gathering additional meta-information during the topic development process to facilitate research on personalised and collaborative IR. However, since no runs were submitted to this track, only preliminary studies were carried out and reported using it.

Within CLEF 2017 we launched the PIR-CLEF benchmark with a pilot study and workshop (PIR CLEF 2017), for the purpose of providing a forum for the exploration of the evaluation of PIR. The PIR-CLEF 2017 Pilot Task was a Web Search task which sought to combine user-centered methods with the

Cranfield evaluation paradigm, with the key potential benefit of producing evaluation results that are easily reproducible. The Pilot task was based on search sessions over a subset of the ClueWeb12 document collection, undertaken by 10 users by using a clearly defined and novel methodology. This collection was distributed to the participants of the PIR-CLEF 2018 [3]. A second collection was also prepared for the PIR-CLEF 2018 lab, but this was not used by any participants. PIR-CLEF at CLEF 2019 continued with the Web Search Task, but also introduced a Medical Search Task.

3   PIR-CLEF 2019 Search Tasks

In this section, we give details of the two tasks offered at PIR-CLEF 2019. We look first at the Web Search Task and then give details of the Medical Search Task.

3.1   Web Search Task

The PIR-CLEF 2019 Web Search task used both of the collections previously developed for PIR-CLEF 2017 and PIR-CLEF 2018. The 2017 data collection was released to PIR-CLEF 2019 participants first as a training dataset, with the 2018 collection released later as a test dataset. The data collection and processing are described in detail in [3]. Here we give summary details of the collection procedure.

- *Data gathering.* This phase involved a group of volunteer users carrying out a task-based search session. Each session was performed by the user on a topic of her choice selected from a provided list of broad topics, and search carried out over a subset of the ClueWeb12 web collection. During this session the activities performed by the user were recorded (e.g, formulated queries, bookmarked documents, etc.). Each search session was composed of a phase of query development, refinement and modification, and associated search with each query on a specific topical domain selected by the user, followed by a relevance assessment phase where the user indicated the relevance of documents returned in response to each query and a short report writing activity based on the search activity undertaken.
- *Data cleaning and preparation.* This phase took place once the data gathering had been completed, and did not involve any user participation. It consisted of filtering and elaborating the information collected in the previous phase in order to prepare a dataset with various kinds of information related to the specific user's preferences. In addition, a bag-of-words representation of the participant's user profile was created to allow comparative evaluation of PIR algorithms using the same simple user model.

The aim of the Web Search task was to use the provided datasets to improve the ranking of a search results list over a baseline ranking of documents judged relevant to the query by the user who entered the query.

The task data provided to registered participants consisted of a set of csv files. They were also provided with access to the search service used in the user search sessions, provided via an API by Dublin City University.

The data provided included the submitted queries, the baseline ranked lists of documents retrieved in response to each query by using a standard search system, the items clicked by the user in the result list, and the documents' relevance assessments provided by the user on a 4-grade scale. The data was extracted and stored in csv format in 7 files in a zip folder. Full details of the files are given in [3].

We encouraged participants to be involved in the task by using existing or new algorithms and/or to explore new ideas. We also welcomed contributions that make an analysis of the task and/or of the dataset.

The metrics and methodology used to evaluate and analyze PIR tasks pose significant challenges, which is one of the key motivations underlying the development of the PIR-CLEF Lab. It is not at all obvious how we might properly compare and contrast the behaviour of alternative methods of integrating personalisation into search sessions. While we can begin by using standard metrics, such as Average Precision (AP) and Normalized Discounted Cumulative Gain (NDCG) these are not sufficient to enable a detailed session based analysis of PIR methods.

As a starting point for the development of formal methodology for analysis and evaluation of our framework for laboratory-based evaluation of PIR in the Web Search task, we developed a prototype evaluation tool described in [3]. This tool has been tested with sample data collected using our session-based framework, and the intention is to analyze participant submissions to the PIR-CLEF 2019 Web Search task using this tool, both to enable detailed analysis of their submissions, but also to enable us to refine the features of the analysis tool itself.

3.2   Medical Search Task

For the new pilot Medical Search task, we challenged participants to work on the task of generating personalised retrieval techniques for the queries posed by patients on viewing their discharge summaries. The discharge summaries and optionally other external resources were to be used in this personalisation process. For this challenge a large collection of web pages was provided, along with patient queries and associated discharge summaries. This test collection was generated in the CLEF eHealth 2013 and 2014 IR challenges [4,5]. Participants were invited to submit any type of run they wanted to the challenge, so long as it was somehow personalised.

The data set for this task consists of a set of medical-related documents, provided by the Khresmoi project[2]. This collection contains documents covering a broad set of medical topics, and does not contain any patient information. The documents in the collection come from several online sources, including the

---

[2] http://www.khresmoi.eu.

Health On the Net organisation certified websites, as well as well-known medical sites and databases (e.g. Genetics Home Reference, ClinicalTrial.gov, Diagnosia). The topic set consists of 50 topics which were previously distributed with CLEF eHealth 2013 IR challenge and 50 topics which were distributed with CLEF eHealth 2014 IR challenge.

The 50 2013 topics were manually generated by medical professionals from highlighted disorders identified in annotated medical discharge summaries. In 2014, the 50 topics were manually generated by medical professionals from the main disorder diagnosed in the discharge summary. A mapping between queries and task 1 matching discharge summary is provided, the participants can get access to the discharge summary (from the MIMIC II database), explained below.

Topics consist of:

- *Title:* text of the query,
- *Description:* longer description of what the query means,
- *Narrative:* expected content of the relevant documents,
- *Profile:* main information on the patient (age, gender, condition),
- *Discharge_summary:* ID of the matching discharge summary

For the 2019 challenge, participants were challenged to use the discharge summaries for personalisation.

The *discharge summaries* consist of deidentified clinical free-text notes from the MIMIC II database, version 2.5[3]. Notes were authored in the ICU setting and note types include discharge summaries, ECG reports, echo reports, and radiology reports (for more information about the MIMIC II database, we refer the reader to the MIMIC User Guide).

The PIR-CLEF organisers did not provide direct access to the discharge summaries, participants were required to follow MIMIC II guidelines to access it[4].

Relevance judgements (qrel files) created by the CLEF eHealth challenge are also used in this year's challenge were provided. Details on how the qrel files were generated are available in [4,5].

Given this year's pilot Medical search task did not offer an interactive personalisation element, standard IR evaluation metrics were used for this task in 2019. Specifically, the focus was on P@5, P@10, NDCG@5, NDCG@10. Evaluation metrics are computed using the trec_eval tool[5].

4   Conclusions and Future Work

This paper described the Web Search and Medical Search Tasks offer at PIR-CLEF 2019. The Web Search task extends the work of the previous PIR-CLEF activities at CLEF 2017 and CLEF 2018, while the Medical Search Task builds

---

[3] http://mimic.physionet.org/.

[4] https://mimic.physionet.org/gettingstarted/access/.

[5] http://trec.nist.gov/trec_eval/.

on previous work in the CLEF eHealth Lab. The purpose of the PIR-CLEF Lab is to enable research groups to work on comparative evaluation methods for the introduction of personalisation in IR and to study its evaluation. Unfortunately, while almost 30 groups registered to participant in the PIR-CLEF 2019 Lab, none of them returned results for either of the available tasks.

References

1. Sanvitto, C., Ganguly, D., Jones, G.J.F., Pasi, G.: A laboratory-based method for the evaluation of personalised search. In: Proceedings of the Seventh International Workshop on Evaluating Information Access (EVIA 2016), A Satellite Workshop of the NTCIR-12 Conference, Tokyo Japan (2016)
2. Pasi, G., Jones, G.J.F., Marrara, S., Sanvitto, C., Ganguly, D., Sen, P.: Overview of the CLEF 2017 personalised information retrieval pilot lab (PIR-CLEF 2017). In: Jones, G.J.F., et al. (eds.) CLEF 2017. LNCS, vol. 10456, pp. 338–345. Springer, Cham (2017). https://doi.org/10.1007/978-3-319-65813-1_29
3. Pasi, G., et al.: Overview of the CLEF 2018 personalised information retrieval lab (PIR-CLEF 2018). In: Proceedings of CLEF 2018, Avignon, France (2018)
4. Goeuriot, L., et al.: ShARe/CLEF eHealth evaluation lab 2013, task 3: information retrieval to address patients' questions when reading clinical reports. In: CLEF 2013 Online Working Notes, 8138 (2013)
5. Goeuriot, L., et al.: ShARe/CLEF eHealth evaluation lab 2014, task 3: user-centred health information retrieval. In: Proceedings of CLEF 2014 (2014)
6. Pasi, G.: Issues in personalising information retrieval. IEEE Intell. Inform. Bull. 11(1), 3–7 (2010)
7. Tamine-Lechani, L., Boughanem, M., Daoud, M.: Evaluation of contextual information retrieval effectiveness: overview of issues and research. Knowl. Inf. Syst. 24(1), 1–34 (2009)
8. Harman, D.: Overview of the fourth text retrieval conference (TREC-4). In: Harman, D.K., (eds.) TREC, volume Special Publication 500–236. National Institute of Standards and Technology (NIST) (1995)
9. Allan, J.: HARD track overview in TREC 2003: high accuracy retrieval from documents. In: Proceedings of The Twelfth Text REtrieval Conference (TREC 2003), Gaithersburg, Maryland, USA, pp. 24–37 (2003)
10. Dean-Hall, A., Clarke, C.L.A., Kamps, J., Thomas, P., Voorhees, E.M.: Overview of the TREC 2012 contextual suggestion track. In Voorhees and Bucklan
11. Carterette, B., Kanoulas, E., Hall, M.M., Clough, P.D.: Overview of the TREC 2014 session track. In: Proceedings of The Twenty-Third Text REtrieval Conference (TREC 2014), Gaithersburg, Maryland, USA (2014)
12. Ganguly, D., Leveling, J., Jones, G.J.F.: Overview of the personalized and collaborative information retrieval (PIR) track at FIRE-2011. In: Majumder, P., Mitra, M., Bhattacharyya, P., Subramaniam, L.V., Contractor, D., Rosso, P. (eds.) FIRE 2010-2011. LNCS, vol. 7536, pp. 227–240. Springer, Heidelberg (2013). https://doi.org/10.1007/978-3-642-40087-2_22
13. Villegas, M., Puigcerver, J., Toselli, A.H., Sanchez, J.A., Vidal, E.: Overview of the ImageCLEF 2016 handwritten scanned document retrieval task. In: Proceedings of CLEF 2016 (2016)
14. Robertson, S.: A new interpretation of average precision. In: Proceedings of the International ACM SIGIR Conference on Research and Development in Information Retrieval (SIGIR 2008), pp. 689–690. ACM, New York (2008)

15. Angiolillo, A.: Comparative Evaluation of Personalised Search Systems. Università degli Studi di Milano Bicocca, Milano (2017)
16. Moffat, A., Zobel, J.: Rank-biased precision for measurement of retrieval effectiveness. ACM Trans. Inf. Syst. (TOIS) **27**(1), 2 (2008)
17. Bai, Q., Chen, J., Hu, Q., He, L.: ECNU at CLEF PIR 2018: evaluation of personalized information retrieval. In: Working Notes of CLEF 2018 - Conference and Labs of the Evaluation Forum, Avignon, France (2018)
18. Andreu-Marín, A., Martnez-Santiago, F., Ureña-López, L.A., Díaz-Galiano, M.C.: PIR Based in explicit and implicit feedback. In: Working Notes of CLEF 2018 - Conference and Labs of the Evaluation Forum, Avignon, France (2018)

Overview of CLEF 2019 Lab ProtestNews: Extracting Protests from News in a Cross-Context Setting

Ali Hürriyetoğlu[✉], Erdem Yörük, Deniz Yüret, Çağrı Yoltar, Burak Gürel, Fırat Duruşan, Osman Mutlu, and Arda Akdemir

Koc University, 34450 Istanbul, Turkey
{ahurriyetoglu,eryoruk,dyuret,cyoltar,bgurel,
fdurusan,omutlu,aakdemir}@ku.edu.tr
http://www.ku.edu.tr

Abstract. We present an overview of the CLEF-2019 Lab ProtestNews on Extracting Protests from News in the context of generalizable natural language processing. The lab consists of document, sentence, and token level information classification and extraction tasks that were referred as task 1, task 2, and task 3 respectively in the scope of this lab. The tasks required the participants to identify protest relevant information from English local news at one or more aforementioned levels in a cross-context setting, which is cross-country in the scope of this lab. The training and development data were collected from India and test data was collected from India and China. The lab attracted 58 teams to participate in the lab. 12 and 9 of these teams submitted results and working notes respectively. We have observed neural networks yield the best results and the performance drops significantly for majority of the submissions in the cross-country setting, which is China.

Keywords: Natural language processing · Information retrieval · Machine learning · Text classification · Information extraction · Event extraction · Computational social science · Generalizability

1 Introduction

We describe a realization of our task set proposal [4] in the scope of CLEF-2019 Lab ProtestNews.[1,2] The task set aims at facilitating development of generalizable natural language processing (NLP) tools that are robust in a cross-context setting, which is cross-country in this lab. Since the performance of NLP tools significantly drop in a context different from the one they are created and validated [1,2,6], measuring and improving state-of-the-art NLP tool development methodology is the primary aim of our efforts.

---

[1] http://clef2019.clef-initiative.eu/.
[2] https://emw.ku.edu.tr/clef-protestnews-2019/.

© Springer Nature Switzerland AG 2019
F. Crestani et al. (Eds.): CLEF 2019, LNCS 11696, pp. 425–432, 2019.
https://doi.org/10.1007/978-3-030-28577-7_32

Comparative social and political science studies facilitate protest information to analyze cross-country similarities, differences, and effect of these actions. Therefore our lab focuses on classifying and extracting protest event information in English local news articles from India and China. We believe our efforts will contribute to enhance the methodologies applied to collect data for these studies. This need was motivated based on the recent results that shows NLP tools, those of text classification and information extraction, have not been satisfactory against the requirements of longer time coverage and working on data from multiple countries [3,7].

This first iteration of our lab attracted 58 teams from all around the world. 12 of these teams submitted their results to one or more tasks on the CodaLab page of the lab.[3] 9 teams described their approach in terms of a working note.

We introduce the task set we tackle, the corpus we have been creating, and the evaluation methodology in Sects. 2, 3, and 4 respectively. We report the results in Sect. 5 and conclude our report in Sect. 6.

2   Task Set

The lab consists of the tasks document classification, event sentence detection and event extraction, which are referred as task 1, task 2, and task 3 respectively, as demonstrated in Fig. 1. The document classification task, which is task 1, requires predicting whether a news article report at least one protest event that has happened or is happening. It is a binary classification task that require to predict whether a news article label should be 1 (positive) or 0 (negative). The sentences that contain any event trigger should be identified in task 2, which is event sentence detection task. Sentence labels are 0 and 1 as well. This task could be handled either as classification or extraction task as we provide order of the sentences in their respective articles. Finally, the event triggers and event information, which are place, facility, time, organizer, participant, and target, should be extracted in task 3. This order of tasks provides a controlled setting that enables error analysis and optimization possibility during annotation and tool development efforts. Moreover, this design enable analyzing steps of the analysis that contributes to explainability of the automated tool predictions.

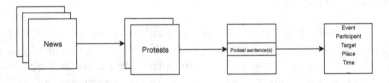

Fig. 1. The lab consists of (a) *Task 1*: Document classification, (b) *Task 2*: Event sentence detection, and (c) *Task 3*: Event extraction.

---

[3] https://competitions.codalab.org/competitions/20318.

3   Data

We provide the number of instances for each task in Table 1 in terms of training, development, test 1, and test 2 data. The training and development data was collected from online local English news from India. Test 1 and test 2 data refer to data from India and China respectively.

Table 1. Number of instances for each task

	Training	Development	Test 1 (India)	Test 2 (China)
Task 1	3, 429	456	686	1, 800
Task 2	5, 884	662	1, 106	1, 234
Task 3	250	36	80	39

A sample from task 1 contains the news article's text, its URL and its label that is assigned by the annotation team. For task 2: sentences, their labels, their order in the article's text they belong, and the URL of their article are available in samples. The release format of the data for task 2 enable participants to treat this task either as classification of individual sentences or extracting event relevant sentences from a document.

The data for task 3 consists of snippets that contain one or more event trigger that refer to the same event. Multiple sentences may occur in a snippet in case these sentences refer to the same event.[4] The tokens in these snippets are annotated using IOB, inside, outside, beginning, scheme. The examples of data is provided in Fig. 2.

There is not any overlap of news articles across tasks. This separation was required in order to avoid any misuse of data from one task to infer the labels for another task without any effort.

3.1   Distribution

We distributed the data set in a way that does not violate copyright of the news sources. This involves only sharing information that is needed to reproduce the corpus from the source for task 1 and task 2 and only relevant snippets for task 3. We released a Docker image that contains the toolbox[5] required to reproduce the news articles on the computer of a participant. The toolbox generates a log of the process that reproduce the data set and we have requested these log files from the participants. The toolbox is a pipeline that scrapes HTMLs, converts HTMLs to text and finally performs specific filling operation for each of task 1 and task 2. To the best of our knowledge, the toolbox succeeded in enabling participants create the data set on their computers. Only one participant from Iran was not able to download the news articles due to restrictions to access online content that are specific to his geolocation.

---

[4] Snippets we share contain information about only a single event.
[5] https://github.com/emerging-welfare/ProtestNews-2019.

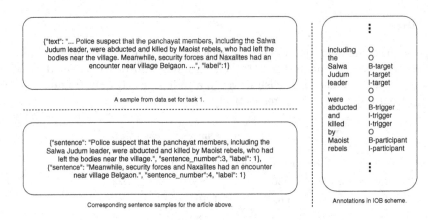

Fig. 2. Data samples for task 1, task 2, and task 3

4   Evaluation Setting

We use macro averaged F1 due to class imbalance present in our data for evaluating the task 1 and task 2. The event extraction task, which is task 3, was evaluated on the average F1 score of all information types that was based on the ratio of the full match between the prediction and the annotations in the test sets, using a python implementation[6] of CoNLL 2003 shared task [5] evaluation script.

We performed two levels of evaluation that were on data from the source country (Test 1) and from target country (Test 2). The participants were informed only about labels of the training and development data from the source country. They did not see labels of any test set. The number of allowed submissions and the period the participants can submit their predictions for Test 1 and Test 2 was determined in a way that restrict the possibility of over-fitting on test data.

We applied three cycles of evaluation. Participants could submit unlimited number of results without being able to see their score. Their last submitted results' scores were announced at the end of each evaluation cycle. First and second cycles aimed at providing feedback to the participants. The third and final cycle was the deadline for submitting results.

Finally, we provided a baseline submission for task 1 and task 2 in order to guide the participants. This baseline was based on predictions of the best scoring machine learning model among Support Vector Machines, Naive Bayes, Rocchio classifier, Ridge Classifier, Perceptron, Passive Aggressive Classifier, Random Forest, K Nearest Neighbors, and Elastic Net on development set. The best scoring model was a linear support vector machines classifier that was trained using stochastic gradient descent.

---

[6] https://github.com/sighsmile/conlleval

5   Results

We facilitated CodaLab platform for managing the submissions and maintain a leaderboard.[7] The leaderboard for task 1 and task 2 is presented in Table 2. The column names has the following format Test <task number>-<test number>, e.g. Test 1-1 stands for the Test 1 of task 1. The results for ProtestLab_Baseline is the aforementioned baseline that was submitted by us.

Table 2. Results that are ranked based on average F1 scores of Test 1 and Test 2 for task 1 and task 2

	Test 1-1	Test 1-2	Test 2-1	Test 2-2	Avg
ASafaya	.81	.63	**.70**	.60	.69
PrettyCrocodile	.79	.60	.65	**.64**	.67
LevelUp Research	**.83**	**.65**	.66	.45	.65
Provos_RUG	.80	.59	.63	.55	.64
GS	.78	.56	.64	.58	.64
Be-LISI	.76	.50	.58	.30	.54
ProtestLab_Baseline	.83	.49	.58	.20	.52
CIC-NLP	.59	.50	.52	.34	.49
SSNCSE1	.38	.15	.56	.35	.36
iAmirSoltani	.69	.36	-	-	.26
Sayeed Salam	.55	.28	-	-	.20
SEDA lab	.58	-	.15	.02	.19

The summary of the approaches and results of each team that participated in task 1 and or task 2 are provided below.[8]

ASafaya (Sakarya University) submitted the best results for task 2 and for average of task 1 and task 2 using Bidirectional Gated Recurrent Unit (GRU) based model. Although this model perform the best in average, the performance of this model drops across the context significantly.

PrettyCrocodile (National Research University HSE) submitted the second best average results that were predicted using Embeddings from Language Models (ELMo). The performance of the model is comparable in the cross-context setting for task 2.

LevelUp Research (University of North Carolina at Charlotte) has applied multi-task learning based on LSTM units using word embeddings

---

[7] https://competitions.codalab.org/competitions/22349#results.

[8] We have not received details of the submissions from CIC-NLP, iAmirSoltani, and Sayeed Salam. The details of other approaches can be found in the respective working notes that were published in proceedings of CLEF 2019 Lab ProtestNews.

from a pre-trained FastText model. This method yielded the best results for task 1.

Provos_RUG (University of Groningen) has implemented a feature based stacked ensemble model based on FastText embeddings and a set of different basic Logistic Regression classifiers that enabled their predictions to rank fourth among the participating teams.

GS (University of Bremen) has stacked the word embeddings such as GloVe and FastText together with the contextualized embeddings generated from Flair language models (LM). This approach was ranked fourth in general and third for task 2.

Be-LISI (Université de Carthage) combined the logistic regression with linguistic processing and expansion of the text with related terms using word embedding similarity. This approach marked a significant difference in terms of overall performance, which is the drop from .64 to .54, in comparison to higher ranked submissions.

SSNCSE1 (Sri Sivasubramaniya College of Engineering) reported results of their bi-directional LSTM that applies Bahdanau, Normed-Bahdanau, Luong, and Scaled-Luong attentions. The submission that uses Bahdanau attention yielded the results reported in Table 2.

SEDA lab (University of Exeter) applied support vector machines and XGBoost classifiers that are combined with various word embedding approaches. Results of this submission showed promising performance in terms of precision on both document and sentence classification tasks.

Task 1 was best solved by. Task 2 best by.
Drastically lower after the fourth.

We analyze task 3 results separate from task 1 and task 2 as it differs from them. The F1 scores for task 3 are presented in Table 2 (Table 3).

Table 3. Results that are ranked based on average score of Test 1 and Test 2 for Task 3

	Test 3-1	Test 3-2	Avg
GS	.604	.532	.568
DeepNEAT	.601	.513	.557
Provos_RUG	.600	.456	.528
PrettyCrocodile	.524	.425	.474
LevelUp Research	.516	.394	.455

GS (University of Bremen) submitted the best results for task 3 using a BiLSTM-CRF model incorporating pooled contextualized flair embeddings, and their model was the best in generalizing.

DeepNEAT (FloodTags & Radboud University) compares the submitted ELMO+BiLSTM model to a traditional CRF and shows that the former is better and more generalizable.

Provos_RUG (University of Groningen) divides the task 3 into two as event trigger detection task and event argument detection task using BiLSTM-CRF model with word embeddings, POS embeddings, and character-level embeddings for both subtasks. He further extends the features for latter subtask with learned embeddings for dependency relations and event triggers.

PrettyCrocodile (National Research University HSE) makes use of ELMO embeddings with different architectures, achieving her best score for task 3 using a BiLSTM.

LevelUp Research (University of North Carolina at Charlotte) implemented a multi-task neural model that require a time-ordered sequence of word vectors representative of a document or sentence. The LSTM layer has been replaced by a layer of bidirectional gated recurrent units (GRU).

6   Conclusion

The results show how text classification and information extraction tool performances drops between two contexts. The scores on data from the target country are significantly lower than on data from the source country. Only the PrettyCrocodile team performed comparatively well across contexts for task 2. Although it is not the best scoring system for neither task 1 nor task 2, PrettyCrocodile team's approach show some promise toward tackling the generalizability of NLP tools.

The generalization of automated tools is an issue that has recently attracted much attention.[9] However, as we have determined in our lab, generalizability is still a challenge for state-of-the-art methodology. Consequently, we will continue our efforts by repeating this practice and extending the data and will be adding data from new countries and languages to our setting. The next iteration will run in the scope of the Workshop on Challenges and Opportunities in Automated Coding of COntentious Political Events (Cope 2019) at European Symposium Series on Societal Challenges in Computational Social Science (Euro CSS 2019).[10,11,12]

Acknowledgments. This work is funded by the European Research Council (ERC) Starting Grant 714868 awarded to Dr. Erdem Yörük for his project Emerging Welfare. We are grateful to our steering committee members for the CLEF 2019 lab Sophia Ananiadou, Antal van den Bosch, Kemal Oflazer, Arzucan Özgür, Aline Villavicencio, and Hristo Tanev. Finally, we thank to Theresa Gessler and Peter Makarov for their contribution in organizing the CLEF lab by reviewing the annotation manuals and sharing their work with us respectively.

---

[9] https://sites.google.com/view/icml2019-generalization/cfp.

[10] https://competitions.codalab.org/competitions/20288.

[11] https://emw.ku.edu.tr/?event=challenges-and-opportunities-in-automated-coding-of-contentious-political-events&event_date=2019-09-02.

[12] http://symposium.computationalsocialscience.eu/2019/.

References

1. Akdemir, A., Hürriyetoğlu, A., Yörük, E., Gürel, B., Yoltar, c., Yüret, D.: Towards generalizable place name recognition systems: analysis and enhancement of NER systems on English news from India. In: Proceedings of the 12th Workshop on Geographic Information Retrieval, GIR 2018, pp. 8:1–8:10. ACM, New York (2018). https://doi.org/10.1145/3281354.3281363
2. Ettinger, A., Rao, S., Daumé III, H., Bender, E.M.: Towards linguistically generalizable NLP systems: a workshop and shared task. In: Proceedings of the First Workshop on Building Linguistically Generalizable NLP Systems, pp. 1–10. Association for Computational Linguistics (2017). http://aclweb.org/anthology/W17-5401
3. Hammond, J., Weidmann, N.B.: Using machine-coded event data for the micro-level study of political violence. Res. Politics 1(2), 2053168014539924 (2014). https://doi.org/10.1177/2053168014539924
4. Hürriyetoğlu, A., et al.: A task set proposal for automatic protest information collection across multiple countries. In: Azzopardi, L., Stein, B., Fuhr, N., Mayr, P., Hauff, C., Hiemstra, D. (eds.) ECIR 2019. LNCS, vol. 11438, pp. 316–323. Springer, Cham (2019). https://doi.org/10.1007/978-3-030-15719-7_42
5. Sang, E.F., De Meulder, F.: Introduction to the CoNLL-2003 shared task: language-independent named entity recognition. arXiv preprint cs/0306050 (2003)
6. Soboroff, I., Ferro, N., Fuhr, N.: Report on GLARE 2018: 1st workshop on generalization in information retrieval: can we predict performance in new domains? In: SIGIR Forum, vol. 52, no. 2, pp. 132–137 (2018). http://sigir.org/wp-content/uploads/2019/01/p132.pdf
7. Wang, W., Kennedy, R., Lazer, D., Ramakrishnan, N.: Growing pains for global monitoring of societal events. Science 353(6307), 1502–1503 (2016). https://doi.org/10.1126/science.aaf6758. http://science.sciencemag.org/content/353/6307/1502

Author Index

Printed in the United States
By Bookmasters